INTRODUCTION TO WORLD PHILOSOPHY

A Multicultural Reader

Daniel Bonevac
University of Texas at Austin
Stephen Phillips
University of Texas at Austin

New York Oxford
OXFORD UNIVERSITY PRESS
2009

Oxford University Press, Inc., publishes works that further Oxford University's objective of excellence in research, scholarship, and education.

Oxford New York
Auckland Cape Town Dar es Salaam Hong Kong Karachi
Kuala Lumpur Madrid Melbourne Mexico City Nairobi
New Delhi Shanghai Taipei Toronto

With offices in
Argentina Austria Brazil Chile Czech Republic France Greece
Guatemala Hungary Italy Japan Poland Portugal Singapore
South Korea Switzerland Thailand Turkey Ukraine Vietnam

Published by Oxford University Press, Inc.
198 Madison Avenue, New York, New York 10016
http://www.oup.com

Oxford is a registered trademark of Oxford University Press

Library of Congress Cataloging-in-Publication Data

Bonevac, Daniel A., 1955–
Introduction to world philosophy: a multicultural reader/Daniel Bonevac and Stephen Phillips.
p. cm.
Includes bibliographical references and index.
ISBN 978-0-19-515231-9
1. Philosophy—Introductions. I. Phillips, Stephen H., 1950– II. Title.
BD21.B66 2009
100—dc22 2008042123

9 8

Printed in Canada
on acid-free paper

Contents

Preface

Introduction to *World Philosophy* includes central sections of works that are classics in various philosophical traditions around the world. In Western philosophy, there is a consensus that Plato, Aristotle, Descartes, Hume, and Kant form the core of a more or less continuous philosophical tradition and that their chief works are philosophical classics. Increasingly, philosophers are aware that there are other more or less continuous philosophical traditions at least as ancient as that tradition. But those traditions are much less familiar, and what counts as a classic is correspondingly more contentious. We have paid close attention to what philosophers working within other traditions treat as classics. We have also, especially in more recent or less continuous traditions, relied on our own judgment of the quality, originality, and importance of works. A major constraint, in addition, has been accessibility. We have sought to include works that those without a deep familiarity with a particular tradition—students and philosophers from other traditions, for example—will find intelligible and important. That has forced us to omit a variety of works that we would otherwise have included.

Our coverage of world philosophy is extensive. We have included the thought of a large number of thinkers—many of whom are women—from almost all areas of the globe. Collecting philosophical classics from around the world is an ambitious project. To keep this project within manageable bounds we have had to restrict our attention in various ways. First, we have limited ourselves to five core areas of philosophy: ethics, philosophy of mind and self, epistemology, metaphysics, and philosophical theology. There are of course philosophical classics that concern political philosophy, aesthetics, the philosophy of language, logic, and other areas. The issue of length has forced us to omit them. We have tried to include classics that address many of the same questions, moreover, to bring works from different philosophical traditions into dialogue with one another. That has been possible only by restricting the questions we have considered. Second, we have included few works written after 1900. Evaluating a work as a philosophical classic requires some perspective, we believe, and that is hard to attain at close range. We have included works written in the twentieth century in a few cases in which they are central to a tradition and relate directly to earlier problems and texts. Third, we have had to omit some philosophers (Spinoza and Kierkegaard, for example) whose work is important but difficult to explain to introductory students or to excerpt in just a few pages.

We have divided the book into five parts, corresponding to the five core areas of philosophy on which we have concentrated. We start with ethics, the most practical and least theory-laden area, and work toward philosophical theology, perhaps the most abstract. Within each part, our organization is both chronological and geographical. We have ordered philosophical traditions in terms of the antiquity of their origins, as follows: Indian philosophy, Chinese philosophy, Greek and Roman philosophy, Christian philosophy, medieval Jewish and Islamic philosophy, early modern philosophy, Kant and post-Kantian philosophy, Spanish and Latin American philosophy, and African philosophy. Not all traditions are represented in every area. Within each tradition, we discuss philosophers chronologically.

We intend this book both for introductory philosophy courses and for readers interested in philosophical classics from around the world. The organization is modular. We have written each part of the book so that it can be read independent of the other parts. This allows readers and teachers great flexibility. Those who see metaphysical questions as primary, for example, and want to start with them can begin with Part IV without any problem. In our own teaching we have sometimes applied the following organizations, which we recommend in addition to the one we have chosen for the book:

Metaphysics (IV), Philosophical Theology (V), Epistemology (III), Mind and Self (II), Ethics (I)

Mind and Self (II), Ethics (I), Epistemology (III), Metaphysics (IV), Philosophical Theology (V)

Metaphysics (IV), Epistemology (III), Philosophical Theology (V), Ethics (I)

Philosophical Theology (V), Metaphysics (IV), Mind and Self (II), Epistemology (III), Ethics (I)

We have also sometimes organized courses around traditions:

Hinduism; Buddhism; Indian Philosophy; Chinese Philosophy; Greek Philosophy; Medieval Jewish, Christian, and Islamic Philosophy; Modern Philosophy; Spanish and Latin American Philosophy; African Philosophy

The book is written so that such an organization works just as well.

There is vastly more material here than can be covered in one course; we encourage instructors to choose what they find most valuable. We have kept our discussions of particular authors and movements as modular as possible so that one can select and omit material flexibly.

We have much supporting material on the book's website, including suggested syllabi, discussion questions, test banks, suggested readings, and PowerPoint-based slides:

http://www.utexas.edu/cola/depts/philosophy/faculty/bonevac/classics/

Please contact us with suggestions for ways to make the book and website more useful.

We are grateful to all those who have supported our work on this project. We have benefited greatly from the enthusiasm and sage advice of Robert Miller at Oxford University Press. Nicholas Asher and David Sosa, successive chairs of the Department of Philosophy at the University of Texas at Austin, have been unfailingly helpful. Joy Carpenter read many chapters and provided extensive comments; her suggestions, large and small, have done much to improve the book. We have profited from the comments of our reviewers, who were exceptionally generous and insightful: Frank X. Ryan, Kent State University; Mark Owen Webb, Texas Tech University; Safro Kwame, Lincoln University; Donna M. Giancola, Suffolk University; Paul Carmona, Cuyamaca College; Kenneth W. Stickkers, Southern Illinois University at Carbondale; Ellen Miller, Rowan University; Daphne M. Rolle, Ball State University; and George Boger, Canisius College. Finally, we are grateful to Beverly Bonevac and Hope Phillips for their patience and their love.

Timeline

Upanishads	800–200 BCE	Udayana	970–1030
Mahavira	599–527 BCE	Avicenna	980–1037
Laozi	580–510 BCE	Anselm	1033–1109
Buddha	563–483 BCE	Al-Ghazali	1058–1111
Confucius	551–479 BCE	Li Qingzhao	1083–1150
Socrates	470–399 BCE	Sun Bu-er	1118–1182
Plato	427–347 BCE	Akka Mahadevi	1120–1180
Aristotle	382–322 BCE	Averroes	1126–1198
Zhuangzi	380–320 BCE	Maimonides	1135–1204
Mencius	372–299 BCE	Peter of Spain	1210–1277
Pyrrho	365–270 BCE	St. Thomas Aquinas	1224–1274
Xunzi	310–212 BCE	Janabai	1270–1350
Rabbinic Judaism	100 BCE–200	Gangesha	1285–1345
Philo	20 BCE–40	Lalla	1320–1390
Wang Chong	27–97	Julian of Norwich	1342–1416
Ban Zhao	48–120	St. Catherine Benicasa	1347–1380
Nagarjuna	120–180	Christine de Pizan	1364–1429
Gautama	170–230	Mirabai	1498–1550
Sextus Empiricus	170–230	St. Teresa of Ávila	1515–1582
St. Augustine	354–430	Francisco Sanches	1551–1623
Vatsyayana	370–430	René Descartes	1596–1650
Dignaga	420–480	Zera Yacob	1599–1692
Dharmapala	439–507	Princess Elizabeth	1618–1680
Xuanzang	596–664	Blaise Pascal	1623–1662
Kumarila	640–700	John Locke	1632–1704
Prabhakara	660–720	Zeb-un-Nissa	1638–1702
Rabi'a Al'-Adiwiyya	741–801	G. W. Leibniz	1646–1716
Yeshe Tsogyal	775–850	George Berkeley	1685–1753
Shankara	788–820	Anton Wilhelm Amo	1703–1759
Yixuan	800–867	David Hume	1711–1776
Yu Xuanji	844–868	Immanuel Kant	1724–1804
Al-Farabi	870–950	William Paley	1743–1805

Jeremy Bentham	1748–1832	Friedrich Nietzsche	1844–1900
Madame de Staël	1766–1817	Miguel de Unamuno	1864–1936
G. W. F. Hegel	1770–1831	Bertrand Russell	1872–1970
John Stuart Mill	1806–1873	José Ortega y Gasset	1883–1955
Charles Sanders Peirce	1839–1914	Jorge Luis Borges	1899–1986

PART I

Ethics

CHAPTER 1

Ethics in the Philosophical Traditions of India

"Free from attachment"

Ancient Indian thinkers developed the earliest ethical theories. Indian ethics arose within religious traditions—Hinduism, Buddhism, and Jainism—and formed central components of those traditions. In classical Indian thought, however, ethical systems also arose outside and in opposition to those traditions.

1.1 *KARMA* AND *DHARMA* IN HINDU THOUGHT

Ethics is about action—about what to do and how to live. All the traditional Indian answers to the questions of the kind of life to lead as well as the kind of person to become center on four conceptions:

1. *Dharma*, duty
2. *Mukti*, liberation or enlightenment, the distinct and highest value
3. *Bhakti*, love of or devotion to God
4. *Karman* (anglicized as *karma*), action or habit

The last is the teaching that virtue is its own reward; we make our future selves by our current action through the development of good or bad dispositions to act. Good actions increase our tendency (not to mention the tendency of others) to do good; bad actions do the reverse. The oldest of the Upanishads, the *Brhadaranyaka*, describes two wise men who, questioned about life after death, "went away and deliberated. What they said was *karma*. What they praised was *karma*. Verily, one becomes good by good action, bad by bad action." The Hindu tradition accepts the possibility of reincarnation; the effects of our actions stretch into future lifetimes.

Even without belief in future lifetimes, it's not hard to see how the idea of karmic virtue could provide moral incentive. What's wrong with being a thief? Well, you're a thief, and you're likely to remain one. Your choice to be a thief binds you to being a thief, a karmic pattern that can determine what you'll be like tomorrow and next month and next year and next decade. A bad choice now may set you on a path that lasts a lifetime.

But the body ages and dies. Can't one steal late in life, when the path that lies ahead is short? Here the possibility of reincarnation plays an important role. I may be choosing to be a thief not only in this lifetime but also in another and perhaps even in endless incarnations. Contrast such a person with one who acts compassionately now and thus begins to become someone who is forever compassionate. Which would you want to be?

Karma and *dharma* are closely related. The laws that maintain cosmic order are laws of karmic justice—another meaning of *dharma*. A person's *karma* reverberates with moral rhythms of the universe. One reaps what one sows. There is karmic payback. The traditional Hindu school of interpretation, Mimamsa, together with texts called *Dharma-sastras*, commissioned by various kings over the centuries to help them make legal decisions, converge around the ethical theme that to live according to *dharma*, the universe's moral backbone, ensures the very best *karma*. By acting in accordance with duty—another primary meaning of *dharma*, "the right way to live"—we turn action into a kind of sacrificial dance that tends to our own self-improvement.

There are many *Dharma-sastras* and many specific sets of ethical codes. Codes of conduct are as much a matter of familial custom as of written law. But certain distinctions apply widely. In addition to caste and gender, stages of life make an ethical difference. A period of (1) being a student or disciple is ideally followed by periods of (2) householding, (3) forest dwelling, and (4) world renunciation as a person prepares for death. The prescriptions for each stage are different. The most greatly elaborated are those for householders, who have more extensive duties to others than those at other stages of life. Not all *dharmas* are relative to a stage of life. Every major world religion includes universal rules for living. Some are virtually universal, found in every religion. (*Do not murder* and *Do not steal*, for example). Others are advanced only by some religions. (*Do not drink alcohol* and *Repay injury with kindness*, for example.) The rules constitute a practical test telling right from wrong.

What makes an act right or wrong? *Divine command theory* holds that God distinguishes right from wrong. What God commands is obligatory; what God allows is permissible; what God forbids is wrong. We know what God commands by way of scripture (the Bible, the Koran, the Veda, etc.), which details rules to use as practical ethical tests. And, according to many divine command theorists, we know God's commands by means of our conscience, which is God's law written on the heart.

The Upanishads constitute the oldest philosophical and ethical texts in India, but it is only much later that their thought is systematized as the Vedanta school. The influence of the Upanishads is pervasive. The ideas about God or Brahman as well as the self (*atman*) influence all later systems of ethics. Yoga (self-discipline) is also introduced in the Upanishads, and a distinctively yogic variety of divine command theory is advanced in the *Bhagavad Gita* (*Song of God*). Traditionally, the *Gita* is not identified as an Upanishad; it does not form part of Vedic literature. But in many Vedantic circles it is treated as an Upanishad, a "secret doctrine," meant to guide yogic practice. The *Gita* expresses the mainstream Hindu view that God's commands—or the Veda, which consists of commands whether or not uttered by God—are right and should be followed. One has to be accomplished in yoga in order to "hear" them in one's highest consciousness. Otherwise, one follows the examples of the "best," the upholders of *dharma* as traditionally conceived.

The *Gita* is a small portion of a long epic poem, the *Mahabharata*, composed at the end of the Upanishadic period, i.e., approximately 400 BCE. The epic is enormous, with more than 100,000 verses; the *Gita* has 900 verses, arranged into eighteen chapters. The main story line of the epic is about princely succession. The rightful heir together with his four brothers and their allies and troops and elephants are arrayed on one side—Arjuna is the third of the five brothers on this side. The usurper together with many venerable sages and heroes are lined up on the other. At the opening of the *Gita*, the warrior Krishna from a neighboring state, who is also here the divine guru (*bhagavad*), joins the battlefront as Arjuna's charioteer. A dialogue takes place between the two just before the fighting begins. In the poem, their conversation is reported by a blind holy man who has the power of being able to hear at a distance.

Arjuna (Everyman), looking across the battlefield at his friends and kin, recoils at the prospect of killing them. Krishna reveals himself as God incarnate and provides a religious and mystical answer to Arjuna's ethical crisis. He urges Arjuna to fight. In part he argues that the soul is immortal and cannot be destroyed. But in part he rests his argument on sacred duty. By practicing the yoga (self-discipline) of action, Krishna says, Arjuna can turn karma (habit) into *dharma* (right action) attuned to God's will. This is the yoga of the *Gita*.

By sacrificing our superficial self-interest and natural desires to act according to God's will, we become part of God's ongoing creative activity, and our consciousness mystically widens to unite with God's (*yoga* in the sense of "union"). Self-sacrifice allows us to participate in God's action. And that promotes our self-interest in a deeper sense. We must do our sacred duty; we must do what God requires. Right and wrong are distinguished, not by the fruits or consequences of action, but by God's command or intention to be known by our conscience, our intuitive sense refined by yoga.

1.1.1 From the *Bhagavad Gita*

Chapter I

Sanjaya said:

Seeing the army of the Pandavas drawn up in battle-array, the prince Duryodhana approached the preceptor, and spoke (these) words: "O preceptor! observe this grand army of the sons of Pandu, drawn up in battle-array by your talented pupil, the son of Drupada. In it are heroes (bearing) large bows, the equals of Bhima and Arjuna in battle." Then seeing (the people of) Dhritarashtra's party regularly marshalled, the son

Source: From the *Bhagavad Gita*, a portion of Book VI of the *Mahabharata*. Translated by Kashinath Trimbak Telang. Volume 8, *The Sacred Books of the East*, 1882.

of Pandu, whose standard is the ape, raised his bow, after the discharge of missiles had commenced, and O king of the earth! spake these words to Hrishikesa: "O undegraded one! station my chariot between the two armies, while I observe those, who stand here desirous to engage in battle, and with whom, in the labours of this struggle, I must do battle. I will observe those who are assembled here and who are about to engage in battle, wishing to do service in battle to the evil-minded son of Dhritarashtra."

Thus addressed by Gudakesa, O descendant of Bharata! Hrishikesa stationed that excellent chariot between the two armies, in front of Bhishma and Drona and of all the kings of the earth, and said, "O son of Pritha! look at these assembled Kauravas." There the son of Pritha saw in both armies, fathers and grandfathers, preceptors, maternal uncles, brothers, sons, grandsons, companions, fathers-in-law, as well as friends. And seeing all those kinsmen standing (there), the son of Kunti was overcome by excessive pity, and spake thus despondingly.

Arjuna said:

Seeing these kinsmen, O Krishna! standing (here) desirous to engage in battle, my limbs droop down; my mouth is quite dried up; a tremor comes on my body; and my hairs stand on end; the Gandiva (bow) slips from my hand; my skin burns intensely. I am unable, too, to stand up; my mind whirls round, as it were; O Kesava! I see adverse omens; and I do not perceive any good (to accrue) after killing (my) kinsmen in the battle. I do not wish for victory, O Krishna! nor sovereignty, nor pleasures: what is sovereignty to us, O Govinda! what enjoyments, and even life? Even those, for whose sake we desire sovereignty, enjoyments, and pleasures, are standing here for battle, abandoning life and wealth—preceptors, fathers, sons as well as grandfathers, maternal uncles, fathers-in-law, grandsons, brothers-in-law, as also (other) relatives. These I do not wish to kill, though they kill (me), O destroyer of Madhu! even for the sake of sovereignty over the three worlds, how much less then for this earth (alone)? What joy shall be ours, O Janardana! after killing Dhritarashtra's sons? Killing these felons we shall only incur sin. Therefore it is not proper for us to kill our own kinsmen, the sons of Dhritarashtra. For how, O Madhava! shall we be happy after killing our own relatives? Although having their consciences corrupted by avarice, they do not see the evils flowing from the extinction of a family, and the sin in treachery to friends, still, O Janardana! should not we, who do see the evils flowing from the extinction of a family, learn to refrain from that sin? . . . Alas! we are engaged in committing a heinous sin, seeing that we are making efforts for killing our own kinsmen out of greed of the pleasures of sovereignty. If the sons of Dhritarashtra, weapon in hand, should kill me in battle, me weaponless and not defending (myself), that would be better for me.

Sanjaya said:

Having spoken thus, Arjuna cast aside his bow together with the arrows, on the battlefield, and sat down in (his) chariot, with a mind agitated by grief.

Chapter II

Sanjaya said:

To him, who was thus overcome with pity, and dejected, and whose eyes were full of tears and turbid, the destroyer of Madhu spoke these words.

The Blessed One said:

How (comes it that) this delusion, O Arjuna! which is discarded by the good, which excludes from heaven, and occasions infamy, has overtaken you in this (place of) peril? Be not effeminate, O son of Pritha! it is not worthy of you. Cast off this base weakness of heart, and arise, O terror of (your) foes!

Arjuna said:

How, O destroyer of Madhu! shall I encounter with arrows in the battle Bhishma and Drona—both, O destroyer of enemies! entitled to reverence? Not killing (my) preceptors—(men) of great glory—it is better to live even on alms in this world. But killing them, though they are avaricious of worldly goods, I should only enjoy blood-tainted enjoyments. Nor do we know which of the two is better for us—whether that we should vanquish them, or that they should vanquish us. Even those, whom having killed, we do not wish to live—even those sons of Dhritarashtra stand (arrayed) against us. With a heart contaminated by the taint of helplessness, with a mind confounded about my duty, I ask you. Tell me what is assuredly good for me. I am your disciple; instruct me, who have thrown myself on your (goodwill). For I do not perceive what is to dispel that grief which will dry up my organs even if I shall have obtained a prosperous kingdom on earth without a foe, or even the sovereignty of the gods.

Sanjaya said:

Having spoken thus to Hrishikesa, O terror of (your) foes! Gudakesa said to Govinda, "I shall not engage in battle;" and verily remained silent. To him thus desponding between the two armies, O descendant of Bharata! Hrishikesa spoke these words with a slight smile.

The Blessed One said:

You have grieved for those who deserve no grief, and you yet talk words of wisdom. Learned men grieve not for the living nor the dead. Never did I not exist, nor you, nor these rulers of men; nor will any one of us ever hereafter cease to be. As, in this body, infancy and youth and old age (come) to the embodied (self), so does the acquisition of another body; a sensible man is not deceived about that. The contacts of the senses, O son of Kunti! which produce cold and heat, pleasure and pain, are not permanent; they are ever coming and going. Bear them, O descendant of Bharata! For, O chief of men! that sensible man whom they (pain and pleasure being alike to him) afflict not, he merits immortality. There is no existence for that which is unreal; there is no nonexistence for that which is real. And the (correct) conclusion about both is perceived by those who perceive the truth.

Know that to be indestructible which pervades all this; the destruction of that inexhaustible (reality) none can bring about. These bodies appertaining to the embodied (self) which is eternal, indestructible, and indefinable, are said to be perishable; therefore do engage in battle, O descendant of Bharata! He who thinks it to be the killer and he who thinks it to be killed, both know nothing. It kills not, is not killed. It is not born, nor does it ever die, nor, having existed, does it come to exist no more. Unborn, everlasting, unchangeable, and primeval, it is not killed when the body is killed.

O son of Pritha! how can that man who knows it thus to be indestructible, everlasting, unborn, and inexhaustible, how and whom can he kill, whom can he cause to be killed? As a man, casting off old clothes, puts on others and new ones, so the embodied (self), casting off old bodies, goes to others and new ones. Weapons do not divide it (into pieces); fire does not burn it, waters do not moisten it; the wind does not dry it up. It is not divisible; it is not combustible; it is not to be moistened; it is not to be dried up. It is everlasting, all-pervading, stable, firm, and eternal. It is said to be unperceived, to be unthinkable, to be unchangeable. Therefore knowing it to be such, you ought not to grieve.

But even if you think that it is constantly born, and constantly dies, still, O you of mighty arms! you ought not to grieve thus. For to one that is born, death is certain; and to one that dies, birth is certain. Therefore about (this) unavoidable thing, you ought not to grieve. The source of things, O descendant of Bharata! is unperceived; their middle state is perceived; and their end again is unperceived. What (occasion is there for any) lamentation regarding them? One looks upon it as a wonder; another similarly speaks of it as a wonder; another too hears of it as a wonder; and even after having heard of it, no one does really know it. This embodied (self), O descendant of Bharata! within every one's body is ever indestructible. Therefore you ought not to grieve for any being. Having regard to your own duty also, you ought not to falter, for there is nothing better for a Kshatriya than a righteous battle. Happy those Kshatriyas, O son of Pritha! who can find such a battle (to fight)—come of itself—an open door to heaven! But if you will not fight this righteous battle, then you will have abandoned your own duty and your fame, and you will incur sin. All beings, too, will tell of your everlasting infamy; and to one who has been honoured, infamy is (a) greater (evil) than death. (Warriors who are) masters of great chariots will think that you abstained from the battle through fear, and having been highly thought of by them, you will fall down to littleness. Your enemies, too, decrying your power, will speak much about you that should not be spoken. And what, indeed, more lamentable than that? Killed, you will obtain heaven; victorious, you will enjoy the earth. Therefore arise, O son of Kunti! resolved to (engage in) battle. Looking alike on pleasure and pain, on gain and loss, on victory and defeat, then prepare for battle, and thus you will not incur sin.

The knowledge here declared to you is that relating to the Samkhya ["understanding"]. Now hear that relating to the Yoga ["self-discipline"]. Possessed of this knowledge, O son of Pritha! you will cast off the bonds of action. In this (path to final emancipation) nothing that is commenced becomes abortive; no obstacles exist; and even a little of this (form of) piety protects one from great danger. There is here, O descendant of Kuru! but one state of mind consisting in firm understanding. But the states of mind of those who have no firm understanding are many-branched and endless. The state of mind consisting in firm understanding regarding steady contemplation does not belong to those, O son of Pritha! who are strongly attached to (worldly) pleasures and power, and whose minds are drawn away by that flowery talk which is full of (ordinances of) specific acts for the attainment of (those) pleasures and (that) power, and which promises birth as the fruit of acts—(that flowery talk) which those unwise ones utter, who are enamoured of Vedic words, who say there is nothing else, who are full of desires, and whose goal is heaven. The Vedas (merely) relate to the effects of the three qualities; do you, O Arjuna! rise above those effects of the three qualities, and be free from the pairs of opposites, always preserve courage, be free from anxiety for new acquisitions or protection of old acquisitions, and be self-controlled. To the instructed Brahmin, there is in all the Vedas as much utility as in a reservoir of water into which waters flow from all sides.

Your business is with action alone; not by any means with fruit. Let not the fruit of action be your motive (to action). Let not your attachment be (fixed) on inaction. Having recourse to yoga, O Dhananjaya! perform actions, casting off (all) attachment, and being equable in success or ill success; (such) equability is called yoga. Action, O Dhananjaya! is far inferior to the yoga of the mind. In that yoga seek shelter. Wretched are those whose motive (to action) is the fruit (of action). He who has obtained yoga in this world casts off both merit and sin.

Therefore apply yourself to yoga; yoga in (all) actions is wisdom. The wise who have obtained yoga cast off the fruit of action; and released from the shackles of (repeated) births, repair to that seat where there is no unhappiness. When your mind shall have crossed beyond the taint of delusion, then will you become indifferent to all that you have heard or will hear. When your mind, confounded by what you have heard, will stand firm and steady in contemplation, then will you acquire yoga.

Arjuna said:

What are the characteristics, O Kesava! of one whose mind is steady, and who is intent on contemplation? How should one of steady mind speak, how sit, how move?

The Blessed One said:

When a man, O son of Pritha! abandons all the desires of his heart, and is pleased in his self only and by his self, he is then called one of steady mind. He whose heart is not agitated in the midst of calamities, who has no longing for pleasures, and from whom (the feelings of) affection, fear, and wrath have departed, is called a sage of steady mind. His mind is steady, who, being without attachments anywhere, feels no exultation and no aversion on encountering the various agreeable and disagreeable (things of this world).

A man's mind is steady, when he withdraws his senses from (all) objects of sense, as the tortoise (withdraws) its limbs from all sides. Objects of sense draw back from a person who is abstinent; not so the taste (for those objects). But even the taste departs from him, when he has seen the Supreme. The boisterous senses, O son of Kunti! carry away by force the mind even of a wise man, who exerts himself (for final emancipation). Restraining them all, a man should remain engaged in yoga, making me his only resort. For his mind is steady whose senses are under his control.

The man who ponders over objects of sense forms an attachment to them; from (that) attachment is produced desire; and from desire anger is produced; from anger results want of discrimination; from want of discrimination, confusion of the memory; from confusion of the memory, loss of reason; and in consequence of loss of reason, he is utterly ruined. But the self-restrained man who moves among objects with senses under the control of his own self, and free from affection and aversion, obtains tranquillity. When there is tranquillity, all his miseries are destroyed, for the mind of him whose heart is tranquil soon becomes steady.

He who is not self-restrained has no steadiness of mind; nor has he who is not self-restrained perseverance in the pursuit of self-knowledge; there is no tranquillity for him who does not persevere in the pursuit of self-knowledge; and whence can there be happiness for one who is not tranquil? For the heart which follows the rambling senses leads away his judgment, as the wind leads a boat astray upon the waters. Therefore, O you of mighty arms! his mind is steady whose senses are restrained on all sides from objects of sense. The self-restrained man is awake, when it is night for all beings; and when all beings are awake, that is the night of the right-seeing sage. He into whom all objects of desire enter, as waters enter the ocean, which, (though) replenished, (still) keeps its position unmoved, he only obtains tranquillity; not he who desires (those) objects of desire. The man who, casting off all desires, lives free from attachments, who is free from egoism, and from (the feeling that this or that is) mine, obtains tranquillity. This, O son of Pritha! is the Absolute state; attaining to this, one is never deluded; and remaining in it in (one's) last moments, one attains (brahma-nirvana) the Absolute bliss.

1.2 THE *BHAKTI* MOVEMENT

Hindu ethical thought develops over the centuries, with different *darshanas* emphasizing different themes but retaining a basis in the Upanishads and the *Bhagavad Gita*. Even within the most influential *darshana*, Vedanta, thinkers stress different elements. Classical Hinduism becomes highly theoretical, leading to advanced studies of rhetoric, aesthetics, logic, and the theory of knowledge. But Hindu ethics retains a strong practical focus. In addition to feudal wars that made life uncertain for many, India suffered Muslim invasions in the twelfth and late fourteenth centuries that resulted in the slaughter of millions, the disruption of India's previously thriving economy and culture, and the destruction of leading universities. Hinduism had to cope with religious conflicts, widespread suffering, and a rising pessimism that led thinkers to question classical Hinduism's assumption that the world harmonizes with the deepest human desires. Nowhere is this tension more evident than in the works of several Indian women, who suffered not only from war, economic depression, and social upheaval but also from discrimination within what remained of the social system. Together, they belong to what is known as the *bhakti* movement; they emphasize *bhakti* yoga—the path of devotion.

Akka Mahadevi (1100s) was born in Karnataka to parents who were followers of the Vira-Shaiva (Hero-Shiva) movement in the twelfth century. From a young age, she worshipped Chenna Mallikarjuna, the beautiful (*chenna*) form of Shiva covered in jasmine (*mallika*). According to myth, the warrior Arjuna fought Shiva to win a powerful weapon from him. When Arjuna's arrows struck Shiva, they were turned into sweet-scented white flowers. Though Mahadevi made it clear to her family that she wanted to pursue an ascetic life ("I have fallen in love with the Beautiful One. Throw into fire husbands who are subject to death and decay"), her great beauty enabled them to arrange a marriage for her with the ruler of the kingdom. She agreed on condition that she could, in accordance with Vira-Shaiva tenets, spend time in meditation, in the company of other devotees, and in the service of her guru. Overcome by jealousy, the king broke all of her conditions.

Mahadevi left him to wander around southwest India composing in Kannada *vacanas* ("sayings") of intense devotion to her beloved Chenna Mallikarjuna. *Vacanas* as a literary form were part of the popular revolt against the Sanskrit-speaking priestly establishment. Mahadevi was called *Akka* ("Older Sister") by other Vira-Shaiva devotees with whom she lived for some time, including Basavanna, one of the founders. She, like male ascetics, often went naked. More than a millennium earlier, Greek thinkers traveling with Alexander the Great wrote of the "naked philosophers" they encountered in India, but nudity for women was uncommon. Finally, Akka Mahadevi retired alone to a holy mountain. Legend reports that she united with the divine in a flash of white light.

Janabai (1260?–1350?) was born to a low-caste family in Maharashtra. Both her parents died when she was a child. She was taken to the temple at Pandharpur, the place of origin of the *Varkari Pantha* (Path). A *varkari* is a devotee of Vitthal (an incarnation of Vishnu). The path, open to all, placed emphasis on devotion over traditional ritual. Janabai was eventually taken into a *varkari* household as a servant. One of the sons, Namdev, grew up to be an important poet. He wrote in the vernacular and stressed the spiritual equality of all people regardless of caste, religious sect, or gender. Janabai cared for Namdev as a child. She remained his servant and disciple her entire life. He inspired her, and she influenced him. Under Namdev's guidance, she reached her goal of union with Vitthal. In her poems, she tells of her suffering as an orphaned, low-caste woman and of transcending suffering through union with the divine. When she sees the divine everywhere, "Jani is *dasi* (servant) no more." According to some sources, Janabai passed away in *samadhi* (yogic trance) at the same time as Namdev.

Lalla (1320?–1390?), born into a family of Brahmins, synthesized many religious ideas of her native Kashmir, including those of various Hindu, Tantric Buddhist, and Sufi groups. She left an unhappy marriage (due mostly to an abusive mother-in-law) to devote herself to the study of Hinduism and Sufism. She traveled throughout Kashmir preaching and teaching. Her writings display extensive knowledge of Hindu scriptures and the practices of yoga. She wrote in the colloquial Kashmiri language, not in philosophical Sanskrit, so that her message of tolerance and love could find a wide audience. She downplays religious rituals and dogmas, arguing that differences between religions are irrelevant to true spirituality, which is a matter of the heart rather than the head. What really matters is ethical behavior—"doing good to others." Lalla was an ascetic, forsaking bodily comforts; according to legend, she usually followed Akka Mahadevi's example and wore no clothing, which was not only startling but remarkable, given Kashmir's climate.

Remembered as a great mystic, she acquired thousands of followers. Even today, about a third of Kashmiri sayings and proverbs come from her work.

Rejecting the claims to exclusiveness of both Brahmin and Muslim, Lalla insisted on the insignificance of distinctions. Hindu, Muslim, or Buddhist, male or female, Brahmin or Shudra, rich or poor—none of this matters; true spirituality knows no boundaries. It is universal, available to anyone. It is internal rather than external. It thus depends on nothing outside the self. Scriptures, rituals or worship, yogic practices, and other techniques may help people to find the divine within themselves. In fact, she outlines *bhakti* yogic practices that she recommends for this purpose. But external manifestations of religion have no other importance.

Mirabai (1498?–1550s?) was born in the rugged land of Rajasthan west of Delhi into the Kshatriya warrior caste of Rajputs. The Afghan empire in northern India was disintegrating. Muslim chiefs fought to carve out kingdoms for themselves. The Rajputs battled back, but plagued by infighting they could not unite. Mirabai's family, the rulers of Merta, arranged a marriage for her to the heir apparent of another Rajput state. She refused to conform to the household customs of her in-laws as she considered herself already married to Krishna, whom she worshipped as her divine husband and protector (Giridhara Nagar). Mirabai's father and her husband were killed in battle. As a widow, she defied convention by bringing holy men into the women's quarters of the palace, dancing in the temple, and composing *padas*, short songs of philosophical and spiritual instruction. Her father-in-law was wounded in a skirmish and later poisoned. The new young king sent a poisoned offering to be placed at the feet of an image of Krishna, knowing that Mirabai would drink the *prasad* according to Hindu practice. In her songs passed from generation to generation, she drank not poison but immortal nectar. Mirabai left the court to wander as a pilgrim, eventually staying at the Ranachor Temple in Gujarat on the Arabian Sea. When members of her family came to find her, she had disappeared. Mirabai argued for *bhakti* yoga, and recognized the pain as well as the splendor of the path of devotion. Only the most extreme devotion liberates us from illusion.

1.2.1 Akka Mahadevi

I do not say it is the Linga,
I do not say it is oneness with the Linga,
I do not say it is union,
I do not say it is harmony,
I do not say it has occurred,
I do not say it has not occurred,
I do not say it is You,
I do not say it is I
After becoming one with the Linga in Chenna
  Mallikarjuna,
I say nothing whatever.

I have fallen in love, O mother, with the
Beautiful One, who knows no death,
knows no decay and has no form;

I have fallen in love, O mother, with the
Beautiful One, who has no middle, has
no end, has no parts and has no
  features;

I have fallen in love, O mother, with the
Beautiful One, who knows no birth and
knows no fear.

I have fallen in love with the Beautiful
One, who is without family, without
country and without peer;
Chenna Mallikarjuna, the Beautiful, is my
husband.
Fling into fire husbands who are subject to death
and decay.

O Lord, listen to me if you will, listen not
if you will not: I cannot rest contented
unless I sing of you.

O Lord, accept me if you will, accept not
if you will not: I cannot rest contented unless
I worship you.

O Lord, love me if you will, love not
if you will not: I cannot rest contented unless I
hold
you in my arms.

O Lord, look at me if you will, look not
if you will not: I cannot rest contented unless
I gaze at you in overpowering longing.

O Lord Chenna Mallikarjuna, I worship you and
revel in delight.

Source: T. N. Sreekantaiya, "Akka Mahadevi," *Women Saints East and West.* Edited by Swami Ghanananda. Hollywood, CA: Vedanta Press, 1979.

(Maya *is illusion, play*; samsara, *the cycle of birth and death.*)

Even if I want to stay apart,
Your *maya* will not leave me;
Even if I struggle against it, this *maya* stays
unbroken;
Your *maya* doesn't leave even if one stands firm;
Those struggling to break this *maya*
Are themselves broken.
To the yogi, your *maya* became the yogini;
To the ascetic, *maya* was the fair woman
ascetic.
For the god, the assumption of monthly
Offerings was the illusion;
If one climbed the mountain, *maya*,
Restless, climbed after.
If one goes into the deep forest, *maya* goes
along;
O *samsara*, it does not leave my back, my hands;
It gives me faith and then makes me forget.
O mercy maker, I am afraid of your *maya*,
O supreme master, Chenna Mallikarjuna,
jasmine-tender,
Have mercy.
What else, O what shall I do, O great god,
O snake-adorned one, do have mercy, O god.

Changing bondage into liberation,
Making the mind a diamond horse, and the soul
the rider,
Not letting it jump up, or leap forward,
Holding back the horse, and dragging it to stand
still on the beautiful petal:
They don't know this
And keep slipping on the coral stone into the
mire.
The jeweler does not see the shining jewel fallen
On the royal road of the marketplace,
And weeps for himself, O lord.
Over the incense-burner of the prime-basis,
Placing the embers of the heart-center,
And stopping the wind by the breath,
The heat of that fire touches the crown-crevice;
The pot of ambrosia breaks and showers onto
the heart-center,
Then the light of the wonderful jewel can be seen.
Who is there to know this, O lord, other than
the egoless devotee,
The devotee who knows the here and the
hereafter,
And knows what the five senses need?
Only the devotee who has left the body...
Who will know you other than your devotee,
Basava,
O Chenna Mallikarjuna, jasmine-tender,
Lord of the holy mountain?

All the Vedas, scriptures and
Sacred lore, canons and codes
Are but grist and husk ground in the mill.
Why grind this, why winnow?
When you behead the mind that
Flows here and there,
O Chenna Mallikarjuna, jasmine-tender,
Then remains eternal space.

What is the use of knowing everything
If one does not know the self?
When one knows in oneself
Why ask others?
Chenna Mallikarjuna, jasmine-tender,
Yourself becoming knowledge,
Showed me the way.
I know you through yourself.

Source: *Songs for Siva: Vacanas of Akka Mahadevi.* Translated by Vinaya Chaitanya; with a foreword by H. S. Shiva Prakash. Walnut Creek, CA: AltaMira Press, 2005.

1.2.2 Janabai

Your wife and mother stay at your feet
and sons are placed proudly in front,

this woman is kept on the doorstep—
no room for the lowly inside.

O God, how I want your embrace!
when will you call *dasi* Jani your own?

I eat God
I drink God
I sleep
on God

I buy God
I count God
I deal
with God

God is here
God is there
void is not
devoid of God

Jani says:
God is within
God is without
and moreover
there is God to spare.

If the Ganga flows to the ocean
and the ocean turns her away,
tell me, O Vitthal,
who would hear her complaint?

Can the river reject its fish?
Can the mother spurn her child?
Jani says,
Lord,
you must accept those
who surrender to you.

Jani has had enough of *samsara*,
but how will I repay my debt?

You leave your greatness behind you
to grind and pound with me.

O Lord you become a woman
washing me and my soiled clothes,

proudly you carry the water
and gather dung with your own two hands.

O Lord, I want
a place at your feet,
says Jani, Namdev's *dasi*.

Source: Sarah Sellergren, "Janabai and Kanhopatra: A Study of Two Women Saints," *Images of Women in Maharashtrian Literature and Religion*. Edited by Anne Feldhaus. Albany: State University of New York Press, 1996. Reprinted by permission of the State University of New York Press, State University of New York.

The bird flies to the end of the horizon
and brings food for its young.
The mother eagle wanders in the sky
but hastens back to her young
Mother is busy with her work
and yet her mind never leaves her child.
Mother monkey jumps over a tree
with her child holding on to her stomach.
Similarly, mother Vitthal watches over Jani
over and over again.

My father and mother passed away,
Now you take care of me Vitthala.

My mind is distressed,
O Hari, truly I have no one of my own.

I see Krishna everywhere.
I look to my left—and see Krishna.
I look to my right—and see Krishna.
If I look down,
Krishna is there.
Everything I see,
moving and unmoving,
is radiating Krishna.
Where am I?
I don't recall anymore.

Jani is *dasi* no more!
The experience was of joy.
The experiencer was joy itself
and the object of experience was also joy.
When this oneness is experienced,
the illusion of separation vanished.

Source: Rajeshwari V. Pandharipande, "Janabai: A Woman Saint of India," *Women Saints in World Religions.* Edited by Arvind Sharma. Albany: State University of New York Press, 2000. Reprinted by permission of the State University of New York Press, State University of New York.

1.2.3 Lalla

My guru gave me only this advice—
From outside transfer the attention within
That became my initiation
That is why I began to wander naked.

I took the reins of the mind-horse
Through practice, I learned breath-control
Then only the orb of moon melted and flowed down into my body
Nothingness merged with nothingness.

She who realized *brahma-randhra mandala* as the abode of the deity
And heard the all-pervasive unobstructed sound through breath-control
And who erased the illusions about herself
As she herself is the deity, whom should she worship?

After traversing six forests, I awakened the orb of the moon
By controlling my breath, I gave up attachment to worldly things
I burned my heart in the fire of love
Thus I found Shankar.

Renouncing cheating, deceit, and hypocrisy
Is the teaching I told my mind to follow
Only One I found in everything
Then what is wrong with eating with people from different castes or religions?

I traversed the field of void alone
And I, Lalla, lost consciousness of myself
I found the secret of my Self
Then the lotus bloomed in the mud for Lalla.

I, Lalla, entered the door to the garden of my mind
I saw Shiva and Shakti in communion
And became immersed in the nectar of bliss
Now life and death are the same to me.

You are the sky and you are the earth
You are the day, the night, and the wind
You are the grain, sandalwood, flowers, and water
You are everything, then what should I offer to you?

Whosoever regards the self and the other as equal
And the day and night as the same
Whose mind is free of duality
She alone has the vision of the lord of creation.

Without discernment, O dear, they read religious books
As parrots recite "Rama" in a cage
Reading the *Gita* becomes an excuse
I have read the *Gita* and I am still reading it.

Why are you groping like the blind
If you are wise, you will turn your attention within
Shiva is there, you need not go anywhere else
Trust my simple words.

Wear those clothes that protect you from cold
Eat that food which satisfies your hunger
Meditate on the Self
O Mind, give your body this advice.

The stone that is on the pedestal and upon the pavement
Is the same stone that comes from the earth
The same stone adorns the grindstone
It is hard to attain Shiva—keep that teaching in mind.

Don't torture your body with thirst and starvation
When the body is exhausted, take care of it
Cursed be your fasts and religious ceremonies
Do good to others, for that is the real religious practice.

I might have known how to scatter southern clouds
Dry up an ocean
Cure a leper
But I never knew how to convince a fool.

Name and fame is like water in a sieve
Whoever has the strength to hold air in a fist
And who can tie an elephant with a strand of hair
She is the one who will attain bliss.

I did not pause for the right moment
I did not trust anything
The wine I, Lalla, drank was my own verses
I caught the inner darkness and gathered it
Tearing it into shreds.

Source: *To The Other Shore: Lalla's Life and Poetry*. Translated with introduction and historical background by Jaishree Kak Odin. New Delhi: Vitasta Publishers, 1999.

1.2.4 Mirabai

O my companion,
I have beheld Shyam, the Son of Nand.
I have lost all consciousness of my surroundings
And worldly shame has fled.
How beautiful are the crescent moons
Shimmering on his peacock-plume crown!
He wears a tilak-mark of saffron
Set between his lovely eyes.
His crocodile-earrings glint against his cheeks,
And his dark locks play in the breeze...
The lord wears the garb of a dancer.
His beauty has charmed the whole world.
Mira would sacrifice her all
To every limb of Lord Giridhara.

Mira has been singing the glories of Govind
And is immersed in joy.
The king sent a snake in a basket:
They came and placed it in Mira's hand.
I washed and came to look at it,
And behold!
It was the Black Stone of Vishnu.
The king sent a cup of poison,
But my lord turned it into nectar.
When I washed my hand and drank,
Behold! It was nectar.
The king sent a mattress of thorns,
Saying: "Give that to Mira to sleep upon."
When evening came and Mira lay down,
Behold! It was a bed of flowers.
Mira's lord ever stands as her protector
And saves her from danger.
She wanders recklessly,
Drunk in adoration,
Offering herself to Giridhara in total sacrifice.

I am mad with love
And no one understands my plight.
Only the wounded
Understand the agonies of the wounded,

When a fire rages in the heart.
Only the jeweler knows the value of the jewel,
Not the one who loses it.
In pain I wandered from door to door,
But could not find a healer.
Mira says: My pain will subside
When Shyam comes as the healer.

My love is only for Giridhara Gopal
And for no one else.
O saints and holy men,
I have seen the world and its ways.
I left brothers and relatives
And all I possessed.
Dispensing with worldly shame,
I came to sit with the holy men.
I felt joy in the company of the devotees,
On beholding the world I wept.
I planted the creeper of love
And watered it with my tears.
I churned the curds
And drew forth the ghee:
The buttermilk I rejected.
The king sent me a cup of poison.
I drank it down with joy.
Mira's love has set in deeply,
She accepts whatever comes.

I dance before my Giridhara.
Again and again I dance
To please that critic
And put his love to the test.
I put on the anklets
Of the love of Shyam
And behold! My Mohan stays true.
Worldly shame and family custom
I have cast to the winds.
I do not forget the beauty of the beloved
Even for an instant.
Mira is dyed deeply in the dye of Hari.

On the banks of the Yamuna
A flute is heard.
The flute-player has captured my heart.
My soul has not strength to withstand
him.
He is dark against the dark waters of the
Yamuna.
On hearing the sound of the flute,
I lose consciousness.
My body is like stone.
Mira says: O Lord Giridhara,
Come quickly and end my pain.

Thou art my companion of many births,
I do not forget thee day or night.
Without thee I can enjoy no peace,
My heart knows it well.
I climbed a high place
To scan thy path.
I suffered sorely and my eyes grew red.
False is the ocean of transmigration,
False is bondage to the world,
False all family ties.
I gaze at thy form every moment
And feel the intoxication of thy beauty.
Mira's lord is Giridhara Nagar,
Her mind is dyed in the feet of Hari.

Come to my house, O Krishna,
Your coming will bring peace.
Great will be my joy when I meet you,
And all my desires will be fulfilled.
You and I are one,
Like the sun and its heat.
Mira's heart cares for nothing else,
Except the beautiful Shyam.

Source: *The Devotional Poems of Mirabai*. Translated with introduction and notes by A. J. Alston. Delhi: Motilal Banarsidass, 1980.

1.3 EARLY BUDDHISM

The Buddha, Siddhartha Gautama (563–483 BCE), a contemporary of Confucius and Laozi, lived in the Ganges valley in what is now Nepal. The Buddha's teaching, as preserved in the earliest records (in the language Pali, a close derivative of the

Sanskrit of the Upanishads), focuses on the practices necessary to attain the highest good.

According to the traditional story of the Buddha's life, the Buddha-to-be was born a prince destined to inherit his father's ruling mantle. As a young man he led a life of pleasure. He was encouraged to enjoy himself by his father, who feared that a prophecy—that his son would become a religious mendicant—would come true. Thus the king tried to protect the boy from all evil. But one day the Buddha-to-be journeyed some distance from the royal gardens and pleasure grounds and encountered first a terribly diseased person, then an old man, wrinkled and decrepit, and finally a corpse. (Buddhists view these conditions as the "three evils.") Inquiring about each in turn, and being told that everyone is subject to such infirmities, the prince renounced his life of pleasure, vowing to search tirelessly for the origin of evil and the power to root it up. The Buddha-to-be tried out various paths of asceticism before arriving at the Middle Way, a way of life he later advocated to his disciples. After a long ordeal in meditation under a Bodhi tree, he achieved the highest good: an extinction of self-regarding desire, *Nirvana*, the end of evil. The Buddha spent the rest of his life traveling and preaching, helping others to reach the supreme good.

An early form of a moral theory based on the control of desire is central to Buddhism. Among the most important teachings presented in Buddhism are the Four Noble Truths:

1. Life is painful (*dukkha*). This Noble Truth characterizes the symptom of the human condition: Life is painful, dislocated, out of joint.
2. The root of pain and suffering is desire, attachment, or personal clinging (*tanha*). This gives the diagnosis: Selfish desire, craving, is the cause of suffering.
3. There is a way to eliminate desire and thereby eliminate suffering, namely Nirvana. This gives the prognosis: There is a way to eliminate suffering. To eliminate suffering, eliminate desire by achieving the highest good.
4. The way to this supreme good is the Eightfold Noble Path: right thought, right resolve, right speech, right conduct, right livelihood, right effort, right mindfulness, and right concentration or meditation. The Eightfold Path is the Buddha's prescription: To eliminate suffering, follow the Eightfold Path.

This is the heart of Buddhist ethics. There is undoubtedly evil in the world; it is real. People suffer, grow old, and die. But we can learn to eliminate pain and suffering by eliminating desire. Why, after all, do pain, infirmity, and death cause us suffering? It is because we want to feel good. We want to be active. We want above all to live. The world thus does not match our desires, and suffering results from the mismatch. So we must either change the world or change ourselves. Prospects for eliminating pain, aging, illness, and death look only slightly better in our day than they did in the Buddha's day. So the best route is to change ourselves, giving up our desires for pleasure, activity, and life.

To eliminate desire, follow the Eightfold Path, which constitutes "the Middle Way, which gives sight and knowledge, and tends to calm, to insight, enlightenment, Nirvana." It has eight components:

1. *Right views.* To eliminate desire, you must know something—in particular, the Four Noble Truths. You must understand your condition and come to the proper diagnosis.
2. *Right intention.* To eliminate desire, you must not only understand your condition but want to eliminate suffering by eliminating desire. You must want to do the right thing and liberate yourself.
3. *Right speech.* You must tell the truth, to others and to yourself. You must also be charitable, recognizing that everyone suffers from the same disease. Lying both stems from and encourages selfish desire.
4. *Right action.* You must overcome selfish desire. In particular, there are five moral precepts you must obey: (a) Do not kill. (b) Do not steal. (c) Do not lie. (d) Do not be unshaven. (e) Do not drink. Killing, lying, stealing, lust, and drinking all stem from selfish desire and further promote it.
5. *Right livelihood.* You must choose an occupation that promotes life and enables you to overcome selfish desire. Certain occupations encourage violations of the foregoing moral precepts. In particular, the Buddha denounces poison peddlers, slave dealers, prostitutes, butchers, brewers, arms makers, tax collectors, and caravan traders—the last, evidently, because a business without a fixed abode is likely to cheat its customers.
6. *Right effort.* Selfish desire stems from human nature. Overcoming it requires constant effort. You must be as steady as an ox, working constantly against your own natural inclinations.
7. *Right mindfulness.* Thought and action are intimately linked; you cannot eliminate selfish desire in your behavior without overcoming it mentally. Only by thinking correctly can you hope to act correctly and escape suffering.
8. *Right concentration.* In the final analysis, only a new mode of experience can allow you to escape selfish desire. You must attain enlightenment, seeing past the boundaries of your self and recognizing the unity between your mind and the world.

1.3.1 The Buddha, from *The First Sermon*

There are two extremes, O monks, which he who has given up the world ought to avoid. What are these two extremes? A life given to pleasures, devoted to pleasures and lusts: this is

Source: The Buddha, from *The First Sermon*, adapted from T. W. Rhys Davids and Herman Oldenberg, trans, *Vinyaya Texts*, in F. Max Müller, ed., *The Sacred Books of the East*, Volume XIII. Oxford: Clarendon Press, 1879–1910.

degrading, sensual, vulgar, ignoble, and profitless; and a life given to mortifications: this is painful, ignoble, and profitless. By avoiding these two extremes, O monks, the Tathagata has gained the knowledge of the Middle Path which leads to insight, which leads to the wisdom which conduces to calm, to knowledge, to enlightenment, to Nirvana.

The Eightfold Path

Which, O monks, is this Middle Path the knowledge of which the Tathagata has gained, which leads to insight, which leads to wisdom, which conduces to calm, to knowledge, to enlightenment, to Nirvana? It is the Noble Eightfold Path, namely,

- Right Belief,
- Right Aspiration,
- Right Speech,
- Right Conduct,
- Right Means of Livelihood,
- Right Endeavor,
- Right Concentration,
- Right Meditation.

This, O monks, is the Middle Path the knowledge of which the Tathagata has gained, which leads to insight, which leads to wisdom, which conduces to calm, to knowledge, to enlightenment, to Nirvana.

The Four Noble Truths

1. This, O monks, is the Noble Truth of Suffering (*dukkha*): Birth is suffering; decay is suffering; illness is suffering; death is suffering. Being around what we hate is suffering; being apart from what we love is suffering; not to obtain what we desire is suffering. Briefly, clinging to existence is suffering.
2. This, O monks, is the Noble Truth of the Cause of suffering: the craving (*tanha*), which leads to rebirth, accompanied by pleasure and lust, finding its delight here and there. This craving is threefold, namely, craving for pleasure, craving for existence, craving for prosperity.
3. This, O monks, is the Noble Truth of the Cessation of suffering: it ceases with the complete cessation of this craving—a cessation which consists in the absence of every passion with the abandoning of this craving, with doing away with it, with the deliverance from it, with the destruction of desire.
4. This, O monks, is the Noble Truth of the Path which leads to the cessation of suffering: that Noble Eightfold Path, that is to say, Right Belief, Right Aspiration, Right Speech, Right Conduct, Right Means of Livelihood, Right Endeavor, Right Concentration, Right Meditation.

As long, O monks, as I did not possess with perfect purity this true knowledge and insight into these Four Noble Truths ... so long, O monks, I knew that I had not yet obtained the highest, absolute enlightenment in the world of men and gods.

But since I possessed, O monks, with perfect purity this true knowledge and insight into these Four Noble Truths ... then I knew, O monks, that I had obtained the highest, universal enlightenment. And this knowledge and insight arose in my mind: The emancipation of my mind cannot be lost; this is my last birth; hence I shall not be born again!

1.3.2 From *The Dhammapada*

1. All that we are is the result of what we have thought: it is founded on our thoughts, it is made up of our thoughts. If a man speaks or acts with an evil thought, pain follows him, as the wheel follows the foot of the ox that draws the carriage.

2. All that we are is the result of what we have thought: it is founded on our thoughts, it is made up of our thoughts. If a man speaks or acts with a pure thought, happiness follows him, like a shadow that never leaves him.

7. He who lives looking for pleasures only, his senses uncontrolled, immoderate in his food, idle, and weak, Mara (the demon tempter) will certainly overthrow him, as the wind throws down a weak tree.

8. He who lives without looking for pleasures, his senses well controlled, moderate in his food, faithful and strong, him Mara will certainly not overthrow, any more than the wind throws down a rocky mountain.

15. The evildoer mourns in this world, and he mourns in the next; he mourns in both. He mourns and suffers when he sees the evil of his own work.

16. The virtuous man delights in this world, and he delights in the next; he delights in both. He delights and rejoices, when he sees the purity of his own work.

21. Earnestness is the path of Nirvana, thoughtlessness the path of death; those who are in earnest do not die, those who are thoughtless are as if dead already.

33. As an archer makes his arrow straight, so a wise man makes straight his trembling and unsteady thought, which is difficult to guard and difficult to hold back.

35. It is good to tame the mind, which is difficult to hold in and flighty, rushing wherever it wishes; a tamed mind brings happiness.

36. Let the wise man guard his thoughts, for they are difficult to perceive, very artful, and they rush wherever they wish: thoughts well guarded bring happiness.

66. Fools of little understanding have themselves for their greatest enemies, for they do evil deeds which must bear bitter fruits.

69. As long as the evil deed done does not bear fruit, the fool thinks it is like honey; but when it ripens, then the fool suffers grief.

90. There is no suffering for him who has finished his journey, and abandoned grief, who has freed himself on all sides, and thrown off all fetters.

92. Men who have no riches, who live on recognized food, who have perceived void and unconditioned freedom (Nirvana), their path is difficult to understand, like that of birds in the air.

96. His (the wise and venerable person: *arhat*) thought is quiet, quiet are his word and deed, when he has obtained freedom by true knowledge, when he has thus become a quiet man.

97. The man who is free from credulity, but knows the uncreated, who has cut all ties, removed temptations, renounced all desires, he is the greatest of men.

100. Even though a speech be a thousand words long, but made up of senseless words, one word of sense is better, which if a man hears, he becomes quiet.

103. If one man conquer in battle a thousand times a thousand men, and if another only conquers himself, he is the greatest of conquerors.

116. If a man would advance towards the good, he should keep his thought away from evil; if a man does what is good slothfully, his mind delights in evil.

121. Let no man think lightly of evil, saying in his heart, It will not come near to me. Even by the falling of water drops is a water pot filled; the fool

Source: From *The Dhammapada*. Translated by Max Müller. Oxford: Clarendon Press, 1881.

becomes full of evil, even if he gathers it little by little.

122. Let no man think lightly of good, saying in his heart, It will not come near to me. Even by the falling of water drops is a water pot filled; the wise man becomes full of good, even if he gathers it little by little.

133. Do not speak harshly to anybody; those who are spoken to will answer you in the same way. Angry speech is painful, blows for blows will touch you.

134. If like a shattered gong, you make no utterance, then you have reached Nirvana; strife is not known to you.

135. As a cowherd with his staff drives his cows into the stable, so do age and death drive the life of men.

136. A fool does not know when he commits his evil deeds; but the wicked man burns by his own deeds, as if by fire.

141. Not nakedness, not matted hair, not dirt, not fasting, or lying on the earth, not rubbing with dust, not sitting motionless, can purify a mortal who has not overcome desires.

145. Canal makers lead the water; archers bend the arrow; carpenters bend a log of wood; good people fashion themselves.

153, 154. Looking for the maker of this tabernacle, I shall have to run through a course of many births, so long as I do not find him; and painful is birth again and again. But now, maker of the tabernacle, you have been seen; you shall not make up this tabernacle again. All your rafters are broken, your ridge pole is sundered; the mind, approaching the eternal has attained to the extinction of all desires.

160. The self is the master of the self, for who else could be its master? With the self well subdued, a man finds a master such as few can find.

163. Bad deeds, and deeds hurtful to ourselves, are easy to do; what is beneficial and good, that is very difficult to do.

165. By oneself the evil is done, by oneself one suffers; by oneself evil is left undone, by oneself one is purified. Purity and impurity belong to oneself; no person can purify another person.

166. Let no one forget his own duty for the sake of another's, however great; let a man, after he has discerned his own duty, be always attentive to his own duty.

170. Look upon the world as a bubble, look upon it as a mirage: the king of death does not see him who thus looks down upon the world.

171. Come. Look at this glittering world, like a royal chariot; the foolish are immersed in it, but the wise do not touch it.

172. He who formerly was reckless and afterwards became sober brightens up this world, like the moon when freed from clouds.

174. This world is dark, few only can see here; a few only go to heaven, like birds escaped from the net.

183. Not to commit any sin, to do good, and to purify one's mind, that is the teaching of the Awakened.

185. Not to blame, not to strike, to live restrained under the law, to be moderate in eating, to sleep and sit alone, and to dwell on the highest thoughts—this is the teaching of the Awakened.

186. There is no satisfying desires, even by a shower of gold pieces; he who knows that desires have a short taste and cause pain, he is wise.

190. He who takes refuge with Buddha, the Law, and the Church; he who, with clear understanding, sees the Four Noble Truths:

191. These four holy truths are: suffering, the origin of suffering, the destruction of suffering, and the Eightfold Noble Path that leads to the quieting of suffering.

192. That is the safe refuge, that is the best refuge; having gone to that refuge, a man is delivered from all suffering.

202. There is no fire like passion; there is no bad gamble like hatred; there is no pain like this body; there is no happiness higher than stillness.

210. Let no man ever look for what is pleasant, or what is unpleasant. Not to see what is pleasant is pain, and it is pain to see what is unpleasant.

306. He who says what is not goes to hell; he who, having done a thing, says he hasn't done that thing also goes to hell. After death, both are equal: they are men with evil deeds in the next world.

367. He who never identifies himself with name and form, and does not grieve over what is no more, he indeed is called a Bhikshu [mendicant].

368. The Bhikshu who acts with kindness, who is calm in the doctrine of Buddha, will reach the quiet place (Nirvana), cessation of natural desires, and happiness.

369. O Bhikshu, empty this boat! If emptied, it will go quickly; having cut off passion and hatred, you will go to Nirvana!

370. Cut off the five senses, leave the five senses, rise above the five senses. A Bhikshu who has escaped from the five chains (i.e., the five senses) is called *oghatinna*: "saved from the flood."

1.4 SONGS OF THE BUDDHIST NUNS

The Buddha's teaching attracted women as well as men. Throughout northern India, with his blessing, communities of women as well as men sprang up to study the Buddha's teachings and convey them to others. These women, known as *theri* (nuns), were sometimes itinerant preachers, but increasingly they lived in monasteries, where they could devote themselves full time to the pursuit of enlightenment. Their chants and sayings were collected into a work known as the *Therigatha*, the *Songs of the Nuns* (or *Psalms of the Sisters*). They became part of the Pali canon. The women who wrote the songs were young and old, of high and low caste, well educated and barely educated; they represented a wide swath of Indian society. The *Songs of the Nuns* thus provides a rare glimpse of a range of expressions of a single philosophy by and for women in various social positions. They do little to advance Buddhism theoretically; their ethical interest is primarily practical. These sayings were the form in which most transmission of the Buddha's doctrines took place. They address everyday, practical concerns, stressing the impermanence of things, the inevitability of frustration, suffering, and death, and the hope of eliminating suffering by eliminating desire. Recognizing the inevitability of suffering and death, far from leading to pessimism, frees us to overcome them.

Each song is headed by the name of the sister who, according to tradition, composed it. Often, the text includes biographical details that aid understanding of the song.

1.4.1 From *Psalms of the Sisters*

VI Dhira

Come, O Dhira, reach up and touch the goal
Where all distractions cease, where sense is stilled,
Where dwells bliss; win Nirvana, win
That sure Salvation which has no beyond.

XIV Sumana

Have you not seen sorrow and ill in all
The springs of life? Come not back to birth!
Cast out the passionate desire again to be.
So shall you go your ways calm and serene.

Source: *Psalms of the Early Buddhists, Volume I: Psalms of the Sisters.* Edited by Mrs. Rhys Davids. London: Henry Frowde, 1909. We have revised the translation for consistency with the rest of this book.

XXVIII Sama

She, too, having made her resolve under former Buddhas, and heaping up good of age-enduring efficacy in this and that state of becoming, being reborn in fortunate conditions, took birth, in this Buddha dispensation, at Kosambi, in the family of an eminent burgess. When her dear friend, the lay disciple Samavati, died, she, in her distress, left the world. But being unable to subdue her grief for her friend, she was unable to grasp the supermundane Way. Now, while she was seated in the sitting room, listening to Elder Ananda preaching, she was established in insight, and, on the seventh day after, attained Arhatship, with thorough grasp of the Dhamma in form and meaning.

And reflecting on what she had won, she expressed it in this psalm:

Four times, nay, five, I sallied from my cell,
And roamed afield to find the peace of mind
I sought in vain, and governance of thoughts
I could not bring into captivity.
To me, even to me, on that eighth day
It came: all craving ousted from my heart.
'Mid many sore afflictions, I had wrought
With passionate endeavour, and had won!
Craving was dead, and the Lord's will was done.

XXXV Sela

. . . An Elder, Sela, lived at Savatthi. And one day she went forth from Savatthi to take siesta in the Dark Grove, and sat down beneath a tree. Then Mara (the tempter), alone and wishing to interrupt her privacy, approached in the guise of a stranger, saying:

Ne'er shall you find escape while in the world!
What profits you then your loneliness?
Take the good things of life while yet you may.
Repentance else too late awaits you.

Then the Sister—thinking: "Verily, 'tis that foolish Mara who would deny me the Nirvana that is revealed to me, and bids me choose the sensuous life. He knows not that I am an Arhat. Now will I tell him and confound him"—recited the following:

Like spears and javelins are the joys of sense
That pierce and rend the mortal frames of us.
These that you call "the good things of life"—
Good of that ilk to me is nothing worth.

On every hand the love of pleasure yields,
And the thick gloom of ignorance is rent
In twain. Know this, O Evil One, avaunt!
Here, O Destroyer, shall you not prevail.

XXXVI Soma

Then, dwelling at Savatthi in the bliss of emancipation, she went forth one day to take siesta in the Dark Grove, and sat down beneath a tree. And Mara, alone, and wishing to interrupt her privacy, approached her, invisible and in the air, saying:

That vantage ground the sages may attain is hard
To reach. With her two-finger consciousness
That is no woman competent to gain!

For women, from the age of 7 or 8, boiling rice at all times, know not the moment when the rice is cooked, but must take some grains in a spoon and press it with two fingers; hence the expression "two-finger" sense. Then the Elder rebuked Mara:

How should the woman's nature hinder us?
Whose hearts are firmly set, who ever move
With growing knowledge onward in the Path?
What can that signify to one in whom
Insight does truly comprehend the Norm?
On every hand the love of pleasure yields,
And the thick gloom of ignorance is rent
In twain. Know this, O Evil One, avaunt!
Here, O Destroyer! shall you not prevail.

To one for whom the question does arise:
Am I a woman in these matters or
Am I a man? or what not am I, then?—
To such a one is Mara fit to talk!

LVI Gutta

Bethink you, Gutta, of that high reward
For which you were content to lose your world,
Renouncing hope of children, lure of wealth.
To that direct and consecrate the mind,
Nor give yourself to sway of truant thoughts.
Deceivers ever are the thoughts of men,
Fain for the haunts where Mara finds his prey;
And running ever on from birth to birth,
To the dread circle bound—a witless world.
But you, O Sister, bound to other goals,
Yours is't to break those fetters five: the lust
Of sense, ill will, delusion of the self,
The taint of rites and ritual, and doubt,
That drag you backward to the hither shore.
'Tis not for you to come again to this!
Get away from life-lust, from conceit,
From ignorance, and from distraction's craze;
Sunder the bonds; so only shall you come
To utter end of ill. Throw off the chain
Of birth and death—you know what they mean.
So, free from craving, in this life on earth,
You shall go on your way calm and serene.

LXIII Kisa-gotami

NOW she was born, when Padumuttara was Buddha, in the city of Hangsavati, in a clansman's family. And one day she heard the Master preach the Dhamma, and assign foremost rank to a Bhikkhuni with respect to the wearing of rough garments. She vowed that this rank should one day be hers. In this Buddha era she was reborn at Savatthi, in a poor family. Gotami was her name, and from the leanness of her body she was called Lean Gotami. And she was disdainfully treated when married, and was called a nobody's daughter. But when she bore a son, they paid her honour. Then, when he was old enough to run about and play, he died, and she was distraught with grief. And, mindful of the change in folks' treatment of her since his birth, she thought: "They will even try to take my child and expose him." So, taking the corpse upon her hip, she went, crazy with sorrow, from door to door, saying: "Give me medicine for my child!" And people said with contempt: "Medicine! What's the use?" She understood them not. But one sagacious person thought: "Her mind is upset with grief for her child. He of the Tenfold Power will know of some medicine for her." And he said: "Dear woman, go to the Very Buddha, and ask him for medicine to give your child." She went to the Vihara at the time when the Master taught the Doctrine, and said: "Exalted One, give me medicine for my child!" The Master, seeing the promise in her, said: "Go, enter the town, and at any house where yet no man has died, thence bring a little mustard seed." " 'Tis well, lord!" she said, with mind relieved; and, going to the first house in the town, said: "Let me take a little mustard, that I may give medicine to my child. If in this house no man has yet died, give me a little mustard." "Who may say how many have not died here?" "With such mustard, then, I have nought to do." So she went on to a second and a third house, until, by the might of the Buddha, her frenzy left her, her natural mind was restored, and she thought: "Even this will be the order of things in the whole town. The Exalted One foresaw this out of his pity for my good." And, thrilled at the thought, she left the town and laid her child in the charnel field, saying:

"No village law is this, no city law,
No law for this clan, or for that alone;
For the whole world—ay, and the gods in heav'n—
This is the Law: ALL IS IMPERMANENT!"

So saying, she went to the Master. And he said: "Gotami, have you gotten the little mustard?" And she said: "Wrought is the work, lord, of the little mustard. Give you me confirmation." Then the Master spoke thus:

"To him whose heart on children and on goods
Is centered, cleaving to them in his thoughts,
Death comes like a great flood in the night,
Bearing away the village in its sleep."

When he had spoken, she was confirmed in the fruition of the First (the Stream-entry) Path, and asked for ordination. He consented, and she, thrice saluting by the right, went to the Sisters, and was ordained. And not long afterwards, studying the causes of things, she caused her insight to grow. Then the Master said a Glory verse:

"The man who, living for an hundred years,
Beholds never the Ambrosial Path,
Had better live no longer than one day,
So he behold within that day the Path."

When he had finished, she attained Arhatship. And becoming preeminent in ascetic habits, she was wont to wear raiment of triple roughness. Then the Master, seated in the Jeta Grove in conclave, and assigning rank of merit to the Sisters, proclaimed her first among the wearers of rough raiment. And she, reflecting on what great things she had won, uttered this Psalm before the Master, in praise of friendship with the elect:

Friendship with noble souls throughout the
world
The sage has praised. A fool, in sooth, grows wise
If he but entertain a noble friend.
Cleave to the men of worth! In them who cleave
Wisdom does grow; and in that pious love
From all your sorrows shall you be released.

Mark sorrow well; mark how it does come,
And how it passes; mark the Eightfold Path
That ends woe, the Four Great Supermundane
Truths.

Woeful is woman's lot! has he declared,
Tamer and driver of the hearts of men:
Woeful when sharing home with hostile wives,
Woeful when giving birth in bitter pain,
Some seeking death, or e'er they suffer twice,
Piercing the throat; the delicate poison take.
Woe too when mother-murdering embryo
Comes not to birth, and both alike find death.

"Returning home to give birth to my child,
I saw my husband in the jungle die.
Nor could I reach my kin ere travail came.
My baby boys I lost, my husband too.
And when in misery I reached my home,
Lo! where together on a scanty pyre,
My mother, father, and my brother burn!"

O wretched, ruined woman! all this weight
Of sorrows have you suffered, shed these tears
Through weary round of many thousand lives.
I too have seen where, in the charnel field,
Devoured was my baby's tender flesh.

Yet she, her people slain, herself outcast,
Her husband dead, has thither come
Where death is not! Lo! I have gone
Up on the supermundane, on the Eightfold Path
That goes to the state ambrosial.
Nirvana have I realized, and gazed
Into the Mirror of the holy Norm.
I, even I, am healed of my hurt,
Low is my burden laid, my task is done,
My heart is wholly set at liberty.
I, sister Kisa-gotami, have uttered this!

1.5 BUDDHIST VIRTUES

The southern branch of Buddhism—sometimes known by the name of the Theravada philosophy—rests its conception of virtue on that of the "Southern Canon." Its ideal is to become an *arhat* (a saint, also called a *pratyeka-buddha*), one who loses all individuality in universal, impersonal bliss, Nirvana. The northern branch of Buddhism, Mahayana Buddhism, recognizes a distinct and later literature as sacred. Its ideal is the *bodhisattva*, "one whose essence is enlightenment," who, unlike the *arhat*, turns back from the final bliss to help others. To achieve Nirvana is no longer the ideal but rather to be enlightened and attain a perfect form.

Mahayana Buddhists sometimes tell a story to illustrate the difference between the *arhat* and the *bodhisattva* and thus between Theravada and Mahayana Buddhism. Four travelers in the desert, about to collapse of thirst, find what appears to be an oasis. But it has a tall wall around it. One offers to climb the wall and report what he finds. He disappears over the wall, and does not call out or come back. The same happens with the second. The third climbs the wall and sees that it is indeed an oasis. He climbs back down and helps boost the fourth over the wall. The fourth calls to him, "Come on!" But he answers, "You go ahead. I'm going to look for others who might be lost in the desert, and direct them here." Three of the four are *arhat*s, who seek their own fulfillment in the oasis. The one who glimpses the oasis but resists entering in order to help others find it is the *bodhisattva*.

Mahayanists try to attain six virtues, or "perfections" (*paramita*s), possessed by the Buddha now thought of as *bodhisattva*. These enable them to promote the welfare of all beings. Thus the Mahayana sect is more world-affirming than Southern Buddhism; it aims to develop individual perfections rather than to extinguish the self in otherworldly bliss. Mahayanists do not deny doctrines of the Southern Canon so much as construe them as the Buddha's way to help people who are not yet ready to appreciate higher truths. In effect, they urge us to look at what the Buddha did as well as what he said. The Buddha himself exemplifies the ideal of the *bodhisattva*, someone who seeks the enlightenment of all. The Buddha did not simply disappear into Nirvana; he spent many years preaching to help others attain the enlightenment that he had achieved.

The six perfections the *bodhisattva* embodies are (1) charity, (2) good moral character (which amounts to concern for others rather than oneself), (3) patience (which involves peace in the face of anger or desire), (4) energy or vigor (for striving for the good), (5) deep concentration, and (6) wisdom.

The *bodhisattva*, that is, is generous, giving to others not just material goods but spiritual gifts that help them toward enlightenment. The benefits of the gift bounce back on the giver, who becomes more deserving of enlightenment as a result of his or her generosity.

The *bodhisattva* concentrates on knowing and helping others. He or she is not in it for the money, or fame, or attention, or gratitude, or respect. In fact the *bodhisattva* has no need of any of these. The *bodhisattva* keeps his or her eyes on the prize of enlightenment without being distracted. But the perfection of morality is more than single-mindedness. The *bodhisattva* is fully compassionate, caring deeply for others. The disciples and *pratyekabuddhas* seek their own enlightenment. They want to eliminate their own suffering. To the extent that you share that perspective and have similar thoughts, you seek your own good rather than that of others. The disciples and *pratyekabuddhas*, in short, are selfish, as is anyone who craves attention, fame, money, respect, or gratitude. The *bodhisattva* is unselfish, desiring the good of others as much as his or her own good.

The *bodhisattva* works tirelessly for the enlightenment of others, thus keeping to the Eightfold Path, which requires right effort. This requires being as steady as an ox, working constantly to overcome desire and inclination.

This reflects another step on the Eightfold Path: right mindfulness. Thought and action are intimately linked; you cannot eliminate selfish desire in your behavior without overcoming it mentally. Only by thinking correctly can you hope to act correctly and escape suffering. The *bodhisattva* has a special temptation over and above those that afflict the rest of us; he or she can choose Nirvana for him- or herself over enlightenment for others. So, anyone who would be a *bodhisattva* must guard especially carefully against "*pratyekabuddha*-thought," that is, his or her own desire for enlightenment.

This relates to the final step on the Eightfold Path, right concentration. The person who has this perfection is enlightened; he or she understands the essential unity between mind and world. He or she has seen through the illusion of a separate ego, recognizing that there is no self. To desire his or her own bliss apart from the bliss of everyone is to fall into the trap of thinking that there is a separate self. The only way to achieve true liberation is to achieve liberation for everyone. These virtues entail others. Anyone who exhibits the six perfections places the good of others above his or her own good. Consequently, the *bodhisattva* is also friendly, compassionate, sympathetic, and impartial, taking joy in the joy of others. In short, the *bodhisattva* is thoroughly altruistic.

How can the *bodhisattva* seek the enlightenment of all without seeking his or her own Nirvana? The key is concentration. The *bodhisattva* remains directed toward others, seeking the highest good for them while transcending his own desires. He seeks these things for others, but "he does not relish them, is not captivated by them." In short, the *bodhisattva* seeks Nirvana only insofar as he is included in "all beings"; he detaches himself from all personal desire.

The Mahayana wisdom literature thus puts forward a conception of virtue that, while distinctly Buddhist, resembles Christian virtues in many ways. The *bodhisattva* sacrifices the quest for his own good to seek the good of others.

The Theravada Buddhist, however, has a response to this ideal. One could argue that the ethical ideal of the *bodhisattva* undermines itself: If the *bodhisattva* helps others toward Nirvana, he or she in effect helps them to become *arhats*, not *bodhisattvas*. So the good *bodhisattva* will teach Theravada, not Mahayana, Buddhism.

From a Mahayana perspective, this response falls into a trap. To achieve enlightenment, one must eliminate cravings—selfish desires—including the desire for Nirvana. The best way to lead people to enlightenment, therefore, is to teach them the *bodhisattva* ideal. Teaching them to be *arhats* encourages them to subjugate most desires to a desire for Nirvana, not to eliminate desire itself.

1.5.1 From *The Lankavatara Sutra*

Chapter XI: Bodhisattvahood and Its Stages

Then said Mahamati to the Blessed One: Will you tell us now about the disciples who are Bodhisattvas?

The Blessed One replied: The Bodhisattvas are those earnest disciples who are enlightened by reason of their efforts to attain self-realisation of Noble Wisdom and who have taken upon themselves the task to enlighten others. They have gained a clear understanding of the truth that

Source: From *The Lankavatara Sutra*. Translated by D. T. Suzuki and D. Goddard. Edited by Dwight Goddard, *The Buddhist Bible*. Boston: Beacon Press, 1938.

all things are empty, unborn, and of a *maya*-like [illusory] nature; they have ceased from viewing things discriminatively and from considering them in their relations; they thoroughly understand the truth of twofold egolessness and have adjusted themselves to it with patient acceptance; they have attained a definite realisation of imagelessness; and they are abiding in the perfect knowledge that they have gained by self-realisation of Noble Wisdom.

Well stamped by the seal of "Suchness" they entered upon the first of the Bodhisattva stages. The first stage is called the stage of joy. Entering this stage is like passing out of the glare and shadows into a realm of "no shadows"; it is like passing out of the noise and tumult of the crowded city into the quietness of solitude. The Bodhisattva feels within himself the awakening of a great heart of compassion and he utters his ten original vows: To honor and serve all Buddhas; to spread the knowledge and practice of the Dharma; to welcome all coming Buddhas; to practise the six Paramitas [perfections]; to persuade all beings to embrace the Dharma; to attain a perfect understanding of the universe; to attain a perfect understanding of tile mutuality of all beings; to attain perfect self-realisation of the oneness of all the Buddhas and Tathagatas [ones who have become *that*, i.e., are fully self-realised] in self-nature, purpose and resources; to become acquainted with all skillful means for the carrying out of these vows for the emancipation of all beings; to realise supreme enlightenment through the perfect self-realisation of Noble Wisdom, ascending the stages and entering Tathagatahood [complete self-realisation].

In the spirit of these vows the Bodhisattva gradually ascends the stages to the sixth. All earnest disciples, masters and Arhats have ascended thus far, but being enchanted by the bliss of the Samadhis [high levels of meditation that break down the distinction between subject and object] and not being supported by the powers of the Buddhas, they pass to their Nirvana. The same fate would befall the Bodhisattvas except for the sustaining power of the Buddhas, by that they are enabled to refuse to enter Nirvana until all beings can enter Nirvana with them. The Tathagatas point out to them the virtues of Buddahood which are beyond the conception of the intellectual mind, and they encourage and strengthen the Bodhisattvas not to give in to the enchantment of the bliss of the Samadhis, but to press on to further advancement along the stages. If the Bodhisattvas had entered Nirvana at this stage, and they would have done so without the sustaining power of the Buddhas, there would have been the cessation of all things and the family of the Tathagatas would have become extinct.

Strengthened by the new strength that comes to them from the Buddhas and with the more perfect insight that is theirs by reason of their advance in self-realisation of Noble Wisdom, they reexamine the nature of the mind system, the egolessness of personality, and the part that grasping and attachment and habit energy play in the unfolding drama of life; they reexamine the illusions of the fourfold logical analysis, and the various elements that enter into enlightenment and self-realisation, and, in the thrill of their new powers of self-mastery, the Bodhisattvas enter upon the seventh stage of Far-going.

Supported by the sustaining power of the Buddhas, the Bodhisattvas at this stage enter into the bliss of the Samadhi of perfect tranquillisation. Owing to their original vows they are transported by emotions of love and compassion as they become aware of the part they are to perform in the carrying out of their vows for the emancipation of all beings. Thus they do not enter into Nirvana, but, in truth, they too are already in Nirvana because in their emotions of love and compassion there is no rising of discrimination; henceforth, with them, discrimination no more takes place. Because of Transcendental Intelligence only one conception is present—the promotion of the realisation of Noble Wisdom. Their insight issues from the Womb of Tathagatahood and they enter into their task with spontaneity and radiancy because it is of the self-nature of Noble Wisdom. This is called the Bodhisattva's

Nirvana—the losing oneself in the bliss of perfect self-yielding. This is the seventh stage, the stage of Far-going.

The eighth stage is the stage of No Recession. Up to this stage, because of the defilements upon the face of Universal Mind caused by the accumulation of habit energy since beginningless time, the mind system and all that pertains to it has been evolved and sustained. The mind system functioned by the discriminations of an external and objective world to which it became attached and by which it was perpetuated. But with the Bodhisattva's attainment of the eighth stage there comes the "turning-about" within his deepest consciousness from self-centered egoism to universal compassion for all beings, by which he attains perfect self-realisation of Noble Wisdom. There is an instant cessation of the delusive activities of the whole mind system; the dancing of the waves of habit energy on the face of Universal Mind are forever stilled, revealing its own inherent quietness and solitude, the inconceivable Oneness of the Womb of Tathagatahood.

Henceforth there is no more looking outward upon an external world by senses and sense minds, nor a discrimination of particularised concepts and ideas and propositions by an intellectual mind, no more grasping, nor attachment, nor pride of egoism, nor habit energy. Henceforth there is only the inner experience of Noble Wisdom which has been attained by entering into its perfect Oneness.

Thus establishing himself at the eighth stage of No Recession, the Bodhisattva enters into the bliss of the ten Samadhis, but avoiding the path of the disciples and masters who yielded themselves up to their entrancing bliss and who passed to their Nirvanas, and supported by his vows and the Transcendental Intelligence which now is his and being sustained by the power of the Buddhas, he enters upon the higher paths that lead to Tathagatahood. He passes through the bliss of the Samadhis to assume the transformation body of a Tathagata that through him all beings may be emancipated. Mahamati, if there had been no Tathagata Womb and no Divine Mind, then there would have been no rising and disappearance of the aggregates that make up personality and its external world, no rising and disappearance of ignorant people nor holy people, and no task for Bodhisattvas; therefore, while walking in the path of self-realisation and entering into the enjoyments of the Samadhis, you must never abandon working hard for the emancipation of all beings and your self-yielding love will never be in vain. To philosophers the conception of Tathagata Womb seems devoid of purity and soiled by these external manifestations, but it is not so understood by the Tathagatas—to them it is not a proposition of philosophy but is an intuitive experience as real as though it was an amalaka fruit held in the palm of the hand.

With the cessation of the mind system and all its evolving discriminations, there is cessation of all strain and effort. It is like a man in a dream who imagines he is crossing a river and who exerts himself to the utmost to do so, who is suddenly awakened. Being awake, he thinks: "Is this real or is it unreal?" Being now enlightened, he knows that it is neither real nor unreal. Thus when the Bodhisattva arrives at the eighth stage, he is able to see all things truthfully and, more than that, he is able to thoroughly understand the significance of all the dreamlike things of his life as to how they came to pass and as to how they pass away. Ever since beginningless time the mind system has perceived multiplicities of forms and conditions and ideas which the thinking mind has discriminated and the empirical mind has experienced and grasped and clung to. From this has risen habit energy that by its accumulation has conditioned the illusions of existence and nonexistence, individuality and generality, and has thus perpetuated the dream state of false imagination. But now, to the Bodhisattvas of the eighth stage, life is past and is remembered as it truly was—a passing dream.

As long as the Bodhisattva had not passed the seventh stage, even though he had attained an intuitive understanding of the true meaning of life and its *maya*-like nature, and as to how the mind carried on its discriminations and attachments, yet, nevertheless, the cherishing of the notions of these things had continued, and, although he no longer experienced within himself any ardent desire for things nor any impulse to grasp them, yet, nevertheless, the notions concerning them persisted and perfumed his efforts to practise the teachings of the Buddhas and to labor for the emancipation of all beings. Now, in the eighth stage, even the notions have passed away, and all effort and striving is seen to be unnecessary. The Bodhisattva's Nirvana is perfect tranquillisation, but it is not extinction nor inertness; while there is an entire absence of discrimination and purpose, there is the freedom and spontaneity of potentiality that has come with the attainment and patient acceptance of the truths of egolessness and imagelessness. Here is perfect solitude, undisturbed by any gradation or continuous succession, but radiant with the potency and freedom of its self-nature, which is the self-nature of Noble Wisdom, blissfully peaceful with the serenity of Perfect Love.

Entering upon the eighth stage, with the turning about at the deepest seat of consciousness, the Bodhisattva will become conscious that he has received the second kind of Transcendental Body (***manomayakaya***). The transition from mortal body to Transcendental Body has nothing to do with mortal death, for the old body continues to function and the old mind serves the needs of the old body, but now it is free from the control of mortal mind. There has been an inconceivable transformation death by which the false imagination of his particularised individual personality has been transcended by a realisation of his oneness with the universalised mind of Tathagatahood, from which realisation there will be no recession. With that realisation he finds himself amply endowed with all the Tathagata's powers, psychic faculties, and self-mastery, and, just as the good earth is the support of all beings in the world of desire (***karma-dhatu***), so the Tathagatas become the support of all beings in the Transcendental World of No Form.

The first seven of the Bodhisattva stages were in the realm of mind and the eighth, while transcending mind, was still in touch with it; but in the ninth stage of Transcendental Intelligence, by reason of his perfect intelligence and insight into the imagelessness of Divine Mind which he had attained by self-realisation of Noble Wisdom, he is in the realm of Tathagatahood. Gradually the Bodhisattva will realise his Tathagata nature and the possession of all its powers and psychic faculties, self-mastery, loving compassion, and skillful means, and by means of them will enter into all the Buddha lands. Making use of these new powers, the Bodhisattva will assume various transformation bodies and personalities for the sake of benefiting others. Just as in the former mental life, imagination had risen from relative knowledge, so now skillful means rise spontaneously from Transcendental Intelligence. It is like the magical gem that reflects instantaneously appropriate responses to one's wishes. The Bodhisattva passes over to all the assemblages of the Buddhas and listens to them as they discourse on the dreamlike nature of all things and concerning the truths that transcend all notions of being and nonbeing, that have no relation to birth and death, nor to eternality nor extinction. Thus facing the Tathagatas as they discourse on Noble Wisdom that is far beyond the mental capacity of disciples and masters, he will attain a hundred thousand Samadhis, indeed, a hundred thousand nyutas of kotis of Samadhis, and in the spirit of these Samadhis he will instantly pass from one Buddha land to another, paying homage to all the Buddhas, being born into all the celestial mansions, manifesting Buddha bodies, and himself discoursing on the Triple Treasure to lesser Bodhisattvas that they too may partake of the fruits of self-realisation of Noble Wisdom.

Thus passing beyond the last stage of Bodhisattvahood, he becomes a Tathagata himself, endowed with all the freedom of the Dharmakaya [embodiment of truth]. The tenth stage belongs to the Tathagatas. Here the Bodhisattva will find himself seated upon a lotuslike throne in a splendid jewel-adorned palace and surrounded by Bodhisattvas of equal rank. Buddhas from all the Buddha lands will gather about him and with their pure and fragrant hands resting on his forehead will give him ordination and recognition as one of themselves. Then they will assign him a Buddha land that he may possess and perfect as his own.

The tenth stage is called the Great Truth Cloud, inconceivable, inscrutable. Only the Tathagatas can realise its perfect Imagelessness and Oneness and Solitude. It is Mahesvara, the Radiant Land, the Pure Land, the Land of Far Distances; surrounding and surpassing the lesser worlds of form and desire (*karma-dhatu*), in which the Bodhisattva will find himself at-one-ment. Its rays of Noble Wisdom, which is the self-nature of the Tathagatas, many-colored, entrancing, auspicious, are transforming the triple world as other worlds have been transformed in the past, and still other worlds will be transformed in the future. But in the Perfect Oneness of Noble Wisdom there is no gradation nor succession nor effort. The tenth stage is the first, the first is the eighth, the eighth is the fifth, the fifth is the seventh: What gradation can there be where perfect Imagelessness and Oneness prevail? And what is the reality of Noble Wisdom? It is the ineffable potency of the Dharmakaya; it has no bounds nor limits; it surpasses all the Buddha lands, and pervades the Akanistha [highest plane of existence] and the heavenly mansions of the Tushita [the heaven where the Buddha resided before being born].

1.6 JAINISM

Various ancient philosophers, both in and beyond the West, anticipated features of utilitarianism. The earliest appeal to pain as a source of moral value occurs in Jainism, one of the ancient philosophies of India. Like other early Indian philosophies, Jainism proclaims a mystical, personal highest good. But the Jain is the most renowned for its ethical commitment to the value of life. Jains are vegetarians; Jain monks have been known to wear masks so that their breathing will not cause injury to microscopic insects. Noninjury, *ahimsa*, an ideal popularized in modern times by Mahatma Gandhi, was propagated in ancient and classical India foremost by Jains.

Like Buddhist scripture, the Jain canon is immense. The following selection, from the *Acaranga Sutra*, concerns *ahimsa* and its justification. Here the practice is justified not simply because it is conducive to one's own good or because it is the teaching of Mahavira ("the Revered One," 599–527 BCE), the founder of Jainism, but because all souls are equally valuable. If I recognize that injury to me is painful for me, I must conclude that injury to others is similarly painful for them. Their souls are as valuable as my own; their pain counts as much as my pain. Therefore, I must refrain from committing injury to others at all times.

Noninjury is for everyone. But, in the details of ethical precepts, monks and laypersons have different duties. The former practice not only asceticism but also prescribed "reflections"—e.g., on the impermanence of things, human helplessness, and the difficulty of enlightenment. Laypeople, "householders," desist from dishonest business practices, lying, illicit sexual relations, and so on, but do not aspire to "liberation" in this lifetime. (Jainism, like Buddhism and other early Indian enlightenment theories, asserts that people are reborn or reincarnated. Jains believe that only the enlightened are liberated, i.e., not reborn.)

The key to ethical living for all, however, is overcoming desire. What leads people to injure other living beings intentionally? Desire—the desire for rich food, for sensual pleasure, for wealth, for self-preservation.

Jains typically maintain that eating vegetables is permissible, but eating animal flesh is not. Why? What is the difference between a carrot and a chicken? A carrot is not sentient; it has no consciousness. It cannot feel pain. A chicken, however, is aware of its surroundings and can feel pain. That is why it, unlike the carrot, merits moral consideration and why it must not be injured. The *Acaranga Sutra* argues that injuring even plants is wrong, though it recognizes that plants have a life cycle and that some human use of plants is acceptable.

Many people draw the line between humans and other animals, not between animals and vegetables or inanimate matter, on the grounds that humans are rational. They recoil at murder but find butchery of animals morally acceptable. From the Jain point of view, however, that is hard to justify. As English philosopher Jeremy Bentham (1748–1832) argues,

> What else is it that should trace the insuperable line? Is it the faculty of reason, or perhaps the faculty of discourse? But a full-grown horse or dog is beyond comparison a more rational, as well as a more conversable animal than an infant of a day or a week or even a month, old. But suppose they were otherwise, what would it avail? The question is not, Can they reason? nor Can they talk? but, Can they suffer?

The capacity for suffering is what gives something a right to moral consideration. If something can suffer, we must take its happiness or unhappiness or, more generally, its welfare, its interests into account. It follows, Jains assert, that injuring any sentient creature is morally wrong.

The Jain argument for noninjury is straightforward. We find suffering painful; we thus have every reason to believe that other sentient creatures find it painful. What makes it wrong to injure another human being? The suffering that results, Jains answer. But then the suffering resulting from injuring any sentient being makes that wrong, too, and for the same reason. All things that are like ourselves in being capable of suffering deserve to be treated with respect. This is the Jain version of what Christians call the Golden Rule: "Do not do unto another what you would not want done to yourself."

Jainism thus sees a creature's ability to suffer, to feel pain, as giving it the right to moral consideration. Alternatively, it is in virtue of being a self that another is due the same respect we naturally and instinctively afford to ourselves. Being a self sets up a moral constraint; we should not treat others in just any old way. What makes an action wrong is the unhappiness it causes whether ours or another's.

The doctrine of noninjury is negative: Do not injure any sentient creature. The doctrine of overcoming desire is also negative. There is no positive obligation to do anything to increase the happiness of one's fellow creatures. Jainism thus allows a great deal of freedom. But Jainism's focus on unhappiness permits no exceptions, no compromises; injuring sentient beings is wrong, period.

1.6.1 From the *Acaranga Sutra*

Lecture One

Second Lesson

The (living) world is afflicted, miserable, difficult to instruct, and without discrimination. In this world full of pain, suffering by their different acts, see the benighted ones cause great pain. See! there are beings individually embodied. See! there are men who control themselves, (whilst others only) pretend to be houseless (i.e., monks, such as the Bauddhas, whose conduct differs not from that of householders), because one destroys this (earth body) by bad and injurious doings, and many other beings, besides, which he hurts by means of earth, through his doing acts relating to earth. About this the Revered One has taught the truth: for the sake of the splendour, honour, and glory of this life, for the sake of birth, death, and final liberation, for the removal of pain, man acts sinfully towards earth, or causes others to act so, or allows others to act so. This deprives him of happiness and perfect wisdom. About this he is informed when he has understood or heard, either from the Revered One or from the monks, the faith to be coveted. There are some who, of a truth, know this (i.e., injuring) to be the bondage, the delusion, the death, the hell. For this a man is longing when he destroys this (earth body) by bad, injurious doings, and many other beings, besides, which he hurts by means of earth, through his doing acts relating to earth. Thus I say. As somebody may cut or strike a blind man (who cannot see the wound), as somebody may cut or strike the foot, the ankle, the knee, the thigh, the hip, the navel, the belly, the flank, the back, the bosom, the heart, the breast, the neck, the arm, the finger, the nail, the eye, the brow, the forehead, the head, as some kill (openly), as some extirpate (secretly), (thus the earth bodies are cut, struck, and killed though their feeling is not manifest).

He who injures these (earth bodies) does not comprehend and renounce the sinful acts; he who does not injure these comprehends and renounces the sinful acts. Knowing them, a wise man should not act sinfully towards earth, nor cause others to act so, nor allow others to act so. He who knows these causes of sin relating to earth, is called a reward-knowing sage. Thus I say.

Sixth Lesson

Thus I say: There are beings called the animate, viz. those who are produced 1. from eggs (birds, etc.), 2. from a fetus (as elephants, etc.), 3. from a fetus with an enveloping membrane (as cows, buffaloes, etc.), 4. from fluids (as worms, etc.), 5. from sweat (as bugs, lice, etc.), 6. by coagulation (as locusts, ants, etc.), 7. from sprouts (as butterflies, wagtails, etc.), 8. by regeneration (men, gods, hell-beings). This is called the Samsara [the cycle of birth and death] for the slow, for the ignorant. Having well considered it, having well looked at it, I say thus: all beings, those with two, three, four senses, plants, those with five senses, and the rest of creation, (experience) individually pleasure or displeasure, pain, great terror, and unhappiness. Beings are filled with alarm from all directions and in all directions. See! there the benighted ones cause great pain. See! there are beings individually embodied.

See! there are men who control themselves; others pretend only to be houseless, for one destroys this (body of an animal) by bad and injurious doings, and many other beings, besides,

---

Source: From the *Acaranga Sutra*, in *Sacred Books of the East*, vol. 22: *Jaina Sutras* Part I, translated by Hermann Jacobi (1884).

which he hurts by means of animals, through his doing acts relating to animals. About this the Revered One has taught the truth: for the sake of the splendour, honour, and glory of this life, for the sake of birth, death, and final liberation, for the removal of pain, man acts sinfully towards animals, or causes others to act so, or allows others to act so. This deprives him of happiness and perfect wisdom. About this he is informed, when he has understood, or heard from the Revered One or from the monks, the faith to be coveted. There are some who, of a truth, know this (i.e., injuring) to be the bondage, the delusion, the death, the hell. For this a man is longing, when he injures this (body of an animal) by bad and injurious doings, and many other beings, besides, which he hurts by means of animals, through acts relating to animals. Thus I say.

Some slay (animals) for sacrificial purposes, some kill (animals) for the sake of their skin, some kill (them) for the sake of their flesh, some kill them for the sake of their blood; thus for the sake of their heart, their bile, the feathers of their tail, their tail, their big or small horns, their teeth, their tusks, their nails, their sinews, their bones; with a purpose or without a purpose. Some kill animals because they have been wounded by them, or are wounded, or will be wounded.

He who injures these (animals) does not comprehend and renounce the sinful acts; he who does not injure these, comprehends and renounces the sinful acts. Knowing them, a wise man should not act sinfully towards animals, nor cause others to act so, nor allow others to act so. He who knows these causes of sin relating to animals, is called a reward-knowing sage. Thus I say.

Lecture Two

Second Lesson

A wise man should remove any aversion (to control); he will be liberated in the proper time. Some, following wrong instruction, turn away (from control). They are dull, wrapped in delusion. While they imitate the life of monks, (saying), "We shall be free from attachment," they enjoy the pleasures that offer themselves. Through wrong instruction the (would-be) sages trouble themselves (for pleasures); thus they sink deeper and deeper in delusion, (and cannot get) to this nor to the opposite shore. Those who are freed (from attachment to the world and its pleasures) reach the opposite shore. Subduing desire by desirelessness, he does not enjoy the pleasures that offer themselves. Desireless, giving up the world, and ceasing to act, he knows, and sees, and has no wishes because of his discernment; he is called houseless.

(But on the contrary) he suffers day and night, works in the right and the wrong time, desires wealth and treasures, commits injuries and violent acts, again and again directs his mind upon these injurious doings; for his own sake, to support or to be supported by his relations, friends, the ancestors, gods, the king, thieves, guests, paupers, Sramanas [wandering monks].

Thus violence is done by these various acts, deliberately, out of fear, because they think "it is for the expiation of sins" or for some other hope. Knowing this, a wise man should neither himself commit violence by such acts, nor order others to commit violence by such acts, nor consent to the violence done by somebody else.

This road (to happiness) has been declared by the noble ones, that a clever man should not be defiled (by sin). Thus I say.

Third Lesson

"Frequently (I have been born) in a high family, frequently in a low one; I am not mean, nor noble, nor do I desire (social preferment)." Thus reflecting, who would brag about his family or about his glory, or for what should he long?

Therefore a wise man should neither be glad nor angry (about his lot): you shouldst know and consider the happiness of living creatures. Carefully conducting himself, he should mind this: blindness, deafness, dumbness, one-eyedness, hunchbackedness, blackness, variety of colour (he will always experience); because of his carelessness he is born in many births, he experiences various feelings.

Not enlightened (about the cause of these ills) he is afflicted (by them), always turns round (in the whirl of) birth and death. Life is dear to many who own fields and houses. Having acquired dyed and coloured (clothes), jewels, ear-rings, gold, and women, they become attached to these things. And a fool who longs for life, and worldly-minded, laments that (for these worldly goods) penance, self-restraint, and control do not avail, will ignorantly come to grief.

Those who are of a steady conduct do not desire this (wealth). Knowing birth and death, one should firmly walk the path (i.e., right conduct), (and not wait for old age to commence a religious life).

For there is nothing inaccessible for death. All beings are fond of life, like pleasure, hate pain, shun destruction, like life, long to live. To all life is dear.

Having acquired it (i.e., wealth), employing bipeds and quadrupeds, gathering riches in the three ways, whatever his portion will be, small or great, he will desire to enjoy it. Then at one time, his manifold savings are a large treasure. Then at another time, his heirs divide it, or those who are without a living steal it, or the king takes it away, or it is ruined in some way or other, or it is consumed by the conflagration of the house. Thus a fool doing cruel deeds which benefit another will ignorantly come thereby to grief.

This certainly has been declared by the sage. They do not cross the flood, nor can they cross it; they do not go to the next shore, nor can they go to it; they do not go to the opposite shore, nor can they go to it.

And though hearing the doctrine, he does not stand in the right place; but the clever one who adopts the true (faith), stands in the right place (i.e., control).

He who sees by himself, needs no instruction. But the miserable, afflicted fool who delights in pleasures, and whose miseries do not cease, is turned round in the whirl of pains. Thus I say.

Lecture Four

First Lesson

The Arhats [saints] and Bhagavats [holy lords] of the past, present, and future all say thus, speak thus, declare thus, explain thus: all breathing, existing, living, sentient creatures should not be slain, nor treated with violence, nor abused, nor tormented, nor driven away.

This is the pure, unchangeable, eternal law, which the clever ones, who understand the world, have declared: among the zealous and the not zealous, among the faithful and the not faithful, among the not cruel and the cruel, among those who have worldly weakness and those who have not, among those who like social bonds and those who do not: "that is the truth, that is so, that is proclaimed in this (creed)."

Having adopted (the law), one should not hide it, nor forsake it. Correctly understanding the law, one should arrive at indifference for the impressions of the senses, and "not act on the motives of the world." "He who is not of this mind, how should he come to the other?"

What has been said here, has been seen (by the omniscient ones), heard (by the believers), acknowledged (by the faithful), and thoroughly understood by them. Those who acquiesce and indulge (in worldly pleasures) are born again and again. "Day and night exerting thyself, steadfast," always having ready wisdom, perceive that the careless (stand) outside (of salvation); if careful, you will always conquer. Thus I say.

Lecture Five

From *Fifth Lesson*

As it would be to you, so it is with him whom you intend to kill. As it would be to you, so it is with him whom you intend to tyrannise over. As it would be to you, so it is with him whom you intend to torment. In the same way (it is with him) whom you intend to punish and to drive away. The righteous man who lives up to these sentiments does therefore neither kill nor cause others to kill (living beings). He should not intentionally cause the same punishment for himself.

The self is the knower (or experiencer), and the knower is the self. That through which one knows is the self. With regard to this (to know) it (the self) is established. Such is he who maintains the right doctrine of self. This subject has truly been explained. Thus I say.

1.7 THE SKEPTICISM AND MATERIALISM OF CHARVAKA

Jainism is not the only classical Indian source of thinking about the moral significance of happiness. The most striking opposition to the religious inspiration for various Jain, Hindu, and Buddhist views comes from a school known as Charvaka, also called *lokayata*, a term meaning "those attached to the ways of the world." Charvaka philosophers are materialists; they believe that physical matter is the only reality. They are also empiricists, holding that we can know only what we perceive through our senses. According to the Charvakas, we cannot assert the validity of any inferences we make about what we perceive. Because they reject inference, the Charvakas are commonly referred to as skeptics.

By arguing that reasoning cannot establish anything—a position that their opponents ridicule as self-refuting!—the Charvakas attack ideas of an immortal soul, rebirth, God, and a mystical enlightenment or liberation. That is to say, by showing that inference is unreliable, whatever the topic, these skeptics seek to strip away all excesses of belief beyond the simple facts of pleasure, pain, and the body. The soul must be identified with the body. And the body exists in an inexplicable material world. The good of the soul must therefore be identified with the good of the body—that is, pleasure.

Consequently, the only values that apply in this world are those arising from pleasure and pain. At least, those are the only values we could possibly know anything about. We can know only what we can immediately sense, and the only things we immediately sense that generate value are pleasure and pain. The Charvakas are thus hedonists: Pleasure and pain in this world are the only possible sources of value.

Opponents retort that the Charvaka attack is self-defeating, for it utilizes the very processes of thinking that it aims to show invalid. The doctrine itself, that is, rests on reasoning. That our only goal is human pleasure is not itself something we perceive. The Charvaka response is that the burden of proof is on the other side and that no other goal can be justified. In any case, the Charvakas are the first philosophers to present something like utilitarianism as the only ethical system compatible with materialism (the view that everything that exists is material) and empiricism (the view that all knowledge comes from experience). Many later utilitarians have similar motivations. They are empiricists who want ethical knowledge to rest on firm foundations. Pleasure and pain establish those foundations, for we undoubtedly experience them.

1.7.1 From *Sarva-Darsana-Samgraha*

The efforts of Charvaka are indeed hard to eradicate, for the majority of living beings endorse the current refrain—

While life is yours live joyously;
No one can avoid Death's searching eye:
When this body of ours is burnt,
How can it ever return again?

In accordance with the dictates of policy and enjoyment, the mass of men consider wealth and satisfaction of desire the only ends of man. They deny the existence of any object belonging to a future world and follow only the doctrine of Charvaka. Hence another name for that school is *Lokayata*—a name well accordant with the thing signified [that only the material world, *loka*, exists].

2. The only end of man is enjoyment produced by sensual pleasures. Nor may you say that such cannot be called the end of man as they are always mixed with some kind of pain, because it is our wisdom to enjoy the pure pleasure as far as we can, and to avoid the pain which inevitably accompanies it. Thus the man who desires fish takes the fish with their scales and bones, and having eaten the parts he wants, desists. Or the man who desires rice takes the rice, straw and all, and, having taken that which he wants, desists. It is not therefore for us, through a fear of pain, to reject the pleasure which our nature instinctively recognizes as congenial. Men do not refrain from sowing rice because there happen to be wild animals to devour it; nor do they refuse to set the cooking pots on the fire because there happen to be beggars to pester us for a share of the contents.

If any one were so timid as to forsake a visible pleasure, he would indeed be foolish like a beast, as has been said by the poet—

> That the pleasure arising to man from contact with sensible objects, is to be relinquished because accompanied by pain—such is the reasoning of fools. The kernels of the paddy, rich with finest white grains, what man, seeking his own true interest, would fling them away because of a covering of husk and dust?

4. Hence it follows that there is no other hell than the mundane pain produced by purely mundane causes, such as thorns and so forth. The only supreme being is the earthly monarch whose existence is proved by all the world's eyesight. And the only liberation is the dissolution of the body. By holding the doctrine that the soul is identical with the body, such phrases as "I am thin," or "I am black," are at once intelligible as the body's attributes of thinness or blackness. In a similar way, self-consciousness will reside in the same subject.

5. In this school the four elements, earth, fire, water, and air, are the original principles. From these alone, when transformed into the body, intelligence is produced—just as the intoxicating power of some herbs is developed from the mixing of certain ingredients. When the body is destroyed, intelligence at once perishes also. They quote the Vedic text for this:

Springing forth from these elements itself
solid knowledge is destroyed
when they are destroyed—
after death no intelligence remains.

Therefore the soul is only the body distinguished by the attribute of intelligence, since there is no evidence for any self distinct from the body. Therefore the existence of such a separate self cannot be proved, because this school holds that perception is the only source of knowledge and does not allow inference as an alternative source.

Source: Adapted from *Sarva-Darsana-Samgraha* by Madhava Acharya. Translated by E. B. Cowell and A. E. Gough. London: Kegan Paul, Trench, and Trubner, 1914.

CHAPTER 2

Chinese Ethics

"From the root grows the Way"

Ancient China consisted of a variety of small states that frequently fought one another. The Warring States period, as it is now known, lasted for more than 250 years, ending in 221 BCE with China's unification. But it witnessed the development of two of the world's most important philosophical systems—Confucianism and Daoism—as well as religious traditions that spring from them.

2.1 THE VIRTUE ETHICS OF CONFUCIUS

Kong Fuzi (K'ung Fu-Tzu)—Grand Master Kong, or, as he became known in the West, Confucius (551–479 BCE)—was a contemporary of Lao Tzu and the Buddha. Born into a poor family in Lu (now Shandong Province in northeastern China), he was completely self-educated. His father died when he was 3. At 19, he married, and he had a son and two daughters. He got a government job, first managing a state granary and then managing herds of cattle and sheep. But at 22 he quit his job and opened up a school. He taught principles of proper living and good government, eventually earning the attention of the Duke of Lu. Living in a time of great political and intellectual upheaval, he was convinced that his teachings could restore order and prosperity. But the chance to put his ideas into practice eluded him. Nevertheless, he rose from poverty and obscurity to become the most influential and revered person in the history of China. For a millennium the Chinese civil service examinations were based on his teachings.

Confucius says much about the superior person (*junzi*, literally, "child of a ruler," but, in Confucius, not one of noble birth but rather one of noble character). The superior person tries to understand the world with an open mind. This understanding can be gained through reflection, though it also requires a thorough knowledge of things in general as well as respect for the traditional social rules that define proper behavior. The superior person seeks clarity, of perception, of thought, and of speech. This requires a focus on virtue—on what we ought to be and do—as well as remaining open to higher laws, principles, and values, "the ordinances of heaven." But we must understand the force of words and understand the world around us to put virtue and general principles into practice. We must "attend to the root of things," seeking true understanding, not merely the accumulation of facts. Only when we understand the underlying principles of things can we understand how we ourselves should act. To do the right thing, we need to think things through, understanding the situation and understanding why we are to act that way.

Confucius gives us sayings rather than dialogues or arguments. The theme of examining oneself runs throughout. We see few examples of the process of examination. Sometimes, however, we glimpse the flavor of what Confucius has in mind. Someone asks about a principle of repaying injury with kindness—"turning the other cheek," in effect. Confucius responds that this principle will erase the difference between the consequences of kindness and injury. Someone hurts you; you respond by being kind. Someone is kind to you; you respond by being kind. You draw no distinctions, and the one who injures suffers no consequences. This reflects a common pattern. Confucius considers a principle and draws out its consequences.

Confucius presents an ethics of virtue, almost 200 years before Aristotle, that has much in common with Aristotle's theory. Nevertheless, Confucius presents a different list of virtues, which has a different structure. Confucian doctrine is sometimes summarized as ethical humanism. Like Aristotle, Confucius begins with the question "What kind of person should I try to become?" and centers his answer on the concept of virtue (*ren*).

Confucius contrasts selfishness, a desire for personal gain, with righteousness (*i* or *yi*), a desire to do what is right just because it is right. The superior person does the right thing for the right reason—because it is the right thing to do—not in order to get something else. In other words, the superior person treats the good as intrinsically valuable.

In developing an ethics of character, Confucius elaborates a system of virtues around "one thread" (4:15, 15:2): "to be true to the principles of our nature and to exercise them benevolently toward others." It may sound as if that one thread comprises two different strands. For Confucius, however, thought and action are intimately linked; being true to the principles of our nature and exercising them in helping others come to the same thing. Because *ren*, virtue, involves both being true to the principles of our nature and acting benevolently toward others, *ren* has often been translated as "humanity" or "benevolence."

Confucius holds that different virtues pertain to different relationships. There are virtues to be displayed toward other people in general, virtues to be displayed to friends and family, and virtues to exhibit to oneself. All are important, but all rest on the virtues of the self, which are central to virtue in general.

The basic virtues toward others are faithfulness and the five key components of *ren*: seriousness, generosity, sincerity, diligence, and kindness. The chief principle for dealing with other people is *zhong*, reciprocity (sometimes translated "altruism" or "likening to oneself"): "What you do not want done to yourself, do not do to others" (5:11, 12:2,

15:23). This so-called "Silver Rule" is a logically weaker cousin of the Golden Rule: "What you would have others do unto you, do so unto them."

The virtues we have discussed so far apply to dealings with family and friends. But there are also virtues special to those relationships that underlie and override more general obligations. Confucius stresses two: filial piety—obedience, reverence, and service to one's parents and elders—and fraternal submission, service, and trustworthiness to one's equals. These virtues are roots of *ren*. We learn how to treat others by learning how to interact with those closest to us.

Most fundamental of all are the virtues of the self. In this respect Confucius and Socrates surely agree that "the unexamined life is not worth living." Knowledge leads to virtuous thought, which leads to virtuous feelings, which leads in turn to virtuous action.

1. *Knowledge:* The superior person knows the Way (*dao*), the right way to act, but also loves learning; without the love of learning, virtues easily transform into their opposites.
2. *Virtues of Thought:* Sincerity and humility are virtues we exhibit to ourselves. They underlie all other virtues. To us, it sounds odd to speak of being sincere or humble with oneself. But we are insincere with others if we do not mean what we say to them. We are likewise insincere with ourselves if we do not mean what we say to ourselves. Insincerity with oneself, in other words, amounts to self-deception. So sincerity to oneself is a form of self-knowledge, of knowing what one thinks and wants and knows.
3. *Virtues of Feeling:* For Confucius, it is not enough to know the Way; one must also love and delight in the Way. The virtuous person not only does the right thing but wants to do it.
4. *Virtues of Action:* The five basic virtues are those of *ren*. The virtuous person is benevolent, kind, generous, and above all balanced, observing the Mean in all things. But Confucius adds other characteristics: he describes the superior person as careful, slow in speech, mild, at ease, composed, warm, satisfied, earnest, respectful, dignified, majestic, and open minded.

Confucius, like Aristotle, thinks of virtue as a mean between extremes; the properly generous person, for example, gives appropriately, neither too much nor too little, to the right person in the right circumstances. Confucian virtues are means between vices, just as in Aristotle. The disposition to virtue, without knowledge and without propriety, leads to vice.

The five virtues of ren:

Too little	*Right amount*	*Too much*
frivolous	serious	somber
stingy	generous	profligate
insincere	sincere	reckless
lazy	diligent	"workaholic"
mean, indifferent	kind	indulgent

Other Confucian virtues:

Too little	*Right amount*	*Too much*
disrespectful	respectful	bustling
careless	cautious	timid
timid	bold	insubordinate
devious	straightforward	rude
weak	strong	extravagant

As in Aristotle, the superior person is at ease with virtue. Proper conduct becomes habitual. It becomes second nature. The superior person not only has strength of will but also avoids inner conflict, for he or she desires to do what is right.

To become virtuous, in Confucius's view, one must associate with the right people (1:8), examine oneself, and above all act with propriety, the observance of proper rites, ceremonies, and principles. Propriety is a crucial component of virtue, for it establishes character. We train ourselves, developing good habits, by obeying the rules of propriety. To become truly virtuous, propriety must become habitual; we must develop a natural ease with, and even love, the rules of propriety. The word he uses is *li*, which means ceremony, rite, ritual, decorum, propriety, principle, and custom. Most often, Confucius uses it to refer to traditional social rules and practices. The rules of propriety are traditional: They are customary and connect us with the past, embodying the wisdom of generations of people who have faced situations similar to those we face. The rules of propriety are social: They concern relations between people in society and constitute a significant part of the social order. Finally, the rules of propriety are rules or practices: They govern how people should behave in certain circumstances. Many features of propriety arise from particular social relations—of parent to child, for example, or friend to friend—but some, such as the rule of reciprocity, are universal.

2.1.1 Confucius, from *The Analects*

1:1. The Master said, "Isn't it pleasant to learn and to apply what you've learned? Isn't it delightful to have friends coming from far away? Isn't he a person of complete virtue who doesn't get angry that others don't appreciate him?"

1:2. Yu said, "Few filial and fraternal people like to offend their superiors, and nobody who doesn't like to offend superiors likes to stir up rebellion. The superior person attends to the root of things. From the root grows the Way [*dao*]. Filial piety and fraternal submission are the root of benevolence [*ren*]."

1:4. Zeng said, "Every day I examine myself on three points: whether, with others, I may have been unfaithful; whether, with friends, I may have been untrustworthy; whether I may have failed

Source: From Confucius, *The Analects*. Translated by James Legge. The translation has been revised for readability and similarity of style to the Chinese.

to master and practice the instructions of my teacher."

1:6. The Master said, "A youth at home should be filial; abroad, respectful to elders. He should be earnest and truthful. He should overflow with love to all and cultivate the friendship of the good. When he has time and opportunity after doing these things, he should study."

1:7. Zi Xia said, "If someone turns from the love of beauty to a sincere love of virtue; if he can serve his parents with all his strength; if he can serve his prince with his life; if his words to his friends are sincere; although people say he has not learned, I will certainly say that he has."

1:8. The Master said, "A scholar who is not serious will not be venerated, and his learning will not be solid. Hold faithfulness and sincerity as first principles. Have no friends not equal to yourself. When you have faults, do not be afraid to abandon them."

1:12. Yu said, "In practicing propriety, a natural ease is best. This is the excellence of the ancient kings, and in things small and great we follow them. Yet it is not to be observed in all cases. Anyone who knows and manifests such ease must regulate it by propriety."

1:14. The Master said, "A superior person doesn't seek gratification or comfort. He's earnest in what he does; he's careful in speech. He associates with people of principle to set himself right. Such a person truly loves to learn."

2:3. The Master said, "If the people are led by laws and restrained by punishments, they will try to avoid them without any sense of shame. If they are led by virtue and restrained by propriety, they will have a sense of shame and become good."

2:4. At 15, I had my mind bent on learning. At 30, I stood firm. At 40, I had no doubts. At 50, I knew the decrees of Heaven. At 60, my ear obeyed truth. At 70, I could follow what my heart desired without transgressing what was right."

2:5. Meng I asked what filial piety was. The Master said, "Not being disobedient." As Fan Qi was driving him, the Master said, "Mang-sun asked me what filial piety was, and I answered, 'Not being disobedient.'" Fan Qi said, "What did you mean?" The Master replied, "Parents, when alive, should be served according to propriety. When dead, they should be buried according to propriety and sacrificed to according to propriety."

2:10. The Master said, "See what a person does. Mark his motives. Examine his habits. How can anyone conceal his character? How can anyone conceal his character?"

2:13. Zi Kong asked what constituted the superior person. The Master said, "He acts before he speaks, and then speaks as he acts."

2:14. The Master said, "The superior person is open minded and not partisan. The mean person is partisan and not open minded."

2:17. The Master said, "Yu, shall I teach you what knowledge is? When you know something, to maintain that you know it; when you don't know something, to admit that you don't know it—this is knowledge."

2:24. The Master said, "...To see what is right and not do it is cowardice."

4:2. The Master said, "Those without virtue can't abide long in a condition of poverty and hardship—or in a condition of enjoyment. The virtuous are at ease with virtue [*ren*]; the wise desire virtue."

4:3. The Master said, "Only the truly virtuous [*ren*] know what to love or hate in others."

4:7. The Master said, "People's faults often reveal their character. By observing someone's character, you may know him to be virtuous."

4:10. The Master said, "The superior person in the world is not for anything or against anything; he follows what is right."

4:11. The Master said, "The superior person thinks of virtue; the small person thinks of comfort. The superior person thinks of the law; the small person thinks of favors."

4:15. The Master said, "Shen, my doctrine is one thread." Zeng replied, "Yes." The Master went out, and the other disciples asked, "What do his words mean?" Zeng said, "Our Master's doctrine is to be true to the principles of our nature and to exercise them benevolently toward others—this and nothing more."

4:16. The Master said, "The superior person's mind is conversant with righteousness [*yi*]; the inferior person's mind is conversant with gain."

4:17. The Master said, "When we see people of worth, we should think of equaling them; when we see people of a contrary character, we should turn inward and examine ourselves."

5:11. Zi Kong said, "What I don't want others to do to me, I also want not to do to others."

6:18. The Master said, "Those who know the Way aren't equal to those who love it, and those who love it aren't equal to those who delight in it."

6:24. Zai Wu asked, "A benevolent person, told someone is in the well, will go in after him, I suppose." Confucius said, "Why should he? A superior person may be made to go into the well, but not to go down into it. One may impose upon him, but not make a fool of him."

6:25. The Master said, "The superior person studies all learning extensively and restrains himself by propriety. So he doesn't swerve from the Way."

6:27. The Master said, "Perfect is the virtue that accords with the Constant Mean! For a long time, its practice has been rare among the people."

6:28. Zi Kong said, "What would you say about someone who benefits people extensively and helps everyone? May he be called perfectly virtuous [*ren*]?" The Master said, "Why only virtuous? Must he not have the qualities of a sage? Even Yao and Shun [legendary rulers who lived as much as two millennia earlier] weren't like this. Someone of perfect virtue [*ren*], wishing to establish himself, establishes others; wishing to enlarge himself, enlarges others. To be able to judge others by what is right in ourselves is the art of virtue [*ren*]."

7:27. The Master said, "Maybe some act without knowing why. I don't. Hearing much, selecting what is good, and following it, seeing much and remembering it, are the second style of knowledge."

8:2. The Master said, "Respectfulness without propriety becomes laborious bustle. Caution without propriety becomes timidity. Boldness without propriety becomes insubordination; straightforwardness without propriety becomes rudeness."

12:1. Yan Yuan asked about perfect virtue [*ren*]. The Master said, "To subdue oneself and return to propriety is virtue. If a man can subdue himself and return to propriety for one day, all under heaven will ascribe virtue to him. Is the practice of virtue from oneself alone, or does it depend on others?" Yan Yuan said, "I want to ask about these steps." The Master replied, "Don't look at what is contrary to propriety; don't listen to what is contrary to propriety; don't speak what is contrary to propriety; don't make a move that is contrary to propriety."

12:2. Zhong Kong asked about perfect virtue [*ren*]. The Master said, "When you travel, act as if you were receiving a great guest. Employ the people as if you were assisting at a great sacrifice. Don't do to others what you wouldn't want done to yourself. Then no one in the country or in your family will complain about you."

12:9. Duke Ai asked Yu Zo, "Suppose the year is one of scarcity and the government faces a deficit. What is to be done?" Yu Zo replied, "Why not demand from the people a tenth of their income?" "With two tenths there isn't enough," said the Duke. "How could I get by on one tenth?" Yu Zo answered, "If the people have plenty, their ruler will not be needy alone. If the people are needy, their ruler can't enjoy plenty alone."

12:17. Qi Kang asked Confucius about government. He replied, "To govern [*cheng*] is to rectify [*cheng*]. If you lead correctly, who will dare to be incorrect?"

13:3. Zi Lu said, "The ruler of Wei is waiting for you to help him govern. What should be done first?" The Master replied, "Rectify names." "Really?" said Zi Lu. "You're wide of the mark. Why rectify names?" The Master said, "How uncultivated you are, Yu! A superior man shows a cautious reserve about what he doesn't know."

13:6. The Master said, "If a ruler acts correctly, he can govern without issuing orders. If he acts incorrectly, his orders won't be followed."

13:13. The Master said, "If a minister makes his own conduct correct, what difficulty will he have in governing? If he can't rectify himself, how can he rectify others?"

13:18. The Duke of She told Confucius, "Some of us are upright. If our father had stolen a sheep, we'd bear witness to it." Confucius said, "In my country the upright are different. The father conceals the misconduct of the son, and the son conceals the misconduct of the father. Uprightness is to be found in this."

14:30. The Master said, "The way of the superior person is threefold, but I am not equal to it. Virtuous [*ren*], he is free from anxieties; wise, he is free from perplexities; bold, he is free from fear." Zi Kong said, "Master, that's you."

14:36. Someone said, "What do you say about the principle of repaying injury with kindness?" The Master said, "How then will you repay kindness? Repay kindness with kindness and injury with justice."

15:17. The Master said, "The superior person takes righteousness [*yi*] to be essential. He practices it according to propriety. He brings it forth in humility. He completes it with sincerity. This is indeed a superior person."

15:20. The Master said, "What the superior person seeks is in himself. What the inferior person seeks is in others."

15:23. Zi Kong asked, "Is there one word to serve as a rule for practice throughout life?" Confucius said, "It is reciprocity. What you don't want done to yourself, don't do to others."

16:10. Confucius said, "The superior person thoughtfully considers nine things: With his eyes, he wants to see clearly. With his ears, he wants to hear distinctly. In countenance, he wants to be warm. In demeanor, he wants to be respectful. In speech, he wants to be sincere. In business, he wants to be careful. When in doubt, he wants to ask others. When angry, he thinks of difficulties that might result. When he sees opportunity for gain, he thinks of righteousness."

17:6. Zi Qang asked Confucius about perfect virtue [*ren*]. Confucius said: "To be able to practice five things everywhere under Heaven constitutes perfect virtue." He begged to know what they were, and was told, "Seriousness, generosity, sincerity, diligence, and kindness. If you're serious, you won't be treated with disrespect. If you're generous, you'll win all hearts. If you're sincere, you'll be trusted. If you're diligent, you'll accomplish much. If you're kind, you'll enjoy the service of others."

17:8. The Master said, "Yu, have you heard the six things followed by the six confusions?" Yu replied, "I haven't." "Sit down and I'll tell you. The love of benevolence without the love of learning leads to an ignorant simplicity. The love of knowledge without the love of learning leads to dissipation of mind. The love of sincerity without the love of learning leads to recklessness. The love of straightforwardness without the love of learning leads to rudeness. The love of boldness without the love of learning leads to insubordination. The love of strength of character without the love of learning leads to extravagance."

20:3. The Master said, "Without recognizing the ordinances of heaven, it's impossible to be a superior person. Without acquaintance with propriety, it's impossible to establish one's character. Without knowing the force of words, it's impossible to know people."

2.2 THE INTUITIONISM OF MENCIUS

Confucius (551–479 BCE) is principally a political and ethical thinker. He takes on challenges about social and political relations, but he says little that is expressly metaphysical. His theory of a self and self-development has a decidedly social spin.

A self is, according to Confucius, self-formed. We construct who we are. We do this by appropriating societal practices, which are conceived as rituals (*li*). This view of a self shaped through socialization provides important backdrop to Confucian ethics. By appropriating societal practices—from language to manners and morals, including arts and crafts, each with internal standards of excellence—we make ourselves in relation to family and community. Not every custom or practice is equally deserving of assimilation and mastery. We use "humanity" (*ren*, also translated as virtue, benevolence, or kindness) as an ultimate touchstone. This universal value provides a counterweight to human malleability.

Confucius refuses to discuss human nature:

> 5:12 Zi Kong said, "We may hear the Master on letters and culture. But we may not hear him on human nature and the way of Heaven."

His vagueness on the relationship between socialization and humanity leads later philosophers to debate the question of whether human nature is essentially good, requiring only nurture like a flower, or evil to some significant degree, such that physical force is called for, like training a horse.

Chinese philosophers of various schools have felt a need to fill in what they see as a gap in Confucius's theory. Mencius argues that human nature is originally and essentially good. Another Confucian, Xunzi, argues the opposite, contending that human nature is evil.

Socrates (470–399 BCE), in his defense against the charge of corrupting the youth of Athens and not believing in the Athenian gods, spoke of an "inner voice" that told him when he was about to go astray and do something wrong. Most people take conscience to be a good practical guide to what to do or, at least, to what not to do. We have a saying: "Let your conscience be your guide." We treat people without adequately developed consciences as sociopaths.

Ethical intuitionism, in its classical form, is the view that conscience is the only reliable practical guide to what to do. Intuitionists, that is, contend that we derive our moral knowledge from our reactions to particular actions and situations. Ethical knowledge is like perceptual knowledge; we perceive things to be right or wrong just as we perceive them to be round or green. And just as we have sense organs that enable us to perceive the perceptual qualities of things, we have a moral sense that enables us to perceive the moral qualities of things. We react to good things with good feelings, feelings of approval, warmth, or even joy. We react to bad things with feelings of disapproval, rejection, and even horror. Our feelings are the best guide to what is right and wrong—indeed, the only guide we need.

Perhaps the first sophisticated version of ethical intuitionism appeared in ancient China. Mencius (372?–289? BCE), originally Mengzi (Meng Tzu, "Master Meng"), was the greatest ancient disciple of Confucius. A contemporary of Aristotle, he lived during the turbulent Warring States period. He abides by the chief doctrines of Confucius but adds to them in some important ways. Confucius refused to talk about human nature. Mencius argues that human nature is originally and essentially good. Anyone seeing a child fall into a well, he observes, would rush to help without thinking. This shows that human nature is altruistic.

Mencius holds that virtues arise from innate (that is, inborn) feelings. We innately feel compassion, which is the beginning of humanity (*ren*); shame and dislike, the beginnings of righteousness or justice (*yi*); modesty, the beginnings of propriety (*li*); and approval and disapproval, the beginnings of knowledge.

Mencius's exposition reflects two additional components of intuitionism: (1) the idea that morality stems from feelings, not from reason alone; and (2) *pluralism*, the idea that morality rests on goods, values, principles, or feelings that differ in kind. Benevolence (*ren*), righteousness (*yi*), propriety (*li*), and knowledge are irreducibly different moral considerations, stemming from different feelings. We acquire virtue not by subjugating our feelings but by developing them. We are innately good; we have an innate capacity to tell right from wrong. Hence, "The path of duty lies in what is near.... The work of duty lies in what is easy." Being good comes naturally to us.

Because the four virtues stem from innate feelings, Mencius places great emphasis on conscience. We are born with a faculty of moral intuition, giving rise to feelings that correspond with the moral character of events. Our faculty of intuition can be developed and clarified, but it can also become clouded by selfish desire. We all have a disposition to virtue, but we must protect and cultivate our intuition to make our feelings good guides to what is right. "The great man," Mencius says, "is he who does not lose his child's-heart," his inborn ability to respond to the moral qualities of what happens around him. Experience, desire, and the demands of life can easily obscure our child's-heart; our ability to tell right and wrong fades if we do not reinforce it. The sights and sounds of the workaday world easily distract us. Hence, we can lose what we had. But we can also find it: "The great end of learning is nothing else but to seek for the lost mind." We must think in order to nourish our innate abilities. We must use reason, in particular, to counteract the force of desire, which beclouds the mind and obscures our natural moral feelings.

Mencius articulates another component of intuitionism, the idea that moral judgment is context dependent. He is suspicious of universal moral principles, maintaining that all have exceptions. There are different moral considerations—*ren, yi, li*, and knowledge—which are independent and stem from different kinds of feelings. They can conflict with each other. How we should resolve these conflicts depends on the context. There is no general rule. Any rule we adopt is bound to ignore many potentially relevant considerations.

2.2.1 From *Mencius*

Chapter 6

Mencius said, "All men have a mind which cannot bear to see the sufferings of others.

"The ancient kings had this commiserating mind, and they, as a matter of course, had likewise a commiserating government. When with a commiserating mind was practised a

Source: From *Mencius*. Translated by James Legge. *The Sacred Books of the East*, Volume II. Transliteration has been converted to Pinyin.

commiserating government, to rule the kingdom was as easy a matter as to make anything go round in the palm.

"When I say that all men have a mind which cannot bear to see the sufferings of others, my meaning may be illustrated thus:—even nowadays, if men suddenly see a child about to fall into a well, they will without exception experience a feeling of alarm and distress. They will feel so, not as a ground on which they may gain the favour of the child's parents, nor as a ground on which they may seek the praise of their neighbours and friends, nor from a dislike for a reputation of having been unmoved by such a thing.

"From this case we may perceive that the feeling of commiseration is essential to man, that the feeling of shame and dislike is essential to man, that the feeling of modesty and complaisance is essential to man, and that the feeling of approving and disapproving is essential to man.

"The feeling of commiseration is the principle of benevolence. The feeling of shame and dislike is the principle of righteousness. The feeling of modesty and complaisance is the principle of propriety. The feeling of approving and disapproving is the principle of knowledge.

"Men have these four principles just as they have their four limbs. When men, having these four principles, yet say of themselves that they cannot develop them, they play the thief with themselves, and he who says of his prince that he cannot develop them plays the thief with his prince.

"Since all men have these four principles in themselves, let them know to give them all their development and completion, and the issue will be like that of fire which has begun to burn, or that of a spring which has begun to find vent. Let them have their complete development, and they will suffice to love and protect all within the four seas. Let them be denied that development, and they will not suffice for a man to serve his parents with."

Mencius said, "Is the arrow maker less benevolent than the maker of armour of defence? And yet, the arrow maker's only fear is lest men should not be hurt, and the armour maker's only fear is lest men should be hurt. So it is with the priest and the coffin maker. The choice of a profession, therefore, is a thing in which great caution is required.

"Confucius said, 'It is virtuous manners which constitute the excellence of a neighbourhood. If a man, in selecting a residence, does not fix on one where such prevail, how can he be wise?' Now, benevolence is the most honourable dignity conferred by Heaven, and the quiet home in which man should dwell. Since no one can hinder us from being so, if yet we are not benevolent;—this is being not wise.

"From the want of benevolence and the want of wisdom will ensue the entire absence of propriety and righteousness;—he who is in such a case must be the servant of other men. To be the servant of men and yet ashamed of such servitude, is like a bowmaker's being ashamed to make bows or an arrow maker's being ashamed to make arrows.

"If he be ashamed of his case, his best course is to practise benevolence.

"The man who would be benevolent is like the archer. The archer adjusts himself and then shoots. If he misses, he does not murmur against those who surpass him. He simply turns round and seeks the cause of his failure in himself."

Mencius said, 'When any one told Ze Lu that he had a fault, he rejoiced.

"When Yu heard good words, he bowed to the speaker.

"The great Shun had a still greater delight in what was good. He regarded virtue as the common property of himself and others, giving up his own way to follow that of others, and delighting to learn from others to practise what was good.

"From the time when he ploughed and sowed, exercised the potter's art, and was a fisherman to the time when he became emperor, he was continually learning from others.

"To take example from others to practise virtue is to help them in the same practice. Therefore, there is no attribute of the superior man greater than his helping men to practise virtue."

Chapter 13

Mencius said, "The power of vision of Li Lao, and skill of hand of Gong Shu, without the compass and square, could not form squares and circles. The acute ear of the music master Kuang, without the pitch tubes, could not determine correctly the five notes. The principles of Yao and Shun, without a benevolent government, could not secure the tranquil order of the kingdom.

"There are now princes who have benevolent hearts and a reputation for benevolence, while yet the people do not receive any benefits from them, nor will they leave any example to future ages;—all because they do not put into practice the ways of the ancient kings.

"Hence we have the saying:—'Virtue alone is not sufficient for the exercise of government; laws alone cannot carry themselves into practice.'

"It is said in the *Book of Poetry*, 'Without transgression, without forgetfulness, following the ancient statutes.' Never has any one fallen into error, who followed the laws of the ancient kings."

Mencius said, "If a man love others and no responsive attachment is shown to him, let him turn inwards and examine his own benevolence. If he is trying to rule others and his government is unsuccessful, let him turn inwards and examine his wisdom. If he treats others politely and they do not return his politeness, let him turn inwards and examine his own feeling of respect.

"When we do not, by what we do, realise what we desire, we must turn inwards, and examine ourselves in every point. When a man's person is correct, the whole kingdom will turn to him with recognition and submission.

"It is said in the *Book of Poetry*, 'Be always studious to be in harmony with the ordinances of God, and you will obtain much happiness.' "

Mencius said, "People have this common saying,—'The kingdom, the State, the family.' The root of the kingdom is in the State. The root of the State is in the family. The root of the family is in the person of its Head."

Mencius said, "The administration of government is not difficult;—it lies in not offending the great families. He whom the great families affect will be affected by the whole State; and he whom any one State affects will be affected by the whole kingdom. When this is the case, such a one's virtue and teachings will spread over all within the four seas like the rush of water."

Chapter 14

Mencius said, "The path of duty lies in what is near, and men seek for it in what is remote. The work of duty lies in what is easy, and men seek for it in what is difficult. If each man would love his parents and show the due respect to his elders, the whole land would enjoy tranquillity."

Mencius said, "When those occupying inferior situations do not obtain the confidence of the sovereign, they cannot succeed in governing the people. There is a way to obtain the confidence of the sovereign:—if one is not trusted by his friends, he will not obtain the confidence of his sovereign. There is a way of being trusted by one's friends:—if one does not serve his parents so as to make them pleased, he will not be trusted by his friends. There is a way to make one's parents pleased:—if one, on turning his thoughts inwards, finds a want of sincerity, he will not give pleasure to his parents. There is a way to the attainment of sincerity in one's self:—if a man does not understand what is good, he will not attain sincerity in himself.

"Therefore, sincerity is the way of Heaven. To think how to be sincere is the way of man.

"Never has there been one possessed of complete sincerity, who did not move others. Never has there been one who had not sincerity who was able to move others."

Mencius said, "Of services, which is the greatest? The service of parents is the greatest. Of charges, which is the greatest? The charge of one's self is the greatest. That those who do not fail to keep themselves are able to serve their parents is what I have heard. But I have never heard of any who, having failed to keep themselves, were able notwithstanding to serve their parents.

"There are many services, but the service of parents is the root of all others. There are many charges, but the charge of one's self is the root of all others."

Chapter 15

Mencius said, "Acts of propriety which are not really proper and acts of righteousness which are not really righteous the great man does not do."

Mencius said, "Those who keep the Mean train up those who do not, and those who have abilities train up those who have not and hence men rejoice in having fathers and elder brothers who are possessed of virtue and talent. If they who keep the Mean spurn those who do not and they who have abilities spurn those who have not, then the space between them—those so gifted and the ungifted—will not admit an inch."

Mencius said, "Men must be decided on what they will NOT do, and then they are able to act with vigour in what they ought to do."

Mencius said, "What future misery have they and ought they to endure who talk of what is not good in others!"

Mencius said, "The great man does not think beforehand of his words that they may be sincere, nor of his actions that they may be resolute;—he simply speaks and does what is right."

Mencius said, "The great man is he who does not lose his child's-heart."

Mencius said, "The superior man makes his advances in what he is learning with deep earnestness and by the proper course, wishing to get hold of it as in himself. Having got hold of it in himself, he abides in it calmly and firmly. Abiding in it calmly and firmly, he reposes a deep reliance on it. Reposing a deep reliance on it, he seizes it on the left and right, meeting everywhere with it as a fountain from which things flow. It is on this account that the superior man wishes to get hold of what he is learning as in himself."

Chapter 16

Mencius said, "That whereby the superior man is distinguished from other men is what he preserves in his heart;—namely, benevolence and propriety.

"The benevolent man loves others. The man of propriety shows respect to others.

"He who loves others is constantly loved by them. He who respects others is constantly respected by them.

"Here is a man, who treats me in a perverse and unreasonable manner. The superior man in such a case will turn round upon himself—'I must have been wanting in benevolence; I must have been wanting in propriety;—how should this have happened to me?'

"He examines himself and is specially benevolent. He turns round upon himself and is specially observant of propriety. The perversity and unreasonableness of the other, however, are still the same. The superior man will again turn round on himself—'I must have been failing to do my utmost.'

"He turns round upon himself and proceeds to do his utmost, but still the perversity and unreasonableness of the other are repeated. On this the superior man says, 'This is a man utterly lost indeed! Since he conducts himself so, what is there to choose between him and a brute? Why should I go to contend with a brute?'

"Thus it is that the superior man has a life-long anxiety and not one morning's calamity. As to what is a matter of anxiety to him, that indeed he has.—He says, 'Shun was a man, and I also am a man. But Shun became an example to all the kingdom, and his conduct was worthy to be handed down after ages, while I am nothing better than a villager.' This indeed is the proper matter of anxiety to him. And in what way is he anxious about it? Just that he maybe like Shun:—then only will he stop. As to what the superior man would feel to be a calamity, there is no such thing.

He does nothing which is not according to propriety. If there should befall him one morning's calamity, the superior man does not account it a calamity."

Chapter 21

The disciple Gong Tu said, "The philosopher Gao says, 'Man's nature is neither good nor bad.'

"Some say, 'Man's nature may be made to practise good, and it may be made to practise evil, and accordingly, under Wan and Wu, the people loved what was good, while under Yu and Li, they loved what was cruel.'

"Some say, 'The nature of some is good, and the nature of others is bad.' Hence it was that under such a sovereign as Yao there yet appeared Hsiang; that with such a father as Gu Sao there yet appeared Shun; and that with Zhao for their sovereign, and the son of their elder brother besides, there were found Qi, the viscount of Wei, and the prince Bi Kan.

"And now you say, 'The nature is good.' Then are all those wrong?"

Mencius said, "From the feelings proper to it, it is constituted for the practice of what is good. This is what I mean in saying that the nature is good.

"If men do what is not good, the blame cannot be imputed to their natural powers.

"The feeling of commiseration belongs to all men; so does that of shame and dislike; and that of reverence and respect; and that of approving and disapproving. The feeling of commiseration implies the principle of benevolence; that of shame and dislike, the principle of righteousness; that of reverence and respect, the principle of propriety; and that of approving and disapproving, the principle of knowledge. Benevolence, righteousness, propriety, and knowledge are not infused into us from without. We are certainly furnished with them. And a different view is simply owing to want of reflection. Hence it is said, 'Seek and you will find them. Neglect and you will lose them.' Men differ from one another in regard to them;—some as much again as others, some five times as much, and some to an incalculable amount:—it is because they cannot carry out fully their natural powers.

"It is said in the *Book of Poetry*, 'Heaven in producing mankind, gave them their various faculties and relations with their specific laws. These are the invariable rules of nature for all to hold, and all love this admirable virtue.' Confucius said, 'The maker of this ode knew indeed the principle of our nature!' We may thus see that every faculty and relation must have its law, and since there are invariable rules for all to hold, they consequently love this admirable virtue.

"Therefore I say,—Men's mouths agree in having the same relishes; their ears agree in enjoying the same sounds; their eyes agree in recognising the same beauty:—shall their minds alone be without that which they similarly approve? What is it then of which they similarly approve? It is, I say, the principles of our nature, and the determinations of righteousness. The sages only apprehended before me that of which my mind approves along with other men. Therefore the principles of our nature and the determinations of righteousness are agreeable to my mind, just as the flesh of grass and grain-fed animals is agreeable to my mouth."

Mencius said, "The trees of the Niu mountain were once beautiful. Being situated, however, in the borders of a large State, they were hewn down with axes and bills;—and could they retain their beauty? Still through the activity of the vegetative life day and night, and the nourishing influence of the rain and dew, they were not without buds and sprouts springing forth, but then came the cattle and goats and browsed upon them. To these things is owing the bare and stripped appearance of the mountain, and when people now see it, they think it was never finely wooded. But is this the nature of the mountain?

"And so also of what properly belongs to man;—shall it be said that the mind of any man was without benevolence and righteousness? The way in which a man loses his proper goodness of mind is like the way in which the trees are denuded by axes and bills. Hewn down day after day, can it—the mind—retain its beauty? But there is a development of its life day and night, and in the calm air of the morning, just between night and day, the mind feels in a degree those desires and aversions which are proper to humanity, but the feeling is not strong, and it is fettered and destroyed by what takes place during the day. This fettering taking place again and again, the restorative influence of the night is not sufficient to preserve the proper goodness of the mind; and when this proves insufficient for that purpose, the nature becomes not much different from that of the irrational animals, and when people now see it, they think that it never had those powers which I assert. But does this condition represent the feelings proper to humanity?

"Therefore, if it receive its proper nourishment, there is nothing which will not grow. If it lose its proper nourishment, there is nothing which will not decay away.

"Confucius said, 'Hold it fast, and it remains with you. Let it go, and you lose it. Its outgoing and incoming cannot be defined as to time or place.' It is the mind of which this is said!"

Chapter 22

Mencius said, "Benevolence is man's mind, and righteousness is man's path.

"How lamentable is it to neglect the path and not pursue it, to lose this mind and not know to seek it again!

"When men's fowls and dogs are lost, they know to seek for them again, but they lose their mind, and do not know to seek for it.

"The great end of learning is nothing else but to seek for the lost mind."

Chapter 25

Mencius said, "When we get by our seeking and lose by our neglecting;—in that case seeking is of use to getting, and the things sought for are those which are in ourselves.

"When the seeking is according to the proper course, and the getting is only as appointed;—in that case the seeking is of no use to getting, and the things sought are without ourselves."

Mencius said, "All things are already complete in us.

"There is no greater delight than to be conscious of sincerity on self-examination.

"If one acts with a vigorous effort at the law of reciprocity, when he seeks for the realization of perfect virtue, nothing can be closer than his approximation to it."

"Those who form contrivances and versatile schemes distinguished for their artfulness, do not allow their sense of shame to come into action.

"When one differs from other men in not having this sense of shame, what will he have in common with them?"

Mencius said, "The ability possessed by men without having been acquired by learning is intuitive ability, and the knowledge possessed by them without the exercise of thought is their intuitive knowledge.

"Children carried in the arms all know to love their parents, and when they are grown a little, they all know to love their elder brothers.

"Filial affection for parents is the working of benevolence. Respect for elders is the working of righteousness. There is no other reason for those feelings;—they belong to all under heaven."

Mencius said, "When Shun was living amid the deep retired mountains, dwelling with the trees and rocks, and wandering among the deer and swine, the difference between him and the rude inhabitants of those remote hills appeared very small. But when he heard a single good word or saw a single good action, he was like a stream or a river bursting its banks and flowing out in an irresistible flood."

Chapter 26

Mencius said, "The principle of the philosopher Yang was—'Each one for himself.' Though he might have benefited the whole kingdom by plucking out a single hair, he would not have done it.

"The philosopher Mo loves all equally. If by rubbing smooth his whole body from the crown to the heel, he could have benefited the kingdom, he would have done it.

"Ze Mo holds a medium between these. By holding that medium, he is nearer the right. But by holding it without leaving room for the exigency of circumstances, it becomes like their holding their one point.

"The reason why I hate that holding to one point is the injury it does to the way of right principle. It takes up one point and disregards a hundred others.

"The superior man draws the bow, but does not discharge the arrow, having seemed to leap with it to the mark; and he there stands exactly in the middle of the path. Those who are able, follow him.

Mencius said, "When right principles prevail throughout the kingdom, one's principles must appear along with one's person. When right principles disappear from the kingdom, one's person must vanish along with one's principles.

"I have not heard of one's principles being dependent for their manifestation on other men."

Chapter 28

Mencius said, "To nourish the mind there is nothing better than to make the desires few. Here is a man whose desires are few:—in some things he may not be able to keep his heart, but they will be few. Here is a man whose desires are many:—in some things he may be able to keep his heart, but they will be few."

2.3 XUNZI'S PESSIMISTIC VIEW OF HUMAN NATURE

Xunzi (also known as Hsün Tsu, 310?–212? BCE) paints a bleak portrait of human nature. Born in Zhao, one of the states that gave the "Warring States" period its name, Xunzi was a talented student who became an accomplished scholar. Having spent several years at the court of Qin (Chin), the most powerful of the warring states, he recognized that a wealthy but intellectually unsophisticated society could be successful and well ordered even though few people exhibited traditional Confucian virtues. Qin attracted good leaders by operating as a meritocracy, advancing those with talent without regard to social class, personal connections, or other factors. Competition among these leaders made for good government.

Xunzi's political views flow from this experience. A good system of government channels people's natural tendencies in productive directions. A bad system allows those tendencies to become destructive. The outcome does not depend on people's exhibiting personal virtues. In fact, Xunzi believes, people are naturally evil. Virtue does not spring from human nature; it is acquired by education, training, and socialization. By nature, we are selfish, envious, lecherous, and combative. Modern commentators point out similarities between Xunzi's view and the theories of human nature put forth by the Westerners Niccolo Machiavelli (1469–1527) and Thomas Hobbes (1588–1679).

Xunzi distinguishes native dispositions from capacities. Prior to training or education, we are disposed to evil. We nevertheless have the capacity for good. That capacity can be nurtured; people can become good in spite of their natures. This requires effort—a point with which Mencius could agree—but also prodding by external forces such as parents, community, and government, to encourage virtue and enforce moral rules. People must be restrained from indulging their naturally vicious tendencies and trained to overcome them.

2.3.1 Xunzi, from "That the Nature Is Evil"

That the Nature Is Evil

The nature of man is evil; the good which it shows is factitious [artificial]. There belongs to it, even at his birth, the love of gain, and as actions are in accordance with this, contentions and robberies grow up, and self-denial and yielding to others are not to be found; there belong to it envy and dislike, and as actions are in accordance with these, violence and injuries spring up, and self-devotedness and faith are not to be found; there belong to it the desires of the ears and the eyes, leading to the love of sounds and beauty, and as the actions are in accordance with these, lewdness and disorder spring up, and righteousness and propriety, with their various orderly displays, are not to be found. It thus appears that to follow man's nature and yield obedience to its feelings will assuredly conduct to contentions and robberies, to the violation of the duties belonging to everyone's lot, and the confounding of all distinctions, till the issue will be in a state of savagism; and that there must be the influence of teachers and laws, and the guidance of propriety and righteousness, from which will spring self-denial, yielding to others, and an observance of the well-ordered regulations of conduct, till the issue will be a state of good government.—From all this it is plain that the nature of man is evil; the good which it shows is factitious.

To illustrate.—A crooked stick must be submitted to the pressing frame to soften and bend it, and then it becomes straight; a blunt knife must be submitted to the grindstone and whetstone, and then it becomes sharp; so the nature of man, being evil, must be submitted to teachers and laws, and then it becomes correct; it must be submitted to propriety and righteousness, and then it comes under government. If men were without teachers and laws, their condition would be one of deflection and insecurity entirely incorrect; if they were without propriety and righteousness, their condition would be one of rebellious disorder, rejecting all government. The sage kings of antiquity, understanding that the nature of man was thus evil, in a state of hazardous deflection, and incorrect, rebellious and disorderly, and refusing to be governed, set up the principles of righteousness and propriety, and framed laws and regulations to straighten and ornament the feelings of that nature and correct them, to tame and change those same feelings and guide them, so that they might all go forth in the way of moral government and in agreement with reason. Now, the man who is transformed by teachers and laws, gathers on himself the ornament of learning and proceeds in the path of propriety and righteousness is a superior man; and he who gives the reins to his nature and its feelings, indulges its resentments, and walks contrary to propriety

Source: Reprinted from *The Works of Mencius.* Edited and translated by James Legge. From *The Chinese Classics*, Volume II. Oxford: Clarendon Press, 1895.

and righteousness is a mean man. Looking at the subject in this way, we see clearly that the nature of man is evil; the good which it shows is factitious.

Mencius said, "Man has only to learn, and his nature appears to be good"; but I reply—It is not so. To say so shows that he had not attained to the knowledge of man's nature, nor examined into the difference between what is natural in man and what is factitious. The natural is what the constitution spontaneously moves toward—it needs not to be learned, it needs not to be followed hard after; propriety and righteousness are what the sages have given birth to:—it is by learning that men become capable of them, it is by hard practice that they achieve them. That which is in man not needing to be learned and striven after is what I call natural; that in man which is attained to by learning and achieved by hard striving is what I call factitious. This is the distinction between those two. By the nature of man, the eyes are capable of seeing and the ears are capable of hearing. But the power of seeing is inseparable from the eyes, and the power of hearing is inseparable from the ears;—it is plain that the faculties of seeing and hearing do not need to be learned. Mencius says, "The nature of man is good, but all lose and ruin their nature, and therefore it becomes bad"; but I say that this representation is erroneous. Man being born with his nature, when he thereafter departs from its simple constituent elements, he must lose it. From this consideration we may see clearly that man's nature is evil. What might be called the nature's being good would be if there were no departing from its simplicity to beautify it, no departing from its elementary dispositions to sharpen it. Suppose that those simple elements no more needed beautifying and the mind's thoughts no more needed to be turned to good than the power of vision which is inseparable from the eyes and the power of hearing which is inseparable from the ears need to be learned, then we might say that the nature is good, just as we say that the eyes see and the ears hear. It is the nature of man, when hungry, to desire to be filled; when cold, to desire to be warmed; when tired, to desire rest:—these are the feelings and nature of man. But now, a man is hungry, and in the presence of an elder he does not dare to eat before him:—he is yielding to that elder; he is tired with labour, and he does not dare to ask for rest:—he is working for some one. A son's yielding to his father and a younger brother to his elder, a son's labouring for his father and a younger brother for his elder:—these two instances of conduct are contrary to the nature and against the feelings; but they are according to the course laid down for a filial son and to the refined distinction of propriety and righteousness. It appears that if there were an accordance with the feelings and the nature, there would be no self-denial and yielding to others. Self-denial and yielding to others are contrary to the feelings and the nature. In this way we come to see how clear it is that the nature of man is evil; the good which it shows is factitious.

An inquirer will ask, "If man's nature be evil, whence do propriety and righteousness arise?" I reply:—All propriety and righteousness are the artificial production of the sages and are not to be considered as growing out of the nature of man. It is just as when a potter makes a vessel from the clay;—the vessel is the product of the workman's art and is not to be considered as growing out of his nature. Or it is as when another workman cuts and hews a vessel out of wood;—it is the product of his art and is not to be considered as growing out of his nature. The sages pondered long in thought and gave themselves to practice, and so they succeeded in producing propriety and righteousness and setting up laws and regulations. Thus it is that propriety and righteousness, laws and regulations, are the artificial product of the sages and are not to be considered as growing properly from the nature of man.

If we speak of the fondness of the eyes for beauty, or of the mouth for pleasant flavours, or of the mind for gain, or of the bones and skin for the enjoyment of ease;—all these grow out of the natural feelings of man. The object is presented and the desire is felt; there needs no effort to produce it. But when the object is presented and the affection does not move till after hard effort, I say that this effect is factitious. Those cases prove the difference between what is produced by nature and what is produced by art.

Thus the sages transformed their nature and commenced their artificial work. Having commenced this work with their nature, they produced propriety and righteousness. When propriety and righteousness were produced, they proceeded to frame laws and regulations. It appears, therefore, that propriety and righteousness, laws and regulations, are given birth to by the sages. Wherein they agree with all other men and do not differ from them is their nature; wherein they differ from and exceed other men is this artificial work.

Now to love gain and desire to get;—this is the natural feeling of men. Suppose the case that there is an amount of property or money to be divided among brothers, and let this natural feeling to love gain and to desire to get come into play;—why, then the brothers will be opposing, and snatching from, one another. But where the changing influence of propriety and righteousness, with their refined distinctions, has taken effect, a man will give up to any other man. Thus it is that if they act in accordance with their natural feelings, brothers will quarrel together; and if they have come under the transforming influence of propriety and righteousness, men will give up to the other men, to say nothing of brothers. Again, the fact that men wish to do what is good is because their nature is bad. The thin wishes to be thick; the ugly wish to be beautiful; the narrow wishes to be wide; the poor wish to be rich; the mean wish to be noble:—when anything is not possessed in one's self, he seeks for it outside himself. But the rich do not wish for wealth; the noble do not wish for position:—when anything is possessed by one's self, he does not need to go beyond himself for it. When we look at things in this way, we perceive that the fact of men's wishing to do what is good is because their nature is evil. It is the case indeed that man's nature is without propriety and benevolence:—he therefore studies them with vigorous effort and seeks to have them. It is the case that by nature he does not know propriety and righteousness:—he therefore thinks and reflects and seeks to know them. Speaking of man, therefore, as he is by birth simply, he is without propriety and righteousness, without the knowledge of propriety and righteousness. Without propriety and righteousness, man must be all confusion and disorder; without the knowledge of propriety and righteousness, there must ensue all the manifestations of disorder. Man, as he is born, therefore, has in him nothing but the elements of disorder, passive and active. It is plain from this view of the subject that the nature of man is evil; the good which it shows is factitious.

When Mencius says that "Man's nature is good," I affirm that it is not so. In ancient times and now, throughout the kingdom, what is meant by good is a condition of correctness, regulation, and happy government; and what is meant by evil, is a condition of deflection, insecurity, and refusing to be under government:—in this lies the distinction between being good and being evil. And now, if man's nature be really so correct, regulated, and happily governed in itself, where would be the use for sage kings? Where would be the use for propriety and righteousness? Although there were the sage kings, propriety, and righteousness, what could they add to the nature so correct, regulated, and happily ruled in itself? But it is not so; the nature of man is bad. It was on this account that anciently the sage kings, understanding that man's nature was bad, in a state of deflection and insecurity, instead of being correct; in a state of rebellious disorder, instead of one of happy rule, set up therefore the majesty of princes and governors to awe it; and set forth propriety and righteousness to change it; and framed laws and statutes of correctness to rule it; and devised severe punishments to restrain it: so that its outgoings might be under the dominion of rule and in accordance with what is good. This is the true account of the governance of the sage kings and the transforming power of propriety and righteousness. Let us suppose a state of things in which there shall be no majesty of rulers and governors, no influences of propriety and righteousness, no rule of laws and statutes, no restraints of punishment:—what would be the relations of men with one another, all under heaven? The strong would be injuring the weak and spoiling them; the many would be tyrannizing over the few and hooting them; a universal disorder and mutual destruction would speedily ensue. When we look at the subject in this way, we see clearly that the nature of man is evil; the good which it shows is factitious.

An inquirer may say again, "Propriety and righteousness, though seen in an accumulation of factitious deeds, do yet belong to the nature of man; and thus it was that the sages were able to produce them." I reply:—It is not so. A potter takes a piece of clay and produces an earthen dish from it; but are that dish and clay the nature of the potter? A carpenter plies his tools upon a piece of wood and produces a vessel; but are that vessel and wood the nature of the carpenter? So it is with the sages and propriety and righteousness; they produced them, just as the potter works with the clay. It is plain that there is no reason for saying that propriety and righteousness, and the accumulation of their factitious actions, belong to the proper nature of man. Speaking of the nature of man, it is the same in all—the same in Yao and Shun and in Chieh and the robber Chih, the same in the superior man and in the mean man. If you say that propriety and righteousness, with the factitious actions accumulated from them, are the nature of man, on what ground do you proceed to ennoble Yao and Yu, to ennoble generally the superior man? The ground on which we ennoble Yao, Yu, and the superior man is their ability to change the nature and to produce factitious conduct. That factitious conduct being produced, out of it there are brought propriety and righteousness. The sages stand indeed in the same relation to propriety and righteousness, and the factitious conduct resulting from them, as the potter does to his clay:—we have a product in either case. This representation makes it clear that propriety and righteousness, with their factitious results, do not properly belong to the nature of man. On the other hand, that which we consider mean in Chieh, the robber Chih, and the mean man generally is that they follow their nature, act in accordance with its feelings, and indulge its resentments, till all its outgoings are a greed of gain, contentions, and rapine—It is plain that the nature of man is bad, the good which it shows is factitious....

What is the meaning of the saying that "Any traveller on the road may become like Yu?" I answer—All that made Yu what he was was his practice of benevolence, righteousness, and his observance of laws and rectitude. But benevolence, righteousness, laws, and rectitude are all capable of being known and being practised. Moreover, any traveler on the road has the capacity of knowing these and the ability to practise them:—it is plain that he may become like Yu. If you say that benevolence, righteousness, laws, and rectitude are not capable of being known and practised, then Yu himself could not have known, could not have practised them. If you will have it that any traveler on the road is really without the capacity of knowing these things and the ability to practise them, then, in his home, it will not be competent for him to know the righteousness that should rule between father and son, and, abroad, it will not be competent for him to know the rectitude that should rule between sovereign and minister. But it is not so. There is no one who travels along the road but may know both that righteousness and that rectitude:—it is plain that the capacity to know and the ability to practise belong to every traveler on the way. Let him, therefore, with his capacity of knowing and ability to practise, take his ground on the knowableness and practicableness of benevolence and righteousness;—and it is clear that he may become like Yu. Yea, let any traveller on the way addict himself to the art of learning with all his heart and the entire bent of his will, thinking, searching, and closely examining;—let him do this day after day, through a long space of time, accumulating what is good, and he will penetrate as far as a spiritual intelligence, he will become a ternion [triad] with Heaven and Earth. It follows that the characters of the sages were what any man may reach by accumulation.

It may be said:—"To be sage may thus be reached by accumulation;—why is it that all men cannot accumulate to this extent?" I reply:—They may do so, but they cannot be made to do so. The mean man might become a superior man, but he is not willing to be a superior man. The superior man might become a mean man, but he is not willing to be a mean man....

There is a knowledge characteristic of the sage; a knowledge characteristic of the scholar and superior man; a knowledge characteristic of the mean man; and a knowledge characteristic of the mere servant. In much speech to show his cultivation and maintain consistency, and though he may discuss for a whole day the reasons of a subject, to have a unity pervading the 10,000 changes of discourse:—this is the knowledge of the sage. To speak seldom and in a brief and sparing manner, and to be orderly in his reasoning, as if its parts were connected with a string:—this is the knowledge of the scholar and superior man. Flattering words and disorderly conduct, with undertakings often followed by regrets:—these mark the knowledge of the mean man. Hasty, officious, smart, and swift but without consistency; versatile, able, of extensive capabilities but without use; decisive in discourse, rapid, exact but the subject unimportant; regardless of right and wrong, taking no account of crooked and straight, to get the victory over others the guiding object:—this is the knowledge of the mere servant.

There is bravery of the highest order; bravery of the middle order; bravery of the lowest order. Boldly to take up his position in the place of the universally acknowledged Mean; boldly to carry into practice his views of the doctrines of the ancient kings; in a high situation not to defer to a bad sovereign, and in a low situation not to follow the current of a bad people; to consider that there is no poverty where there is virtue and no wealth or honour where virtue is not; when appreciated by the world, to desire to share in all men's joys and sorrows; when unknown by the world, to stand up grandly alone between heaven and earth and have no fears:—this is the bravery of the highest order. To be reverently observant of propriety and sober-minded; to attach importance to adherence to fidelity and set little store by material wealth; to have the boldness to push forward men of worth and exalt them, to hold back undeserving men and get them deposed:—this is the bravery of the middle order. To be devoid of self-respect and set a great value on wealth; to feel complacent in calamity and always have plenty to say for himself; saving himself in any way, without regard to right and wrong; whatever be the real state of a case, making it his object to get the victory over others:—this is the bravery of the lowest order....

So it is with man:—granted to him an excellent capacity of nature and the faculty of intellect, he must still seek for good teachers under whom to place himself and make choice of friends with whom he may be intimate. Having got good masters and placed himself under them, what he will hear will be the doctrines of Yao, Shun, Yu, and Tang; having got good friends and become intimate with them, what he will see will be deeds of self-consecration, fidelity, reverence, and complaisance:—he will go on from day to day to benevolence and righteousness, without being conscious of it: a natural following of them will make him do so. On the other hand, if he lives with bad men, what he will hear will be the language of deceit, calumny, imposture, and hypocrisy; what he will see will be conduct of filthiness, insolence, lewdness, corruptness, and greed:—he will be going on from day to day to punishment and disgrace, without being conscious of it; a natural following of them will make him do so.

The Record says, "If you do not know your son, look at his friends; if you do not know your prince, look at his confidants." All is the influence of association! All is the influence of association!

2.4 CONFUCIAN AND NEO-CONFUCIAN WOMEN WRITERS

Throughout Chinese history, philosophy was mostly the province of men. Many women, especially those born into high social positions, nevertheless received excellent educations and wrote literature of various kinds, including philosophy. Often, inspired in part by the example of the *Dao-De-Jing*, they wrote philosophy in the form of poetry.

Two such writers raise important questions within Confucianism—questions never raised by the men whose work constitutes much of the Confucian and later neo-Confucian traditions. The first is Ban Zhao (Pan Chao; 48–120), who was born into a family of scholars with royal connections. Married at 14, she lost her husband just a few years later. She spent the rest of her life as a scholar, teacher, tutor to the royal family, and, ultimately, close friend and advisor to Empress Deng. Her father had begun a history of the Han dynasty, the *Han shu*. Her brother wrote the majority of the book, with her help; she, at royal request, finished the project, writing perhaps a fourth of the whole. When she died, she received an honor rare for anyone outside the royal family: The Empress went into mourning for her.

Ban Zhao wrote a number of poems and letters, in addition to *Precepts for my Daughters*, a text on the education and upbringing of women that inspired many imitators over the centuries. Philosophically, it raises some intriguing questions. Is virtue the same for men and for women? What is it to be a good man? What is it to be a good woman? Should those questions receive the same answer? If not, are masculinity and feminity themselves virtues? Ban Zhao responds that being a virtuous woman is *not* the same as being a virtuous man. In part, her answer reflects the different and in many ways inferior position women occupied in ancient China. In part, however, it reflects the *yin/yang* dichotomy that influenced much Chinese thinking. *Yin* and *yang* are basic forces of the universe, opposing yet complementary. They correspond to the distinctions between passive and active, dark and light, feminine and masculine, night and day. In each case, the two terms are opposites, but one cannot exist without the other. They are explanatory principles; everything that happens can be understood in terms of their interaction, manifested in the behavior of the five material agents (wood, fire, earth, metal, and water). Virtue, therefore, must be understood by distinguishing its *yin* and *yang* components. They are different, and even opposite, but neither could exist without the other, and virtue itself could not exist without their duality.

The *yin/yang* dichotomy that underlies Ban Zhao's thought is not part of classical Confucianism itself. As is appropriate for a historian of the Han dynasty, her work reflects the combination of Confucian, Daoist, and other traditional aspects of Chinese thought known as the Han synthesis. The universe has a unity, captured in the Daoist notion of the Dao and the *I-Ching*'s notion of the Great Ultimate. But then why are there distinct things? Why is there opposition, conflict, and change? *Yin* and *yang* provide the answer.

They may seem, however, to provide too good an answer. If *yin, yang*, and the five material agents explain all change, what place is left for human freedom? What place is left for virtue? Daoism stresses submission to the forces of the universe; Confucianism, striving to channel them. How can they be reconciled? Ban Zhao addresses the question in a poem, "Traveling Eastward"—written after one of her brothers had been executed and she herself was fleeing, doubting that she would ever see her home again—that affirms a limited freedom within bounds against which we are persistently driven to rebel.

A second woman writer, working a thousand years later, raises another set of questions. Li Qingzhao (Li Ch'ing-chao, 1083?–1150?) was born into a talented and well-connected, though by no means affluent, family in Shandong during the Song dynasty, when medieval China was at the height of its scientific, literary, and artistic achievements. She and her husband married while still students; they wrote and collected antiquities, mostly old books. He became a government official. When she was about 40, invaders conquered the capital, burned their house, captured the royal family, and set up a new government. Her husband died shortly thereafter. Li was forced to flee, losing almost everything she owned. She nevertheless wrote poetry, edited a compilation of inscriptions she had copied from her collection of old books, and published her husband's work.

Her surviving poems paint a vivid portrait of loss and struggle against overwhelming forces. Their poignant beauty almost leads one to overlook the profound challenge she raises for Confucianism and her response to that challenge. Confucian virtues go hand in hand with a well-ordered society. What becomes of virtue when society breaks down, order collapses, people flee for their lives, and intellectual pursuits are but a haunting memory? The Confucian conception of virtue may seem a curiosity, a tender, fragile way of life contingent on fortunate circumstances. Aspects of it are exactly that, she concedes, recalling her previous life and wistfully declaring, "I would have been glad to grow old in such a world." But there is virtue even in the midst of chaos, she affirms. Indeed, the virtues most highly to be prized in difficult circumstances are precisely those of traditional Confucianism.

2.4.1 Ban Zhao, from *Lessons for My Daughters*

Introduction

Now that my son is a man and able to plan his own life, I need not again have concern for him. But I do grieve that you, my daughters, just now at the age for marriage, have not at this time had gradual training and advice; that you still have not learned the proper customs for married women. I fear that by failure in good manners in other families you will humiliate both your ancestors and your clan. I am now seriously ill, life is uncertain. As I have thought of you all in so untrained a state, I have been uneasy many a time for you. At hours of leisure I have composed these instructions under the title, "Lessons for Women."

Source: Nancy Lee Swann, *Pan Chao: Foremost Woman Scholar of China*. New York: Century Company, 1932. Reprinted by permission of The East Asian Library and the Gest Collection, Princeton University.

Humility

On the third day after the birth of a girl the ancients observed three customs: first to place the baby below the bed; second to give her a potsherd [a piece of broken pottery] with which to play; and third to announce her birth to her ancestors by an offering. Now, to lay the baby below the bed plainly indicated that she is lowly and weak and should regard it as her primary duty to humble herself before others. To give her potsherds with which to play indubitably signified that she should practice labor and consider it her primary duty to be industrious. To announce her birth before her ancestors clearly meant that she ought to esteem as her primary duty the continuation of the observance of worship in the home.

These three ancient customs epitomize woman's ordinary way of life and the teachings of the traditional ceremonial rites and regulatons. Let a woman modestly yield to others; let her respect others; let her put others first, herself last. Should she do something good, let her not mention it; should she do something bad let her not deny it. Let her bear disgrace; let her even endure when others speak or do evil to her. Always let her seem to tremble and to fear. When a woman follows such maxims as these, then she may be said to humble herself before others.

Let a woman retire late to bed but rise early to duties; let her nor dread tasks by day or by night. Let her not refuse to perform domestic duties whether easy or difficult. That which must be done, let her finish completely, tidily, and systematically. When a woman follows such rules as these, then she may be said to be industrious.

Let a woman be correct in manner and upright in character in order to serve her husband. Let her live in purity and quietness of spirit, and attend to her own affairs. Let her love not gossip and silly laughter. Let her cleanse and purify and arrange in order the wine and the food for the offerings to the ancestors. When a woman observes such principles as these, then she may be said to continue ancestral worship.

No woman who observes these three fundamentals of life has ever had a bad reputation or has fallen into disgrace. If a woman fail to observe them, how can her name be honored; how can she but bring disgrace upon herself?

Husband and Wife

The Way of husband and wife is intimately connected with Yin and Yang and relates the individual to gods and ancestors. Truly it is the great principle of Heaven and Earth and the great basis of human relationships. Therefore the "Rites" honor union of man and woman; and in the "Book of Poetry" the "First Ode" manifests the principle of marriage. For these reasons the relationship cannot but be an important one.

If a husband be unworthy, then he possesses nothing by which to control his wife. If a wife be unworthy, then she possesses nothing with which to serve her husband. If a husband does not control his wife, then the rules of conduct manifesting his authority are abandoned and broken. If a wife does not serve her husband, then the proper relationship between men and women and the natural order of things are neglected and destroyed. As a matter of fact the purpose of these two [the controlling of women by men, and the serving of men by women] is the same.

Now examine the gentlemen of the present age. They only know that wives must be controlled and that the husband's rules of conduct manifesting his authority must be established. They therefore teach their boys to read books and study histories. But they do not in the least understand that husbands and masters must also be served and that the proper relationship and the rites should be maintained. Yet only to teach men and not to teach women—is that not ignoring the essential relation between them? According to the "Rites," it is the rule to begin to teach children to read at the age of 8 years, and by the age of 15 years they ought then to be ready for cultural training. Only, why should it not be that girls' education as well as boys' be according to this principle?

Respect and Caution

As Yin and Yang are not of the same nature, so man and woman have different characteristics. The distinctive quality of the Yang is rigidity; the function of the Yin is yielding. Man is honored for strength; a woman is beautiful on account of her gentleness. Hence there arose the common saying: "A man though born like a wolf may, it is feared, become a weak monstrosity; a woman though born like a mouse may, it is feared, become a tiger."

Now, for self-culture nothing equals respect for others. To counteract firmness nothing equals compliance. Consequently it can be said that the Way of respect and acquiescence is woman's most important principle of conduct. So respect may be defined as nothing other than holding on to that which is permanent; and acquiescence nothing other than being liberal and generous. Those who are steadfast in devotion know that they should stay in their proper places; those who are liberal and generous esteem others and honor and serve them.

If husband and wife have the habit of staying together, never leaving one another, and following each other around within the limited space of their own rooms, then they will lust after and take liberties with one another. From such action improper language will arise between the two. This kind of discussion may lead to colicentiousness. But of licentiousness will be born a heart of disrespect to the husband. Such a result comes from not knowing that one should stay in one's proper place.

Furthermore, affairs may be either crooked or straight; words may be either right or wrong. Straightforwardness cannot lead to quarreling; crookedness cannot but lead to accusation. If there are really accusations and quarrels, then undoubtedly there will be angry affairs. Such a result comes from not esteeming others and not honoring and serving them.

If wives suppress not contempt for husbands, then it follows that such wives rebuke and scold their husbands. If husbands stop not short of anger, then they are certain to beat their wives. The correct relationship between husband and wife is based upon harmony and intimacy, and conjugal love is grounded in proper union. Should actual blows be dealt, how could matrimonial relationship be preserved? Should sharp words be spoken, how could conjugal love exist? If love and proper relationship both be destroyed, then husband and wife are divided.

Womanly Qualifications

A woman ought to have four qualifications: (1) womanly virtue; (2) womanly words; (3) womanly bearing; and (4) womanly work. Now, what is called womanly virtue need not be brilliant ability, exceptionally different from others. Womanly words need be neither clever in debate nor keen in conversation. Womanly appearance requires neither a pretty nor a perfect face and form. Womanly work need not be work done more skillfully than that of others.

To guard carefully her chastity; to control circumspectly her behavior; in every motion to exhibit modesty; and to model each act on the best usage, this is womanly virtue.

To choose her words with care; to avoid vulgar language; to speak at appropriate times; and not to weary others with much conversation may be called the characteristics of womanly words.

To wash and scrub filth away; to keep clothes and ornaments fresh and clean; to wash the head and bathe the body regularly; and to keep the person free from disgraceful filth may be called the characteristics of womanly bearing.

With whole-hearted devotion to sew and to weave; to love not gossip and silly laughter; in cleanliness and order to prepare the wine and food for serving guests may be called the characteristics of womanly work.

These four qualifications characterize the greatest virtue of a woman. No woman can afford to be without them. In fact they are very easy to possess if a woman only treasure them in her heart. The ancients had a saying: "Is love afar off? If I desire love, then love is at hand!" So can it be said of these qualifications.

2.4.2 Ban Zhao, "Traveling Eastward"

It is the seventh year of Yung-ch'u;
I follow my son in his journey eastward.
It is an auspicious day in Spring's first moon;
We choose this good hour, and are about to start.

Now I arise to my feet and ascend my carriage.
At eventide we lodge at Yen-shih:
Already we leave the old and start for the new.
I am uneasy in mind, and sad at heart.

Dawn's first light comes, and yet I sleep not;
My heart hesitates as though it would fail me.
I pour out a cup of wine to relax my thoughts.

Suppressing my feelings, I sigh and blame myself:
I shall not need to dwell in nests, nor (eat) worms from dead trees.
Then how can I not encourage myself to press forward?

And further, am I different from other people?
Let me but hear heaven's command and go its way.

Throughout the journey we follow the great highway.
If we seek shortcuts, whom shall we follow?
Pressing forward, we travel on and on;
In abandonment our eyes wander, and our spirits roam....

Secretly I sigh for the capital city I love, (but)
To cling to one's native place characterizes a small nature,
As the histories have taught us....

When we enter K'uang City I recall far distant events.
I am reminded of Confucius' straightened activities
In that decadent, chaotic age which knew not the Way,
And which bound and awed even him, that holy man!

In fact genuine virtue cannot die;
Though the body decay, the name lives on....

I know that man's nature and destiny rests with Heaven,
But by effort we can go forward and draw near to love.
Stretched, head uplifted, we tread onward to the vision....

The thoughts of the princely man
Ought to be written down.
But why should one not voice his own opinion?
As we admire the ancients, (so I attest to that)
Every action of that virtuous one (my father)
Meant literary creation.
Even though I am not wise,
I dare not but follow him.

Honour and dishonour, poverty and wealth,
These may not be sought.
With body erect, let us walk the Way!
And bide the proper time.
Our life may be long or short.
The stupid and the wise are alike in this.
Let us be quietly reverential; resigned to our destiny,
Regardless of whether it be good or evil.

Source: Nancy Lee Swann, *Pan Chao: Foremost Woman Scholar of China*. New York: Century Company, 1932. Reprinted by permission of The East Asian Library and the Gest Collection, Princeton University.

Let us respect, be careful, and not be indolent;
Let us think being humble and temperate;
Let us be pure and calm and want little,
Like the Master Gongchao.

2.4.3 Li Qingzhao, from *Hou Hsu*

Epilogue

In 1101 [aged 17/18],... I came as a bride to the Zhao household. At that time my father was a division head in the Ministry of Rites, and my father-in-law, later a Grand Counselor, was an executive in the Ministry of Personnel. My husband was then 21 and a student in the Imperial Academy.

In those days our two families, the Zhaos and the Lis, were not well-to-do and we were always frugal. On the first and fifteenth day of every month, my husband would... "pawn some clothes"... [and] buy fruit and rubbings of inscriptions. When he brought these home, we would sit facing one another, rolling them out before us, examining and munching. And we thought ourselves persons of the age of Ge-tian [an age of contentment].

When, two years later, he went to take up a post, we lived on rice and vegetables and dressed in common cloth; but he would search out the most... ancient writing and unusual scripts.... [I]n the Imperial Libraries... one might find many ancient poems omitted from the Classic of Poetry, unofficial histories, and writings never before seen, works hidden in walls and recovered from tombs....

I recall that... a man came with a painting of peonies by Xu Li [900s] and asked 20,000 cash for it. In those days 20,000 was a hard sum to raise, even for children of the nobility. We kept the painting with us for a few days, and having thought of no plan by which we could purchase it, we returned it. For several days afterward my husband and I faced each other in deep depression.

Later we lived privately at home for ten years, gathering what we could here and there to have enough food and clothing.... When he got hold of a piece of calligraphy, a painting, a goblet, or a tripod, we would go over it at our leisure, pointing out faults and flaws, setting for our nightly limit the time it took one candle to burn down. Thus our collection came to surpass all others in fineness of paper and the perfection of the characters.

I happen to have an excellent memory, and every evening after we had finished eating, we would... make tea. Pointing to the heaps of books and histories, we would guess on which line of which page in which chapter of which book a certain passage could be found. Success in guessing determined who got to drink his or her tea first. Whenever I got it right, I would raise the teacup, laughing so hard that the tea would spill in my lap, and I would get up, not having been able to drink any of it at all. I would have been glad to grow old in such a world.

At that point an imperial decree arrived, ordering my husband to take charge of Hu-Zhou and to proceed to an audience with the Emperor before he took up the office.... He had the boats [containing the remaining treasure] pulled up onto the shore... and took his leave.

Source: Li Qing-zhao's *Epilogue to Records on Metal and Stone.* Reprinted by permission of the publisher from *Remembrances: The Experience of the Past in Classical Chinese Literature* by Stephen Owen, pp. 82, 84–87, 89–90, 92–98. Cambridge, MA: Harvard University Press,

I was terribly upset. I shouted to him, "If I hear the city is in danger, what should I do?"

He answered from afar...: "Follow the crowd. If you can't do otherwise, abandon the household goods first, then the clothes, then the books and scrolls, then the old bronzes—but carry the sacrificial vessels for the ancestral temple yourself. Live or die with them; don't give them up!"

With this he galloped off on his horse.

In February that winter, the Jin invaders sacked Hong-Zhao and all was lost. Those books, which... it took a string of boats to ferry across the Yangzi, were scattered into clouds of smoke....

Since I could no longer go upriver, and since the movements of the invaders were unpredictable, I was going to stay with my brother, a reviser of edicts. By the time I reached Tai-Zhou, the governor of the place had already fled. Proceeding on to Shan through Mu-Zhou, we left the clothing and linen behind. Hurrying to Yellow Cliff, we hired a boat to take us toward the sea, following the fleeing court....

[E]arly in 1131, all the officials of the government were released from their posts.

All that remained were six or so baskets of books, paintings, ink and inkstones that I hadn't been able to part with. I always kept these under my bed and opened them with my own hands.

I still have a few volumes from three or four sets, none complete, and some very ordinary pieces of calligraphy, yet I treasure them as if I were protecting my own head—foolish person that I am!

Nowadays when I chance to look over these books, it's like meeting old friends.... It is so sad—today the ink of his writing seems still fresh, but the trees on his grave have grown to an armspan in girth....

When there is possession, there must be loss of possession; when there is a gathering together, there must be a scattering—this is the constant principle in things. Someone loses a bow; another person finds a bow; what's so special in that? The reason why I have recorded this story... is to let it serve as a warning for scholars and collectors in later generations.

2.4.4 Li Qingzhao, from *Complete Poems*

From "To Lord Hu"

We shall not ask for the precious pearl of the
 Duke of Sui,
nor for the priceless jade disk of Master Ho.
We merely ask for the recent news of our
 homeland.
The palace of spiritual illumination must be still
 there, surrounded by desolation.
What's happened to the stone statues buried
 deep in the grass,
still guarding the imperial tombs?
Is it true that our people left behind in the
 occupied territories
are still planting mulberry trees and hemp?
Is it true that the rear guard of the barbarians
only patrols the city walls?

This widow's father and grandfather were born
 in Shantung.
Although they never held high office, their fame
 spread far and wide.

Source: *Li Ch'ing-chao, Complete Poems.* Translated and edited by Kenneth Rexroth and Ling Chung. New York: New Directions Publishing Corp., 1979 by Kenneth Rexroth and Ling Chung. Reprinted by permission of New Directions Publishing Corp.

I remember when they carried on animated discussions
with other scholars by the city gate.
The listeners were so crowded that their sweat fell like rain.
Their offspring crossed the Yangtse River to the south many years ago.
Drifting in the rapids, they mingled with refugees.

I send blood-stained tears to the mountains and rivers of home,
And sprinkle a cup of earth on East Mountain.
I imagine when Your Lordship, His Majesty's envoy, upholding the imperial spirit,
passes through our two capitals, K'ai Feng and Lo Yang,
Thousands of people would line the streets and present tea and broth to welcome you....

Announce that the emperor's heart aches for the suffering people—
they are his own children.
Let them understand that the Will of Heaven remembers all living beings.
Our sagacious emperor offers his trust which is as brilliant as the sun.
There is no need to negotiate many times after the long chaos of the years.

"A Morning Dream"

This morning I dreamed I followed
Widely spaced bells, ringing in the wind,
And climbed through mists to rosy clouds.
I realized my destined affinity
With An Ch'i-sheng the ancient sage.
I met unexpectedly O Lu-hua
The heavenly maiden.

... Together we saw lotus roots as big as boats.
Together we ate jujubes as huge as melons.
We were the guests of those on swaying lotus seats.
They spoke in splendid language,
Full of subtle meanings.
The argued with sharp words over paradoxes.
We drank tea brewed on living fire.

Although this might not help the emperor to govern,
It is endless happiness.
The life of men could be like this.
Why did I have to return to my former home,
Wake up, dress, sit in meditation,
Cover my ears to shut out the disgusting racket?
My heart knows I can never see my dream come true.
At least I can remember
That world and sigh.

2.5 THE VIRTUE ETHICS OF DAOISM

Laozi (LAO-dzih, Lao Tzu), the founder of Daoism (Taoism), was a contemporary of Confucius and the Buddha in the sixth century BCE. According to legend, he composed the *Dao-de-Jing* (*Tao-te-Ching*), literally, the "Way-Virtue-Classic," upon his retirement, though many scholars believe that several people compiled the book over roughly two centuries. Daoism opposes Confucianism in many respects. Confucius emphasizes traditional social rules, activity, and social relationships; Laozi stresses nonconformity, tranquility, and individual transcendence. But Laozi, too, can be seen as outlining an ethics of character. Daoist virtues, however, differ strikingly from those advocated by Confucius or Aristotle.

Confucius, in elaborating his account of the superior person, refuses to say anything about human nature, the nature of the universe, or God. He treats Dao, the Way, as a purely ethical concept: the right way to live. Laozi, in contrast, begins with metaphysical speculation about Dao, which he takes as the way the universe works and identifies with the One, which underlies everything but admits no description. Laozi nevertheless takes the Dao as having moral force. Dao, embodied in an individual thing, is the thing's *de*—its power, force, nature, character, or virtue. It is an active principle guiding the thing. It also determines what the thing ought to do and be. The excellence of a thing thus stems from its Dao.

This twofold character of *de*—power and virtue, or, in different terminology, moving and regulating principle, causal force and norm—leads to the distinctive ethical principles of Daoism. What a thing is and what it ought to be are intertwined. Things naturally tend toward what they ought to be. *De* flows both from and toward the Dao.

Laozi therefore advocates inaction. If things naturally tend toward what they ought to be, we should leave them alone; our interference is more likely to do harm than good. Laozi therefore recommends simplicity and tranquillity. It might seem that he recommends passivity and laziness. But the inaction (*wuwei*) he recommends is that of letting nature take its course. We should let the guiding principles of things guide them without interference. The Dao flows naturally, spontaneously, underpinning a world in which things naturally tend toward what they ought to be. The coincidence of guiding and regulating principles in *de* means that things naturally tend to their own states of excellence. Interference with this natural process prevents them from attaining excellence. The individual should adopt a policy of noninterference.

The Daoist case for noninterference rests partly on the assumption that people are naturally good. Things naturally tend toward what they ought to be, and so do people. Consequently, for normal people, at any rate, becoming good requires no special effort. If you relax and do what comes naturally, you will naturally tend toward what is good. This leads Laozi to criticize Confucian ideas directly in various passages, maintaining that virtue (*ren*), righteousness (*yi*), and propriety (*li*) are signs of desperation and decline. All result from self-examination and training. But if our moving and regulating principles converge—if people, that is, naturally tend to be good and become what they ought to be—then none of this is necessary. We do not need to examine ourselves unless there is something wrong with us. We do not need to be trained unless something has disrupted our natural tendencies. Laozi thus advocates virtues of inactivity, passivity, humility, and spontaneity. Above all, we are to act naturally. He advises acceptance rather than desire, cooperation rather than competition, understanding rather than knowledge.

The Daoist ideal is the uncarved block (*pu*), which simply is what it is and does not try to be anything else. It avoids superfluous actions and makes no attempt to go beyond what it is and ought to be (its nature, *de*) by cultivating an excess or artificial nature (*yu de*). Similarly, because we cannot describe the Dao, we should not seek enlightenment through language. In thinking, we draw distinctions. Language, reason, reflection, and other forms of intellectual activity thus lead us away from the ultimate truth, from recognizing the world's unity.

Daoism is therefore anti-intellectual. Ordinarily, we think in order to understand. We reflect in order to answer questions arising from reason or experience. For Confucius, knowledge is the root of all virtue. Even those who would not go quite so far as that—Aristotle, for example—think that knowledge is good and a vital component of practical wisdom.

In Laozi's view, however, thinking leads us away from understanding. We understand most clearly when we set reason, language, and thinking aside. This anti-intellectual aspect of Daoism has had significant influence on the Chinese and Japanese form of Buddhism known as Zen.

2.5.1 Laozi, from *Dao-de-Jing*

1

The Dao that can be trodden is not the eternal Dao.
The name that can be named is not the eternal name.
Nameless, it is the origin of heaven and earth.
Named, it is the mother of ten thousand things.

2

Therefore the sage manages affairs without acting, and teaches without speech.
Ten thousand things spring up and show themselves,
They grow and he does not claim them,
They mature and he does not expect reward.
The sage accomplishes without resting on his laurels.
He works imperceptibly, so his power continues.

4

The Dao is the emptiness of a bowl; beware fullness.
Deep and unfathomable, it seems to be the ancestor of ten thousand things.
Blunt the sharp, unravel the knots, temper the bright, and become dark.
The Dao is pure and still.

5

Heaven and earth are not benevolent [*ren*];
They treat the ten thousand things like straw dogs.
The sage is not benevolent;
He treats the people like straw dogs.

8

The highest excellence is like water,
Which benefits all things, without contending with any.

10

In concentrating your breath to make it soft,
Can you become like a baby?
In cleansing your mind of the dark,
Can you make it spotless?
In loving the people and governing the state,
Can you practice inaction?
In opening and shutting heaven's gate,

Source: Laozi, *Dao-de-Jing*, from *The Texts of Taoism*. Translated by James Legge. Oxford: Oxford University Press, 1891. We have altered the translation significantly to bring out the poetic quality of the original and to accord with the Pinyin transliteration system.

Can you be the female?
In understanding all,
Can you be without knowledge?

To produce, to nourish, to produce without claiming,
To act without boasting, to preside without control,
This is called the dark virtue.

When De is lost, benevolence [*ren*] appears.
When benevolence is lost, righteousness [*yi*] appears.
When righteousness is lost, propriety [*li*] appears.
Propriety is the thin edge of loyalty and good faith,
And the beginning of disorder;
Intelligence is the flower of Dao,
And the beginning of ignorance.

Great people abide in the solid and reject the flimsy;
Abide in the fruit and not in the flower.
Thus they put away one and choose the other.

16

Reach the height of Emptiness; strive for stillness.
Ten thousand things flourish together and then return.
Things grow luxuriously and then return to the root.
To return to the root is to achieve stillness.
To achieve stillness is to reach the goal.

17

The best rulers, the people don't even know that they're there.
The next best, they love and praise.
The next best, they fear.
The worst, they despise.
When rulers lose faith in their people,
People lose faith in their rulers.

Words matter.
Work done, things accomplished,
The people say, "We did these things ourselves."

18

When the great Dao ceases to be observed,
There are benevolence [*ren*] and righteousness [*yi*].

When wisdom and cleverness appear,
There is great hypocrisy.

When the six kinships are not in harmony,
There is filial piety.

When the nations and clans fall into disorder,
There are loyal ministers.

19

Renounce sagacity, discard wisdom,
People will profit a hundredfold.

Renounce benevolence [*ren*], discard righteousness [*yi*],
People will again practice filial piety.

Renounce artistry, discard profit-seeking,
There will be no robbers and thieves.

These three pairs adorn inadequacy.
Therefore, let there be the advice:
Look to the undyed silk, hold on to the uncarved wood [*pu*],
Reduce your selfishness and your desires.

20

Renounce learning and have no troubles.
Yes and no, how far apart are they?
Good and evil, how far apart are they?

25

There was something indefinite existing before heaven and earth.
Still, formless, alone, unchanging,

Reaching everywhere without becoming exhausted,
It may be called the mother of ten thousand things.

I do not know its name; I call it Dao.
If pressed, I call it "great."
"Great," it flows constantly.
Flowing, it goes far away.
Far away, it returns.

Therefore Dao is great,
Heaven is great,
Earth is great,
The king is also great.
In the universe four are great,
And the king is one of them.

Humans take their law from the earth,
Earth takes its law from heaven;
Heaven takes its law from Dao,
Dao takes its law from what it is.

37

Dao does nothing, yet there is nothing it does not do.
If kings and princes can hold to it,
The ten thousand things will transform themselves.

If I desire this transformation,
I will express it by the nameless uncarved wood.
The nameless uncarved wood has no desires.
Without desire, at rest and still,
The ten thousand things will order themselves.

38

Those of high De do not display De, so they have De.
Those of low De cling to De, so they lack De.

Those of high De do not act, for they have no need to.
Those of low De act, and need to.

Those of high benevolence [*ren*] act, but have no need to.
Those of high righteousness [*yi*] act, and need to.

Those of high propriety [*li*] act, but, getting no response,
Bare their arms and march.

Thus when Dao is lost, De appears.

47

Without stepping out the door, understand all under the sky.
Without looking out the window, see the Dao of Heaven.
The farther you go out, the less you know.

Therefore sages know without traveling,
Name things without seeing them,
Accomplish without trying.

56

One who knows does not speak,
One who speaks does not know.

57

Govern by rectifying; fight cleverly.
Take the kingdom without trying.

How do I know?
The more prohibitions there are, the poorer the people.
The more tools there are, the greater the disorder.
The more cleverness there is, the more contrivances there are.
The more laws there are, the more criminals there are.

Therefore a sage says:
I do nothing, and the people transform themselves.
I love stillness, and the people correct themselves.

I have no business, and the people prosper themselves;
I have no ambition, and the people attain the uncarved wood themselves.

58

When the government is dull, the people are good.
When the government is meddling, the people are disappointed.

63

Act without acting,
Manage affairs without trouble,
Taste without tasting.
Consider the small great, the few many.
Repay injury with De.

Plan difficult things while they are easy.
Accomplish great things while they are small.
Difficult things of the world start easy.
Great things of the world start small.
Because the sage never does great things,
He can accomplish great things.

He who promises lightly keeps few promises.
He who thinks things easy finds them difficult.
Therefore even the sage takes even easy things to be difficult,
So that they are not difficult.

71

From knowing to not knowing is best.
From not knowing to knowing is sickness.
By being sick of sickness, you keep from being sick.

2.6 DAOIST WOMEN WRITERS

Yu Xuanji (Yu Hsuan-chi; 844?–868?) was born in Tang dynasty's capital city of Xian. According to a questionable tenth-century account, she was second wife of a government official. His first wife demanded that he abandon her. He did. Yu Xuanji survived as a courtesan and became a Daoist priestess. But her temper was compatible neither with being a priestess nor with the tenets of Daoism. In rage, she struck a servant, killing her. As a result, she was executed. Whether or not this account is correct, she appears to have traveled a great deal, maintained contacts with other writers, and become known for her poetry during her lifetime.

Yu Xuanji develops an existential side of Daoism. High-spirited, she rebels against the calm acceptance that the *Dao-de-jing* seems to recommend. If everything is and is directed by Dao, who am I? How should I conceive of my life? What should I do with it? As a woman, she finds herself shut out of roles that would be natural for her. As a Daoist, she sees life as a "dream of joy and sorrow," but finds herself without direction, "a loosed boat floating a thousand miles." When times are good, it is easy to display Daoist virtues. When times are hard, however—and human relationships often make them hard—virtue becomes difficult. "How do we get the life we want?" she asks, without finding an answer.

Sun Bu-er (Sun Pu-erh, 1119?–1182?), a contemporary of Li Qingzhao and the neo-Confucian philosopher Zhu Xi, was born during the Song dynasty in a time of great scientific, literary, and philosophical accomplishment—but also a time of great political turmoil. She married and raised three children. Inspired perhaps by the chaos around her, she then devoted herself to the study of Daoism, becoming a noted teacher and priestess. Founder of the Purity and Tranquillity School, tradition considers her one of the Seven Immortals of Daoism.

Sun Bu-er is best remembered for her poetry, which conveys Daoist themes in beautifully precise images. Her chief innovation was the development of her teacher Wang Chongyang's theory of "Inner Alchemy," a way of transforming the self influenced by yoga and by Zen Buddhism as well as traditional Daoist teachings. Combining the idea of self-transformation with the female/male division of the *yin/yang* theory, she distinguished female alchemy from male alchemy. She analyzed the former process into fourteen steps: (1) concentrate one's mind, subdue one's thoughts and fancies, and focus on the "Elixir Field"; (2) nourish one's breath, practice breathing, and return to "Pre-existence," a blank mind; (3) concentrate one's spirit and circulate one's breath, bringing mind and body into harmony; (4) "cut the dragon," which means to control one's bodily functions; (5) cultivate one's "elixir," fixing attention and guarding "the jade pass," maintaining mind and body in this state; (6) breathe "embryonically," eliminating illusions, not only harmonizing mind and body but also returning to the Dao, where *yin* and *yang* are unified; (7) keep the spirit clear and quiet, persistently; (8) receive the "Inner Elixir," which needs careful nurture; (9) refine the spirit, leaving the worldly realm; (10) absorb the essence of the sky, earth, sun, and moon; (11) abstain from grains and cooked food; (12) meditate in a small shrine; (13) form the Original Spirit into a "body outside the body"; (14) ascend to the realm of Immortality. Sun Bu-er thus develops a Daoist notion of meditation containing strong elements of the supernatural.

2.6.1 Yu Xuanji, from *Poems*

"Seeing the new listing of successful Degree Candidates"

(After each civil service test, the results were posted at various temples. Skill at writing poetry played a large part in success on these government tests. Women were ineligible to try.)

Cloudy peaks fill the eyes,
far from the lightness of spring;
silver spools of calligraphy
take shape beneath my hand.

Too bad my silken woman's dress
obscures my poetry;
looking up, I uselessly
envy the names on the list I see.

"Reply to a friend"

Though we live on the same street,
you haven't passed by all year.
Fine poetry pleased your former lady,
distinguished laurels, your new degree.

A Daoist nature cares not at all
for the cold of ice and snow,
a Buddhist heart laughs aloud
at ostentatious silk;
since you rose to rank at court,
we have no chance to meet—
having climbed to the lofty sky,
no more is there a way to receive
the misty waves below.

"To a neighbor girl"

The shyness of the daytime's covered
by a silken sleeve;
the melancholy of spring makes it
hard to rise and dress.
A priceless gem's more easily found
than a man who has a heart.

Hidden tears on the pillow,
secret sorrows among the flowers;
if one could glimpse a righteous man,
why lament a mere playboy?

"An allegory"

Rosy peaches everywhere
presenting the colors of spring,
on emerald willows at every house
the moonlight glow is agleam.

Freshly groomed, she awaits upstairs
the coming of the night;
in the bedroom, sitting alone,
she keeps her feelings inside.

Fishes frolic under the leaves
of the lotus flowers;
the twittering of sparrows calls
on the rainbow'd horizon.

Human life is but a dream,
a dream of joy and sorrow;
how can one be able to join
the company of immortals?

Source: *Autumn Willows: Poetry by Women of China's Golden Age*. Translated from the original Chinese by Bannie Chow and Thomas Cleary. Ashland, OR: Story Line Press, 2003.

"Selling ruined peonies"

(A peony was a conventional image for a courtesan.)

Sigh, in the wind fall flowers, their petals dance.
Their secret fragrance dies in spring's decay.

Too costly: no one bought them.
Too sweet for butterflies.

If these red blooms had grown in a palace
Would they now be stained by dew and dust?
If they grew now in a forbidden garden
Princes would covet what they could not buy.

"At the end of spring"

Deep lanes, poor families; I have few friends.
He stayed behind only in my dreams.

Fragrant silk scents the breeze: whose party?
A song comes carried in the wind: from where?

Drums in the street wake me at dawn.
In the courtyard, magpies mourn a spoiled
spring.

How do we get the life we want?
I am a loosed boat floating a thousand miles.

"Staying in the mountains in summer"

I've moved here to the Immortal's place:
Flowers everywhere we didn't plant before.

The courtyard trees are bent like clotheshorses.
At the feast, wine cups float in a new spring.

Dark balcony. Path through deep bamboo.
Long summer dress. Confusion of books.

I sing in the moonlight and ride a painted boat,
Trusting the wind to blow me home again.

Source: *A Book of Women Poets from Antiquity to Now*. Edited by Aliki Barnstone and Willis Barnstone. Rev. ed. New York: Schocken Books, 1992.

"By the Yangtze River"

(This alludes to Zhuangzi's question: "Was I then a man, dreaming I was a butterfly, or am I now a butterfly, dreaming I am a man?")

Our boat slants across the wide river
to Wuchang city
past Parrot Island,
home to 10,000 households,
and I dream myself a butterfly
searching for a flower.

"A poem in reply, matching the form"

Dashing red and purple,
the clatter of official carriages
fills the streets.

Walking behind
my crude wicker gate
I chance upon a poem:

these white flowers
so undeserving
of my poor verses.

In my tender life,
the thirst for company
has passed,
pine trees are content
to live their lives
on high mountain slopes.

Source: Justin Hill, *Passing Under Heaven*. London: Abacus, 2004.

2.6.2 Sun Bu-er, from *Poems*

"Precious treatise on preservation of unity on the great way"

The Tao is uncontrived, yet there is nothing it does not do.
It can be witnessed by the mind, not known by knowledge.
What is "knowing"? What is "witness"?
Knowledge dismisses knowledge.

Witness only responds.
Response comes from nowhere.

Mind then penetrates.
Penetrate the One, and all tasks are done.

The One is the root.
The task is the door.
When the task returns to One, the One is ever present.

The presence should not be reified;
provisionally we speak of keeping it.

Keep open selflessness and naturally be eternal.

"Refining the spirit"

The relic from before birth
Enters one's heart one day.
Be as careful as if you were holding a full vessel,
Be as gentle as if you were caressing an infant.
The gate of earth should be shut tight,
The portals of heaven should be first opened.
Wash the yellow sprouts clean,
And atop a mountain is thunder shaking the earth.

"The beginning of the sustenance of life"

The beginning of the sustenance of life
Is all in *yin* and *yang*.
The limitless can open up
The light of the great limit.
Diligently polished, the mirror of mind
Is bright as the moon;
The universe in a grain
May rise or it may hide.

"Gathering the mind"

Before our body existed,
One energy was already there.
Like jade, more lustrous as it's polished
Like gold, brighter as it's refined,
Sweep clear the ocean of birth and death,
Stay firm by the door of total mastery,
A particle at the point of open awareness,
The gentle firing is warm.

Source: *Immortal Sisters*: *Secret Teachings of Taoist Women*. Translated and edited by Thomas Cleary. Boston: Shambhala Publications, 1989.

"You need companions to travel"

You need companions to travel
To the Isle of Immortals—
It is hard to climb
The azure cliffs alone.
If you take dead stillness for refinement,
The weak water brimming
Will lack a convenient boat.

"A springlike autumn's balmy breeze reaches afar"

A springlike autumn's balmy breeze reaches afar.
The sun shines on the house of a recluse
South of the river;
They encourage the December apricots
To burst into bloom:
A simple-hearted person
Faces the simple-hearted flowers.

"Cultivating the elixir"

Tie up the tiger and return it to the true lair;
Bridle the dragon and gradually increase the elixir.
Nature should be as clear as water,
Mind should be as still as a mountain.
Turning the breath, gather it into the gold crucible;
Stabilizing the spirit, guard the jade pass.
If you can increase the grain of rice day by day,
You will be rejuvenated.

"Facing a wall"

All things finished,
You sit still in a little niche.
The light body rides on violet energy,
The tranquil nature washes in a pure pond.
Original energy is unified, *yin* and *yang* are one;
The spirit is the same as the universe.
When the work is done, you pay court to the Jade Palace;
A long whistle gusts a misty gale.

"Projecting the spirit"

There is a body outside the body,
Which has nothing to do with anything produced by magical arts.
Making this aware energy completely pervasive
Is the living, active, unified original spirit.
The bright moon congeals the gold liquid,
Blue lotus refines jade reality.
When you've cooked the marrow of the sun and moon,
The pearl is so bright you don't worry about poverty.

CHAPTER 3

Ancient Greek Ethics

"The unexamined life is not worth living"

Western philosophy begins in ancient Greece. Plato (427–347 BCE), student of Socrates, teacher of Aristotle, and the first great systematic philosopher of the West, develops two accounts of virtue. In his early dialogues, such as the *Apology, Euthyphro*, and *Laches*, Socrates appears as a character and treats virtue as a kind of knowledge. He subtly argues that the virtues are ultimately one. Probably these views are close to those of the historical Socrates. In the *Republic*, from Plato's middle period, the soul is treated as having three parts or aspects: the rational, appetitive, and spirited elements. Virtue is a proper balance of the parts. This theory seems to be distinctively Plato's. Aristotle advances a third theory, distinguishing intellectual from moral virtue, which is a mean between extremes.

3.1 SOCRATES ON VIRTUE

Plato's early dialogues are essentially plays; Plato never speaks in his own voice. The central character is Socrates, Plato's teacher. (The relation of the character to the historical Socrates is a matter of some dispute.) Socrates typically encounters a small group of people involved in a discussion, one of whom eventually makes a claim about someone having or lacking a certain virtue: courage, self-control, piety, or beauty, for example. Socrates then asks, "What is courage?" (or self-control or piety, etc.). Someone typically gives an example, and Socrates points out that an example is not a definition. The person then proposes a definition, and Socrates shows that it is either too broad (including things that do not fall under the term) or too narrow (failing to include things that do fall under the term). The interlocutor amends the definition, or someone else proposes a different one, and the process continues. Socrates never advances his own definition.

He professes to have no answers, but maintains that wisdom begins with recognition of one's own ignorance. A wise person realizes how little he or she knows.

In the *Laches*, for example, the initial conversation concerns educating young people. Socrates points out that the young should be raised to be virtuous, and everyone agrees. But what, he asks, is virtue? To make the question easier, he proposes to examine a particular virtue, courage. Laches, a Greek general, proposes a definition: Courage is staying at your post and fighting. Socrates observes that he has defined only one kind of courage, that of a soldier in a particular type of situation. So Laches's definition is far too narrow. Socrates poses the question again.

Laches's second definition is that courage is a sort of endurance of the soul. Now it is not clear that this is a definition at all. *What* sort of endurance is courage? A wise endurance, Laches answers. Now Socrates shows that defining courage as wise endurance of the soul does not work either. It is too broad; it counts too many things as courage. Worse, it often appears that the person who endures foolishly is braver than the person who endures wisely.

Nicias takes over the argument and defines courage as knowing the grounds of hope and fear. Socrates attacks this definition in a different way. He argues that, on this account, courage is not just one of the virtues but all of virtue. He begins by noting that hope and fear are directed toward the future. But there is no division between wisdom about the past, wisdom about the present, and wisdom about the future; the same quality of good judgment underlies all of them. So knowledge of the grounds of hope and fear is just knowledge of good and evil—knowing what to do and what not to do, what to seek and what to avoid, what to admire and what to deplore—which is virtue in general.

This is a common theme in the early dialogues. Every particular virtue turns out to be indistinguishable from the knowledge of good and evil, which, Socrates asserts, is virtue in general. He then declares defeat. But another way to view the result is that, at root, virtues are all identical. Socrates seems to be relying on a thesis of the unity of the virtues; courage, wisdom, self-control, justice, piety, and so on are really the same thing: a kind of knowledge—the knowledge of good and evil, of right and wrong, of what to pursue and what to avoid. Some interpret him as endorsing the weaker position that knowledge is necessary for virtue though not always sufficient. In any case, at least part of that virtue lies in the pursuit of its definition.

3.1.1 Plato, from *Laches*

Socrates: Aren't our two friends, Laches, at this very moment inviting us to consider how to give their sons the gift of virtue to improve their minds?

Laches: Definitely.

Socrates: Then mustn't we first know the nature of virtue? For how can we tell anyone how to attain something we know nothing about?

Laches: I don't think we can, Socrates.

Source: Plato, *Laches*, from *The Dialogues of Plato*. Translated by Benjamin Jowett. New York: Oxford University Press, 1892. We have revised the translation for readability.

Socrates: Then, Laches, we must know the nature of virtue?

Laches: Yes.

Socrates: And what we know we must surely be able to tell?

Laches: Certainly.

Socrates: My friend, I don't think we should start by asking about the whole of virtue. That may be more than we can accomplish. Let's first start with a part; that should be easier for us.

Laches: Let's do as you say, Socrates.

Socrates: Then what parts of virtue should we choose? How about the virtue the art of fighting in armour is supposed to produce? Isn't that generally thought to be courage?

Laches: Yes, certainly.

Socrates: Then, Laches, suppose we first try to figure out the nature of courage. After that we can ask how young people can attain it. Tell me, if you can, what courage is.

Laches: Socrates, that's easy. A man of courage is one who doesn't run away but remains at his post and fights the enemy. There can be no mistake about that.

Socrates: Very good, Laches. But I'm afraid that I didn't express myself clearly. So you've answered a question other than the one I meant to ask.

Laches: What do you mean, Socrates?

Socrates: I'll try to explain. You'd call a man courageous who remains at his post and fights with the enemy?

Laches: Certainly.

Socrates: So would I. But what would you say about someone who fights flying, instead of remaining?

Laches: What do you mean, "flying"?

Socrates: Why, as they say the Scythians fight, flying as well as pursuing. Homer says, praising the horses of Aeneas, that they knew "how to pursue, and fly quickly here and there"; and he passes an encomium on Aeneas himself, as having a knowledge of fear or flight, and calls him "an author of fear or flight."

Laches: Yes, Socrates. Homer is right. He was speaking of chariots, as you were speaking of the Scythian cavalry. They fight that way. But the heavy-armed Greek foot soldier fights by remaining in his rank.

Socrates: And yet, Laches, the Lacedaemonians at Plataea were an exception. When they came upon the light shields of the Persians, they say, they weren't willing to stand and fight. They fled. But when the Persian ranks broke, they turned upon them like cavalry and won the battle of Plataea.

Laches: That's true.

Socrates: That's what I meant when I said that I was to blame for putting my question badly. That's why you answered badly. For I meant to ask you not only about the courage of heavy-armed soldiers, but about the courage of cavalry and every other style of soldier; not only who are courageous in war, but who are courageous in perils by sea, in disease, in poverty, or again in politics; and not only who are courageous against pain or fear, but who are mighty in fighting desires and pleasures—either fixed in their rank or turning upon their enemy. There is this sort of courage, isn't there, Laches?

Laches: Certainly, Socrates.

Socrates: All these are courageous—some in pleasures, and some in pains: some in desires, and some in fears. Some are cowards under the same conditions.

Laches: Very true.

Socrates: Now, I was asking about courage and cowardice in general. I'll begin with courage, and once more ask, What's the common quality called *courage*, which is the same in all these cases? Now do you understand what I mean?

Laches: Not very well.

Socrates: It's like this: Suppose I were to ask what that quality is that's called quickness, which is found in running, playing the lyre, speaking, learning, and many other, similar actions, and which we can possess in nearly every action of arms, legs, mouth, voice, mind that's worth mentioning. Wouldn't you apply the term *quickness* to all of them?

Laches: Of course.

Socrates: And suppose someone were to ask me: What is that common quality, Socrates, which, in all these uses of the word, you call *quickness*? I should say the quality which accomplishes much in a little time—whether in running, speaking, or in any other sort of action.

Laches: You'd be right.

Socrates: And now, Laches, try to tell me: What's the common quality called *courage* that includes all the various uses of the term when applied to both pleasure and pain and in all other cases?

Laches: I'd say that courage is a sort of endurance of the soul, if I'm to speak of the universal nature which pervades them all.

Socrates: But that's what we have to do to answer the question. And yet I can't say that every kind of endurance ought to be called courage. Let me explain. I'm sure, Laches, that you'd consider courage to be a very noble quality.

Laches: Most noble, certainly.

Socrates: And you'd say that a wise endurance is also good and noble?

Laches: Very noble.

Socrates: But what would you say about a foolish endurance? Shouldn't that to be regarded as evil and hurtful?

Laches: Yes.

Socrates: And is anything noble that's evil and hurtful?

Laches: I should say not, Socrates.

Socrates: Then you wouldn't count that sort of endurance to be courage—for it isn't noble, but courage is noble?

Laches: You're right.

Socrates: Then, according to you, only wise endurance is courage?

Laches: Yes.

Socrates: But as to the epithet "wise,"—wise in what? In all things small as well as great? For example, if a man displays endurance in spending his money wisely, knowing that by spending he'll acquire more in the end, do you call him courageous?

Laches: Definitely not.

Socrates: Or, for example, if a man is a physician, and his son or some patient of his has inflammation of the lungs and begs that he may be allowed to eat or drink something, and the doctor is firm and refuses; is that courage?

Laches: No; that's not courage at all, any more than the last.

Socrates: Again, take the case of someone who endures in war, is willing to fight, and wisely calculates and knows that others will help him and that there will be fewer and inferior men against him than there are with him. Suppose that he has also advantages of position. Who is braver: someone who endures with all this wisdom and preparation, or some man in the opposing army who is in the opposite circumstances and yet endures and remains at his post?

Laches: I'd say that the latter, Socrates, was braver.

Socrates: But, surely, this is a foolish endurance in comparison with the other?

Laches: That's true.

Socrates: Then you'd say that someone with a knowledge of horsemanship who endures in a cavalry engagement isn't as courageous as someone who endures without such knowledge?

Laches: So I should say.

Socrates: And someone who endures, knowing how to use the sling or the bow or any other weapon, isn't as courageous as someone who endures without such knowledge?

Laches: True.

Socrates: And someone who descends into a well, and dives and holds out in this kind of action without any knowledge of diving, is more courageous than those who do so with this knowledge?

Laches: Why, Socrates, what else can a man say?

Socrates: Nothing, if that's what he thinks.

Laches: But that is what I think.

Socrates: And yet men who thus run risks and endure are foolish, Laches, compared to those who do the same things and have the skill to do them.

Laches: That's true.

Socrates: But foolish boldness and endurance appeared before to be base and hurtful to us.

Laches: Quite true.

Socrates: But we agreed that courage is a noble quality.

Laches: True.

Socrates: And now on the contrary we're saying that foolish endurance, which was before held in dishonour, is courage.

Laches: Very true.

Socrates: And are we right in saying so?

Laches: Indeed, Socrates, I'm sure that we're not right.

Socrates: Then, according to your statement, you and I, Laches, are not attuned to the Dorian mode, which is a harmony of words and deeds. Our deeds do not match our words. Anyone would say that we had courage who saw us in action, but not, I imagine, he who heard us talking about courage just now.

Laches: That's true.

Socrates: And is this condition of ours satisfactory?

Laches: Quite the reverse.

Socrates: Suppose, however, that we admit the principle we're talking about—to a certain extent.

Laches: To what extent? What principle do you mean?

Socrates: The principle of endurance. We too must endure and persevere in our enquiry. Then courage won't laugh at our faintheartedness in searching for courage. After all, it may, very likely, be endurance.

Laches: I'm ready to go on, Socrates. I'm not used to investigations of this sort. But the spirit of controversy has been aroused in me. I'm really grieved that I can't express my meaning, for I think that I do know the nature of courage. Somehow or other, however, she's slipped away from me, and I can't get hold of her and tell her nature.

Socrates: My good friend, shouldn't the good sportsman follow the track and not be lazy?

Laches: Certainly, he should.

Socrates: Let's invite Nicias to join us. He may be better at the sport than we are. What do you say?

Laches: I'd like that.

Socrates: Come here, Nicias. Do what you can to help your friends. They're tossing on the waves of argument, and at their last gasp. You see our extremity. Maybe you can save us, and also settle your own opinion, if you tell us what you think about courage.

Nicias: I've been thinking, Socrates, that you and Laches aren't defining courage in the right way. You've forgotten an excellent saying which I've heard from your own lips.

Socrates: What is it, Nicias?

Nicias: I've often heard you say that "Every man is good when he is wise and bad when he is unwise."

Socrates: That's certainly true, Nicias.

Nicias: And so, if the brave man is good, he's also wise.

Socrates: Do you hear him, Laches?

Laches: Yes, I hear him, but I don't understand him very well.

Socrates: I think I understand him. He appears to me to mean that courage is a sort of wisdom.

Laches: What can he possibly mean, Socrates?

Socrates: That's a question you should ask him.

Laches: Yes.

Socrates: Tell him, Nicias, what you mean by wisdom. You surely don't mean the wisdom that plays the flute?

Nicias: Certainly not.

Socrates: Nor the wisdom that plays the lyre?

Nicias: No.

Socrates: But what is this knowledge then? What is it knowledge *of*?

Laches: I think you put the question to him very well, Socrates. I'd like him to explain the nature of this knowledge or wisdom.

Nicias: I mean to say, Laches, that courage is the knowledge of what inspires fear or confidence—in war or in anything.

Laches: How strangely he's talking, Socrates!

Socrates: Why do you say so, Laches?

Laches: Why, surely courage is one thing and wisdom another.

Socrates: That's just what Nicias denies.

Laches: Yes, that is what he denies. But that's silly!

Socrates: Suppose we instruct instead of abusing him?

Nicias: Laches doesn't want to instruct me, Socrates. But, having been proved to be talking nonsense himself, he wants to prove that I've been doing the same.

Laches: Very true, Nicias; and you *are* talking nonsense, as I'll endeavour to show. Let me ask you a question: Don't physicians know the dangers of disease? Or do the courageous know them? Or are the physicians the same as the courageous?

Nicias: Not at all.

Laches: No more than the husbandmen who know the dangers of husbandry—or than other craftsmen, who have a knowledge of what inspires them with fear or confidence in their own arts. Yet they aren't courageous a bit more for that.

Socrates: What is Laches saying, Nicias? He seems to be saying something important.

Nicias: Yes, he's saying something, but it isn't true.

Socrates: How so?

Nicias: Why, because he doesn't see that the physician's knowledge only extends to the nature of health and disease. He can tell the sick man no more than this. Do you imagine, Laches, that the physician knows whether health or disease is more terrible to a man? Many a man is better off never getting up from his sick bed. I'd like to know whether you think that life is always better than death. Isn't death often the better of the two?

Laches: Yes, certainly so in my opinion.

Nicias: And do you think that the same things are terrible to those who are better off dying and to those who are better off living?

Laches: Certainly not.

Nicias: Do you suppose that the physician or any other artist knows this? Does anyone, other than one who is skilled in the grounds of fear and hope? That's who I call courageous.

Socrates: Do you understand his meaning, Laches?

Laches: Yes; I suppose that, in his way of speaking, the soothsayers are courageous. For who but one of them can know who is better off living or dying? And yet, Nicias, would you allow that you are yourself a soothsayer? Or are you neither a soothsayer nor courageous?

Nicias: What! do you mean to say that the soothsayer ought to know the grounds of hope or fear?

Laches: Indeed I do: who else?

Nicias: The person I'm talking about! A soothsayer ought to know only the signs of things that are about to come to pass, whether death or disease, loss of property, victory, or defeat in war or in any sort of contest. But who is better off suffering or not suffering these things? That can no more be decided by the soothsayer than by one who is no soothsayer.

Laches: I can't understand what Nicias is doing, Socrates. For he represents the courageous man as neither a soothsayer, nor a physician, nor anything else, unless he means to say that he is a god. My opinion is that he doesn't want to confess honestly that he's talking nonsense. He shuffles up and down to conceal the difficulty he's got himself into. You and I, Socrates, could have practiced a similar shuffle just now, if we had only wanted to avoid the appearance of inconsistency. If we had been arguing in a court of law, there might have been reason to do that. But why should a man deck himself out with vain words at a meeting of friends such as this?

Socrates: I quite agree with you, Laches, that he shouldn't. But perhaps Nicias is serious, and not merely talking for the sake of talking. Let's ask him just to explain what he means. If he has reason on his side, we'll agree with him; if not, we'll instruct him.

Laches: Ask him, if you like, Socrates: I think I've asked enough.

Socrates: I don't see why I shouldn't. My question will do for both of us.

Laches: Very good.

Socrates: Then tell me, Nicias, or rather tell us, for Laches and I are partners in the argument: Do you mean to affirm that courage is the knowledge of the grounds of hope and fear?

Nicias: I do.

Socrates: And not every man has this knowledge; the physician and the soothsayer don't; and they won't be courageous unless they acquire it—that's what you were saying?

Nicias: I was.

Socrates: Then this is certainly not a thing that every pig would know, as the proverb says. So he couldn't be courageous.

Nicias: I think not.

Socrates: Clearly not, Nicias; not even such a big pig as the Crommyonian sow would be called by you courageous. I say this not as a joke, but because I think that one who assents to your doctrine—that courage is the knowledge of the grounds of fear and hope—can't allow that any wild beast is courageous, unless he admits that a lion, or a leopard, or perhaps a boar, or any other animal, has such a degree of wisdom that he knows things so difficult that only a few human beings ever know them. One who takes your view of courage must affirm that a lion, a stag, a bull, and a monkey have equally little pretensions to courage.

Laches: Capital, Socrates! By the gods, that is truly good! And I hope, Nicias, that you'll tell us whether these animals, which we all admit to be courageous, are really wiser than mankind; or whether you will have the boldness, in the face of universal opinion, to deny their courage.

Nicias: Why, Laches, I don't call animals or anything else courageous if they have no fear of dangers only because they aren't aware of them. They're merely fearless and senseless. Do you imagine that I'd call little children courageous if they fear no dangers only because they know none? There's a difference, to my way of thinking, between fearlessness and courage. I think that thoughtful courage is a quality possessed by very few. Rashness, boldness, and fearlessness, which require no forethought, are very common qualities possessed by many men, women, children, and animals. And you, and men in general, call "courageous" actions I call rash. My courageous actions are wise actions.

Laches: Look, Socrates, how admirably, as he thinks, he decks himself out in words while seeking to deprive of the honor of courage those all the world acknowledges to be courageous.

Nicias: That's not true, Laches, but don't be alarmed. I'm quite willing to say that you, Lamachus, and many other Athenians are courageous and therefore wise.

Laches: I could answer that; but I wouldn't have you throw in my face that I am a haughty Aexonian.

Socrates: Don't answer him, Laches; I doubt you're aware of the source of his wisdom. He got all this from my friend Damon, and Damon is always with Prodicus, who, of all the Sophists, is considered best at pulling words of this sort to pieces.

Laches: Yes, Socrates. Examining such niceties is a much more suitable employment for a Sophist than for a great statesman the city chooses to preside over her.

Socrates: Yes, my sweet friend, but a great statesman is likely to have great intelligence. And I think that the view implied in Nicias' definition of courage is worth examining.

Laches: Then examine for yourself, Socrates.

Socrates: That's what I'm going to do, my good friend. But don't suppose I'll let you out of our partnership, for I'll expect you to apply your mind and join with me in considering the question.

Laches: I will if you think I should.

Socrates: Yes, I do; but I must beg you, Nicias, to begin again. You remember that we originally considered courage to be a part of virtue.

Nicias: Very true.

Socrates: And you yourself said that it was a part; and there were many other parts, all of which taken together are called virtue.

Nicias: Certainly.

Socrates: Do you agree with me about the parts? For I say that justice, temperance, and the like are all parts of virtue just as courage is. Wouldn't you say the same?

Nicias: Certainly.

Socrates: Well then, so far we're agreed. Now let's proceed a step and try to arrive at a similar agreement about the fearful and the hopeful. I don't want you to be thinking one thing while I think another. Let me tell you my own opinion. If I'm wrong, you'll set me straight. In my opinion, the terrible and the hopeful are the things that do or do not create fear. Fear is not of the present, nor of the past. It's of future and expected evil. Don't you agree, Laches?

Laches: Yes, Socrates, entirely.

Socrates: That's my view, Nicias; the terrible things are the evils in the future. The hopeful are the good, or at any rate not evil things, in the future. Do you agree with me?

Nicias: I agree.

Socrates: And the knowledge of these things you call courage?

Nicias: Precisely.

Socrates: Now let me see whether you agree with Laches and myself on a third point.

Nicias: What's that?

Socrates: I'll tell you. He and I have a notion that there's not one knowledge or science of the past, another of the present, a third of what is likely to be best and what will be best in the future. There is one science of all three. For example, there is one science of medicine. It's concerned with the health in all times equally, present, past, and future. There is one science of husbandry, similarly, which is concerned with producing things from the earth in all times. As to the art of the general: You yourselves will be my witnesses that he has an excellent foreknowledge of the future. He claims to be the master and not the servant of the soothsayer, because he knows better what is happening or is likely to happen in war. Accordingly, the law places the soothsayer under the general, and not the general under the soothsayer. Isn't that right, Laches?

Laches: Quite right.

Socrates: And do you too, Nicias, acknowledge that the same science gives understanding of the same things, whether future, present, or past?

Nicias: Yes, indeed Socrates; that is my opinion.

Socrates: And courage, my friend, is, as you say, a knowledge of the fearful and of the hopeful?

Nicias: Yes.

Socrates: And the fearful and the hopeful are admitted to be future goods and future evils?

Nicias: True.

Socrates: And the same science has to do with the same things in the future or at any time?

Nicias: That's true.

Socrates: Then courage isn't the science concerned with the fearful and hopeful, for they are future only. Courage, like the other sciences, is concerned with good and evil not only in the future but in the present and past and in any time?

Nicias: That, I suppose, is true.

Socrates: Then the answer you've given, Nicias, includes only a third of courage. But our question extended to the whole nature of courage. According to your view—that is, according to your present view—courage is not only the knowledge of the hopeful and the fearful, but seems to include nearly every good and evil, without reference to time. What do you say to that alteration in your statement?

Nicias: I agree, Socrates.

Socrates: But then, my good friend, if a man knew all good and evil, and how they are, have been, and will be produced, wouldn't he be perfect, lacking no virtue, whether justice, temperance, or holiness? He'd possess them all. He'd know what was dangerous and what wasn't. He'd guard against dangers whether they were supernatural or natural. He'd do good things, for he'd know how to deal both with gods and with men.

Nicias: I think, Socrates, that there's a great deal of truth in what you say.

Socrates: But then, Nicias, courage, according to this new definition of yours, instead of being a part of virtue only, will be all of virtue?

Nicias: It seems so.

Socrates: But we were saying that courage is one of the parts of virtue?

Nicias: Yes, that was what we were saying.

Socrates: And that contradicts our present view?

Nicias: Apparently.

Socrates: Then, Nicias, we haven't discovered what courage is.

Nicias: We haven't.

3.2 PLATO'S CONCEPTION OF VIRTUE

The view that virtue is a kind of knowledge has an important consequence: Weakness of will is either impossible or irrelevant. Paul gives the classic characterization of weakness of will in his letter to the Romans:

> For what I do, I do not allow. What I want to do, I don't do. What I hate, I do. If then I do what I don't want to do, I consent to the law that it is good.... The will to do good is present in me. But I can't figure out how to perform what is good. For the good that I want to do, I do not; but the evil that I do not want to do—that I do. (Romans 7:15–19)

Weakness of will, in short, is knowing the better and doing the worse. It is knowing what you ought to do and nevertheless not doing it. The smoker who knows she ought to quit but can't and the dieter who knows he shouldn't eat the cake but does anyway both display weakness of will.

If virtue is simply a matter of knowing good and evil, however, weakness of will is unintelligible. For then virtue is knowing the better; someone who knows the better and does the worse would be virtuous. But that seems absurd. As philosophers such as Aristotle and Kant have stressed, self-control, strength of character, and willpower are themselves virtues. Turning this around, on Socrates's view, all vice is ignorance. But we do not tend to think that the person who is weak of will is simply ignorant. The only way to defend the thesis that virtue is knowledge is to maintain either that weakness of will is impossible or that the person displaying weakness of will is ignorant in some significant way. But neither option seems very plausible. Cases of weakness of will are commonplace. And they do not seem to involve ignorance. The sinner trying to reform may be all too aware of the evils of sin.

Plato offers a very different account of virtue in the *Republic*, where Socrates (the character) for the first time offers his own definition of a virtue. The question is "What is justice?" Socrates answers, "Doing one's own"—an answer that rests on an analysis both of the state and of the soul. According to Plato, each has three parts: the rational, the appetitive, and the spirited. A person is just when his or her soul is in balance, when, that is, each part of the soul is playing its proper role.

The soul, then, contains a rational principle and an appetitive principle. There is also a third passionate or spirited principle. It cannot be identified with appetite or reason.

There are, then, three parts of the soul—the rational, appetitive, and spirited elements (or, in other words, reason, desire, and passion)—each of which has an essential role to play. In a just person, each element plays its proper role. The rational element rules over the other two, restraining both desires and passions.

On this account, it is easy to explain weakness of will, which poses problems for Socrates's view. A person may face a conflict between reason and desire, or reason and passion, or passion and desire. She may know which ought to triumph. But she may or may not be strong enough to make it triumph. The smoker, for example, may know it would be best for her to quit smoking. Her rational element directs her to stop. But her appetitive element calls for her to smoke. If she is strong, the rational element wins. If not, the appetitive element does.

Plato, in short, offers us two theories of virtue. In his early dialogues, Socrates treats the virtues as unified. Virtue is a kind of knowledge, specifically, the knowledge of good and evil. That makes weakness of will impossible or irrelevant. In the *Republic*, Plato puts forward an account of virtue as a balance of the parts of the soul. A person is virtuous when reason, desire, and passion each play their proper role. That makes weakness of will easy to understand; it occurs when reason loses a conflict with desire or passion.

3.2.1 Plato, from the *Republic*

We won't, I said, be overly positive just yet. But if, on trial, this conception of justice can be verified in the individual as well as in the State, there will be no longer any room for doubt. If it is not verified, we must start a fresh enquiry. First let's complete the old investigation, which we began, you remember, under the impression that, if we could first examine justice on a larger scale, it would be easier to recognize justice in an individual. That larger example appeared to be the State. Accordingly we constructed as good a State as we could, knowing well that in the good State justice would be found. Let's apply the discovery we made to the individual—if they agree, we'll be satisfied; or, if there be a difference in the individual, we'll come back to the State and have another trial of the theory. The friction of the two when rubbed together might strike a light in which justice will shine forth, and the vision then revealed we'll fix in our souls.

That sounds good; let's do as you say.

I proceeded to ask: When two things, a greater and a less, are called by the same name, are they like or unlike insofar as they are called the same?

Like, he replied.

The just man, then, if we regard the idea of justice alone, will be like the just State?

He will.

And we thought a State just when the three classes in the State each did its own business. We thought it temperate and valiant and wise by reason of certain other characteristics of these same classes?

True, he said.

And so of the individual. We may assume that he has the same three principles in his own soul which are found in the State. He may be rightly described in the same terms, because he is affected in the same manner?

Certainly, he said.

Once more, then, my friend, we've alighted upon an easy question—whether the soul has these three principles or not.

An easy question! No, Socrates, the proverb holds that hard is the good.

Very true, I said; and I don't think that the method we're employing is at all adequate to the accurate solution of this question. The true method is another and a longer one. Still we may arrive at a solution not below the level of the previous enquiry.

May we not be satisfied with that? he said. Under the circumstances, I'm quite content.

I too, I replied, shall be extremely well satisfied.

Source: Plato, *Republic*. Translated by Benjamin Jowett. New York: Charles Scribner's Sons, 1871. We have altered the translation for readability.

Then don't faint in pursuing the speculation, he said.

Mustn't we acknowledge, I said, that in each of us there are the same principles and habits that there are in the State; and that from the individual they pass into the State? How else can they get there? Take the quality of passion or spirit; it would be ridiculous to imagine that this quality, when found in States, is not derived from the individuals who are supposed to possess it, e.g., the Thracians, the Scythians, and in general the northern nations. The same may be said of the love of knowledge, which is the special characteristic of our part of the world. Or of the love of money, which may, with equal truth, be attributed to the Phoenicians and Egyptians.

Exactly so, he said.

There's no difficulty in understanding this.

None whatever.

But the question isn't quite so easy when we proceed to ask whether these principles are three or one; whether, that is to say, we learn with one part of our nature, are angry with another, and with a third part desire the satisfaction of our natural appetites; or whether the whole soul comes into play in each sort of action—to determine that is the difficulty.

Yes, he said; there lies the difficulty.

Then let us now try to determine whether they are the same or different.

How can we? he asked.

I replied as follows: The same thing clearly can't act or be acted upon in the same part or in relation to the same thing at the same time in contrary ways. Therefore, whenever this contradiction occurs in things apparently the same, we know that they are really not the same but different.

Good.

For example, I said, can the same thing be at rest and in motion at the same time in the same part?

Impossible.

Still, I said, let's have a more precise statement of terms, so we don't end up falling by the wayside. Imagine the case of a man who is standing and also moving his hands and his head. Suppose someone says that one and the same person is in motion and at rest at the same moment. We'd object to such a mode of speech. We'd rather say that one part of him is in motion while another is at rest.

Very true.

And suppose the objector to refine this still further and to draw the nice distinction that not only parts of tops, but whole tops, when they spin round with their pegs fixed on the spot, are at rest and in motion at the same time. (He may say the same of anything which revolves in the same spot.) We wouldn't admit his objection, because in such cases things aren't at rest and in motion in the same parts of themselves. We'd rather say that they have both an axis and a circumference. The axis stands still, for there is no deviation from the perpendicular. The circumference goes round. But if, while revolving, the axis inclines either to the right or the left, forwards or backwards, then from no point of view can they be at rest.

That's the right way to describe them, he replied.

Then none of these objections will confuse us, or incline us to believe that the same thing at the same time, in the same part or in relation to the same thing, can act or be acted upon in contrary ways.

Certainly not, according to my way of thinking.

Yet, I said, so we don't have to examine all such objections and prove at length that they are untrue, let's assume their absurdity and go forward on the understanding that hereafter, if this assumption turns out to be wrong, we'll withdraw all the consequences that follow.

Yes, he said, that will be the best way.

Well, I said, wouldn't you allow that assent and dissent, desire and aversion, attraction and repulsion, are all of them opposites, whether we regard them as active or passive (for that makes no difference in the fact of their opposition)?

Yes, he said, they are opposites.

Well, I said, and hunger and thirst, and the desires in general, and again willing and wishing—all these you'd refer to the classes already mentioned. You would say—wouldn't you?—that the soul of one who desires is seeking after the object of his desires; that he is drawing to himself the thing he wishes to possess: or again, when a person wants anything to be given to him, his mind, longing for the realization of his desires, intimates his wish to have it by a nod of assent, as if he had been asked a question?

Very true.

And what would you say of unwillingness and dislike and the absence of desire; shouldn't these be referred to the opposite class of repulsion and rejection?

Certainly.

Admitting this to be true of desire generally, let's take a particular class of desires. Out of these let's select hunger and thirst, as they are called, which are the most obvious of them.

Let's take that class, he said.

The object of one is food and of the other drink?

Yes.

And here's the point: Isn't thirst the desire the soul has for drink, and for drink only? Not of drink qualified by anything else—for example, warm or cold, or much or little, or, in a word, drink of any particular sort—but if the thirst be accompanied by heat, then the desire is for cold drink; or, if accompanied by cold, then for warm drink; or, if the thirst is excessive, then the drink desired will be excessive; or, if not great, the quantity of drink will also be small. But thirst pure and simple will desire drink pure and simple, which is the natural satisfaction of thirst, as food is of hunger?

Yes, he said; the simple desire is, as you say, in every case for the simple object and the qualified desire for the qualified object.

But here a confusion may arise; and I wish to guard against an opponent starting up and saying that no man desires drink only, but good drink, or food only, but good food. For good is the universal object of desire, and thirst, being a desire, will necessarily be thirst after good drink; and the same is true of every other desire.

Yes, he replied, the opponent might have something to say.

Nevertheless I'd still maintain that of relatives some have a quality attached to either term of the relation; others are simple and have their correlatives simple.

I don't know what you mean.

Well, you know of course that the greater is relative to the less?

Certainly.

And the much greater to the much less?

Yes.

And the sometime greater to the sometime less, and the greater that is to be to the less that is to be?

Certainly, he said.

And so of more and less, and of other correlative terms, such as double and half, or again, heavier and lighter, swifter and slower; and of hot and cold, and of any other relatives;—is not this true of all of them?

Yes.

And doesn't the same principle hold in the sciences? The object of science is knowledge (assuming that to be the true definition), but the object of a particular science is a particular kind of knowledge. I mean, for example, that the science of house building is a kind of knowledge defined and distinguished from other kinds and is therefore termed *architecture*.

Certainly.

Because it has a particular quality nothing else has?

Yes.

And it has this particular quality because it has an object of a particular kind. This is true of the other arts and sciences?

Yes.

Now, then, if I've made myself clear, you'll understand my original meaning in what I said about relatives. My meaning was that if one term of a relation is taken alone, the other is taken alone; if one term is qualified, the other is also qualified. I don't mean to say that relatives may not be disparate, or that the science of health is healthy, or of disease necessarily diseased, or that the sciences of good and evil are therefore good and evil; but only that, when the term *science* is no longer used absolutely but has a qualified object, which in this case is the nature of health and disease, it becomes defined and is hence called not merely *science*, but the *science of medicine.*

I quite understand, and I think as you do.

Wouldn't you say that thirst is one of these essentially relative terms, having clearly a relation—

Yes, thirst is relative to drink.

And a certain kind of thirst is relative to a certain kind of drink; but thirst taken alone is neither of much nor little, nor of good nor bad, nor of any particular kind of drink, but of drink only?

Certainly.

Then the soul of the thirsty one, insofar as he is thirsty, desires only drink; for this he yearns and tries to obtain it?

That is plain.

And if you suppose something which pulls a thirsty soul away from drink, that must be different from the thirsty principle which draws him like a beast to drink; for, as we were saying, the same thing can't at the same time with the same part of itself act in contrary ways about the same thing.

Impossible.

No more than you can say that the hands of the archer push and pull the bow at the same time, but what you say is that one hand pushes and the other pulls.

Exactly so, he replied.

And might a man be thirsty and yet unwilling to drink?

Yes, he said, it constantly happens.

And in such a case what is one to say? Wouldn't you say that there was something in the soul bidding a man to drink, and something else forbidding him, which is other and stronger than the principle which bids him?

I'd say so.

And the forbidding principle is derived from reason, and that which bids and attracts proceeds from passion and disease?

Clearly.

Then we may fairly assume that they are two and that they differ from one another. The one with which a man reasons, we may call the *rational* principle of the soul. The other, with which he loves and hungers and thirsts and feels the flutterings of any other desire, may be termed the irrational or *appetitive*, the ally of sundry pleasures and satisfactions?

Yes, he said, we may fairly assume them to be different.

Then let's finally determine that there are two principles existing in the soul. And what of passion, or spirit? Is it a third, or akin to one of the preceding?

I'd be inclined to say—akin to desire.

Well, I said, there's a story I remember and in which I put faith. The story is that Leontius, the son of Aglaion, coming up one day from the Piraeus, under the north wall on the outside, observed some dead bodies lying on the ground at the place of execution. He felt a desire to see them and also a dread and abhorrence of them. For a time he struggled and covered his eyes. But at length the desire got the better of him. Forcing them open, he ran up to the dead bodies, saying, "Look, you wretches, take your fill of the fair sight!"

I've heard the story myself, he said.

The moral of the tale is that anger at times goes to war with desire, as though they were two distinct things.

Yes, that's the meaning, he said.

And aren't there many other cases in which we observe that when a man's desires violently prevail over his reason, he reviles himself, and is angry at the violence within him? In this struggle, which is like the struggle of factions in a State, his spirit is on the side of his reason. But for the passionate or spirited element to take the side of desires when reason decides that she shouldn't be opposed is a sort of thing which, I believe, you never observed occurring in yourself, nor, as I should imagine, in anyone else?

Certainly not.

Suppose that a man thinks he's done a wrong to another. The nobler he is, the less able he is to feel indignant at any suffering, such as hunger or cold or any other pain the injured person may inflict upon him. These he deems to be just, and, as I say, his anger refuses to be excited by them.

True, he said.

But when he thinks that he is the sufferer of the wrong, then he boils and chafes and is on the side of what he believes to be justice. Because he suffers hunger or cold or other pain he is only the more determined to persevere and conquer. His noble spirit will not be quelled until he either slays or is slain; or until he hears the voice of the shepherd, that is, reason, bidding his dog bark no more.

The illustration is perfect, he replied; and in our State, as we were saying, the auxiliaries were to be dogs, and to hear the voice of the rulers, who are their shepherds.

I perceive, I said, that you quite understand me; there is, however, a further point I wish you to consider.

What point?

You remember that passion or spirit appeared at first sight to be a kind of desire. But now we should say quite the contrary; for in the conflict of the soul spirit is arrayed on the side of the rational principle.

Most assuredly.

But a further question arises: Is passion different from reason too, or only a kind of reason? In the latter case, instead of three principles in the soul, there will only be two, the rational and the concupiscent. Or rather, as the State was composed of three classes, traders, auxiliaries, counsellors, so may there not be in the individual soul a third element which is passion or spirit, that when not corrupted by bad education is the natural auxiliary of reason?

Yes, he said, there must be a third.

Yes, I replied, if passion, which has already been shown to be different from desire, turns out also to be different from reason.

But that's easily proved:—We may observe even in young children that they're full of spirit almost as soon as they're born, whereas some of them never seem to attain to the use of reason, and most of them late enough.

Excellent, I said, and you may see passion equally in brute animals, which is a further proof of the truth of what you're saying. And we may once more appeal to the words of Homer, which have been already quoted by us,

> "He smote his breast, and thus rebuked his soul";

for in this verse Homer has clearly supposed the power that reasons about the better and worse to be different from the unreasoning anger rebuked by it.

Very true, he said.

3.3 ARISTOTLE ON VIRTUE

Aristotle (384–322 BCE), student of Plato, tutor of Alexander the Great, and contemporary of Euclid, develops the classic theory of virtue in the Western philosophical tradition. He distinguishes intrinsic goods, which are desired for their own sake, from instrumental goods, which are desired as means to other things. To justify any answers to questions of justification, we must appeal to intrinsic goods. To respond to questions asking for justification successfully, we must invoke something good for its own sake.

Aristotle contends that people desire only one thing for its own sake and never for the sake of something else: happiness. What is happiness? We tend to think that people are happy when they feel good. Aristotle would agree that happiness has something to do with feelings. But that is only part of the story. To be happy, for Aristotle, is to succeed at life; to flourish; to be fulfilled; to live well.

What is it to live well? Some people—according to some feminist philosophers, especially men—tend to think of success, of living well, in purely material terms. Aristotle thinks that material well-being and outright luck are important factors; it's hard to be happy, he points out, if you are starving or if your loved ones have been killed. But there is more to happiness than prosperity and luck. What more is required to live well? Aristotle's answer relies on the idea that human beings have a function. Just as a good knife cuts well and a good teacher teaches well, a good person fulfills the function of a human being well.

But what is the function of a person? According to Aristotle, it is what is most distinctive of human beings. It is what distinguishes us from other animals. As philosophers over the ages have pointed out, we differ from other animals in many ways: We use language; we can conceive of beings such as God who are greater than anything we experience; we buy and sell; we control what Marx calls "the means of production"; we construct institutions such as schools, hospitals, markets, and governments. Dogs and cats do not talk, pray, trade, or farm. But what underlies all these differences is our ability to reason. Undoubtedly, other animals have some cognitive abilities; they learn to trot into the kitchen at the sound of the can opener. In general, they act rationally in some respects. It is not easy to say what is distinctive about human reason that enables us to do the things we alone can do. But, whatever it is, it enables us not only to act rationally in particular situations but also to construct rational plans for our lives. That, Aristotle contends, is our function: to live according to a rational plan.

A good person acts in accordance with virtue, and to act virtuously is to act in accordance with a rational plan. A good person consistently does the right thing at the right time, in the right way, and for the right reason. There is no rule for becoming good or for distinguishing good from bad, right from wrong; a person of practical wisdom has a highly refined ability to draw the right distinctions and tell right from wrong whatever the particular circumstances.

How does a person become virtuous? How, in other words, can someone become practically wise? Not by abstract thought, Aristotle says, but by doing virtuous things. One becomes good not by intellectual discovery but by apprenticeship to good role models. If you do brave things, for example—initially, by forcing yourself to do them, by imitating a brave person, by pretending to be brave—you gradually develop the habit of doing brave things. When the habit is ingrained to the point of being second nature, you are brave. In general, people become good by doing good things.

A good person, we've seen, does the right thing at the right time, in the right way, and for the right reason. Virtue is thus a mean between extremes. The ability to find that mean Aristotle calls practical wisdom (*phronesis*). To fear too much is cowardly, but to fear too little is rash. Someone who forgets a bungee cord and leaps into a river with construction cable tied around his ankle is not brave but foolish. Courage is fearing what ought to be feared, when it ought to be feared, to the extent that it ought to be feared, and for the appropriate reason.

Right and wrong are defined in terms of virtue: an act is good if it is something a virtuous person would do.

We can think of virtues, for Aristotle, as corresponding to human drives and emotions. A virtue constrains a drive or emotion—at the right times, in the right ways, and for the right reasons. Any virtue, then, has two related vices. One consists in not constraining the drive or emotion enough, the other, in constraining it too much. These are the virtues and vices Aristotle describes:

Drive or Emotion	*Too unconstrained*	*Virtuous*	*Too constrained*
fear	cowardly	courageous	rash
pleasure	self-indulgent	self-controlled	insensitive
material goods	stingy	generous	extravagant
spending	grudging, mean	magnificent	vulgar, profligate
self-esteem	vain	high-minded	small-minded
drive for honor	ambitious	[unnamed]	unambitious
anger	short-tempered	gentle	apathetic
social relations	obsequious	friendly	grouchy
boasting	boastful	truthful	self-depreciating
humor	clownish	witty	boorish

In sum, all virtues are means between constraining a drive too much and not enough. To act as we ought is to find that mean. Correct action therefore requires practical wisdom.

Virtue is a means between extremes: One must do the right thing, to the right person, to the right extent, at the right time, with the right motive, in the right way, in the right circumstances, and for the right reasons. How do you find the intermediate in all these respects? There is no rule, Aristotle says; you must develop judgment, that is, the ability to see what to do. He takes the analogy between moral and perceptual knowledge seriously. For Aristotle, practical wisdom is the product of experience, training, and reflection. Reason itself is not enough to determine what ought to be done in particular situations. It follows that precise rules for ethical behavior are impossible. The best we can do is give rules true for the most part.

3.3.1 Aristotle, from *Nicomachean Ethics*

Book I

1. Every art and every inquiry, and similarly every action and pursuit, is thought to aim at some good; and for this reason the good has rightly been declared to be that at which all things aim. But a certain difference is found among ends; some are activities, others are products apart from the activities that produce them. Where there are ends apart from the actions, it is the nature of the products to be better than the activities. Now, as there are many actions, arts, and sciences, their ends also are many; the end of the medical art is health, that of shipbuilding a vessel, that of strategy victory, that of economics wealth. But where such arts fall under a single capacity—as bridle-making and the other arts concerned with the equipment of horses fall under the art of riding, and this and every military action under strategy, in the same way other arts fall under yet others—in all of these the ends of the master arts are to be preferred to all the subordinate ends; for it is for

Source: Aristotle, *Nicomachean Ethics*. Translated by W. D. Ross. Oxford: Clarendon Press, 1908.

the sake of the former that the latter are pursued. It makes no difference whether the activities themselves are the ends of the actions, or something else apart from the activities, as in the case of the sciences just mentioned.

3. Our discussion will be adequate if it has as much clearness as the subject-matter admits of, for precision is not to be sought for alike in all discussions, any more than in all the products of the crafts. Now fine and just actions, which political science investigates, admit of much variety and fluctuation of opinion, so that they may be thought to exist only by convention, and not by nature. And goods also give rise to a similar fluctuation because they bring harm to many people; for before now men have been undone by reason of their wealth, and others by reason of their courage. We must be content, then, in speaking of such subjects and with such premisses to indicate the truth roughly and in outline, and in speaking about things which are only for the most part true and with premisses of the same kind to reach conclusions that are no better. In the same spirit, therefore, should each type of statement be received; for it is the mark of an educated man to look for precision in each class of things just so far as the nature of the subject admits; it is evidently equally foolish to accept probable reasoning from a mathematician and to demand from a rhetorician scientific proofs.

Now each man judges well the things he knows, and of these he is a good judge. And so the man who has been educated in a subject is a good judge of that subject, and the man who has received an all-round education is a good judge in general. Hence a young man is not a proper hearer of lectures on political science; for he is inexperienced in the actions that occur in life, but its discussions start from these and are about these; and, further, since he tends to follow his passions, his study will be vain and unprofitable, because the end aimed at is not knowledge but action. And it makes no difference whether he is young in years or youthful in character; the defect does not depend on time, but on his living, and pursuing each successive object, as passion directs. For to such persons, as to the incontinent, knowledge brings no profit; but to those who desire and act in accordance with a rational principle knowledge about such matters will be of great benefit.

These remarks about the student, the sort of treatment to be expected, and the purpose of the inquiry, may be taken as our preface.

4. Let us resume our inquiry and state, in view of the fact that all knowledge and every pursuit aims at some good, what it is that we say political science aims at and what is the highest of all goods achievable by action. Verbally there is very general agreement; for both the general run of men and people of superior refinement say that it is happiness, and identify living well and doing well with being happy; but with regard to what happiness is they differ, and the many do not give the same account as the wise. For the former think it is some plain and obvious thing, like pleasure, wealth, or honour; they differ, however, from one another—and often even the same man identifies it with different things, with health when he is ill, with wealth when he is poor; but, conscious of their ignorance, they admire those who proclaim some great ideal that is above their comprehension. Now some thought that apart from these many goods there is another which is self-subsistent and causes the goodness of all these as well. To examine all the opinions that have been held were perhaps somewhat fruitless; enough to examine those that are most prevalent or that seem to be arguable.

Let us not fail to notice, however, that there is a difference between arguments from and those to the first principles. For Plato, too, was right in raising this question and asking, as he used to do, "Are we on the way from or to the first principles?" There is a difference, as there is in a racecourse between the course from the judges to the turning-point and the way back. For, while we must begin with what is known, things are objects of knowledge in two senses—some to us, some without qualification. Presumably, then, we must begin with things known to us. Hence anyone who is to listen intelligently to lectures about what is noble and just, and generally, about the subjects of political science must have been brought up in good habits. For the fact is the starting-point, and if this is sufficiently plain to him, he will not at the start need the reason as well; and the man who has been well brought up has or can easily get starting-points. And as for him who neither has nor can get them, let him hear the words of Hesiod:

> Far best is he who knows all things himself;
> Good, he that hearkens when men counsel right;
> But he who neither knows, nor lays to heart
> Another's wisdom, is a useless wight.

7. Let us again return to the good we are seeking, and ask what it can be. It seems different in different actions and arts; it is different in medicine, in strategy, and in the other arts likewise. What then is the good of each? Surely that for whose sake everything else is done. In medicine this is health, in strategy victory, in architecture a house, in any other sphere something else, and in every action and pursuit the end, for it is for the sake of this that all men do whatever else they do. Therefore, if there is an end for all that we do, this will be the good achievable by action, and if there are more than one, these will be the goods achievable by action.

So the argument has by a different course reached the same point; but we must try to state this even more clearly. Since there is evidently more than one end, and we choose some of these (e.g., wealth, flutes, and in general instruments) for the sake of something else, clearly not all ends are final ends; but the chief good is evidently something final. Therefore, if there is only one final end, this will be what we are seeking, and if there is more than one, the most final of these will be what we are seeking. Now we call that which is in itself worthy of pursuit more final than that which is worthy of pursuit for the sake of something else, and that which is never desirable for the sake of something else more final than the things that are desirable both in themselves and for the sake of that other thing, and therefore we call final without qualification that which is always desirable in itself and never for the sake of something else.

Now such a thing happiness, above all else, is held to be; for this we choose always for self and never for the sake of something else, but honour, pleasure, reason, and every virtue we choose indeed for themselves (for if nothing resulted from them we should still choose each of them), but we choose them also for the sake of happiness, judging that by means of them we shall be happy. Happiness, on the other hand, no one chooses for the sake of these, nor, in general, for anything other than itself.

From the point of view of self-sufficiency the same result seems to follow; for the final good is thought to be self-sufficient. Now by self-sufficient we do not mean that which is sufficient for a man by himself, for one who lives a solitary life, but also for parents, children, wife, and in general for his friends and fellow citizens, since man is born for citizenship. But some limit must be set to this; for if we extend our requirement to ancestors and descendants and friends' friends we are in for an infinite series. Let us examine this question, however, on another occasion; the self-sufficient we now define as that which when isolated makes life desirable and lacking in nothing; and such we think happiness to be; and further we think it most desirable of all things, without being counted as one good thing among others—if it were so counted it would clearly be made more desirable by the addition of even the least of goods; for that which is added becomes an excess of goods, and of goods the greater is always more desirable. Happiness, then, is something final and self-sufficient, and is the end of action.

Presumably, however, to say that happiness is the chief good seems a platitude, and a clearer account of what it is still desired. This might perhaps be given, if we could first ascertain the function of man. For just as for a flute-player, a sculptor, or an artist, and, in general, for all things that have a function or activity, the good and the "well" is thought to reside in the function, so would it seem to be for man, if he has a function. Have the carpenter, then, and the tanner certain functions or activities, and has man none? Is he born without a function? Or as eye, hand, foot, and in general each of the parts evidently has a function, may one lay it down that man similarly has a function apart from all these? What then can this be? Life seems to be common even to plants, but we are seeking what is peculiar to man. Let us exclude, therefore, the life of nutrition and growth. Next there would be a life of perception, but it also seems to be common even to the horse, the ox, and every animal. There remains, then, an active life of the element that has a rational principle; of this, one part has such a principle in the sense of being obedient to one, the other in the sense of possessing one and exercising thought. And, as "life of the rational element" also has two meanings, we must state that life in the sense of activity is what we mean; for this seems to be the more proper sense of the term. Now if the function of man is an activity of soul which follows or implies a rational principle, and if we say "so-and-so" and "a good so-and-so" have a function which is the same in kind, e.g., a lyre and a good lyre player, and so without qualification in all cases, eminence in respect of goodness being added to the name of the function (for the function of a lyre-player is to play the lyre, and that of a good lyre-player is to do so well): if this is the case, and we state the function of man to be a certain kind of life, and this to be an activity or actions of the soul implying a rational principle, and the function of a good man to be the good and noble performance of these, and if any action is well performed when it is performed in accordance with the appropriate excellence: if this is the case, human good turns out to be activity of soul in accordance with virtue, and if there is more than one virtue, in accordance with the best and most complete.

But we must add "in a complete life." For one swallow does not make a summer, nor does one day; and so too one day, or a short time, does not make a man blessed and happy.

13. Since happiness is an activity of soul in accordance with perfect virtue, we must consider the nature of virtue; for perhaps we shall thus see better the nature of happiness. The true student of politics, too, is thought to have studied virtue above all things, for he wishes to make his fellow citizens good and obedient to the laws. As an example of this we have the lawgivers of the Cretans and the Spartans, and any others of the kind that there may have been. And if this inquiry belongs to political science, clearly the pursuit of it will be in accordance with our original plan. But clearly the virtue we must study is human virtue, for the good we were seeking was human good and the happiness human happiness. By human virtue we mean not that of the body but that of the soul; and happiness also we call an activity of soul. But if this is so, clearly the student of politics must know somehow the facts about soul, as the man who is to heal the eyes or the body as a whole must know about the eyes or the body; and all the more since politics is more prized and better than medicine; but even among doctors the best educated spend much labour on acquiring knowledge of the body. The student of politics, then, must study the soul, and must study it with these objects in view, and do so just to the extent which is sufficient for the questions we are discussing, for further precision is perhaps something more laborious than our purposes require.

Some things are said about it, adequately enough, even in the discussions outside our school, and we must use these, e.g., that one element in the soul is irrational and one has a rational principle. Whether these are separated as the parts of the body or of anything divisible are, or are distinct by definition but by nature inseparable, like convex and concave in the circumference of a circle, does not affect the present question.

Of the irrational element one division seems to be widely distributed, and vegetative in its nature, I mean that which causes nutrition and growth, for it is this kind of power of the soul that one must assign to all nurslings and to embryos, and this same power to full-grown creatures; this is more reasonable than to assign some different power to them. Now the excellence of this seems to be common to all species and not specifically human; for this part or faculty seems to function most in sleep, while goodness and badness are least manifest in sleep (whence comes the saying that the happy are not better off than the wretched for half their lives;

and this happens naturally enough, since sleep is an inactivity of the soul in that respect in which it is called good or bad), unless perhaps to a small extent some of the movements actually penetrate to the soul, and in this respect the dreams of good men are better than those of ordinary people. Enough of this subject, however; let us leave the nutritive faculty alone, since it has by its nature no share in human excellence.

There seems to be also another irrational element in the soul—one which in a sense, however, shares in a rational principle. For we praise the rational principle of the continent man and of the incontinent, and the part of their soul that has such a principle, since it urges them aright and towards the best objects; but there is found in them also another element naturally opposed to the rational principle, which fights against and resists that principle. For exactly as paralysed limbs when we intend to move them to the right turn on the contrary to the left, so is it with the soul; the impulses of incontinent people move in contrary directions. But while in the body we see that which moves astray, in the soul we do not. No doubt, however, we must nonetheless suppose that in the soul too there is something contrary to the rational principle, resisting and opposing it. In what sense it is distinct from the other elements does not concern us. Now, even this seems to have a share in a rational principle, as we said; at any rate in the continent man it obeys the rational principle, and presumably in the temperate and brave man it is still more obedient, for in him it speaks, on all matters, with the same voice as the rational principle.

Therefore the irrational element also appears to be two-fold. For the vegetative element in no way shares in a rational principle, but the appetitive and in general the desiring element in a sense shares in it, insofar as it listens to and obeys it; this is the sense in which we speak of "taking account" of one's father or one's friends, not that in which we speak of "accounting" for a mathematical property. That the irrational element is in some sense persuaded by a rational principle is indicated also by the giving of advice and by all reproof and exhortation. And if this element also must be said to have a rational principle, that which has a rational principle (as well as that which has not) will be twofold, one subdivision having it in the strict sense and in itself, and the other having a tendency to obey as one does one's father.

Virtue too is distinguished into kinds in accordance with this difference, for we say that some of the virtues are intellectual and others moral, philosophic wisdom and understanding and practical wisdom being intellectual, liberality and temperance moral. For in speaking about a man's character we do not say that he is wise or has understanding but that he is good-tempered or temperate; yet we praise the wise man also with respect to his state of mind; and of states of mind we call those which merit praise virtues.

Book II

1. Virtue, then, being of two kinds, intellectual and moral, intellectual virtue in the main owes both its birth and its growth to teaching (for which reason it requires experience and time), while moral virtue comes about as a result of habit, whence also its name (*ethike*) is one that is formed by a slight variation from the word *ethos* (habit). From this it is also plain that none of the moral virtues arises in us by nature, for nothing that exists by nature can form a habit contrary to its nature. For instance, the stone which by nature moves downwards cannot be habituated to move upwards, not even if one tries to train it by throwing it up ten thousand times; nor can fire be habituated to move downwards, nor can anything else that by nature behaves in one way be trained to behave in another. Neither by nature, then, nor contrary to nature do the virtues arise in us; rather we are adapted by nature to receive them, and are made perfect by habit.

Again, of all the things that come to us by nature we first acquire the potentiality and later exhibit the activity (this is plain in the case of the senses, for it was not by often seeing or often hearing that we got these senses, but on the contrary we had them before we used them, and did not come to have them by using them); but the virtues we get by first exercising them, as also happens in the case of the arts as well. For the things we have to learn before we can do them, we learn by doing them; e.g., men become builders by building and lyre players by playing the lyre; so too we become just by doing just acts, temperate by doing temperate acts, brave by doing brave acts.

This is confirmed by what happens in states; for legislators make the citizens good by forming habits in them, and this is the wish of every legislator, and those who do not effect it miss their mark, and it is in this that a good constitution differs from a bad one.

Again, it is from the same causes and by the same means that every virtue is both produced and destroyed, and similarly every art, for it is from playing the lyre that both good and bad lyre-players are produced. And the corresponding statement is true of builders and of all the rest; men will be good or bad builders as a result of building well or badly. For if this were not so, there would have been no need of a teacher, but all men would have been born good or bad at their craft. This, then, is the case with the virtues also; by doing the acts that we do in our transactions with other men we become just or unjust, and by doing the acts that we do in the presence of danger, and being habituated to feel fear or confidence, we become brave or cowardly. The same is true of appetites and feelings of anger; some men become temperate and good-tempered, others self-indulgent and irascible, by behaving in one way or the other in the appropriate circumstances. Thus, in one word, states of character arise out of like activities. This is why the activities we exhibit must be of a certain kind; it is because the states of character correspond to the differences between these. It makes no small difference, then, whether we form habits of one kind or of another from our very youth; it makes a very great difference, or rather all the difference.

2. Since, then, the present inquiry does not aim at theoretical knowledge like the others (for we are inquiring not in order to know what virtue is, but in order to become good, since otherwise our inquiry would have been of no use), we must examine the nature of actions, namely how we ought to do them; for these determine also the nature of the states of character that are produced, as we have said. Now, that we must act according to the right rule is a common principle and must be assumed—it will be discussed later, i.e., both what the right rule is, and how it is related to the other virtues. But this must be agreed upon beforehand, that the whole account of matters of conduct must be given in outline and not precisely, as we said at the very beginning that the accounts we demand must be in accordance with the subject-matter; matters concerned with conduct and questions of what is good for us have no fixity, any more than matters of health. The general account being of this nature, the account of particular cases is yet more lacking in exactness; for they do not fall under any art or precept but the agents themselves must in each case consider what is appropriate to the occasion, as happens also in the art of medicine or of navigation.

But though our present account is of this nature, we must give what help we can. First, then, let us consider this, that it is the nature of such things to be destroyed by defect and excess, as we see in the case of strength and of health (for to gain light on things imperceptible we must use the evidence of sensible things); both excessive and defective exercise destroys the strength, and similarly drink or food which is above or below a certain amount destroys the health, while that which is proportionate both produces and increases and preserves it. So too is it, then, in the case of temperance and courage and the other virtues. For the man who flies from and fears everything and does not stand his ground against anything becomes a coward, and the man who fears nothing at all but goes to meet every danger becomes rash; and similarly the man who indulges in every pleasure and abstains from none becomes self-indulgent, while the man who shuns every pleasure, as boors do, becomes in a way insensible; temperance and courage, then, are destroyed by excess and defect, and preserved by the mean.

But not only are the sources and causes of their origination and growth the same as those of their destruction, but also the sphere of their actualization will be the same; for this is also true of the things which are more evident to sense, e.g., of strength; it is produced by taking much food and undergoing much exertion, and it is the strong man that will be most able to do these things. So too is it with the virtues; by abstaining from pleasures we become temperate, and it is when we have become so that we are most able to abstain from them; and similarly too in the case of courage, for by being habituated to despise things that are terrible and to stand our ground against them we become brave, and it is when we have become so that we shall be most able to stand our ground against them.

4. The question might be asked, what we mean by saying that we must become just by doing just acts, and temperate by doing temperate acts; for if men do just and temperate acts, they are already just and temperate, exactly as, if they do what is in accordance with the laws of grammar and of music, they are grammarians and musicians....

Again, the case of the arts and that of the virtues are not similar, for the products of the arts have their goodness in themselves, so that it is enough that they should have a certain character, but if the acts that are in accordance with the virtues have themselves a certain character it does not follow that they are done justly or temperately. The agent also must be in a certain condition when he does them; in the first place he must have knowledge, secondly he must choose the acts, and choose them for their own sakes, and thirdly his action must proceed from a firm and unchangeable character. These are not reckoned in as conditions of the possession of the arts, except the bare knowledge, but as a condition of the possession of the virtues knowledge has little or no weight, while the other conditions count not for a little but for everything, i.e., the very conditions which result from often doing just and temperate acts.

Actions, then, are called just and temperate when they are such as the just or the temperate man would do; but it is not the man who does these that is just and temperate, but the man who also does them as just and temperate men do them. It is well said, then, that it is by doing just acts that the just man is produced, and by doing temperate acts the temperate man; without doing these no one would have even a prospect of becoming good.

But most people do not do these, but take refuge in theory and think they are being philosophers and will become good in this way, behaving somewhat like patients who listen attentively to their doctors, but do none of the things they are ordered to do. As the latter will not be made well in body by such a course of treatment, the former will not be made well in soul by such a course of philosophy.

6. We must, however, not only describe virtue as a state of character, but also say what sort of state it is. We may remark, then, that every virtue or excellence both brings into good condition the thing of which it is the excellence and makes the work of that thing be done well; e.g., the excellence of the eye makes both the eye and its work good, for it is by the excellence of the eye that we see well. Similarly the excellence of the horse makes a horse both good in itself and good at running and at carrying its rider and at awaiting the attack of the enemy. Therefore, if this is true in every case, the virtue of man also will be the state of character which makes a man good and which makes him do his own work well.

How this is to happen we have stated already, but it will be made plain also by the following consideration of the specific nature of virtue. In everything that is continuous and divisible it is possible to take more, less, or an equal amount, and that either in terms of the thing itself or relatively to us; and the equal is an intermediate between excess and defect. By the intermediate in the object I mean that which is equidistant from each of the extremes, which is one and the same for all men; by the intermediate relatively to us that which is neither too much nor too little—and this is not one, nor the same for all. For instance, if ten is many and two is few, six is the intermediate, taken in terms of the object; for it exceeds and is exceeded by an equal amount; this is intermediate according to arithmetical proportion. But the intermediate relatively to us is not to be taken so; if ten pounds are too much for a particular person to eat and two too little, it does not follow that the trainer will order six pounds; for this also is perhaps too much for the person who is to take it, or too little—too little for Milo, too much for the beginner in athletic exercises. The same is true of running and wrestling. Thus a master of any art avoids excess and defect, but seeks the intermediate and chooses this—the intermediate not in the object but relatively to us.

If it is thus, then, that every art does its work well—by looking to the intermediate and judging its works by this standard (so that we often say of good works of art that it is not possible either to take away or to add anything, implying that excess and defect destroy the goodness of works of art, while the mean preserves it; and good artists, as we say, look to this in their work), and if, further, virtue is more exact and better than any art, as nature also is, then virtue must have the quality of aiming at the intermediate. I mean moral virtue, for it is this that is concerned with passions and actions, and in these there is excess, defect, and the intermediate. For instance, both fear and confidence and appetite and anger and pity and in general pleasure and pain may be felt both too much and too little, and in both cases not well; but to feel them at the right times, with reference to the right objects, towards the right people, with the right motive, and in the right way, is what is both intermediate and best, and this is characteristic of virtue. Similarly with regard to actions also there is excess, defect, and the intermediate. Now virtue is concerned with passions and actions, in which excess is a form of failure, and so is defect, while the intermediate is praised and is a form of success; and being praised and being successful are both characteristics of virtue. Therefore virtue is a kind of mean, since, as we have seen, it aims at what is intermediate.

Again, it is possible to fail in many ways (for evil belongs to the class of the unlimited, as the Pythagoreans conjectured, and good to that of the limited), while to succeed is possible only in one way (for which reason also one is easy and the other difficult—to miss the mark easy, to hit it difficult); for these reasons also, then, excess and defect are characteristic of vice, and the mean of virtue, for men are good in but one way, but bad in many.

Virtue, then, is a state of character concerned with choice, lying in a mean, i.e., the mean relative to us, this being determined by a rational principle and by that principle by which the man of practical wisdom would determine it. Now, it is a mean between two vices, that which depends on excess and that which depends on defect; and again it is a mean because the vices respectively fall short of or exceed what is right in both passions and actions, while virtue both finds and chooses that which is intermediate. Hence in respect of its substance and the definition which states its essence, virtue is a mean with regard to what is best and right and extreme.

But not every action nor every passion admits of a mean, for some have names that already imply badness, e.g., spite, shamelessness, envy, and in the case of actions adultery, theft, murder, for all of these and suchlike things imply by their names that they are themselves bad and not the excesses or deficiencies of them. It is not possible, then, ever to be right with regard to them; one must always be wrong. Nor does goodness or badness with regard to such things depend on committing adultery with the right woman, at the right time, and in the right way, but simply to do any of them is to go wrong. It would be equally absurd, then, to expect that in unjust, cowardly, and voluptuous action there should be a mean, an excess, and a deficiency, for at that rate there would be a mean of excess and of deficiency, an excess of excess, and a deficiency of deficiency. But as there is no excess and deficiency of temperance and courage because what is intermediate is in a sense an extreme, so too of the actions we have mentioned there is no mean nor any excess and deficiency, but however they are done they are wrong, for in general there is neither a mean of excess and deficiency nor excess and deficiency of a mean.

CHAPTER 4

Medieval Christian, Jewish, and Islamic Ethics

"The true perfection of man"

Central to Judaism is the Torah, the five books of the Hebrew scriptures that constitute the Law. These books—Genesis, Exodus, Leviticus, Numbers, and Deuteronomy—not only tell the early history of God's relationship with Israel but outline the law revealed by God to govern it. The law is complex, consisting not only of the famous Ten Commandments but also of 603 others, though all are thought to follow from two basic commandments: Love the Lord your God with all your heart, soul, mind, and strength (Deuteronomy 6:5), and Love your neighbor as yourself (Leviticus 19:18).

Christianity has played a critical role in the development of Western civilization. Christian ethics, in particular, has affected the behavior not only of individuals but of entire peoples. Much of the ethical thinking that has taken place in the West throughout the past 2,000 years has occurred in the context of Christianity. Jesus of Nazareth (4? BCE–29? CE), the founder of Christianity, was a Jew living in a Hellenized Middle East during the Golden Age of Rome. Christianity began as a sect of Judaism. The New Testament—comprising the Gospels and writings by Paul and other Apostles—intends to fulfill and transcend Hebrew scripture with a new teaching of reliance on God through Jesus and an ethics of brotherly love. Jesus, like Confucius and the Buddha, wrote nothing. But his ethical stance inspired his followers to construct ethical theories and to engage in philosophical discussion. The problem of temptation and the contrast between ethical behavior as rule following and as love have been central to Christian ethics.

The Koran, a compilation of sayings that God is said to have revealed to Mohammed, details an even more complex law than that of Judaism. Islam is perhaps the only major world religion that specifies a detailed code of law without enunciating a few fundamental ethical principles from which the rest can be derived. That has posed a special challenge for Muslim philosophers looking to understand the basis for the Koran's commands.

Christian, Jewish, and Muslim philosophical traditions include attempts to construct a moral theory that explains and justifies the status of the revealed Law. Oral traditions and Greek philosophy—especially the philosophy of Aristotle—play important roles in shaping those traditions of ethical reflection.

4.1 THE ETHICS OF THE FATHERS

For centuries, rabbis (teachers) studied the Torah and taught it to others, training future rabbis. A tradition of scholarship thus arose and was transmitted orally from rabbi to rabbi. It was not written down until the fall of Jerusalem in 70 CE, when the diaspora threatened to disrupt the transmission of Jewish culture and scholarship. The discourses of the rabbis were recorded in the Talmud. The Jerusalem Talmud, the first compilation, was completed in the fourth century; the more comprehensive Babylonian Talmud was completed about a century later.

The ethical system presented in the Talmud is unsystematic, consisting of the sayings (singular *Mishna*, plural *Mishnayoth*) of many rabbis over a period of several centuries and then commentary on them by other rabbis (here omitted). There are detailed rules for observing the sabbath, holding religious festivals, adjudicating civil and criminal cases, and other matters. The moral core of the Talmud, however, is the section known as "The Ethics of the Fathers," which collects the ethical maxims the rabbis took as fundamental. They are quite different from the Ten Commandments or other ethical principles found in the Torah. They stress the importance of deliberation, of study, and of the Law itself. One of the fundamental rules is to build ramparts around the Law, protecting it (and oneself) from people and forces that might corrupt it. Our understanding of the Law changes over time; it can become better or worse. It is important to establish traditions and practices that make our understanding of the proper way to live richer and deeper rather than poorer and shallower.

Since a code of 613 commandments, supplemented with many volumes of detailed rules, is difficult for anyone who is not an expert to understand and follow, the rabbis concentrate especially on general principles and attitudes that will help people do the right thing. Judge others by their good qualities; love work; pursue peace; love everyone; love God; and work at your own moral improvement. Especially well known are these principles (translated somewhat differently later):

- Rabbi Hillel: "What is hateful to you, do not do to your fellow. That is the whole Torah; the rest is explanation. Go and learn."
- Rabbi Jehudah the Prince: "Be as scrupulous about the lightest command as about the weightiest, for no one knows the result of his actions."
- Rabbi Gamaliel: "Beautiful is the study of the Law together with the ways of the world."
- Rabbi Aqiba: "Tradition is the rampart around the Law."
- Rabbi Aqabia ben Mahalallel: "Consider three things, and you will not stray: Know where you come from, where you are going, and before whom you must give account."

- Rabbi Hillel: "If I am not for myself, who will be for me? But if I am for myself alone, what am I? And if not now, when?"

4.1.1 From the *Babylonian Talmud*

Chapter I

MISHNA A. Moses received the Law on Sinai and delivered it to Joshua; Joshua in turn handed it down to the Elders (not to the seventy Elders of Moses' time but to the later Elders who have ruled Israel, and each of them delivered it to his successor); from the Elders it descended to the prophets (beginning with Eli and Samuel), and each of them delivered it to his successors until it reached the men of the Great Assembly. The last named originated three maxims: "Be not hasty in judgment; bring up many disciples; and erect safeguards for the Law."

MISHNA B. Simeon the Just was one of the remnants of the Great Assembly. His motto was: "The order of the world rests upon three things: on law, on worship, and on bestowal of favors."

MISHNA C. Antigonus of Socho, who received it from Simeon the Just, was in the habit of saying: "Be not like slaves who serve their master for the sake of the compensation; be like such servants as labor for their master without reward; and let the fear of Heaven be upon you."

MISHNA D. Jose b. Joezer of Zereda and Jose b. Johanan of Jerusalem received from them. Jose b. Joezer used to say: "Let thy house be the meeting place of the wise; sit gladly at their feet, and drink in their words with avidity."

MISHNA F. Joshua b. Pera'hia and Nithai the Arbelite received from them. The former used to say: "Get thee a wise teacher, acquire a comrade, and judge everyone by his good qualities (i.e., from his favorable side)."

MISHNA G. Nithai the Arbelite was accustomed to say: "Keep aloof from a wicked neighbor, associate not with a sinner, and never consider thyself exempt from God's chastisement."

MISHNA I. Shemayah and Abtalion received from them. The former was in the habit of saying: "Love work and hate to attain superiority, and see to it that your name be not known to the government."

MISHNA K. Hillel and Shammai received from them. Hillel said: "Be a disciple of Aaron, love peace, pursue peace, love all men too, and bring them nigh unto the Law."

MISHNA L. He [Rabbi Hillel] also used to say: "A name made great is a name destroyed; he who increases not, decreases; and he who will not learn from his masters is not worthy to live; and he who uses his knowledge as a tiara perishes."

MISHNA M. He also used to say: "If I do not look to myself, who will do so? But if I look only to myself, what am I? And if not now, when?"

Source: The *Babylonian Talmud*. Translated by Michael L. Rodkinson. New York: New Talmud Publishing Company, 1918.

MISHNA N. Shammai was in the habit of saying: "Fix a time for study; promise little, and do much to receive everyone with friendly countenance."

MISHNA O. Rabban Gamaliel said: "Make to thyself a master, and free thyself of doubt, and tithe not much by estimation."

MISHNA P. Simeon his son was wont to say: "All the days of my life have been passed among the sages, and I have never found anything better for a man than silence; and the discussion of the Law is not of such import as is the practice thereof. He who talks much, cannot avoid sin."

MISHNA Q. He also said: "Three things support the world—law, truth, and peace—as it is written [Zechariah, viii. 16]: 'Truth and the judgment of peace, judge ye in your gates.' "

Chapter II

MISHNA A. Rabbi (Jehudah the Prince) was in the habit of saying: "In choosing the right path, see that it is one which is honorable to thyself and without offence to others. Be as scrupulous about the lightest command as about the weightiest, for no man knoweth the result of his actions. Weigh the present temporal disadvantages of a dutiful course against the reward of the future, and the present desirable fruits of a sinful deed against the injury to thine immortal soul. In general, consider three things and thou wilt never fall into sin: Remember that there is above thee an all-seeing eye, an all-hearing ear, and a record of all thine actions."

MISHNA B. Rabban Gamaliel, the son of R. Jehudah the Prince, was wont to say: "Beautiful is the study of the Law when conjoined with a worldly avocation, for the efforts demanded by both stifle all inclination to sin. But study which is not associated with some worldly pursuit must eventually cease, and may lead to iniquity. All who occupy themselves with communal affairs should do it in the name of Heaven, for the merit of their fathers sustains them and their righteousness stands forever. And ye yourselves shall have reward reckoned unto you, as if ye had wrought it."

MISHNA C. "Be cautious with those in authority, for they let not a man approach them but for their own purposes; and they appear like friends when it is to their advantage, and stand not by a man in the time of his need."

MISHNA D. He also used to say: "Do His will as if it were thy own, that He may do thy will as if it were His. Annul thy will before His, that He may annul the will of others before thy will."

MISHNA E. Hillel was in the habit of saying: "Do not isolate thyself from the community and its interest. Do not rely upon thy spiritual strength until the day of thy death. Pass not judgment upon thy neighbor until thou hast put thyself in his place. Say not a thing which must not be heard, because eventually it will be heard. Say never, 'Sometime or other, when I enjoy leisure, I will attend to my spiritual advancement'; perhaps thou wilt then never have the leisure."

MISHNA F. He also said: "The boor can never fear sin, the ignorant can never be truly pious. Whoso is ashamed to ask will never learn; no irritable man can be a teacher. He whose mind is given to worldly gain will not acquire wisdom. Where a man is needed, endeavor that thou be the man."

MISHNA G. Moreover, he saw a skull which floated on the face of the water, and he said to it: "Because thou drownedst they drowned thee, and in the end they that drowned thee will be drowned."

MISHNA H. He furthermore said: "The more feasting the more food for worms; the more wealth the more cares; more women, more witchcraft; more maid-servants, more lewdness; more men-servants, more theft. But the more knowledge, the more food for life; the more study, the more wisdom; the more reflection the better the counsel; the more charity the more peace. He who earns a good name gains something that can never be taken away. He who has gotten to himself words of Law has gotten to himself the life of the world to come."

MISHNA I. Rabban Johanan b. Zakkai received it from Hillel and Shammai. He was wont to say: "If thou hast learned much, do not boast of it, for it is for that that thou wast created."

MISHNA K. He [Johanan b. Zakkai] said to them once: "Go out and find what is the best thing to cultivate." R. Eliezer said: "A generous eye"; R. Joshua said: "A loyal friend"; R. Jose said: "A good neighbor"; R. Simeon thought: "Prudence and foresight"; R. Elazar said: "A good heart." Thereupon the Master said: "I consider R. Elazar b. Arach's judgment the best, for in his all of yours are included."

He said to them again: "Go and find out which is the evil way a man should shun." R. Eliezer said: "An evil eye"; R. Joshua said: "An evil companion"; R. Jose said: "An evil neighbor"; and R. Simeon said: "He that borrowed and repayeth not; he that borrows from a man is the same as if he borroweth from the Omnipotent, as it is written [Ps. xxxvii. 21]: 'The wicked borroweth and repayeth not, but the righteous is beneficent and giveth.' " R. Elazar said: "An evil heart." Thereupon the Master said: "I consider R. Elazar b. Arach's judgment the best, for in his all of yours are included."

MISHNA L. Each of these disciples had three maxims. R. Eliezer: "Thy fellow man's honor must be as dear to thee as thine own. Do not allow thyself to be easily angered. Repent one day before thy death." (He also said:) "Warm thyself before the light of the wise, but beware of their embers, perchance thou mayest be singed, for their bite is the bite of a fox, and their sting the sting of a scorpion, and their hiss is that of a fiery-serpent; and all their words are as coals of fire."

MISHNA M. R. Joshua: "An envious eye, sinful propensities, and misanthropy drive a man out of the world."

MISHNA N. R. Jose: "Thy neighbor's property must be as sacred as thine own. Set thyself to learn the Law, for it is not an heirloom unto thee. Let noble purpose underlie thine every action."

MISHNA O. R. Simeon: "Be careful in reading the Shema, and, in prayer; do not look upon the prayer as an obligatory task, but as a privilege granted by mercy and grace before God, for it is written [Joel, ii. 13]: 'For gracious and merciful is he, long-suffering and of great kindness, and he bethinketh himself of the evil.' Never think thyself too great a sinner to approach Him."

MISHNA P. R. Elazar: "Be most zealous in the pursuit of study; be prepared always to answer a scoffer; remember in whose service thou laborest." (He also added:) "Know who is thy Master, that he may be trusted to recompense thee for thy work."

MISHNA Q. R. Tarphon was in the habit of saying: "The day is short, the work is great, the workmen are slothful, the reward is rich, and the Master is urgent."

MISHNA R. He also said: "It is not incumbent on thee to complete the whole task, but thou art not at liberty therefore to neglect it entirely. If thou hast learned much Law, thou wilt be given much reward; and faithful is the Master of thy work, who will pay thee the reward of thy work; and know also that the gift of the recompense of the righteous is for the world to come."

Chapter III

MISHNA A. Aqabia b. Mahalallel used to say: "Consider three things, and thou wilt not fall into transgression: Know whence thou comest, whither thou art going, and before whom thou art about to give account and reckoning; know whence thou comest—from a fetid drop, and whither thou art going—to worm and maggot; and before whom thou art about to give account and reckoning: before the King of the kings of kings, the Holy One, blessed be He."

MISHNA B. R. Haninah, the Segan of the high-priest, said: "Pray always for the welfare of the government; were it not for the fear of it, men would swallow each other alive." R. Haninah b. Phradyon said: "Two that sit together and do not discuss any portion of the Law, their sitting is considered that of scorners, as it is written [Ps. i. 1]: 'And sitteth not in the seat of scorners'; but two that sit together and are discussing some words of the Law have the Shekhina among them, as it is written [Mal. iii. 16]: 'Then conversed they that feared the Lord one with the other; and the Lord listened and heard it,' etc."

This is as to two. Whence is it deduced of even one who occupies himself with the study of the Law, that the Holy One, blessed be He, fixes his reward? It is written [Sam. iii. 28]: "That he sit in solitude and be silent; because He hath laid it upon him."

MISHNA J. R. Hanina b. Dosa said: "He in whom fear of sin precedes his wisdom, (may be sure that) his wisdom will endure; and he in whom wisdom precedes his fear of sin, (may be sure that) his wisdom will not endure."

He also used to say: "He whose works are in excess of his wisdom, (it is certain that) his wisdom will endure; and he whose wisdom is in excess of his works, (it is certain that) his wisdom will not endure."

He also said: "He who has earned man's esteem and love, will also receive the favor of Heaven; but he who is not worthy of such esteem, cannot expect to find favor with God."

MISHNA K. R. Dosa b. Horkhinas said: "Sleeping away the morning, carousing at noonday, childish trifling, and the company of the vulgar waste a man's life away."

MISHNA N. R. Aqiba said: "Mockery and frivolity are the forerunners of immorality. Tradition is the rampart about the Law; tithes (charity) are the rampart of wealth; good resolutions are the preservative of abstinence; and the safeguard of wisdom is—silence."

MISHNA R. "Everything is foreseen and freewill is given. And the world is judged by grace; and every one is judged according to the majority of his deeds" (i.e., if one has done more good than evil, he is judged more favorably—Rashi).

MISHNA T. R. Elazar b. Azariah was wont to say: "Without knowledge of religion there can be no true culture, and without true culture there is no knowledge of religion. Where there is no wisdom, there is no fear of God; and without fear of God there is no wisdom. Without learning there can be no counsel, and without counsel there will be lack of learning. Where there is a dearth of bread, culture cannot thrive, and lack of culture causes dearth of bread."

Chapter IV

MISHNA A. Ben Zoma was in the habit of saying: "Who is a wise man? He who learns from everybody, as it is written [Ps. cxix. 99]: 'Above all my teachers have I obtained intelligence!' Who is a hero? He who conquers his passions, as it is written [Prov. xvi. 32]: 'One that is slow to anger is better than a hero; and he that ruleth his spirit, than the conqueror of a city.' Who is a rich man? He who is satisfied with his lot, as it is written [Ps. cxxviii. 2]: 'For thou eatest the labor of thy hands: then wilt thou be happy, and it shall be well with thee.' 'Wilt thou be happy' in this world, 'it shall be well with thee' in the world to come. Who is honored? He who honors his fellow men, as it is written [I Samuel ii. 30]: 'For those that honor me will I honor, and those that despise me shall be lightly esteemed.' "

MISHNA B. Ben Azai was in the habit of saying: "Hasten to fulfill the commandment of little importance as if it were of much importance, and flee from all manner of sin, for the fulfillment of one precept brings about that of another, and one transgression brings about another; for the reward of virtue is virtue itself, and the reward of sin is sin." He likewise said: "Despise no man, and consider nothing as too far removed to come to pass; for there is no man but hath his day, and no event that may not come."

MISHNA F. R. Jose said: "Whosoever honors the Torah is himself held in honor, and whosoever dishonors the Torah is himself dishonored with men."

MISHNA I. R. Jonathan said: "Whosoever fulfills the Law in poverty will at length fulfill it in wealth, and whosoever neglects the Law in wealth will at length neglect it in poverty."

MISHNA J. R. Meir said: "Lessen your business, that you have more time for the study of the Law, and be lowly in spirit unto every man; and if thou idlest away thy time without study of the Law, thou wilt have many idlers against thee; and if thou laborest in the Law, He hath much reward to give unto thee."

MISHNA K. R. Eliezer b. Jacob said: "He who performs one precept has acquired unto himself one advocate, and he who commits one transgression has gotten to himself one accuser. Repentance and good deeds are as a shield against punishment."

MISHNA L. R. Jehudah the Sandlar said: "Whatsoever congregation is for the sake of Heaven will in the end succeed; and that which is not for a divine purpose will in the end not succeed."

MISHNA M. R. Elazar b. Shamna said: "Let the honor of thy disciple be as dear unto thee as the honor of thine associate; and the honor of thine associate as the fear of thy master; and the fear of thy master as the fear of Heaven."

MISHNA N. R. Jehudah said: "Be careful in thy study, for error in study counts for an intentional sin."

MISHNA O. R. Simeon was wont to say: "There are three crowns—the crown of the Law, the crown of the priesthood, and the crown of royalty. But the crown of a fair name excelleth them all."

MISHNA P. R. Nehorai said: "Betake thyself to a place of Torah, and say not that it will come after thee, because thine associates will confirm it unto thee, and (moreover) lean not unto thine own understanding."

MISHNA Q. R. Janai said: "Neither the security of the wicked nor the afflictions of the righteous are within the grasp of our understanding."

MISHNA R. R. Mathia b. Heresh was in the habit of saying: "Be beforehand in saluting every man! Be the lion's tail rather than the fox's head!"

MISHNA S. R. Jacob said: "This world is, as it were, the antechamber of the world hereafter; therefore, prepare thyself in the antechamber, that thou mayest be admitted into the banqueting hall!"

MISHNA T. He used to say: "Better is one hour of repentance and good deeds in this world than all the life of the world to come, though one hour of refreshment of spirit in the world to come is better than all the life in this world."

MISHNA U. R. Simeon b. Elazar said: "Do not seek to appease thy friend in the hour of his passion, and do not seek to console him in the hour when his dead is laid out before him; and do not interrogate him in the hour of his vow, and strive not to see him in the hour of his disgrace."

MISHNA V. Samuel the Little used always to repeat the following passage [Prov. xxiv. 17, 18]: "At the fall of thy enemy do not rejoice, and at his stumbling let not thy heart be glad, lest the Lord see it, and it be displeasing in his eyes, and he turn away from him his wrath."

MISHNA Z. Rabbi Eliezer the Kapar said, "Envy, sensuality, and ambition destroy life."

MISHNA AA. He likewise said: "Those born unto the world are destined to die; the dead to live on again; and those who enter the eternal life, to be judged. Therefore let it be recognized, understood, and remembered that He the Almighty, the Creator, Architect, He is the counsellor, He the judge, He the witness, He the accuser. He is always ready to give judgment; blessed be He! for, before Him there is no injustice, no oversight, no regard for rank, no bribery. Know that all will appear in the account! Accept not the assurance of thy passions, that the grave will be a place of refuge for thee. For without thy consent wert thou created, wert born into the world without thy choice; thou art now living without thine own volition, without thine approval thou wilt have to die; so likewise without thy consent thou wilt have to render account before the Supreme King, the Holy One, blessed be He!"

4.2 AUGUSTINE ON WEAKNESS OF WILL

St. Augustine (354–430), born Aurelius Augustinus, by far the best known of the Christian platonists, was born to a Christian family in North Africa as the Roman Empire began to crumble. He had little interest in school as a child. Although he learned Latin and a little Greek, by his own account he excelled mostly on the playground. At 16, after his father died, Augustine went to Carthage to study rhetoric. He acquired a mistress, had an illegitimate child, and renounced Christianity. At 18, he read the *Hortensius*, a lost dialogue of Cicero's, and decided to search for wisdom. He became a teacher of rhetoric, setting up a school in Carthage at age 20. At 29, he went to Rome. Disappointed by the students there, he became professor of rhetoric at Milan. Not too long after, however, he resigned his post, converted to Christianity, and was baptized by Bishop Ambrose. He planned to return to Africa. His mother died in Italy awaiting a return passage, however, and his son died shortly after they reached Africa. He devoted the rest of his life to the Church, becoming Bishop of Hippo, where he died as the Vandals laid seige to the city.

Augustine developed Plato's philosophy into a comprehensive Christian philosophical worldview. He advanced innovative theories in many areas of philosophy as well as in theology. In ethics, he developed a new perspective on the problem of weakness of will.

Socrates argues that virtue is knowledge. No matter what virtue we try to analyze—courage, piety, temperance, and so on—we are led to the conclusion that virtue is knowing what to do and what not to do. This implies that weakness of will is impossible, for there can be no divide between knowing what to do and doing it. Plato, finding this implausible, rejects the Socratic position, distinguishing three parts of the soul and construing weakness of will as an imbalance in the soul. A person is weak of will when he or she knows what to do—by virtue of the soul's rational element—but does not do it, following instead the direction of the appetitive or spirited part of the soul. Plato's premise is that nothing can have contrary qualities. The soul, which feels pulled toward the right thing but also, even more strongly, toward the wrong thing, must consist of distinct parts.

Augustine rejects that reasoning. If we were to distinguish different parts of the soul every time we experience conflict, we would end up with thousands of parts of the soul. Desires can come into conflict with one another. I might want to go to the theater and to the market but be unable to do both. Feelings, too, can conflict; consider Catullus's famous poem, *Odi et amo*: "I hate and I love." Even rational conclusions can conflict. In thinking about the ancient liar paradox—*This sentence is false*—I may reason that it is false (if it were true, it would be false) but also that it is true. (Suppose it were false. It says it is false; so what it says is true.) The soul may have three functions, but it is one indivisible thing. If Plato were to pursue his strategy consistently, therefore, each desire, each emotion, and each conclusion of reason would have to constitute its own part of the soul.

The soul, Augustine affirms, is unified. Whatever else I am, I am one thing. My desires, my feelings, and my thoughts are all mine. If we think of a conflict as having the form "I want to do A and also not A," we can see no reason why one choice rather than another should be considered weak. The real tension, he writes, is between higher-order and lower-order attitudes. Conflicts have the form "I want to do A, but I don't want to want to do A." I might want to eat a piece of cake, for example, but, trying to lose weight, I don't want to want to eat it. Tempted to do wrong, I find that I want to do the wrong thing, even though I don't want to want it; I want to want to do the right thing. Weakness of will consists in letting my lower-order desire—my wanting to do the wrong thing—triumph over my higher-order desire (my wanting not to want to do it).

The soul is nevertheless not simple. It changes, and only what is manifold can change. Our thoughts, desires, and feelings are in a sense components of the soul. But they are components of the same thing.

Augustine's most famous work is his *Confessions*, a remarkable autobiography that is mostly about his inner, spiritual life. He describes his spiritual turmoil and his conversion to Christianity, pausing at various stages to outline a view of weakness of will, a theory of time, and an analysis of God and the creation of the universe.

4.2.1 Augustine, from *Confessions*

Chapter VIII.—The Conversation with Alypius Ended, He Retires to the Garden, Where His Friend Follows Him

19. In the midst, then, of this great strife of my inner dwelling—which I had strongly raised up against my soul in the chamber of my heart (Isa. xxvi. 20, and Matt. vi. 6)—troubled both in mind and countenance, I seized Alypius and exclaimed: "What's wrong with us? What is this? What did you hear? (The unlearned start up and 'take' heaven, Matt. xi. 12.) We, with our learning but

Source: Augustine, *Confessions*. Translated by J. G. Pilkington, in Philip B. Schaff (ed.), *Nicene and Post-Nicene Fathers*, Volume I. Edinburgh: T & T Clark, 1886. We have revised the translation for readability.

wanting heart—see where we wallow in flesh and blood! Because others have preceded us, are we ashamed to follow, or ashamed at not following?" Some such words I uttered. In my excitement I flung myself away from him. He gazed on me in silent astonishment, for I didn't speak in my usual tone. My brow, cheeks, eyes, color, and tone of voice all expressed my emotion more than my words.

There was a little garden where we were living. We had the use of it, as well as the whole house. The master, our landlord, didn't live there. The tempest within my breast hurried me there, where no one might impede the fiery battle I was waging with myself. Eventually it came to the issue you knew, though I didn't. But I was mad that I might be whole, and dying that I might have life. I knew what evil thing I was; I didn't know what good thing I was shortly to become. Into the garden, then, I retired. Alypius followed my steps. His presence was no bar to my solitude. How could he desert me so troubled? We sat down as far from the house as we could. I was disquieted in spirit. I was most impatient with myself that I didn't enter into Your will and covenant, O my God. All my bones cried out to me to enter, extolling it to the skies. We don't enter therein by ships, chariots, or feet; no, nor by going so far as I had come from the house to that place where we were sitting. For not only to go, but to enter there, was nothing but to will to go, resolutely and thoroughly; not to stagger and sway this way and that—a changeable and half-wounded will, wrestling, with one part falling as another rose.

20. Finally, in the very fever of my irresolution, I made many of those motions with my body which men sometimes desire to do, but cannot, if they don't have limbs or their limbs are bound with fetters, weakened by disease, or hindered in some other way. Thus, if I tore my hair, struck my forehead, or if, entwining my fingers, I clasped my knee, this I did because I willed it. But I might have willed and not done it, if the power of motion in my limbs had not responded. So many things, then, I did, when to have the will was not to have the power. I didn't do what, with an unequaled desire, I longed more to do. Shortly, when I'd will to do it, I'd have the power to do it; because, shortly, when I'd will it, I'd will thoroughly. For in such things the power was one with the will. To will was to do—and yet was it not done. More readily did the body obey the slightest wish of the soul in the moving its limbs at the order of the mind than the soul obeyed itself to accomplish what it wills most—in the will alone.

Chapter IX.—That the Mind Commands the Mind, but It Doesn't Will Entirely

21. Whence is this monstrous thing? And why is it? Let Your mercy shine on me, that I may ask; the hiding-place of man's punishment and the darkest contritions of the sons of Adam, may answer me. Whence is this monstrous thing? and why is it? The mind commands the body, and it obeys right away. The mind commands itself, and meets resistance. The mind commands the hand to be moved, and such readiness is there that the command is hard to distinguish from the obedience. Yet the mind is mind, and the hand is body. The mind commands the mind to will, and yet, though it commands itself, it does not obey. Whence this monstrous thing? and why is it? I repeat, it commands itself to will, and wouldn't give the command unless it willed. Yet what it commands doesn't happen. But it doesn't will *entirely*; therefore it doesn't command entirely. For it commands as it wills. If the thing commanded isn't done, it doesn't will. For the will commands that there be a will—not another, but itself. But it doesn't command entirely, therefore what it commands doesn't happen. For were it entire, it wouldn't need to command it to be, because it would already be. It is, therefore, no monstrous thing partly to will, partly to be unwilling; it's an infirmity of the mind that it doesn't wholly rise—sustained by truth, pressed down by custom. And so there are two wills, because one of them is not entire. The one has what the other needs.

Chapter X.—He Refutes the Opinion of the Manicheans as to Two Kinds of Minds—One Good and the Other Evil

22. Let them perish from Your presence (Ps. lxviii. 2), O God, as "vain talkers and deceivers" (Titus i. 10) of the soul perish, who, observing that there were two wills in deliberating, affirm that there are two kinds of minds in us—one good, the other evil. They say, therefore, that they are not responsible for their evil deeds—for it is not they that sin, but the nature of evil in them. They themselves really are evil when they hold these evil opinions. They'll become good when they hold the truth and consent to it. Your apostle may say unto them, "Ye were sometimes darkness, but now are ye light in the Lord" (Eph. v. 8). But, they, desiring to be light, not "in the Lord" but in themselves, conceive the nature of the soul to be the same as God's. They are made darker, for out of a shocking arrogance they went farther from You, "the true Light, which lights every man that comes into the world" (John i. 9). Take heed what you say, and blush for shame. Draw near to Him and be "lightened," and your faces won't be "ashamed" (Ps. xxxiv. 5). When I was deliberating on serving the Lord my God now, as I had long planned—it was I who willed, and I who was unwilling. It was I, even I myself. I neither willed entirely, nor was entirely unwilling. Therefore was I at war with myself, and destroyed by myself. This destruction overtook me against my will. Yet it showed not the presence of another mind but the punishment of my own. "Now, then, it is no more I that do it, but sin that dwells in me" (Rom. vii. 17)—the punishment of a more unconfined sin, in that I was a son of Adam.

23. For if there are as many contrary natures as there are conflicting wills, there will not now be only two natures, but many. If any one deliberates whether he should go to their conventicle, or to the theatre, those men, The Manicheans, at once cry out, "Behold, here are two natures,—one good, drawing this way, another bad, drawing back that way; for whence else is this indecision between conflicting wills?" But I reply that both are bad—that which draws to them, and that which draws back to the theatre. But they don't believe that will to be other than good which draws to them. Supposing, then, one of us should deliberate, and through the conflict of his two wills should waver whether he should go to the theatre or to our church; wouldn't these also waver what to answer? For either they must confess, which they are not willing to do, that the will which leads to our church is good, as well as that of those who have received and are held by the mysteries of theirs, or they must imagine that there are two evil natures and two evil minds in one man, at war one with the other; and that will not be true which they say, that there is one good and another bad; or they must be converted to the truth, and no longer deny that where anyone deliberates, there is one soul fluctuating between conflicting wills.

24. Let them no more say, then, when they perceive two wills to be antagonistic to each other in the same man, that the contest is between two opposing minds, of two opposing substances, from two opposing principles, the one good and the other bad. For Thou, O true God, disprove, check, and convince them; just as when both wills are bad, one deliberates whether he should kill a man by poison or by the sword; whether he should take possession of this or that estate of another's, when he cannot both; whether he should purchase pleasure by prodigality or retain his money by covetousness; whether he should go to the circus or the theatre, if both are open on the same day; or, thirdly, whether he should rob another man's house, if he have the opportunity; or, fourthly, whether he should commit adultery, if at the same time he have the means of doing so,—all these things concurring in the same point of time, and all being equally longed for, although impossible to be enacted at one time. For they rend the mind amid four, or even (among the vast variety of things men desire) more antagonistic wills, nor do they yet affirm that there are so many different substances. Thus

also is it in wills which are good. For I ask them, is it a good thing to have delight in reading the apostle, or good to have delight in a sober psalm, or good to discourse on the gospel? To each of these they will answer, "It is good." What, then, if all equally delight us, and all at the same time? Do not different wills distract the mind, when a man is deliberating which he should rather choose? Yet are they all good, and are at variance until one be fixed upon, whither the whole united will may be borne, which before was divided into many. Thus, also, when above eternity delights us, and the pleasure of temporal good holds us down below, it is the same soul which does not will that or this with an entire will, and is therefore torn asunder with grievous perplexities, while out of truth it prefers that, but out of custom forbears not this.

Chapter XII.—Having Prayed to God, He Pours Forth a Shower of Tears, and, Admonished by a Voice, He Opens the Book and Reads the Words in Rom. XIII. 13; by Which, Being Changed in His Whole Soul, He Discloses the Divine Favour to His Friend and His Mother

28. But when a profound reflection had, from the secret depths of my soul, drawn together and heaped up all my misery before the sight of my heart, there arose a mighty storm, accompanied by as mighty a shower of tears. Which, that I might pour forth fully, with its natural expressions, I stole away from Alypius; for it suggested itself to me that solitude was fitter for the business of weeping. So I retired to such a distance that even his presence could not be oppressive to me. Thus was it with me at that time, and he perceived it; for something, I believe, I had spoken, wherein the sound of my voice appeared choked with weeping, and in that state had I risen up. He then remained where we had been sitting, most completely astonished. I flung myself down, how, I know not, under a certain fig-tree, giving free course to my tears, and the streams of mine eyes gushed out, an acceptable sacrifice unto Thee (1 Pet. ii. 5). And, not indeed in these words, yet to this effect, spoke I much unto Thee,—"But Thou, O Lord, how long?" (Ps. vi. 3) "How long, Lord? Wilt Thou be angry forever? Oh, remember not against us former iniquities" (Ps. lxxix. 5, 8), for I felt that I was enthralled by them. I sent up these sorrowful cries,—"How long, how long? Tomorrow, and tomorrow? Why not now? Why is there not this hour an end to my uncleanness?"

29. I was saying these things and weeping in the most bitter contrition of my heart, when, lo, I heard the voice as of a boy or girl, I know not which, coming from a neighbouring house, chanting, and oft repeating, "Take up and read; take up and read." Immediately my countenance was changed, and I began most earnestly to consider whether it was usual for children in any kind of game to sing such words; nor could I remember ever to have heard the like. So, restraining the torrent of my tears, I rose up, interpreting it no other way than as a command to me from Heaven to open the book, and to read the first Chapter I should light upon. For I had heard of Antony, that, accidentally coming in whilst the gospel was being read, he received the admonition as if what was read were addressed to him, "Go and sell that thou hast, and give to the poor, and thou shalt have treasure in heaven; and come and follow me" (Matt. xix. 21). And by such oracle was he forthwith converted unto Thee. So quickly I returned to the place where Alypius was sitting; for there had I put down the volume of the apostles, when I rose thence. I grasped, opened, and in silence read that paragraph on which my eyes first fell,—"Not in rioting and drunkenness, not in chambering and wantonness, not in strife and envying; but put ye on the Lord Jesus Christ, and make not provision for the flesh, to fulfill the lusts thereof" (Rom. xiii. 13, 14). No further would I read, nor did I need; for instantly, as the sentence ended,—by a light, as it were, of security infused into my heart,—all the gloom of doubt vanished away.

30. Closing the book, then, and putting either my finger between, or some other mark, I now with a tranquil countenance made it known to Alypius. And he thus disclosed to me what was wrought in him, which I knew not. He asked to look at what I had read. I showed him; and he looked even further than I had read, and I knew not what followed. This it was, verily, "Him that is weak in the faith, receive ye" (Rom. xiv. 1), which he applied to himself and discovered to me. By this admonition was he strengthened; and by a good resolution and purpose, very much in accord with his character (wherein, for the better, he was always far different from me), without any restless delay he joined me. Thence we go in to my mother. We make it known to her,—she rejoices. We relate how it came to pass,—she leaps for joy, and triumphs, and blesses You, who are "able to do exceeding abundantly above all that we ask or think" (Eph. iii. 20), for she perceived You to have given her more for me than she used to ask by her pitiful and most doleful groanings. For You so converted me unto Yourself that I sought neither a wife nor any other of this world's hopes,—standing in that rule of faith in which You, so many years before, had showed me unto her in a vision. And You turned her grief into a gladness (Ps. xxx. 11), much more plentiful than she had desired, and much dearer and chaster than she used to crave, by having grandchildren of my body.

4.2.2 Augustine, from *On the Trinity*

Chapter 6.—How God Is a Substance Both Simple and Manifold

8. But if it is asked how that substance is both simple and manifold: consider, first, why the creature is manifold, but in no way really simple. And first, all that is body is composed certainly of parts; so that therein one part is greater, another less, and the whole is greater than any part whatever or how great soever. For the heaven and the earth are parts of the whole bulk of the world; and the earth alone, and the heaven alone, is composed of innumerable parts; and its third part is less than the remainder, and the half of it is less than the whole; and the whole body of the world, which is usually called by its two parts, viz. the heaven and the earth, is certainly greater than the heaven alone or the earth alone. And in each several body, size is one thing, color another, shape another; for the same color and the same shape may remain with diminished size; and the same shape and the same size may remain with the color changed; and the same shape not remaining, yet the thing may be just as great, and of the same color. And whatever other things are predicated together of body can be changed either all together, or the larger part of them without the rest. And hence the nature of body is conclusively proved to be manifold, and in no respect simple. The spiritual creature also, that is, the soul, is indeed the more simple of the two if compared with the body; but if we omit the comparison with the body, it is manifold, and itself also not simple. For it is on this account more simple than the body, because it is

Source: Augustine, *On the Trinity*, VI, 6 (from Philip Schaff (ed.), *Nicene and Post-Nicene Fathers*, Volume III: St. Augustine, On the Holy Trinity, Doctrinal Treatises, Moral Treatises; New York: Christian Literature Publishing Co., 1890).

not diffused in bulk through extension of place, but in each body, it is both whole in the whole, and whole in each several part of it; and, therefore, when anything takes place in any small particle whatever of the body, such as the soul can feel, although it does not take place in the whole body, yet the whole soul feels it, since the whole soul is not unconscious of it. But, nevertheless, since in the soul also it is one thing to be skillful, another to be indolent, another to be intelligent, another to be of retentive memory; since cupidity is one thing, fear another, joy another, sadness another; and since things innumerable, and in innumerable ways, are to be found in the nature of the soul, some without others, and some more, some less; it is manifest that its nature is not simple, but manifold. For nothing simple is changeable, but every creature is changeable.

4.3 AL-FARABI ON HAPPINESS

Al-Farabi (Abu Nasr Muhammad al-Farabi, 870?–950), of Turkish descent, was born in Transoxania, now part of Uzbekistan in central Asia. He studied in Khorasan (covering parts of present-day Iran and Afghanistan) and Baghdad. Many of his teachers were from the Alexandrian school, which moved to Antioch and then Harran after the Muslim conquest of Alexandria. He combined elements from Plato, Aristotle, and neo-Platonic philosophers into the first of several great philosophical systems produced by medieval Islamic philosophers.

Socrates and Aristotle both stress the importance of virtue. But they offer different accounts of it. For Socrates, virtue is a kind of knowledge, the knowledge of good and evil. The good person knows what to pursue and what to shun, and does it. Vice is a kind of ignorance: bad people do wrong because they don't know any better. For Aristotle, this is not so. It is possible for people to exhibit weakness of will, to know what is right but not do it. Virtue requires knowledge, but it also requires action. Plato assumes that all goods and evils are comparable, but Aristotle does not. There are many different goods that constitute happiness. There is no rule for comparing them. Virtue thus requires training. A good person must develop the ability to perceive what is right and wrong in particular situations. A person with political virtue can do this in political matters, involving the welfare of the entire community.

Al-Farabi combines these accounts into his own distinctive philosophy. Aristotle distinguishes intellectual virtues, which involve knowledge and can be taught, from practical or moral virtues, which involve putting knowledge into practice and cannot strictly speaking be taught. What is the link between these virtues? What, that is, takes us from knowledge to action? Aristotle's answer is deliberation. Al-Farabi agrees, speaking of the deliberative faculty. He gives a Socratic account of it. The deliberative faculty, he says, is "the skill and the faculty by which one discovers and discerns the variable accidents of the intelligibles whose particular instances are made to exist by the will." In different language, it is *the ability to recognize the properties of the results of actions.* Deliberative virtue is a kind of foresight. As al-Farabi elaborates the point, deliberation requires knowing what ends to pursue and what means will achieve those ends. To deliberate, in other words, you need to know what you want to accomplish and what you can do to accomplish it.

Al-Farabi's definition has the consequence that deliberation is a kind of knowledge. Since deliberation provides the link between knowledge and action, deliberative virtue—excellence at deliberation—is all you need for practical or moral virtue. Moral virtue is deliberative virtue, and deliberative virtue is knowledge. Thus, moral virtue itself becomes a kind of knowledge. Intellectual virtue, deliberative virtue, and moral virtue all go hand-in-hand. This makes sense from the perspective of Socrates's view as expressed in Plato's early dialogues. There, virtue is a kind of knowledge. So, al-Farabi's understanding of deliberative virtue seems to have led him from Aristotle back to Socrates.

This, however, seems puzzling. We sought the link between knowledge and action and seem to have found more knowledge. Does deliberative virtue really suffice for moral virtue? How does the knowledge involved in deliberation trigger action? There must, al-Farabi concludes, be some other kind of virtue that combines with deliberative virtue to produce good action. Since reasoning about means does seem to be a matter of knowledge, this other kind of virtue comes into play in thinking about ends. We are innately disposed to pursue certain ends. Someone with *natural virtue* pursues good ends. Natural virtue combines with deliberation to produce action. So, the ultimate link between knowledge and action is not deliberation as such but natural virtue.

Just as lions tend to act courageously, and foxes tend to act cunningly, humans tend to pursue certain ends. But people differ in which ends they are disposed to pursue and how strongly and persistently they tend to pursue them. Some people are thus more naturally virtuous than others.

Great moral virtue, then, requires excellence in knowledge—intellectual or theoretical virtue, and also deliberative virtue—as well as great natural virtue. Aristotle would insist that one could excel at one of these without the other. Someone who is weak of will, for example, might excel at intellectual virtue without excelling at deliberative or natural virtue. Someone who is kind-hearted but confused might excel at natural virtue without excelling at the others. Al-Farabi gives no argument against this possibility, but he rejects it. He holds that each kind of virtue presupposes all the others. In any case one must excel at all the kinds of virtue to have superior moral virtue overall.

Al-Farabi sees important political consequences as following from this portrait of virtue. He follows Plato's argument for philosopher-kings in the *Republic*. An ideal ruler would be able to make decisions that benefit the community. That requires moral virtue, which requires theoretical, deliberative, and natural excellence. If the philosopher is one who excels in theoretical virtue, then, the ruler should be a philosopher. But being a philosopher is not enough. One must be inclined to pursue the right ends (natural virtue); know how to achieve them in general (intellectual virtue); know how to make decisions in particular cases (deliberative virtue); and carry out those decisions.

Can any one person excel in all these respects? If so, who? Here, al-Farabi's thought takes a religious turn. There is one excellence from which all the others follow: knowledge of God. One who truly knows God knows what ends to pursue, knows how to pursue them, and is inclined to pursue them. So, the religious leader, the Imam, is the ideal ruler. He is "one whose example is followed and who is well received." But being well-received requires full use of the talents of the philosopher, religious leader, and supreme ruler. The true philosopher and the supreme ruler are thus the same. Moreover, persuasion requires the use of images as well as arguments, and this, al-Farabi observes, is the role of religion. The ideal ruler persuades people to do what they can do to promote the happiness of the community, and this requires an excellence at prompting the religious imagination as well as excellence at rational persuasion.

Al-Farabi's combination of Socratic, Platonic, and Aristotelian elements thus yields a political philosophy that vests ultimate power in a single person, the person who most excels in intellectual virtues, practical virtues, and the understanding of religion and religious imagery. He provides the theoretical underpinnings of theocratic rule, which still exerts great influence in Islamic countries around the globe.

4.3.1 Al-Farabi, from *The Attainment of Happiness*

Chapter 1

...It is incumbent on man to investigate... the things that realize for man his objective through the intellectual principles that are in him, and by which he achieves that perfection that became known in natural science. It will become evident concomitantly that these rational principles are not mere causes by which man attains the perfection for which he is made. Moreover, he will know that these rational principles also supply many things to natural beings other than those supplied by nature. Indeed man arrives at the ultimate perfection (whereby he attains that which renders him truly substantial) only when he labors with these principles toward achieving that perfection. Moreover, he cannot labor toward this perfection except by exploiting a large number of natural beings and until he manipulates them to render them useful to him for arriving at the ultimate perfection he should achieve. Furthermore, it will become evident to him in this science that each man achieves only a portion of that perfection, and what he achieves of this portion varies in its extent, for an isolated individual cannot achieve all the perfections by himself and without the aid of many other individuals. It is the innate disposition of every man to join another human being or other men in the labor he ought to perform: this is the condition of every single man. Therefore, to achieve what he can of that perfection, every man needs to stay in the neighborhood of others and associate with them. It is also the innate nature of this animal to seek shelter and to dwell in the neighborhood of those who belong to the same species, which is why he is called the social and political animal. There emerges now another science and another inquiry that investigates these intellectual principles and the acts and states of character with which man labors toward this perfection. From this, in turn, emerge the science of man and political science....

...He should continue this investigation until he finally reaches a being that cannot possess any of these principles at all (what something is or from what it is) but is itself the first principle of all the aforementioned beings: It is itself that by which, from which, and for which they are, in the most perfect modes in which a thing can be a principle for the beings, modes free from all defects. Having understood this, he should investigate next what properties the other beings

Source: From *Alfarabi's Philosophy of Plato and Aristotle*. Translated with introduction by Muhsin Mahdi. New York: The Free Press, 1962.

possess as a consequence of their having this being as their principle and the cause of their being. He should begin with the being whose rank is higher than the rest (that is, the one nearest to the first principle), until he terminates in the being whose rank is inferior to the rest (that is, the one furthest from the first principle). He will thus come to know the ultimate causes of the beings. This is the divine inquiry into them. For the first principle is the divinity, and the principles that come after it—and are not bodies or in bodies—are the divine principles.

Then he should set out next upon the science of man and investigate the what and the how of the purpose for which man is made, that is, the perfection that man must achieve. Then he should investigate all the things by which man achieves this perfection or that are useful to him in achieving it. These are the good, virtuous, and noble things. He should distinguish them from things that obstruct his achieving this perfection. These are the evils, the vices, and the base things. He should make known what and how every one of them is, and from what and/or what it is, until all of them become known, intelligible, and distinguished from each other. This is political science. It consists of knowing the things by which the citizens of cities attain happiness through political association in the measure that innate disposition equips each of them for it....

Chapter II

Things of this sort are not covered by the theoretical sciences, which cover only the intelligibles that do not vary at all. Therefore another faculty and another skill is required with which to discern the voluntary intelligibles, [not as such but] insofar as they possess these variable accidents: that is, the modes according to which they can be brought into actual existence by the will at a determined time, in a determined place, and when a determined event occurs. That is the deliberative faculty. It is the skill and the faculty by which one discovers and discerns the variable accidents of the intelligibles whose particular instances are made to exist by the will, when one attempts to bring them into actual existence by the will at a determined time, in a determined place, and when a determined event takes place, whether the time is long or short, whether the locality is large or small.

Things are *discovered* by the deliberative faculty only insofar as they are found to be useful for the attainment of an end and purpose. The discoverer first sets the end before himself and then investigates the means by which that end and that purpose are realized. The deliberative faculty is most perfect when it discovers what is most useful for the attainment of these ends. The ends may be truly good, may be evil, or may be only believed to be good. If the means discovered are the most useful for a virtuous end, then they are noble and fair. If the ends are evil, then the means discovered by the deliberative faculty are also evil, base, and bad. And if the ends are only believed to be good, then the means useful for attaining and achieving them are also only believed to be good....

It is obvious that the one who possesses a virtue by which he discovers what is most useful and noble, and this for the sake of a virtuous end that is good (irrespective of whether what is discovered is a true good that he wishes for himself, a true good that he wishes someone else to possess, or something that is believed to be good by whomever he wishes it for), cannot possess this faculty without possessing a moral virtue. For if a man wishes the good for others, then he is either truly good or else believed to be good by those for whom he wishes the good although he is not good and virtuous. Similarly he who wishes the true good for himself has to be good and virtuous, not in his deliberation, but in his moral character and in his acts. It would seem that his virtue, moral character, and acts, have to correspond to his power of deliberation and ability to discover what is most useful and noble. Hence if he discovers by his deliberative virtue only those most useful and noble means that are of great force (such as what is most useful for a virtuous end common to a whole nation, to many nations, or to a whole city, and does not vary except over a long period), then his moral virtues ought to be of a comparable measure. Similarly, if his deliberative virtues are confined to means that are most useful for a restricted end when a specific event occurs, then this is the measure of his [moral] virtue also. Accordingly, the more perfect the authority and the greater the power of these deliberative virtues, the stronger the authority and the greater the power of the moral virtues that accompany them....

Therefore one ought to investigate which virtue is the perfect and most powerful virtue. Is it the combination of all the virtues? Or, if one virtue (or a number of virtues) turns out to have a power equal to that of all the virtues together, what ought to be the distinctive mark of the virtue that has this power and is hence the most powerful virtue? This virtue is such that when a man decides to fulfill its functions, he cannot do so without making use of the functions of all the other virtues. If he himself does not happen to possess all of these virtues—in which case he cannot make use of the functions of particular virtues present in him when he decides to fulfill the functions of that virtue—that virtue of his will be a moral virtue in the exercise of which he exploits the acts of the virtues possessed by all others, whether they are nations, cities within a nation, groups within a city, or parts within each group. This, then, is the leading virtue that is not surpassed by any other in authority....

It is evident that the deliberative virtue with the highest authority can only be subordinate to the theoretical virtue, for it merely discerns the accidents of the intelligibles that, prior to having these accidents as their accompaniments, are acquired by the theoretical virtue. If it is determined that the one who possesses the deliberative virtue should discover the variable accidents and states of only those intelligibles of which he has personal insight and personal knowledge (so as not to make discoveries about things that perhaps ought not to take place), then the deliberative virtue cannot be separated from the theoretical virtue. It follows that the theoretical virtue, the leading deliberative virtue, the leading moral virtue, and the leading practical art are inseparable from each other; otherwise the latter [three] will be unsound, imperfect, and without complete authority.

But if, after the theoretical virtue has caused the intellect to perceive the moral virtues, the latter can only be made to exist if the deliberative virtue discerns them and discovers the accidents that must accompany their intelligibles so that they can be brought into existence, then the deliberative virtue is anterior to the moral virtues. If it is anterior to them, then he who possesses the deliberative virtue discovers by it only such moral virtues as exist independent of the deliberative virtues. Yet if the deliberative virtue is independent of the moral virtue, then he who has the capacity for discovering the (good) moral virtues will not himself be good, not even in a single virtue. But if he himself is not good, how then does he seek out the good or wish the true good for himself or for others? And if he does not wish the good, how is he capable of discovering it without having set it before himself as an end? Therefore, if the deliberative virtue is independent of the moral virtue, it is not possible to discover the moral virtue with it. Yet if the moral virtue is inseparable from the deliberative, and they coexist, how could the deliberative virtue discover the moral and join itself to it? For if they are inseparable, it will follow that the deliberative virtue did not discover the moral virtue; while if the deliberative virtue did discover the moral virtue, it will follow that the deliberative virtue is independent of the moral virtue. Therefore either the deliberative virtue itself is the virtue of goodness, or one should assume that the deliberative virtue is accompanied by some other virtue, different from the moral virtue that is discovered by the deliberative faculty. If that other moral virtue is formed by the will also, it follows that the deliberative virtue discovered it—thus the original doubt recurs. It follows, then, that there must be some other moral virtue—other, that is, than the one discovered by the deliberative virtue—which accompanies the deliberative virtue and enables the possessor of the deliberative virtue to wish the good and the virtuous end. *That* virtue must be *natural* and must come into being by nature, and it must be coupled with a certain deliberative virtue [that is, cleverness] which comes into being by nature and discovers the moral virtues formed by the will. The virtue formed by the will will then be the human virtue by which man, after acquiring it in the way in which he acquires voluntary things, acquires the *human* deliberative virtue.

But one ought to inquire what manner of thing that *natural* virtue is. Is it or is it not identical with this voluntary virtue? Or ought one to say that it *corresponds* to this virtue, like the states of character that exist in irrational animals?—just as it is said that courage resides in the lion, cunning in the fox, shiftiness in the bear, thievishness in the magpie, and so on. For it is possible that every man is innately so disposed that his soul has a power such that he generally moves more easily in the direction of the accomplishment of a certain virtue or of a certain state of character than in the direction of doing the opposite act. Indeed man moves first in the direction in which it is easier for him to move, provided he is not compelled to do something else. For instance, if a man is innately so disposed that he is more prone to stand his ground against dangers than to recoil before them, then all he needs is to undergo the experience a sufficient number of times and this state of character become voluntary. Prior to this, he possessed the corresponding *natural* state of character. If this is so in particular moral virtues that accompany particular deliberative virtues, it must also be the case with the highest moral virtues that accompany the highest deliberative virtues. If this is so, it follows that there are some men who are innately disposed to a [*natural* moral] virtue that corresponds to the highest [*human* moral] virtue and that is joined to a naturally superior deliberative power, others just below them, and so on. If this is so, then not every chance human being will possess art, moral virtue, and deliberative virtue with great power.

Therefore the prince occupies his place by nature and not merely by will. Similarly, a subordinate occupies his place primarily by nature and only secondarily by virtue of the will, which perfects his natural equipments. This being the case, the theoretical virtue, the highest deliberative virtue, the highest moral virtue, and the highest practical art are realized in those equipped for them by nature: that is, in those who possess superior natures with very great potentialities.

Chapter IV

...[N]ations and the citizens of cities are composed of some who are the elect and others who are the vulgar. The vulgar confine themselves, or should be confined, to theoretical cognitions that are in conformity with unexamined common opinion. The elect do not confine themselves in any of their theoretical cognitions to what is in conformity with unexamined common opinion but reach their conviction and knowledge on the basis of premises subjected to thorough scrutiny. Therefore whoever thinks that he is not confined to what is in conformity with unexamined common opinion in his inquiries, believes that in them he is of the "elect" and that everybody else is vulgar. Hence the competent practitioner of every art comes to be called one of the "elect" because people know that he does not confine himself, with respect to the objects of his art, to what is in conformity with unexamined common opinion, but exhausts them and scrutinizes them thoroughly. Again, whoever does not hold a political office or does not possess an art that establishes his claim to a political office, but either possesses no art at all or is enabled by his art to hold only a subordinate office in the city, is said to be "vulgar"; and whoever holds a political office or else possesses an art that enables him to aspire to a political office is of the "elect." Therefore, whoever thinks that he possesses an art that qualifies him for assuming a political office or thinks that his position has the same status as a political office (for instance, men with prominent ancestors and many who possess great wealth) calls himself one of the "elect" and a "statesman."

Whoever has a more perfect mastery of the art that qualifies him for assuming an office is more appropriate for inclusion among the elect. Therefore it follows that the most elect of the elect is the supreme ruler. It would appear that this is so because he is the one who does not confine himself in anything at all to what is in conformity with unexamined common opinion. He must hold the office of the supreme ruler and be the most elect of the elect because of his state of character and skill....

When the theoretical sciences are isolated and their possessor does not have the faculty for exploiting them for the benefit of others, they are defective philosophy. To be a truly perfect philosopher one has to possess both the theoretical sciences and the faculty for exploiting them for the benefit of all others according to their capacity. Were one to consider the case of the true philosopher, he would find no difference between him and the supreme ruler. For he who possesses the faculty for exploiting what is comprised by the theoretical matters for the benefit of all others possesses the faculty for making such matters intelligible as well as for bringing into actual existence those of them that depend on the will. The greater his power to do the latter, the more perfect is his philosophy. Therefore he who is truly perfect possesses with sure insight, first, the theoretical virtues and subsequently the practical. Moreover, he possesses the capacity for bringing them about in nations and cities in the manner and the measure possible with reference to each. Since it is impossible for him to possess the faculty for bringing them about except by employing certain demonstrations, persuasive methods, as well as methods that represent things through images, and this either with the consent of others or by compulsion, it follows that the true philosopher is himself the supreme ruler.

Every instruction is composed of two things: (a) making what is being studied comprehensible and causing its idea to be established in the soul and (b) causing others to assent to what is comprehended and established in the soul. There are two ways of making a thing comprehensible: first, by causing its essence to be perceived by the intellect, and second, by causing it to be imagined through the similitude that imitates it. Assent, too, is brought about by one of two methods, either the method of certain demonstration or the method of persuasion. Now when one acquires knowledge of the beings or receives instruction in them, if he perceives their ideas themselves with his intellect, and his assent to them is by means of certain demonstration, then the science that comprises these cognitions is philosophy. But if they are known by imagining them through similitudes that imitate them, and assent to what is imagined of them is caused by persuasive methods, then the ancients call what comprises these cognitions religion. And if those intelligibles themselves are adopted, and *persuasive* methods are used, then the religion comprising them is called *popular, generally accepted*, and *external* philosophy. Therefore, according to the ancients, religion is an imitation of philosophy. Both comprise the same subjects and both give an account of the ultimate principles of the beings. For both supply knowledge about the first principle and cause of the beings, and both give an account of the ultimate end for the sake of which man is made—that is, supreme happiness—and the ultimate end of every one of the other beings. In everything of which philosophy gives an account based on intellectual perception or conception, religion gives an account based on imagination. In everything demonstrated by philosophy, religion employs persuasion. Philosophy gives an account of the ultimate principles (that is, the essence of the first principle and the essences of the incorporeal second principles), as they are perceived by the intellect. Religion sets forth their images by means of similitudes of them taken from corporeal principles and imitates them by their likenesses among political offices. It imitates the divine acts by means of the functions of political offices. It imitates the actions of natural powers and principles by their likenesses among the faculties, states, and arts that have to do with the will, just as Plato does in the *Timaeus*. It imitates the intelligibles by their likenesses among the sensibles: For instance, some imitate matter by *abyss* or *darkness* or *water*, and *nothingness* by *darkness*.

It imitates the classes of supreme happiness—that is, the ends of the acts of the human virtues—by their likenesses among the goods that are believed to be the ends. It imitates the classes of true happiness by means of the ones that are believed to be happiness. It imitates the ranks of the beings by their likenesses among spatial and temporal ranks. And it attempts to bring the similitudes of these things as close as possible to their essences. Also, in everything of which philosophy gives an account that is demonstrative and certain, religion gives an account based on persuasive arguments. Finally, philosophy is prior to religion in time.

Again, it is evident that when one seeks to bring into actual existence the intelligibles of the things depending on the will supplied by practical philosophy, he ought to prescribe the conditions that render possible their actual existence. Once the conditions that render their actual existence possible are prescribed, the voluntary intelligibles are embodied in laws. Therefore the legislator is he who, by the excellence of his deliberation, has the capacity to find the conditions required for the actual existence of voluntary intelligibles in such a way as to lead to the achievement of supreme happiness. It is also evident that only after perceiving them by his intellect should the legislator seek to discover their conditions, and he cannot find their conditions that enable him to guide others toward supreme happiness without having perceived supreme happiness with his intellect. Nor can these things become intelligible (and the legislative craft thereby hold the supreme office) without his having beforehand acquired philosophy. Therefore, if he intends to possess a craft that is authoritative rather than subservient, the legislator must be a philosopher. Similarly, if the philosopher who has acquired the theoretical virtues does not have the capacity for bringing them about in all others according to their capacities, then what he has acquired from them has no validity. Yet he cannot find the states and the conditions by which the voluntary intelligibles assume actual existence, if he does not possess the deliberative virtue; and the deliberative virtue cannot exist in him without the practical virtue. Moreover, he cannot bring them about in all others according to their capacities except by a faculty that enables him to excel in persuasion and in representing things through images.

It follows, then, that the idea of *Imam*, Philosopher, and Legislator is a single idea. However, the name *philosopher* signifies primarily theoretical virtue. But if it be determined that the theoretical virtue reach its ultimate perfection in every respect, it follows necessarily that he must possess all the other faculties as well. *Legislator* signifies excellence of knowledge concerning the conditions of practical intelligibles, the faculty for finding them, and the faculty for bringing them about in nations and cities. When it is determined that they be brought into existence on the basis of knowledge, it will follow that the theoretical virtue must precede the others—the existence of the inferior presupposes the existence of the higher. The name *prince* signifies sovereignty and ability. To be completely able, one has to possess the power of the greatest ability. His ability to do a thing must not result only from external things; he himself must possess great ability because his art, skill, and virtue are of exceedingly great power. This is not possible except by great power of knowledge, great power of deliberation, and great power of [moral] virtue and art. Otherwise he is not truly able nor sovereign. For if his ability stops short of this, it is still imperfect. Similarly, if his ability is restricted to goods inferior to supreme happiness, his ability is incomplete and he is not perfect. Therefore the true prince is the same as the philosopher-legislator. As to the idea *Imam* in the Arabic language, it signifies merely the one whose example is followed and who is well received: That is, either his perfection is well received or his purpose is well received. If he is not well received in all the infinite activities, virtues, and arts, then he is not truly well received. Only when all other arts, virtues, and activities seek to realize his purpose and no other, will his art be the most powerful art, his [moral] virtue the most powerful virtue, his deliberation the most powerful deliberation, and his science the most powerful science. For with all of these powers he will be exploiting the powers of others so as to accomplish his own purpose. This is not possible without the theoretical sciences, without the greatest of all deliberative virtues, and without the rest of those things that are in the philosopher.

So let it be clear to you that the idea of the Philosopher, Supreme Ruler, Prince, Legislator, and *Imam* is but a single idea. No matter which one of these words you take, if you proceed to look at what each of them signifies among the majority of those who speak our language, you will find that they all finally agree by signifying one and the same idea.

4.4 MAIMONIDES ON HAPPINESS AND VIRTUE

Maimonides (1135? 1138?–1204) offers a version of consequentialism, the doctrine that moral value depends solely on consequences of actions. Like Averroës, his contemporary, he was born in Córdoba, Spain. His father was a distinguished Jewish scholar. The family fled Córdoba, already under Muslim control, when an intolerant Islamic sect conquered it and forced all non-Muslims to choose conversion, exile, or death. They eventually settled in Morocco, where he attended the University of Al Karaouine. Maimonides became a court physician in Egypt. He served as a leader of the Jewish community there, becoming a great authority on Jewish law.

Maimonides wrote many volumes on Jewish law, medicine, and other topics. His chief work of philosophy is *The Guide of the Perplexed*, a long treatise written in Arabic on the meaning of various Hebrew words. Maimonides addresses his work to people torn between what they see as the competing claims of philosophy and religion. (Such people, called "the perplexed," are among the "weeds" of the ideal city described by al-Farabi in *The Political Regime*.) Maimonides recognizes that many people think that reason and religious belief conflict. He tries to reconcile them, showing that reason supports religion. In his view, shallow thought challenges religion, but profound thought strengthens it.

In ethics, Maimonides tries to show that the 613 commandments in the Torah are all consistent with reason; all that pertain to relations between humans, he contends, are actually required by reason. All the commandments pertaining to human relations, he argues, are justified because they benefit humanity.

Maimonides's consequentialism is distinctive in two ways. First, the good includes virtue as well as happiness. Happiness is intrinsically good; people seek happiness for its own sake. But virtue is also intrinsically good; people seek virtues for their own sakes. Virtues are independent of and may even conflict with happiness. In benefiting people, then, we must promote not only people's *feeling* good but people's *being* good. Many rules, Maimonides argues, aim at maximizing being good rather than feeling good. Virtue, as Aristotle says, requires moderation. That in turn requires restraint. Many rules are designed to develop the needed restraint. Those rules do not promote feeling good; often they have the opposite effect. The purpose of the Law is to promote both the perfection of the body and the perfection of the soul—to prevent people from harming each other and to inculcate virtue and ultimately knowledge, especially the highest knowledge, which is knowledge of God.

Second, Maimonides treats ***kinds*** of actions as fundamental. He stresses the importance of rules in moral deliberation. He justifies the rules of the Torah by arguing that they benefit humanity and then judges individual actions by those rules. This arguably makes Maimonides something like a ***rule-utilitarian***, who judges particular actions indirectly by appeal to rules that are themselves justified as maximizing the good.

In most cases, act-utilitarians—who judge individual actions directly by their effects on the amount of good—agree with rule-utilitarians. They disagree, however, whenever it would be possible to do better by breaking the rules. "Do not murder," for example, is a good rule; following it maximizes the good. In some circumstances, however, murder might actually produce more good, or less evil, than refraining from murder. (Consider the possible assassination of a tyrant such as Hitler.) The principle of utility, in this sort of case, conflicts with the rule it generally justifies. Which takes priority: the rule the principle of utility justifies ("Do not murder") or the principle of utility itself?

Act-utilitarians argue that the principle of utility takes priority. They find it bizarre to say that we should follow the rule rather than the underlying principle—"Maximize good"—since the rule derives its moral force solely from the justification the principle of utility provides. But rule-utilitarians hold that the rule must take priority. Maimonides, for example, argues that rules are essential to moral thinking and moral education. We cannot calculate what to do in every individual case. We simply do not know enough about what the effects of individual acts will be and what the good in particular situations amounts to. If we try to set aside the rules when we think we can do better, we will make mistakes far more often than we will get things right. (Think about what happened to those who attempted Hitler's assassination.) And our vices will tempt us to break the rules more effectively than our virtues will tempt us to transcend them. The result will be moral chaos. So there is a consequentialist justification for following the rules even when we think we might be better off breaking them.

4.4.1 Moses Maimonides, from *Guide of the Perplexed*

Book III

Chapter XXVII

The general object of the Law is twofold: the well-being of the soul, and the well-being of the body. The well-being of the soul is promoted by correct opinions communicated to the people according to their capacity. Some of these opinions are therefore imparted in a plain form, others allegorically: because certain opinions are in their plain form too strong for the capacity of the common people. The well-being of the body is established by a proper management of the relations in which we live one to another. This we can attain in two ways: first by removing all violence from our midst: that is to say, that we do not do everyone as he pleases, desires, and is able to do; but every one of us does that which contributes towards the common welfare. Secondly, by teaching every one of us such good morals as must produce a good social state. Of these two objects, the one, the well-being of the

Source: Moses Maimonides, *Guide of the Perplexed*. Translated by M. Friedländer. New York: Dover, 1904.

soul, or the communication of correct opinions, comes undoubtedly first in rank, but the other, the well-being of the body, the government of the state, and the establishment of the best possible relations among men, is anterior in nature and time. The latter object is required first; it is also treated [in the Law] most carefully and most minutely, because the well-being of the soul can only be obtained after that of the body has been secured. For it has already been found that man has a double perfection: the first perfection is that of the body, and the second perfection is that of the soul. The first consists in the most healthy condition of his material relations, and this is only possible when man has all his wants supplied, as they arise; if he has his food, and other things needful for his body, e.g., shelter, bath, and the like. But one man alone cannot procure all this; it is impossible for a single man to obtain this comfort; it is only possible in society, since man, as is well known, is by nature social.

The second perfection of man consists in his becoming an actually intelligent being; i.e., he knows about the things in existence all that a person perfectly developed is capable of knowing. This second perfection certainly does not include any action or good conduct, but only knowledge, which is arrived at by speculation, or established by research.

It is clear that the second and superior kind of perfection can only be attained when the first perfection has been acquired; for a person that is suffering from great hunger, thirst, heat, or cold, cannot grasp an idea even if communicated by others, much less can he arrive at it by his own reasoning. But when a person is in possession of the first perfection, then he may possibly acquire the second perfection, which is undoubtedly of a superior kind, and is alone the source of eternal life. The true Law, which as we said is one, and beside which there is no other Law, viz., the Law of our teacher Moses, has for its purpose to give us the twofold perfection. It aims first at the establishment of good mutual relations among men by removing injustice and creating the noblest feelings. In this way the people in every land are enabled to stay and continue in one condition, and every one can acquire his first perfection. Secondly, it seeks to train us in faith, and to impart correct and true opinions when the intellect is sufficiently developed. Scripture clearly mentions the twofold perfection, and tells us that its acquisition is the object of all the divine commandments. "And the Lord commanded us to do all these statutes, to fear the Lord our God, for our good always, that he might preserve us alive as it is this day" (Deut. vi. 24). Here the second perfection is first mentioned because it is of greater importance, being, as we have shown, the ultimate aim of man's existence. This perfection is expressed in the phrase, "for our good always." You know the interpretation of our sages, "'that it may be well with thee' (ibid. xxii. 7), namely, in the world that is all good, 'and that thou mayest prolong thy days' (ibid.), i.e., in the world that is all eternal." In the same sense I explain the words, "for our good always," to mean that we may come into the world that is all good and eternal, where we may live permanently; and the words, "that he might preserve us alive as it is this day," I explain as referring to our first and temporal existence, to that of our body, which cannot be in a perfect and good condition except by the cooperation of society, as has been shown by us.

Chapter XXVIII

It is necessary to bear in mind that Scripture only teaches the chief points of those true principles which lead to the true perfection of man, and only demands in general terms faith in them. Thus Scripture teaches the Existence, the Unity, the Omniscience, the Omnipotence, the Will, and the Eternity of God. All this is given in the form of final results, but they cannot be understood fully and accurately except after the acquisition of many kinds of knowledge. Scripture further demands belief in certain truths, the belief in which is indispensable in regulating our social relations: Such is the belief that God is angry with those who disobey Him, for it leads us to the fear and dread of disobedience [to the will of God]. There are other truths in reference to the whole of the universe which form the substance of the various and many kinds of speculative sciences, and afford the means of verifying the above-mentioned principles as their final result. But Scripture does not so distinctly prescribe the belief in them as it does in the first case; it is implied in the commandment, "to love the Lord" (Deut. xi. 13). It may be inferred from the words, "And thou shalt love the Lord thy God with all thy heart, and with all thy soul, and with all thy might" (ibid. vi. 5) what stress is laid on this commandment to love God. We have already shown in the *Mishneh-torah* (*Yes. ha-torah* ii. 2) that this love is only possible when we comprehend the real nature of things, and understand the divine wisdom displayed therein. We have likewise mentioned there what our sages remark on this subject.

The result of all these preliminary remarks is this: The reason of a commandment, whether positive or negative, is clear, and its usefulness evident, if it directly tends to remove injustice, or to teach good conduct that furthers the well-being of society, or to impart a truth which ought to be believed either on its own merit or as being indispensable for facilitating the removal of injustice or the teaching of good morals. There is no occasion to ask for the object of such commandments: for no one can, e.g., be in doubt as to the reason why we have been commanded to believe that God is one, why we are forbidden to murder, to steal, and to take vengeance, or to retaliate, or why we are commanded to love one another. But there are precepts concerning which people are in doubt, and of divided opinions, some believing that they are mere commands, and serve no purpose whatever, whilst others believe that they serve a certain purpose, which, however, is unknown to man. Such are those precepts which in their literal meaning do not seem to further any of the three above-named results: to impart some truth, to teach some moral, or to remove injustice. They do not seem to have any influence upon the well-being of the soul by imparting any truth, or upon the well-being of the body by suggesting such ways and rules as are useful in the government of a state, or in the management of a household. Such are the prohibitions of wearing garments containing wool and linen; of sowing divers seeds, or of boiling meat and milk together; the commandment of covering the blood [of slaughtered beasts and birds], the ceremony of breaking the neck of a calf [in case of a person being found slain, and the murderer being unknown]; the law concerning the first-born of an ass, and the like. I am prepared to tell you my explanation of all these commandments, and to assign for them a true reason supported by proof, with the exception of some minor rules, and of a few commandments, as I have mentioned above. I will show that all these and similar laws must have some bearing upon one of the following three things, viz., the regulation of our opinions, or the improvement of our social relations, which implies two things, the removal of injustice, and the teaching of good morals. Consider what we said of the opinions [implied in the laws]; in some cases the law contains a truth which is itself the only object of that law, as, e.g., the truth of the Unity, Eternity, and Incorporeality of God; in other cases, that truth is only the means of securing the removal of injustice, or the acquisition of good morals; such is the belief that God is angry with those who oppress their fellow-men, as it is said, "Mine anger will be kindled, and I will slay," etc. (Exod. xxii. 23); or the belief that God hears the crying of the oppressed and vexed, to deliver them out of the hands of the oppressor and tyrant, as it is written, "And it shall come to pass, when he will cry unto me, that I will hear, for I am gracious" (Exod. xxii. 25).

Chapter XXXI

There are persons who find it difficult to give a reason for any of the commandments, and consider it right to assume that the commandments and prohibitions have no rational basis whatever. They are led to adopt this theory by a certain disease in their soul, the existence of which they perceive, but which they are unable to discuss or to describe. For they imagine that these precepts, if they were useful in any respect, and were commanded because of their usefulness, would seem to originate in the thought and reason of some intelligent being. But as things which are not objects of reason and serve no purpose, they would undoubtedly be attributed to God, because no thought of man could have produced them. According to the theory of those weak-minded persons, man is more perfect than his Creator. For what man says or does has a certain object, whilst the actions of God are different; He commands us to do what is of no use to us, and forbids us to do what is harmless. Far be this! On the contrary, the sole object of the Law is to benefit us. Thus we explained the Scriptural passage "for our good always, that He might preserve us alive, as it is this day" (Deut. vi. 24). Again, "which shall hear all those statutes (*hukkim*), and say, surely this great nation is a wise and understanding people" (ibid. iv. 6). He thus says that even every one of these "statutes" convinces all nations of the wisdom and understanding it includes. But if no reason could be found for these statutes, if they produced no advantage and removed no evil, why then should he who believes in them and follows them be wise, reasonable, and so excellent as to raise the admiration of all nations? But the truth is undoubtedly as we have said, that every one of the six hundred and thirteen precepts serves to inculcate some truth, to remove some erroneous opinion, to establish proper relations in society, to diminish evil, to train in good manners or to warn against bad habits. All this depends on three things: opinions, morals, and social conduct. We do not count words, because precepts, whether positive or negative, if they relate to speech, belong to those precepts which regulate our social conduct, or to those which spread truth, or to those which teach morals. Thus these three principles suffice for assigning a reason for every one of the divine commandments.

Chapter XXXIV

It is also important to note that the Law does not take into account exceptional circumstances; it is not based on conditions which rarely occur. Whatever the Law teaches, whether it be of an intellectual, a moral, or a practical character, is founded on that which is the rule and not on that which is the exception: It ignores the injury that might be caused to a single person through a certain maxim or a certain divine precept. For the Law is a divine institution, and [in order to understand its operation] we must consider how in nature the various forces produce benefits which are general, but in some solitary cases they cause also injury. This is clear from what has been said by ourselves as well as by others. We must consequently not be surprised when we find that the object of the Law does not fully appear in every individual; there must naturally be people who are not perfected by the instruction of the Law, just as there are beings which do not receive from the specific forms in nature all that they require. For all this comes from one God, is the result of one act: "they are all given from one shepherd" (Eccles. xii. 11). It is impossible to be otherwise; and we have already explained (chap. xv) that that which is impossible always remains impossible and never changes. From this consideration it also follows that the laws cannot like medicine vary according to the different conditions of persons and times; whilst the cure of a person depends on his particular constitution at the particular time, the divine guidance contained in the Law must be certain and general, although it may be effective in some cases and ineffective in others. If the Law depended on the varying conditions of man, it would be imperfect in its totality, each precept being left indefinite. For this reason it would not be right to make the fundamental principles of the Law dependent on a certain time or a certain place; on the contrary, the statutes and the judgments must be definite, unconditional, and general, in accordance with the divine words: "As for the congregation, one ordinance shall be for you and for the stranger" (Num. xv. 15); they are intended, as has been stated before, for all persons and for all times.

4.5 AQUINAS ON LAW AND VIRTUE

St. Thomas Aquinas (1224–1274), perhaps the greatest of all Catholic theologians and philosophers, was born in Roccasecca, Italy, and studied at Naples, Paris, and Cologne. At age 32 he was awarded a doctorate in theology at Paris; he joined the faculty there the next year. Starting in 1259 he spent a decade teaching at various Dominican monasteries near Rome, returning to Paris to teach in 1268. In 1272, at 48, he joined the faculty in Naples; he died just two years later.

Aquinas bases his views on ethics on those of Aristotle. But he adds many innovations, blending Aristotelian insights into a Christian worldview. He develops a comprehensive theory of natural law that remains influential today.

Aquinas begins with Aristotle's idea that human good depends on human nature. To live well—to excel or flourish—is to fulfill one's function well. Just as an excellent knife cuts well, and an excellent eye sees well, an excellent human being displays excellence in rational activity. As these examples suggest, different things have different functions. In general, the function of a thing depends on its nature. So what something ought to do and be depends on its function, which in turn depends on its nature.

Aquinas adds God to this Aristotelian picture. God establishes the order of nature, determining the natures of things. God thus indirectly establishes not only the physical laws that constitute the order of nature but also the natural laws that free beings ought to obey. Since human nature is distinctively rational, law itself is essentially a matter of reason.

Aquinas distinguishes several different kinds of law. Eternal law is the law of nature, established by God, that governs the entire universe. Everything in the universe obeys eternal law, and does so necessarily. Science investigates eternal law and tries to describe it. Natural law is normative; it prescribes what things should do and be. Since a thing's nature determines its function and, thus, its virtue—what it ought to do and be—eternal law determines natural law. Natural law is the manifestation of eternal law in creatures capable of rational choice and activity.

Natural law manifests the eternal law by way of "the light of natural reason." God imprints on us the natural ability to tell right from wrong. Aquinas also distinguishes natural law from human law. Natural law is fully general and universal, but human law must apply to particular circumstances in specific ways. Natural law relates to human law as principles relate to conclusions drawn from them. One can think of natural law, then, as comprising the axioms of the moral law in general. Natural law consists of first principles, the starting points for practical reasoning. Because natural law serves as a set of axioms of the moral law, it must be self-evident; it cannot be a conclusion from some other premise. Precepts of natural law must be both general and obvious. Precepts of natural law are true universally and necessarily. Ordinary moral principles derived from them are not, for they rely on practical connections between means and ends, and those are frequently neither universal nor necessary.

It might seem that natural law, as Aquinas outlines it, has little content. Pursue good; avoid evil. Everyone can agree to that. But what is good? What is evil? Aquinas appeals to human nature. As Aristotle argued, human excellence depends on our characteristic function, which depends in turn on our nature. What we are determines what we ought to do and be. The universe is ordered so that we naturally tend to pursue good and avoid evil. Our own dispositions thus provide a test. We are naturally disposed to pursue good and avoid evil. The natural law is in us in the form of the "light of natural reason."

Aquinas contends that four factors determine whether an act is good or bad, right or wrong:

1. Its genus, that is, its being an action
2. Its species, that is, the kind of action it is; its essential properties
3. Its circumstances; its accidental properties
4. Its end

Good actions are good in all four respects. They accord with reason. Wrong actions are in some respect against reason. They may be intrinsically irrational; they may be irrational in the circumstances in which they are done; they may be aimed at an irrational goal.

4.5.1 St. Thomas Aquinas, from *Summa Theologica*

Question 18

Article 4. Whether a human action is good or evil from its end?

Objection 1. It would seem that the good and evil in human actions are not from the end. For Dionysius says (*Div. Nom.* iv) that "nothing acts with a view to evil." If therefore an action were good or evil from its end, no action would be evil. Which is clearly false.

Objection 2. Further, the goodness of an action is something in the action. But the end is an extrinsic cause. Therefore an action is not said to be good or bad according to its end.

Objection 3. Further, a good action may happen to be ordained to an evil end, as when a man gives an alms from vainglory; and conversely, an evil action may happen to be ordained to a good end, as a theft committed in order to give something to the poor. Therefore an action is not good or evil from its end.

On the contrary, Boethius says (*De Differ. Topic.* ii) that "if the end is good, the thing is good, and if the end be evil, the thing also is evil."

I answer that, The disposition of things as to goodness is the same as their disposition as to being. Now in some things the being does not depend on another, and in these it suffices to consider their being absolutely. But there are things the being of which depends on something else, and hence in their regard we must consider their being in its relation to the cause on which it depends. Now just as the being of a thing depends on the agent, and the form, so the goodness of a thing depends on its end. Hence in the Divine Persons, Whose goodness does not depend on another, the measure of goodness is not taken from the end. Whereas human actions, and other things, the goodness of which depends on something else, have a measure of goodness from the end on which they depend, besides that goodness which is in them absolutely.

Source: *The Summa Theologica of St. Thomas Aquinas.* Translated by Fathers of the English Dominican Province, 1920.

Accordingly a fourfold goodness may be considered in a human action. First, that which, as an action, it derives from its genus; because as much as it has of action and being so much has it of goodness, as stated above. Secondly, it has goodness according to its species; which is derived from its suitable object. Thirdly, it has goodness from its circumstances, in respect, as it were, of its accidents. Fourthly, it has goodness from its end, to which it is compared as to the cause of its goodness.

Reply to Objection 1. The good in view of which one acts is not always a true good; but sometimes it is a true good, sometimes an apparent good. And in the latter event, an evil action results from the end in view.

Reply to Objection 2. Although the end is an extrinsic cause, nevertheless due proportion to the end, and relation to the end, are inherent to the action.

Reply to Objection 3. Nothing hinders an action that is good in one of the ways mentioned above, from lacking goodness in another way. And thus it may happen that an action which is good in its species or in its circumstances is ordained to an evil end, or vice versa. However, an action is not good simply, unless it is good in all those ways: since "evil results from any single defect, but good from the complete cause," as Dionysius says (*Div. Nom.* iv).

Article 5. Whether a human action is good or evil in its species?

Objection 1. It would seem that good and evil in moral actions do not make a difference of species. For the existence of good and evil in actions is in conformity with their existence in things, as stated above. But good and evil do not make a specific difference in things; for a good man is specifically the same as a bad man. Therefore neither do they make a specific difference in actions.

Objection 2. Further, since evil is a privation, it is a non-being. But non-being cannot be a difference, according to the Philosopher (*Metaph.* iii, 3). Since therefore the difference constitutes the species, it seems that an action is not constituted in a species through being evil. Consequently good and evil do not diversify the species of human actions.

Objection 3. Further, acts that differ in species produce different effects. But the same specific effect results from a good and from an evil action: thus a man is born of adulterous or of lawful wedlock. Therefore good and evil actions do not differ in species.

Objection 4. Further, actions are sometimes said to be good or bad from a circumstance, as stated above. But since a circumstance is an accident, it does not give an action its species. Therefore human actions do not differ in species on account of their goodness or malice.

On the contrary, According to the Philosopher (*Ethic* ii. 1) "like habits produce like actions." But a good and a bad habit differ in species, as liberality and prodigality. Therefore also good and bad actions differ in species.

I answer that, Every action derives its species from its object, as stated above. Hence it follows that a difference of object causes a difference of species in actions. Now, it must be observed that a difference of objects causes a difference of species in actions, according as the latter are referred to one active principle, which does not cause a difference in actions, according as they are referred to another active principle. Because nothing accidental constitutes a species, but only that which is essential; and a difference of object may be essential in reference to one active principle, and accidental in reference to another. Thus to know color and to know sound, differ essentially in reference to sense, but not in reference to the intellect.

Now in human actions, good and evil are predicated in reference to the reason; because as Dionysius says (*Div. Nom.* iv), "the good of man is to be in accordance with reason," and evil is "to be against reason." For that is good for a thing which suits it in regard to its form; and evil, that which is against the order of its form. It is therefore evident that the difference of good and evil considered in reference to the object is an essential difference in relation to reason; that is to say, according as the object is suitable or unsuitable to reason. Now certain actions are called human or moral, inasmuch as they proceed from the reason. Consequently it is evident that good and evil diversify the species in human actions; since essential differences cause a difference of species.

Reply to Objection 1. Even in natural things, good and evil, inasmuch as something is according to nature, and something against nature, diversify the natural species; for a dead body and a living body are not of the same species. In like manner, good, inasmuch as it is in accord with reason, and evil, inasmuch as it is against reason, diversify the moral species.

Reply to Objection 2. Evil implies privation, not absolute, but affecting some potentiality. For an action is said to be evil in its species, not because it has no object at all; but because it has an object in disaccord with reason, for instance, to appropriate another's property. Wherefore insofar as the object is something positive, it can constitute the species of an evil act.

Reply to Objection 3. The conjugal act and adultery, as compared to reason, differ specifically and have effects specifically different; because the other deserves praise and reward, the other, blame and punishment. But as compared to the generative power, they do not differ in species; and thus they have one specific effect.

Reply to Objection 4. A circumstance is sometimes taken as the essential difference of the object, as compared to reason; and then it can specify a moral act. And it must needs be so whenever a circumstance transforms an action from good to evil; for a circumstance would not make an action evil, except through being repugnant to reason.

Question 20

Article 1. Whether goodness or malice is first in the action of the will, or in the external action?

Objection 1. It would seem that good and evil are in the external action prior to being in the act of the will. For the will derives goodness from its object, as stated above. But the external action is the object of the interior act of the will: for a man is said to will to commit a theft, or to will to give an alms. Therefore good and evil are in the external action, prior to being in the act of the will.

Objection 2. Further, the aspect of good belongs first to the end: since what is directed to the end receives the aspect of good from its relation to the end. Now whereas the act of the will cannot be an end, as stated above, the act of another power can be an end. Therefore good is in the act of some other power prior to being in the act of the will.

Objection 3. Further, the act of the will stands in a formal relation to the external action, as stated above. But that which is formal is subsequent; since form is something added to matter. Therefore good and evil are in the external action, prior to being in the act of the will.

On the contrary, Augustine says (*Retract.* i, 9) that "it is by the will that we sin, and that we behave aright." Therefore moral good and evil are first in the will.

I answer that, External actions may be said to be good or bad in two ways. First, in regard to their genus, and the circumstances connected with them: thus the giving of alms, if the required conditions be observed, is said to be good. Secondly, a thing is said to be good or evil, from its relation to the end: thus the giving of alms for vainglory is said to be evil. Now, since the end is the will's proper object, it is evident that this aspect of good or evil, which the external action derives from its relation to the end, is to be found first of all in the act of the will, whence it passes to the external action. On the other hand, the goodness or malice which the external action has of itself, on account of its being about due matter and its being attended by due circumstances, is not derived from the will, but rather from the reason. Consequently, if we consider the goodness of the external action, insofar as it comes from reason's ordination and apprehension, it is prior to the goodness of the act of the will: but if we consider it insofar as it is in the execution of the action done, it is subsequent to the goodness of the will, which is its principle.

Reply to Objection 1. The exterior action is the object of the will, inasmuch as it is proposed to the will by reason, as good apprehended and ordained by reason: and thus it is prior to the good in the act of the will. But inasmuch as it is found in the execution of the action, it is an effect of the will and is subsequent to the will.

Reply to Objection 2. The end precedes in the order of intention, but follows in the order of execution.

Reply to Objection 3. A form as received into matter is subsequent to matter in the order of generation, although it precedes it in the order of nature: but inasmuch as it is in the active cause, it precedes in every way. Now the will is compared to the exterior action, as its efficient cause. Wherefore the goodness of the act of the will, as existing in the active cause, is the form of the exterior action.

Whether law is something pertaining to reason?

Objection 1. It would seem that law is not something pertaining to reason. For the Apostle says (Romans 7:23): "I see another law in my members," etc. But nothing pertaining to reason is in the members; since the reason does not make use of a bodily organ. Therefore law is not something pertaining to reason.

Objection 2. Further, in the reason there is nothing else but power, habit, and act. But law is not the power itself of reason. In like manner, neither is it a habit of reason: because the habits of reason are the intellectual virtues of which we have spoken above. Nor again is it an act of reason: because then law would cease, when the act of reason ceases, for instance, while we are asleep. Therefore law is nothing pertaining to reason.

Objection 3. Further, the law moves those who are subject to it to act aright. But it belongs properly to the will to move to act, as is evident from what has been said above. Therefore law pertains, not to the reason, but to the will; according to the words of the Jurist (*Lib.* i, ff., *De Const. Prin. leg.* i): "Whatsoever pleaseth the sovereign, has force of law."

On the contrary, it belongs to the law to command and to forbid. But it belongs to reason to command, as stated above. Therefore law is something pertaining to reason.

I answer that, Law is a rule and measure of acts, whereby man is induced to act or is restrained from acting: for *lex* [law] is derived from *ligare* [to bind], because it binds one to act. Now the rule and measure of human acts is the reason, which is the first principle of human acts, as is evident from what has been stated above; since it belongs to the reason to direct to the end, which is the first principle in all matters of action, according to the Philosopher (*Phys.* ii). Now that which is the principle in any genus is the rule and measure of that genus: for instance, unity in the genus of numbers, and the first movement in the genus of movements. Consequently it follows that law is something pertaining to reason.

Reply to Objection 1. Since law is a kind of rule and measure, it may be in something in two ways. First, as in that which measures and rules: and since this is proper to reason, it follows that, in this way, law is in the reason alone. Secondly, as in that which is measured and ruled. In this way, law is in all those things that are inclined to something by reason of some law: so that any inclination arising from a law, may be called a law, not essentially but by participation as it were. And thus the inclination of the members to concupiscence is called "the law of the members."

Reply to Objection 2. Just as, in external action, we may consider the work and the work done, for instance the work of building and the house built; so in the acts of reason, we may consider the act itself of reason, i.e., to understand and to reason, and something produced by this act. With regard to the speculative reason, this is first of all the definition; secondly, the proposition; thirdly, the syllogism or argument. And since also the practical reason makes use of a syllogism in respect of the work to be done, as stated above and since as the Philosopher teaches (*Ethic.* vii, 3); hence we find in the practical reason something that holds the same position in regard to operations, as, in the speculative intellect, the proposition holds in regard to conclusions. Suchlike universal propositions of the practical intellect that are directed to actions have the nature of law. And these propositions are sometimes under our actual consideration, while sometimes they are retained in the reason by means of a habit.

Reply to Objection 3. Reason has its power of moving from the will, as stated above: for it is due to the fact that one wills the end, that the reason issues its commands as regards things ordained to the end. But in order that the volition of what is commanded may have the nature of law, it needs to be in accord with some rule of reason. And in this sense is to be understood the saying that the will of the sovereign has the force of law; otherwise the sovereign's will would savor of lawlessness rather than of law.

Whether there is in us a natural law?

Objection 1. It would seem that there is no natural law in us. Because man is governed sufficiently by the eternal law: for Augustine says (*De Lib. Arb.* i) that "the eternal law is that by which it is right that all things should be most orderly." But nature does not abound in superfluities as neither does she fail in necessaries. Therefore no law is natural to man.

Objection 2. Further, by the law man is directed, in his acts, to the end, as stated above. But the directing of human acts to their end is not a function of nature, as is the case in irrational creatures, which act for an end solely by their natural appetite; whereas man acts for an end by his reason and will. Therefore no law is natural to man.

Objection 3. Further, the more a man is free, the less is he under the law. But man is freer than all the animals, on account of his free-will, with which he is endowed above all other animals. Since therefore other animals are not subject to a natural law, neither is man subject to a natural law.

On the contrary, A gloss on Rm. 2:14: "When the Gentiles, who have not the law, do by nature those things that are of the law," comments as follows: "Although they have no written law, yet they have the natural law, whereby each one knows, and is conscious of, what is good and what is evil."

I answer that, As stated above, law, being a rule and measure, can be in a person in two ways: in one way, as in him that rules and measures; in another way, as in that which is ruled and measured, since a thing is ruled and measured, insofar as it partakes of the rule or measure. Wherefore, since all things subject to Divine providence are ruled and measured by the eternal law, as was stated above; it is evident that all things partake somewhat of the eternal law, in so far as, namely, from its being imprinted on them, they derive their respective inclinations to their proper acts and ends. Now among all others, the rational creature is subject to Divine providence in the most excellent way, insofar as it partakes of a share of providence, by being provident both for itself and for others. Wherefore it has a share of the Eternal Reason, whereby it has a natural inclination to its proper act and end: and this participation of the eternal law in the rational creature is called the natural law. Hence the Psalmist after saying (Psalm 4:6): "Offer up the sacrifice of justice," as though someone asked what the works of justice are, adds: "Many say, Who showeth us good things?" in answer to which question he says: "The light of Thy countenance, O Lord, is signed upon us"; thus implying that the light of natural reason, whereby we discern what is good and what is evil, which is the function of the natural law, is nothing else than an imprint on us of the Divine light. It is therefore evident that the natural law is nothing else than the rational creature's participation of the eternal law.

Reply to Objection 1. This argument would hold, if the natural law were something different from the eternal law: whereas it is nothing but a participation thereof, as stated above.

Reply to Objection 2. Every act of reason and will in us is based on that which is according to nature, as stated above: for every act of reasoning is based on principles that are known naturally, and every act of appetite in respect of the means is derived from the natural appetite in respect of the last end. Accordingly the first direction of our acts to their end must needs be in virtue of the natural law.

Reply to Objection 3. Even irrational animals partake in their own way of the Eternal Reason, just as the rational creature does. But because the rational creature partakes thereof in an intellectual and rational manner, therefore the participation of the eternal law in the rational creature is properly called a law, since a law is something pertaining to reason, as stated above. Irrational creatures, however, do not partake thereof in a rational manner, wherefore there is no participation of the eternal law in them, except by way of similitude.

Whether the natural law contains several precepts, or only one?

Objection 1. It would seem that the natural law contains, not several precepts, but one only. For law is a kind of precept, as stated above. If therefore there were many precepts of the natural law, it would follow that there are also many natural laws.

Objection 2. Further, the natural law is consequent to human nature. But human nature, as a whole, is one; though, as to its parts, it is manifold. Therefore, either there is but one precept of the law of nature, on account of the unity of nature as a whole; or there are many, by reason of the number of parts of human nature. The result would be that even things relating to the inclination of the faculty of desire belong to the natural law.

Objection 3. Further, law is something pertaining to reason, as stated above. Now reason is but one in man. Therefore there is only one precept of the natural law.

On the contrary, The precepts of the natural law in man stand in relation to practical matters, as the first principles to matters of demonstration. But there are several first indemonstrable principles. Therefore there are also several precepts of the natural law.

I answer that, As stated above, the precepts of the natural law are to the practical reason, what the first principles of demonstrations are to the speculative reason, because both are self-evident principles. Now a thing is said to be self-evident in two ways: first, in itself; secondly, in relation to us. Any proposition is said to be self-evident in itself, if its predicate is contained in the notion of the subject: although, to one who knows not the definition of the subject, it happens that such a proposition is not self-evident. For instance, this proposition, "Man is a rational being," is, in its very nature, self-evident, since who says "man," says "a rational being": and yet to one who knows not what a man is, this proposition is not self-evident. Hence it is that, as Boethius says (*De Hebdom.*), certain axioms or propositions are universally self-evident to all; and such are those propositions whose terms are known to all, as, "Every whole is greater than its part," and, "Things equal to one and the same are equal to one another." But some propositions are self-evident only to the wise, who understand the meaning of the terms of such propositions: thus to one who understands that an angel is not a body, it is self-evident that an angel is not circumscriptively in a place: but this is not evident to the unlearned, for they cannot grasp it.

Now a certain order is to be found in those things that are apprehended universally. For that which, before aught else, falls under apprehension, is "being," the notion of which is included in all things whatsoever a man apprehends. Wherefore the first indemonstrable principle is that "the same thing cannot be affirmed and denied at the same time," which is based on the notion of "being" and "not-being": and on this principle all others are based, as is stated in *Metaph.* iv, text. 9. Now as "being" is the first thing that falls under the apprehension simply, so "good" is the first thing that falls under the apprehension of the practical reason, which is directed to action: since every agent acts for an end under the aspect of good. Consequently the first principle of practical reason is one founded on the notion of good, viz. that "good is that which all things seek after." Hence this is the first precept of law, that "good is to be done and pursued, and evil is to be avoided." All other precepts of the natural law are based upon this: so that whatever the practical reason naturally apprehends as man's good (or evil) belongs to the precepts of the natural law as something to be done or avoided.

Since, however, good has the nature of an end, and evil, the nature of a contrary, hence it is that all those things to which man has a natural inclination, are naturally apprehended by reason as being good, and consequently as objects of pursuit, and their contraries as evil, and objects of avoidance. Wherefore according to the order of natural inclinations, is the order of the precepts of the natural law. Because in man there is first of all an inclination to good in accordance with the nature which he has in common with all substances: inasmuch as every substance seeks the preservation of its own being, according to its nature: and by reason of this inclination, whatever is a means of preserving human life, and of warding off its obstacles, belongs to the natural law. Secondly, there is in man an inclination to things that pertain to him more specially, according to that nature which he has in common with other animals: and in virtue of this inclination, those things are said to belong to the natural law, "which nature has taught to all animals" [*Pandect. Just.* I, tit. i], such as sexual intercourse, education of offspring and so forth. Thirdly, there is in man an inclination to good, according to the nature of his reason, which nature is proper to him: thus man has a natural inclination to know the truth about God, and to live in society: and in this respect, whatever pertains to this inclination belongs to the natural law; for instance, to shun ignorance, to avoid offending those among whom one has to live, and other such things regarding the above inclination.

Reply to Objection 1. All these precepts of the law of nature have the character of one natural law, inasmuch as they flow from one first precept.

Reply to Objection 2. All the inclinations of any parts whatsoever of human nature, e.g., of the concupiscible and irascible parts [desire and emotion], insofar as they are ruled by reason, belong to the natural law and are reduced to one first precept, as stated above: so that the precepts of the natural law are many in themselves, but are based on one common foundation.

Reply to Objection 3. Although reason is one in itself, yet it directs all things regarding man; so that whatever can be ruled by reason, is contained under the law of reason.

4.6 ST. CATHERINE OF SIENA ON THE PARADOXES OF WISDOM

St. Catherine Benincasa (1347–1380), the youngest child of a large lower-middle-class family in Siena, Italy, began to see visions and live ascetically at a young age. At 19 she had an especially powerful mystical experience and devoted her life to helping the poor and tending the sick. She was known for her extraordinary charm, happiness, and wisdom, even though she often ate nothing other than the sacraments. At 23 she received a vision telling her to enter public life. She wrote to Pope Gregory XI, imploring him to leave Avignon and seek peace. Shortly thereafter, war broke out in Italy, and the Pope sent her on a mission to secure the neutrality of several of the Papal States. When Catherine was 31, Pope Urban VI summoned her to Rome, where she remained, working closely with him, until her death just two years later. Catherine is one of only three women recognized as Doctors of the Church.

Catherine's ethics emerge in her letters, where she advises her correspondents, in quite un-Aristotelian fashion, to love immoderately. You must love God completely and likewise love people. But that, perhaps surprisingly, requires limiting your interaction with people. To achieve perfection, it is necessary to set your life in order and be disciplined in interacting with others. It is easy to be distracted from what really matters by everyday concerns. You must know and understand yourself well to be able to set your life in order. Without a commensurate knowledge of God, however, this is not enough. In fact, it leads to a distortion of the self, for humility is a key virtue, and reflecting on the self apart from God leads away from it. There are two wills—in Paul's language, the will of the flesh and the will of the spirit—and the latter must dominate the former. Only by placing the love of God first can you turn yourself into the person you ought to be.

4.6.1 Letter to Monna Alessa Dei Saracini

In the Name of Jesus Christ crucified and of sweet Mary:

Dearest daughter in Christ sweet Jesus: I Catherine, thy poor unworthy mother, want thee to attain that perfection for which God has chosen thee. It seems to me that one wishing so to attain should walk with and not without moderation. And yet every work of ours ought to be done both without and with moderation: It befits us to love God without moderation, putting to that love neither limit nor measure nor rule, but loving Him immeasurably. And if thou wish to reach the perfection of love, it befits thee to set thy life in order. Let thy first rule be to flee the conversation of every human being, in so far as it is simply conversation, except as deeds of charity may demand; but to love people very much, and talk with few of them. And know how to talk in moderation even with those whom thou lovest with spiritual love; reflect that if thou didst not do this, thou wouldst place a limit before perceiving it to that limitless love which thou oughtest to bear to God, by placing the finite creature between you: for the love which thou shouldst place in God thou wouldst place in the creature, loving it without moderation; and this would hinder thy perfection. Therefore thou shouldst love it spiritually, in a disciplined way.

Be a vase, which thou fillest at the source and at the source dost drink from. Although thou hadst drawn thy love from God, who is the Source of living water, didst thou not drink it continually in Him thy vase would remain empty. And this shall be the sign to thee that thou dost not drink wholly in God: when thou sufferest from that which thou lovest, either by some talk thou didst hold, or because thou wast deprived of some consolation thou wast used to receiving, or for some other accidental cause. If thou sufferest, then, from this

---

Source: *Saint Catherine of Siena as Seen in Her Letters.* Translated and edited with introduction by Vida D. Scudder. London: J. M. Dent, 1905.

or anything else except wrong against God, it is a clear sign to thee that this love is still imperfect and drawn far from the Source. What way is there, then, to make the imperfect perfect? This way: to correct and chastise the movements of thy heart with true self-knowledge, and with hatred and distaste for thy imperfection, that thou art such a peasant as to give to the creature that love which ought to be given wholly to God, loving the creature without moderation and God moderately. For love toward God should be without measure, and that for the creature should be measured by that for God and not by the measure of one's own consolations, either spiritual or temporal. So do, then, that thou lovest everything in God, and correct every inordinate affection.

Make two homes for thyself, my daughter. One actual home in thy cell, that thou go not running about into many places, unless for necessity, or for obedience to the prioress, or for charity's sake; and another spiritual home, which thou art to carry with thee always—the cell of true self-knowledge, where thou shalt find within thyself knowledge of the goodness of God. These are two cells in one, and when abiding in the one it behoves thee to abide in the other, for otherwise the soul would fall into either confusion or presumption. For didst thou rest in knowledge of thyself, confusion of mind would fall on thee; and didst thou abide in the knowledge of God alone, thou wouldst fall into presumption. The two, then, must be built together and made one same thing; if thou dost this, thou wilt attain perfection. For from self-knowledge thou wilt gain hatred of thine own fleshliness, and through hate thou wilt become a judge, and sit upon the seat of thy conscience, and pass judgment; and thou wilt not let a fault go without giving sentence on it.

From such knowledge flows the stream of humility; which never seizes on mere report, nor takes offence at anything, but bears every insult, every loss of consolation, and every sorrow, from whatever direction they may come, patiently, with joy. Shames appear glory, and great persecutions refreshment; and it rejoices in all, seeing itself punished for that perverse law of self-will in its members which for ever rebels against God; and it sees itself conformed with Christ Jesus crucified, the way and the doctrine of truth.

In the knowledge of God thou shalt find the fire of divine charity. Where shalt thou rejoice? Upon the Cross, with the Spotless Lamb, seeking His honour and the salvation of souls, through continual, humble prayer. Now herein is all our perfection. There are many other things also, but this is the chief, from which we receive so much light that we cannot err in the lesser works that follow.

Rejoice, my daughter, to conform thee to the shame of Christ. And watch over the impulse of the tongue, that the tongue may not always respond to the impulse of the heart; but digest what is in thy heart, with hatred and distaste for thyself. Do thou be the least of the least, subject in humility and patience to every creature through God; not making excuses, but saying: the fault is mine. Thus are vices conquered in thy soul and in the soul of him to whom thou shouldest so speak: through the virtue of humility.

Order thy time: the night to vigil, when thou hast paid the debt of sleep to thy body; and the morning in church with sweet prayer; do not spend it in chatting until the appointed hour. Let nothing except necessity, or obedience, or charity, as I said, draw thee away from this or anything else. After the hour of eating, recollect thyself a little, and then do something with thy hands, as thou mayest need. At the hour of vespers, do thou go and keep quiet; and as much as the Holy Spirit enjoins on thee, that do. Then go back and take care of thy old mother without negligence, and provide what she needs; be thine this burden. More when I return. So do that thou mayest fulfill my desire. I say no more. Remain in the holy and sweet grace of God. Sweet Jesus, Jesus Love.

4.6.2 Letter to the Venerable Religious Brother Antonio of Nizza, of the Order of the Hermit Brothers of St. Augustine at the Wood of the Lake

In the Name of Jesus Christ crucified and of sweet Mary:

To you, most beloved and dearest father and brother in Christ Jesus: I Catherine, servant and slave of the servants of Jesus Christ, write and commend me in the Precious Blood of the Son of God, with desire to see you kindled and inflamed in the furnace of divine charity and your own self-will—the will that robs us of all life—consumed therein. Let us open our eyes, dearest brother, for we have two wills–one of the senses, which seeks the things of sense, and the other the self-will of the spirit, which, under aspect and colour of virtue, holds firm to its own way. And this is clear when it wants to choose places and seasons and consolations to suit itself, and says: "Thus I wish in order to possess God more fully." This is a great cheat, and an illusion of the devil; for not being able to deceive the servants of God through their first will—since the servants of God have already mortified it so far as the things of sense go—the devil catches their second will on the sly with things of the spirit. So many a time the soul receives consolation, and then later feels itself deprived thereof by God; and another experience will harrow it, which will give less consolation and more fruit. Then the soul, which is inspired by what gives sweetness, suffers when deprived of it, and feels annoyance. And why annoyance? Because it does not want to be deprived; for it says, "I seem to love God more in this way than in that. From the one I feel that I bear some fruit, and from the other I perceive no fruit at all, except pain and ofttimes many conflicts; and so I seem to wrong God."

Son and brother in Christ Jesus, I say that this soul is deceived by its self-will. For it would not be deprived of sweetness; with this bait the devil catches it. Frequently men lose time in longing for time to suit themselves, for they do not employ what they have otherwise than in suffering and gloominess.

Once our sweet Saviour said to a very dear daughter of His, "Dost thou know how those people act who want to fulfill My will in consolation and in sweetness and joy? When they are deprived of these things, they wish to depart from My will, thinking to do well and to avoid offence; but false sensuality lurks in them, and to escape pains it falls into offence without perceiving it. But if the soul were wise and had the light of My will within, it would look to the fruit and not to the sweetness. What is the fruit of the soul? Hatred of itself and love of Me. This hate and love are the issue of self-knowledge; then the soul knows its faulty self to be nothing, and it sees in itself My goodness, which keeps its will good; and it sees what a person I have made it, in order that it may serve Me in greater perfection, and judges that I have made it for the best, and for its own greatest good. Such a man as this, dearest daughter, does not wish for time to suit himself, because he has learned humility; knowing his infirmity, he does not trust in his own wish, but is faithful to Me. He clothes him in My highest and eternal will, because he sees that I neither give nor take away, save for your sanctification; and he sees that love alone impels Me to give you sweetness and to take it from you. For this cause he cannot grieve over any consolation that might be taken from him within or without, by

Source: *Saint Catherine of Siena as Seen in Her Letters.* Translated and edited with introduction by Vida D. Scudder. London: J. M. Dent, 1905.

demon or fellow-creature—because he sees that, were this not for his good, I should not permit it. Therefore this man rejoices because he has light within and without, and is so illumined that when the devil approaches his mind with shadows to confuse him, saying, 'This is for thy sins,' he replies like a person who shrinks not from suffering, saying, 'Thanks be to my Creator, who has remembered me in the time of shadows, punishing me by pain in finite time. Great is this love, which will not punish me in the infinite future.' Oh, what tranquillity of mind has this soul, because it has freed itself from the self-will which brings storm! But not thus does he whose self-will is lively within, seeking things after his own way! For he seems to think that he knows what he needs better than I. Many a time he says, 'It seems to me that I am wronging God in this: Free me from wrong, and let what He wills be done.'

"This is a sign that you are freed from wrong, when you see in yourself both goodwill not to want to wrong God, and displeasure with sin; thence ought you to take hope. Although all external activities and inward consolations should fail, let goodwill to please God ever remain firm. Upon this rock is founded grace. If thou sayest, I do not seem to have it, I say that this is false, for if thou hadst it not, thou wouldst not fear to wrong God. But it is the devil who makes things look so, in order that the soul may fall into confusion and disordered sadness, and hold firm its self-will, by wanting consolations, times and seasons in its own way. Do not believe him, dearest daughter, but let your soul be always ready to endure sufferings in howsoever God may inflict them. Otherwise you would do like a man who stands on the threshold with a light in his hand, who reaches his hand out and casts light outside, and within it is dark. Such is a man who is already united in outward things with the will of God, despising the world; but within, his spiritual self-will is living still, veiled in the colour of virtue." Thus spoke God to that servant of His spoken of above.

Therefore I said that I wished and desired that your will should be absorbed and transformed in Him, while we hold ourselves always ready to bear pains and toils howsoever God chooses to send them to us. So we shall be freed from darkness and abide in light. Amen. Praised be Jesus Christ crucified and sweet Mary.

4.7 CHRISTINE DE PIZAN'S FEMINISM

Christine de Pizan (1364?–1429?), born in Venice, lived most of her life in Paris during the Hundred Years' War. She married a royal secretary and had three children. When she was 24, her husband died. Lawsuits about his property kept her and her children in poverty for years. In her 30s she began writing poems, at first giving them as gifts and then accepting commissions. She quickly established herself as one of France's leading intellectuals. She was in her mid-50s when the British defeated the French at Agincourt. She fled Paris, staying thereafter as a lay resident of a convent.

Christine de Pizan has been called the first feminist. Certainly she argued that women were intellectually and morally equal to men, defending, in a poem, Eve's virtue in giving Adam the forbidden fruit in the Garden of Eden. She became famous for arguing that the thirteenth-century satire of conventions of courtly love, *Romance of the Rose*, depicted women unfairly. One of her major works, *The Book of the City of Ladies*, describes a city of equality between the sexes where women are respected as equals. She urges women to seek peace, playing a mediating role in social conflicts, and to develop their abilities to speak and write effectively to persuade others. She describes many different social positions that women might occupy and details the virtues and obligations appropriate to each position. Though these details differ, the three primary virtues, reason, rectitude, and justice, apply universally.

4.7.1 Christine de Pizan, from *The Treasury of the City of Ladies*

Book I

Here is what you must do if you want to be saved. The Scriptures tell of the two ways which lead to Heaven: the contemplative life and the active life. Without following these paths it is impossible to enter there. What do they entail? The contemplative life is a manner and a state of serving God wherein one loves Our Lord so greatly and so ardently that she totally forgets father, mother, children, everyone, even herself, because of the great, consuming thought she devotes endlessly to her Creator. She never thinks of other things; nothing else is important to her. No poverty, tribulation, nor suffering (which, indeed, might damage another) hinders her heart, the heart of the true contemplative. Her manner of life completely disdains everything in the world and all its fleeting joys. She remains solitary, apart from others, knees to the ground, joined hands pointing heavenward, heart raised up in such elevated thought that in contemplation she ascends to the presence of God. Through divine inspiration she sees the Holy Trinity and the Court of Heaven and all of its joys.

The perfect contemplative often is so ravished that she seems other than herself, and the consolation, sweetness, and pleasure she experiences can scarcely be told, nor can any earthly joy be compared with them. She feels and tastes the glories and joys of Paradise. She sees God in spirit through her contemplation. Her burning love gives perfect sufficiency in this world because she feels no other desire. God delights his servant, offering the sweets of His Holy Paradise. Pure, holy, heavenly thoughts give perfect hope of joining that joyous company. No other exultation compares; those who have tried the contemplative way know this. To my regret, I cannot speak of that exultation any more than a blind man can describe colors. But this is the way, above all others, manifestly agreeable to God. Certain holy contemplatives are said to have risen physically, soaring above the earth in their contemplation, by God's miracle, as if the body were following the thought as it rose toward Heaven. I am not worthy to speak of this holy, elevated life, nor to describe it as adequately as it deserves. But the Holy Scriptures are filled with words on it for anyone who wishes to learn more.

The active life is the other way of serving God. The one following this way is so charitable that if she could, she would serve all for the love of God. So she serves in hospitals, visiting the sick and the poor, aiding with her own wealth and her own efforts, generously, for the love of God. She has such great pity for the creatures she sees in sin, misery, or tribulation that she weeps as if the trouble were her own. She seeks her neighbor's good as if it were her own; and since she always is striving to do good, she never is idle. Her ardent desire to accomplish charitable works is unceasing; she devotes all her energies to them. Such a woman bears all trials and tribulations patiently

Source: *Christine de Pizan, A Medieval Woman's Mirror of Honor. The Treasury of the City of Ladies.* Translated by Charity Cannon Willard; edited by Madeleine Pelner Cosman.

for the love of Our Lord. This active life, as you can see, serves the world more than the other.

Although both ways are excellent, Our Lord Jesus Christ gave his opinion as to the more perfect of the two: the figure of the contemplative life, seated herself at His feet, as one who had no heart for anything else and was totally consumed by holy love. Martha, her sister, the example of the active life, was the hostess of Our Lord, busying herself to serve Him and the apostles; she complained to Him because her sister did not help her. Our Lord excused Mary, saying: "Martha, you are very diligent, and your work is of great excellence and necessary for the aid and succor of others. Nevertheless, the contemplative life represents the abandonment of the whole world and all its demands only to meditate on Him. That is of greater dignity and more perfect."

For this reason holy men long ago established religious orders, for that life is the nearest estate to God. Those wishing to love in contemplation can separate themselves from the world for the service of God without other cares. Along with pleasing themselves, such contemplatives greatly please God when they are faithful to their duty....

The good princess will do even more than tread the pathway of charity. She will personify Saint Basil's words to the rich: "Your temporal possessions come from God." You have more of them than others more deserving. Was God not just in dividing them unequally? Not at all. By sharing with the poor you can merit God's gifts to you; and because of their suffering, the poor will be crowned with a diadem of patience. Do not let the bread of the hungry mildew in your larder! Do not let moths eat the poor man's cloak. Do not store the shoes of the barefoot. Do not hoard the money of the needy. Things you possess in too great abundance belong to the poor and not to you. You are the thief who steals from God if you are able to help your neighbor and refuse to do it....

The noble lady will send her almoner secretly to these poor, good people so that even they themselves will not know whence the help is coming; that was what Saint Nicholas counseled. Nor will the good lady, accompanied by her ladies, be ashamed occasionally to visit hospitals and the poor in their homes. Speaking to the poverty-stricken and the ill, touching them and gently comforting them, she will be distributing the greatest charity of all. For the poor feel especially comforted and prefer the kind word, the visit, and the attention of the great and powerful personage over anything else. They think the world despises them. If someone of importance deigns to visit and speak with them, they thereby recover a certain self-respect, which everyone naturally desires.

So doing, the princess or great lady acquires greater merit than a lesser person who performs the same good deed. Three reasons justify that disparity. First, the more exalted the donor, the deeper comfort the poor person receives. Second, the greater the person, the more she must humble herself, and thus the more profound the virtue. Third, and most important, she sets a good example for those who see a good work performed with such spirit of humility. Nothing so well instructs subjects as observation of their lord or lady. Therefore, it is as great a benefit when the highborn or others in authority are graciously well-bred as it is a great misfortune when the opposite is true. No lady is so important that it is shameful or unsuitable for her to go devoutly and humbly to pardons or to visit churches or holy places. A lady ashamed to do good is ashamed to work for her own salvation.

Perhaps you will ask me how a great lady can give alms if she has no money, for I have already said that it is dangerous to amass worldly treasure. But, of course, there is no inevitable harm in the princess gathering treasure through revenues or income rightfully her own and gotten without extortion. The question is what she does with these treasures. Certainly God does not oblige her to give all to the poor if she does not want to. She can rightfully use it for her own necessities, to preserve her worldly station, to pay her servants, to give suitable gifts, and to pay her debts. Debts must be paid even before alms are distributed, for there is no merit in giving as alms what truly is due another. The good lady, however, should avoid the temptation of extravagances. Denying herself numerous robes and superfluous jewels and using her money instead for alms is true generosity. Admirable is she who so acts!...

In short, then, charity (joined to other noble virtues in her heart) will provide the benevolent princess with such good will that she will celebrate other people's worthiness as greater than her own and rejoice in their welfare as if it were her own. Their good reputation also will delight her. Accordingly, she will encourage the good to persevere in their virtue and the wicked to desist....

Worldly prudence's teachings and advice do not depart greatly from God's, but rather arise from them and depend on them. Therefore, we shall speak of the wise governance of life according to prudence, who will teach the princess or noble lady to cherish honor and good reputation above all things in this earthly world. Prudence also will say that God is not in the least displeased with a creature living morally in the world, and she who lives the moral life will love the good renown called *honor*. Saint Augustine's *Book of Corrections* tells us that two things necessary for living well are conscience and good repute. Similarly, the wise author of the Book of Ecciesiasticus exhorts: "Cherish good repute for it will endure longer than any other treasure."

Agreeing that, above all earthly things, nothing so suits the noble as honor, the good princess will ask what qualities belong to true honor. Certainly not worldly riches, at least not according to the world's normal habits. Riches are of meager value in perfecting honor. What things, then, are suitable? Good morals. What in the world is the use of good morals? They perfect the noble creature, achieving the good repute wherein lies perfect honor. No matter what wealth a prince or princess possesses, if she does not lead a life of reputation and praise through doing good, she lacks honor regardless of the blandishments of her entourage to suggest that she has it. True honor must be above reproach. How greatly should the noble lady love honor? Certainly more than her life, for she would pay more dearly for the loss of it. The reason for this is clear. Whoever dies well is saved, but the one who is dishonored suffers reproach, living or dead, so long as she is remembered.

Good reputation is the greatest treasure a princess or noble lady can acquire. No other is so great or should be sought more eagerly. Ordinary treasure is useful only in the locale in which she finds herself, but the treasure which is the reputation of her honor serves her in lands near and far. Like the odor of sanctity, good repute is a sweet fragrance from the body wafting across the world so that everyone is aware of it. The fragrance of good repute thus goes forth from a worthy person so that everyone else may sense her good example.

After this admonishment by prudence, the princess might well ask what she must do to put these ideas into practice. Her life will pivot around two particular points. One is the morals she will observe and abide by, and the other is the style of life which will direct her. Two moral considerations are especially necessary for women who desire honor, for without them it is unattainable:namely, sobriety and chastity.

Sobriety, the first, does not concern merely eating and drinking, but indeed all else serving to restrain and moderate excess.... The same sobriety will duly correct her tongue, for her speech must be free from extravagances so unbecoming to great ladies, and, indeed, to all worthy women. Heartily despising the vice of falsehood, she will prefer truth, which will be so habitual in her mouth that always what she says will be believed and respected. She will be known as a person who never lies. The virtue of truth is more necessary in the mouths of princes and princesses than in others because everyone must trust them. Sobriety also will prevent her from speaking words she has not carefully considered in advance, especially in those places where they will be weighed or reported.

Prudence and sobriety teach a lady well-ordered speech and wise eloquence. She never will be coy, but will speak well-considered words, soft and rather low-pitched, uttered with a pleasant face and without excessive motion of the hands or body, nor facial grimaces. She will avoid excessive or uncalled-for laughter. Refraining from speaking ill of others, she will not blame, but rather will encourage goodness. Gladly she will keep in check vague, dishonest words, nor will she permit others to speak them to her. Her humor also will be discreet.

Book III

The first chapter explains how all that has already been said can apply to some women as well as to others, and it speaks of the kind of management a woman of position should observe in her household.

At the beginning of this third part, having followed the path of the princesses, and the ladies and demoiselles both at court and away from it, we will speak to the women of importance in cities: those who are married to clerks, to the counsellors of kings or princes, or to guardians of justice and other officials, as well as to women married to the burghers, who live in cities and large towns and are considered, in certain countries, to be noble if they belong to ancient families. Thereafter, we will speak to other women so that all may hear our doctrine.

As we have repeatedly stated, whatever we have said regarding virtues and the proper manner of life can pertain to any woman, whatever her estate. On these subjects, what is specifically suitable for some may also be suitable for others. Each can take from our teachings whatever she finds useful. Do not imitate certain foolish people, who only listen to a sermon when the preacher speaks of subjects or situations in which they have no stake. These they note well, saying his words are true and well-expressed. But when it comes to what really affects them or pertains directly to their own lives, they lower their heads and close their ears. As if their own imperfections were too trivial to mention, they ignore them and concentrate only on the foibles of others. For this reason, the wise preacher should know what sort of people are present at his sermon. If he speaks directly to some, he should touch the others in such way that they will neither mock one another nor murmur against each other.

4.8 VIRTUE IN ST. TERESA OF ÁVILA

St. Teresa of Ávila (Teresa Sachez Cepeda Davila y Ahumada, 1515–1582), prominent monastic reformer and mystic, is one of only three women recognized as Doctors of the Church. She was deeply pious even as a child, trying to run away from home to fight the Moors when she was only 7. She succeeded in running away to a Carmelite monastery at 20. She quickly became ill and spent her time studying mystical writings. Teresa reported a number of powerful mystical visions, one of which lasted for two years. She established monasteries devoted to absolute poverty and spiritual development throughout Spain, and devoted much of her life to mystical reflection and writing.

As the title of Teresa's chief ethical work, *The Ways of Perfection*, suggests, her ethical theory is a form of perfectionism. She outlines an ethical ideal that few people are capable of following. But some are capable of following it, and one person who is, she contends, can do more good than many who only approximate it. Even for those who cannot achieve it, the ideal provides a measure for action and a guide for becoming the people we ought to be.

Teresa's ethics centers on three principles:

- Love everyone with a pure, spiritual love.
- Detach oneself from all created things.
- Become truly humble.

She explores what these precepts mean for various human relationships, developing an ethical system rooted in the ancient command to "love your neighbor as yourself" (Leviticus 19:18; Matthew 22:39; Mark 12:31; Luke 10:27; Romans 13:9; Galatians 5:14).

4.8.1 St. Teresa of Ávila, from *The Ways of Perfection*

Chapter 4

Now, daughters, you have looked at the great enterprise which we are trying to carry out. What kind of persons shall we have to be if we are not to be considered over-bold in the eyes of God and of the world? It is clear that we need to labour hard and it will be a great help to us if we have sublime thoughts so that we may strive to make our actions sublime also. If we endeavour to observe our Rule and Constitutions in the fullest sense, and with great care, I hope in the Lord that He will grant our requests. I am not asking anything new of you, my daughters—only that we should hold to our profession, which, as it is our vocation, we are bound to do, although there are many ways of holding to it.

Our Primitive Rules tell us to pray without ceasing. Provided we do this with all possible care (and it is the most important thing of all) we shall not fail to observe the fasts, disciplines, and periods of silence which the Order commands; for, as you know, if prayer is to be genuine it must be reinforced with these things—prayer cannot be accompanied by self-indulgence.

It is about prayer that you have asked me to say something to you. As an acknowledgment of what I shall say, I beg you to read frequently and with a good will what I have said about it thus far, and to put this into practice. Before speaking of the interior life—that is, of prayer—I shall speak of certain things which those who attempt to walk along the way of prayer must of necessity practise. So necessary are these that, even though not greatly given to contemplation, people who have them can advance a long way in the Lord's service, while, unless they have them, they cannot possibly be great contemplatives, and, if they think they are, they are much mistaken. May the Lord help me in this task and teach me what I must say, so that it may be to His glory. Amen.

Do not suppose, my friends and sisters, that I am going to charge you to do a great many things; may it please the Lord that we do the things which our holy Fathers ordained and practised and by doing which they merited that name. It would be wrong of us to look for any other way or to learn from anyone else. There are only three things which I will explain at some length and which are taken from our Constitution itself. It is essential that we should understand how very important they are to us in helping us to preserve that peace, both inward and outward, which the Lord so earnestly recommended to us. One of these is love for each other; the second, detachment from all created things; the third, true humility, which,

Source: St. Teresa of Ávila, from *The Ways of Perfection*. Translated and edited by E. Allison Peers, 1852.

although I put it last, is the most important of the three and embraces all the rest.

With regard to the first—namely, love for each other—this is of very great importance; for there is nothing, however annoying, that cannot easily be borne by those who love each other, and anything which causes annoyance must be quite exceptional. If this commandment were kept in the world, as it should be, I believe it would take us a long way towards the keeping of the rest; but, what with having too much love for each other or too little, we never manage to keep it perfectly. It may seem that for us to have too much love for each other cannot be wrong, but I do not think anyone who had not been an eye-witness of it would believe how much evil and how many imperfections can result from this. The devil sets many snares here which the consciences of those who aim only in a rough-and-ready way at pleasing God seldom observe—indeed, they think they are acting virtuously—but those who are aiming at perfection understand what they are very well: little by little they deprive the will of the strength which it needs if it is to employ itself wholly in the love of God.

This is even more applicable to women than to men, and the harm which it does to community life is very serious. One result of it is that all the nuns do not love each other equally: some injury done to a friend is resented; a nun desires to have something to give to her friend or tries to make time for talking to her, and often her object in doing this is to tell her how fond she is of her, and other irrelevant things, rather than how much she loves God. These intimate friendships are seldom calculated to make for the love of God; I am more inclined to believe that the devil initiates them so as to create factions within religious orders. When a friendship has for its object the service of His Majesty, it at once becomes clear that the will is devoid of passion and indeed is helping to conquer other passions.

Where a convent is large I should like to see many friendships of that type; but in this house, where there are not, and can never be, more than thirteen nuns, all must be friends with each other, love each other, be fond of each other and help each other. For the love of the Lord, refrain from making individual friendships, however holy, for even among brothers and sisters such things are apt to be poisonous and I can see no advantage in them; when they are between other relatives, they are much more dangerous and become a pest. Believe me, sisters, though I may seem to you extreme in this, great perfection and great peace come of doing what I say and many occasions of sin may be avoided by those who are not very strong. If our will becomes inclined more to one person than to another (this cannot be helped, because it is natural—it often leads us to love the person who has the most faults if she is the most richly endowed by nature), we must exercise a firm restraint on ourselves and not allow ourselves to be conquered by our affection. Let us love the virtues and inward goodness, and let us always apply ourselves and take care to avoid attaching importance to externals.

Let us not allow our will to be the slave of any, sisters, save of Him Who bought it with His blood. Otherwise, before we know where we are, we shall find ourselves trapped, and unable to move. God help me! The puerilities which result from this are innumerable. And, because they are so trivial that only those who see how bad they are will realize and believe it, there is no point in speaking of them here except to say that they are wrong in anyone, and, in a prioress, pestilential.

In checking these preferences we must be strictly on the alert from the moment that such a friendship begins and we must proceed diligently and lovingly rather than severely. One effective precaution against this is that the sisters should not be together except at the prescribed hours, and that they should follow our present custom in not talking with one another, or being alone together, as is laid down in the Rule: each one should be alone in her cell. There must be no workroom at Saint Joseph's; for, although it is a praiseworthy custom to have one, it is easier to keep silence if one is alone, and getting used to solitude is a great help to prayer. Since prayer must be the foundation on which this house is built, it is necessary for us to learn to like whatever gives us the greatest help in it.

Returning to the question of our love for one another, it seems quite unnecessary to commend this to you, for where are there people so brutish as not to love one another when they live together, are continually in one another's company, indulge in no conversation, association or recreation with any outside their house and believe that God loves us and that they themselves love God since they are leaving everything for His Majesty? More especially is this so as virtue always attracts love, and I hope in God that, with the help of His Majesty, there will always be love in the sisters of this house. It seems to me, therefore, that there is no reason for me to commend this to you any further.

With regard to the nature of this mutual love and what is meant by the virtuous love which I wish you to have here, and how we shall know when we have this virtue, which is a very great one, since Our Lord has so strongly commended it to us and so straitly enjoined it upon His Apostles—about all this I should like to say a little now as well as my lack of skill will allow me; if you find this explained in great detail in other books, take no notice of what I am saying here, for it may be that I do not understand what I am talking about.

There are two kinds of love which I am describing. The one is purely spiritual, and apparently has nothing to do with sensuality or the tenderness of our nature, either of which might stain its purity. The other is also spiritual, but mingled with it are our sensuality and weakness; yet it is a worthy love, which, as between relatives and friends, seems lawful. Of this I have already said sufficient.

It is of the first kind of spiritual love that I would now speak. It is untainted by any sort of passion, for such a thing would completely spoil its harmony....

Chapter 6

Let us now return to the love which it is good [and lawful] for us to feel. This I have described as purely spiritual; I am not sure if I know what I am talking about, but it seems to me that there is no need to speak much of it, since so few, I fear, possess it; let any one of you to whom the Lord has given it praise Him fervently, for she must be a person of the greatest perfection. It is about this that I now wish to write. Perhaps what I say may be of some profit, for if you look at a virtue you desire it and try to gain it, and so become attached to it.

God grant that I may be able to understand this, and even more that I may be able to describe it, for I am not sure that I know when love is spiritual and when there is sensuality mingled with it, or how to begin speaking about it. I am like one who hears a person speaking in the distance and, though he can hear that he is speaking, cannot distinguish what he is saying. It is just like that with me: sometimes I cannot understand what I am saying, yet the Lord is pleased to enable me to say it well. If at other times what I say is [ridiculous and] nonsensical, it is only natural for me to go completely astray.

Now it seems to me that, when God has brought someone to a clear knowledge of the world, and of its nature, and of the fact that another world (or, let us say, another kingdom) exists, and that there is a great difference between the one and the other, the one being eternal and the other only a dream; and of what it is to love the Creator and what to love the creature (this must be discovered by experience, for it is a very different matter from merely thinking about it and believing it); when one understands by sight and experience what can be gained by the one practice and lost by the other, and what the Creator is and what the creature, and many other things which the Lord teaches to those who are willing to devote themselves to being taught by Him in prayer, or whom His Majesty wishes to teach—then one loves very differently from those of us who have not advanced thus far.

It may be, sisters, that you think it irrelevant for me to treat of this, and you may say that you already know everything that I have said. God grant that this may be so, and that you may indeed know it in the only way which has any meaning, and that it may be graven upon your inmost being, and that you may never for a moment depart from it, for, if you know it, you will see that I am telling nothing but the truth when I say that he whom the Lord brings thus far possesses this love. Those whom God brings to this state are, I think, generous and royal souls; they are not content with loving anything so miserable as these bodies, however beautiful they be and however numerous the graces they possess. If the sight of the body gives them pleasure they praise the Creator, but as for dwelling upon it for more than just a moment—no! When I use that phrase "dwelling upon it," I refer to having love for such things. If they had such love, they would think they were loving something insubstantial and were conceiving fondness for a shadow, they would feel shame for themselves and would not have the effrontery to tell God that they love Him, without feeling great confusion.

You will answer me that such persons cannot love or repay the affection shown to them by others. Certainly they care little about having this affection. They may from time to time experience a natural and momentary pleasure at being loved; yet, as soon as they return to their normal condition, they realize that such pleasure is folly save when the persons concerned can benefit their souls, either by instruction or by prayer. Any other kind of affection wearies them, for they know it can bring them no profit and may well do them harm; nonetheless they are grateful for it and recompense it by commending those who love them to God. They take this affection as something for which those who love them lay the responsibility upon the Lord, from Whom, since they can see nothing lovable in themselves, they suppose the love comes, and think that others love them because God loves them; and so they leave His Majesty to recompense them for this and beg Him to do so, thus freeing themselves and feeling they have no more responsibility. When I ponder it carefully, I sometimes think this desire for affection is sheer blindness, except when, as I say, it relates to persons who can lead us to do good so that we may gain blessings in perfection.

It should be noted here that, when we desire anyone's affection, we always seek it because of some interest, profit or pleasure of our own. Those who are perfect, however, have trodden all these things beneath their feet—[and have despised] the blessings which may come to them in this world, and its pleasures and delights—in such a way that, even if they wanted to, so to say, they could not love anything outside God, or unless it had to do with God. What profit, then, can come to them from being loved themselves?

When this truth is put to them, they laugh at the distress which had been assailing them in the past as to whether their affection was being returned or no. Of course, however pure our affection may be, it is quite natural for us to wish it to be returned. But, when we come to evaluate the return of affection, we realize that it is insubstantial, like a thing of straw, as light as air and easily carried away by the wind. For, however dearly we have been loved, what is there that remains to us? Such persons, then, except for the advantage that the affection may bring to their souls (because they realize that our nature is such that we soon tire of life without love), care nothing whether they are loved or not. Do you think that such persons will love none and delight in none save God? No; they will love others much more than they did, with a more genuine love, with greater passion and with a love which brings more profit; that, in a word, is what love really is. And such souls are always much fonder of giving than of receiving, even in their relations with the Creator Himself. This [holy affection], I say, merits the name of *love*, which name has been usurped from it by those other base affections.

Do you ask, again, by what they are attracted if they do not love things they see? They do love what they see and they are greatly attracted by what they hear; but the things which they see are everlasting. If they love anyone they immediately look right beyond the body (on which, as I say, they cannot dwell), fix their eyes on the soul and see what there is to be loved in that. If there is nothing, but they see any suggestion or inclination which shows them that, if they dig deep, they will find gold within this mine, they think nothing of the labour of digging, since they have love. There is nothing that suggests itself to them which they will not willingly do for the good of that soul since they desire their love for it to be lasting, and they know quite well that that is impossible unless the loved one has certain good qualities and a great love for God. I really mean that it is impossible, however great their obligations and even if that soul were to die for love of them and do them all the kind actions in its power; even had it all the natural graces joined in one, their wills would not have strength enough to love it nor would they remain fixed upon it. They know and have learned and experienced the worth of all this; no false dice can deceive them. They see that they are not in unison with that soul and that their love for it cannot possibly last; for, unless that soul keeps the law of God, their love will end with life—they know that unless it loves Him they will go to different places.

Those into whose souls the Lord has already infused true wisdom do not esteem this love, which lasts only on earth, at more than its true worth—if, indeed, at so much. Those who like to take pleasure in worldly things, delights, honours and riches, will account it of some worth if their friend is rich and able to afford them pastime and pleasure and recreation; but those who already hate all this will care little or nothing for such things. If they have any love for such a person, then, it will be a passion that he may love God so as to be loved by Him; for, as I say, they know that no other kind of affection but this can last, and that this kind will cost them dear, for which reason they do all they possibly can for their friend's profit; they would lose a thousand lives to bring him a small blessing. Oh, precious love, forever imitating the Captain of Love, Jesus, our Good!

Chapter 7

It is strange to see how impassioned this love is; how many tears, penances and prayers it costs; how careful is the loving soul to commend the object of its affection to all who it thinks may prevail with God and to ask them to intercede with Him for it; and how constant is its longing, so that it cannot be happy unless it sees that its loved one is making progress. If that soul seems to have advanced, and is then seen to fall some way back, her friend seems to have no more pleasure in life: she neither eats nor sleeps, is never free from this fear and is always afraid that the soul whom she loves so much may be lost, and that the two may be parted forever. She cares nothing for physical death, but she will not suffer herself to be attached to something which a puff of wind may carry away so that she is unable to retain her hold upon it. This, as I have said, is love without any degree whatsoever of self-interest; all that this soul wishes and desires is to see the soul [it loves] enriched with blessings from Heaven. This is love, quite unlike our ill-starred earthly affections—to say nothing of illicit affections, from which may God keep us free.

These last affections are a very hell, and it is needless for us to weary ourselves by saying how evil they are, for the least of the evils which they bring are terrible beyond exaggeration. There is no need for us ever to take such things upon our lips, sisters, or even to think of them, or to remember that they exist anywhere in the world; you must never listen to anyone speaking of such affections, either in jest or in earnest, nor allow them to be mentioned or discussed in your presence. No good can come from our doing this and it might do us harm even to hear them mentioned. But with regard to the lawful affections which, as I have said, we may have for each other, or for relatives and friends, it is different. Our whole desire is that they should not die: if their heads ache, our souls seem to ache too; if we see them in distress, we are unable (as people say) to sit still under it; and so on.

This is not so with spiritual affection. Although the weakness of our nature may at first allow us to feel something of all this, our reason soon begins to reflect whether our friend's trials are not good for her, and to wonder if they are making her richer in virtue and how she is bearing them, and then we shall ask God to give her patience so that they may win her merit. If we see that she is being patient, we feel no distress—indeed, we are gladdened and consoled. If all the merit and gain which suffering is capable of producing could be made over to her, we should still prefer suffering her trial ourselves to seeing her suffer it, but we are not worried or disquieted.

I repeat once more that this love is a similitude and copy of that which was borne for us by the good Lover, Jesus. It is for that reason that it brings us such immense benefits, for it makes us embrace every kind of suffering, so that others, without having to endure the suffering, may gain its advantages. The recipients of this friendship, then, profit greatly, but their friends should realize that either this intercourse—I mean, this exclusive friendship—must come to an end or that they must prevail upon Our Lord that their friend may walk in the same way as themselves, as Saint Monica prevailed with Him for Saint Augustine. Their heart does not allow them to practise duplicity: if they see their friend straying from the road, or committing any faults, they will speak to her about it; they cannot allow themselves to do anything else. And if after this the loved one does not amend, they will not flatter her or hide anything from her. Either, then, she will amend or their friendship will cease; for otherwise they would be unable to endure it, nor is it in fact endurable. It would mean continual war for both parties. A person may be indifferent to all other people in the world and not worry whether they are serving God or not, since the person she has to worry about is herself. But she cannot take this attitude with her friends: nothing they do can be hidden from her; she sees the smallest mote in them. This, I repeat, is a very heavy cross for her to bear.

Happy the souls that are loved by such as these! Happy the day on which they came to know them! O my Lord, wilt Thou not grant me the favour of giving me many who have such love for me? Truly, Lord, I would rather have this than be loved by all the kings and lords of the world—and rightly so, for such friends use every means in their power to make us lords of the whole world and to have all that is in it subject to us. When you make the acquaintance of any such persons, sisters, the Mother Prioress should employ every possible effort to keep you in touch with them. Love such persons as much as you like. There can be very few of them, but nonetheless it is the Lord's will that their goodness should be known. When one of you is striving after perfection, she will at once be told that she has no need to know such people—that it is enough for her to have God. But to get to know God's friends is a very good way of "having" Him; as I have discovered by experience, it is most helpful. For, under the Lord, I owe it to such persons that I am not in hell; I was always very fond of asking them to commend me to God, and so I prevailed upon them to do so.

Let us now return to what we were saying. It is this kind of love which I should like us to have; at first it may not be perfect but the Lord will make it increasingly so. Let us begin with the methods of obtaining it. At first it may be mingled with emotion, but this, as a rule, will do no harm. It is sometimes good and necessary for us to show emotion in our love, and also to feel it, and to be distressed by some of our sisters' trials and weaknesses, however trivial they may be. For on one occasion as much distress may be caused by quite a small matter as would be caused on another by some great trial, and there are people whose nature it is to be very much cast down by small things. If you are not like this, do not neglect to have compassion on others; it may be that Our Lord wishes to spare us these sufferings and will give us sufferings of another kind which will seem heavy to us, though to the person already mentioned they may seem light. In these matters, then, we must not judge others by ourselves, nor think of ourselves as we have been at some time when, perhaps without any effort on our part, the Lord has made us stronger than they; let us think of what we were like at the times when we have been weakest.

Note the importance of this advice for those of us who would learn to sympathize with our neighbours' trials, however trivial these may be. It is especially important for such souls as have been described, for, desiring trials as they do, they make light of them all. They must therefore try hard to recall what they were like when they were weak, and reflect that, if they are no longer so, it is not due to themselves. For otherwise, little by little, the devil could easily cool our charity toward our neighbours and make us think that what is really a failing on our part is perfection. In every respect we must be careful and alert, for the devil never slumbers. And the nearer we are to perfection, the more careful we must be, since his temptations are then much more cunning because there are no others that he dare send us; and if, as I say, we are not cautious, the harm is done before we realize it. In short, we must always watch and pray, for there is no better way than prayer of revealing these hidden wiles of the devil and making him declare his presence.

Contrive always, even if you do not care for it, to take part in your sisters' necessary recreation and to do so for the whole of the allotted time, for all considerate treatment of them is a part of perfect love. It is a very good thing for us to take compassion on each other's needs. See that you show no lack of discretion about things which are contrary to obedience. Though privately you may think the prioress' orders harsh ones, do not allow this to be noticed or tell anyone about it (except that you may speak of it, with all humility, to the prioress herself), for if you did so you would be doing a great deal of harm. Get to know what are the things in your sisters which you should be sorry to see and those about which you should sympathize with them; and always show your grief at any notorious fault which you may see in one of them. It is a good proof and test of our love if we can bear with such faults and not be shocked by them. Others, in their turn, will bear with your faults, which, if you include those of which you are not aware, must be much more numerous. Often commend to God any sister who is at fault and strive for your own part to practise the virtue which is the opposite of her fault with great perfection. Make determined efforts to do this so that you may teach your sister by your deeds what perhaps she could never learn by words nor gain by punishment.

The habit of performing some conspicuously virtuous action through seeing it performed by another is one which very easily takes root. This is good advice: do not forget it. Oh, how true and genuine will be the love of a sister who can bring profit to everyone by sacrificing her own profit to that of the rest! She will make a great advance in each of the virtues and keep her Rule with great perfection. This will be a much truer kind of friendship than one which uses every possible loving expression (such as are not used, and must not be used, in this house): "My life!" "My love!" "My darling!" and suchlike things, one or another of which people are always saying. Let such endearing words be kept for your Spouse, for you will be so often and so much alone with Him that you will want to make use of them all, and this His Majesty permits you. If you use them among yourselves they will not move the Lord so much; and, quite apart from that, there is no reason why you should do so. They are very effeminate; and I should not like you to be that, or even to appear to be that, in any way, my daughters; I want you to be strong men. If you do all that is in you, the Lord will make you so manly that men themselves will be amazed at you. And how easy is this for His Majesty, Who made us out of nothing at all!

It is also a very clear sign of love to try to spare others household work by taking it upon oneself and also to rejoice and give great praise to the Lord if you see any increase in their virtues. All such things, quite apart from the intrinsic good they bring, add greatly to the peace and concord which we have among ourselves, as, through the goodness of God, we can now see by experience. May His Majesty be pleased ever to increase it, for it would be terrible if it did not exist, and very awkward if, when there are so few of us, we got on badly together. May God forbid that.

If one of you should be cross with another because of some hasty word, the matter must at once be put right and you must betake yourselves to earnest prayer. The same applies to the harbouring of any grudge, or to party strife, or to the desire to be greatest, or to any nice point concerning your honour. (My blood seems to run cold, as I write this, at the very idea that this can ever happen, but I know it is the chief trouble in convents.) If it should happen to you, consider yourselves lost. Just reflect and realize that you have driven your Spouse from His home: He will have to go and seek another abode, since you are driving Him from His own house. Cry aloud to His Majesty and try to put things right; and if frequent confessions and communions do not mend them, you may well fear that there is some Judas among you.

For the love of God, let the prioress be most careful not to allow this to occur. She must put a stop to it from the very outset, and, if love will not suffice, she must use heavy punishments, for here we have the whole of the mischief and the remedy. If you gather that any of the nuns is making trouble, see that she is sent to some other convent and God will provide them with a dowry for her. Drive away this plague; cut off the branches as well as you can; and, if that is not sufficient, pull up the roots. If you cannot do this, shut up anyone who is guilty of such things and forbid her to leave her cell; far better this than that all the nuns should catch so incurable a plague. Oh, what a great evil is this! God deliver us from a convent into which it enters: I would rather our convent caught fire and we were all burned alive. As this is so important I think I shall say a little more about it elsewhere, so I will not write at greater length here, except to say that, provided they treat each other equally, I would rather that the nuns showed a tender and affectionate love and regard for each other, even though there is less perfection in this than in the love I have described, than that there were a single note of discord to be heard among them. May the Lord forbid this, for His own sake. Amen.

CHAPTER 5

Ethics in Modern Philosophy

"The dignity of rational nature"

Ethics in Western philosophy rested almost entirely on ancient theories for well over a thousand years. Medieval Jewish, Christian, and Islamic writers followed Platonic and then increasingly Aristotelian models. Starting in the thirteenth century, ancient Greek texts that had been lost to the West for centuries began to reemerge. They included not only Platonic dialogues and Aristotle's *Metaphysics* and *Nicomachean Ethics* but also, by the seventeenth century, works by ancient Stoics, Skeptics, and Epicureans. These influenced early modern philosophers profoundly. Inspired by the new perspectives on ethics they provided, early modern thinkers raised fundamental questions about the nature of right action, the good life, and moral knowledge and developed dramatically new theories in response to them.

5.1 PRINCESS ELIZABETH'S CRITIQUE OF REASON IN ETHICS

René Descartes (1596–1650), the father of modern philosophy, wrote relatively little on ethics. Deeply influenced by Stoicism, his views are thoroughly rationalist:

- The goal of human life is happiness.
- Happiness is mental flourishing, contentment, and tranquillity: "to love life without fearing death."
- Happiness requires a healthy mind.
- The "true health of the mind" consists in developing wisdom, which is "true and sound judgment."

- Wisdom requires knowledge and the use of reason.
- Reason must, in particular, control the passions and "examine and consider without passion" our options and ends so that "we shall always choose the better."
- Virtue is reasoning constantly and well: "a firm and constant will to bring about everything we judge to be the best and to employ all the force of our intellect in judging well."

Choosing the right course of action and, in general, living well are primarily intellectual tasks, carried out by reason.

Princess Elizabeth of Bohemia (1618–1680), also known as Elizabeth von der Pfalz or Princess Palatine, raises objections to Descartes's ethics and in fact inspires him to write *The Passions of the Soul* is response to her objections. Princess Elizabeth was the eldest daughter of King Frederick of Bohemia as well as the granddaughter of King James I of England. But she hardly lived the pampered life that description might suggest. Her father lost his throne and fled to Germany before Elizabeth turned 2. She was 9 before she was able to rejoin her family in exile in Holland. Two years later, her eldest brother drowned; her father, overcome with grief, died two years after that. Elizabeth, an ardent Protestant, gave up any hope of marriage after rejecting a betrothal to the Catholic King of Poland. She received an outstanding education, becoming fluent in six languages and earning a reputation as a scholar of Greek and Latin. At 24, she read Descartes's *Meditations.* Descartes, hearing of this, sought her out and introduced himself to her. That began a seven-year correspondence that ended when Descartes died in Sweden. At 49 the Princess became abbess of Herford, where she sheltered religious dissidents such as William Penn, hosted prominent visitors such as Gottfried Leibniz, and became widely known and respected for her justice and tolerance in a Europe still torn by religious wars.

Elizabeth objects to Descartes's ethics on a number of grounds. First, she doubts whether happiness, as described by Descartes, is achievable, for reason and feeling are not so easily distinguished. She points to physical illnesses that disrupt the use of reason, observing that rational control is not a purely mental phenomenon. (This is part of her general attack on Descartes's philosophy of mind.) But neither is morality just a matter of health. If all moral error is illness, then we have an all-purpose excuse; we can no more be blamed for immorality than we can for being sick. But morality is not therapy. We have free will. There is more to ethics than health, knowledge, and intelligence.

Good judgment, moreover, depends on experience. Experience does more than provide premises from which reason can deduce conclusions. It trains our senses and our passions, making us sensitive to the right things and enabling us to feel the right emotions. Thinking about moral problems and making moral choices is at least as much a matter of feeling as of reason. We frequently act on the basis of conscience, which ratifies our passions to reason, declaring them as acceptable or unacceptable. Reason, in short, acts on premises that conscience provides. Reason thus cannot act independent of feeling. Conscience and some passions play important roles in moral thinking.

In civic life, moreover, we must make decisions knowing that many people involved are not very rational in their approach to matters. In politics, Elizabeth argues, experience is a better guide than reason.

Elizabeth worries about any moral theory that treats the consequences of actions as critical to determining what ought to be done. Assessing consequences requires knowing what the consequences of an act will or might be, at an indefinite distance into the future. It also requires knowing how the values of all those potential consequences compare with one another. The knowledge required to reach moral conclusions on such a theory must be infinite. It would follow that moral knowledge is impossible. Plainly, however, it is not. So moral reasoning cannot require detailed assessment of consequences and thus cannot require the use of reason in anything like the way Descartes supposes.

The contrast between Elizabeth and Descartes persists throughout the early modern period in European philosophy. To what extent is ethics rational? To what extent must we understand the consequences of actions to reach moral conclusions? These questions echo for several centuries and remain important today.

5.1.1 Elizabeth to Descartes—The Hague, August 16, 1645

Mr. Descartes,

I found, by examining the book that you recommended to me [Seneca's *On the Happy Life*], a quantity of beautiful sentences well designed to incline me to a pleasant meditation—but not to instruct me on what it treats, since those sentences are without method and the author does not follow through on what he had proposed. For instead of showing the shortest way to happiness, he is satisfied to show that its richnesses and luxury are not inaccessible. I was obliged to write to you so that you do not think that I have come to this opinion by prejudice or idleness. I also do not ask that you continue to correct Seneca, because your way of reasoning is more extraordinary, but also because it is more natural that I encounter him myself. He seems to teach me nothing new, except to draw from my own spirit of knowledge what I had not yet seen. And thus I would still like to know—I am still troubled by doubt about whether one can arrive at the happiness you describe without the assistance of what does not depend absolutely on the will, since there are diseases which completely remove the capacity to reason.

Consequently, to enjoy a reasonable satisfaction, other factors that decrease the force [of reason] and prevent a person from following the maxims that good sense will have forged, and which incline the most moderate person to be carried away with his passions and become less able to detach himself from accidents of fortune, require a prompt resolution. When Epicurus lied on his deathbed, to ensure his friends that he did not feel bad, instead of crying out like an ordinary man, he carried out the life of philosopher, not that of a prince, captain or courtier. He knew that nothing arriving from outside could make him forget his role and fail to detach himself according to the rules of his philosophy.

And it is on these occasions that repentance seems inevitable to me, without the knowledge to defend us that it is as natural for a man to fail as to be sick. For one could thus excuse every particular fault. But I am sure that you will clear up these difficulties for me, and a quantity of others that

Source: Elizabeth to Descartes—The Hague, August 16, 1645. Translated by Daniel Bonevac.

do not occur to me at this hour, when you teach me the truths that must be known to facilitate the use of the virtue. Thus do not lose, I beg you, the intention to oblige me by your precepts. Trust that I value them as much as they deserve. For eight days my sick brother's bad mood has prevented me from making this request of you. I have been obliged, by the kindness he has for me, to remain near him, to get him to follow the doctor's orders, or to give him mine, while trying to divert him, since he is convinced that I am capable. I wish to assure you that I will be all my life, Mr. Descartes,

Your very affectionate friend, at your service,
Elizabeth

5.1.2 Elizabeth to Descartes—The Hague, September 13, 1645

Mr. Descartes,

If my conscience remained as satisfied with the excuses you give as with remedies for my ignorance, I would be much obliged and would be free of repenting to have so badly employed the time I have enjoyed the use of reason. That has been longer for me than for others my age, for my birth and my fortune forced me to employ my judgment at an earlier time, to manage a life rather painful and free of prosperity that kept me from thinking of myself, as if required to put my faith in the prudence of a governess.

It is not, however, prosperity or the accompanying flatteries that I think absolutely able to remove the fortitude of spirit of well-born hearts and to prevent them from bearing a change of fortune philosophically. But I am convinced that the multitude of accidents that surprise the people governing the public, without their taking the time to examine the most useful expedient, are often the gateway (no matter how virtuous they are) to actions which cause afterward the regret that you call one of the principal obstacles to happiness. It is true that a practice of valuing goods according to whether they can contribute to satisfaction, and measuring this satisfaction according to perfections which give birth to pleasures, and judging without passion these perfections and these pleasures, will guard against a quantity of faults. But, to value goods thus, they should be known perfectly; and to know all those among which one is constrained to make a choice in an active life, we would have to have an infinite science.

You will say that one may not be satisfied until conscience testifies that one has taken all possible precautions. But that never happens, when its account is not found. For one always revises what remains to be considered. To measure satisfaction according to the perfection that causes it, it would be necessary to see the value of each one clearly, whether those that are useful only for us or those that remain useful for others are preferable. The latter seem to be valued more roughly than those of value only to oneself. And nevertheless each of them supports its inclination of reasons strongly enough to make it continue all throughout life.

It is thus other perfections of the body and of the spirit that a tacit feeling ratifies to reason. That feeling should not be called a passion, for it was born with us. Thus tell me, please, to what extent

Source: Elizabeth to Descartes—The Hague, September 13, 1645. Translated by Daniel Bonevac.

it is necessary to follow it (being a gift of nature) and how to correct it.

I would still like to see you defining passions, to know them well; for those that name disturbances of the soul would persuade me that their force consists only in dazzling and subjugating reason, if experience did not show me that there are some that carry us to reasonable actions. But I am sure that you will shed more light when you explain how the force of passions renders them all the more useful when they are subject to reason.

I will receive this favour at Riswyck, where we will remain, until this house here is cleaned, in the house of the Prince of Orange; but you do not need to change the address of your letters to

Your very affectionate friend, at your service,
Elizabeth

5.1.3 Elizabeth to Descartes—Riswyck, September 30, 1645

Mr. Descartes,

Though your observations on Seneca's views of the supreme good made my reading more profitable than it would have been otherwise, I don't mind changing them for truths so necessary that those who understand them strengthen their understanding of how to distinguish what is the best in all the actions of life, provided that you still add to it the explanation, which my stupidity needs, concerning the utility of the knowledge that you propose. That the existence of God and his attributes can comfort us in facing misfortunes that come from the ordinary course of nature and the order established there—like losing goods in a storm, health by an infection in the air, or friends in death—but not those imposed on us by men, whose will appears entirely free to us. We have only faith alone to persuade us that God takes care to govern our wills, and that he determined the fortune of each person before the creation of the world. The immortality of the soul, and knowing that it is much nobler than the body, can make us seek death as well as scorn it, since we cannot doubt that we will live more fortunately, free of the diseases and sufferings of the body. And I am astonished that those who were said to be persuaded of this truth and lived without the revealed law preferred a painful life to an advantageous death.

The great extent of the universe, which you showed in the third book of your *Principles*, is used to detach our affections from what we see. But it also differentiates this particular providence, which is the basis of theology, from the idea that we have of God.

The consideration that we are part of the whole of which we must seek the advantage is the source of all generous actions; but I find many difficulties in the conditions that you prescribe for them. How can one measure the evils one suffers for the public against the good which will come from doing so without those evils appearing larger to us—the more so as their idea is more distinct? And what rule will we have for comparing things that are not known to us, such as our own merit and that of those with which we live? A natural arrogance will always tilt the balance to one side, and modesty will be valued less than it is worth.

To benefit from the particular truths of which you speak, it is necessary to know exactly all the passions and all the concerns to which the majority are insensitive. By observing the manners of the

---

Source: Elizabeth to Descartes—Riswyck, September 30, 1645. Translated by Daniel Bonevac.

countries where we are, we sometimes find very unreasonable what it is necessary to follow to avoid greater disadvantages.

Since I am here, I make quite an annoying test of this; for I hoped to benefit from staying in the country while I dedicated myself to study, and I have encountered there, without comparison, less leisure than I had in The Hague, by the diversions of those things only it can provide; and no matter how very unjust it may be to deprive me of real goods in exchange for imaginary ones, I am forced to yield to the impertinent laws of civility that are established to avoid making enemies. Since I wrote that, I was stopped more than seven times by inconvenient visits. It is your excessive kindness that guarantees my letters to present a similar predicament for you, and which obliges you to put your knowledge into practice by communicating it to a disobedient person like

Your very affectionate, at your service,
Elizabeth

5.1.4 Elizabeth to Descartes—The Hague, April 25, 1646

Mr. Descartes,

... But I find it less difficult to understand all that you say about the passions than to practice the remedies you order against their excesses. For how can we envisage all the countless accidents that can occur in life? And how can we help wishing with ardor for things that necessarily tend to our preservation (like health and the means to live), which nevertheless don't depend on the will? For the knowledge of the truth would justify a desire that is naturally in everyone; but it would be necessary to have an infinite knowledge to know the right value of the goods and evils disposed to move us, since there is much more than one person alone could imagine. It would be necessary to know all the things in the world perfectly.

Since you already told me the principal ones for an individual life, I would still like to know your maxims for civic life, which depends on people who are not very reasonable. Up to now, for things relating to it, I have always found experience to serve me better than reason.

I was so often interrupted in writing to you that I am forced to send you my draft and to use Alcmar's messenger, having forgotten the name of the friend to whom you wanted me to address my letters. I do not dare to return your treatise to you until I remember it. I cannot entrust to the hands of a drunkard an item of such great value, which gave so much satisfaction to

Your very affectionate friend, at your service,
Elizabeth

5.2 HUME'S EMPIRICIST ETHICS: FROM *IS* TO *OUGHT*

David Hume (1711–1776), a contemporary of Voltaire, Rousseau, Handel, Bach, and fellow Scotsman Adam Smith, entered the University of Edinburgh at age 12. After dabbling at careers in law and business, he went to France and wrote *A Treatise of*

Source: Elizabeth to Descartes—The Hague, April 25, 1646. Translated by Daniel Bonevac.

Human Nature, his greatest philosophical work, when still in his 20s. He argued for a skeptical empiricism, maintaining that all knowledge comes from sense experience and that, therefore, we can have no knowledge of anything beyond experience.

In ethics, Hume stresses the importance of feeling as opposed to reason. There is a gulf between *is* and *ought*; factual premises can never yield a moral conclusion on their own. The fact that something is a murder, for example, does not itself imply that it is wrong; we need a moral principle such as "Murder is wrong." Moreover, purely rational motives can never provide a motive for action. Reason can lead us to conclusions, but it cannot make us want to do anything. In morality and in other areas where we seek to go beyond sense experience, "reason is, and ought to be, the slave of the passions."

Hume advances a novel argument for the intuitionistic thesis that morality stems from feelings rather than reason. Morality is not a matter of reason. Nor is it a matter of fact. But if morality stems from neither reason nor facts, where does it have its root? Hume's answer: in the passions. Morality is a matter of feeling, not of reason or fact. Moreover, its source is within us. To use a contemporary term, morality is response-dependent: To say that something is bad is simply to say that a normal person, all other things being equal, would disapprove of it. Moral qualities are secondary qualities like colors and sounds, not primary qualities like lengths and velocities. They pertain to the relation between the object and the perceiver or moral agent, not to the object alone. An act is right if it causes a certain kind of pleasure in a normal observer; it is wrong if it causes a certain kind of uneasiness in a normal observer.

Some philosophers have interpreted Hume as holding that morality is purely subjective, something we impose on the world. In a sense that is right; the grounds of morality are in us. But they are also in the world. Color is in a sense subjective, contributed by our perceptual faculties, but we are responding systematically to objective features of the world. So, for Hume, we give the world its "moral color," but we do so by responding systematically to objective features of the world. We cannot will murder to be right any more than we can will grass to be red.

5.2.1 David Hume, from *A Treatise of Human Nature*

Of Virtue and Vice in General

Moral distinctions not deriv'd from reason

It has been observ'd that nothing is ever present to the mind but its perceptions; and that all the actions of seeing, hearing, judging, loving, hating, and thinking, fall under this denomination. The mind can never exert itself in any action, which we may not comprehend under the term of perception; and consequently that term is no less applicable to those judgments, by which we distinguish moral good and evil, than to every other operation of the mind. To approve of one character, to condemn another, are only so many different perceptions.

Source: David Hume, *A Treatise of Human Nature*, 1739.

Now as perceptions resolve themselves into two kinds, viz. impressions and ideas, this distinction gives rise to a question with which we shall open up our present enquiry concerning morals. Whether 'tis by means of our ideas or impressions we distinguish betwixt vice and virtue and pronounce an action blameable or praiseworthy? This will immediately cut off all loose discourses and declamations and reduce us to something precise and exact on the present subject.

Those who affirm that virtue is nothing but a conformity to reason; that there are eternal fitnesses and unfitnesses of things, which are the same to every rational being that considers them; that the immutable measures of right and wrong impose an obligation, not only on human creatures, but also on the Deity himself: All these systems concur in the opinion, that morality, like truth, is discern'd merely by ideas, and by their juxtaposition and comparison. In order, therefore, to judge of these systems, we need only consider whether it be possible, from reason alone, to distinguish betwixt moral good and evil, or whether there must concur some other principles to enable us to make that distinction.

If morality had naturally no influence on human passions and actions, 'twere in vain to take such pains to inculcate it; and nothing wou'd be more fruitless than that multitude of rules and precepts with which all moralists abound. Philosophy is commonly divided into speculative and practical; and as morality is always comprehended under the latter division, 'tis supposed to influence our passions and actions and to go beyond the calm and indolent judgments of the understanding. And this is confirm'd by common experience, which informs us that men are often govern'd by their duties and are deterr'd from some actions by the opinion of injustice and impell'd to others by that of obligation.

Since morals, therefore, have an influence on the actions and affections, it follows that they cannot be deriv'd from reason; and that because reason alone, as we have already prov'd, can never have any such influence. Morals excite passions and produce or prevent actions. Reason of itself is utterly impotent in this particular. The rules of morality, therefore, are not conclusions of our reason. No one, I believe, will deny the justness of this inference; nor is there any other means of evading it than by denying that principle, on which it is founded. As long as it is allow'd that reason has no influence on our passions and action, 'tis in vain to pretend that morality is discover'd only by a deduction of reason. An active principle can never be founded on an inactive; and if reason be inactive in itself, it must remain so in all its shapes and appearances, whether it exerts itself in natural or moral subjects, whether it considers the powers of external bodies or the actions of rational beings.

It would be tedious to repeat all the arguments by which I have prov'd that reason is perfectly inert and can never either prevent or produce any action or affection. 'Twill be easy to recollect what has been said upon that subject. I shall only recall on this occasion one of these arguments, which I shall endeavour to render still more conclusive and more applicable to the present subject.

Reason is the discovery of truth or falshood. Truth or falshood consists in an agreement or disagreement either to the real relations of ideas or to real existence and matter of fact. Whatever, therefore, is not susceptible of this agreement or disagreement is incapable of being true or false and can never be an object of our reason. Now 'tis evident our passions, volitions, and actions are not susceptible of any such agreement or disagreement; being original facts and realities, compleat in themselves, and implying no reference to other passions, volitions, and actions. 'Tis impossible, therefore, they can be pronounced either true or false and be either contrary or conformable to reason.

This argument is of double advantage to our present purpose. For it proves directly that actions do not derive their merit from a conformity to reason nor their blame from a contrariety to it; and it proves the same truth more indirectly, by shewing us that as reason can never immediately prevent or produce any action by contradicting or approving of it, it cannot be the source of moral good and evil which are found to have that influence. Actions may be laudable or blameable, but they cannot be reasonable: Laudable or blameable, therefore, are not the same as reasonable or unreasonable. The merit and demerit of actions frequently contradict and sometimes control our natural propensities. But reason has no such influence. Moral distinctions, therefore, are not the offspring of reason. Reason is wholly inactive and can never be the source of so active a principle as conscience or a sense of morals.

Thus upon the whole 'tis impossible that the distinction betwixt moral good and evil can be made to reason; since that distinction has an influence upon our actions, of which reason alone is incapable. Reason and judgment may, indeed, be the mediate cause of an action, by prompting or by directing a passion: But it is not pretended that a judgment of this kind, either in its truth or falshood, is attended with virtue or vice. And as to the judgments which are caused by our judgments, they can still less bestow those moral qualities on the actions, which are their causes.

Nor does this reasoning only prove that morality consists not in any relations that are the objects of science; but if examin'd, will prove with equal certainty that it consists not in any matter of fact which can be discover'd by the understanding. This is the second part of our argument; and if it can be made evident, we may conclude that morality is not an object of reason. But can there be any difficulty in proving that vice and virtue are not matters of fact whose existence we can infer by reason? Take any action allow'd to be vicious: Willful murder, for instance. Examine it in all lights, and see if you can find that matter of fact, or real existence, which you call vice. In whichever way you take it, you find only certain passions, motives, volitions and thoughts. There is no other matter of fact in the case. The vice entirely escapes you as long as you consider the object. You never can find it, till you turn your reflection into your own breast, and find a sentiment of disapprobation, which arises in you, towards this action. Here is a matter of fact; but 'tis the object of feeling, not of reason. It lies in yourself, not in the object. So that when you pronounce any action or character to be vicious, you mean nothing but that from the constitution of your nature you have a feeling or sentiment of blame from the contemplation of it. Vice and virtue, therefore, may be compar'd to sounds, colours, heat and cold, which, according to modern philosophy, are not qualities in objects but perceptions in the mind: And this discovery in morals, like that other in physics, is to be regarded as a considerable advancement of the speculative sciences; tho', like that too, it has little or no influence on practice. Nothing can be more real, or concern us more, than our own sentiments of pleasure and uneasiness; and if these be favourable to virtue, and unfavourable to vice, no more can be requisite to the regulation of our conduct and behaviour.

I cannot forbear adding to these reasonings an observation, which may, perhaps, be found of some importance. In every system of morality, which I have hitherto met with, I have always remark'd, that the author proceeds for some time in the ordinary way of reasoning, and establishes the being of a God, or makes observations concerning human affairs; when of a sudden I am surpriz'd to find that instead of the usual copulations of propositions, is and is not, I meet with no proposition that is not connected with an ought, or an ought not. This change is imperceptible; but is, however, of the last consequence. For as this ought, or ought not, expresses some new relation or affirmation, 'tis necessary that it shou'd be observ'd and explain'd; and at the same time that a reason should be given, for what seems altogether inconceivable, how this new relation can be a deduction from others which are entirely different from it. But as authors do not commonly use this precaution, I shall presume to recommend it to the readers; and am persuaded that this small attention wou'd subvert all the vulgar systems of morality and let us see that the distinction of vice and virtue is not founded merely on the relations of objects nor is perceiv'd by reason.

Moral distinctions deriv'd from a moral sense

Thus the course of the argument leads us to conclude that since vice and virtue are not discoverable merely by reason or the comparison of ideas, it must be by means of some impression or sentiment they occasion, that we are able to mark the difference betwixt them. Our decisions concerning moral rectitude and depravity are evidently perceptions; and as all perceptions are either impressions or ideas, the exclusion of the one is a convincing argument for the other. Morality, therefore, is more properly felt than judg'd of; tho' this feeling or sentiment is commonly so soft and gentle that we are apt to confound it with an idea, according to our common custom of taking all things for the same which have any near resemblance to each other.

The next question is, Of what nature are these impressions, and after what manner do they operate upon us? Here we cannot remain long in suspense but must pronounce the impression arising from virtue to be agreeable, and that proceding from vice to be uneasy. Every moment's experience must convince us of this. There is no spectacle so fair and beautiful as a noble and generous action; nor any which gives us more abhorrence than one that is cruel and treacherous. No enjoyment equals the satisfaction we receive from the company of those we love and esteem; as the greatest of all punishments is to be oblig'd to pass our lives with those we hate or contemn. A very play or romance may afford us instances of this pleasure, which virtue conveys to us, and pain, which arises from vice.

Now since the distinguishing impressions by which moral good or evil is known are nothing but particular pains or pleasures, it follows that in all enquiries concerning these moral distinctions it will be sufficient to shew the principles, which make us feel a satisfaction or uneasiness from the survey of any character, in order to satisfy us why the character is laudable or blameable. An action, or sentiment, or character is virtuous or vicious; why? because its view causes a pleasure or uneasiness of a particular kind. In giving a reason, therefore, for the pleasure or uneasiness, we sufficiently explain the vice or virtue. To have the sense of virtue is nothing but to feel a satisfaction of a particular kind from the contemplation of a character. The very feeling constitutes our praise or admiration. We go no farther; nor do we enquire into the cause of the satisfaction. We do not infer a character to be virtuous because it pleases: But in feeling that it pleases after such a particular manner, we in effect feel that it is virtuous. The case is the same as in our judgments concerning all kinds of beauty, and tastes, and sensations. Our approbation is imply'd in the immediate pleasure they convey to us.

5.3 KANT'S DEONTOLOGY

Immanuel Kant (1724–1804), a contemporary of Bentham, Blake, Goethe, and Mozart, was born in Königsberg, East Prussia, the son of a saddlemaker and grandson of a Scottish immigrant. Kant attended the University of Königsberg, from which he graduated at 22. He worked as a private tutor and then a *Privatdozent*, an unpaid lecturer who collects fees from his students, until he was appointed to a chair of logic and metaphysics at the university at age 46. At 57, Kant published the *Critique of Pure Reason*, which earned him fame and which is still regarded as one of the greatest works of the Western philosophical tradition. Over the next ten years he wrote four more books, primarily on ethics. Though known for his wit, conversational skill, and dinner parties, Kant never married and never traveled more than a few miles from the place of his birth. His habits were so regular that, according to legend, neighbors would set their clocks by his afternoon walks.

Kant begins by asking what is good without qualification. The only unqualified good, he answers, is a good will. Virtues, material things, power, and even happiness are not good if pressed into service for the wrong end. An "impartial rational spectator," as Kant puts it, would never delight in the courage, wealth, power, or happiness of an evil tyrant. What matters from a moral point of view is not happiness but worthiness to be happy. That is a matter of the will, not of happiness, virtue, or any external sign.

What makes a will good, Kant says, is acting on the basis of universal considerations rather than subjective, particular determinations: "the proper and inestimable worth of an absolutely good will consists just in this, that the principle of action is free from all influence of contingent grounds." Take a paradigm case of a good action—Smith, at significant risk to her own life, jumping into an icy river to save someone calling for help. Why does she do it? The act truly has moral worth, Kant says, if she does it to save a life or, more generally, to help someone in distress. These are universal considerations that apply no matter who Smith is, what kind of person she is, what she wants, likes, or dreams, or whom she is trying to save. It lacks moral worth, however, if she does it just to show off for some bystanders, or just because the person in trouble is a friend, or just because she is feeling warm and the thought of a plunge into the river sounds invigorating. These considerations are subjective, depending on her state of mind. They are also particular, in that they relate to specific aspects of the circumstances that have no moral relevance. A person manifests a good will, and acts in a way that has moral worth, when he or she acts from duty, out of respect for the moral law.

The moral quality of an act, Kant maintains, does not depend on consequences. We judge Smith's action admirable even if she fails to save the person crying for help—even, indeed, if she herself perishes in the attempt. Kant's theory is thus deontological, and in a strong form: consequences play no role whatever. We judge acts as right or wrong according to the agent's intentions. The maxim of an act is "a subjective principle of action," a rule it falls under that captures the agent's intention, but abstracts from morally irrelevant details. Smith's intention is to jump into the river, swim to the person in danger of drowning, and pull him to safety. Most of this is morally irrelevant; it does not matter whether she is jumping into a river or rushing into a burning building or running along the railroad tracks with the train in view. What matters from a moral point of view is that she is trying to save someone in danger. So, the maxim of Smith's act is, "Try to save someone in danger." Kant judges acts as right or wrong by judging their maxims.

Kant's test he calls the categorical imperative. An imperative, in general, expresses a command or obligation. Hypothetical imperatives, such as "You ought to work hard if you want to succeed," contain an "if" and depend on circumstances or someone's goals and desires. The command "You ought to work hard" as a hypothetical imperative, for example, applies only if you want to succeed; otherwise, it has no force. Categorical imperatives, in contrast, apply universally, without regard to circumstances, goals, or desires.

This distinction relates interestingly to the distinction between qualified and unqualified goods. Hypothetical imperatives are appropriate to qualified goods. Categorical imperatives are appropriate to unqualified goods. Hard work, for instance, is not good without qualification; it is good because it brings success. So, the imperative appropriate to it is hypothetical: "You ought to work hard if you want to succeed." A good will is good without qualification; the imperative "You ought to have a good will" is thus categorical. Indeed, it is in a sense the only possible categorical imperative, for a good will is the only unqualified good.

Aristotle, of course, would argue that happiness is intrinsically good, indeed the only thing always desired for its own sake and never for the sake of something else. So, he might take "You ought to be happy" as a categorical imperative, and take hypothetical imperatives of the form "If you want to be happy, then you should..." as constituting morality's primary subject matter. But that is not at all how Kant sees it. Though he agrees that a desire for happiness is universal, he sees it as having no intrinsic moral worth. The imperatives of the form "If you want to be happy, then you should..." constitute the subject matter, not of morality, but of prudence. Happiness, then, cannot constitute the basis for a categorical imperative.

Since the only unqualified good, for Kant, is a good will, the only categorical imperative is "You ought to have a good will." But a good will responds solely on the basis of universal considerations, acting out of respect for the moral law. So, we might also frame the categorical imperative as "You ought to respect the moral law"—which by itself has little content—or, more informatively, as "You ought to act on the basis of universal considerations." This gives us Kant's first formulation of the categorical imperative:

> There is therefore but one categorical imperative, namely, this: Act only on that maxim whereby thou canst at the same time will that it should become a universal law.

He quickly gives a second and, he holds, equivalent formulation:

> Act as if the maxim of thy action were to become by thy will a universal law of nature.

Act, in other words, as if everyone were going to act according to your maxims. If you want other people to respect your property, you ought to respect theirs. If you would want other people to save you when you were in danger, you should save them in such circumstances. Kant sees his imperative as a more precise form of the Golden Rule: "Treat others as you would want them to treat you."

Kant maintains that the categorical imperative is the one moral axiom from which other moral imperatives can be derived as theorems: "all imperatives of duty can be deduced from this one imperative." He discusses four examples to show how the categorical imperative works to distinguish right from wrong. The general pattern: To test whether action *A* would be right or wrong, (a) identify *A*'s maxim; (b) ask whether that maxim could become a universal law; and (c) if it could, ask whether you can will it as universal law.

Kant first gives examples of perfect duties—duties that are specific, involving specific obligations to specific people, and giving those people rights that the duty be performed. Smith, for instances, should not kill Jones. This is specific, directed at a specific person (though it is an instance of a quite general obligation not to kill others). Jones has a correlative right not to be killed. So, the obligation not to kill is perfect. Less dramatically, suppose that Smith borrows money from Jones. She has a perfect obligation to pay it back, and Jones has a right to receive it. The obligation to repay debts is thus also perfect. One may have perfect duties to oneself as well as to others. In such cases, Kant holds, the maxim ("kill" or "don't repay debts") fails part (b) of the test. The maxim could not hold as a universal law.

Imperfect duties are general, allowing an agent choice about when and how to perform them. The classic example is charity. You may be obliged to help the less fortunate without being obliged to do anything in particular for any specific person. Whom you help, and how you help them, is up to you. Consequently, nobody else has any right to your help. In the case of imperfect obligations, a maxim fails part (c) of Kant's test. The maxim could be a universal law—there is no contradiction—but it could not be willed as universal law. You are a rational being; you cannot help but will not only your own survival but also your own rationality. That means that you cannot will to be ignorant, or stupid, or ineffective. Nor can you will that others fail to help you when you need their help.

Another way of putting Kant's point in the categorical imperative is this: Do not make an exception of yourself. People who do something wrong do not will that everyone should act that way; they will that other people obey the moral law. The thief does not want to be robbed; the murderer does not want to be killed. The liar does not want to be deceived; the adulterer does not want to be cuckolded. Instead, they want others to follow the rules, but make an exception for themselves. This is what gets them into trouble.

Though there is only one categorical imperative, commanding that we have a good will, Kant offers different formulations of it, to bring out different aspects of having a good will. The idea that a good will acts on the basis of universal considerations rather than subjective, particular, and morally irrelevant factors generates the formulations we have seen so far. But Kant develops another formulation to stress that a good will also acts out of respect—respect for the moral law, which stems from respect for others as rational beings. Recall that a categorical imperative is appropriate only for an intrinsic good. A good will is the only intrinsic good. But a good will is nothing other than a moral agent. So, we may also think of the categorical imperative as commanding, "You ought to respect moral agents." In this formulation, the categorical imperative is "Treat people as ends, never only as means." In other words, "Respect people; don't use them." This permits a more direct and intuitive evaluation of acts as right or wrong.

The categorical imperative differs from other, earlier principles of morality, Kant says, for it is a command we give ourselves as moral agents. Acting in accord with it, we are bound only by the rules we set for ourselves as rational beings. In living by the rules we establish for ourselves we exhibit our autonomy. The heteronomous person follows someone else's command; the autonomous person follows his or her own. Autonomy is what gives human beings dignity.

5.3.1 Immanuel Kant, from *Fundamental Principles of the Metaphysics of Morals*

Nothing can possibly be conceived in the world, or even out of it, that can be called good without qualification except a good will. Intelligence, wit, judgement, and the other talents of the mind, however they may be named, or courage, resolution, perseverance, as qualities of temperament, are undoubtedly good and desirable in many respects. But these gifts of nature may also become extremely bad and mischievous if the will that is to make use of them, and which, therefore, constitutes what is called character, is not good. It is the same with the gifts of fortune. Power, riches, honour, even health, and the general well-being and contentment with one's condition which is called happiness, inspire pride, and often presumption, if there is not a good will to correct the influence of these on the mind, and with this also to rectify the whole principle of acting and adapt it to its end. The sight of a being who is not adorned with a single feature of a pure and good will, enjoying unbroken prosperity, can never give pleasure to an impartial rational spectator. Thus a good will appears to constitute the indispensable condition even of being worthy of happiness.

There are even some qualities which are of service to this good will itself and may facilitate its action, yet which have no intrinsic unconditional value but always presuppose a good will. This qualifies the esteem that we justly have for them and does not permit us to regard them as absolutely good. Moderation in the affections and passions, self-control, and calm deliberation are not only good in many respects, but even seem to constitute part of the intrinsic worth of a person. But they are far from deserving to be called good without qualification, although they have been unconditionally praised as such by the ancients. For without the principles of a good will, they may become extremely bad. The coolness of a villain not only makes him far more dangerous, but also directly makes him more abominable in our eyes than he would have been without it.

A good will is good not because of what it performs or effects, nor by its aptness for the attainment of some proposed end, but simply by virtue of the volition itself. That is, it is good in itself. Considered by itself, it is to be esteemed much higher than all that can be brought about by it in favour of any inclination—even of the sum total of all inclinations. Even if it should happen that, owing to special disfavour of fortune, or the niggardly provision of a step-motherly nature, this will should wholly lack power to accomplish its purpose—if with its greatest efforts it should yet achieve nothing, and there should remain only the good will (not, to be sure, a mere wish, but the summoning of all means in our power)—then, like a jewel, it would still shine by its own light as a thing that has its whole value in itself. Its usefulness or fruitfulness can neither add nor take away anything from this value. It would be, as it were, only the setting that would enable us to handle it more conveniently in common commerce, or to attract to it the attention of those who are not yet connoisseurs, but not to recommend it to true connoisseurs, or to determine its value....

The concept of an objective principle, insofar as it is obligatory for a will, is called a *command* (of reason), and the formula of the command is called an *imperative.*

All imperatives are expressed by the word *ought* [or *should*], and thereby indicate the relation of an objective law of reason to a will. Its subjective constitution is not necessarily determined by it.

Source: Immanuel Kant, from *Fundamental Principles of the Metaphysics of Morals.* Translated by Thomas Kingsmill Abbott. London: Longmans, Green, 1909. We have revised the translation for readability.

They say that something would be good to do or to forbear. But they say it to a will that does not always do a thing because it is thought to be good to do it. What is practically good, however, determines the will by means of the concepts of reason, and consequently not from subjective causes, but objectively—that is, on principles valid for every rational being as such. It is distinguished from the pleasant, as that which influences the will only by means of sensation from merely subjective causes, valid only for the sense of this or that one, and not as a principle of reason, which holds for everyone.

Now all imperatives command either *hypothetically* or *categorically*. The former represent the practical necessity of a possible action as means to something else that is willed (or at least that one might possibly will). The categorical imperative would be one that represented an action as necessary of itself without reference to another end, i.e., as objectively necessary.

Every practical law represents a possible action as good and, on this account, as necessary, for a subject whose actions are determined by reason. So, all imperatives are formulae determining an action that is necessary according to the principle of a will good in some respects. If now the action is good only as a means to something else, then the imperative is hypothetical. If it is conceived as good in itself and consequently as being necessarily the principle of a will which of itself conforms to reason, then it is categorical.

Finally, there is an imperative which commands a certain conduct immediately, without having as its condition any other purpose to be attained by it. This imperative is categorical. It concerns not the matter of the action, or its intended result, but its form and the principle of which it is itself a result. What is essentially good in it consists in the mental disposition, let the consequence be what it may. This imperative may be called that of morality.

When I conceive a hypothetical imperative, in general I do not know beforehand what it will contain until I am given the condition. But when I conceive a categorical imperative, I know at once what it contains. For as the imperative contains, besides the law, only the necessity that the maxims shall conform to this law—while the law contains no conditions restricting it—there remains nothing but the general statement that the maxim of an action should conform to a universal law. It is this conformity alone that the imperative properly represents as necessary.

[Note:] A *maxim* is a subjective principle of action. It must be distinguished from an objective principle, namely, a practical law. The former contains the practical rule set by reason according to the conditions of the subject (often its ignorance or its inclinations). It is the principle on which the subject acts. But the law is the objective principle valid for every rational being. It is the principle on which such a being ought to act that is an imperative.

There is therefore but one categorical imperative, namely, this:

> Act only on a maxim you can will to become a universal law.

Now if all imperatives of duty can be deduced from this one imperative as from their principle, then—although it should remain undecided whether what is called duty is not merely a vain notion—yet at least we shall be able to show what we understand by it and what this notion means.

The universality of the law according to which effects are produced constitutes what is properly called nature in the most general sense (as to form). That is the existence of things so far as it is determined by general laws. So, the imperative of duty may be expressed thus:

> Act as if the maxim of your action were to become, by your will, a universal law of nature.

We will now enumerate a few duties, adopting the usual division of them into duties to ourselves and to others, and into perfect and imperfect duties.

1. A man reduced to despair by a series of misfortunes feels weary of life. But he is still so far in possession of his reason that he can ask himself whether it would not be contrary to his duty to himself to take his own life. Now he inquires

whether the maxim of his action could become a universal law of nature. His maxim is: "From self-love I adopt it as a principle to shorten my life when its longer duration is likely to bring more evil than satisfaction." We then ask simply whether this principle founded on self-love can become a universal law of nature. Now we see at once that a system of nature of which it should be a law to destroy life by means of the very feeling whose special nature it is to impel to the improvement of life would contradict itself. It therefore could not exist as a system of nature. Hence that maxim cannot possibly exist as a universal law of nature. Consequently, it would be wholly inconsistent with the supreme principle of all duty.

2. Another finds himself forced by necessity to borrow money. He knows that he will not be able to repay it. But he sees as well that nothing will be lent to him unless he promises stoutly to repay it in a definite time. He desires to make this promise. But he still has so much conscience as to ask himself: "Is it not unlawful and inconsistent with duty to get out of a difficulty in this way?" Suppose however that he resolves to do so. Then the maxim of his action would be: "When I think myself in need of money, I will borrow money and promise to repay it although I know that I never can do so." Now this principle of self-love, or of one's own advantage, may be consistent with my whole future welfare. But the question now is, "Is it right?" I then change the suggestion of self-love into a universal law, and state the question thus: "How would it be if my maxim were a universal law?" Then I see at once that it could never hold as a universal law of nature. It would necessarily contradict itself. For suppose it to be a universal law that everyone, when he thinks himself in a difficulty, should be able to promise whatever he pleases with the purpose of not keeping his promise. The promise itself would become impossible as well as the end that one might have in view in it. For no one would consider that anything was promised to him, but would ridicule all such statements as vain pretences.

3. A third finds in himself a talent which, with the help of some cultivation, might make him a useful man in many respects. But he finds himself in comfortable circumstances and prefers to indulge in pleasure rather than to take pains in enlarging and improving his happy natural capacities. He asks, however, whether his maxim of neglect of his natural gifts, besides agreeing with his inclination to indulgence, agrees also with what is called duty. He sees then that a system of nature could indeed subsist with such a universal law. People (like the South Sea islanders) could let their talents rest and resolve to devote their lives merely to idleness, amusement, and propagation of their species—in a word, to enjoyment. But he cannot possibly *will* that this should be a universal law of nature, or be implanted in us as such by a natural instinct. For, as a rational being, he necessarily wills that his faculties be developed, since they serve him and have been given him for all sorts of possible purposes.

4. A fourth is prosperous, but sees that others have to contend with great wretchedness and that he could help them. He thinks: "What concern is it of mine? Let everyone be as happy as Heaven pleases, or as he can make himself. I will take nothing from him nor even envy him. But I do not wish to contribute anything to his welfare or to his assistance in distress!" Now no doubt if such a mode of thinking were a universal law, the human race might very well subsist—doubtless even better than in a state in which everyone talks of sympathy and good-will, or even takes care occasionally to put it into practice, but, on the other side, also cheats when he can, betrays the rights of men, or otherwise violates them. But although a universal law of nature could exist in accordance with that maxim, it is impossible to will that such a principle should have the universal validity of a law of nature. For a will that resolved this would contradict itself. Many cases might occur in which one would have need of the love and sympathy of others. In these cases, by such a law of nature, sprung from his own will, he would deprive himself of all hope of the aid he desires.

These are a few of the many actual duties, or at least what we regard as such, that obviously fall into two classes on the one principle that we have laid down. We must be able to will that a maxim of our action should be a universal law. This is the canon of the moral appreciation of the action generally. Some actions are of such a character that their maxim cannot without contradiction even be conceived as a universal law of nature—far from it being possible that we should will that it should be so. In others this intrinsic impossibility is not found, but still it is impossible to will that their maxim should be raised to the universality of a law of nature, since such a will would contradict itself. It is easily seen that the former violate perfect, strict, or rigorous (inflexible) duty; the latter only imperfect (meritorious) duty. Thus it has been completely shown how all duties depend, as regards the nature of their obligation (not the object of their action), on the same principle.

If we now attend to ourselves on occasion of any transgression of duty, we shall find that we in fact do not will that our maxim should be a universal law. That is impossible for us. On the contrary, we will that the opposite should remain a universal law. We only assume the liberty of making an exception in our own favor or (just for this time only) in favor of our inclination. Consequently, if we considered all cases from one and the same point of view, namely, that of reason, we should find a contradiction in our own will: that a certain principle should be objectively necessary as a universal law, and yet subjectively should not be universal but admit of exceptions. We at one moment, however, regard our action from the point of view of a will wholly conformed to reason. Then we look at the same action again from the point of view of a will affected by inclination. There is not really any contradiction. But there is an antagonism of inclination to the precept of reason. The universality of the principle is changed into a mere generality, so that the practical principle of reason meets the maxim halfway. Now, although this cannot be justified in our own impartial judgement, it proves that we do really recognize the validity of the categorical imperative. With all respect for it, we allow ourselves only a few exceptions, which we think unimportant and forced from us.

The will is conceived as a faculty of determining oneself to action in accordance with the concept of certain laws. And such a faculty can be found only in rational beings. Now what serves the will as the objective ground of its self-determination is the end. If this is assigned by reason alone, it must hold for all rational beings. On the other hand, what merely contains the ground of possibility of the action of which the effect is the end is called the means. The subjective ground of desire is the spring. The objective ground of the volition is the motive: hence the distinction between subjective ends, which rest on springs, and objective ends, which depend on motives valid for every rational being. Practical principles are formal when they abstract from all subjective ends. They are material when they assume these ends and, therefore, particular springs of action. The ends a rational being proposes to himself at pleasure as effects of his actions (material ends) are all only relative. For it is only their relation to the particular desires of the subject that gives them their worth. They therefore cannot furnish principles universal and necessary for all rational beings and for every volition—that is to say, practical laws. Hence all these relative ends can give rise only to hypothetical imperatives.

Suppose, however, that there were something whose existence has in itself an absolute worth—something that, being an end in itself, could be a source of definite laws. Then in this and this alone would lie the source of a possible categorical imperative, that is, a practical law.

Now I say: man and generally any rational being exists as an end in himself, not merely as a means to be arbitrarily used by this or that will. In all his actions, whether they concern himself or other rational beings, he must always be regarded at the same time as an end. All objects of the inclinations have only a conditional worth. For if the inclinations and the wants founded on them did not exist, then their object would be without value. But the inclinations, themselves being sources of desire, are so far from having an absolute worth for which they should be desired that, on the contrary, the universal wish of every rational being must be to be wholly free from them. Thus the worth of any object to be acquired by our action is always conditional. Beings whose existence depends not on our will but on nature's have nevertheless, if they are irrational beings, only a relative value as means, and are therefore called things. Rational beings, on the contrary, are called persons, because their very nature points them out as ends in themselves—that is, as something that must not be used merely as means, and so far therefore restricts freedom of action and is an object of respect. These, therefore, are not merely subjective ends whose existence has a worth for us as an effect of our action. They are objective ends, that is, things whose existence is an end in itself. Their existence is an end moreover for which no other can be substituted, which they should subserve merely as means. For otherwise nothing whatever would possess absolute worth. But if all worth were conditioned and therefore contingent, then there would be no supreme practical principle of reason whatever.

If, then, there is a supreme practical principle or, in respect of the human will, a categorical imperative, it must be one which—being drawn from the concept of what is necessarily an end for everyone because it is an end in itself—constitutes an objective principle of will. It can therefore serve as a universal practical law. The foundation of this principle is: Rational nature exists as an end in itself. Man necessarily conceives his own existence as being so. So far, then, this is a subjective principle of human actions. But every other rational being regards its existence similarly, just on the same rational principle that holds for me. So, it is at the same time an objective principle, from which, as a supreme practical law, all laws of the will must be capable of being deduced. Accordingly the practical imperative will be as follows:

> Treat humanity in every case, whether in your own person or in that of anyone else, as an end, never only as a means.

We will now inquire whether this can be practically carried out.

To abide by the previous examples: First, under the head of necessary duty to oneself: He who contemplates suicide should ask himself whether his action can be consistent with the idea of humanity as an end in itself. If he destroys himself in order to escape from painful circumstances, he uses a person merely as a mean to maintain a tolerable condition up to the end of life. But a man is not a thing, that is to say, something which can be used merely as means. He must in all his actions always be considered as an end in himself. I cannot, therefore, dispose in any way of the man in my own person so as to mutilate, damage, or kill him. (It belongs to ethics proper to define this principle more precisely, so as to avoid all misunderstanding, for example, as to amputating limbs to save myself, exposing my life to danger to preserve it, etc. This question is therefore omitted here.)

Second, in regard to necessary duties, or those of perfect obligation, towards others: He who is thinking of making a lying promise to others will see at once that he would be using another man merely as a means, not as an end in himself. For he whom I propose by such a promise to use for my own purposes cannot possibly assent to my mode of acting towards him. He therefore cannot himself contain the end of this action. This violation of the principle of humanity in other men is more obvious if we consider examples of attacks on the freedom and property of others. For then it is clear that he who transgresses the rights of men intends to use the person of others merely as a means, without considering that as rational beings they ought always to be esteemed also as ends—that is, as beings who must be capable of containing in themselves the end of the very same action.

Third, in regard to imperfect (meritorious) duties to oneself: It is not enough that the action does not violate humanity in our own person as an end in itself. It must also harmonize with it. Now there are in humanity capacities of greater perfection that belong to the end that nature has in view, in regard to the humanity in ourselves as agents. To neglect these might perhaps be consistent with the *maintenance* of humanity as an end in itself, but not with the *advancement* of this end.

Fourth, in regard to meritorious duties toward others: The natural end that all men have is their own happiness. Now humanity might indeed subsist, even though no one contributed anything to the happiness of others, provided he did not intentionally withdraw anything from it. But, after all, it would harmonize only negatively, not positively, with humanity as an end in itself, if every one does not also endeavour, as far as in him lies, to forward the ends of others. For the ends of any subject who is an end in himself ought, as far as possible, to be my ends also, if that conception is to have its full effect with me.

This principle, that humanity and generally every rational nature is an end in itself—which is the supreme limiting condition of every man's freedom of action—is not borrowed from experience. First, it is universal. It applies as it does to all rational beings whatever. Experience is not capable of determining anything about them. Second, it does not present humanity as an end to men (subjectively), that is, as an object which men themselves actually adopt as an end. It presents it as an objective end, which must as a law constitute the supreme limiting condition of all our subjective ends, let them be what we will. It must therefore spring from pure reason. In fact the objective principle of all practical legislation lies (according to the first principle) in the rule and its form of universality which makes it capable of being a law (say, e.g., a law of nature). But the subjective principle is in the end. Now by the second principle the subject of all ends is each rational being, inasmuch as it is an end in itself. Hence follows the third practical principle of the will, which is the ultimate condition of its harmony with universal practical reason: the idea of the will of every rational being as a universally legislative will.

On this principle all maxims are rejected which are inconsistent with the will being itself universal legislator. Thus the will is not subject simply to the law, but so subject that it must be regarded as itself giving the law and, on this ground only, subject to the law (of which it can regard itself as the author).

Looking back now on all previous attempts to discover the principle of morality, we need not wonder why they all failed. It was seen that man was bound to laws by duty. But it was not observed that the laws to which he is subject are only those of his own giving. At the same time they are universal. He is only bound to act in conformity with his own will—a will, however, designed by nature to give universal laws. For when one has conceived man only as subject to a law (no matter what), then this law required some interest, either by way of attraction or constraint, since it did not originate as a law from his own will, but this will was according to a law obliged by something else to act in a certain manner. Now by this necessary consequence all the labor spent in finding a supreme principle of duty was irrevocably lost. For men never elicited duty, but only a necessity of acting from a certain interest. Whether this interest was private or otherwise, in any case the imperative must be conditional and could not by any means be capable of being a moral command. I will therefore call this the principle of autonomy of the will, in contrast with every other which I accordingly reckon as heteronomy.

The concept of the will of every rational being is one that must consider itself as giving, in all the maxims of its will, universal laws, so as to judge itself and its actions from this point of view. This concept leads to another which depends on it and is very fruitful, namely that of a kingdom of ends.

By a *kingdom* I understand the union of different rational beings in a system by common laws. Now it is by laws that ends are determined in regard to their universal validity. Hence, if we abstract from the personal differences of rational beings and, likewise, from all the content of their private ends, we shall be able to conceive all ends combined in a systematic whole—including both rational beings as ends in themselves, and also the special ends which each may propose to himself—that is to say, we can conceive a kingdom of ends, which on the preceding principles is possible.

For all rational beings come under the law that each of them must treat itself and all others never merely as means, but in every case at the same time as ends in themselves. From this results a systematic union of rational beings by common objective laws. This kingdom may be called a kingdom of ends, since what these laws have in view is just the relation of these beings to one another as ends and means. It is certainly only an ideal.

A rational being belongs as a member to the kingdom of ends when, although giving universal laws in it, he is also himself subject to these laws. He belongs to it as sovereign when, while giving laws, he is not subject to the will of any other.

A rational being must always regard himself as giving laws either as member or as sovereign in a kingdom of ends rendered possible by the freedom of will. He cannot, however, maintain the latter position merely by the maxims of his will, but only in case he is a completely independent being without wants and with unrestricted power adequate to his will.

Morality consists then in referring all action to the legislation which alone can render a kingdom of ends possible. This legislation must be capable of existing in every rational being and of emanating from his will. The principle of this will is never to act on any maxim that could not without contradiction be also a universal law. Accordingly, we must always act so that the will could at the same time regard itself as giving, in its maxims, universal laws. If now the maxims of rational beings are not by their own nature coincident with this objective principle, then the necessity of acting on it is called practical necessitation, i.e., duty. Duty does not apply to a sovereign in the kingdom of ends, but rather to every member of it and to all in the same degree.

The practical necessity of acting on this principle, that is, duty, does not rest at all on feelings, impulses, or inclinations. It rests solely on the relation of rational beings to one another. The will of a rational being must always be regarded as legislative. Otherwise it could not be conceived as an end in itself. Reason then refers every maxim of the will, regarding it as legislating universally, to every other will and also to every action towards itself. This is not on account of any other practical motive or any future advantage. It comes from the idea of the dignity of a rational being, obeying no law but that which he himself also gives.

In the kingdom of ends everything has either a price or a dignity. Whatever has a price can be replaced by something else that is equivalent. Whatever, on the other hand, is above all price, and therefore admits of no equivalent, has a dignity.

Whatever has reference to the general inclinations and desires of mankind has a market value. Whatever, without presupposing a desire, corresponds to a certain taste, that is, to a satisfaction in the mere purposeless play of our faculties, has a fancy value. But that which constitutes the condition under which alone anything can be an end in itself has not merely a relative worth, that is, a price, but an intrinsic worth, that is, dignity.

Now morality is the condition under which alone a rational being can be an end in himself. By this alone is it possible that he should be a legislating member in the kingdom of ends. Thus morality, and humanity as capable of it, alone have dignity. Skill and diligence in labor have a market value. Wit, lively imagination, and humor, have fancy value. On the other hand, fidelity to promises and benevolence from principle (not from instinct) have intrinsic worth. Neither nature nor art contains anything that, in default of these, it could put in their place. Their worth consists not in the effects which spring from them, nor in the use and advantage which they secure, but in a disposition of mind, that is, the maxims of the will that are ready to manifest themselves in such actions, even if they do not have the desired effect. These actions also need no recommendation from any subjective taste or sentiment that they may be looked on with immediate favour and satisfaction. They need no immediate propension or feeling for them. They exhibit the will that performs them as an object of an immediate respect. Nothing but reason is required to impose them on the will—not to flatter it into them, which, in the case of duties, would be a contradiction. This estimation therefore shows that the worth of such a disposition is dignity. It places it infinitely above all value, with which it cannot for a moment be brought into comparison or competition without as it were violating its sanctity.

What then is it which justifies virtue or the morally good disposition in making such lofty claims? It is nothing less than the privilege it secures to the rational being of participating in the giving of universal laws. That qualifies him to be a member of a possible kingdom of ends—a privilege to which he was already destined by his own nature as being an end in himself and, on that account, legislating in the kingdom of ends. He is free in regard to all laws of physical nature, and obeys only those he himself gives. His maxims belong to a system of universal law to which at the same time he submits himself. For nothing has any worth except what the law assigns it. Now the legislation itself which assigns the worth of everything must for that very reason possess dignity, that is, an unconditional incomparable worth. The word *respect* alone supplies a becoming expression for the esteem which a rational being must have for it. Autonomy, then, is the basis of the dignity of human and of every rational nature.

5.4 MADAME DE STAËL ON THE PASSIONS

Madame de Staël, Baroness de Staël-Holstein (1766–1817), was born Anne-Louise-Germaine Necker in Paris. Her parents were Swiss Protestants; her father was King Louis XVI's finance minister. Even as a child, she met many famous Enlightenment intellectuals, including Edward Gibbon, Denis Diderot, and Jean d'Alembert. At 20 she married the Swedish ambassador to France. She earned a reputation as an intellectual in her own right when she published *Letters on Rousseau* at 22. Her marriage did not last, and she had a series of affairs with prominent men, including Talleyrand and Benjamin Constant (a famous opponent of Kant's). She established a well-known literary salon, becoming one of Paris's leading citizens, but, at 27, had to flee the Reign of Terror. Just two years later, Napoleon exiled her for her belief in liberty and her opposition to militarism. She settled at Coppett, her family's estate in Switzerland, which she made famous as a literary center. She also traveled extensively throughout Europe, writing a series of novels as well as philosophical works. Her emphasis on the passions marks her as one of the earliest Romantic thinkers. After Napoleon's defeat at Waterloo, she returned to Paris and began campaigning against the slave trade, but died three years later, at 51.

Sometimes called "the Empress of Mind" and often described as the most brilliant woman of her time—which was, after all, a remarkable time, at once the height of the Age of Reason and the advent of Romanticism—Madame de Staël rebelled against the dominance of reason, insisting on the importance of enthusiasm, which "leads us to recognize the value and beauty in all things." A political activist, she championed freedom of thought, tolerance, constitutional monarchy, and the rights of women. She also served as a model of what women could accomplish, inspiring writers from George Sand to Willa Cather.

Influence of the Passions upon the Happiness of Individuals and of Nations, published when she was 30, treats the passions as the greatest obstacle to human happiness. With the image of the French Revolution and the Reign of Terror fresh in her mind, she recognizes the passions as hugely important in human affairs and also as potentially hugely destructive. The very thing that gives life its greatest meaning and vibrancy also threatens it. Plato, in his metaphor of the chariot, saw the spirited horse as working in general in harmony with reason. Madame de Staël sees it as even more disruptive and unruly than desire. The chief task of ethics must be to restrain the passions, to allow reason to direct us to what we ought to do. Intriguingly, she argues that the best means to happiness is not to worry about happiness.

5.4.1 Madame de Staël, from *Influence of the Passions upon the Happiness of Individuals and of Nations*

From the passions, that impulsive force which domineers over the will of man, arises the principal obstacle to individual and political happiness. Without the interference of the passions, governments would be a machine fully as simple as the different levers whose power is proportioned to the weight they are to raise, and the destiny of man would exactly result from a just equilibrium between his desires and his means of gratifying them. I shall therefore consider morals and politics only inasmuch as they experience difficulties from the operation of the passions. Characters uninfluenced by the passions naturally place themselves in the situation that best befits them, which is generally the one pointed out to them by chance; or if they introduce any change in it, it is only that which was easily and immediately within their reach. Let us not disturb their happy calm; they want not our assistance; their happiness is as varied in appearance as the different lots which their destiny has drawn; but the basis of that happiness is invariably the same, viz. the certainty of never being either agitated or overruled by any emotion beyond the compass of their resistance. The lives of these impassible beings are doubtless as much exposed as those of other men to the operation of material accidents, which may destroy their fortunes, impair their health, etc.

But afflictions of this nature are prevented or removed not by sensible or moral thoughts, but by positive computations. The happiness of *impassioned* characters being, on the contrary, wholly dependent on what passes within them, they alone can derive consolation from the reflexions which are awakened in their souls; and as the natural bent of their inclinations exposes them to the most cruel calamities, they stand peculiarly in need of a system whose object it is to avoid pain. In a word, it is your impassioned characters only who, by means of certain traits of resemblance, may, in their aggregate, become the subject of the same general considerations. Persons of the other cast of character live, as it were, one by one, without either analogy or variety, in a monotonous kind of existence, though each of them pursues a different end and presents as many varying shades as there are individuals: it is impossible, however, to discover in them any real characteristic colour. If in a treatise on individual happiness I touch only on impassioned characters, it is still more natural to analyze governments in relation to the play they give to the influence of the passions. An individual may be considered as exempt from passions; but a collective body of men is composed of a certain number of characters of every cast, which yield a result nearly similar: and it ought to be

Source: Madame de Staël, *Influence of the Passions upon the Happiness of Individuals and of Nations*. London: George Cawthorn, 1798.

observed that circumstances the most dependent on chance may be the subject of a positive calculation whenever the chances are multiplied. In the Canton of Berne, for example, it has been observed that every ten years nearly the same number of divorces took place; and there are several towns in Italy where an exact calculation is made of the number of murders that are regularly committed every year. Thus events, which link with a multitude of various combinations, have their periodical return, and preserve a fixed proportion, when our observations on them are the result of a great number of chances. Hence we may be led to believe that political science may one day acquire the force of geometrical evidence. The science of morals, when applied to a particular individual, may be wholly erroneous with regard to him, but the organization of a constitution is invariably grounded on data that are fixed, as the greater number in everything affords results that are always similar and always foreseen. That the greatest difficulty which obstructs the march of governments arises from the passions, is a truth that needs no illustration; and it is pretty evident that all the despotic social combinations would prove equally suitable to those listless and inert dispositions that are satisfied to remain in the situation which chance has allotted them, and that the most purely abstract democratical theory might be reduced to practice among wise men whose sole rule of conduct would be the dictates of their reason. You might, therefore, solve whatever is problematical in constitutions if you could but discover to what degree the passions may be incited or repressed without endangering the public happiness.

But before I proceed further, it may perhaps be expected that I attempt a definition of happiness. Happiness, then, such as we aspire after, is the reunion of all the contraries. For individuals, it is hope without fear, activity without solicitude, celebrity without detraction, love without inconstancy; that glow of imagination that embellishes to the eye of fancy whatever we possess, and dims the recollection of whatever we may have lost; in a word, the very reverse of moral nature, the pure perfection of every condition, of every talent, of every pleasure, unmixed and unadulterated with the ills that usually attend them. The happiness of nations must likewise result from the well-tempered combination of republican liberty with monarchical quiet; of the rivalry of talents with the inactivity of factions; of the pride of military glory abroad with submissive obedience to the laws at home. Happiness, such as the mind of man endeavours to conceive, is an object beyond the reach of human efforts; and happiness that is attainable can only be accomplished by a patient study of the surest means that can shield us from the greater ills of life. To the investigation of these means the present treatise is devoted.

And in this attempt, two works may be blended into one. The first considers man in his relations to himself; the other views him in the social relations of all the individuals to each other. Nor are the principal ideas of these two works without some analogy; because a nation exhibits the character of a man and the force of a government acts upon a nation as an individual is acted on by the force of his own reason. The wish of the philosopher is to give permanency to the transient will of reflexion, while the social art tends to perpetuate the actions of wisdom. In a word, what is great is discoverable in what is little; together with the same exactness of proportions. The whole of the universe is reflected in each of its parts, and the more it appears the result of one grand idea, the greater is the admiration it inspires.

There is a wide difference, however, between the system of Individual Happiness and that of the Happiness of Nations: in the former, we may aspire to the most perfect moral independence; that is, to the subjection of all the passions, every man having it in his power to make the experiment on himself: but in the latter, political liberty must be calculated on the positive and indestructible existence of a certain number of impassioned dispositions, which constitute a part of the people who are to be governed....

I have marked out an imported sketch of the work which I projected. The first part which I now deliver to the public is founded upon the study of our own heart and upon the observations made upon the character of mankind in every age. In the study of government we must propose happiness as the end and liberty as the means. In the moral science of man, independence of mind is the principal object to be cultivated; the happiness to be enjoyed is the consequence which it may afford. The man who should devote his life to the pursuit of perfect felicity would be the most wretched of beings; the nation which should only direct its efforts to the attainment of the highest abstract point of metaphysical liberty, would be the most miserable nation in the universe. Legislators then ought to calculate and to direct circumstances; individuals should endeavour to render themselves independent of them: governments should aim at the real happiness of all; and moralists ought to teach individuals to dispense with happiness.

In the very order of things some good is necessarily produced for the mass, and yet there is no felicity for individuals. Everything concurs to the preservation of the species, everything conspires to oppose the desires of the individual; and governments, in some respects representatives of the scheme which obtain in the system of nature, may attain that perfection of which the general order furnishes the example. But moralists, addressing themselves, as I conceive, to men singly, to all those individual beings carried along in the universal moment, cannot promise them personally any enjoyment but that which ever depends upon themselves. There is considerable advantage to be obtained from proposing, as the object of our efforts upon ourselves, the most perfect philosophical independence. Even useless attempts leave behind them some salutary effects. Acting at once upon the whole of the being which constitutes ourselves, we are not startled by the apprehension, as in experiments upon nations, of disjoining, of separating, of opposing to each other the various component parts of the body politic. In our breasts we have no compromise to make with external obstacles. We calculate our own strength, we triumph, or we abandon the contest. Everything is simple; everything even is possible; for if it is allowed to consider a whole nation as a people of philosophers, it is true that every individual may aspire to that character and flatter himself with its attainment.

I am prepared for the various objections of feeling and of argument which may be urged against the system inculcated in this first part. Nothing, it is true, is more repugnant to the first emotions of youth than the idea of rendering ourselves independent of the affections of others. The earliest impulse is to consecrate life to acquire the love of friends and to captivate the favour of the public. At that period of life we seem to think that we have never dedicated enough of our time to please those we love, that we have never sufficiently proved how necessary their welfare is to our existence. Unwearied industry, incessant services, are but poor displays of that ardour of soul, that irresistible necessity which impels us to devote our whole attention, to surrender our whole being to others. We figure to ourselves a futurity wholly composed of those ties which we have formed, we rely with the more implicit confidence upon their duration, because we ourselves are incapable of ingratitude. We are conscious of possessing right to acknowledgement, we depend upon friendship thus constituted more than upon any other tie in nature: everything is means, this alone is the end. We wish likewise to obtain the esteem of the public, and our friends seem pledges for the attainment of our wishes. We have done everything to promote their advantage; they know it, they confess it. Why then will truth, the truth impressed by experience, fail to convince the world of our sincerity? What! can it fail to be ultimately recognised? The innumerable proofs which from every quarter conspire to establish its reality must at length triumph over the fabrications of calumny. Our words, our accents, the air we breathe, all seem to you to bear the impression of what we really are, and we deem it impossible to be long exposed to erroneous interpretations. It is with a feeling of unlimited confidence like this that we launch with flying sails into the ocean of life. All that knowledge has witnessed, all that report has communicated to you, of the bad dispositions of a great number of men appears in your mind like history, like the lessons in morality which we are taught but never have experienced. We never think of applying any of these general ideas to our particular situation. Everything that befalls us, everything which we observe around us is classed as exception. The talent we may possess obtains no influence upon our conduct. The voice of the heart, the impulse of the soul, is alone felt and obeyed. Those fads which we ourselves have never experienced are known only to our understanding without ever entering into life and guiding our actions.

At the age of 25, however, precisely at that period when life ceases to enlarge, when our being is fixed, a severe change takes place in our existence. Men begin to judge of our situation. All then is not future in our destiny. In many respects our lot is fixed, and men then reflect whether it be for their advantage to connect their fortune with ours. If such a union present to their view fewer advantages than they had imagined, if in any manner their expectation is disappointed, at the moment they have resolved to separate themselves from you, they are anxious to justify to their own minds, by some pretext, the injury to you which they are about to commit. They pry into your character, they endeavour to discover a thousand defects in it, in order to acquit themselves of the greatest defect by which a man can be disgraced. The friends who incur the guilt of ingratitude endeavour to degrade you in order to justify themselves; they deny the sincerity of your attachment, they charge you with officiousness: in a word, they employ separate and contradictory means to throw over your conduct, and their own, a kind of uncertain and equivocal character, which every man will explain as he affects. What a multitude of painful feelings then assails the heart of him who had indulged the fond wish and cherished the delightful plan of living in the affections of others, and finds himself deceived in this illusion!

Your system of life is attacked, every successive blow shakes to its foundations the unity of the whole arrangement. *And he too abandons me*, is a painful idea which gives to the last tie which is broken a value and an interest it had not till then possessed. The public also, whose favour had been experienced, loses all the indulgence it had testified. It loves that success which it anticipates, it becomes hostile to that of which itself is the cause. What it formerly had supported by its authority it now attacks; what it formerly had encouraged by its protection, it now labours to destroy. This injustice, of which opinion is guilty in a thousand ways, at once excites agonizing sensations. This individual who defames you with malignity is too unworthy for you to regret his suffrage; but every petty detail of a great vexation, the history of which unfolds to your view, renews your anguish and your suffering; though aware of its inevitable term, you nevertheless experience some painful emotion at every step of the progress. In a word, the affections of the heart are withered, the gay colouring of life fades away. Faults are contracted, which disgust us equally with ourselves and with others, which discourage us from the prosecution of that system of perfection with which our bosoms once proudly swelled. Henceforth we know not to what source we ought to repair, what course we ought to pursue. Once having trusted without discretion, we are disposed to suspect without cause. Is it sensibility, is it virtue, that is nothing but a phantom? And does that sublime complaint which Brutus uttered in the fields of Philippi infer either that we ought to abandon that rigid morality, which we had imposed upon our conduct, or does it prescribe to us self-murder?

At this fatal epoch the earth, as it were, seems to sink under our feet. More uncertain of the future than even when the prospect was dimmed by the clouds of infancy; we entertain doubts of all that we imagined we had known and anew begin our existence; with this difference, that we no longer have hope as a companion to cheer us in the journey. It is at that period of life when the circle of enjoyment has been explored, and the third part of life hardly attained, that this book is calculated to be useful. It is not fit to be read sooner; for I myself did not begin, or even conceive the design of this work, till I had reached that age. It, perhaps, may be objected to me likewise that in attempting to subdue the passions I am labouring to extinguish the principle of the most glorious of human actions, sublime discoveries, and generous sentiments. Although I am not entirely of this opinion, I admit that there is something elevated in passion; that while it continues, it adds to the superiority of man; that under its dominion he is able to accomplish whatever he proposes; so much is firm and persevering *will* an active force in the moral order of things. Man, then, hurried away by something more powerful than himself, wastes his life but employs it with greater energy. If the soul is to be considered only as an impulse, this impulse is more lively when excited by passion. If men destitute of passions must be roused by the interest of some grand spectacle, if the gladiators must mutually murder each other before their eyes, while they are to be nothing more than the spectators of these shocking combats, it unquestionably is necessary to enflame by every possible contrivance these unfortunate beings whose impetuous feelings are destined to animate or to desolate the theatre of the world. But what advantage can they derive from this course, what general happiness can be obtained by the encouragement thus given to the passions of the soul? Every emotion necessary to social life, every impulse necessary to virtue, might exist without this destructive spring.

But it may be said that it is to guide, not to conquer, these passions that our efforts ought to be directed. For my part, I do not understand how it is possible to direct that which only exists while it governs without control. Man is capable but of two states. Either he can rely upon governing within his own breast, and then there are no passions, or he is conscious that there reigns within him a power superior to himself; and upon this, then, he must be wholly dependent. All these compromises with passion are completely imaginary. Like real tyrants, it must either be enthroned in power or subdued in fetters. It never was my intention, however, to devote this work to the extinction of all the passions; men are imbued with them at their birth. Still, it has been my principal endeavour to present a system of life which should not be wholly destitute of pleasurable feelings at that period when the hopes of positive happiness in this state of existence disappear. That system is suited only to those whose character is naturally subject to the influence of passion and who have struggled to regain the empire of themselves. Many of its enjoyments belong only to souls originally ardent, and the necessity of its sacrifices cannot be felt but by those who have been unhappy. Indeed, if man were not born with passions, what should he have to fear, what efforts should he be called upon to exert, what could the feelings of his mind present to occupy the moralist, or fill him with apprehension for the fate of human kind? Am I liable also to the reproach of having failed to treat separately of the enjoyments attached to the performance of our duties, and the anguish inflicted by the remorse which attends the commission of wrong, or the guilt of having neglecled those duties to which we stand engaged?

These two primary ideas of our existence apply equally to all situations, to all characters; and the point which I was principally anxious to demonstrate is the relation which obtains between the passions of man and the agreeable or painful impressions of which he is conscious in his heart. In the prosecution of this plan, I conceive, at the same time, that I have proved that there is no happiness without virtue. That we arrive at this conclusion by every path we pursue is a fresh evidence of its truth. In the analysis of the various moral affections of man, allusions will sometimes occur to the revolution of France. Every remembrance which the mind preserves is tinged with this terrible event. It was my wish likewise to render this first part useful to the second, to prepare, by the examination of men individually, to enter upon the calculation of the effects of their union in societies. I cherished the hope, I again repeat, that by labouring to promote the moral independence of man we should facilitate the attainment of his political liberty, since every restriction which it is necessary to impose upon this liberty is always prescribed by the effervescence of some one of the human passions.

In a word, whatever opinion may be formed of my plan, so much is certain, that my only object has been to combat misery under every appearance it may assume; to study the thoughts, the feelings, the institutions which produce pain to mankind; to investigate what are the reflections, the employments, the combinations which are calculated to diminish in any degree the severity of the sufferings to which the human soul is exposed. The image of misfortune, in whatever aspect it appears, haunts my imaginatlon and tears my heart. Alas! I myself have experienced so bitterly what it is to be miserable that a susceptibility inexpressibly tender, a disquietude mingled with sorrow, steals upon my heart at the idea of the sufferings which any fellow creature endures. I am penetrated with sympathetic emotions at the prospect of those inevitable vexations, of the torments which spring from the imagination, the disappointments which the just man undergoes, and even the remorse which the guilty suffers; at the view of those wounds of the heart, of all griefs the most poignant, and those bitter regrets which we blush to own without ceasing less acutely to feel. In a word, I am penetrated with sorrow at the prospect of those evils which draw forth the tears of anguish, those tears which the ancients collected in a consecrated urn. Such was the veneration with which they viewed the august spectacle of human sorrow. Alas! It is not enough to have sworn that within the limits which bound our existence whatever injustice, whatever injury, we may be doomed to suffer we should never voluntarily occasion a painful sensation to any human being: we likewise should never voluntarily forego the possibility of solacing a single woe. We ought also to try whether any shadow of talent, whether any power of meditation we possess, may not contribute to the discovery of that language with which melancholy gently agitates the soul; whether we might not assist to discover that philosophic height which is beyond the reach of the weapons which annoy. In a word, if time and study can unfold any doctrine by which we may be enabled to demonstrate political principles with that evidence which in future will rescue them from being the subject of two religions and, consequently, of the most sanguinary of all furies, it should seem that the world would be then furnished with a complete example of all those moral shields which protect the fate of man from the dominion of misfortune.

5.5 UTILITARIANISM

How can we tell right from wrong? What makes right actions right and wrong actions wrong? The answer, many philosophers have held, is what makes people happy. Happiness, as Aristotle noted, is intrinsically good. It is a small step to saying that right actions are right because they promote human happiness. Wrong actions are wrong because they detract from it. We can tell right from wrong by observing what makes people happy.

The most influential form of this answer is utilitarianism, a view implicit in various ancient and medieval thinkers, advocated explicitly by Francis Hutcheson (1694–1746) and William Paley (1743–1805) in the eighteenth century and brought to full development by Jeremy Bentham and John Stuart Mill. Jeremy Bentham (1748–1832), a prolific writer on law and public policy, was born in London. The most important utilitarian of the Enlightenment, Bentham was a contemporary of Immanuel Kant, Edmund Burke, William Paley, and Mary Wollstonecraft. Like another contemporary, Mozart, Bentham was a prodigy; he entered Oxford at 12 and graduated at 15. He studied law and was admitted to the bar at 19. But Bentham was so appalled by English law that he never practiced it, even for a day. Instead, he devoted his life to legal reform. He wrote thousands of pages and founded a group of influential thinkers, the philosophical radicals, which included James Mill, economist David Ricardo, and legal theorist John Austin. They advocated representative democracy, universal suffrage, and a scientific approach to philosophy. Bentham also founded the *Westminster Review*, a political journal, and University College, London, where his embalmed body still rests, seated in a glass case in the library.

John Stuart Mill (1806–1873), a contemporary of Charles Darwin, Charles Dickens, Karl Marx, and Leo Tolstoy, was the most influential philosopher of the English-speaking world in the nineteenth century. His father, James Mill (1773–1836), a friend and fellow "philosophical radical" of Jeremy Bentham, was the son of a Scottish shoemaker. He educated young John Stuart Mill at home, teaching him to read Greek by age 3 and Latin just a few years later. The younger Mill was well read in classical literature and history by 8, and studied philosophy, mathematics, and economics before reaching his teens. For thirty-five years he worked in the East India Company, which governed India under charter from the British government. In 1865 he won election to Parliament, despite his refusal to campaign or defend his views.

Bentham's *An Introduction to the Principles of Morals and Legislation* appeared in 1789, the year of the French Revolution. Bentham objects strongly to views of morality and politics that stress individual conscience or religious conviction; both, in his view, are little more than prejudice in disguise. Bentham also rejects doctrines of natural rights, such as those invoked by the French revolutionaries, calling them "nonsense on stilts."

Bentham proposes to base ethics and politics on a single principle, the principle of utility. Roughly, Bentham's version of this principle says that a good action increases the balance of pleasure over pain in the community of people affected by it; a bad action decreases it. The principle of utility approves actions in proportion to their tendency to increase the happiness of the people affected. The best actions, then, are those that maximize happiness. From this principle, together with the facts about the effects of actions, Bentham maintains, all correct moral and political judgments follow. Bentham is an individualist: He holds that the good of the community is nothing but the sum of the goods of its members. We may calculate the effects on the community, therefore, by adding up the effects on its members. This holds for individual actions, for laws or other rules, and for acts of government. Bentham outlines a method of computing the moral value of possible actions called the moral (or felicific) calculus.

Applying the moral calculus can be complicated. Utilitarianism, however, can be summarized in two words: Maximize good. Utilitarians hold that all of ethics and political philosophy reduces to that one maxim, the principle of utility. As Bentham outlines the principle in *The Constitutional Code*:

> the greatest happiness of the whole community, ought to be the end or object of pursuit, in every branch of the law—of the political rule of action, and of the constitutional branch in particular.... The right and proper end of government in every political community is the greatest happiness of all the individuals of which it is composed, say, in other words, the greatest happiness of the greatest number.

The principle seems simple, but it has a number of far-reaching consequences. Utilitarians evaluate actions by the extent to which they maximize good. They evaluate actions, therefore, solely in terms of their consequences. To determine whether an action is right or wrong, we need only to ask, Is it for the best? What effect does it have on the total amount of good? Utilitarians are thus consequentialists, who hold that the moral value of an action depends entirely on its consequences.

Another implication of utilitarianism is universalism: We must consider the consequences of an action on everyone it affects. We cannot consider ourselves alone, or just our friends, or the people in our community, or our fellow citizens; we must consider everyone. Fortunately, most decisions affect only a small number of people. Political decisions, however, may affect millions or even billions of people. Nevertheless, we must take the good of everyone affected into account. Moreover, we cannot show favoritism; we must consider everyone equally. To evaluate an action, we must judge its effects on the total amount of good in the universe. It makes no difference in the calculation who in particular has what amount of good; only the total matters.

Commonsense ethical reasoning does not appear to be universalist in this sense. We typically show favoritism toward our friends, our family, our neighbors, and our fellow citizens. Parents support their children, buy them gifts, pay for their educations, etc., not because they think that doing these things for their children maximizes the amount of good in the universe but because they want to do good for their children. In short, parents care more about their children's welfare than they care about the welfare of others. On the face of it, at least, this violates utilitarianism, which implies that everyone's good should be considered equally.

Some utilitarians are revisionists, holding that we ought to revise commonsense moral thinking to accord with the principle of utility. More, however, hold that the principle in fact supports common sense. It is good, they maintain, that parents show favoritism toward their children, that friends show favoritism toward friends, and so on. Family relationships, friendship, and love make us all better off. There are thus good utilitarian, universalist reasons for people not to treat everyone's good as equally valuable to them in their personal lives. Utilitarianism, in short, explains why most people, in most situations, should not think like utilitarians. They can act in accordance with the principle of utility without consciously meaning to do so.

Finally, utilitarianism requires an independent theory of the good. The principle of utility tells us to maximize good, but it does not tell us what the good is. What should we maximize? The most common answer—the answer many take to define utilitarianism—is happiness. Jeremy Bentham and John Stuart Mill are, more specifically, hedonists: They believe that pleasure and pain are the only sources of value. The good, for both, is happiness, and happiness is pleasure and the absence of pain. In their view, the principle of utility tells us to maximize the balance of pleasure over pain—in short, to maximize happiness.

Mill's version of utilitarianism remains very close to Bentham's. Mill highlights, however, several aspects of the theory. Mill stresses that pleasures and pains differ in quality as well as quantity. Thomas Carlyle had called Bentham's utilitarianism "a philosophy fit for swine," contending that it encouraged people to live like pigs, pursuing pleasure by any means possible. If the only good is feeling good, Carlyle had argued, human beings are no better than pigs. Mill answers, "It is better to be a human being dissatisfied than a pig satisfied," for human beings are capable of much better pleasures than pigs are. How can we rank pleasures in quality? How can we tell whether the pleasure of a cold beer on a summer's day is of higher or lower quality than the pleasure of a beautiful sunset or a good conversation with a friend or a good book? We consult those who are familiar with the pleasures in question and see what they prefer.

Even if some pleasures were not intrinsically more valuable than others, however, utilitarianism would not be "pig philosophy"; the development and use of our higher faculties would be virtuous solely by virtue of their benefits to others.

Mill emphasizes that the principle of utility justifies right actions. It explains what makes them right. But it does not have to be a conscious motive; it does not even have to be a practical test of what is right or wrong. Most right acts are done from other motives. And most people facing moral decisions rely on commonsense moral rules rather than utilitarian calculation.

Mill stresses the importance of secondary principles, commonsense rules such as "Do not murder," "Do not steal," and so on, that give us moral guidance. There is not time to do the moral calculus in the face of every decision. Nor is there any need to, for we can rely on tradition, "the whole past duration of the human species," as Mill puts it, to have determined, in general, the tendencies of certain kinds of actions to produce good or ill effects. "Whatever we adopt as the fundamental principle of morality, we require subordinate principles to apply it by." These secondary, commonsense moral principles are the core of ordinary moral decision making and moral education. They are justified by the principle of utility; following them maximizes the good. Utility also gives us a basis for reforming tradition, for we may find, in some cases, that traditional rules need to be modified or rejected outright. We need to appeal to the principle of utility directly only when secondary principles conflict.

Plato describes a classic case of moral conflict. You've borrowed a knife from a friend, offering to return it whenever he needs it. He shows up at your door, crazed with anger, and says he needs the knife to kill a neighbor who insulted him. Do you return it? Your obligation to keep your promise conflicts with your obligation to save a life.

Plato and Confucius each discuss another sort of conflict: You learn that your father has done something criminal. Do you turn him in? Your obligation to a family member conflicts with your obligation as a citizen.

Kant describes yet another case. A child knocks on your door and says an ax-wielding madman is chasing her. You let her in and hide her in a closet. A moment later the madman bangs on the door and demands to know where the child is. Do you tell him? This time, your obligation to tell the truth conflicts with your obligation to save a life.

Normally, Mill says, we can rely on secondary principles such as "Keep your promises," "Tell the truth," "Report crimes," and "Save lives," which the principle of utility justifies as maximizing happiness. When they conflict, however, we must appeal directly to utility, looking in detail at the consequences. You should probably break your promise (in Plato's case) and tell a lie (in Kant's case), since the consequences of keeping the promise and telling the truth include an innocent person's death.

Bentham generalizes this into an argument for utilitarianism. Traditional moral rules, whether advanced by religion or common sense, have exceptions. "Thou shalt not kill"—but would the assassination of Hitler been an immoral act? "Thou shalt not steal"—but would it be wrong to steal bread to feed your starving family? That, he thinks, is evidence that they are not fundamental principles. When we face a conflict between two or more such principles, traditional theories provide no guidance. But we still think there is a right way and a wrong way to resolve such conflicts; we think the knife should not be returned, even if it means breaking a promise, and the child should be hidden, even if it means telling a lie. There must be a fundamental principle that allows us to weigh the competing considerations in cases of moral conflict—a principle that does not have exceptions and allows us to compare different kinds of moral factors. That, of course, is the principle of utility.

5.5.1 John Stuart Mill, from *Utilitarianism*

The creed which accepts as the foundation of morals, Utility, or the Greatest Happiness Principle, holds that actions are right in proportion as they tend to promote happiness, wrong as they tend to produce the reverse of happiness. By happiness is intended pleasure and the absence of pain; by unhappiness, pain and the privation of pleasure. To give a clear view of the moral standard set up by the theory, much more requires to be said; in particular, what things it includes in the ideas of pain and pleasure; and to what extent this is left an open question. But these supplementary explanations do not affect the theory of life on which this theory of morality is grounded—namely, that pleasure, and freedom from pain, are the only things desirable as ends; and that all desirable things (which are as numerous in the utilitarian as in any other scheme) are desirable either for the pleasure inherent in themselves or as means to the promotion of pleasure and the prevention of pain.

Now, such a theory of life excites in many minds, and among them in some of the most estimable in feeling and purpose, inveterate dislike. To suppose that life has (as they express it) no higher end than pleasure—no better and nobler object of desire and pursuit—they designate as utterly mean and groveling; as a doctrine worthy only of swine, to whom the followers of Epicurus were, at a very early period, contemptuously likened; and modern holders of the doctrine are occasionally made the subject of equally polite comparisons by its German, French, and English assailants.

When thus attacked, the Epicureans have always answered, that it is not they, but their accusers, who represent human nature in a degrading light; since the accusation supposes human beings to be capable of no pleasures except those of which swine are capable. If this supposition were true, the charge could not be gainsaid, but would then be no longer an imputation; for if the sources of pleasure were precisely the same to human beings and to swine, the rule of life which is good enough for the one would be good enough for the other. The comparison of the Epicurean life to that of beasts is felt as degrading precisely because a beast's pleasures do not satisfy a human being's conceptions of happiness. Human beings have faculties more elevated than the animal appetites, and when once made conscious of them, do not regard anything as happiness which does not include their gratification. I do not, indeed, consider the Epicureans to have been by any means faultless in drawing out their scheme of consequences from the utilitarian principle. To do this in any sufficient manner, many Stoic, as well as Christian elements require to be included. But there is no

Source: John Stuart Mill, *Utilitarianism*. London: Parker, Son and Bourn, 1863.

known Epicurean theory of life which does not assign to the pleasures of the intellect, of the feelings and imagination, and of the moral sentiments, a much higher value as pleasures than to those of mere sensation. It must be admitted, however, that utilitarian writers in general have placed the superiority of mental over bodily pleasures chiefly in the greater permanency, safety, uncostliness, etc., of the former—that is, in their circumstantial advantages rather than in their intrinsic nature. And on all these points utilitarians have fully proved their case; but they might have taken the other and, as it may be called, higher ground, with entire consistency. It is quite compatible with the principle of utility to recognize the fact that some kinds of pleasure are more desirable and more valuable than others. It would be absurd that while, in estimating all other things, quality is considered as well as quantity, the estimation of pleasures should be supposed to depend on quantity alone.

If I am asked, what I mean by difference of quality in pleasures, or what makes one pleasure more valuable than another, merely as a pleasure, except its being greater in amount, there is but one possible answer. Of two pleasures, if there be one to which all or almost all who have experience of both give a decided preference, irrespective of any feeling of moral obligation to prefer it, that is the more desirable pleasure. If one of the two is, by those who are competently acquainted with both, placed so far above the other that they prefer it, even though knowing it to be attended with a greater amount of discontent, and would not resign it for any quantity of the other pleasure which their nature is capable of, we are justified in ascribing to the preferred enjoyment a superiority in quality so far outweighing quantity as to render it, in comparison, of small account.

Now it is an unquestionable fact that those who are equally acquainted with, and equally capable of appreciating and enjoying, both do give a most marked preference to the manner of existence which employs their higher faculties. Few human creatures would consent to be changed into any of the lower animals for a promise of the fullest allowance of a beast's pleasures; no intelligent human being would consent to be a fool, no instructed person would be an ignoramus, no person of feeling and conscience would be selfish and base, even though they should be persuaded that the fool, the dunce, or the rascal is better satisfied with his lot than they are with theirs. They would not resign what they possess more than he for the most complete satisfaction of all the desires which they have in common with him. If they ever fancy they would, it is only in cases of unhappiness so extreme that to escape from it they would exchange their lot for almost any other however undesirable in their own eyes. A being of higher faculties requires more to make him happy, is capable probably of more acute suffering, and certainly accessible to it at more points, than one of an inferior type; but in spite of these liabilities, he can never really wish to sink into what he feels to be a lower grade of existence. We may give what explanation we please of this unwillingness; we may attribute it to pride, a name which is given indiscriminately to some of the most and to some of the least estimable feelings of which mankind are capable: we may refer it to the love of liberty and personal independence, an appeal to which was with the Stoics one of the most effective means for the inculcation of it; to the love of power, or to the love of excitement, both of which do really enter into and contribute to it: but its most appropriate appellation is a sense of dignity, which all human beings possess in one form or other, and in some, though by no means in exact, proportion to their higher faculties, and which is so essential a part of the happiness of those in whom it is strong that nothing which conflicts with it could be, otherwise than momentarily, an object of desire to them. Whoever supposes that this preference takes place at a sacrifice of happiness—that the superior being, in anything like equal circumstances, is not happier than the inferior—confounds the two very different ideas, of happiness and content. It is indisputable that the being whose capacities of enjoyment are low has the greatest chance of having them fully satisfied; and a highly endowed being will always feel that any happiness which he can look for, as the world is constituted, is imperfect. But he can learn to bear its imperfections, if they are at all bearable; and they will not make him envy the being who is indeed unconscious of the imperfections but only because he feels not at all the good which those imperfections qualify. It is better to be a human being dissatisfied than a pig satisfied; better to be Socrates dissatisfied than a fool satisfied. And if the fool, or the pig, are a different opinion, it is because they only know their own side of the question. The other party to the comparison knows both sides. It may be objected that many who are capable of the higher pleasures occasionally, under the influence of temptation, postpone them to the lower. But this is quite compatible with a full appreciation of the intrinsic superiority of the higher. Men often, from infirmity of character, make their election for the nearer good, though they know it to be the less valuable; and this no less when the choice is between two bodily pleasures than when it is between bodily and mental. They pursue sensual indulgences to the injury of health, though perfectly aware that health is the greater good. It may be further objected that many who begin with youthful enthusiasm for everything noble, as they advance in years sink into indolence and selfishness. But I do not believe that those who undergo this very common change voluntarily choose the lower description of pleasures in preference to the higher. I believe that before they devote themselves exclusively to the one, they have already become incapable of the other. Capacity for the nobler feelings is in most natures a very tender plant, easily killed, not only by hostile influences, but by mere want of sustenance; and in the majority of young persons it speedily dies away if the occupations to which their position in life has devoted them, and the society into which it has thrown them, are not favourable to keeping that higher capacity in exercise. Men lose their high aspirations as they lose their intellectual tastes, because they have not time or opportunity for indulging them; and they addict themselves to inferior pleasures, not because they deliberately prefer them, but because they are either the only ones to which they have access or the only ones which they are any longer capable of enjoying. It may be questioned whether anyone who has remained equally susceptible to both classes of pleasures ever knowingly and calmly preferred the lower; though many, in all ages, have broken down in an ineffectual attempt to combine both.

From this verdict of the only competent judges, I apprehend there can be no appeal. On a question which is the best worth having of two pleasures, or which of two modes of existence is the most grateful to the feelings apart from its moral attributes and from its consequences, the judgment of those who are qualified by knowledge of both, or, if they differ, that of the majority among them, must be admitted as final. And there needs be the less hesitation to accept this judgment respecting the quality of pleasures, since there is no other tribunal to be referred to even on the question of quantity. What means are there of determining which is the acutest of two pains, or the intensest of two pleasurable sensations, except the general suffrage of those who are familiar with both? Neither pains nor pleasures are homogeneous, and pain is always heterogeneous with pleasure. What is there to decide whether a particular pleasure is worth purchasing at the cost of a particular pain except the feelings and judgment of the experienced? When, therefore, those feelings and judgment declare the pleasures derived from the higher faculties to be preferable in kind, apart from the question of intensity, to those of which the animal nature, disjoined from the higher faculties, is susceptible, they are entitled on this subject to the same regard.

I have dwelt on this point as being a necessary part of a perfectly just conception of Utility or Happiness, considered as the directive rule of human conduct. But it is by no means an indispensable condition to the acceptance of the utilitarian standard; for that standard is not the agent's own greatest happiness, but the greatest amount of happiness altogether; and if it may possibly be doubted whether a noble character is always the happier for its nobleness, there can be no doubt that it makes other people happier, and that the world in general is immensely a gainer by it. Utilitarianism, therefore, could only attain its end by the general cultivation of nobleness of character, even if each individual were only benefited by the nobleness of others and his own, so far as happiness is concerned, were a sheer deduction from the benefit. But the bare enunciation of such an absurdity as this last renders refutation superfluous.

According to the Greatest Happiness Principle, as above explained, the ultimate end, with reference to and for the sake of which all other things are desirable (whether we are considering our own good or that of other people), is an existence exempt as far as possible from pain and as rich as possible in enjoyments, both in point of quantity and quality; the test of quality, and the rule for measuring it against quantity, being the preference felt by those who in their opportunities of experience, to which must be added their habits of self-consciousness and self-observation, are best furnished with the means of comparison. This being, according to the utilitarian opinion, the end of human action is necessarily also the standard of morality; which may accordingly be defined, the rules and precepts for human conduct, by the observance of which an existence such as has been described might be, to the greatest extent possible, secured to all mankind, and not to them only, but, so far as the nature of things admits, to the whole sentient creation.

I must again repeat, what the assailants of utilitarianism seldom have the justice to acknowledge, that the happiness which forms the utilitarian standard of what is right in conduct is not the agent's own happiness but that of all concerned. As between his own happiness and that of others, utilitarianism requires him to be as strictly impartial as a disinterested and benevolent spectator. In the golden rule of Jesus of Nazareth, we read the complete spirit of the ethics of utility. To do as you would be done by, and to love your neighbour as yourself, constitute the ideal perfection of utilitarian morality. As the means of making the nearest approach to this ideal, utility would enjoin, first, that laws and social arrangements should place the happiness, or (as speaking practically it may be called) the interest, of every individual as nearly as possible in harmony with the interest of the whole; and secondly, that education and opinion, which have so vast a power over human character, should so use that power as to establish in the mind of every individual an indissoluble association between his own happiness and the good of the whole, especially between his own happiness and the practice of such modes of conduct, negative and positive, as regard for the universal happiness prescribes; so that not only he may be unable to conceive the possibility of happiness to himself consistently with conduct opposed to the general good, but also that a direct impulse to promote the general good may be in every individual one of the habitual motives of action, and the sentiments connected therewith may fill a large and prominent place in every human being's sentient existence. If the impugners of the utilitarian morality represented it to their own minds in this its true character, I know not what recommendation possessed by any other morality they could possibly affirm to be wanting to it, what more beautiful or more exalted developments of human nature any other ethical system can be supposed to foster, or what springs of action, not accessible to the utilitarian, such systems rely on for giving effect to their mandates.

The objectors to utilitarianism cannot always be charged with representing it in a discreditable light. On the contrary, those among them who entertain anything like a just idea of its disinterested character sometimes find fault with its standard as being too high for humanity. They say it is exacting too much to require that people shall always act from the inducement of promoting the general interests of society. But this is to mistake the very meaning of a standard of morals and confound the rule of action with the motive of it. It is the business of ethics to tell us what are our duties, or by what test we may know them; but no system of ethics requires that the sole motive of all we do shall be a feeling of duty; on the contrary, ninety-nine hundredths of all our actions are done from other motives, and rightly so done, if the rule of duty does not condemn them. It is the more unjust to utilitarianism that this particular misapprehension should be made a ground of objection to it, inasmuch as utilitarian moralists have gone beyond almost all others in affirming that the motive has nothing to do with the morality of the action, though much with the worth of the agent. He who saves a fellow creature from drowning does what is morally right, whether his motive be duty or the hope of being paid for his trouble; he who betrays the friend that trusts him is guilty of a crime, even if his object be to serve another friend to whom he is under greater obligations. But to speak only of actions done from the motive of duty and in direct obedience to principle: it is a misapprehension of the utilitarian mode of thought to conceive it as implying that people should fix their minds upon so wide a generality as the world or society at large. The great majority of good actions are intended not for the benefit of the world, but for that of individuals, of which the good of the world is made up; and the thoughts of the most virtuous man need not on these occasions travel beyond the particular persons concerned, except so far as is necessary to assure himself that in benefiting them he is not violating the rights, that is, the legitimate and authorized expectations, of anyone else. The multiplication of happiness is, according to the utilitarian ethics, the object of virtue: The occasions on which any person (except one in a thousand) has it in his power to do this on an extended scale, in other words to be a public benefactor, are but exceptional; and on these occasions alone is he called on to consider public utility; in every other case, private utility, the interest or happiness of some few persons, is all he has to attend to. Those alone the influence of whose actions extends to society in general need concern themselves habitually about so large an object. In the case of abstinences—indeed of things which people forbear to do from moral considerations, though the consequences in the particular case might be beneficial—it would be unworthy of an intelligent agent not to be consciously aware that the action is of a class which, if practiced generally, would be generally injurious, and that this is the ground of the obligation to abstain from it. The amount of regard for the public interest implied in this recognition is no greater than is demanded by every system of morals, for they all enjoin to abstain from whatever is manifestly pernicious to society.

Again, defenders of utility often find themselves called upon to reply to such objections as this—that there is not time, previous to action, for calculating and weighing the effects of any line of conduct on the general happiness. This is exactly as if anyone were to say that it is impossible to guide our conduct by Christianity because there is not time, on every occasion on which anything has to be done, to read through the Old and New Testaments. The answer to the objection is that there has been ample time, namely, the whole past duration of the human species. During all that time, mankind have been learning by experience the tendencies of actions, on which experience all the prudence, as well as all the morality of life, are dependent. People talk as if the commencement of this course of experience had hitherto been put off, and as if, at the moment when some man feels tempted to meddle with the property or life of another, he had to begin considering for the first time whether murder and theft are injurious to human happiness. Even then I do not think that he would find the question very puzzling; but, at all events, the matter is now done to his hand. It is truly a whimsical supposition that, if mankind were agreed in considering utility to be the test of morality, they would remain without any agreement as to what is useful, and would take no measures for having their notions on the subject taught to the young and enforced by law and opinion. There is no difficulty in proving any ethical standard whatever to work ill, if we suppose universal idiocy to be conjoined with it; but on any hypothesis short of that, mankind must by this time have acquired positive beliefs as to the effects of some actions on their happiness; and the beliefs which have thus come down are the rules of morality for the multitude, and for the philosopher until he has succeeded in finding better. That philosophers might easily do this, even now, on many subjects; that the received code of ethics is by no means of divine right; and that mankind have still much to learn as to the effects of actions on the general happiness, I admit, or rather, earnestly maintain. The corollaries from the principle of utility, like the precepts of every practical art, admit of indefinite improvement, and, in a progressive state of the human mind, their improvement is perpetually going on. But to consider the rules of morality as improveable is one thing; to pass over the intermediate generalizations entirely and endeavour to test each individual action directly by the first principle is another. It is a strange notion that the acknowledgment of a first principle is inconsistent with the admission of secondary ones. To inform a traveler respecting the place of his ultimate destination is not to forbid the use of landmarks and direction-posts on the way. The proposition that happiness is the end and aim of morality does not mean that no road ought to be laid down to that goal, or that persons going thither should not be advised to take one direction rather than another. Men really ought to leave off talking a kind of nonsense on this subject, which they would neither talk nor listen to on other matters of practical concernment. Nobody argues that the art of navigation is not founded on astronomy because sailors cannot wait to calculate the Nautical Almanac. Being rational creatures, they go to sea with it ready calculated; and all rational creatures go out upon the sea of life with their minds made up on the common questions of right and wrong as well as on many of the far more difficult questions of wise and foolish. And this, as long as foresight is a human quality, it is to be presumed they will continue to do. Whatever we adopt as the fundamental principle of morality, we require subordinate principles to apply it by; the impossibility of doing without them, being common to all systems, can afford no argument against any one in particular; but gravely to argue as if no such secondary principles could be had, and as if mankind had remained till now, and always must remain, without drawing any general conclusions from the experience of human life is as high a pitch, I think, as absurdity has ever reached in philosophical controversy.

The remainder of the stock arguments against utilitarianism mostly consist in laying to its charge the common infirmities of human nature and the general difficulties which embarrass conscientious persons in shaping their course through life. We are told that a utilitarian will be apt to make his own particular case an exception to moral rules, and, when under temptation, will see a utility in the breach of a rule greater than he will see in its observance. But is utility the only creed which is able to furnish us with excuses for evil doing and means of cheating our own conscience? They are afforded in abundance by all doctrines which recognize as a fact in morals the existence of conflicting considerations; which all doctrines do that have been believed by sane persons. It is not the fault of any creed, but of the complicated nature of human affairs, that rules of conduct cannot be so framed as to require no exceptions, and that hardly any kind of action can safely be laid down as either always obligatory or always condemnable. There is no ethical creed which does not temper the rigidity of its laws by giving a certain latitude, under the moral responsibility of the agent, for accommodation to peculiarities of circumstances; and under every creed, at the opening thus made, self-deception and dishonest casuistry get in. There exists no moral system under which there do not arise unequivocal cases of conflicting obligation. These are the real difficulties, the knotty points both in the theory of ethics and in the conscientious guidance of personal conduct. They are overcome practically, with greater or with less success, according to the intellect and virtue of the individual; but it can hardly be pretended that anyone will be the less qualified for dealing with them from possessing an ultimate standard to which conflicting rights and duties can be referred. If utility is the ultimate source of moral obligations, utility may be invoked to decide between them when their demands are incompatible. Though the application of the standard may be difficult, it is better than none at all: while in other systems, the moral laws all claiming independent authority, there is no common umpire entitled to interfere between them; their claims to precedence one over another rest on little better than sophistry, and unless determined, as they generally are, by the unacknowledged influence of considerations of utility, afford a free scope for the action of personal desires and partialities. We must remember that only in these cases of conflict between secondary principles is it requisite that first principles should be appealed to. There is no case of moral obligation in which some secondary principle is not involved; and if only one, there can seldom be any real doubt which one it is, in the mind of any person by whom the principle itself is recognized.

CHAPTER 6

African Ethics

"The light of the heart"

The tendency to wonder about the origin and nature of the world, the foundations of knowledge, the best way to live, and the meaning of life are universal. Philosophy comes naturally to us. A developed and continuous philosophical tradition, however, requires certain conditions: a level of affluence permitting some people to spend significant amounts of time in reflection; a culture that values writing; institutions dedicated to passing down to future generations what has been thought and written in the past; and enough stability in such institutions and their political surroundings to allow that transmission to succeed. Those conditions have been met in many cultures, at many periods of time, but have gone unmet in many more. They have only rarely been met in Africa. We have extensive works by ancient Egyptians as well as North Africans such as Augustine, Maimonides, and Averroes, but we knew little of sub-Saharan philosophy until quite recently. Fortunately, we do have records of seventeenth-century Ethiopian philosophy. And contemporary African thinkers have developed ethical theory in novel and important directions.

6.1 THE ETHIOPIAN ENLIGHTENMENT

Seventeenth-century philosophical works from Ethiopia survive and document an Ethiopian enlightenment. Like the philosophers of the European Enlightenment, the authors of these works stress the primacy of reason and the possibility of knowledge of the world through its use.

Zera Yacob (1599–1692), the greatest of these philosophers—a contemporary of Descartes, Pascal, Locke, and Leibniz—was born near Aksum, the religious center of Ethiopia. The son of a poor farmer, he attended traditional schools, studying the Psalms, sacred music, and Ethiopian literature. Such schools encouraged questions and discussions, teaching reflection, criticism, and the power of thought. Following a period of devastation brought about by foreign invasion, Ethiopia was undergoing a religious revival and suffering various religious conflicts. In 1626, in the midst of these upheavals, the king converted to Catholicism and summarily ordered obedience to Rome. A rival priest from Aksum denounced Zera Yacob as a traitor, claiming that he was inciting revolution against the Catholics and the king. Only 27 years old, Zera Yacob fled for his life, taking nothing but a small amount of gold and his copy of the Psalms to a cave in a beautiful valley, where he stayed for two years and formulated the basic ideas of his philosophy, which he recorded later in *The Treatise of Zera Yacob.* Fearing persecution, he never published it. He lived in Enfraz, happily and prosperously, until his death at age 93.

The book's original Geez title, *Hatata*, comes from a root meaning "to question, search, investigate, or examine." The *Treatise* champions reason as a tool for understanding the world and for understanding religion. Zera Yacob argues that reason, applied to the available evidence, supports the conclusion that the world, God's creation, is essentially good. His ethics rests on this foundation. Because creation is essentially good, enjoying it is also good. Zera Yacob thus opposes traditional Ethiopian asceticism, a philosophy of denial, fasting, and monastic life, in favor of involvement with the secular world.

Zera Yacob calls reason the "light of the heart." He uses it to criticize the ethical prescriptions of various religions. He argues that Jewish law, Christian morality, and Islamic rules of conduct imply that the order of nature itself is wrong. Moses, for example, considers sexual intercourse impure; but since people naturally have a disposition to desire it and the survival of humanity depends on it, Moses's attitude indicts the whole order of creation. For the same reason, Zera Yacob criticizes the Christian preference for a monastic life as unnatural and contrary to the law of God. Sexual desire is natural, so it cannot in itself be wrong or unclean. He attacks Islam for permitting polygamy, which leaves many men without wives. Nature has proportioned the number of boys and girls as approximately equal, and so polygamy violates natural law. He also assails Islam for allowing slavery. Yearning for freedom is natural, so slavery is wrong. He criticizes all three for insisting on rituals of fasting. Since hunger is natural, fasting should not be obligatory. Rules that restrain our natural dispositions may be acceptable, but those that contradict them cannot be.

Reason thus serves as a foundation for morality and as a test for religious beliefs. Any religion that teaches that some part of the natural order or some natural disposition is wrong cannot be correct.

Underlying Zera Yacob's assault on particular religious tenets is a general skepticism about deriving ethical conclusions from religious revelation. *Divine command theorists* take God's will as itself making some acts right and others wrong. Many other religious thinkers have believed that God reveals moral truth and that we can know that truth only because God reveals it to us. Zera Yacob argues that neither can be correct. Defenders of each religion claim that they know the only true way. Obviously, not all can be right. How can we decide who is right? How, that is, can we judge which alleged revelations really come from God? Zera Yacob argues that we cannot—we have no way to tell true revelations from pretenders—except by using reason to discover moral truth and judging the claims of religions by the light of reason.

6.1.1 Zera Yacob, from *The Treatise of Zera Yacob*

Chapter IV/ The Investigation of Faith and of Prayer

Later on I thought, saying to myself: "Is everything that is written in the Holy Scriptures true?" Although I thought much about these things I understood nothing, so I said to myself: "I shall go and consult scholars and thinkers; they will tell me the truth." But afterwards I thought, saying to myself: "What will men tell me other than what is in their heart?" Indeed each one says: "My faith is right, and those who believe in another faith believe in falsehood, and are the enemies of God." These days the Frang [foreigners] tell us: "Our faith is right, yours is false." We on the other hand tell them: "It is not so; your faith is wrong, ours is right." If we also ask the Mohammedans and the Jews, they will claim the same thing, and who would be the judge for such a kind of argument? No single human being can judge: for all men are plaintiffs and defendants between themselves. Once I asked a Frang scholar many things concerning our faith; he interpreted them all according to his own faith. Afterwards I asked a well-known Ethiopian scholar and he also interpreted all things according to his own faith. If I had asked the Mohammedans and the Jews, they also would have interpreted according to their own faith; then, where could I obtain a judge that tells the truth? As my faith appears true to me, so does another one find his own faith true; but truth is one. While thinking over this matter, I said: "O my creator, wise among the wise and just among the just, who created me with an intelligence, help me to understand, for men lack wisdom and truthfulness; as David said: 'No man can be relied upon.' "

I thought further and said: "Why do men lie over problems of such great importance, even to the point of destroying themselves?" and they seemed to do so because although they pretend to know all, they know nothing. Convinced they know all, they do not attempt to investigate the truth. As David said: "Their hearts are curdled like milk." Their heart is curdled because they assume what they have heard from their predecessors and they do not inquire whether it is true or false. But I said: "O Lord! who strike me down with such torment, it is fitting that I know your judgement. You chastise me with truth and admonish me with mercy. But never let my head be anointed with the oil of sinners and of masters in lying: make me understand, for you created me with intelligence." I asked myself: "If I am intelligent, what is it I understand?" And I said: "I understand there is a creator, greater than all creatures, since from his overabundant greatness, he created things that are so great. He is intelligent who understands all, for he created us as intelligent from the abundance of his intelligence; and we ought to worship him, for he is the master of all things. If we pray to him, he will listen to us; for he is almighty." I went on saying in my thought: "God did not create me intelligent without a purpose, which is to look for him and to grasp him and his wisdom in the path he has opened for me and to worship him as long as I live." And still thinking on the same subject, I said to myself: "Why is it that all men do not adhere to truth, instead of believing falsehood?" The cause seemed to be the nature of man, which is weak and sluggish. Man aspires to know truth and the hidden things of nature, but his endeavour is difficult and can only be attained with great labour and patience, as Soloman said: "With the help of wisdom I have been at pains to

---

Source: From *The Treatise of Zera Yacob, The Source of African Philosophy: The Ethiopian Philosophy of Man*. Edited by Claude Sumner. Stuttgart (Germany): Franz Steiner Verlag, 1986.

study all that is done under heaven; oh, what a weary task God has given mankind to labour at!" Hence people hastily accept what they have heard from their fathers and shy from any critical examination. But God created man to be the master of his own actions, so that he will be what he wills to be, good or bad. If a man chooses to be wicked he can continue in this way until he receives the punishment he deserves for his wickedness. But being carnal, man likes what is of the flesh; whether they are good or bad, he finds ways and means through which he can satisfy his carnal desire. God did not create man to be evil, but to choose what he would like to be, so that he may receive his reward if he is good or his condemnation if he is bad. If a liar, who desires to achieve wealth or honours among men, needs to use foul means to obtain them, he will say he is convinced this falsehood was for him a just thing. To those people who do not want to search, this action seems to be true, and they believe in the liar's strong faith. I ask you in how many falsehoods do our people believe? They believe wholeheartedly in astrology and other calculations, in the mumbling of secret words, in omens, in the conjuration of devils and in all kinds of magical art and in the utterances of soothsayers. They believe in all these because they did not investigate the truth but listened to their predecessors. Why did these predecessors lie unless it was for obtaining wealth and honours? Similarly those who wanted to rule the people said: "We were sent by God to proclaim the truth to you"; and the people believed them. Those who came after them accepted their fathers' faith without question: rather, as a proof of their faith, they added to it by including stories of signs and omens. Indeed they said: "God did these things"; and so they made God a witness of falsehood and a party to liars.

Chapter V / The Law of Moses and the Meditation of Mohammed

To the person who seeks it, truth is immediately revealed. Indeed he who investigates with the pure intelligence set by the creator in the heart of each man and scrutinizes the order and laws of creation will discover the truth. Moses said: "I have been sent by God to proclaim to you his will and his law"; but those who came after him added stories of miracles that they claimed had been wrought in Egypt and on Mount Sinai and attributed them to Moses. But to an inquisitive mind they do not seem to be true. For in the Books of Moses, one can find a wisdom that is shameful and that fails to agree with the wisdom of the creator or with the order and the laws of creation. Indeed by the will of the creator, and the law of nature, it has been ordained that man and woman would unite in a carnal embrace to generate children, so that human beings will not disappear from the earth. Now this mating, which is willed by God in his law of creation, cannot be impure since God does not stain the work of his own hands. But Moses considered that act as evil; but our intelligence teaches us that he who says such a thing is wrong and makes his creator a liar. Again they said that the law of Christianity is from God, and miracles are brought forth to prove it. But our intelligence tells and confirms to us with proofs that marriage springs from the law of the creator; and yet monastic law renders this wisdom of the creator ineffectual, since it prevents the generation of children and extinguishes mankind. The law of Christians which propounds the superiority of monastic life over marriage is false and cannot come from God. How can the violation of the law of the creator stand superior to his wisdom, or can man's deliberation correct the word of God? Similarly Mohammed said: "The orders I pass to you are given to me by God"; and there was no lack of writers to record miracles proving Mohammed's mission, and people believed in him. But we know that the teaching of Mohammed could not have come from God; those who will be born both male and female are equal in number; if we count men and women living in an area, we find as many women as men; we do not find eight or ten women for every man; for the law of creation orders one man to marry one woman. If one man marries ten women, then nine men will be without wives. This violates the order of creation and the laws of nature and it ruins the usefulness of marriage; Mohammed, who taught in the name of God, that one man could marry many wives, is not sent from God. These few things I examined about marriage.

Similarly when I examine the remaining laws, such as the Pentateuch, the law of the Christians and the law of Islam, I find many things which disagree with the truth and the justice of our creator that our intelligence reveals to us. God indeed has illuminated the heart of man with understanding by which he can see the good and evil, recognize the licit and the illicit, distinguish truth from error, "and by your light we see the light, O Lord"! If we use this light of our heart properly, it cannot deceive us; the purpose of this light which our creator gave us is to be saved by it, and not to be ruined by it. Everything that the light of our intelligence shows us comes from the source of truth, but what men say comes from the source of lies and our intelligence teaches us that all that the creator established is right. The creator in his kind wisdom has made blood to flow monthly from the womb of women. And the life of a woman requires this flow of blood in order to generate children; a woman who has no menstruation is barren and cannot have children, because she is impotent by nature. But Moses and Christians have denied the wisdom of the creator; Moses even considers impure all the things that such a woman touches; this law of Moses impedes marriage and the entire life of a woman and it spoils the law of mutual help, prevents the bringing up of children and destroys love. Therefore this law of Moses cannot spring from him who created woman. Moreover, our intelligence tells us that we should bury our dead brothers. Their corpses are impure only if we follow the wisdom of Moses; they are not, however, if we follow the wisdom of our creator, who made us out of dust that we may return to dust. God does not change into impurity the order he imposes on all creatures with great wisdom, but man attempts to render it impure that he may glorify the voice of falsehood.

The Gospel also declares: "He who does not leave behind father, mother, wife and children is not worthy of God." This forsaking corrupts the nature of man. God does not accept that his creature destroy itself, and our intelligence tells us that abandoning our father and our mother helpless in their old age is a great sin; the Lord is not a god that loves malice; those who desert their children are worse than the wild animals, which never forsake their offspring. He who abandons his wife abandons her to adultery and thus violates the order of creation and the laws of nature. Hence what the Gospel says on this subject cannot come from God. Likewise the Mohammedans said that it is right to go and buy a man as if he were an animal. But with our intelligence we understand that this Mohammedan law cannot come from the creator of man who made us equal, like brothers, so that we call our creator our father. But Mohammed made the weaker man the possession of the stronger and equated a rational creature with irrational animals; can this depravity be attributed to God?

God does not order absurdities, nor does he say: "Eat this, do not eat that; today eat, tomorrow do not eat; do not eat meat today, eat it tomorrow," unlike the Christians who follow the laws of fasting. Neither did God say to the Mohammedans: "Eat during the night, but do not eat during the day," nor similar and like things. Our reason teaches us that we should eat of all things which do no harm to our health and our nature, and that we should eat each day as much as is required for our sustenance. Eating one day, fasting the next endangers health; the law of fasting reaches beyond the order of the creator who created food for the life of man and wills that we eat it and be grateful for it; it is not fitting that we abstain from his gifts to us. If there are people who argue that fasting kills the desire of the flesh, I shall answer them: "The concupiscence of the flesh by which a man is attracted to a woman and a woman to a man springs from the wisdom of the creator, it is improper to do away with it; but we should act according to the well-known law that God established concerning legitimate intercourse. God did not put a purposeless concupiscence into the flesh of men and of all animals; rather he planted it in the flesh of man as a root of life in this world and a stabilizing power for each creature in the way destined for it. In order that this concupiscence lead us not to excess, we should eat according to our needs, because overeating and drunkenness result in ill health and shoddiness in work. A man who eats according to his needs on Sunday and during the fifty days does not sin, similarly he who eats on Friday and on the days before Easter does not sin. For God created man with the same necessity for food on each day and during each month. The Jews, the Christians and the Mohammedans did not understand the work of God when they instituted the law of fasting; they lie when they say that God imposed fasting upon us and forbade us to eat; for God our creator gave us food that we support ourselves by it, not that we abstain from it.

Chapter VII / The Law of God and The Law of Man

I said to myself: "Why does God permit liars to mislead his people?" God has indeed given reason to all and everyone so that they may know truth and falsehood, and the power to choose between the two as they will. Hence if it is truth we want, let us seek it with our reason which God has given us so that with it we may see that which is needed for us from among all the necessities of nature. We cannot, however, reach truth through the doctrine of man, for all men are liars. If on the contrary we prefer falsehood, the order of the creator and the natural law imposed on the whole of nature do not perish thereby, but we ourselves perish by our own error. God sustains the world by his order which he himself has established and which man cannot destroy, because the order of God is stronger than the order of men. Therefore those who believe that monastic life is superior to marriage are they themselves drawn to marriage because of the might of the order of the creator; those who believe that fasting brings righteousness to their soul eat when they feel hungry; and those who believe that he who has given up his goods is perfect are drawn to seek them again on account of their usefulness, as many of our monks have done. Likewise all liars would like to break the order of nature: but it is not possible that they do not see their lie broken down. But the creator laughs at them, the Lord of creation derides them. God knows the right way to act, but the sinner is caught in the snare set by himself. Hence a monk who holds the order of marriage as impure will be caught in the snare of fornication and of other carnal sins against nature and of grave sickness. Those who despise riches will show their hypocrisy in the presence of kings and of wealthy persons in order to acquire these goods. Those who desert their relatives for the sake of God lack temporal assistance in times of difficulty and in their old age, they begin to blame God and men and to blaspheme. Likewise all those who violate the law of the creator fall into the trap made by their own hands. God permits error and evil among men because our souls in this world live in a land of temptation, in which the chosen ones of God are put to the test, as the wise Solomon said: "God has put the virtuous to the test and proved them worthy to be with him; he has tested them like gold in a furnace, and accepted them as a holocaust." After our death, when we go back to our creator, we shall see how God made all things in justice and great wisdom and that all his ways are truthful and upright. It is clear that our soul lives after the death of our flesh; for in this world our desire for happiness is not fulfilled; those in need desire to possess, those who possess desire more, and though man owned the whole world, he is not satisfied and craves for more. This inclination of our nature shows us that we are created not only for this life, but also for the coming world; there the souls which have fulfilled the will of the creator will be perpetually satisfied and will not look for other things. Without this inclination the nature of man would be deficient and would not obtain that of which it has the greatest need. Our soul has the power of having the concept of God and of seeing him mentally; likewise it can conceive of immortality. God did not give this power purposelessly; as he gave the power, so did he give the reality. In this world complete justice is not achieved: Wicked people are in possession of the goods of this world in a satisfying degree, the humble starve; some wicked men are happy, some good men are sad, some evil men exult with joy; some righteous men weep. Therefore, after our death there must needs be another life and another justice, a perfect one, in which retribution will be made to all according to their deeds, and those who have fulfilled the will of the creator revealed through the light of reason and have observed the law of their nature will be rewarded. The law of nature is obvious, because our reason clearly propounds it, if we examine it. But men do not like such inquiries; they choose to believe in the words of men rather than to investigate the will of their creator.

Chapter VIII / The Nature of Knowledge

The will of God is known by this short statement from our reason that tells us: "Worship God your creator and love all man as yourself." Moreover our reason says: "Do not do unto others that which you do not like done to you, but do unto others as you would like others to do unto you." The decalogue of the Pentateuch expresses the will of the creator excepting the precept about the observance of the Sabbath, for our reason says nothing of the observance of the Sabbath. But the prohibitions of killing, stealing, lying, adultery: our reason teaches us these and similar ones. Likewise the six precepts of the Gospel are the will of the creator. For indeed we desire that men show mercy to us; it therefore is fitting that we ourselves show the same mercy to the others, as much as it is within our power. It is the will of God that we keep our life and existence in this world. It is the will of the creator that we come into and remain in this life, and it is not right for us to leave it against his holy will. The creator himself wills that we adorn our life with science and work; for such an end did he give us reason and power. Manual labour comes from the will of God, because without it the necessities of our life cannot be fulfilled. Likewise marriage of one man with one woman and education of children. Moreover there are many other things which agree with our reason and are necessary for our life or for the existence of mankind. We ought to observe them, because such is the will of our creator, and we ought to know that God does not create us perfect but creates us with such a reason as to know that we are to strive for perfection as long as we live in this world, and to be worthy for the reward that our creator has prepared for us in his wisdom. It was possible for God to have created us perfect and to make us enjoy beatitude on earth; but he did not will to create us in this way; instead he created us with the capacity of striving for perfection, and placed us in the midst of the trials of the world so that we may become perfect and deserve the reward that our creator will give us after our death; as long as we live in this world we ought to praise our creator and fulfill his will and be patient until he draws us unto him, and beg from his mercy that he will lessen our period of hardship and forgive our sins and faults which we committed through ignorance, and enable us to know the laws of our creator and to keep them.

Now as to prayer, we always stand in need of it because our rational nature requires it. The soul endowed with intelligence that is aware that there is a God who knows all, conserves all, rules all, is drawn to him so that it prays to him and asks him to grant things good and to be freed from evil and sheltered under the hand of him who is almighty and for whom nothing is impossible, God great and sublime who sees all that is above and beneath him, holds all, teaches all, guides all, our Father, our creator, our Protector, the reward for our souls, merciful, kind, who knows each of our misfortunes, takes pleasure in our patience, creates us for life and not for destruction, as the wise Solomon said: "You, Lord, teach all things, because you can do all things and overlook men's sins so that they can repent. You love all that exists, you hold nothing of what you have made in abhorrence, you are indulgent and merciful to all." God created us intelligent so that we may meditate on his greatness, praise him and pray to him in order to obtain the needs of our body and soul. Our reason which our creator has put in the heart of man teaches all these things to us. How can they be useless and false?

6.2 THE COMMUNITARIAN UTILITARIANISM OF THE AKAN

The Akan tribe lives in Ghana, on the west African coast that yielded many of the African natives brought by slave traders to North America. Contemporary African philosopher Kwame Gyekye, himself an Akan, has written about the Akan view of causality, metaphysics, religion, and ethics.

Gyekye describes a version of *consequentialism*, the view that all moral value depends solely on the consequences of actions. Good acts are those that bring about the well-being of society; bad actions work against it. The Akan thus evaluate actions by their consequences. But their view differs from that of most Western consequentialists, who treat the good of a community as the sum of the goods of its members. The Akan maintain that the good of the community cannot be reduced to individual goods. According to their *communitarian* consequentialism, good acts promote the well-being of society. The Akan understand social well-being in terms of social welfare, solidarity, harmony, and other features of the social order itself. The good of the community, while it does not reduce to individual well-being, nevertheless is not independent of it. Certain character traits are more conducive to social well-being than others and are therefore considered virtues: kindness, faithfulness, compassion, and hospitality, for example. Akan ethics judges actions and character traits by appeal to their effect on social good.

Akan ethics groups unethical actions into two categories: ordinary and extraordinary evils. Extraordinary evils bring suffering to the whole community, not just to individual members of it. Theft, adultery, lying, and backbiting are ordinary evils; they harm specific people but do little to affect people not immediately connected to the act. Murder, rape, incest, cursing the chief, and stealing from a deity, in contrast, are extraordinary evils. They affect the entire community, undermining a people's sense of community. Performing an extraordinarily evil act, the Akan think, has religious ramifications, for it angers the gods. Still, it is the disastrous consequences for the well-being of the community that make the evil extraordinary, not the gods' disapproval.

For the Akan, people are essentially social. One can speak of the good of an individual only in terms of the good of the society he or she inhabits. People cannot achieve the good on their own; they must rely upon others. Consequently, individual good depends on the good of the community. Gyekye concludes that each must work for the good of all.

Gyekye seeks to reconcile this view with individualism. People have basic needs for food, shelter, health, equality of opportunity, and liberty. The common good includes these things, which are essential to human beings as human beings. He argues that the common good cannot oppose the individual good of any member of society; individual and common goods depend on each other.

Individuals, while responsible for the welfare of all, are also responsible for their own welfare. They cannot rely on the group for all their needs and desires. They must seek the good on their own. Nevertheless, social good is something over and above individual goods. A good society contains happy people, but also exhibits other specifically collective virtues: harmony, peace, mutual concern, and solidarity.

6.2.1 Kwame Gyekye, *An Essay in African Philosophy: The Akan Conceptual Scheme*

The Concepts of Good and Evil

I shall begin with the Akan moral concepts of good (or goodness: *papa*) and evil (*bone*), which are fundamental in the moral thought and practice of any culture. In Akan thought goodness is not defined by reference to religious beliefs or supernatural beings. What is morally good is not that which is commanded by God or any spiritual being; what is right is not that which is pleasing to a spiritual being or in accordance with the will of such being. In the course of my field research none of my discussants referred to Onyame (God) or other spiritual entities in response to the questions "What is good?" "What is evil?" None of them held that an action was good or evil because Onyame had said so. On the contrary, the views that emerge in discussions of these questions reveal an undoubted conviction of a nonsupernaturalistic—a humanistic—origin of morality. Such views provide insight into the Akan conception of the criterion of moral value.

In Akan moral thought the sole criterion of goodness is the welfare or well-being of the community. Thus, in the course of my field research, the response I had to the question, "What do the Akan people mean by 'good' (or, goodness)?" invariably included a list of goods, that is, a list of deeds, habits, and patterns of behavior considered by the society as worthwhile because of their consequences for human well-being. The list of such goods invariably included: kindness (generosity), faithfulness (honesty, truthfulness), compassion, hospitality, that which brings peace, happiness, dignity, and respect and so on. The good comprehends all the above, which is to say that the good (*papa*) is explained in terms of the qualities of things (actions, behavioral patterns). Generosity, hospitality, justice are considered (kinds of) good. Generosity is a good thing, but it is not identical with goodness. Goodness (or the good), then, is considered in Akan moral thinking as a concept comprehending a number of acts, states, and patterns of behavior that exemplify certain characteristics.

On what grounds are some acts (etc.) considered good? The answer is simply that each of them is supposed (expected or known) to bring about or lead to social well-being. Within the framework of Akan social and humanistic ethics, what is morally good is generally that which promotes social welfare, solidarity, and harmony in human relationships. Moral value in the Akan system is determined in terms of its consequences for mankind and society. "Good" is thus used of actions that promote human interest. The good is identical with the welfare of the society, which is expected to include the welfare of the individual. This appears to be the meaning or definition of "good" in Akan ethics. It is clear that this definition does not at all refer to the will or commands of God. That which is good is decreed not by a

Source: Kwame Gyekye, *An Essay on African Philosophical Thought: The Akan Conceptual Scheme*. Cambridge: Cambridge University Press, 1987.

supernatural being as such, but by human beings within the framework of their experiences in living in society. So that even though an Akan maxim says I am doing the good (thing) so that my way to the world of spirits might not be blocked (*mereye papa na ankosi me nsaman kwan*), what constitutes the good is determined not by spiritual beings but by human beings.

Just as the good is that action or pattern of behavior which conduces to well-being and social harmony, so the evil (*bone*; that is, moral evil) is that which is considered detrimental to the well-being of humanity and society. The Akan concept of evil, like that of good, is definable entirely in terms of the needs of society. Thus, even though one often hears people say, "God does not like evil," yet what constitutes evil is determined by the members of the community, not by Onyame.

Akan ethics recognizes two categories of evil, *bone* and *musuo*, although *bone* is the usual word for evil. The first category, *bone*, which I shall call "ordinary," includes such evils as theft, adultery, lying, backbiting and so on. The other category of evil, *musuo*, I shall call "extraordinary." As described by a group of discussants, "*musuo* is an evil which is great and which brings suffering to the whole community, not just to the doer alone." Another discussant also stated that "the consequences of committing *musuo* affect the whole community." *Musuo* was also defined as an "uncommon evil," and as an "indelible evil," "remembered and referred to by people even many years after the death of the doer." Thus, *musuo* is generally considered to be a great, extraordinary moral evil; it is viewed by the community with particular abhorrence and revulsion because its commission is believed not only to bring shame to the whole community, but also, in the minds of many ordinary people, to invite the wrath of the supernatural powers....

Religion, Sanctions, and Moral Practice

...Akan thought conceives the human being as a social animal and society as a necessary condition for human existence.... This thought is expressed in the proverb

> When a man descends from heaven, he descends into human society.

But the person who descends into human society has desires, aims, interests, and will, and these have to be reconciled with those of others. An Akan proverb such as

> One man's curse is another man's fortune (lit.: What appears sour on one man's palate appears sweet on another man's palate)

indicates the view that the desires, interests, and passions of individual members of a society differ and may conflict with one another. One often hears the ordinary Akan say *obi mpe a obi pe*: "If one does not desire it, the other does"; that is, people have different desires, preferences, and choices. One Akan motif shows a "siamese" crocodile with two heads but a common stomach. The saying that goes with the symbol is that, although they have one stomach, the heads fight over the food that will eventually nourish both of them. The symbol ... points to the conflicts that result from the existence of individual desires and needs. The problem is how to minimize such conflicts and at the same time allow room for the realization of individual desires and needs. The need for a system of rules to regulate the conduct of individuals and, consequently, for social harmony and cooperative living, thus becomes urgent. It is this social need that gives rise to morality, according to Akan ethics.

Thus considerations for human well-being and for an ideal type of social relationships—both of which are generated by the basic existential conditions of man—these, not divine pronouncements, constitute the crucible in which Akan morality is fashioned. Whatever the moral virtues possessed by, or ascribed to, God and the other spiritual powers, it should now be clear that the compelling reason of the Akan for pursuing the good is not that it is pleasing to the supernatural beings or approved by them, but rather that it will lead to the attainment of human well-being. This *humanistic* moral outlook of the Akan is something that, I think, is worth being cherished, for its goal, from the moral point of view, is ultimate and, thus, self-justifying.

The Centrality of Character (*suban*) in Akan Ethics

Morality is generally concerned with right and wrong conduct or behavior and good and bad character. We speak not only of a moral act but also of a moral person; we speak not only of an honest or generous or vicious act but also of an honest or generous or vicious person. When a person is generally honest or generous the Akans judge him or her to be a good person, by which they mean that he or she has a good character (*owo suban papa*), and when the person is wicked or dishonest they judge him or her to be a bad person, that is, to have a bad character. It is on the basis of a person's conduct (deeds, *nneyee*) that the Akans judge one to be good or bad, to have good character or bad character. According to them, the character of a person is basic. The performance of good or bad acts depends on the state of one's character; inasmuch as good deeds reflect good character, character (*suban*) appears as the focal point of the ethical life. It is, in Akan moral thought, the crucial element in morality, for it profits a society little if its moral system is well articulated intellectually and the individuals in that system nevertheless have bad character and so do the wrong things. A well-articulated moral system does not necessarily produce good character; neither does knowledge of moral rules make one a good person or produce good character.

For the Akans, and perhaps also for the Greeks and Arabs, ethics has to do principally with character. Ethics, according to Akan thinkers, deals essentially with the quality of the individual's character. This is a remarkable assertion, for after all the ethical response, that is, the response or attitude to a moral rule, is an individual, private affair. All that a society can do regarding morality is to provide or impart moral knowledge to its members, making them aware of the moral rules that are applicable to all living in it. But granted this, it does not follow that the individual members of the society will lead lives in conformity with the moral rules. A man may know and may even accept a moral rule such as, say, it is wrong to seduce someone's wife. But he may fail to apply this rule to a particular situation. He is not able to effect the transition from knowledge to action. According to the Akan thinkers, to be able to act in accord with the moral rules of the society requires the possession of a good character (*suban*).

What, then, is character? How do Akan thinkers define character? The root of *suban* is *su* or *esu*, meaning nature, which might imply that character is associated with a person's nature, that character develops from a set of inborn traits.... Overall, one might conclude that character is a state or condition of the soul which "causes" it to perform its actions spontaneously and easily. This implies that the moral habits are innate, that we are born virtuous and are not responsible for our character. That impression, however, is false. Despite its etymological link with nature, the *suban* of a person is not wholly innate....

Akan thinkers define character in terms of habits, which originate from a person's deeds or actions; character is the configuration of (individual) acts. Thus, several of my discussants opined that "Character is your deeds"; "Character comes from your deeds." Moreover, sometimes the Akans use the sentence, "He has a bad character" when they want to say "He does bad things." The thought here is that moral virtues arise through habituation, which is consonant with the empirical orientation of Akan philosophy. This is, I think, the reason for the teaching of moral values embedded in proverbs and folktales to children in the process of their socialization; the moral instructions are meant to habituate them to moral virtues. If moral habits were thought to be acquired by nature or through birth it would be senseless to pursue moral instruction. But it is believed and expected that the narratives are one way by which children acquire and internalize moral virtues.

I hold the view that in general society presents us with a variety of modes of behavior. We see and are told what is good behavior and what is bad, what is praiseworthy and what is blameworthy. We are given a choice. To acquire virtue, a person must practice good deeds so that they become habitual. The newly acquired good habit must be strengthened by repetition. A single good deed may initiate further good deeds, and in this way virtue is acquired. Over time such an acquired virtue becomes a habit. This is the position of Akan philosophy, for this is what they mean by saying *aka ne ho*, "It is left (or has remained) with him," "It has become part of him," "It has become his habit." Such practice and performance emphasize the relevance and importance of action in the acquisition of virtue. To be just, for instance, one must first behave in a just manner. The emphasis placed by Akan thinkers on the influence of actions on character illustrates their conviction that one is in some sense responsible for the sort of person one is; the person is responsible for the state of his or her character. The unjust man may be held responsible for becoming unjust, because his character is the result of repeated voluntary acts of injustice. He had the choice between committing acts of injustice and refraining from such acts.

The emphasis on the relevance of actions for states of character is reflected in the way that abstract terms for "goodness," "virtue," are formed. The usual words for "goodness" in Akan are *yieye* and *papaye* (the latter also appears sometimes as *papa*). The last syllable of each word means to do or perform. Thus, the two words literally mean "good-doing" (that is, doing good).

This analysis of the Akan concept of character supports, as far as the Akan position goes, Mbiti's view that "the essence of African morality is that it is a morality of 'conduct' rather than a morality of 'being'... [A] person is what he is because of what he does, rather than that he does what he does because of what he is." This view is repeated by Bishop Sarpong: "For it would appear that for the Akan what a man is is less important than what a man does. To put it more concretely, a person is what he is because of his deeds. He does not perform those deeds because of what he is." The emphasis on deeds (*nneyee*) is appropriate, for it agrees with the Akan belief that a person is not born virtuous or vicious. The previously quoted proverb

> One is not born with a bad "head," but one takes it on the earth

implies, among other things, that a bad habit is not an inborn characteristic, but one that is acquired. The Akan position thus is that the original nature of human beings was morally neutral. If this were not the case, there would be no such thing as a moral person. The person's original moral neutrality later comes to be affected by actions, habits, responses to moral instruction, and so on. Consequently, what a person does or does not do is crucial to the formation of the character. A virtuous character is the result of the performance of virtuous acts....

... But then the question is: If a person is not born virtuous, how can he or she perform virtuous acts? The answer is through moral instruction, which in traditional Akan society was normally done by means of ethical proverbs and folktales. In this way the growing child and young adult become aware of what is a virtuous or vicious act and become virtuous by performing virtuous acts.

6.3 EAST AFRICAN ISLAMIC ETHICS

Both Islam and traditional African beliefs have shaped ethical thought in East Africa. Islam came to East Africa in the eighth century and spread along trade routes, meshing with traditional beliefs to yield a conceptual framework embedded in the Swahili language and culture. The key concept is *utu*, *humanity* or *goodness*, which, like the English word *humanity*, has descriptive and normative dimensions. Descriptively, it simply refers to the essence of human beings—what makes us *human*. Normatively, it refers to what makes us *humane*. The distinction, then, is between what we are and what we ought to be. These are associated, for humanity is the sphere of moral goodness; what we are determines what we ought to be. As beings that essentially think, decide, and act, furthermore, normativity itself is essential to us. To choose is to distinguish what ought to be done.

A number of traditional Swahili proverbs reveal aspects of *utu*. "A human being is *utu*," and "What defines a person is *utu*" is in one sense a tautology—what is essential to us is our humanity—but in another sense it expresses the thought that we are essentially moral beings. "*Utu* is action" stresses that humanity and morality are expressed in what we do. Those who violate moral norms are said to lack *utu*. That we are essentially rational and therefore moral beings implies that we deserve moral respect, and that we are equally deserving of moral respect. The moral view that emerges thus has much in common with that of Immanuel Kant in Western philosophy. *Utu* contrasts with *kitu*; according to another saying, "A human being is not a thing (*mtu si kitu*)." People must not be used, but must be respected as moral agents.

6.3.1 Kai Kresse, from *Philosophising in Mombasa*

Salim

Salim, of Baluchi family background and about thirty years old, explained that *utu* is very much based on *imani* (good faith, trust or religious belief). He reasoned this out in the following way. *Imani* could be seen as an inner guideline to treat people in a good and proper way. Nothing bad could result from *imani*, because *imani* itself was linked to and defined by the word of God (in the Qur'an). He specifically exemplified this by focusing on the treatment of other people, using the popular saying *mtu si kitu* (a human being is not a thing), which stresses that fellow human beings must never be treated as things. This position, he claimed, is already part of *imani*: acting out of good faith makes it impossible to treat a fellow human being like a thing. It can be seen that the two sayings *mtu ni utu* and *mtu si kitu* complement each other, stating the same principle in a positive and in a negative form. *Mtu si kitu* implies a warning against an instrumental orientation towards other people. *Mtu ni utu* is a positive reminder, pointing at the shared sphere of human beings, humanity, and thereby it implies a moral demand similar to the

Source: Kai Kresse, *Philosophising in Mombasa: Knowledge, Islam, and Intellectual Practice on the Swahili Coast*. London: Edinburgh University Press (www.eupublishing.com) for the International African Institute, 2007.

golden rule: treat others as you would have them treat you. *Imani*, then, as the source of good intention for any action performed, assures *utu* or compliance with *utu*. Concluding his explanation, Salim told me that *utu* would result in *heshima* (respect, honour). *Heshima* is obviously less a moral but rather a social category, signifying a publicly acknowledged social status that someone has, and implying a corresponding behaviour toward that person. To respect someone else (*kumheshimu mtu*) in the appropriate way and display this in the form appropriate to one's own status has been one of the ever-present tasks in Swahili social life (expressed in greetings, behaviour, language used, etc.). To prepare for this is one of the earliest tasks of childhood education, where the children are taught *adabu* (good manners). When a child (or an adult) has misbehaved, others may comment *hana adabu, yeye* (he/she has no manners).

In this particular discussion, I tried to obtain a better sense of the religious tones in Salim's explanation and about their implications. When asked about the religious significance of *imani* in his explanantion of *utu* and whether *utu* was an Islamic concept, Salim emphasised that *utu* was strongly connected to religion but not determined by it. The most important thing for him was that *utu* shows itself in all good deeds that are performed, irrespective of the actor's faith. Non-Muslims as well as Muslims are capable of doing good (having *utu*), and he agreed that it was possible, though surely not the rule, that a non-Muslim might display more *utu* than a Muslim. This stress on deeds rather than on religious identity for the qualification of an action as good, i.e., showing *utu*, is based on another popular saying which Salim mentioned at this stage: *utu ni vitendo* (goodness is deeds). This highlights the performative character of goodness: morality shows itself only in good deeds, not in good thoughts or talk alone, nor in high social status, wealth, descent or religious allegiance. However, religion can be taken as a guideline in order to perform good deeds, and in such a way the usage of *imani* above should be understood. From this, the relation between Islam and *utu* in general could be described as one of correspondence, not of consequence. It is not the Islamic doctrine as such which necessitates good deeds, but rather the good faith of an individual's intention when performing an action that makes the action a morally good one. Something performed out of good faith, treating others as fellow human beings and not as things, can be called a good action, displaying *utu*, regardless of the religious belief involved. Thus in Salim's explanation of *utu*, two different theoretical approaches can be identified: a morality of intention, as his last comments suggest, and a morality of performance, as the earlier emphasis on *kitendo* implies.

There was, however, one last question which I put to Salim: if not in the Qur'an, in God's word, where and by whom is the fundamental distinction between good and bad ultimately defined? But if it is defined in the Qur'an, is then the concept of *utu* not necessarily derived from it in the last instance, and is it thus an Islamic concept? This seemed difficult to answer, and Salim stuck with what he had stated before. It was true indeed, he said, that the ultimate reliable distinction between good and bad could only be found in the Qur'an as the only imaginable source of criteria for moral goodness. On the other hand, he insisted that *utu* was not a religious concept as such, while there was an overlap between *utu* and Islam.

Two Brothers

On another occasion, I asked two friends to explain *utu* to me. They were two brothers in their late twenties from an Arab family background and they highlighted two things initially. Firstly, they said that *utu* marks the equality of all people: *watu wote ni sawasawa* (all people are equal). Secondly, statements made about the *utu* of a person *(yeye ana utu*, i.e., he/she has *utu*) were positive acknowledgements, a declaration that the respective person was honourable (*yule ni mwungwana*). *Utu* was described as a kind of religious (or religiously originated) command of Islam, to respect others (*kuwaheshimu wengine*) and to treat them as human beings. People following this command would show their *utu*. They insisted that *utu* was equally applicable to people from all parts of the world, no matter what religion they adhered to. *Utu* was thus presented as a universal moral concept. Even though it was conceded that the specific rules of behaviour that counted as *utu*-like were determined from within the Swahili context, it was claimed that in principle *utu* was still applicable to people from other cultures and religions. To say that someone has *utu* is to highlight that person as reliable and trustworthy.

I then referred to the two possible layers of meaning and ways of understanding *utu* which are inherent in the saying *mtu ni utu*. I asked the brothers whether I was correct in thinking that *utu* can be understood descriptively, in regard to the totality of all human beings as living creatures, as well as normatively, referring to the quality of moral goodness, linked to the group of proven good moral actors. They said that both these levels exist, but it was emphasised that the second, moral, connotation dominates common usage of *utu*. In everyday life, the whole point of using the term is in regard to the moral order: advising people to behave better, or praising others for having done good and holding them up as an example to others. As one of the brothers pointed out very clearly, "There is no bad *utu*" (*hakuna utu mbaya*). If the first, descriptive, connotation prevailed, bad *utu* would be conceivable in everyday usage, but since the moral understanding dominates, it usually makes no sense to speak of bad *utu*.

In fact, it was stated, bad actions which grossly violated the principle of *utu* would relegate the doer from the realm of humanity (*utu*) to the sphere of animals, bestiality (*unyama*). Thus in popular discourse, people committing atrocities or gross evil are situated outside the human sphere and are referred to as animals (*wanyama*) rather than as human beings (*watu*). But this might not only be a dismissive label used out of contempt and disgust. Again, the principle of *vitendo* (agency, actions) can be applied: one could also say *unyama ni vitendo*. By committing such a gross violation of moral rules, the perpetrators *situate themselves* outside of humanity, beyond the community of mutual moral obligation.

Outside the moral sphere of humanity, there is only bestiality (*unyama*), the sphere of creatures deemed incapable of distinguishing good from bad. By contrast, human beings were endowed by God with the capacity to distinguish good and evil. From this point, it seems logical that the performance of bad actions indicates an earlier choice to do bad, i.e., an intention to violate the moral principles governing human life. At this point one can say that performers of evil have situated themselves outside the moral community of which they should have been part. Thus the issue of responsibility for one's own wrongdoing is touched upon. This might be crucial for a more detailed discussion of morality in popular (and also intellectual) discourse, since it establishes a link to the concept of freedom which again marks a difference between morality and custom.

My friends finally gave me two positive characterisations of *utu* as a moral concept, which I will call *utu* as command and *utu* as reward. As a moral command, all human beings are subject to *utu* in the same way. They are required to do good, i.e., to treat all other human beings with respect (*heshima*). Thus goodness would be expressed by their actions and be observable in actions that comply with the command. Another aspect of *utu* is highlighted when viewing it as reward or praise. Then it is the outcome of the compliance with the moral command that is referred to. *Utu* here marks the achievement of moral status, which is expressed in the praise *ana utu* (he/she has *utu*). Not all human beings earn this praise but only those who performed good deeds, who followed the "command of God" (*amri ya Mungu*), as one of my friends said, or, one could say, who followed *utu* as moral command. Thus it seems to be the notion of *vitendo* that links the two relevant levels highlighted in this discussion of *utu*. Good moral conduct in every performed action is firstly demanded, and secondly rewarded, by *utu*. And the moral praise also leads to social recognition, since, as I was told, an increase of respect (*heshima*) is the outcome. Both levels, of course, are also strongly linked to religion. It is God who demands morality and sets the standards for it, accessible for human beings via Prophet Muhammad and the Qur'an. Also, the moral reward, which is achieved by following God's word, ultimately secures a higher position, according to my friends, not only religiously, in the eyes of God, but also socially, in terms of respect and recognition....

Common Basics: *Utu* in the Dimension of Social Knowledge

Perhaps the most striking commonality in all these different elaborations of *utu* by young men of Kibokoni is the claim to its universality as a moral concept. *Utu* is not regarded as simply a local notion restricted to the Swahili context. On the contrary, it was continually and forcefully said that the Swahili model of *utu* is applicable to the evaluation of morality in human actions anywhere in the world. But still, this can be clarified some more. Here the characterisations so far given are summarised, before introducing and discussing further information on the popular social conception.

While making a case for a moral theory that transcends the Swahili context from which it is formulated, all the positions looked at so far have emphasised a link with religion, and particularly Islam. Religion, and God as an ultimate point of reference, are at the basis of this universalism. The moral equality of human creatures is secured by a God who created them as equal. And a universalist position is made possible by the fact that *utu* itself is a formal, abstract concept, referring to a moral quality (goodness) that can be recognised or assessed in any concrete action performed. People would argue that in every case, viewing the action in context, it is possible to say whether the action was a morally good one or not. The criteria for what is morally good then have to be part of the understanding of *utu* itself.

But this understanding seems already presumed as part of common knowledge in society: the criteria for a morally good action are not explicated, but the morally good way of acting is expected to be known or identified intuitively within the context of social action. Members of society are supposed to know what good moral behaviour is, and the only criteria that have been given so far, namely to act out of inner good faith and to respect everybody, seem to be regarded as ample guidelines for this. If this is correct, it seems as if serious moral conflict between opposed and even incompatible views that are all equally based on the sources of good faith and respect is not reckoned with. Does this mean that the moral qualities of *utu* are, after all, regarded as inherently culture-specific (goodness depending on the concrete specifics of the Swahili area), although the reported statements emphasise that *utu* applies to all human beings?

Summarising, the claim of *utu* as a valid moral concept for all human beings could be observed in all the collected statements. This seems based on the particularly human quality of knowing the distinction between good and evil, and the ability to orient one's actions accordingly. The moral equality of all human beings has also been stressed: goodness has firmly been linked to the performance of good actions, irrespective of the social or economic status of the actor. Finally, some differing but not exclusive bits of further information can be summarised from the three different explanations:

1. *Utu* has been characterised as mediating between an inner (possibly religiously inspired) motivating force for action, the *imani* (good faith) within the individual, and the subsequent outer sphere of social recognition expressed through *heshima* (respect). As such, the action-bound moral sphere can be understood to mediate between the personal and the social.
2. As a sign of moral equality among human beings, *utu* has been linked to a general command to show respect to everyone; as

a sign of acknowledgement of good deeds, *utu* has been characterised as a reward, to earn respect from everyone (having followed the command). This can be called a kind of moral circle of humanity from which each individual actor can expel himself at any time through ignoring or violating the moral demands; he will no longer belong to *utu* (humanity, the moral sphere) anymore, but consign himself to *unyama* (the sphere of bestiality).

3. Several different levels of *utu* are said to exist. This would mean that moral goodness is not understood rigidly as an absolute quality which is there or not, but is seen as a matter of degree (one can be more and less moral).

PART II

Philosophy of Mind and Self

CHAPTER 7

The Self in Indian Philosophy

"The light of man"

The central questions of philosophy—what there is, how we know it, and what we should do about it—require us to reflect on how minds relate to the world. Nowhere, however, is it more difficult to see how things hang together than in the philosophy of mind, the area of philosophy that asks about what we are. What is it to be a human being? Human beings have minds; we think, consider, doubt, know, see, fear, hope, and wonder. We also have bodies. That much is uncontroversial. But how do our minds relate to our bodies? Do we in addition have souls? Is any part of us capable of surviving death?

7.1 THE UPANISHADS ON A HIGHER SELF

The earliest philosophical texts in India, called Upanishads ("mystic teachings," from as early as 800 BCE), say yes. "Some say that when someone dies the person continues. Others deny this. What is the truth?" a teenager named Naciketas asks Yama, the God of Death, in the Katha Upanishad. The Upanishads articulate doctrines of a soul, a spiritual self that transcends the body and survives death.

Centuries later, Indian philosophy expands in what is known as the classical period (150–1800 CE) to include a wide variety of views about what it is to be a self or person. At one extreme lies the position that one's true self is God, the supreme being—infinite, immortal, self-existent, self-aware, and intrinsically blissful. At the other lies the materialist theory that a person is just a material thing, a living human body that disintegrates at death. ("Consciousness is an adventitious attribute of the body, like the intoxicating power of fermented grain," says the Charvaka philosopher.) A rich diversity of opinion and argument marks this area of Indian thought.

The Upanishads repeatedly affirm that each of us is in some way a soul (in Sanskrit, *atman*), a spiritual self that has, or is capable of, awareness superior to our everyday consciousness. This, our "higher self," is continuous with our "surface consciousness" or "waking consciousness"—or continuous, at least, with the *best* of our everyday awareness. What is that? Our *self*-awareness—our awareness of being aware. Reflecting on our own consciousness and nature brings us closer to our higher self.

We can discover the reality of the soul in meditation by practicing yoga. Something in us survives death and is either reborn or reabsorbed into an absolute consciousness or self. The long-running classical Hindu systems of Vedanta, Samkhya, and Yoga center on belief in a hidden, true, or supreme self.

The mind, on these views, is distinct from the soul. The self thus has distinct parts. Psychological theories about these parts and their relationships are spread throughout the Upanishads, which contain several different pictures of a self's components. These stem from metaphysical views about the nature of a greater reality and the way one ought to relate to it. What are the parts of a self? The answer depends on what is supremely real and how it is known.

The Upanishads assert that at the height of a self's consciousness is a supreme being, termed *Brahman*. It is variously interpreted as the Absolute, the Ground of Being, or God. We can experience Brahman. Mystical discovery of Brahman lies at the end of a series of changes in experience. For example, we might be able to progress through a series of dream and deep-sleep states; we might be able to progress through a series of "bodies," ranging from a physical body to so-called "sheaths" or spiritual containers: one incorporating life and mind, one incorporating a "higher mind," and one, the final, most essential sheath, "made out of bliss."

Our feelings and thoughts are distinctively mental; they are contained in something other than our material frames. The *Katha Upanishad*, through the image of a chariot, arranges the parts of a self in a hierarchy from the body through the senses and mind to the self and then, finally, to a divine Person. Like the "sheath" psychology of the *Tattiriya Upanishad*, the image suggests that the self can separate from the body and even the mind, just as a charioteer may step up into a chariot and step down again. The self may be reincarnated in a different body and mind. It can also, through yogic practice, know itself as separate from its lower instruments, thus achieving *mukti*, "liberation" or "enlightenment."

7.1.1 From the *Brhadaranyaka Upanishad*

Now, when Yajnavalkya was going to enter upon another state, he said: "Maitreyi, I'm going away from this, my house, into the forest. Let me make a settlement between you and Katyayani (my other wife)."

Source: Translated by Max Müller. *Sacred Books of the East*, volume 15, part II, 1883. We have revised the translation for readability.

Maitreyi said: "My Lord, if the whole earth, full of wealth, belonged to me, tell me, would it make me immortal?"

"No, replied Yajnavalkya; you would live the life of rich people. But there's no hope of immortality by wealth."

And Maitreyi said: "What should I do with that which doesn't make me immortal? What you know of immortality, tell me."

Yajnavalkya replied: "You're truly dear to me; you speak dear words. Come, sit down, I'll explain it to you. Mark well what I say."

And he said: "Surely, a husband is not dear, that you may love the husband; but that you may love the Self [*atman*], therefore a husband is dear. Surely, a wife is not dear, that you may love the wife; but that you may love the self, therefore a wife is dear. Surely, sons are not dear, that you may love the sons; but that you may love the self, therefore sons are dear. Surely, wealth is not dear, that you may love wealth; but that you may love the self, therefore wealth is dear. Surely, the Brahman class is not dear, that you may love the Brahman class; but that you may love the self, therefore the Brahman class is dear. Surely, the worlds are not dear, that you may love the worlds; but that you may love the self, therefore the worlds are dear. Surely, creatures are not dear, that you may love the creatures; but that you may love the self, therefore are creatures dear. Surely, everything is not dear that you may love everything; but that you may love the self, therefore everything is dear. Surely, the self is to be seen, to be heard, to be perceived, to be marked, O Maitreyi! When we see, hear, perceive, and know the self, then all this is known.

"Whosoever looks for the Brahman class elsewhere than in the self was abandoned by the Brahman class. Whosoever looks for the worlds elsewhere than in the self was abandoned by the worlds. Whosoever looks for creatures elsewhere than in the self was abandoned by the creatures. Whosoever looks for anything elsewhere than in the self was abandoned by everything. This Brahman class, these worlds, these creatures, this everything—all is that self."

Janaka Vaideha said: "When the sun has set, O Yajnavalkya, and the moon has set, and the fire is gone out, and the sound hushed, what is then the light of man?"

Yajnavalkya said: "The self indeed is his light; for, having the self alone as his light, man sits, moves about, does his work, and returns."

Janaka Vaideha said: "Who is that self?"

Yajnavalkya replied: "He who is within the heart, surrounded by the senses, the person of light, consisting of knowledge. He, remaining the same, wanders along the two worlds, as if thinking, as if moving. During sleep, in dreams, he transcends this world and all that is perishable.

"On being born, that person, taking on his body, becomes united with all evils; when he departs and dies, he leaves all evils behind.

"And there are two states for that person: the one here in this world, the other in the other world—and, as a third, intermediate state, the state of sleep. When in that intermediate state, he sees both those states together, the one here in this world and the other in the other world. Now, whatever his admission to the other world may be, having gained that admission, he sees both the evils and the blessings. And when he falls asleep, then after having taken away with him the material from the whole world, destroying and building it up again, he dreams by his own light. In that state the person is self-illuminated.

"There are no real chariots in that state—no horses, no roads—but he himself creates chariots, horses, and roads. There are no blessings there—no happiness, no joys—but he himself creates blessings, happiness, and joys. There are no bodies of water there—no lakes, no rivers—but he himself creates bodies of water, lakes, and rivers. He indeed is the maker.

"On this there are these verses:

After having subdued by sleep
all that belongs to the body,
he, not asleep himself,
looks down upon the sleeping senses.

Having assumed light,
he goes again to his place,

the golden person,
the lonely bird.

Guarding with his life the lower nest,
the immortal moves away from the nest;
that immortal one goes wherever he likes,
the golden person,
the lonely bird.

Going up and down in his dream,
the god makes manifold shapes for himself,
either rejoicing together with women,
or laughing with his friends,
or seeing terrible sights.
People may see his playground,
but himself no one ever sees.

"An ocean is that one seer without any duality; this is the Brahma world, O King." Thus did Yajnavalkya teach him. This is his highest goal; this is his highest success; this is his highest world; this is his highest bliss. All other creatures live on a small portion of that bliss.

7.1.2 From the *Chandogya Upanishad*

All this is Brahman. Let a man meditate on the visible world as beginning, ending, and breathing in it—Brahman. Now, man is a creature of will. What his will is in this world, so will he be when he has departed this life. Let him therefore have this will and belief:

The intelligent, whose body is spirit, whose form is light, whose thoughts are true, whose nature is like ether, omnipresent and invisible, from whom all works, all desires, all sweet odors and tastes proceed; he who embraces all this, who never speaks, and is never surprised.

He is my self within the heart, smaller than a corn of rice, smaller than a corn of barley, smaller than a mustard seed, smaller than a canary seed or the kernel of a canary seed. He also is my self within the heart, greater than the earth, greater than the sky, greater than heaven, greater than all these worlds.

He from whom all works, all desires, all sweet odors and tastes proceed, who embraces all this, who never speaks and who is never surprised, he, my self within the heart, is that Brahman. When I shall have departed from hence, I shall obtain him. He who has this faith has no doubt.

Those whose conduct has been good will quickly attain some good birth. But those whose conduct has been evil will quickly attain an evil birth: the birth of a dog or a hog. Hence let a man take care!...

Prajapati said: "The self which is free from sin, free from old age, from death and grief, from hunger and thirst, which desires nothing but what it ought to desire, and imagines nothing but what it ought to imagine—that's what we must search out, that's what we must try to understand. He who has searched out that self and understands it obtains all worlds and all desires."

The gods and demons both heard these words, and said: "Well, let us search for that self by which, if one has searched it out, all worlds and all desires are obtained."

Thus saying Indra went from the gods, Virochana from the demons, and both, without having communicated with each other, approached Pragapati, holding fuel in their hands,

Source: Translated by Max Müller. *Sacred Books of the East*, volume 15, part I, 1883. We have revised the translation for readability.

as is the custom for pupils approaching their master. They dwelt there as pupils for thirty-two years. Then Pragapati asked them: "Why have you both dwelt here?"

They replied: "A saying of yours is being repeated: 'the self which is free from sin, free from old age, from death and grief, from hunger and thirst, which desires nothing but what it ought to desire, and imagines nothing but what it ought to imagine, that's what we must search out, that's what we must try to understand. He who has searched out that Self and understands it obtains all worlds and all desires.' Now we both have dwelt here because we wish for that self."

Pragapati said to them: "The person seen in the eye—that is the self. This is what I have said. That is the immortal, the fearless—that is Brahman."

They asked: "Sir, he who is perceived in the water, and he who is perceived in a mirror—who is he?"

He replied: "He himself indeed is seen in all these."

7.1.3 From the *Mundaka Upanishad*

Manifest, near, moving in the cave of the heart is the great Being. In it is centered everything you know as moving, breathing, and blinking—as being and not-being, as adorable, as the best—that is beyond the understanding of creatures.

That which is brilliant, smaller than small, that on which the worlds are founded, and their inhabitants—that is the indestructible Brahman. That is the breath, speech, mind; that is the true; that is the immortal. That is our target. Hit it, my friend!

Having taken the Upanishad as the bow, as the great weapon, let him place on it an arrow sharpened by yoga! Then, having drawn it with a thought directed to what is, hit the mark, my friend—that which is the Indestructible!

Om is the bow; the self is the arrow. Brahman is its aim. It is to be hit by a man who is not thoughtless; and then, as the arrow becomes one with the target, he will become one with Brahman.

In him the heaven, the earth, and the sky are woven, the mind also with all the senses. Know him alone as the self, and leave off other words! He is the bridge of the Immortal.

He moves about, becoming manifold within the heart, where the arteries meet like spokes fastened to the hub of a wheel. Meditate on the self as *Om*! Hail to you, that you may cross beyond the sea of darkness!

He who understands all and who knows all, he to whom all this glory in the world belongs—the self—is placed in the ether, in the heavenly city of Brahman. He assumes the nature of mind and becomes the guide of the body of the senses. He subsists in food, in close proximity to the heart. The wise who understand this behold the Immortal which shines forth full of bliss.

The fetter of the heart is broken, all doubts are solved, and all his works and their effects perish when He who is high and low, cause and effect, has been seen.

In the highest golden sheath there is Brahman, without passions and without parts. That is pure,

---

Source: Translated by Max Müller. *Sacred Books of the East*, volume 15, part II, 1883. We have revised the translation for readability.

the light of lights; that is what they know, who know the self.

The sun does not shine there, nor do the moon and the stars. Nor does the lightning, much less this fire. When he shines, everything shines after him; his light lights the whole world.

That immortal Brahman is before, behind, right, and left. It has gone forth below and above; Brahman alone is the whole world, the best.

Two birds, inseparable friends, cling to the same tree. One of them eats the sweet fruit, the other looks on without eating.

On the same tree man sits grieving, immersed, bewildered by his own impotence. But when he sees the other contented and knows his glory, then his grief passes away.

When the seer sees the brilliant maker and lord of the world as the person who has his source in Brahman, then he is wise, and, shaking off good and evil, he reaches the highest oneness, free from passions.

For he is the life shining forth in all beings, and he who understands this becomes truly wise, not a talker only. He revels in the self; he delights in the self. And, having performed his works, he rests, firmly established in Brahman—the best of those who know Brahman.

By truthfulness, austerity [*tapas*, an early word for yoga], right knowledge, and abstinence must that self be gained; the self whom spotless anchorites gain is pure, and like a light within the body.

The true prevails, not the untrue; by the true the path is laid out, the way of the gods, on which the old sages, satisfied in their desires, trod, where there is that highest place of the True One.

That true Brahman shines forth grand, divine, inconceivable, smaller than small; it is far beyond what is far and yet near here; it is hidden in the cave of the heart among those who see it even here.

He is not apprehended by the eye, nor by speech, nor by the other senses, nor by austerity or good works. When a man's nature has become purified by the serene light of knowledge, then he sees him, meditating on him as without parts.

That subtle self is to be known by thought, there where breath has entered fivefold; for every thought of men is interwoven with the senses, and when thought is purified, then the self arises.

Whatever state a man whose nature is purified imagines, he conquers; whatever desires he desires for himself or for others, he obtains. Therefore let every man who desires happiness honor the man who knows the self.

7.1.4 From the *Svetasvatara Upanishad*

If a wise man holds his body with chest, neck, and head even and turns his senses with the mind towards the heart, he will then, in the boat of Brahman, cross all the torrents of fear. Compressing his breathings, let him who has subdued all motions breathe forth through the nose with gentle breath. Let the wise man without fail restrain his mind—that chariot yoked with vicious horses. Let him perform his exercises in a place that is level, pure, free from pebbles, fire, and

Source: Translated by Max Müller. *Sacred Books of the East*, volume 15, part II, 1883. We have revised the translation for readability.

dust—delightful by its sounds, its water, and bowers, not painful to the eye, and full of shelters and caves.

When yoga is being performed, the forms that come first, producing apparitions in Brahman, are those of misty smoke, sun, fire, wind, fireflies, lightning, and a crystal moon. When, as earth, water, light, heat, and ether arise, the fivefold quality of yoga takes place, then there is no longer illness, old age, or pain for him who has obtained a body produced by the fire of yoga.

The first results of yoga they call lightness, healthiness, steadiness, a good complexion, an easy pronunciation, a sweet odor, and slight excretions. As a mirror tarnished by dust shines bright again after it has been cleaned, so is the one incarnate person satisfied and free from grief after he has seen the real nature of the self.

And when by means of the real nature of his self he sees, as by a lamp, the real nature of Brahman, then, having known the unborn, eternal god who is beyond all natures, he is freed from all fetters.

He indeed is the god who pervades all regions: he is the first-born and he is in the womb. He has been born and he will be born. He stands behind all persons, looking everywhere.

The god who is in the fire, the god who is in the water, the god who has entered into the whole world, the god who is in plants, the god who is in trees—adoration be to that god, adoration!

7.1.5 From the *Maitri Upanishad*

The Valakhilyas said to Prajapati Kratu: "O saint, if you thus show the greatness of that self, then who is that other different one, also called self, who, really overcome by bright and dark fruits of action, enters on a good or bad birth? Downward or upward is his course, and overcome by the pairs [distinctions between hot and cold, pleasure and pain, etc.] he roams about."

Prajapati Kratu replied: "There is indeed that other different one, called the elemental self, who, overcome by bright and dark fruits of action, enters on a good or bad birth: Downward or upward is his course, and overcome by the pairs he roams about. And this is his explanation: The five senses are called *bhuta*, as are the five gross elements. Then the aggregate of all these is called the body. And lastly he who dwells in the body is called the elemental self. Thus his immortal self is like a drop of water on a lotus leaf, and he himself is overcome by the qualities of nature. Then, because he is thus overcome, he becomes bewildered, and, because he is bewildered, he sees not the creator, the holy Lord, abiding within himself. Carried along by the waves of the qualities, darkened in his imaginations, unstable, fickle, crippled, full of desires, vacillating, he enters into belief, believing 'I am he,' 'this is mine;' he binds his self by his self, as a bird with a net, and overcome afterwards by the fruits of what he has done, he enters on a good and bad birth; downward or upward is his course, and overcome by the pairs he roams about."

They asked: "Which is it?" And he answered them:

Source: Translated by Max Müller. *Sacred Books of the East*, volume 15, part II, 1883. We have revised the translation for readability.

"This also has elsewhere been said: He who acts is the elemental self; he who causes to act by means of the organs is the inner man. Now, as even a ball of iron, heated by fire and hammered by smiths, assumes different forms, the elemental Self, pervaded by the inner man and hammered by the qualities, becomes manifold. And the four tribes (mammals, birds, reptiles, and fish), the fourteen worlds, with all the number of beings, multiplied eighty-four times—all this appears as manifoldness. And those multiplied things are impelled by the conscious being as the wheel by the potter. And as when the ball of iron is hammered, the fire is not overcome, so the inner man is not overcome, but the elemental self is overcome, because it has united itself with the elements.

"And it has been said elsewhere: Bewilderment, fear, grief, sleep, sloth, carelessness, decay, sorrow, hunger, thirst, niggardliness, wrath, infidelity, ignorance, envy, cruelty, folly, shamelessness, meanness, pride, changeability—these are the results of the quality of darkness (*tamas*). Inward thirst, fondness, passion, covetousness, unkindness, love, hatred, deceit, jealousy, vain restlessness, fickleness, unstableness, emulation, greed, patronizing of friends, family pride, aversion to disagreeable objects, devotion to agreeable objects, whispering, prodigality—these are the results of the quality of passion (*rajas*). By these he is filled, by these he is overcome, and therefore this elemental self assumes manifold forms—yes, manifold forms."

7.1.6 From the *Taittiriya Upanishad*

Hari, *Om*! May it (Brahman) protect us both! May it enjoy us both! May we acquire strength together! May our knowledge become bright! May we never quarrel! Peace! peace! peace!

He who knows the Brahman attains the highest—Brahman. On this the following verse is recorded: "He who knows Brahman, which is, which is conscious, which is without end, as hidden in the depth of the heart, in the highest ether—he enjoys all blessings, at one with the omniscient Brahman."

Different from [the body], which consists of the essence of food, is the other, the inner self, which consists of breath. The inner self fills the body. It also has the shape of man. Like the human shape of the body is the human shape of the inner self.

There is also an inner self that consists of mind. "He who knows the bliss of Brahman, from whence all speech, with the mind, turns away, unable to reach it—he never fears!" The embodied self of what consists of mind is the same as that of what consists of breath.

Different from what consists of mind is another inner self, which consists of understanding. "If a man knows understanding as Brahman, and if he does not swerve from it, he leaves all evils behind in the body and attains all his wishes." The embodied self of what consists of understanding is the same as that of what consists of mind.

Different from what consists of understanding is still another inner self, which consists of bliss.

Source: Translated by Max Müller. *Sacred Books of the East*, volume 15, part II, 1883. We have revised the translation for readability.

7.1.7 From the *Katha Upanishad*

The context: The god of Death, Yama, has granted Nachiketas three wishes.

Nachiketas said: "There is doubt, when a man is dead—some saying, he is; others, he is not. This I should like to know."

Death said: "On this point even the gods used to doubt; it is not easy to understand. That subject is subtle. Choose another wish, O Nachiketas; do not press me. Let me off that request."

Nachiketas said: "On this point even the gods have doubted, and, indeed, you, Death, have declared it to be hard to understand. Another teacher like you is not to be found. Surely no other wish is like this."

Death said: "Choose sons and grandsons who shall live a hundred years, herds of cattle, elephants, gold, and horses. Choose the wide abode of the earth, and live as many harvests as you desire. If you can think of any wish equal to that, choose wealth, and long life. Be king, Nachiketas, of the entire earth. I will satisfy all your desires. Whatever desires are difficult to attain among mortals, ask for them according to your wish. These fair maidens with their chariots and musical instruments—such are indeed not to be obtained by men—be waited on by them. I will give them to you. But do not ask me about dying."

Nachiketas said: "These things last only till tomorrow, O Death, for they wear out the vigor of all the senses. Even the whole of life is short. Keep your horses; keep dance and song for yourself. No man can be made happy by wealth. Shall we possess wealth, when we see you? Shall we live, as long as you rule? My wish is the only thing I want.

"What mortal, slowly decaying here below, and knowing, after having approached them, the freedom from decay enjoyed by the immortals, would delight in a long life after he has pondered on the pleasures which arise from beauty and love?

"No, that on which there is this doubt, O Death, tell us what there is in the great Hereafter. Nachiketas does not choose another wish but that which enters into the hidden world."

[Death replied:] "Know the self to be sitting in the chariot, the body to be the chariot, the intellect the charioteer, and the mind the reins.

"The senses they call the horses, the objects of the senses their roads. When he (the Highest Self) is in union with the body, the senses, and the mind, then wise people call him the Enjoyer.

"He who has no understanding and whose mind is never firmly held, his senses are unmanageable, like vicious horses of a charioteer.

"But he who has understanding and whose mind is always firmly held, his senses are under control, like good horses of a charioteer.

"He who has no understanding, who is unmindful and always impure, never reaches that place, but enters into the round of births.

"But he who has understanding, who is mindful and always pure, reaches indeed that place from whence he is not born again.

"But he who has understanding for his charioteer and who holds the reins of the mind, he reaches the end of his journey, and that is the highest place of Vishnu.

"Beyond the senses there are the objects, beyond the objects there is the mind, beyond

Source: Translated by Max Müller. *Sacred Books of the East*, volume 15, part II, 1883. We have revised the translation for readability.

the mind there is the intellect, the 'great self' is beyond the intellect.

"Beyond the great there is the 'undeveloped', beyond the undeveloped there is the 'person' (*purusha*). Beyond the person there is nothing—this is the goal, the highest road.

"That self is hidden in all beings and does not shine forth, but it is seen by subtle seers through their sharp and subtle intellect.

"A wise man should keep down speech and mind; he should keep them within the self which is knowledge; he should keep knowledge within the self which is the great; and he should keep that (the great) within the self which is the quiet."

7.2 VEDANTA, SAMKHYA, AND YOGA: HINDU PATHS TO SELF-AWARENESS

The term *Hindu* gained prominence in India only after invasions from the west, first by Muslims and then by European traders and colonialists. Several ancient and classical philosophies are mainstays for the umbrella religion that we call Hinduism today. They include Vedanta but also Samkhya, Yoga, and Mimamsa ("Exegesis").

Vedanta derives its name from an epithet for the Upanishads. *Vedanta* literally means the end of the Veda; the Upanishads were appended to the Veda, an even older collection of verses or mantras viewed as sacred and revealed. Advaita Vedanta is a classical Vedanta school that upholds the identity, or nonduality (*advaita*), between the individual consciousness and the supreme self, or Brahman, who is all-inclusive. Advaita Vedanta, that is, holds that the soul is identical with God. Shankara (c. 700) is Advaita's most famous advocate. Other Vedanta schools hold views on the self and the person that combine some aspects of the Advaita theory of consciousness with realist views about the everyday person and the body.

All these schools belong to the period of classical philosophy, defined by the prominence of philosophical argument. The Upanishads and early epic literature contain relatively few arguments, most of which are implicit. Classical Indian philosophy, however, centers on argument. It stands to earlier texts roughly as Socrates and Plato stand to pre-Socratic philosophers in ancient Greece.

Of Vedanta schools, we shall take up only Advaita in this section. According to the Advaita of Shankara, the world of everyday experience is a dream—an illusion, a projection (*maya*) of a single self. Except for our self-awareness, our everyday sense of ourselves as having a body, as belonging to a family, as having property and occupying a social position, is a false identification with aspects of a world that is a cosmic illusion.

Even in our everyday state, our self-awareness—the gateway to Brahman—is "self-illumining," transparent to itself. We do not really have bodies; we do not really own property; we do not really hold jobs. But we really are conscious beings. Our awareness that we are aware is not an illusion. Unlike our perception of external objects, we are conscious of ourselves in a direct, unmediated way. Meditation (*jnana* yoga) develops our self-awareness, allowing it to extend to the higher self—to the soul and, thus, to God.

Samkhya ("analysis") proposes careful understanding of nature (*prakrti*), including not only her organizing principles but also her subtle presentations of herself as thoughts and emotions. Through such understanding we come to recognize that we are distinct from our body and our mind. Samkhya sees mental occurrences as parts of nature and, more surprisingly, as external to the true person. Nature thus includes mind and thought. But it excludes consciousness, the awareness of thoughts and emotions, which is a separate substance—the real person. What am I, really? Samkhya answers: *consciousness.* External events, thoughts, feelings, and so on all happen to *me.* I am, essentially, the inner person, the consciousness to whom they happen. I am thus transcendent. I am not merely a part of nature. I lie beyond it.

Western philosophers concerned with criteria of personal identity debate the question of nature versus nurture: How much of our personality, of who we are, is inborn, and how much is developed, acquired, or shaped by our environment? Indian philosophers bring an interesting perspective to this problem. An individual may have distinct or multiple personalities during different stages of life; there are of course dramatic cases of people with multiple identities. According to Samkhya, all personality is a mask. We have various personas that the true person identifies with for a time. In doing that, the true person thereby alienates himself (or herself or itself: the true person has no gender) from its native state of self-absorption and bliss. Moreover, the true person does not create these masks. Nature presents them to us. By understanding them, we can more easily discover ourselves as the transcendent beings we are. Because we are really transcendent, inner selves, we are not really shaped by nature; indeed, we can think of nature as serving us. In essence, we are free.

Yoga as a school of philosophy has much in common with Samkhya; both view nature as real but as alien to the true individuals we are. Both describe true individuals similarly. But Samkhya lays out principles of nature in a comprehensive worldview. Yoga is thoroughly practical. It is the philosophy of the *Yogasutra*, a handbook on yogic practices—postures, breath control, meditation exercises, and so on. By practicing yoga ("self-discipline"), we can discover a higher self. Postures and breath control remove physical distractions. Meditation removes mental distractions; we concentrate to achieve complete mental silence. We thereby find or achieve a transcendent consciousness. What is that transcendent consciousness, that true self, like? It is just what Samkhya philosophers hold it to be. But note that philosophers of other persuasions (Vedantins and Buddhists, for example) advocate the yogic practices of the *Yogasutra* while conceiving of the self differently.

There is a puzzle about who practices yoga. It is evidently not the true self. How can a transcendent, free self be deluded, falsely identifying itself with mind and body? Later advocates struggle with these questions, sometimes inventing rather ingenious answers. The *Samkhya-Karika* draws out and celebrates what might seem to be an odd ramification of the view: Nature makes the effort, the text says at the end. This threatens to turn consciousness into a passive observer of a world completely foreign to it.

There are common themes among Advaita Vedanta, Samkhya, and Yoga. Who am I? What am I? All three answer that I am a higher consciousness than I might realize. Desire, will, and effort are extraneous to me. Not all Indian philosophers agree. Theistic Vedanta, Nyaya, and Mimamsa all defend what they consider our commonsense conception of ourselves as having bodies, having thoughts and desires, and generally being part of nature.

Advaita, Samkhya, and Yoga all hold that consciousness is "self-illumining." There is a kind of consciousness—self-consciousness—that is aware of itself. It is its own subject and object. But it is not divided, as that formulation might suggest; it is "nondual." It is unified, immediate, and intrinsic, an awareness of awareness. It is nonconceptual and independent of all thought, even thought about it. It is also supposed to be independent of the material world, even of the brain. It does not imply possession of a concept of self or the ability to use such a concept in thinking about oneself. Indeed, the connection goes the other way; our concept of ourselves presupposes our awareness of awareness.

The expression "self-illumining consciousness" first occurs in the *Brhadaranyaka Upanishad* (circa 800 BCE), in a passage about transformations of consciousness in dreams and mystic trances. A person first dreams by her "own light." She then becomes "self-illuminated." Light illumines itself. A lamp lets us see objects other than itself. But it also lets us see it; we do not need another lamp to see it.

The Advaitin Shankara says explicitly that some consciousness is "nondual," *advaita*. It knows itself just by being what it is. It knows itself immediately, nonreflectively, in a nonintellectual, nonobservational manner. Shankara appears to have in mind a consciousness whose content is itself. It is a "state" consciousness: It is not a consciousness of anything. It is, to put the point grammatically, not a transitive consciousness but a, so to say, intransitive one. Alternatively, we could say that this is a consciousness of itself.

Shankara argues for the existence of the soul. What we experience could turn out to be an illusion. We might, for example, see a rope as a snake and jump back from it. All objects of experience could turn out to be something other than what they seem to be. But self-consciousness is not like that. We might misidentify an object lit by a lamp, but we cannot misidentify its light.

What makes a perceptual illusion possible? A perception presents an object as qualified by a property. But the object might not really have that property. Thus, we see something as a snake; looking more closely, when it does not move, we see that it is only a rope.

Self-illumining consciousness is not like that. It is not awareness of itself as having a property. So, it cannot be nonveridical or mistaken. It thus differs from all perception and indeed from all thinking (remembering, inferring, understanding what someone has said, etc.) All those kinds of cognition are consciousness of something as being such and such. Self-illuming consciousness is not. Thus self-illumining consciousness is self-authenticating. To itself, self-illumining consciousness stands self-revealed.

7.2.1 Shankara, from the *Brahmasutra Commentary*

It is a matter not requiring any proof that the object and the subject whose respective spheres are the notion of the "thou" (the non-ego) and the "ego," and which are opposed to each other as much as darkness and light are, cannot be identified. All the less can their respective attributes be identified. Hence it follows that it is wrong to superimpose upon the subject—whose self is intelligence and which has for its sphere the notion of the ego—the object whose sphere is the notion of the non-ego and the attributes of the object, and, vice versa, to superimpose the subject and the attributes of the subject on the object. In spite of this it is on the part of man a natural procedure—which has its cause in wrong knowledge—not to distinguish the two entities (object and subject) and their respective attributes, although they are absolutely distinct, but to superimpose upon each the characteristic nature and the attributes of the other and thus, coupling the real and the unreal, to make use of expressions such as "That am I," "That is mine."—But what have we to understand by the term "superimposition?"—The apparent presentation, in the form of remembrance, to consciousness of something previously observed, in some other thing....

With reference again to that kind of activity which is founded on the Veda (sacrifices and the like), it is true indeed that the reflecting man who is qualified to enter on it does so not without knowing that the self has a relation to another world; yet that qualification does not depend on the knowledge, derivable from the Vedanta texts, of the true nature of the self as free from all wants, raised above the distinctions of the Brahmana and Kshattriya classes and so on, transcending transmigratory existence. For such knowledge is useless and even contradictory to the claim (on the part of sacrificers, etc. to perform certain actions and enjoy their fruits). And before such knowledge of the self has arisen, the Vedic texts continue in their operation, to have for their object that which is dependent on nescience. For such texts as the following, "A Brahmana is to sacrifice," are operative only on the supposition that on the self are superimposed particular conditions such as caste, stage of life, age, outward circumstances, and so on. That by superimposition we have to understand the notion of something in some other thing we have already explained. (The superimposition of the non-self will be understood more definitely from the following examples.) Extrapersonal attributes are superimposed on the self, if a man considers himself sound and entire, or the contrary, as long as his wife, children, and so on are sound and entire or not. Attributes of the body are superimposed on the self, if a man thinks of himself (his self) as stout, lean, fair, as standing, walking, or jumping. Attributes of the sense organs, if he thinks "I am mute, or deaf, or one-eyed, or blind." Attributes of the internal organ when he considers himself subject to desire, intention, doubt, determination, and so on. Thus the producer of the notion of the ego (i.e., the internal organ) is superimposed on the interior self, which, in reality, is the witness of all the modifications of the internal organ, and vice versa the interior self, which is the witness of everything, is superimposed on the internal organ, the senses, and so on. In this way there goes on this natural beginning- and

Source: Shankara, *Brahmasutrabhasya (The Brahmasutra Commentary)*, in *The Vedanta Sutras of Badarayana.* Translated by Georg Thibaut. *Sacred Books of the East*, 1890.

endless superimposition, which appears in the form of wrong conception, is the cause of individual souls appearing as agents and enjoyers (of the results of their actions), and is observed by everyone.

With a view to freeing one's self from that wrong notion which is the cause of all evil and attaining thereby the knowledge of the absolute unity of the self, the study of the Vedanta texts is begun.

7.2.2 Ishvarakrishna, from *Verses on the Analysis of Nature (Samkhya-karika)*

I. Because of the torment of the threefold suffering, (there arises) the desire to know the means of counteracting it. If (it is said that) this (desire—i.e., inquiry) is useless because perceptible (means of removal are available), (we say) no, since perceptible means are not final or abiding.

II. The revealed (or scriptural) means of removing the torment are like the perceptible (i.e., ultimately ineffective), for they are connected with impurity, destruction and excess; a superior method, different from both, is the (discriminative) knowledge of the manifest, the unmanifest and the knowing one (or knower—i.e., *purusa*).

III. Primordial nature is uncreated. The seven—the great one, etc.—are both created and creative. The sixteen are created. *Purusa* is neither created nor creative.

IV. The attainment of reliable knowledge is based on determining the means of correct knowledge. The accepted means of correct knowledge are three because (these three) comprehend all means of correct knowledge. These three means (are as follows): (a) perception, (b) inference, (c) reliable authority.

V. Perception is the selective ascertainment of particular sense-objects. Inference, which is of three kinds, depends upon a characteristic mark and that which bears the mark. Reliable authority is trustworthy verbal testimony.

VI. The understanding of things beyond the senses is by means of (or from) inference by analogy. That which is beyond even inference, is established by means of reliable authority.

VII. (Perception may be impossible due to the following): (a) because something is too far away; (b) because something is too close; (c) because of an injured sense-organ; (d) because of inattention; (e) because of being exceedingly subtle; (f) because of intervention (of an object between an organ and the object to be perceived); (g) because of suppression (i.e., seeing the sun but no planets); (h) because of intermixture with what is similar.

VIII. The non-perception (of *prakrti*) is because of its subtlety—not because of its non-existence. Its apprehension is because of (or by means of) its effect. Its effect—the great one—is different from yet similar to *prakrti*.

IX. The effect exists (before the operation of cause) (a) because of the non-productivity of non-being; (b) because of the need for an (appropriate) material cause; (c) because of the impossibility of all things coming from all things; (d) because something can only produce what it is capable of producing; (e) because of the nature of the cause (or, because the effect is non-different from the cause)....

XI. (Both) the manifest and unmanifest are (a) (characterized by the) three *gunas*

Source: Gerald Larson, *Classical Samkhya*. Delhi: Motilal Banarsidass, 1979.

("constituents" or "strands"); (b) undiscriminated; (c) objective; (d) general; (e) non-conscious; (f) productive; the *purusa* is the opposite of them, although similar.

XII. The *gunas*, whose natures are pleasure, pain, and indifference, (serve to) manifest, activate, and limit. They successively dominate, support, activate, and interact with one another.

XIII. *Sattva* is buoyant and shining; *rajas* is stimulating and moving; *tamas* is heavy and enveloping. They function for the sake of the *purusa* like a lamp.

XIV. Lack of discrimination, etc., is established because of (the manifest) having the three *gunas* and because of the absence (of the *gunas*) in the opposite of that (i.e., in the *purusa*). The unmanifest is likewise established because of the *guna*-nature in the cause of the effect (or because the effect has the same qualities as the cause)....

XVIII. The plurality of *purusas* is established, (a) because of the diversity of births, deaths, and faculties; (b) because of actions or functions (that take place) at different times; (c) and because of differences in the proportions of the three *gunas* (in different entities).

XIX. And, therefore, because (the *purusa*) (is) the opposite (of the unmanifest), it is established that *purusa* is (a) a witness; (b) possessed of isolation or freedom; (c) indifferent; (d) a spectator; (e) and inactive.

XX. Because of the proximity (or association) of the two—i.e., *prakrti* and *purusa*—the unconscious one appears as if characterized by consciousness. Similarly, the indifferent one appears as if characterized by activity, because of the activities of the three *gunas*.

XXI. The proximity (or association) of the two, which is like that of a blind man and a lame man, is for the purpose of seeing the *pradhana* [*prakrti*] and for the purpose of the isolation of the *purusa*. From this (association) creation proceeds.

XXII. From *prakrti* (emerges) the great one; from that (comes) self-awareness; from that (comes) the group of sixteen. Moreover, from five of the sixteen (come) the five gross elements.

XXIII. The *buddhi* ("will" or "intellect") is (characterized by) ascertainment or determination. Virtue, knowledge, non-attachment, and possession of power are its *sattvika* form. Its *tamasa* form is the opposite (of these four).

7.2.3 From the *Yoga Sutras of Patanjali*

1.1. Now instruction in yoga.

1.2. Yoga is the stilling of fluctuations of thought and emotion (*citta*).

1.3. Then the seer (the conscious being, *purusa*) rests in its true form.

1.4. At other times, fluctuations are identified with.

1.5. Fluctuations are of five types, and are detrimental or non-detrimental (to the practices of yoga).

1.6. The five are knowledge sources (and knowledge), the opposite, thought and imagination, sleep (and dreaming), and memory.

1.7. The knowledge sources (along with the veridical awarenesses to which they give rise) are perception, inference, and testimony (including scriptural tradition).

1.8. The opposite to the knowledge sources amounts to misapprehension indicating that something is what it is not.

Source: *The Yoga Sutras of Patanjali.* Translated by Stephen H. Phillips.

1.9. Thought and imagination (*vikalpa*, the third item on the list of five), which are devoid of real objects, are dependent on words and concepts.

1.10. Sleep (along with dreaming) comprises the mental fluctuation whose object is a stream of ideas about things not present.

1.11. Memory is not letting experienced objects escape.

1.12. Restriction of them (of all five types of fluctuation) is accomplished through practice and disinterestedness.

1.13. Practice is effort to hold fast the restriction.

1.14. Effort becomes firmly established when it is put forth for a long time continuously.

1.15. Disinterestedness is the consciousness of being in control (of appetites), on the part of someone who has no thirst for objects directly perceived or reported.

1.16. Superior to that is (the absolute disinterestedness of) lack of desire for (manifest or unmanifest) phenomena (*guna*, "qualities") because of perception of the *purusa* ("true person").

1.17. *Samadhi* ("mystic trance" or "mystic accomplishment") has two forms, one of which is supported by wisdom in accordance with reasoning, discrimination, bliss, and sense of identity ("I-am-ness").

1.18. The other, in which only mental dispositions (*samskara*) remain, is preceded by effort to hold steady ideas intent on contentment.

1.33. Calming illumination of the mind (*citta*) is furthered through practicing (or, enlivening), towards objects pleasant, painful, virtuous, and full of vice, (respectively the balancing attitudes of) friendship, compassion, gladness, and indifference.

1.34. Or, it (calming illumination, stilling of the *citta*) can be brought about by controlled exhalation and holding of the breath.

1.35. Or, (it arises from) the advent of sense-object-centered activity binding the sensuous mentality (*manas*).

1.36. Or, (it arises with) activity that is free from sorrow and luminous (such as concentration on the heart center or the center between the eyebrows).

1.37. Or, when the mind (*citta*) contemplates beings who have transcended passion.

1.38. Or, (another means is) the mind brought to knowledge of sleep and dreams.

1.39. Or, from meditation in accordance with (an individual's) proclivities.

1.41. The person whose mental fluctuations have become attenuated achieves "yogic balance," with respect to things subjective, sensational, and objective, like a polished jewel that takes on the color of that on which it lies.

1.43. The type of "yogic balance," called "beyond the rational," occurs after the memory has been purified, shining in pure awareness of whatever object, devoid of self-consciousness, as it were.

1.45. Content can be subtler and subtler until it is the "unmanifest" (i.e., nature undifferentiated).

1.46. All these (stages and types of mental balance) are called *samadhi* "with seed."

1.47. After becoming expert in non-discursive mental balance and *samadhi*, the spiritual opens its light.

2.3. Afflictions are spiritual ignorance, I-identification, liking, disliking, and the proclivity to remain in one's own form (or, clinging to life).

2.4. Spiritual ignorance is the field for the others (to flourish) in degrees from dormancy and attenuatedness to suppression and expression outright.

2.5. To be spiritually ignorant is to mistake the non-eternal, impure, painful, and non-self for the eternal, pure, delightful, and true self.

2.6. I-identification is the seeming-one-and-the-same on the part of the distinct powers of the seer (the conscious being, *purusa*) and the seeing (nature, *prakrti*).

2.7. Liking follows pleasure.

2.8. Disliking follows pain.

2.9. Proclivity to remain in one's own form (clinging to life) is sustained by its own relishing, being self-perpetuating even for the learned.

2.10. Subtle (though they be in their disturbances), these afflictions can be banished by countermeasures (swimming upstream creating counterflow).

2.11. These detrimental fluctuations can be banished through meditation.

2.12. (Action-inducing) karmic latencies, which are to be experienced in the current or a future birth, are rooted in these afflictions.

2.13. So long as the root endures, its fruit will endure, the (triple) fruit, namely, of birth, life, and enjoyment.

2.14. These three bring joy or suffering according to moral merit or lack thereof (in accumulated karmic latencies).

2.15. And because of conflicting fluctuations of qualities, there is suffering in change, in anxious, feverish states of mind, and in mental dispositions (*samskara*). Thus the person of discriminating judgment sees all as suffering.

2.16. Future suffering is to be banished.

2.17. That which is to be banished stands caused by a conjunction of the seer (the conscious being) and that to be seen (nature).

2.18. What is to be seen (i.e., nature) is characterized by the (three qualities or strands of) (a) intelligence, (b) activity, and (c) stability or inertia (*sattva*, *rajas*, and *tamas*); it includes the gross elements and the sense organs and has as its raison dêtre enjoyment for, or liberation of, the conscious being.

2.19. The (three) qualities (of which nature is comprised) are expressed in distinct stages, that is to say, stages where predominate: (a) individuals, (b) general forms, (c) subtle forms, and (d) the trans-subtle.

2.20. The seer (the conscious being), although pure (i.e., although pure consciousness), appears to see through thoughts and ideas.

2.21. Only for the sake of the seer is the seen in its essence.

2.22. Although destroyed (for the liberated) yogin whose purpose is accomplished, nature is not destroyed for others (who are not liberated), because she is common to everyone.

2.23. The conjunction between the powers of phenomena and the powers of their controller (the conscious being) is caused by perception of (the two's) identity.

2.24. Spiritual ignorance is its cause (i.e., the reason the conjunction endures).

2.25. When spiritual ignorance is no longer, the conjunction is no longer. This is the relinquishment, the "aloneness" (*kaivalya*, i.e., the highest good) of the seer (the conscious being).

2.26. Unbroken practice of discriminative discernment is the way to that relinquishment.

2.27. For such a yogin, sevenfold wisdom and insight are the boundary of his attainment.

2.28. By practice of the "limbs of yoga" impurity is attenuated. Cognition is illuminated up to discriminative discernment.

2.29. Ethical restraints, personal constraints, *asanas*, breath-control, withdrawal of the senses from their objects, (and three stages of meditation) *dharana* (concentration in movement), *dhyana* (meditation proper), and *samadhi* are the eight "limbs of yoga."

2.30. The restraints (*yama*) are nonharmfulness (non-injury, *ahimsa*), truthfulness, non-stealing, sexual restraint, and non-possessiveness.

2.31. These practiced universally irrespective of station and circumstance of time and place constitute the "great vow."

2.32. The personal constraints are cleanliness, contentment, asceticism, self-study (in the light of a sacred text), and opening to the Lord (or, meditation on the Lord).

3.1. Concentration (in movement) is binding the *citta* down to the spot (of movement).

3.2. Of the three (stages of meditation), "meditation" (proper, *dhyana*) is a single ideational focus.

3.3. "Mystic accomplishment," *samadhi*, is illumination of an object as object only, bereft, as it were, of its being anything other than object of consciousness.

3.4. The three together are called "conscious identification."

3.5. Through its mastery comes the light of wisdom and insight.

3.49. The yogin whose awareness is restricted to perception of the difference between (the strand of nature called) intelligence (*sattva*) and the conscious being achieves mastery over all states of (inner) being and knowledge of it all as well.

3.50. Through disinterest in that achievement, too, arises "aloneness" (*kaivalya*) in the attenuation of the seeds of defects.

3.51. On being called by divinities, a yogin should not let the attention give rise to pride or attachment, since that could lead again to unwanted consequences.

3.52. From *samyama* (self-projecting concentration) on moments (the units of time) and their succession (in the flow of fluctuations of *citta*), comes cognition born of discrimination (of the conscious being from nature).

3.53. From that comes understanding by differentiation of each thing though identical with another with respect to type, characteristics, and place.

3.54. The cognition born of discrimination carries to the further shore with everything as its object in every fashion and non-sequentially.

3.55. When the intelligence (strand, i.e., *sattva*) and the conscious being are equal in purity, "aloneness" (*kaivalya*) ensues.

4.7. Karma is neither good nor bad that belongs to the yogin. For others, it is of three types (good, bad, or a mix).

4.8. "Mental dispositions (across births, *vasana*)," manifest just according to the ripening (in good or bad deeds as well as in moral payback) that results from the (moral) types of karma.

4.13. Particulars are manifest or subtle. They are of the nature (of combinations) of the strands (the three *gunas*).

4.14. The truth or particularity of a thing is due to a unique transformation (of nature, a unique combination of *gunas*).

4.15. Since with regard to one and the same thing, *citta* differs (on different occasions of perception, or from the perspectives of two different perceivers), the two (*citta* and objects) have a distinct mode of being.

4.16. And (to exist) a thing does not depend on a single mind or awareness (*citta*). When it is not cognized by that mind, what then would it be?

4.17. Something remains known or unknown to a particular mind, according to its conditioning or expectation.

4.18. The fluctuations of mind are always known to their lord, the conscious being, the *purusa*, inasmuch as the *purusa* is unchanging.

4.19. That (the *citta*) is not self-luminous, because it is something to be perceived.

4.20. And there is no possibility of (*citta*) cognizing both (objects and itself) at the same time.

4.21. It would be absurd to assume that different *citta* is required to grasp *citta*, because of the impossible regress of one cognition after another being required (in order that any be known). This would also mean memory's (impossibility because of) confusion.

4.22. Self-awareness—consciousness of self and of cognition—occurs when the *citta*, (now) unfluctuating, assumes the form of that (the conscious being).

4.23. *Citta* that is conditioned both by awareness of the seer and that to be seen is capable of cognizing anything.

4.24. Although the *citta* is moved by countless deep mental dispositions, it works by unifying (diversities) for the sake of the other (the conscious being).

4.25. For one who sees the distinction (between nature and the conscious being), the projection of sense of self in nature ceases.

4.26. Then the *citta*, settling into deep discrimination, is carried on towards (reflecting) the aloneness (of the conscious being).

4.27. In the gaps (or weaknesses) of discrimination, other ideational presentations (i.e., distractions) may arise by force of (unexhausted) mental dispositions.

4.28. These are to be banished, like the afflictions, in the ways explained.

4.29. The *samadhi* called Cloud of Dharma occurs for a person who has no interest even in elevated awareness, whose awareness is in every way directed to discrimination (of the conscious being from nature).

4.30. Thence afflictions and karma cease.

4.31. Then, since awareness is unlimited when parted from coverings and impurities, what remains to be known is trivial.

4.32. Thence the completion of processes of transformation on the part of the strands (*gunas*), their purpose fulfilled.

4.33. Process, which is relative to the units of time, is apprehensible at the end of a transformation.

4.34. Aloneness (*kaivalya*, the highest good) entails the reversal of the course of the strands or qualities of nature (*gunas*), now empty of meaning and value for the conscious being. Or, it may be understood as the power of consciousness returned and established in its own true self.

7.3 INDIAN BUDDHISM: NO-SELF, BUNDLE SELF, AND IMPERMANENCE

The Buddha (c. 500 BCE) taught that the supreme goal of life is *nirvana*, an "extinction" or "blowing out" of suffering and desire and an awakening to what is most real. In Sanskrit, the word *buddha* literally means "awakened." The Buddha, Siddhartha Gautama, was a historical person. But he did not write anything. We are left to reconstruct his teachings from his disciples' reports.

Almost all Buddhists see the Four Noble Truths as the heart of the Buddha's message: (1) Life is suffering. (2) Desire, craving, or clinging is the cause of suffering. (3) Nirvana extinguishes craving and hence suffering. (4) The path to nirvana is the Eightfold Noble Path. Accompanying the Four Noble Truths are several further core doctrines, notably, that there is no soul or self (*anatman*—no soul), that what we call the self is really just a bundle (*skandhas*), and that everything is impermanent. These positions underpin the possibility of enlightenment.

The doctrine that there is no soul or self contradicts Vedanta, the generally accepted philosophy in the sixth century BCE Ganges valley where the Buddha preached. Vedanta asserts a "great self," *atman*. But we should not exaggerate the difference. The Buddha teaches that we must avoid false identification with the body and the mind. Advaita recognizes a transcendent self similarly prone to false identification.

"No-self" is supposed to guide a mystic practice. It helps us avoid identifying with elements we commonly take to be ourselves—the body, thoughts, desires, and emotions. It thus helps us eliminate desire. Enlightenment is *nirvana*, an "extinguishing" of selfish desire, where something, or perhaps Nothing, indescribably wonderful is awakened and set free.

The Questions of King Milinda presents the Buddhist monk Nagasena debating King Milinda (in Greek, Menander), who ruled from 160 to 135 BCE in Sagala, an affluent and beautiful city with a mixed Greek and Indian population in what would today be northern Pakistan. Menander was a popular ruler of a sizable kingdom; Plutarch, the famous Greek historian, wrote,

> Menander was a king noted for justice who enjoyed such popularity with his subjects that upon his death, which took place in camp, diverse cities contended for the possession of his ashes. The dispute was settled by the representatives of the different cities agreeing to divide the relics, and then erecting separate monuments to his memory.

The debate concerns the nature of objects and the nature of the self. The mind in both cases creates a false image of unity. A chariot has no essence; it is just a collection of parts. The same is true of us. Concepts of ourselves are convenient fictions. Indeed, the Buddhist often maintains that all concepts are convenient fictions reflecting no underlying reality.

7.3.1 From *Questions to King Milinda*

The Chariot

And King Milinda asked the monk Nagasena: "How is Your Reverence known, and what is your name, sir?"

"As Nagasena I am known, O Great King, and as Nagasena do my fellow monks habitually address me. But although parents give a name such as Nagasena, nevertheless this word 'Nagasena' is just a denomination, a designation, a conceptual term, a temporary appellation, a mere name. There is no real person here to be apprehended."

But King Milinda explained: "Now listen, you 500 Greeks and 80,000 monks, this Nagasena tells me that he is not a real person! How can I be expected to agree with that!" And to Nagasena he said: "If, Most Reverend Nagasena, no person can be apprehended in reality, who then, I ask you, gives you what you need by way of robes, food, lodging, and medicines? Who is it that guards morality, practises meditation, and realizes the [four] paths and their fruits and thereafter Nirvana? Who is it that commits the five deadly sins—that kills living beings, takes what is not given, commits sexual misconduct, tell lies, drinks intoxicants? For, if there were no person, there could be no merit and no demerit; no doer of meritorious or demeritorious deeds, and no agent behind them; no fruit of good and evil deeds; and no reward or punishment for them. If someone should kill you, O Venerable Nagasena, he would not kill a real teacher, or instructor, or ordained monk! You just told me that your fellow religious habitually address you as 'Nagasena.' Then what is this 'Nagasena'? Are perhaps the hairs of the head 'Nagasena'?"

"No, Great King!"

"Or perhaps the nails, teeth, skin, muscles, sinews, bones, marrow, kidneys, heart, liver, serous membranes, spleen, lungs, intestines, mesentery, stomach, excrement, the bile, phlegm, pus, blood, grease, fat, tears, sweat, spittle, snot, fluid of the joints, urine, or the brain in the skull—are they this 'Nagasena'?"

"No, Great King!"

"Or is 'Nagasena' a form, or feelings, or perceptions, or impulses, or consciousness?"

Source: *Questions to King Milinda* (*Milindapanha*), from *Buddhism in Translations*. Translated by Henry Clarke Warren. Cambridge, MA: Harvard University Press, 1896. Revisions have been made for readability.

"No, Great King!"

"Then is it the combination of form, feelings, perceptions, impulses, and consciousness?"

"No, Great King!"

"Then is it outside the combination of form, feelings, perceptions, impulses, and consciousness?"

"No, Great King!"

"Then, ask as I may, I can discover no Nagasena at all. This 'Nagasena' is just a mere sound, but who is the real Nagasena? Your Reverence has told a lie, has spoken a falsehood! There is really no Nagasena!"

Thereupon, the Venerable Nagasena said to King Milinda: "As a king you have been brought up in great refinement and you avoid roughness of any kind. If you would walk at midday on this hot, burning, and sandy ground, then your feet would have to tread on the rough and gritty gravel and pebbles, and they would hurt you, your body would get tired, your mind impaired, and your awareness of your body would be associated with pain. How then did you come—on foot or on a mount?"

"I did not come, sir, on foot, but on a chariot."

"If you have come on a chariot, then please explain to me what a chariot is. Is the pole the chariot?"

"No, Reverend Sir!"

"Is then the axle the chariot?"

"No, Reverend Sir!"

"Is it then the wheels, or the framework, or the flagstaff, or the yoke, or the reins, or the goadstick?"

"No, Reverend Sir!"

"Then is it the combination of poke, axle, wheels, framework, flagstaff, yoke, reins, and goad which is the 'chariot'?"

"No, Reverend Sir!"

"Then is this 'chariot' outside the combination of poke, axle, wheels, framework, flagstaff, yoke, reins and goad?"

"No, Reverend Sir!"

"Then, ask as I may, I can discover no chariot at all. This 'chariot' is just a mere sound. But what is the real chariot? Your Majesty has told a lie, has spoken a falsehood! There is really no chariot! Your Majesty is the greatest king in the whole of India. Of whom then are you afraid that you do not speak the truth?" And he exclaimed: "Now listen, you 500 Greeks and 80,000 monks, this King Milinda tells me that he has come on a chariot. But when asked to explain to me what a chariot is, he cannot establish its existence. How can one possibly approve of that?"

The 500 Greeks thereupon applauded the Venerable Nagasena and said to King Milinda: "Now let Your Majesty get out of that if you can!"

But King Milinda said to Nagasena: "I have not, Nagasena, spoken a falsehood. For it is in dependence on the pole, the axle, the wheels, the framework, the flagstaff, etc., that there takes place this denomination 'chariot,' this designation, this conceptual term, a current appellation and a mere name."

"Your Majesty has spoken well about the chariot. It is just so with me. In dependence on the thirty-two parts of the body and the five *skandhas*, there takes place this denomination 'Nagasena,' this designation, this conceptual term, a current appellation and a mere name. In ultimate realtiy, however, this person cannot be apprehended. And this has been said by our sister Vajira when she was face to face with the Lord Buddha:

"Where all constituent parts are present, the word 'chariot' is applied. So, likewise, where the *skandhas* are, the term 'being' commonly is used."

"It is wonderful, Nagasena, it is astonishing, Nagasena! Most brilliantly have these questions been answered! Were the Lord Buddha himself here, He would approve what you have said. Well spoken, Nagasena! Well spoken!"

Personal Identity and Rebirth

The king asked: "When someone is reborn, Venerable Nagasena, is he the same as the one who just died, or is he another?"

The elder replied: "He is neither the same nor another."

"Give me an illustration!"

"What do you think, Great King? When you were a tiny infant, newly born and quite soft, were you then the same as the one who is now grown up?"

"No, that infant was one; I, now grown up, am another."

"If that is so, then, Great King, you have had no mother, no father, no reading, no schooling! Do we then take it that there is one mother for the embryo in the first stage, another for the second stage, another for the third, another for the fourth, another for the baby, another for the grown-up man? Is the schoolboy one person and the one who has finished school another? Does one commit a crime, but the hands and feet of another are cut off?"

"Certainly not! But what would you say, Reverend Sir, to all that?"

The elder replied: "I was neither the tiny infant, newly born and quite soft, nor am I now the grown-up man; but all these are comprised in one unit depending on this very body."

"Give me a simile!"

"If a man were to light a lamp, could it give light throughout the whole night?"

"Yes, it could."

"Is now the flame which burns in the first watch of the night the same as the one which burns in the second?"

"It is not the same."

"Or is the flame which burns in the second watch the same as the one which burns in the last one?"

"It is not the same."

"Do we then take it that there is one lamp in the first watch of the night, another in the second, and another again in the third?"

"No, it is just because the light of the lamp shines throughout the night."

"Even so must we understand the collocation of a series of successive *dharmas*. At rebirth one *dharma* arises while another stops; but the two processes take place almost simultaneously (i.e., they are continous). Therefore, the first act of consciousness in the new existence is neither the same as the last act of consciousness in the previous existence, nor is it another."

"Give me another simile!"

"Milk, once the milking is done, turns after some time into curds; from curds it turns into fresh butter; and from fresh butter into ghee. Would it now be correct to say that the milk is the same thing as the curds, or the fresh butter, or the ghee?"

"No, it would not. But they have been produced because of it."

"Just so must be understood the collocation of a series of successive *dharmas*."

7.4 EXEGESIS, LOGIC, AND MATERIALISM: THE EVERYDAY SELF

Classical Indian philosophy asks what a self is, what its distinguishing marks are, and how it relates to external objects. How, for example, are perception and purposive action, which are crucial to human knowledge and accomplishment, possible? Three schools that take "deflationary" positions on these concerns, defending common sense, are Mimamsa, Nyaya, and Charvaka.

Mimamsa, "Exegesis," is a major player in classical debates of all periods. Its most famous advocates were separated by just one generation: Kumarila (c. 670) and his renegade pupil, Prabhakara (c. 700). They turn first to Vedic literature but also try to follow common sense. Traditionally, Exegetes are most interested in questions of *dharma*, "duty" or "right practice." They understand this as the performance of certain rituals and, by extension, as one's entire conduct in life. We incur particular duties from our age, sex, and social position. Mimamsakas see human actions and reactions as governed by laws that maintain cosmic order. A person's *karma* (in Sanskrit, *karman*; in Pali, *kamma*)—actions and dispositions to act—reverberate throughout the moral rhythms of the universe. Understanding *dharma*, the universe's moral backbone, enables a person to develop the very best *karma* and thus to stand in right relation with the world as a whole.

What is *karma*? The concept is pan-Indian; it is not restricted to Exegete philosophy. It includes a psychological thesis and a thesis of moral cosmology. Psychologically, any action creates a tendency—a habit, if you like—to repeat it. Thus our *karma*—our dispositions, formed by our previous acts—determine much of our lives. Virtue is its own reward. Vice is its own punishment.

According to the moral cosmology, actions have external consequences that invariably embrace a moral dimension. There is moral payback. What goes around comes around. You get what you deserve, if not in this life then in a future lifetime. Fortunately, by performing actions in accordance with duty, *dharma*, "the right way to live," we can develop good dispositions, securing virtue and status in this lifetime and in lifetimes to come.

We cannot review in all its rich detail the reflection of Exegetes on the nature of a self. But note the task they shoulder. They must spell out what a self is—a self in the precise sense of a person who can follow *dharma*, accrue karmic dispositions, and be reborn in a position and status according to moral law. The theory of a self that captures all this must also conform to everyday usages. Exegetes are ingenious at bringing linguistic evidence to bear on issues. A self is as much a doer as a knower. Dave as a self is a lot more than one who experiences: Dave is an agent. Awareness itself is an act, not something that happens or simply occurs.

Exegetes contribute much to classical discussions about the self and its place in the world. The great Exegetes are great reasoners, particularly in refuting Buddhist positions and arguments. Excerpted here are passages from Kumarila, who has a protracted discussion of the self and the falsity of Buddhist contentions. Kumarila critiques the views of Dharmakirti as well as the ultra-deflationary views of the "Materialists."

The Charvaka "Materialist" school vehemently opposes any mystical, inflated notion of a self. The self is just the body. Charvaka philosophers make fun of the religious rituals championed by Mimamsakas. They mock beliefs in karma and rebirth. Others argue that phrases such as "my body" imply that there is something, a spiritual self that *has* a body. Charvaka philosophers claim that this is only metaphorical.

Charvakas are materialists; they believe that physical matter is the only reality. They are also radical empiricists, holding that we can know only what we perceive through our senses. They go so far as to hold that we cannot assert the validity of any inference we make about what we perceive. They thereby rule out all inferences to a self. We perceive only bodies.

By arguing that reasoning cannot establish anything—a position ridiculed by others as self-refuting!—the Charvakas attack ideas of an immortal self, rebirth, Brahman, and a mystical enlightenment. That is to say, by insisting that inference is unreliable, whatever the topic, these skeptics seek to strip away all excesses of belief beyond the simple facts of pleasure, pain, and the body. The self is the living body, which exists in an inexplicable material world.

Nyaya, commonly rendered "Logic," is a school of classical philosophy whose texts span almost 2,000 years. Nyaya philosophers include some of the greatest minds of classical India, with positions as wide-ranging as those of any classical system. Nyaya's primary focus is on knowledge, the means thereto, and right procedures in debate and critical inquiry. The school largely accepts the ontology (concerning what is real and interrelations among realities) of a sister school, "Atomism," Vaisheshika. Vaisheshika posits seven fundamental categories all of which are utilized in the analyses of Nyaya authors. About the self, Nyaya says that it is a substance and locus of psychological properties, a substance that endures while its properties change. Each of us is an immortal self reborn until liberation.

Vatsyayana (c. 400) in his commentary on the *Nyaya-sutra* (c. 150 CE) puts forth two arguments for endurance (against Buddhists) and the Nyaya conception of a self as distinct from the body (against Charvaka materialists): (1) We can see the same thing through different sense modalities, sight and touch, for example, and (2) We can recognize something perceived previously ("This is the same Jane Smith that I saw yesterday"), called recognition (*pratyabhijnana*).

The learned Nyaya philosopher of a much later day, Udayana (c. 1000), presents other arguments and refinements of these two: (a) properties exhibited by physical things are not signs of things conscious but of things unconscious; (b) since the precise material composition of the body is all the time changing, the body could not be that which remembers something the person experienced in the past; (c) an amputee remembers experiences mediated by the severed limb, and so the bodily part is not crucial to remembering; and (d) the causal link established through invariable positive and negative correlation between effort and action, on the one hand, and previous experience, on the other, requires postulation of previous experience whose subject is clearly not the body in the case of a newborn child's effort to get milk.

7.4.1 Kumarila, from *Notes on the Verses*

1–3. Authoritativeness and nonauthoritativeness,—virtue and vice and the effects thereof—the assumptions of the objects of injunctions, eulogistic passages, mantras, and names,—in short, the very existence of the various chapters (of the Sutra) based upon the various proofs,—the differentiation of the Question from the Reply, by means of distinctions in the style of expression,—the relation between actions and their results in this world, as well as beyond this world, etc.,—all these would be groundless (unreasonable), if ideas (or cognitions) were devoid of (corresponding) objects (in the external world).

Source: Kumarila, *Notes on the Verses* (*Slokavartika*). Translated by Ganganatha Jha. Calcutta: Bibliotheca India, 1908.

4. Therefore those who wish (to know) duty should examine the question of the existence or nonexistence of (external) objects, by means of proofs accepted (as such) by people,—for the sake of the (accomplishment of) actions.

5. [A Buddhist:] "Even if only the 'idea' (or sensation) is accepted (to be a real entity), all this (which is ordinarily known as the 'external world') may be explained as 'Samvriti Reality'; and as such it is useless for you to persist in holding the reality of the (external) object."...

8–9. Thus, then, the words "*samvriti*" and "*mithya*" (false) being synonymous [as the Buddhists suppose], the assumption (of "*Samvriti* [empirical] Reality") is only meant to hoodwink ordinary men, just like the word "*vaktrasava*" (mouth-wine) as used with reference to the saliva.... And so is also their theory of the assumed reality (of external objects); because there can be no assumption of the indivisible (consciousness which alone is real, for the Buddhist) in the void (i.e., the external world, whose existence is denied by the Buddhist).

10. Therefore it must be admitted that that which does not exist does not exist; and that which really exists is real, while all else is unreal; and therefore there can be no assumption of two kinds of reality.

11. There is a theory current (among the Buddhists) that the experiences (of heaven, etc.) are similar to the experiences of a dream; and it is for the refutation of this theory that we seek to prove the reality of external objects.

12–13. It cannot be for the mere pleasures of a dream that people engage in the performance of duty. Dream coming to a man spontaneously, during sleep, the learned would only lie down quietly, instead of performing sacrifices, etc., when desirous of obtaining real results. For these reasons, we must try our best, by arguments, to establish (the truth of) the conception of external objects (as realities).

14–16. (Among the Buddhists) the Yogacaras hold that "ideas" are without corresponding realities (in the external world); and those that hold the Madhyamika doctrine deny the reality of the idea also. In both of these theories, however, the denial of the external object is common....

17–18. The denial of the external object is of two kinds: One is based upon an examination of the object itself, and another is based upon reasoning. Of these, that which is based upon a consideration of the object may be laid aside for the present; that which is based upon reasoning, and as such is the root (of the theory), is what is here examined.

18–19. Here, too, the denial has been introduced in two ways: at first through inference, and then, after an examination of the applicability of sense-perception, through its inapplicability (to external objects)....

20–22. Objection: "(I). It has been declared that 'sense-perception' is only that which is produced by a contact (of the sense) with the particular object; but there is no relation between the objects and the sense organ, in reality; while, as for an assumed contact, this is present in a dream also; therefore it is not possible to have any such differentiation (in reality) as that into (cognitions) produced by such contact and (those) not so produced. (2) And again, it has been said that falsity is only of two kinds and not more; but here it is added that all (cognition) is false; why, then, should there be any such specification?"

23. "The cognition of a pole is false, because it is a cognition; because whatever is a cognition has always been found to be false,—f.i. the cognitions in a dream."...

24–25." ... And further, because of the acceptance (by the Buddhists) of the reality of the idea of the cognition itself, what is here denied is only the reality of the external objects of perception."...

34. It is only the denial of an object, comprehended by means of a faulty cognition, that can be correct. If there be a denial of every conception, then your own theory too cannot be established....

36. If the cognition of the subject and predicate as belonging to the speaker and

the hearer were without corresponding realities, then both of them would stand self-contradicted. [They could not communicate but they do.]

37. Nor would any differentiation be possible between the subject and the predicate. For these reasons the declaration of your conclusion cannot be right.

38. "But we do not admit of any such entity, as the character of having no real corresponding object; therefore it is not right to raise any questions as to the absence or otherwise of such entities."

39. If cognition is not a real entity, then in what way do you wish to explain it to us? Or how do you yourself comprehend it?

39–40. If it be urged that "we assume its existence and then seek to prove it," then (we reply), how can there be an assumption of something that does not exist? And even if it is assumed, it comes (by the mere fact of this assumption) to be an entity.

7.4.2 Madhava, from *Compendium of Philosophy*

THE CHARVAKA SYSTEM. [We have said in our preliminary invocation "Salutation to Shiva, the abode of eternal knowledge, the storehouse of supreme felicity,"] but how can we attribute to the Divine Being the giving of supreme felicity when such a notion has been utterly abolished by Charvaka, the crest gem of the atheistical school, the follower of the doctrine of Brahaspati? The efforts of Charvaka are indeed hard to be eradicated, for the majority of living beings hold by the current refrain—

While life is yours, live joyously;
None can escape Death's searching eye:
When once this frame of ours they burn,
How shall it e'er again return?

The mass of men, in accordance with the sastras of policy and enjoyment, considering wealth and desire the only ends of man, and denying the existence of any object belonging to a future world, are found to follow only the doctrine of Charvaka. Hence another name for that school is Lokayata,—a name well accordant with the thing signified [*loka* means "world"].

In this school the four elements, earth, etc., are the original principles; from these alone, when transformed into the body, intelligence is produced, just as the inebriating power is developed from the mixing of certain ingredients; and when these are destroyed, intelligence at once perishes also. They quote the *sruti* for this [*Brhad. Up.* ii. 4, 12], "Springing forth from these elements, itself solid knowledge, it is destroyed when they are destroyed,—after death no intelligence remains." Therefore the soul is only the body distinguished by the attribute of intelligence, since there is no evidence for any soul distinct from the body, as such cannot be proved, since this school holds that perception is the only source of knowledge and does not allow inference, etc.

The only end of man is enjoyment produced by sensual pleasures. Nor may you say that such cannot be called the end of man as they are always mixed with some kind of pain, because it is our wisdom to enjoy the pure pleasure as far as we can and to avoid the pain which inevitably accompanies it; just as the man who desires fish takes the fish with their scales and bones and, having taken

Source: Madhava, *Compendium of Philosophy (The Sarva-Darsana-Samgraha)*. Translated by E. B. Cowell and A. E. Gough. London: Kegan Paul, Trench, Trubner, 1914.

as many as he wants, desists; or just as the man who desires rice takes the rice, straw and all, and having taken as much as he wants, desists. It is not therefore for us, through a fear of pain, to reject the pleasure which our nature instinctively recognises as congenial. Men do not refrain from sowing rice because forsooth there are wild animals to devour it; nor do they refuse to set the cooking pots on the fire because forsooth there are beggars to pester us for a share of the contents. If anyone were so timid as to forsake a visible pleasure, he would indeed be foolish like a beast, as has been said by the poet—

> The pleasure which arises to men from contact with sensible objects, is to be relinquished as accompanied by pain,—such is the reasoning of fools. The berries of paddy, rich with the finest white grains, what man, seeking his true interest, would fling away because covered with husk and dust?

If you object that, if there be no such thing as happiness in a future world, then how should men of experienced wisdom engage in the *agnihotra* and other sacrifices, which can only be performed with great expenditure of money and bodily fatigue, your objection cannot be accepted as any proof to the contrary, since the *agnihotra*, etc., are only useful as means of livelihood, for the Veda is tainted by the three faults of untruth, self-contradiction, and tautology; then again the impostors who call themselves Vaidic pundits are mutually destructive, as the authority of the *jnana-khanda* [i.e., the Upanishads] is overthrown by those who maintain that of the *karma-khanda* [i.e., Vedic texts about ritual], while those who maintain the authority of the *jnana-khanda* reject that of the *karma-khanda*; and lastly, the three Vedas themselves are only the incoherent rhapsodies of knaves, and to this effect runs the popular saying—

> The *agnihotra*, the three Vedas, the ascetic's three staves, and smearing oneself with ashes,—Brahaspati says, these are but means of livelihood for those who have no manliness nor sense.

Hence it follows that there is no other hell than mundane pain produced by purely mundane causes, as thorns, etc.; the only Supreme is the earthly monarch, whose existence is proved by all the world's eyesight; and the only liberation is the dissolution of the body. By holding the doctrine that the soul is identical with the body, such phrases as "I am thin," "I am black," etc., are at once intelligible, as the attributes of thinness, etc., and self-consciousness will reside in the same subject [the body]; and the use of the phrase "my body" is metaphorical. All this has been thus summed up—

> In this school there are four elements, earth, water, fire, and air; And from these four elements alone is intelligence produced,—just like the intoxicating power from *kinva* [a type of grain], etc., mixed together; since in "I am fat," "I am lean," these attributes abide in the same subject; and since fatness, etc., reside only in the body, it alone is the soul and no other; and such phrases as "my body" are only significant metaphorically.

"Be it so," says the opponent; "your wish would be gained if inference, etc., had no force of proof; but then they have this force; else, if they had not, then how, on perceiving smoke, should the thoughts of the intelligent immediately proceed to fire; or why, on hearing another say, "There are fruits on the bank of the river," do those who desire fruit proceed at once to the shore?"

All this, however, is only the inflation of the world of fancy.

Those who maintain the authority of inference accept the sign or middle term [smoke] as the causer of knowledge, which middle term must be found in the minor [a mountain as inferential subject] and be itself invariably connected with the major [fire]. Now, this invariable connection must be a relation destitute of any condition accepted or disputed; and this connection does not possess its power of causing inference by virtue of its existence, as the eye, etc., are the cause of perception, but by virtue of its being known. What, then, is the means of this connection's being known?

"We will first show that it is not perception. Now, perception is held to be of two kinds, external and internal [i.e., as produced by the external senses or by the inner sense, mind]. The former is not the required means; for although it is possible that the actual contact of the senses and the object will produce the knowledge of the particular object thus brought in contact, yet, as there can never be such contact in the case of the past or the future, the universal proposition which was to embrace the invariable connection of the middle and major terms in every case becomes impossible to be known. Nor may you maintain that this knowledge of the universal proposition has the general class as its object, because if so, there might arise a doubt as to the existence of the invariable connection in this particular case [as, for instance, in this particular smoke as implying fire].

Nor is internal perception the means, since you cannot establish that the mind has any power to act independently towards an external object, since all allow that it is dependent on the external senses, as has been said by one of the Logicians, "The eye, etc., have their objects as described; but mind externally is dependent on the others."

Nor can inference be the means of the knowledge of the universal proposition, since in the case of this inference we should also require another inference to establish it, and so on, and hence would arise the fallacy of an *ad infinitum* retrogression.

Nor can testimony be the means thereof, since we may either allege in reply, in accordance with the Vaisesika doctrine of Kanada, that this is included in the topic of inference; or else we may hold that this fresh proof of testimony is unable to leap over the old barrier that stopped the progress of inference, since it depends itself on the recognition of a sign in the form of the language used in the child's presence by the old man; and, moreover, there is no more reason for our believing on another's word that smoke and fire are invariably connected than for our receiving the *ipse dixit* of Manu, etc. [which, of course, we Charvakas reject].

And again, if testimony were to be accepted as the only means of the knowledge of the universal proposition, then in the case of a man to whom the fact of the invariable connection between the middle and major terms had not been pointed out by another person, there could be no inference of one thing [as fire] on seeing another thing [as smoke]; hence, on your own showing, the whole topic of inference for oneself would have to end in mere idle words.

Then, again, comparison, etc., must be utterly rejected as the means of the knowledge of the universal proposition, since it is impossible that they can produce the knowledge of the unconditioned connection [i.e., the universal proposition], because their end is to produce the knowledge of quite another connection, viz., the relation of a name to something so named.

Again, this same absence of a condition [governing the connection, as wet fuel governs the connection between fire and smoke such that from mere fire smoke cannot be inferred], which has been given as the definition of an invariable connection [i.e., a universal proposition], can itself never be known; since it is impossible to establish that all conditions must be objects of perception; and therefore, although the absence of perceptible things may be itself perceptible, the absence of nonperceptible things must be itself nonperceptible; and thus, since we must here too have recourse to inference, etc., we cannot leap over the obstacle which has already been planted to bar them....

But since the knowledge of the condition must here precede the knowledge of the condition's absence, it is only when there is the knowledge of the condition that the knowledge of the universality of the proposition is possible, i.e., a knowledge in the form of such a connection between the middle term and major term as is distinguished by the absence of any such condition; and on the other hand, the knowledge of the condition depends upon the knowledge of the invariable connection. Thus we fasten on our opponents as with adamantine glue the thunderbolt-like fallacy of reasoning in a circle. Hence by the impossibility of knowing the universality of a proposition it becomes impossible to establish inference, etc.

The step which the mind takes from the knowledge of smoke, etc., to the knowledge of fire, etc., can be accounted for by its being based on a former perception or by its being an error; and that in some cases this step is justified by the result is accidental, just like the coincidence of effects observed in the employment of gems, charms, drugs, etc.

From this it follows that fate, etc., do not exist, since these can only be proved by inference. But an opponent will say, if you thus do not allow [the existence of unseen forces], the various phenomena of the world become destitute of any cause.

But we cannot accept this objection as valid, since these phenomena can all be produced spontaneously from the inherent nature of things. Thus it has been said—

> The fire is hot, the water cold, refreshing cool
> the breeze of morn. By whom came this variety?
> From their own nature was it born.

And all this has been also said by Brihaspati—

> "There is no heaven, no final liberation, nor any soul in another world; nor do the actions of the four castes, orders, etc., produce any real effect. The *agnihotra*, the three Vedas, the ascetic's three staves, and smearing one's self with ashes were made by nature as the livelihood of those destitute of knowledge and manliness.
>
> "If a beast slain in the *jyotishtoma* rite will itself go to heaven, why then does not the sacrificer forthwith offer his own father?
>
> "If the *shraddha* produces gratification to beings who are dead, then here, too, in the case of travelers when they start, it is needless to give provisions for the journey. If beings in heaven are gratified by our offering the *shraddha* here, then why not give the food down below to those who are standing on the housetop?
>
> "While life remains let a man live happily, let him feed on ghee even though he runs in debt. When once the body becomes ashes, how can it ever return?
>
> "If he who departs from the body goes to another world, how is it that he comes not back again, restless for love of his kindred?
>
> "Hence it is only as a means of livelihood that Brahmins have established here all these ceremonies for the dead—there is no other fruit anywhere. The three authors of the Vedas were buffoons, knaves, and demons.
>
> "All the well-known formulas of the pandits, *jarphari*, *tuphari*, etc., and all the obscene rites for the queen commanded in the *ashvamedha*, these were invented by buffoons; and so all the various kinds of presents to the priests, while the eating of flesh was similarly commanded by night-prowling demons."

Hence in kindness to the mass of living beings must we fly for refuge to the doctrine of Charvaka. Such is the pleasant consummation.

7.4.3 From the *Nyaya Sutra*

[*Commentary*:] Is the self a mere assemblage of body, sense-organs, mind, knowledge and feelings (of pleasure and pain)? Or, is it something different (from such an assemblage)?

Sutra 3.1.1: Because (the same knower) knows the same object through the visual as well as the tactual senses-organs.

Source: From *Nyaya Philosophy: Gautama's Nyaya-sutra and Vatsyayana's Bhashya.* Translated by Mrinalkanti Gangopadhyaya. Calcutta: Indian Studies, 1967.

Bhashya [*Commentary*]: An object is perceived by the visual sense. The same object is perceived by the tactual sense. (We have experiences in the form) "I am now perceiving through the tactual sense the same object which I previously perceived through the visual sense," and "I am now perceiving through the visual sense the same object which I previously perceived through the tactual sense." These two perceptions of the same object are apprehended (by a further internal perception in the form of recognition or *pratyabhijnana*) as having an identical agent and not as having for their agents the aggregate of body, etc., nor as having for their identical agent any sense-organ. Therefore, the self as a distinct category is that which is the knower of the same object through the visual as well as the tactual sense and which recognises these two perceptions that are obtained through different sense-organs which have an identical agent and which have for themselves an identical object.

But why are these two perceptions not apprehended as having for their identical agent the sense-organ? Because, each sense-organ is capable of apprehending its own appropriate object and hence, can have recognition of only that which is not due to any other sense-organ. No sense-organ can apprehend an object which is not appropriate for it.

But why are these two perceptions not apprehended as having for their agent the aggregate of body, etc.? Because the knower, which is one and the same, can apprehend the two perceptions that are obtained through different sense-organs and which perceptions are, moreover, recognised by itself (i.e., the same knower); but an aggregate cannot (thus apprehend). Why? Because, no member in an aggregate can have the recognition of the apprehension of a different object (i.e., of an object apprehended by a different member of the aggregate), just as in the case of a different sense-organ (which cannot have recognition of the perception of an object apprehended through another sense-organ)....

The self is distinct from the body, etc., also because of the ground, namely—

> *Sutra* 3.1.7: Because of the recognition (*pratyabhijnana*) of an object by the other (i.e., the right) eye (which was) "perceived by the left eye".

Bhashya [*Commentary*]: Recognition (*pratyabhijnana*) means that two pieces of knowledge, one acquired earlier and the other later, are known as being related to the same object. As for example: I now perceive the same object which I perceived before,—this object is identical with that (i.e., the object previously perceived). (The *sutra* means) Because of the recognition of an object by the other (i.e., the right) eye (which was) perceived by the left eye in the form: I am now perceiving that which I perceived before. On the assumption of the sense-organ being itself conscious, there cannot be any explanation of such recognition, because one cannot have recognition of what is perceived by another. However, such recognition being a fact, the conscious self is distinct from the sense-organ.

7.4.4 Udayana, from *Atmatattvaviveka*

Opponent: Isn't it the case that this attribution (of recognition and the required psychology) is not proved (to hold of a selfsame self) since it is just the body that has consciousness?

Udayana: Don't think like that. For, (the body is not a locus of consciousness inasmuch as it is the locus of) being-a-body, being-of-determinate-shape, being-material, possessing-color-and-the-like, and other such (properties not correlate with things that are conscious).

Furthermore, it is not the case that a precise composite of material elements is the possessor of consciousness, since, the composite being different everyday, there would be no memory of something experienced at this or that time previously.

Moreover, the consciousness (exhibited in memory of something or other mediated by a particular bodily part, as a thorn in a toe) is not dependent on the precise bodily part. For, in that case it would not be possible to remember it given a severance of the hand or foot or whatever limb (whereas in fact an amputee can remember the previous experience).

And, if it were the body that has consciousness, then a (newborn) child would not be able for a first time to make effort (to acquire something desired or to avoid something disliked). For, without desire or aversion, effort makes no sense. And without recognition (*pratisandhana*, "recognitive synthesis") of how the desired is to be acquired, desire makes no sense. Inasmuch as (under the circumstances) there would be no memory (on the part of the newborn child) of the connection which has not been experienced in the current lifetime, such recognition (*pratisandhana*) would not happen (whereas in fact the newborn desiring milk reaches for the breast of its mother). And with respect to what has been experienced in another birth, the experiencer (presuming, *ex hypothesi*, that it is the physical body), having (been cremated and) turned to ashes, there would be no remembering by another (body, that is, still supposing counterfactually that it is the body that is the locus of consciousness). Furthermore, in this very lifetime the causal relation between experiences at the one end and effort (and action) at the other is known with certainty. And so, in the absence of the one (experience, etc.), there is absence of the other (desire, etc.)—a proposition that is easy to grasp. (However, there is desire, etc., and so there must have been experience, etc.) Otherwise, there would be untoward consequences (as pointed out).

Source: Udayana, *Atmatattvaviveka*. Translated by Stephen H. Phillips, "Self as Locus/Substratum (*adhikarana*) of Psychological Continuities and Discontinuities," *American Philosophical Association Newsletter* 05(1). Fall 2005.

CHAPTER 8

The Self in Chinese Buddhism

"Flowers in the air"

Buddhism came to China in the first century CE through contacts along the Silk Road. By the beginning of the sixth century it had grown to rival Daoism as one of China's leading religions. Philosophers of the Consciousness-Only School, influenced by idealist forms of Buddhism from India, argue that there is nothing independent of consciousness and that there is no such thing as a mind or self. There are only mental entities—*dharmas*—that are objects of consciousness and out of which we construct the world of experience. This no-self view shapes the attitude toward the self characteristic of Zen Buddhism, a highly influential Buddhist school starting in the ninth century.

8.1 CHINESE BUDDHISM: THE CONSCIOUSNESS-ONLY SCHOOL

Early Buddhist texts spell out a no-soul doctrine. They argue that, when we introspect, we find no self. We become aware only of particular thoughts, sensations, desires, and other mental states. The self cannot be identified with any object, part, or aspect of it nor with any combination of them.

The Chinese Consciousness-Only school develops this tradition. Xuanzang (Hsüan-tsang, 596–664 CE) was born to a Buddhist family near the end of the fifth century. He entered a Buddhist monastery at 13; at 22, he began traveling to monasteries throughout China to study various doctrines. He then left China, against imperial order, to study in India for sixteen years. He spent much of his time at Nalanda University, one of the world's first universities—established in 450 CE and devastated in

1193 by Muslim invaders—which in the seventh century had an extensive library, about 2,000 faculty members, and 10,000 students from as far away as Korea, Indonesia, and Turkey.

At 49, Xuanzang returned to China with 657 Buddhist works previously unavailable there. The emperor, despite Xuanzang's disobedience, gave him a grand welcome and supported him and a large group of assistants. The emperor commissioned from them the largest translation project in Chinese history. When Xuanzang died at age 68, the emperor canceled all his meetings for three days to mourn.

Most of the texts Xuanzang and his assistants translated were of the Yogachara school of Buddhist idealism. Dharmapala (439–507 CE) wrote commentaries on the early Indian Yogacarin Vasabandhu that exerted great influence on Xuanzang's *Treatise on the Establishment of the Doctrine of Consciousness-Only*, which, together with the notes of his student Kwei Zhi (K'uei-chi), articulate a Chinese version of Buddhist idealism.

Xuanzang analyzes the mind into eight consciousnesses: the five senses (sight, smell, hearing, taste, and touch), a sense-center consciousness that coordinates the senses and forms concepts, a thought-center consciousness that wills and reasons, and storehouse consciousness, that is, roughly, memory, which serves as a mental warehouse storing materials for later use. All eight are in constant flux. Storehouse consciousness receives sensations and thoughts from other consciousnesses and emits "manifestations," that is, memories, associations, and other thoughts. Thought-center consciousness interacts with storehouse consciousness, using its materials for purposes of intellectual deliberation. Sense-center consciousness combines the five senses into a coherent picture of the external world.

Laws of cause and effect govern these interactions. Objects (*dharmas*, here meaning not duties but objects of thought) are constructions from these eight forms of consciousness. Some *dharmas*—for example, qualities—are purely illusory or imaginary and do not exist. Some depend on other *dharmas* and so exist only temporarily. Some, finally, have their own independent natures and truly exist. Their "perfect reality" is the ultimate reality revealed in *nirvana* experience.

Xuanzang advocates the no-soul doctrine: "The self and *dharmas* are merely constructions based on false ideas and have no reality of their own." Why? "Because neither the real self nor the real *dharma* is possible."

Xuanzang critiques theories of the self that treat it as unified. Where is this unified self? There are only three possible answers. It may be universal, "as extensive as empty space," that is, existing outside the bounds of any particular body. It may be coextensive with the body. Or it may be within the body.

Suppose that the self (or soul) is transcendental, existing outside the bounds of any particular body. Then its interaction with the body becomes inexplicable. And we lack any compelling way to individuate selves: Why should we count people as different selves when they have different bodies? Why can't this old man and that young girl have or be the same self?

Suppose that the self is coextensive with the body. Aristotle, who construes the soul as the form of the body, might have sympathy with such a view. But Xuanzang finds it to be "like child's play." Say Jones gains weight. Does his soul expand? Say he cuts his hair; does he lose part of himself? Moreover, if the soul is coextensive with the body, it is divisible. But how, then, can it be *one* self?

Finally, suppose that the self is within the body. (For example, suppose one identifies the self with the brain, or the nervous system, or neural impulses.) Xuanzang finds it implausible that a small part of the body could cause the entire body to move. Moreover, he worries that the self, on this view, is neither one nor eternal, for there is no unity—on all these options, the self is divisible—and, being material, perishes. And if there is no unity, there is no self.

To summarize these arguments: If mind is separate from body, it cannot interact with the body. If mind is part or whole of the body, it lacks unity, and there is no self.

Next, consider the view that the self is an aggregate of matter, sensation, thought, disposition, and/or consciousness. Again, the self would be neither one nor eternal. The senses, furthermore, can be restricted (as by wearing a blindfold) or injured without changing who a person is. Thoughts and sensations are not continuous, but the self is. A person in a deep, dreamless sleep hardly ceases to exist. In general, all the components—matter, sensation, thought, etc.—depend on external causes. But the self does not. If the cat hadn't walked into the room, Smith would not have thought about feeding it. But we do not want to say that, if her cat hadn't walked into the room, she wouldn't have been herself.

Xuanzang raises other objections. Thought is *intentional*, in the sense that it is about things. A thought is a thought *of* something. But matter isn't *of* anything. So thought isn't matter. The self can take things as its objects; matter cannot. So the self cannot simply be matter.

8.1.1 Xuanzang, from *The Treatise on the Establishment of the Doctrine of Consciousness-Only*

1. The Nonexistence of the Self

1. Because the ideas of the self (*atman*) and *dharmas* are [constructions produced by causes and therefore] false,

> Their characters of all kinds arise.
>
> These characters are [constructions] based on the transformations of consciousness, which are of three kinds.

2a. They are the consciousness (the eighth, or storehouse, consciousness) whose fruits (retribution) ripen at later times, the consciousness (the seventh or thought-center consciousness) that deliberates, and the consciousness (the sense-center consciousness and the five-sense consciousness) that discriminates spheres of objects.

The *Treatise* says:

Both the world and sacred doctrines declare that the self and *dharmas* are merely constructions based on false ideas and have no reality of their own. ...On what basis are [the self and *dharmas*] produced? Their characters are all constructions

Source: Hsüan-tsang, *The Treatise on the Establishment of the Doctrine of Consciousness-Only*, from Wing-Tsit Chan (ed.), *A Source Book in Chinese Philosophy*. Princeton, NJ: Princeton University Press, 1963, 1991 renewed PUP. Reprinted by permission of Princeton University Press.

based on the evolution and transformation of consciousness. . . .

How do we know that there is really no sphere of objects but only inner consciousness which produces what seem to be the external spheres of objects? Because neither the real self nor the real *dharma* is possible.

Why is the real self impossible? Theories of the self held by the various schools may be reduced to three kinds. The first holds that the substance of the self is eternal, universal, and as extensive as empty space. It acts anywhere and as a consequence enjoys happiness or suffers sorrow. The second holds that although the substance of the self is eternal, its extension is indeterminate, because it expands or contracts according to the size of the body. The third holds that the substance of the self is eternal and infinitesimal like an atom, lying deeply and moving around within the body and thus acts.

The first theory is contrary to reason. Why? If it is held that the self is eternal, universal, and as extensive as empty space, it should not enjoy happiness or suffer sorrow along with the body. Furthermore, being eternal and universal, it should be motionless. How can it act along with the body? Again, is the self so conceived the same or different among all sentient beings? If it is the same, when one being acts, receives the fruits of action, or achieves salvation, all beings should do the same. But this would of course be a great mistake. If it is different, then the selves of all sentient beings would universally penetrate one another and their substance would be mixed, and since the field of abode of all selves is the same, the acts of one being or the fruits of action received by him should be the act or fruits of all beings. If it is said that action and fruits belong to each being separately and there would not be the mistake just described, such a contention is also contrary to reason, because action, fruits, and body are identified with all selves and it is unreasonable for them to belong to one self but not to another. When one is saved, all should be saved, for the Dharma (truth) practiced and realized would be identical with all selves.

The second theory is also contrary to reason. Why? If in substance the self always remains in the same state, it should not expand or contract along with the body. If it expands or contracts like wind in a bag or a pipe, it is not always remaining in the same state. Furthermore, if the self follows the body, it would be divisible. How can it be held that the substance of the self is one? What this school says is like child's play.

The last theory is also contrary to reason. Why? Since the self is infinitesimal like an atom, how can it cause the whole big body to move? If it is said that although it is small it goes through the body like a whirling wheel of fire so that the whole body seems to move, then the self so conceived is neither one nor eternal, for what comes and goes is neither eternal nor one.

Furthermore, there are three additional theories of the self. The first holds that the self is identical with the aggregates (namely, matter, sensation, thought, disposition, and consciousness). The second holds that it is separated from the aggregates. And the third holds that it is neither identical with nor separated from the aggregates. The first theory is contrary to reason, for the self would be like the aggregates and is therefore neither eternal nor one. Furthermore, the internal matters (the five senses) are surely not the real self, for they are physically obstructed (or restricted) like external matters. The mind and mental qualities are not the real self either, for they are not always continuous and depend on various causes to be produced. Other conditioned things and matters are also not the real self, for like empty space they are without intelligence.

The second theory is also contrary to reason, for the self would then be like empty space, which neither acts nor receives fruits of action.

The last theory is also contrary to reason. This theory allows that the self is based on the aggregates but is neither identical with nor separated from them. The self would then be like a vase [which depends on clay] and has no reality of its own. Also, since it is impossible to say whether it is produced from causes or not produced from causes, it is also impossible to say whether it is a self or not. Therefore the real self conceived in the theory cannot be established.

Again, does the substance of the real self conceived by the various schools think or not? If it does, it would not be eternal, because it does not think all the time. If it does not, it would be like empty space, which neither acts nor receives fruits of action. Therefore on the basis of reason, the self conceived by the theory cannot be established.

Again, does this substance of the real self conceived by the various schools perform any function or not? If it does, it would be like hands and feet and would not be eternal. If it does not, it would be like [illusory] horns of a hare and not the real self. Therefore in either case, the self conceived by them cannot be established.

Again, is the substance of the real self conceived by the various schools an object of the view of the self or not? If it is not, how do advocates of the theory know that there is really a self? If it is, then there should be a view of the self that does not involve any perversion, for that would be knowledge of what really is. In that case, how is it that the perfectly true doctrines believed in by those holding the theory of the self all denounce the view of the self and praise the view of the non-self? [Advocates of the theory themselves] declare that the view of the non-self will lead to Nirvana while clinging to the view of the self will lead to sinking in the sea of life and death (transmigration). Does an erroneous view ever lead to Nirvana and a correct view, on the contrary, lead to transmigration?

Again, the various views of the self [actually] do not take the real self as an object, because it has objects [which are not itself] like the mind takes others [such as external matters] as objects. The object of the view of the self is certainly not the real self, because it [the view] is an object like other *dharmas*. Therefore the view of the self does not take the real self as an object. Only because the various aggregates are transformed and manifested by inner consciousness, all kinds of imagination and conjecture result in accordance with one's own erroneous opinions. ...

6. Consciousness-Only

... Therefore everything produced from causes, everything not produced from causes, and everything seemingly real or unreal, are all inseparable from consciousness. The word "only" is intended to deny that there are real things separated from consciousness, but not to deny that there are mental qualities, *dharmas*, and so forth inseparable from consciousness. The word "transform" means that the various inner consciousnesses transform and manifest the characters which seem to be the external spheres of the self and *dharmas*. This process of transformation and change is called *discrimination* because it is its own nature to make erroneous discriminations [that things are real]. It refers to the mind and mental qualities in the three worlds. These, what it holds to be spheres of objects, are called *objects of discrimination*, that is, the self and *dharmas* which it erroneously holds to be real. Because of this discrimination, which evolves characters which seem to be the external spheres of the false self and *dharmas*, what is discriminated as the real self and *dharmas* are all absolutely nonexistent. This theory has been extensively refuted by the doctrines [of our teachers] already cited.

Therefore everything is consciousness-only, because erroneous discrimination in itself is admitted as a fact. Since "only" does not deny the existence of *dharmas* not separated from consciousness, therefore true Emptiness and so forth have the nature of being. In this way we steer far away from the two extremes of holding that *dharmas* are real [although they have no nature of their own] or holding that *dharmas* are unreal [although they do function as causes and effects], establish the principle of Consciousness-Only, and hold correctly to the Middle Path.

8.2 TIBETAN BUDDHISM: THE SELF AS TRANSCENDENT

Buddhism reached Tibet in 173 CE and became deeply ingrained into Tibetan life. Kings of Tibet sent people to India to learn Sanskrit and study Buddhism; they also invited prominent Indian thinkers, including Shankara and Nagarjuna. In the ninth century, King Trisong Deutsen (790–844) commissioned teams of scholars—108 brought from India, together with a comparable number from Tibet—to translate Buddhist texts into Tibetan and invited many famous Buddhist teachers, including Padmasambhava, to come to Tibet to teach. He built a monastery and teaching center, Samye, saw the first monks ordained there, and established Buddhism as the state religion. When Padmasambhava arrived in Tibet, the king gave him a remarkably beautiful young woman as a gift, to be his assistant and consort. She was a noble's daughter who had repeatedly rejected marriage proposals; having thus made many enemies, she was under the king's protection. That young woman, Yeshe Tsogyal (late 700s–mid-800s), became Padmasambhava's foremost student. She helped to make the king's dream of a temple complex a reality by gaining the support of many of Tibet's leading women. Eventually, she became a noted Buddhist teacher in her own right, traveling throughout the country and collecting many followers. Her primary means of teaching—indeed, in her view, the only fully legitimate form of teaching—was direct and oral. (This marks Tsogyal's Buddhism as *esoteric*, something that can be transmitted only by direct personal contact.) Concerned about the future, however, she wrote down many of Padmasambhava's teachings as well as her own and hid them in temples and other sacred spots. Most of the hidden texts remained secret for centuries, being discovered only 300 to 800 years after her death.

Yeshe Tsogyal's Buddhism is in the *Vajrayana* ("Lightning" or "Diamond" Raft) tradition, also known as Mantrayana or Tantric Buddhism. It adds to early Buddhist teachings the study of methods for accelerating enlightenment. These Tantra techniques are designed to produce enlightenment within a single lifetime. Tantric Buddhists do not reject Theravada and Mahayana doctrines; they accept those paths but maintain that more direct, faster routes are possible. Those faster routes depend on the Four Purities:

1. Seeing your body as the body of the deity
2. Seeing your environment as the *mandala*, the "pure land" of the deity
3. Seeing your enjoyments as the pleasures of the deity
4. Acting only for the benefit of others.

Those who exhibit the Four Purities are *bodhisattvas*.

The central concept of Tantric Buddhism as taught by Padmasambhava and Tsogyal is *dzogchen*, "great perfection," which is the natural and original state of every sentient being. It is a primordial, undifferentiated, "intrinsic" awareness that has no form of its own. This awareness can take on forms, representing anything within it without changing its nature. It is a mirror reflecting the world. The secret to enlightenment—to overcoming desire, overcoming suffering, and hence to nirvana experience—is maintaining this sort of awareness.

Known as "pure experience" by Japanese philosophers of the Kyoto School and as "clear mind" by other Zen thinkers, this state of awareness is achieved in three stages. First, the teacher must introduce the student to the great perfection, teaching him or her to recognize intrinsic awareness. Second, the teacher must train the student to investigate, gaining familiarity and confidence with this state. Finally, the teacher must train the student to maintain this state in the face of inevitable distractions. The goal is "the View," an unbroken contemplation manifesting intrinsic awareness continuously. Those who achieve this and are capable of teaching it to others are "gurus," or *Lamas*. Tantric Buddhists teach a variety of techniques for achieving this, including meditation, chanting, concentration on *mandalas*, visualization, and sexual practices.

8.2.1 Yeshe Tsogyal, from *Autobiography*

Tsogyel's *Dzokchen* Instruction

(A ***dakini*** *is a sky dancer or sky walker, a minor goddess.)*
Then Odren Zhonnu Pel made this petition:

O Yeshe Tsogyelma!
When you go to the land of Orgyen
How should we incorrigible creatures
Practice Vision Meditation and Action?
I beg you for a little advice.

In response I gave this instruction:

Listen, faithful Zhonnu Pel.
The fledgling *dakini*-bird nesting in a crag
Could not conceive how easy was flight
Until her skill in the six vehicles was perfected;
But her potential realised, wings beating with hidden strength,
Breaking the back of even the razor-edged wind,
She arrived at whatever destination she chose.
It was like that with me, the girl Tsogyel;
Although I longed for Buddhahood I was forced to wait
Until I had perfected my skill in meditation practice.
Practising to perfection the creative and fulfilment processes and *dzokchen*,
This corporeal bundle dissolved in light,
And now I go into the presence of Orgyen Guru.
But I will leave you with these few words of testament.

"Vision" is but a quality of all meditative existence;
Yet absorbed in reality, experiencing its nature,
You find no mere emptiness for there is awareness and radiance,
Yet nothing permanent for all is intrinsically empty.
That essential insight is called "Vision."
What are the modes of Vision?
In the creative mode it is the deity;

Source: Excerpts from *Sky Dancer: The Secret Life and Songs of the Lady Yeshe Tsogyel.* Translated with commentary by Keith Dowman. London: Routledge & Kegan Paul, 1984. Reprinted with permission of Snow Lion Publications, www.snowlionpub.com.

When you practise radiation and re-absorption, it is compassion;
When you practise the fulfilment process, it is *mahamudra* (direct access to the nature of experience),
The essence without permanence or flux.
Turn your eyes inwards upon your own reality
And you see yourself, but you see nothing:
That visionary perception in itself,
That is what is designated "Vision."

"Meditation" is the basis of all meditative existence;
When absorbed in reality, experiencing its nature,
Intent upon seeing the essential Vision,
Focusing an unwavering attention free of any limitation,
That is called meditative absorption.
And what are the modes of meditation?
Whether you practise the creative or fulfilment process
Peak experience shows you the ineffable reality—
You may practise any of the innumerable modes of meditation.
In truth, whatever your technique, the creative or fulfilment process,
In a condition free from depression, torpor and mental fog,
Registering undistracted silence,
If you focus upon universal sameness, you practise "Meditation."

"Action" is the dynamic form of meditative existence;
When absorbed in its reality, experiencing its nature,
Sure in clarity of Vision, Meditation an ineradicable habit,
In a state of imperturbable relaxation,
You will see yourself perform a variety of actions.
What are the specific modes of Action?
Whatever the variable form of your activity,
Based in primal purity there is no conflict with meditative experience,
Which is intensified and elevated.
In truth, working, sleeping, coming, going,
Eating, sitting—in the performance of every activity
Is the quality of "Action."
Because Action is an integral function of meditation practice—
Creative and fulfilment processes and *dzokchen*, etc.
There is nothing else to say.

The Supreme Being Is the Dakini Queen of the Lake of Awareness!

The Supreme Being is the *dakini* queen of the lake of awareness!
I have vanished into fields of lotus-light, the plenum of dynamic space,
To be born in the inner sanctum of an immaculate lotus;
Do not despair, have faith!
When you have withdrawn attachment to this rocky defile,
This barbaric Tibet, full of war and strife,
Abandon unnecessary activity and rely on solitude.
Practice energy control, purify your psychic nerves and seed-essence,
And cultivate *mahamudra* and *dzokchen*.

The Supreme Being is the *dakini* queen of the lake of awareness!
Attaining humility, through Guru Pema Jungne's compassion I followed him,
And now I have finally gone into his presence;
Do not despair, but pray!
When you see your karmic body as vulnerable as a bubble,
Realising the truth of impermanence, and that in death you are helpless,
Disabuse yourself of fantasies of eternity,
Make your life a practice of *sadhana* (spiritual practice),
And cultivate the experience that takes you to the place where *ati* (the highest form of yoga) ends.

8.3 ZEN BUDDHISM: THE SELF AS EMPTY

Zen Buddhism originated in China, and spread to much of East Asia. Zen offers a hard-to-classify theory of self. The Japanese word *zen* derives from the Chinese *chan*, which, in turn, derives from the Sanskrit *dhyana* ("meditation"). In China, however, the Indian idea of meditation blended with a Daoist idea of concentration and attunement to Dao.

Theravada Buddhism, an early Buddhist philosophy and still the dominant school in southeast Asia, stresses the monastic life. Mahayana Buddhism, which today is prevalent in China, Japan, and Korea, developed as early as the first century CE, stressing the universal possibility of enlightenment. Indeed, *mahayana* means "Great Vehicle," a path for all to achieve *nirvana*. Mahayana Buddhism split into five schools in China, one of which became Zen. Other schools stressed gradual enlightenment based on a process of eliminating error and establishing mental quietude. Zen, a southern subschool, stressed sudden enlightenment. The Buddha is everywhere; anything can bring about the realization of Buddha Nature, a state of mind in which reality becomes transparent and crystalline.

Central to the development of Zen is the Mahayana tradition of patriarchs and lineages. According to Chinese texts, Bodhidharma came to China in 520, met with Emperor Wu, and stayed in the Shaolinsi monastery for nine years. He brought to China a special "transmission outside the scriptures." The Buddha, near the end of his life, delivered what is called the Flower Sermon. He said nothing; he simply held up a single flower and smiled. Two disciples, Kashyapa and Ananda, understood the Buddha's meaning and becoming "awakened." These patriarchs—including, most importantly for China, Bodhidharma, the first Chinese patriarch and the twenty-eighth of India—passed along a special vector of enlightenment not to be transmitted by words. Sometimes called a *message*, it is said to lie beyond the scriptures.

Nevertheless, some doctrines cluster around this vector, including, for both Indian and Chinese Mahayanins:

- *Interdependent origination*: The view that all things interrelate and affect one another. Each *dharma*—in Buddhist usage, each object or "quality," each little bit of experience, including an individual moment of self-consciousness—cannot be understood except in relation to other *dharmas*.
- *Emptiness*: The nature of the *dharmas* is Emptiness. The ultimate truth of the world is Emptiness (in Sanskrit, taken over into Japanese, *sunyata*).

The *locus classicus* of the emptiness doctrine is the *Heart Sutra*, written originally in Sanskrit but translated by Xuanzang into Chinese and influential primarily on east Asian Buddhist thinkers.

Zen's doctrine of unity and inseparability of mind or consciousness implies that all distinctions are unfounded. Normally the mind thinks by discriminating, telling one thing from another. But this leads to suffering. The mind discriminates through being shackled and put in the service of desire. The Four Noble Truths teach that desire and suffering are inextricably linked. To escape suffering, we must eliminate desire. To do that, we must recognize that everything is empty. We must recognize that all differentiations are ultimately meaningless impositions or projections of the mind. As the *Avatamsaka Sutra* has it, "If you wish to understand thoroughly all the Buddhas of the past, present, and future, then you should view the nature of the whole universe as being created by the mind alone."

Zen masters sometimes use extreme methods to transcend the dividing mind. Yixuan (I-Hsüan, d. 867) founded the Linji (Lin-chi) school. Called *Rinzai* in Japanese, it was the most radical of the ninth-century Zen schools. It encouraged the "lightning" method of shouting and beating to prepare the mind for enlightenment. (Yixuan himself is often called Linji or Rinzai.) *Koan*, paradoxes, help the mind transcend everyday concepts as mediated by language: "What is the sound of one hand clapping?" "What was your face before you were born?" A seeker strives to solve the puzzle and thereby to break the mind's attachments.

8.3.1 From the *Heart Sutra*

Om Homage to the Perfection of Wisdom the Lovely, the Holy!

Avalokita, the Holy Lord and Bodhisattva, was moving in the deep course of the wisdom which has gone beyond. He looked down from on high, he beheld but five heaps, and he saw that in their own-being they were empty.

Here, O Sariputra, form is emptiness and the very emptiness is form; emptiness does not differ from form, form does not differ from emptiness, whatever is emptiness, that is form, the same is true of feelings, perceptions, impulses, and consciousness.

Here, O Sariputra, all *dharmas* are marked with emptiness; they are not produced or stopped, not defiled or immaculate, not deficient or complete.

Therefore, O Sariputra, in emptiness there is no form nor feeling, nor perception, nor impulse, nor consciousness;

No eye, ear, nose, tongue, body, mind; no forms, sounds, smells, tastes, touchables or objects of mind; no sight-organ element, and so forth, until we come to:

No mind-consciousness element; there is no ignorance, no extinction of ignorance, and so forth, until we come to: There is no decay and death, no extinction of decay and death. There is no suffering, no origination, no stopping, no path. There is no cognition, no attainment and no non-attainment.

Therefore, O Sariputra, it is because of his non-attainmentness that a Bodhisattva, through having relied on the Perfection of Wisdom (*prajna-paramita*), dwells without thought-coverings. In the absence of thought-coverings he has not been made to tremble, he has overcome what can upset, and in the end he attains to Nirvana.

All those who appear as Buddhas in the three periods of time fully awake to the utmost, right and perfect Enlightenment because they have relied on the Perfection of Wisdom.

Therefore one should know the Perfection of Wisdom as the great mantra, the mantra of great knowledge, the utmost mantra, the unequalled mantra, allayer of all suffering, in truth—for what

---

Source: *Buddhist Wisdom Books: Containing the Diamond Sutra and the Heart Sutra*. Translated by Edward Conze. London: George Allen & Unwin, Ltd., 1958.

could go wrong? By the *prajna-paramita* has this mantra been delivered. It runs like this:

gate gate paragate parasamgate bodhi svaha.

(Gone, gone, gone beyond, gone altogether beyond, O what an awakening, *svaha*!)

This completes the Heart of perfect Wisdom.

8.3.2 From *The Recorded Conversations of Zen Master Yixuan*

A monk asked, "What is the basic idea of the Law preached by the Buddha?" Thereupon the Master shouted at him. The monk paid reverence.

The Master said, "The Master and the monk can argue all right."

Question: "Master, whose tune are you singing? Whose tradition are you perpetuating?"

The Master said, "When I was a disciple of Huang-po, I asked him three times and I was beaten three times."

As the monk hesitated about what to say, the Master shouted at him and then beat him, saying, "Don't nail a stick into empty space."

2. The Master ascended the hall and said, "Over a lump of reddish flesh there sits a pure man who transcends and is no longer attached to any class of Buddhas or sentient beings. He comes in and out of your sense organs all the time. If you are not yet clear about it, look, look!"

At that point a monk came forward and asked, "What is a pure man who does not belong to any class of Buddhas or sentient beings?" The Master came right down from his chair and, taking hold of the monk, exclaimed, "Speak! Speak!" As the monk deliberated what to say, the Master let him go, saying, "What dried human excrement-removing stick is the pure man who does not belong to any class of Buddhas or sentient beings!" Thereupon he returned to his room.

3. The Master ascended the hall. A monk asked, "What is the basic idea of the Law preached by the Buddha?" The Master lifted up his swatter. The monk shouted, and the Master beat him.

[The monk asked again], "What is the basic idea of the Law preached by the Buddha?" The Master again lifted up his swatter. The monk shouted, and the Master shouted also. As the monk hesitated about what to say, the Master beat him.

Thereupon the Master said, "Listen, men. Those who pursue after the Law will not escape from death. I was in my late Master Huang-po's place for twenty years. Three times I asked him about the basic idea of the Law preached by the Buddha and three times he bestowed upon me the staff. I felt I was struck only by a dried stalk. Now I wish to have a real beating. Who can do it to me?"

One monk came out of the group and said, "I can do it."

The Master picked up the staff to give him. As he was about to take it over, the Master beat him.

5. The Master told the congregation: "Seekers of the Way. In Buddhism no effort is necessary. All one has to do is to do nothing, except to move his bowels, urinate, put on his clothing, eat his meals, and lie down if he is tired. The stupid will laugh at

Source: *The Recorded Conversations of Zen Master I-Hsüan*, from Wing-Tsit Chan (ed.), *A Source Book in Chinese Philosophy*. Princeton, NJ: Princeton University Press, 1963, 1991 renewed PUP. Reprinted by permission of Princeton University Press.

him, but the wise one will understand. An ancient person said, 'One who makes effort externally is surely a fool.' "

6. Question: "What is meant by the mind's not being different at different times?"

The Master answered, "As you deliberated to ask the question, your mind has already become different. Therefore the nature and character of *dharmas* have become differentiated. Seekers of the Way, do not make any mistake. All mundane and supramundane *dharmas* have no nature of their own. Nor have they the nature to be produced [by causes]. They have only the name Emptiness, but even the name is empty. Why do you take this useless name as real? You are greatly mistaken! ...If you seek after the Buddha, you will be taken over by the devil of the Buddha, and if you seek after the patriarch, you will be taken over by the devil of the patriarch. If you seek after anything, you will always suffer. It is better not to do anything. Some unworthy priests tell their disciples that the Buddha is the ultimate and that he went through three infinitely long periods, fulfilled his practice, and then achieved Buddhahood. Seekers of the Way, if you say that the Buddha is the ultimate, why did he die lying down sidewise in the forest in Kusinagara after having lived for eighty years? Where is he now? ...Those who truly seek after the Law will have no use for the Buddha. They will have no use for the *bodhisattvas* or *arhats*. And they will have no use for any excellence in the three worlds (of desires, matter, and pure spirit). They will be distinctly free and not bound by material things. Heaven and earth may turn upside down but I shall have no more uncertainty. The Buddhas of the ten cardinal directions may appear before me and I shall not feel happy for a single moment. The three paths (of fire, blood, and swords) to hell may suddenly appear, but I shall not be afraid for a single moment. Why? Because I know that all *dharmas* are devoid of characters. They exist when there is transformation [in the mind] and cease to exist when there is no transformation. The three worlds are but the mind, and all *dharmas* are consciousness only. Therefore [they are all] dreams, illusions, and flowers in the air. What is the use of grasping and seizing them? ...

"Kill anything that you happen on. Kill the Buddha if you happen to meet him. Kill a patriarch or an *arhat* if you happen to meet him. Kill your parents or relatives if you happen to meet them. Only then can you be free, not bound by material things, and absolutely free and at ease. ..."

"I have no trick to give people. I merely cure disease and set people free. ...My views are few. I merely put on clothing and eat meals as usual, and pass my time without doing anything. You people coming from the various directions have all made up your minds to seek the Buddha, seek the Law, seek emancipation, and seek to leave the three worlds. Crazy people! If you want to leave the three worlds, where can you go? 'Buddha' and 'patriarchs' are terms of praise and also bondage. Do you want to know where the three worlds are? They are right in your mind which is now listening to the Law."

7. Ma-ku came to participate in a session. As he arranged his seating cushion, he asked, "Which face of the twelve-face Kuan-yin faces the proper direction?"

The Master got down from the rope chair. With one hand he took away Ma-ku's cushion and with the other he held Ma-ku, saying, "Which direction does the twelve-face Kuan-yin face?"

Ma-ku turned around and was about to sit in the rope chair. The Master picked up the staff and beat him. Ma-ku having grasped the staff, the two dragged each other into the room.

8. The Master asked a monk: "Sometimes a shout is like the sacred sword of the Diamond King. Sometimes a shout is like a golden-haired lion squatting on the ground. Sometimes a shout is like a rod or a piece of grass [used to attract fish]. And sometimes a shout is like one which does not function as a shout at all. How do you know which one to use?"

As the monk was deliberating what to say, the Master shouted.

9. When the Master was among Huang-po's congregation, his conduct was very pure. The senior monk said with a sigh, "Although he

is young, he is different from the rest!" He then asked, "Sir, how long have you been here?"

The Master said, "Three years."

The senior monk said, "Have you ever gone to the head monk (Huang-po) and asked him questions?"

The Master said, "I have not. I wouldn't know what to ask."

The senior monk said, "Why don't you go and ask the head monk what the basic idea of the Law preached by the Buddha clearly is?"

The Master went and asked the question. But before he finished, Huang-po beat him. When he came back, the senior monk asked him how the conversation went. The Master said, "Before I finished my question, he already had beaten me. I don't understand. The senior monk told him to go and ask again."

The Master did and Huang-po beat him again. In this way he asked three times and got beaten three times. ...Huang-po said, "If you go to Ta-yu's place, he will tell you why."

The Master went to Ta-yu, who asked him, "Where have you come from?"

The Master said, "I am from Huang-po's place."

Ta-yu said, "What did Huang-po have to say?"

The Master said, "I asked three times about the basic idea of the Law preached by the Buddha and I was beaten three times. I don't know if I was mistaken."

Ta-yu said, "Old kindly Huang-po has been so earnest with you and you still came here to ask if you were mistaken!"

As soon as the Master heard this, he understood and said, "After all, there is not much in Huang-po's Buddhism."

CHAPTER 9

Ancient Greek Philosophy of Mind

"The pilot of the soul"

Philosophy did not begin in Greece, as was commonly said only a generation ago, but Western awareness of traditions of philosophy not derivative from Greek philosophy is recent. The English word *philosophy* comes from two Greek words, *philos* and *sophia*, which compounded mean "love of wisdom." Many issues in contemporary philosophy—as well as, indeed, in the distant traditions of ancient China and India—were debated by Greek philosophers from about 500 BCE. The Greek language remained the lingua franca of Western philosophy until Latin replaced it upon the rise of the Roman Empire. Central to Greek philosophy was the problem of the self. Who am I? What kind of thing am I? How does what I am relate to what I ought to be?

9.1 PLATO: THE ETERNAL, TRIPARTITE SOUL

Within the Greek tradition, Socrates (469–399 BCE) may be said to be the first philosopher, though there were predecessors, called pre-Socratics, fragments of whose speculations have survived. A contemporary of the Greek playwrights Sophocles, Euripedes, and Aristophanes as well as of the historians Thucydides and Herodotus, Socrates was a historical person. But we know of him almost exclusively through the writings of his follower Plato (427–347 BCE). Plato's dialogues generally seem fictional, like plays. Thus the life and philosophy of the historical Socrates are subjects of some controversy. Nevertheless, the character Socrates in Plato's early dialogues gives us a sense of a person embodying the spirit of philosophy perhaps better than anyone anywhere before or since.

Socrates' philosophical spirit comes out in the sorts of questions he asks—about friendship, love, and justice, for example—in his humility about his beliefs, and in his fantastic talent for argument. He was utterly authentic and devoted to what Buddhists call right living. Plato depicts him as a man of courage and loyalty as well as wit. Plato makes us love and admire this hero of clear thought, the Sherlock Holmes of abstract inquiry.

For Socrates, philosophical inquiry is abstract, focused on definitions. He seeks criteria for what it is in general for something to count as *X* (love, justice, the good). The direction of inquiry flows from Socrates' dedication to a certain kind of knowledge. Plato's teacher seeks the essential truths about ourselves as ethical agents and as knowers. Plato comes to endorse answers to these questions. He adopts a view of the nature of the self. But, in Plato's early dialogues, Socrates rarely gives answers. He raises questions and subjects possible answers to rigorous criticism. In Plato's later dialogues, in contrast, the character called Socrates becomes a mouthpiece for Plato's own views.

Philosophical argument distinguishes Socrates from earlier thinkers. We can usually reconstruct their views from fragments and later commentaries. But it is difficult to discern their reasons for holding those views. In contrast, Socrates focuses primarily on having reasons and testing their worth. Plato's teacher ingeniously draws out presuppositions and ramifications of theories we are hardly aware we hold.

Plato's early dialogues follow a pattern. Socrates puts forward no particular theory of his own. He clarifies and investigates a question by drawing out entailments of the answers given by one or more interlocutors, his fellow characters in the play. Such examination is sometimes called the Socratic method or Socratic dialectic. For example, Socrates asks what piety or courage or friendship or justice is. Someone answers. The philosopher then analyzes the definition by asking further questions. He leads the parties to see what has to be true if the definition is correct. This usually leads them to renounce it. Thus, he says, he prepares the mind for genuine knowledge by clearing away false or unwarranted beliefs.

Sometimes the proposed definition is unclear; sometimes it includes too much or too little. Sometimes it leads to a contradiction or an infinite regress. Sometimes the reasons advanced in its favor are circular or show another defect. Someone then proposes another definition, and the process continues. In the early dialogues, the results seem entirely negative. In what scholars call Plato's middle dialogues, in contrast, Plato does have the character Socrates (who is less richly depicted from a literary point of view) endorse and defend positions. We are presented with positive theories, not just refutations of an interlocutor's views. The excerpts presented next are from a transitional dialogue, the *Phaedo*, and from two middle dialogues, the *Phaedrus* and the *Republic*. The positive theories Socrates presents in the latter two dialogues are the mature Plato's views of self, person, and soul. They seem to differ somewhat from the views of the historical Socrates.

Plato believes that the soul is immortal. He divides it into parts. In the *Republic* he distinguishes three parts of the soul: the rational part, the appetitive part, and the spirited part. The first thinks; the second desires; the third feels. In the *Phaedrus*, Plato (like the Upanishads) uses the image of a chariot to describe their relation to one another. The charioteer is the rational part of the soul. The noble horse is the spirited element, the part that feels; the ignoble horse is desire, the appetitive element, the part that craves. Virtue consists in subjecting the horses, especially the ignoble, rebellious horse, to the firm control of the driver. The rational element must, Plato insists, dominate the others for a person to be virtuous and happy.

Plato intends this account to explain both how psychological conflict is possible and how it ought to be resolved. Conflict occurs when parts of the soul pull in different directions. It ought to be resolved by the control of the rational part of the soul. When the charioteer has the horses well under control, the chariot rides smoothly and effectively. Just so, when the rational part of the soul dominates the others, the person is happy as well as virtuous. When the charioteer loses control of one or both of the horses, the chariot itself is out of control and becomes a danger to the charioteer and the horses as well as to others. Similarly, when a person loses control of the spirited or appetitive element, the person endangers him- or herself in addition to others. This explains why Plato sees virtue and happiness as going together; both result from the rational elements' control of the other elements of the soul.

9.1.1 Plato, from *Phaedo*

[Socrates:] And now I'll answer you, O my judges, and show that he who has lived as a true philosopher has reason to be of good cheer when he's about to die and that after death he may hope to receive the greatest good in the other world. And how this may be, Simmias and Cebes, I'll endeavor to explain. For I think that the true disciple of philosophy is likely to be misunderstood by other men. They don't perceive that he's ever pursuing death and dying. If this is true, why, having desired death all his life long, should he grumble at the arrival of that which he has been always pursuing and desiring?

Simmias laughed and said: Though not in a laughing humor, I swear that I can't help laughing when I think what the wicked world will say when they hear this. They'll say that this is very true. Our people at home will agree with them in saying that the life philosophers desire is truly death and that they have found them out to be deserving of the death which they desire.

And they're right, Simmias, in saying this, with the exception of the words "They have found them out," for they haven't found out the nature of this death the true philosopher desires or how he deserves or desires death. But let's leave them and have a word with ourselves: Do we believe that there's such a thing as death?

To be sure, replied Simmias.

And is this anything but the separation of soul and body? And being dead is the attainment of this separation; when the soul exists in herself and is parted from the body and the body is parted from the soul—that's death?

Exactly: that and nothing else, he replied.

And what do you say of another question, my friend, about which I'd like to have your opinion. The answer will probably throw light on our present inquiry. Do you think that the philosopher ought to care about the pleasures—if they are to be called pleasures—of eating and drinking?

Certainly not, answered Simmias.

Source: Plato, *Phaedo*. Translated by Benjamin Jowett. New York: Charles Scribner's Sons, 1871. We have revised the translation for readability.

And what do you say of the pleasures of love—should he care about them?

By no means.

And will he think much of the other ways of indulging the body—for example, the acquisition of costly raiment, or sandals, or other adornments of the body? Instead of caring about them, doesn't he rather despise anything more than nature needs? What do you say?

I'd say the true philosopher would despise them.

Wouldn't you say that he's entirely concerned with the soul and not with the body? He'd like, as far as he can, to be rid of the body and turn to the soul.

That's true.

In matters of this sort philosophers, above all other men, may be observed in every sort of way to dissever the soul from the body.

That's true.

Simmias, the rest of the world thinks that a life that has no bodily pleasures and no part in them isn't worth having. But he who thinks nothing of bodily pleasures is almost as though he were dead.

That's quite true.

What again shall we say of the actual acquiring of knowledge? Is the body, if invited to share in the inquiry, a hinderer or a helper? I mean to say, have sight and hearing any truth in them? Aren't they, as the poets are always telling us, inaccurate witnesses? And yet, if even they are inaccurate and indistinct, what's to be said of the other senses? For you'll allow that they are the best of them?

Certainly, he replied.

Then when does the soul attain truth? For in attempting to consider anything in company with the body, she is obviously deceived.

Yes, that's true.

Then mustn't existence be revealed to her in thought, if at all?

Yes.

And thought is best when the mind is gathered into herself and none of these things trouble her—neither sounds nor sights nor pain nor any pleasure—when she has as little as possible to do with the body and has no bodily sense or feeling, but is aspiring after being?

That's true.

And in this the philosopher dishonors the body; his soul runs away from the body and desires to be alone and by herself?

That's true.

Well, but there's another thing, Simmias: Is there or is there not an absolute justice?

Assuredly there is.

And an absolute beauty and absolute good?

Of course.

But did you ever behold any of them with your eyes?

Certainly not.

Or did you ever reach them with any other bodily sense? (And I speak not of these alone, but of absolute greatness, and health, and strength, and of the essence or true nature of everything.) Have you ever perceived the reality of them through your bodily organs? Or rather, isn't the nearest approach to the knowledge of their several natures made by one who so orders his intellectual vision as to have the most exact conception of the essence of that which he considers?

Certainly.

And he attains to the knowledge of them in their highest purity who goes to each of them with the mind alone. He doesn't allow, when in the act of thought, the intrusion or introduction of sight or any other sense in the company of reason. But with the very light of the mind in her clearness, he penetrates into the very light of truth in each. He has got rid, as far as he can, of eyes and ears and of the whole body, which he conceives of only as a disturbing element, hindering the soul from the acquisition of knowledge when in company with her. Isn't this the sort of man who, if ever a man did, is likely to attain the knowledge of existence?

There's admirable truth in that, Socrates, replied Simmias.

And when they consider all this, mustn't true philosophers make a reflection? They'll speak of it to one another in such words as these: We've found, they'll say, a path of speculation that seems to bring us and the argument to the conclusion that while we're in the body and while the soul is mingled with this mass of evil, our desire for truth won't be satisfied. For the body is a source of endless trouble to us merely because it requires food. It's also liable to diseases, which overtake and impede us in the search after truth. By filling us so full of loves, and lusts, and fears, and fancies, and idols, and every sort of folly, it prevents our ever having, as people say, so much as a thought. For whence come wars, and fightings, and factions? whence but from the body and its lusts? For wars are occasioned by the love of money, and money has to be acquired for the sake and in the service of the body. Consequently, the time that ought to be given to philosophy is lost. Moreover, if there's time and an inclination toward philosophy, the body still introduces turmoil, confusion, and fear into the course of speculation. It hinders us from seeing the truth. All experience shows that if we want pure knowledge of anything we must get rid of the body. The soul in herself must behold all things in themselves. Then, I suppose, we'll attain what we desire and what we say we love—wisdom—not while we live, but after death, as the argument shows. For if the soul cannot have pure knowledge while in company with the body, one of two things seems to follow—either knowledge is not to be attained at all or, if at all, after death. For then, and not till then, the soul will be in herself alone and without the body. In this present life, I reckon that we make the nearest approach to knowledge when we have the least possible concern for or interest in the body and aren't saturated with the bodily nature, but remain pure until the hour when God himself is pleased to release us. And then the foolishness of the body will be cleared away. We'll be pure and converse with other pure souls. We ourselves will know the clear light everywhere—the light of truth. For no impure thing is allowed to approach the pure. These are the sort of words, Simmias, that the true lovers of wisdom can't help saying to one another, and thinking. You will agree with me in that?

Certainly, Socrates.

But if this is true, my friend, then there's great hope that, going where I go, I'll be satisfied with what has been our chief concern in our past lives. And now that the hour of departure is appointed to me, this is the hope with which I depart—and not I only, but every man who believes that he has his mind purified.

Certainly, replied Simmias.

And what is purification but the separation of the soul from the body, as I was saying before? The habit of the soul gathering and collecting herself into herself, out of all the courses of the body; the dwelling in her own place alone, as in another life, so also in this, as far as she can; the release of the soul from the chains of the body?

Very true, he said.

And what is death, but this very separation and release of the soul from the body?

To be sure, he said.

And the true philosophers, and they only, study and are eager to release the soul. Isn't the separation and release of the soul from the body their special study?

That's true.

And as I was saying at first, there would be a ridiculous contradiction in men studying to live as nearly as they can in a state of death and yet complaining when death comes.

Certainly.

Then, Simmias, as the true philosophers are ever studying death, to them, of all men, death is the least terrible. Look at the matter this way: How inconsistent of them to have always been enemies of the body and wanting to have the soul alone and, when this is granted to them, to be trembling and complaining. Instead of rejoicing at their departing to that place where, when they arrive, they hope to gain what they loved in life—wisdom—and at the same time to be rid of the company of their enemy. Many a man has been willing to go to the world below in the hope of seeing there an earthly love, or wife, or son, and conversing with them. And will he who is a true lover of wisdom and is persuaded in like manner that only in the world below he can worthily enjoy her still complain at death? Won't he depart with joy? Surely he will, my friend, if he's a true philosopher. For he'll have a firm conviction that there only, and nowhere else, he can find wisdom in her purity. And if this is true, he'd be very absurd, as I was saying, if he were to fear death.

Now, the compound or composite may be supposed to be naturally capable of being dissolved just as it was compounded. But what is uncompounded, and that only, must be indissoluble, if anything is.

Yes; that's what I'd imagine, said Cebes.

And the uncompounded may be assumed to be the same and unchanging, where the compound is always changing and never the same?

That I also think, he said.

Then now let's return to the previous discussion. Is that idea or essence, which in the dialectical process we define as the essence of true existence—whether essence of equality, beauty, or anything else—are these essences, I say, liable at times to some degree of change? Or are they each of them always what they are, having the same simple, self-existent, and unchanging forms, and not admitting of variation at all, or in any way, or at any time?

They must be always the same, Socrates, replied Cebes.

And what would you say of the many beautiful things—whether men, horses, garments, or any other things that may be called equal or beautiful—are they all unchanging and the same always, or quite the reverse? May they not rather be described as almost always changing and hardly ever the same either with themselves or with one another?

The latter, replied Cebes; they're always in a state of change.

And these you can touch, see, and perceive with the senses. But the unchanging things you can only perceive with the mind—they're invisible and aren't seen?

That's very true, he said.

Well, then, he added, let's suppose that there are two sorts of existences, one seen, the other unseen.

Let's suppose them.

The seen is the changing, and the unseen is the unchanging.

That also may be supposed.

And, further, is not one part of us body and the rest of us soul?

To be sure.

And to which class may we say that the body is more alike and akin?

Clearly to the seen: no one can doubt that.

And is the soul seen or not seen?

Not by man, Socrates.

And by "seen" and "not seen" we mean what is or is not visible to the eye of man?

Yes, to the eye of man.

And what do we say of the soul? Is that seen or not seen?

Not seen.

Unseen then?

Yes.

Then the soul is more like to the unseen and the body to the seen?

That's most certain, Socrates.

And weren't we saying long ago that the soul, when using the body as an instrument of perception, that is to say, when using the sense of sight or hearing or some other sense (for the meaning of perceiving through the body is perceiving through the senses)—weren't we saying that the soul too is then dragged by the body into the region of the changeable and wanders and is confused; the world spins round her, and she is like a drunkard when under their influence?

Very true.

But when returning into herself she reflects; then she passes into the realm of purity, and eternity, and immortality, and unchangeableness, which are her kindred, and with them she ever lives, when she is by herself, unhindered. Then she ceases from her erring ways and, being in communion with the unchanging, is unchanging. And this state of the soul is called wisdom?

That's well and truly said, Socrates, he replied.

And to which class is the soul more nearly alike and akin, as far as may be inferred from this argument as well as from the preceding one?

I think, Socrates, that, in the opinion of everyone who follows the argument, the soul will be infinitely more like the unchangeable. Even the most stupid person won't deny that.

And the body is more like the changing?

Yes.

Yet consider the matter once more in this light: When the soul and the body are united, then nature orders the soul to rule and govern and the body to obey and serve.

Now which of these two functions is akin to the divine? And which to the mortal? Doesn't the divine appear to you to be what naturally orders and rules and the mortal what is subject and servant?

True.

And which does the soul resemble?

The soul resembles the divine and the body the mortal—there can be no doubt of that, Socrates.

Then reflect, Cebes: Isn't the conclusion of the whole matter this?—that the soul is in the very likeness of the divine, immortal, intelligible, uniform, indissoluble, and unchangeable; and the body is in the very likeness of the human, mortal, unintelligible, multiform, dissoluble, and changeable. Can this, my dear Cebes, be denied?

No, indeed.

But if this is true, then isn't the body liable to speedy dissolution? Isn't the soul almost or altogether indissoluble?

Certainly.

And do you further observe that after a man is dead, the body, which is the visible part of man and has a visible framework called a corpse, which would naturally be dissolved, decomposed, and dissipated, is not dissolved or decomposed at once, but may remain for a good while, if its constitution is sound at the time of death and the season of the year favorable? For the body when shrunk and embalmed, as is the custom in Egypt, may remain almost entire through infinite ages; and even in decay, still there are some portions, such as the bones and ligaments, which are practically indestructible. You allow that?

Yes.

And are we to suppose that the soul, which is invisible, in passing to the true Hades, which like her is invisible, and pure, and noble, and on her way to the good and wise God, to which, if God wills, my soul is also soon to go—that the soul, I repeat, if this is her nature and origin, is blown away and perishes immediately on quitting the body as the many say? That can never be, dear Simmias and Cebes. The truth rather is that the soul that is pure at departing draws after her no bodily taint, having never voluntarily had connection with the body, which she is ever avoiding, herself gathered into herself (for such abstraction has been the study of her life). And what does this mean except that she's been a true disciple of philosophy and has practised how to die easily? And isn't philosophy the practise of death?

Certainly.

That soul, I say, herself invisible, departs to the invisible world to the divine, immortal, and rational: Arriving there, she lives in bliss and is released from the error and folly of men, their fears and wild passions and all other human ills, and forever dwells, as they say of the initiated, in company with the gods. Isn't this true, Cebes?

Yes, said Cebes, beyond a doubt.

But the soul that has been polluted is impure at the time of her departure, is the companion and servant of the body always, and is in love with and fascinated by the body and by the desires and pleasures of the body, until she is led to believe that the truth only exists in a bodily form, which a man may touch and see and taste and use for the purposes of his lusts—the soul, I mean, accustomed to hate and fear and avoid the intellectual principle, which to the bodily eye is dark and invisible and can be attained only by philosophy—do you suppose that such a soul as this will depart pure and unalloyed?

That's impossible, he replied.

She's engrossed by the corporeal, which the continual association and constant care of the body have made natural to her.

Very true.

And this, my friend, may be conceived to be that heavy, weighty, earthy element of sight by which such a soul is depressed and dragged down again into the visible world, because she is afraid of the invisible and of the world below—prowling about tombs and sepulchres, in the neighborhood of which, as they tell us, are seen certain ghostly apparitions of souls which have not departed pure, but are cloyed with sight and therefore visible.

That is very likely, Socrates.

Yes, that is very likely, Cebes; and these must be the souls, not of the good, but of the evil, who are compelled to wander about such places in payment of the penalty of their former evil way of life; and they continue to wander until the desire which haunts them is satisfied and they are imprisoned in another body. And they may be supposed to be fixed in the same natures which they had in their former life.

What natures do you mean, Socrates?

I mean to say that men who have followed after gluttony, and wantonness, and drunkenness, and have had no thought of avoiding them, would pass into asses and animals of that sort. What do you think?

I think that's exceedingly probable.

And those who have chosen the portion of injustice, and tyranny, and violence will pass into wolves, or into hawks and kites; where else can we suppose them to go?

Yes, said Cebes; that's doubtless the place of natures such as theirs. And there's no difficulty, he said, in assigning to all of them places answering to their several natures and propensities?

There isn't, he said.

Even among them some are happier than others. The happiest both in themselves and their place of abode are those who have practised the civil and social virtues which are called temperance and justice and are acquired by habit and attention without philosophy and mind.

Why are they the happiest?

Because they may be expected to pass into some gentle, social nature which is like their own, such as that of bees or ants, or even back again into the form of man, and just and moderate men spring from them.

That isn't impossible.

But he who is a philosopher or lover of learning and is entirely pure at departing is alone permitted to reach the gods. And this is the reason, Simmias and Cebes, why the true votaries of philosophy abstain from all fleshly lusts and endure and refuse to give themselves up to them—not because they fear poverty or the ruin of their families, like the lovers of money, and the world in general; nor like the lovers of power and honor, because they dread the dishonor or disgrace of evil deeds.

No, Socrates, that wouldn't become them, said Cebes.

No, indeed, he replied; and therefore they who have a care of their souls and don't merely live in the fashions of the body say farewell to all this. They won't walk in the ways of the blind. When philosophy offers them purification and release from evil, they feel that they shouldn't resist her influence. To her they incline, and wherever she leads they follow her.

9.1.2 Plato, from *Phaedrus*

The soul through all her being is immortal, for that which is ever in motion is immortal. But what moves another and is moved by another, in ceasing to move, ceases also to live. Only the self-moving,

Source: Plato, *Phaedrus*. Translated by Benjamin Jowett. New York: Charles Scribner's Sons, 1871. We have revised the translation for readability.

never leaving itself, never ceases to move and is the fountain and beginning of motion to all that moves besides. Now, the beginning is unbegotten, for that which is begotten has a beginning. But the beginning is begotten of nothing, for if it were begotten of something, then the begotten would not come from a beginning. But if unbegotten, it must also be indestructible; for if beginning were destroyed, there could be no beginning out of anything, nor anything out of a beginning; and all things must have a beginning. And therefore the self-moving is the beginning of motion. This can neither be destroyed nor begotten, or else the whole heavens and all creation would collapse and stand still and never again have motion or birth. But if the self-moving is proved to be immortal, he who affirms that self-motion is the very idea and essence of the soul won't suffer confusion. For the body moved from without is soulless. But what is moved from within has a soul, for such is the nature of the soul. But if this is true, must not the soul be self-moving and therefore of necessity unbegotten and immortal? Enough of the soul's immortality.

Of the nature of the soul, though her true form is ever a theme of large and more than mortal discourse, let me speak briefly and in a figure. And let the figure be composite—a pair of winged horses and a charioteer. Now, the winged horses and the charioteers of the gods are all noble and of noble descent, but those of other races are mixed. The human charioteer drives his in a pair. One of them is noble and of noble breed; the other is ignoble and of ignoble breed. Driving them of necessity gives a great deal of trouble to him.

I'll endeavour to explain to you how the mortal differs from the immortal creature. The soul in her totality has the care of inanimate being everywhere and traverses the whole heaven appearing in diverse forms. When perfect and fully winged she soars upward and orders the whole world. The imperfect soul, losing her wings and drooping in her flight, at last settles on the solid ground. There, finding a home, she receives an earthly frame that appears to be self-moved but is really moved by her power. This composition of soul and body is called a living and mortal creature. For no such union can be reasonably believed to be immortal, although fancy, not having seen or known the nature of God, may imagine an immortal creature having both a body and also a soul united throughout all time. Let that, however, be as God wills, and be spoken of acceptably to him. And now let's ask why the soul loses her wings!

The wing is the corporeal element most akin to the divine. By nature it tends to soar aloft and carry what gravitates downwards into the upper region, which is the habitation of the gods. The divine is beauty, wisdom, goodness, and the like. By these the wing of the soul is nourished and grows apace. But when fed upon evil and foulness and the opposite of good, it wastes and falls away. Zeus, the mighty lord, holding the reins of a winged chariot, leads the way in heaven, ordering all and taking care of all. There follows him the array of gods and demigods, marshaled in eleven bands. Hestia alone abides at home in the house of heaven; of the rest they who are reckoned among the princely twelve march in their appointed order. They see many blessed sights in the inner heaven. There are many ways to and fro, along which the blessed gods are passing, every one doing his own work. He may follow who will and can, for jealousy has no place in the celestial choir. But when they go to banquet and festival, then they move up the steep to the top of the vault of heaven. The chariots of the gods in even poise, obeying the rein, glide rapidly. But the others labour, for the vicious steed goes heavily, weighing down the charioteer to the earth when his steed has not been thoroughly trained. This is the hour of agony and extremest conflict for the soul. For the immortals, when they are at the end of their course, go forth and stand upon the outside of heaven. The revolution of the spheres carries them round, and they behold the things beyond. But of the heaven which is above the heavens, what earthly poet ever did or ever will sing worthily? I'll describe it, for I must dare to speak the truth, when truth is my theme. There abides the very being with which true knowledge is concerned: the colourless, formless, intangible essence, visible only to mind, the pilot of the soul. The divine intelligence, being nurtured upon mind and pure knowledge, and the intelligence of every soul capable of receiving the food proper to it, rejoices at beholding reality and once more gazing upon truth. She is replenished and made glad until the revolution of the worlds brings her round again to the same place. In the revolution she beholds justice, and temperance, and knowledge absolute, not in the form of generation or of relation, which men call existence, but knowledge absolute in existence absolute. Beholding the other true existences in like manner and feasting upon them, she passes down into the interior of the heavens and returns home. There the charioteer, putting up his horses at the stall, gives them ambrosia to eat and nectar to drink.

Such is the life of the gods. But of other souls, that which follows God best and is likest to him lifts the head of the charioteer into the outer world and is carried round in the revolution, troubled indeed by the steeds, and with difficulty beholding true being; while another only rises and falls, and sees, and again fails to see by reason of the unruliness of the steeds. The rest of the souls are also longing after the upper world and they all follow. But not being strong enough they are carried round below the surface, plunging, treading on one another, each striving to be first. There is confusion and perspiration and the extremity of effort. Many of them are lamed or have their wings broken through the ill-driving of the charioteers. All of them, after a fruitless toil, not having attained to the mysteries of true being, go away and feed upon opinion. The reason why the souls exhibit this exceeding eagerness to behold the plain of truth is that pasturage suited to the highest part of the soul is found there. The wing on which the soul soars is nourished with this. And there is a law of Destiny, that the soul that attains any vision of truth in company with a god is preserved from harm until the next period, and if attaining always is always unharmed. But when she is unable to follow, and fails to behold the truth, and through some mishap sinks beneath the double load of forgetfulness and vice, and her wings fall from her and she drops to the ground, then the law ordains that this soul shall at her first birth pass, not into any other animal, but only into man. The soul that has seen the most of truth shall be born as a philosopher, or artist, or some musical and loving nature. Whoever has seen truth in the second degree shall be some righteous king or warrior chief. The soul of the third class shall be a politician, or economist, or trader. The fourth shall be lover of gymnastic toils, or a physician. The fifth shall lead the life of a prophet or hierophant. To the sixth the character of poet or some other imitative artist will be assigned. To the seventh, the life of an artisan or husbandman. To the eighth, that of a sophist or demagogue. To the ninth, that of a tyrant. All these are states of probation, in which he who does righteously improves and he who does unrighteously deteriorates his lot.

Ten thousand years must elapse before the soul of each one can return to the place from which she came, for she cannot grow her wings in less. Only the soul of a philosopher, guileless and true, or the soul of a lover, who is not devoid of philosophy, may acquire wings in the third of the recurring periods of a thousand years. He is distinguished from the ordinary good man who gains wings in 3,000 years. And they who choose this life three times in succession have wings given to them and go away at the end of 3,000 years. But the others receive judgment when they have completed their first life. After the judgment they go, some of them to the houses of correction under the earth, and are punished. Others go to some place in heaven to which they are lightly borne by justice. There they live in a manner worthy of the life they led here when in the form of men. And at the end of the first thousand years the good souls and also the evil souls both come to draw lots and choose their second life, and they may take any one they please. The soul of a man may pass into the life of a beast, or from the beast return again into the man. But the soul which has never seen the truth will not pass into the human form. For a man must have intelligence of universals and be able to proceed from the many particulars of sense to one conception of reason. This is the recollection of those things which our soul once saw while following God—when regardless of what we now call being she raised her head up towards the true being. And therefore the mind of the philosopher alone has wings. This is just, for he is always, according to the measure of his abilities, clinging in recollection to those things in which God abides. In beholding them He is what He is. And he who employs aright these memories is ever being initiated into perfect mysteries and alone becomes truly perfect. But, as he forgets earthly interests and is rapt in the divine, the vulgar deem him mad and rebuke him; they do not see that he is inspired.

As I said at the beginning of this tale, I divided each soul into three—two horses and a charioteer. One of the horses was good and the other bad. The division may remain, but I have not yet explained in what the goodness or badness of either consists, and to that I will proceed. The right-hand horse is upright and cleanly made; he has a lofty neck and an aquiline nose. His colour is white, and his eyes dark; he is a lover of honour and modesty and temperance and the follower of true glory. He needs no touch of the whip, but is guided by word and admonition only. The other is a crooked lumbering animal, put together any which way; he has a short thick neck; he is flat-faced and of a dark colour, with grey eyes and blood-red complexion, the mate of insolence and pride, shag-eared and deaf, hardly yielding to whip and spur. Now, when the charioteer beholds the vision of love, has his whole soul warmed through sense, and is full of the prickings and ticklings of desire, the obedient steed, then as always under the government of shame, refrains from leaping on the beloved. But the other, heedless of the pricks and of the blows of the whip, plunges and runs away, giving all manner of trouble to his companion and the charioteer, whom he forces to approach the beloved and to remember the joys of love. They at first indignantly oppose him and will not be urged on to do terrible and unlawful deeds. But at last, when he persists in plaguing them, they yield and agree to do as he bids them.

9.2 ARISTOTLE ON THE SELF AND HUMAN FUNCTION

Aristotle (384–322 BCE) was born in Stigara near Macedonia. His father, Nichomachus, was court physician to the Macedonian king. At 17, Aristotle traveled to Athens and became a student in Plato's school, the Academy, where he remained the next twenty years. The Macedonian king called him to return home to educate a young prince named Alexander. Alexander became one of the greatest generals and empire builders ever to live—Alexander the Great. Aristotle came back to Athens upon the ascendency of Alexander and set up his own school, the Lyceum. There he lectured on almost the entire span of philosophical and scientific questions during the period when the culture of classical Greece was at its highest point. He also wrote voluminously, not so elegantly as Plato, in the works that have survived, but in a style that shows that he had learned a lot about good reasoning from Socrates and the intellectual revolution Socrates brought about. Indeed, a contemporary of Euclid, Aristotle was an early codifier of principles of reasoning, the founder of logic in the West. His writings were so important to medieval philosophers in Europe that they called him simply "the philosopher."

Here we shall look at his ideas about the self. Aristotle says that a self is a primary substance. It has a function. The self is sui generis; it does not reduce to a sum of its parts. It is not merely a mixture or combination. The self has both mental and physical properties. A soul or person is fundamentally a unity of material and mental properties; it is impossible to analyze that unity into something more primitive.

A soul, Aristotle says, is a cause or source of a living body. The soul is not just the body; it is not itself physical. It has an essential connection to life: It is that by virtue of which the body lives. More specifically, it gives the body the power to grow, move, perceive, and think.

Though the soul is not the body, it does have an essential connection to the body. So, Aristotle says, the soul cannot exist without the body. We might think of it as the form of the body; soul and body stand in a relation not unlike that of form to matter.

9.2.1 Aristotle, from *De Anima*

1

Let the foregoing suffice as our account of the views concerning the soul which have been handed on by our predecessors; let us now dismiss them and make as it were a completely fresh start, endeavouring to give a precise answer to the question What is soul?, i.e., to formulate the most general possible definition of it.

We are in the habit of recognizing, as one determinate kind of what is, substance, and that in several senses, (a) in the sense of matter or that which in itself is not "a this," and (b) in the sense of form or essence, which is that precisely in virtue of which a thing is called "a this," and thirdly (c) in the sense of that which is compounded of both (a) and (b). Now matter is potentiality, form actuality; of the latter there are two grades related to one another as, e.g., knowledge to the exercise of knowledge.

Among substances are by general consent reckoned bodies and especially natural bodies; for they are the principles of all other bodies. Of natural bodies some have life in them, others not; by life we mean self-nutrition and growth (with its correlative decay). It follows that every natural body which has life in it is a substance in the sense of a composite.

But since it is also a body of such and such a kind, viz. having life, the body cannot be soul; the body is the subject or matter, not what is attributed to it. Hence the soul must be a substance in the sense of the form of a natural body having life potentially within it. But substance is actuality, and thus soul is the actuality of a body as above characterized. Now the word *actuality* has two senses corresponding respectively to the possession of knowledge and the actual exercise of knowledge. It is obvious that the soul is actuality in the first sense, viz. that of knowledge as possessed, for both sleeping and waking presuppose the existence of soul, and of these waking corresponds to actual knowing, sleeping to knowledge possessed but not employed, and, in the history of the individual, knowledge comes before its employment or exercise.

That is why the soul is the first grade of actuality of a natural body having life potentially in it. The body so described is a body which is organized. The parts of plants in spite of their extreme

Source: Aristotle, *On the Soul*. From *De Anima*, Book II. Translated by J. A. Smith. Oxford: Oxford University Press, 1931.

simplicity are "organs"; e.g., the leaf serves to shelter the pericarp, the pericarp to shelter the fruit, while the roots of plants are analogous to the mouth of animals, both serving for the absorption of food. If, then, we have to give a general formula applicable to all kinds of soul, we must describe it as the first grade of actuality of a natural organized body. That is why we can wholly dismiss as unnecessary the question whether the soul and the body are one: it is as meaningless as to ask whether the wax and the shape given to it by the stamp are one, or generally the matter of a thing and that of which it is the matter. Unity has many senses (as many as "is" has), but the most proper and fundamental sense of both is the relation of an actuality to that of which it is the actuality.

We have now given an answer to the question, What is soul?—an answer which applies to it in its full extent. It is substance in the sense which corresponds to the definitive formula of a thing's essence. That means that it is "the essential whatness" of a body of the character just assigned. Suppose that what is literally an "organ," like an axe, were a natural body, its "essential whatness," would have been its essence, and so its soul; if this disappeared from it, it would have ceased to be an axe, except in name. As it is, it is just an axe; it wants the character which is required to make its whatness or formulable essence a soul; for that, it would have had to be a natural body of a particular kind, viz. one having in itself the power of setting itself in movement and arresting itself. Next, apply this doctrine in the case of the "parts" of the living body. Suppose that the eye were an animal—sight would have been its soul, for sight is the substance or essence of the eye which corresponds to the formula, the eye being merely the matter of seeing; when seeing is removed the eye is no longer an eye, except in name—it is no more a real eye than the eye of a statue or of a painted figure. We must now extend our consideration from the "parts" to the whole living body, for what the departmental sense is to the bodily part which is its organ, that the whole faculty of sense is to the whole sensitive body as such.

We must not understand by that which is "potentially capable of living" what has lost the soul it had, but only what still retains it; but seeds and fruits are bodies which possess the qualification. Consequently, while waking is actuality in a sense corresponding to the cutting and the seeing, the soul is actuality in the sense corresponding to the power of sight and the power in the tool; the body corresponds to what exists in potentiality; as the pupil plus the power of sight constitutes the eye, so the soul plus the body constitutes the animal.

From this it indubitably follows that the soul is inseparable from its body, or at any rate that certain parts of it are (if it has parts) for the actuality of some of them is nothing but the actualities of their bodily parts. Yet some may be separable because they are not the actualities of any body at all. Further, we have no light on the problem whether the soul may not be the actuality of its body in the sense in which the sailor is the actuality of the ship.

This must suffice as our sketch or outline determination of the nature of soul.

2

We resume our inquiry from a fresh starting-point by calling attention to the fact that what has soul in it differs from what has not, in that the former displays life. Now, this word has more than one sense, and provided any one alone of these is found in a thing we say that thing is living. Living, that is, may mean thinking or perception or local movement and rest, or movement in the sense of nutrition, decay and growth. Hence we think of plants also as living, for they are observed to possess in themselves an originative power through which they increase or decrease in all spatial directions; they grow up and down, and everything that grows increases its bulk alike in both directions or indeed in all, and continues to live so long as it can absorb nutriment.

This power of self-nutrition can be isolated from the other powers mentioned, but not they from it—in mortal beings at least. The fact is obvious in plants; for it is the only psychic power they possess.

This is the originative power the possession of which leads us to speak of things as living at all, but it is the possession of sensation that leads us for the first time to speak of living things as animals; for even those beings which possess no power of local movement but do possess the power of sensation we call animals and not merely living things.

The primary form of sense is touch, which belongs to all animals. Just as the power of self-nutrition can be isolated from touch and sensation generally, so touch can be isolated from all other forms of sense. (By the power of self-nutrition we mean that departmental power of the soul which is common to plants and animals: all animals whatsoever are observed to have the sense of touch.) What the explanation of these two facts is, we must discuss later. At present we must confine ourselves to saying that soul is the source of these phenomena and is characterized by them, viz. by the powers of self-nutrition, sensation, thinking, and motivity.

Is each of these a soul or a part of a soul? And if a part, a part in what sense? A part merely distinguishable by definition or a part distinct in local situation as well? In the case of certain of these powers, the answers to these questions are easy, in the case of others we are puzzled what to say. Just as in the case of plants which when divided are observed to continue to live though removed to a distance from one another (thus showing that in their case the soul of each individual plant before division was actually one, potentially many), so we notice a similar result in other varieties of soul, i.e., in insects which have been cut in two; each of the segments possesses both sensation and local movement; and if sensation, necessarily also imagination and appetition; for, where there is sensation, there is also pleasure and pain, and, where these, necessarily also desire.

We have no evidence as yet about mind or the power to think; it seems to be a widely different kind of soul, differing as what is eternal from what is perishable; it alone is capable of existence in isolation from all other psychic powers. All the other parts of soul, it is evident from what we have said, are, in spite of certain statements to the contrary, incapable of separate existence though, of course, distinguishable by definition. If opining is distinct from perceiving, to be capable of opining and to be capable of perceiving must be distinct, and so with all the other forms of living above enumerated. Further, some animals possess all these parts of soul, some certain of them only, others one only (this is what enables us to classify animals); the cause must be considered later. A similar arrangement is found also within the field of the senses; some classes of animals have all the senses, some only certain of them, others only one, the most indispensable, touch.

Since the expression "that whereby we live and perceive" has two meanings, just like the expression "that whereby we know"—that may mean either (a) knowledge or (b) the soul, for we can speak of knowing by or with either, and similarly that whereby we are in health may be either (a) health or (b) the body or some part of the body; and since of the two terms thus contrasted knowledge or health is the name of a form, essence, or ratio, or if we so express it an actuality of a recipient matter—knowledge belongs to what is capable of knowing, health to what is capable of being made healthy (for the operation of that which is capable of originating change terminates and has its seat in what is changed or altered); further, since it is the soul by or with which primarily we live, perceive, and think: It follows that the soul must be a ratio or formulable essence, not a matter or subject. For, as we said, the word *substance* has three meanings—form, matter, and the complex of both—and of these three what is called matter is potentiality, what is called form actuality. Since then the complex here is the living thing, the body cannot be the actuality of the soul; it is the soul which is the actuality of a certain kind of body. Hence the rightness of the view that the soul cannot be without a body, while it cannot be a body; it is not a body but something relative to a body. That is why it is in a body, and a body of a definite kind. It was a mistake, therefore, to do as former thinkers did, merely to fit it into a body without adding a definite specification of the kind or character of that body. Reflection confirms the observed fact; the actuality of any given thing can only be realized in what is already potentially that thing, i.e., in a matter of its own appropriate to it. From all this it follows that soul is an actuality or formulable essence of something that possesses a potentiality of being besouled.

4

The soul is the cause or source of the living body. The terms cause and source have many senses. But the soul is the cause of its body alike in all three senses which we explicitly recognize. It is (a) the source or origin of movement, it is (b) the end (*telos*), it is (c) the essence of the whole living body.

CHAPTER 10

Mind and Body in Early Modern Philosophy

"A thing that thinks"

René Descartes (1596–1650), the father of modern philosophy, begins his *Meditations on First Philosophy* by subjecting his beliefs to skeptical challenge. Traditional skeptical arguments—the reality of illusions, the possibility that he is dreaming—lead him to doubt the evidence of his senses. The possibility of an evil deceiver leads him to doubt even the truths of logic. But he finds one thing he cannot doubt: that he thinks and thus that he exists. *Cogito ergo sum*, he writes: "I think, therefore I am." I am a thing that thinks. Descartes thus moves theory of knowledge to center stage in philosophy, brings a thoroughly new paradigm to the philosophy of mind, and defines the problems that would occupy philosophers for the next several centuries.

10.1 DESCARTES' DUALISM OF MIND AND BODY

What is a thing that thinks? "It is a thing which doubts, understands, [conceives], affirms, denies, wills, refuses, which also imagines and feels," Descartes says. He develops a catalog of properties or capacities peculiar to selves and constituting their essence. Each of us is essentially a thing that thinks: doubts, understands, affirms, denies, wills, feels, and so on.

Descartes points out that these are mental properties or states, not physical properties. Mental states cannot be divided in the way that a material object can. Furthermore, each of us can know his or her own mind more directly and securely than we can know anything physical. We cannot be sure even about our own bodies. We could be dreaming; we could be brains in vats. We can, however, have certainty about our thoughts. As Descartes concludes, "I see clearly that there is nothing which is easier for me to know than my mind." He thus distinguishes mind from body.

We do have bodies, according to Descartes, although we do not know them directly in the way that we know ourselves. We know them through our senses, though we could be deceived. In fact, we are not, because God, our Creator, is good and cannot be a deceiver. The notion of a deceiver God would contradict our clear and distinct idea that God is perfect.

So we are things that think. We also have bodies fundamentally distinct from our minds. But then how does a body relate to a mind? They seem closely linked, for the mind receives sensory impressions—sights, sounds, and so on—from the body. A person's mental decision to walk results, moreover, in movements of his or her limbs. If mind and body are fundamentally different, as Descartes argues, then how is their "union and apparent intermingling" possible?

This is a form of the "mind/body problem" that has remained prominent in Western philosophy, including the contemporary period, since Descartes. Is there a causal relationship between mind and body? But then how can a mental act cause physical motion? And how can a physical object give rise to a thought or sensation in the mind? Descartes's reflection shows us a mind/body problem, but his view of their interaction as learned "by means of ordinary life and conversations," not by philosophical reflection, seems to miss the point. The problem is not whether mind and body do interact; it is how it is possible that they do, given their fundamental difference. The unity of a person as a composite of body and mind seems, on Descartes's account, to remain a mystery.

10.1.1 René Descartes, from *Meditations on First Philosophy*

Meditation II: Of the Nature of the Human Mind; and That It Is More Easily Known than the Body

The Meditation of yesterday filled my mind with so many doubts that it is no longer in my power to forget them. And yet I do not see in what manner I can resolve them; and, just as if I had all of a sudden fallen into very deep water, I am so disconcerted that I can neither make certain of setting my feet on the bottom, nor can I swim and so support myself on the surface. I shall nevertheless make an effort and follow anew the same path as that on which I yesterday entered, i.e., I shall proceed by setting aside all that in which the least doubt could be supposed to exist, just as if I had discovered that it was absolutely false; and I shall ever follow in this road until I have met with something which is certain, or at least, if I can do nothing else, until I have learned for certain that there is nothing in the world that is certain. Archimedes, in order that he might draw the terrestrial globe out of its place and transport it elsewhere, demanded only that one point should be fixed and immovable; in the same way I shall have the right to conceive high hopes if I am happy enough to discover one thing only which is certain and indubitable.

Source: René Descartes, *Meditations on First Philosophy*. Translated by Elizabeth S. Haldane, in *The Philosophical Works of Descartes*. Cambridge: Cambridge University Press, 1911.

I suppose, then, that all the things that I see are false; I persuade myself that nothing has ever existed of all that my fallacious memory represents to me. I consider that I possess no senses; I imagine that body, figure, extension, movement and place are but the fictions of my mind. What, then, can be esteemed as true? Perhaps nothing at all, except that there is nothing in the world that is certain.

But how can I know there is not something different from those things that I have just considered, of which one cannot have the slightest doubt? Is there not some God, or some other being by whatever name we call it, who puts these reflections into my mind? That is not necessary, for is it not possible that I am capable of producing them myself? I myself, am I not at least something? But I have already denied that I had senses and body. Yet I hesitate, for what follows from that? Am I so dependent on body and senses that I cannot exist without these? But I was persuaded that there was nothing in all the world, that there was no heaven, no earth, that there were no minds, nor any bodies: was I not then likewise persuaded that I did not exist? Not at all; of a surety I myself did exist since I persuaded myself of something [or merely because I thought of something]. But there is some deceiver or other, very powerful and very cunning, who ever employs his ingenuity in deceiving me. Then without doubt I exist also if he deceives me, and let him deceive me as much as he will, he can never cause me to be nothing so long as I think that I am something. So that after having reflected well and carefully examined all things, we must come to the definite conclusion that this proposition: I am, I exist, is necessarily true each time that I pronounce it, or that I mentally conceive it.

But I do not yet know clearly enough what I am, I who am certain that I am; and hence I must be careful to see that I do not imprudently take some other object in place of myself, and thus that I do not go astray in respect of this knowledge that I hold to be the most certain and most evident of all that I have formerly learned. That is why I shall now consider anew what I believed myself to be before I embarked upon these last reflections; and of my former opinions I shall withdraw all that might even in a small degree be invalidated by the reasons which I have just brought forward, in order that there may be nothing at all left beyond what is absolutely certain and indubitable.

What then did I formerly believe myself to be? Undoubtedly I believed myself to be a man. But what is a man? Shall I say a reasonable animal? Certainly not; for then I should have to inquire what an animal is, and what is reasonable; and thus from a single question I should insensibly fall into an infinitude of others more difficult; and I should not wish to waste the little time and leisure remaining to me in trying to unravel subtleties like these. But I shall rather stop here to consider the thoughts which of themselves spring up in my mind, and which were not inspired by anything beyond my own nature alone when I applied myself to the consideration of my being. In the first place, then, I considered myself as having a face, hands, arms, and all that system of members composed on bones and flesh as seen in a corpse which I designated by the name of body. In addition to this I considered that I was nourished, that I walked, that I felt, and that I thought, and I referred all these actions to the soul: but I did not stop to consider what the soul was, or if I did stop, I imagined that it was something extremely rare and subtle like a wind, a flame, or an ether, which was spread throughout my grosser parts. As to body I had no manner of doubt about its nature, but thought I had a very clear knowledge of it; and if I had desired to explain it according to the notions that I had then formed of it, I should have described it thus: By the body I understand all that which can be defined by a certain figure: something which can be confined in a certain place, and which can fill a given space in such a way that every other body will be excluded from it; which can be perceived either by touch, or by sight, or by hearing, or by taste, or by smell; which can be moved in many ways not, in truth, by itself, but by something which is foreign to it, by which it is touched [and from which it receives impressions]: for to have the power of self-movement, as also of feeling or of thinking, I did not consider to appertain to the nature of body: on the contrary, I was rather astonished to find that faculties similar to them existed in some bodies.

But what am I, now that I suppose that there is a certain genius which is extremely powerful, and, if I may say so, malicious, who employs all his powers in deceiving me? Can I affirm that I possess the least of all those things which I have just said pertain to the nature of body? I pause to consider, I revolve all these things in my mind, and I find none of which I can say that it pertains to me. It would be tedious to stop to enumerate them. Let us pass to the attributes of soul and see if there is any one which is in me? What of nutrition or walking [the first mentioned]? But if it is so that I have no body it is also true that I can neither walk nor take nourishment. Another attribute is sensation. But one cannot feel without body, and besides I have thought I perceived many things during sleep that I recognised in my waking moments as not having been experienced at all. What of thinking? I find here that thought is an attribute that belongs to me; it alone cannot be separated from me. I am, I exist, that is certain. But how often? Just when I think; for it might possibly be the case if I ceased entirely to think, that I should likewise cease altogether to exist. I do not now admit anything which is not necessarily true: to speak accurately I am not more than a thing which thinks, that is to say a mind or a soul, or an understanding, or a reason, which are terms whose significance was formerly unknown to me. I am, however, a real thing and really exist; but what thing? I have answered: a thing which thinks.

And what more? I shall exercise my imagination [in order to see if I am not something more]. I am not a collection of members which we call the human body: I am not a subtle air distributed through these members, I am not a wind, a fire, a vapour, a breath, nor anything at all which I can imagine or conceive; because I have assumed that all these were nothing. Without changing that supposition, I find that I only leave myself certain of the fact that I am somewhat. But perhaps it is true that these same things which I supposed were non-existent because they are unknown to me, are really not different from the self which I know. I am not sure about this, I shall not dispute about it now; I can only give judgment on things that are known to me. I know that I exist, and I inquire what I am, I whom I know to exist. But it is very certain that the knowledge of my existence taken in its precise significance does not depend on things whose existence is not yet known to me; consequently it does not depend on those which I can feign in imagination. And indeed the very term *feign in imagination* proves to me my error, for I really do this if I imagine myself a something, since to imagine is nothing else than to contemplate the figure or image of a corporeal thing. But I already know for certain that I am, and that it may be that all these images, and, speaking generally, all things that relate to the nature of body are nothing but dreams [and chimeras]. For this reason I see clearly that I have as little reason to say, I shall stimulate my imagination in order to know more distinctly what I am, than if I were to say, I am now awake, and I perceive something that is real and true: but because I do not yet perceive it distinctly enough, I shall go to sleep of express purpose so that my dreams may represent the perception with greatest truth and evidence. And, thus, I know for certain that nothing of all that I can understand by means of my imagination belongs to this knowledge which I have of myself, and that it is necessary to recall the mind from this mode of thought with the utmost diligence in order that it may be able to know its own nature with perfect distinctness.

But what then am I? A thing which thinks. What is a thing which thinks? It is a thing which doubts, understands, [conceives], affirms, denies, wills, refuses, which also imagines and feels.

Certainly it is no small matter if all these things pertain to my nature. But why should they not so pertain? Am I not that being who now doubts nearly everything, who nevertheless understands certain things, who affirms that one only is true, who denies all the others, who desires to know more, is averse from being deceived, who imagines many things, sometimes indeed despite his will, and who perceives many likewise, as by the intervention of the bodily organs? Is there nothing in all this which is as true as it is certain that I exist, even though I should always sleep and though he who has given me being employed all his ingenuity in deceiving me? Is there likewise any one of these attributes which can be distinguished from my thought, or which might be said to be separated from myself? For it is so evident of itself that it is I who doubts, who understands, and who desires, that there is no reason here to add anything to explain it. And I have certainly the power of imagining likewise; for although it may happen (as I formerly supposed) that none of the things which I imagine are true, nevertheless this power of imagining does not cease to be really in use, and it forms part of my thought. Finally, I am the same who feels, that is to say, who perceives certain things, as by the organs of sense, since in truth I see light, I hear noise, I feel heat. But it will be said that these phenomena are false and that I am dreaming. Let it be so; still it is at least quite certain that it seems to me that I see light, that I hear noise, and that I feel heat. That cannot be false; properly speaking it is what is in me called feeling; and used in this precise sense that is no other thing than thinking.

From this time I begin to know what I am with a little more clearness and distinction than before; but nevertheless it still seems to me, and I cannot prevent myself from thinking, that corporeal things, whose images are framed by thought, which are tested by the senses, are much more distinctly known than that obscure part of me which does not come under the imagination. Although really it is very strange to say that I know and understand more distinctly these things whose existence seems to me dubious, which are unknown to me, and which do not belong to me, than others of the truth of which I am convinced, which are known to me and which pertain to my real nature, in a word, than myself. But I see clearly how the case stands: my mind loves to wander, and cannot yet suffer itself to be retained within the just limits of truth. Very good, let us once more give it the freest rein, so that, when afterwards we seize the proper occasion for pulling up, it may the more easily be regulated and controlled.

Let us begin by considering the commonest matters, those which we believe to be the most distinctly comprehended, to wit, the bodies which we touch and see; not indeed bodies in general, for these general ideas are usually a little more confused, but let us consider one body in particular. Let us take, for example, this piece of wax: it has been taken quite freshly from the hive, and it has not yet lost the sweetness of the honey which it contains; it still retains somewhat of the odour of the flowers from which it has been culled; its colour, its figure, its size are apparent; it is hard, cold, easily handled, and if you strike it with the finger, it will emit a sound. Finally all the things which are requisite to cause us distinctly to recognise a body, are met with in it. But notice that while I speak and approach the fire what remained of the taste is exhaled, the smell evaporates, the colour alters, the figure is destroyed, the size increases, it becomes liquid, it heats, scarcely can one handle it, and when one strikes it, now sound is emitted. Does the same wax remain after this change? We must confess that it remains; none would judge otherwise. What then did I know so distinctly in this piece of wax? It could certainly be nothing of all that the senses brought to my notice, since all these things which fall under taste, smell, sight, touch, and hearing, are found to be changed, and yet the same wax remains.

Perhaps it was what I now think, viz. that this wax was not that sweetness of honey, nor that agreeable scent of flowers, nor that particular whiteness, nor that figure, nor that sound, but simply a body which a little while before appeared to me as perceptible under these forms, and which is now perceptible under others. But what, precisely, is it that I imagine when I form such conceptions? Let us attentively consider this, and, abstracting from all that does not belong to the wax, let us see what remains. Certainly nothing remains excepting a certain extended thing which is flexible and movable. But what is the meaning of flexible and movable? Is it not that I imagine that this piece of wax being round is capable of becoming square and of passing from a square to a triangular figure? No, certainly it is not that, since I imagine it admits of an infinitude of similar changes, and I nevertheless do not know how to compass the infinitude by my imagination, and consequently this conception which I have of the wax is not brought about by the faculty of imagination. What now is this extension? Is it not also unknown? For it becomes greater when the wax is melted, greater when it is boiled, and greater still when the heat increases; and I should not conceive [clearly] according to truth what wax is, if I did not think that even this piece that we are considering is capable of receiving more variations in extension than I have ever imagined. We must then grant that I could not even understand through the imagination what this piece of wax is, and that it is my mind alone which perceives it. I say this piece of wax in particular, for as to wax in general it is yet clearer. But what is this piece of wax which cannot be understood excepting by the [understanding or] mind? It is certainly the same that I see, touch, imagine, and finally it is the same which I have always believed it to be from the beginning. But what must particularly be observed is that its perception is neither an act of vision, nor of touch, nor of imagination, and has never been such although it may have appeared formerly to be so, but only an intuition of the mind, which may be imperfect and confused as it was formerly, or clear and distinct as it is at present, according as my attention is more or less directed to the elements which are found in it, and of which it is composed.

Yet in the meantime I am greatly astonished when I consider [the great feebleness of mind] and its proneness to fall [insensibly] into error; for although without giving expression to my thought I consider all this in my own mind, words often impede me and I am almost deceived by the terms of ordinary language. For we say that we see the same wax, if it is present, and not that we simply judge that it is the same from its having the same colour and figure. From this I should conclude that I knew the wax by means of vision and not simply by the intuition of the mind; unless by chance I remember that, when looking from a window and saying I see men who pass in the street, I really do not see them, but infer that what I see is men, just as I say that I see wax. And yet what do I see from the window but hats and coats which may cover automatic machines? Yet I judge these to be men. And similarly solely by the faculty of judgment which rests in my mind, I comprehend that which I believed I saw with my eyes.

A man who makes it his aim to raise his knowledge above the common should be ashamed to derive the occasion for doubting from the forms of speech invented by the vulgar; I prefer to pass on and consider whether I had a more evident and perfect conception of what the wax was when I first perceived it, and when I believed I knew it by means of the external senses or at least by the common sense as it is called, that is to say by the imaginative faculty, or whether my present conception is clearer now that I have most carefully examined what it is, and in what way it can be known. It would certainly be absurd to doubt as to this. For what was there in this first perception which was distinct? What was there which might not as well have been perceived by any of the animals? But when I distinguish the wax from its external forms, and when, just as if I had taken from it its vestments, I consider it quite naked, it is certain that although some error may still be found in my judgment, I can nevertheless not perceive it thus without a human mind.

But finally what shall I say of this mind, that is, of myself, for up to this point I do not admit in myself anything but mind? What then, I who seem to perceive this piece of wax so distinctly, do I not know myself, not only with much more truth and certainty, but also with much more distinctness and clearness? For if I judge that the wax is or exists from the fact that I see it, it certainly follows much more clearly that I am or that I exist myself from the fact that I see it. For it may be that what I see is not really wax, it may also be that I do not possess eyes with which to see anything; but it cannot be that when I see, or (for I no longer take account of the distinction) when I think I see, that I myself who think am nought. So if I judge that the wax exists from the fact that I touch it, the same thing will follow, to wit, that I am; and if I judge that my imagination, or some other cause, whatever it is, persuades me that the wax exists, I shall still conclude the same. And what I have here remarked of wax may be applied to all other things which are external to me [and which are met with outside of me]. And further, if the [notion or] perception of wax has seemed to me clearer and more distinct, not only after the sight or the touch, but also after many other causes have rendered it quite manifest to me, with how much more [evidence] and distinctness must it be said that I now know myself, since all the reasons which contribute to the knowledge of wax, or any other body whatever, are yet better proofs of the nature of my mind! And there are so many other things in the mind itself which may contribute to the elucidation of its nature, that those which depend on body such as these just mentioned, hardly merit being taken into account.

But finally here I am, having insensibly reverted to the point I desired, for, since it is now manifest to me that even bodies are not properly speaking known by the senses or by the faculty of imagination, but by the understanding only, and since they are not known from the fact that they are seen or touched, but only because they are understood, I see clearly that there is nothing which is easier for me to know than my mind. But because it is difficult to rid oneself so promptly of an opinion to which one was accustomed for so long, it will be well that I should halt a little at this point, so that by the length of my meditation I may more deeply imprint on my memory this new knowledge.

10.2 PRINCESS ELIZABETH'S CRITIQUE OF DESCARTES' DUALISM

Princess Elizabeth of Bohemia (1618–1680) raises objections to Descartes' dualism. If mind and body are distinct, how can they interact? Elizabeth thus raises, perhaps for the first time, what has become known as *the mind–body problem.* It comprises two problems:

- *Sensation.* How is it possible for the body to affect the mind? How do excitations of the eyes, ears, etc., produce mental events such as sensations?
- *Mental causation.* How is it possible for the mind to affect the body? How can a mental event—a decision to raise my arm, for example—produce a physical motion in my limb?

Elizabeth not only raises these questions but advances sophisticated arguments that the soul cannot be distinct from the body. One, addressed especially to mental causation, rests on the completeness of physics. We have an account of what causes physical motions—namely, other physical motions. The physical motions occurring in the world, together with the laws of physics that govern such motions, seem to fix completely the physical motions that result. If so, there seems to be no space left in which mental events such as decisions or intentions might cause physical motions. Another argument concerns the nature of causation itself. How can something cause a physical motion in space and time if it is not itself extended in space? Our concept of causation includes combinations of events, such as one billiard ball striking and moving another, for the motions occur in space and time and are in fact contiguous in space and time. Gravity stretches our concept, for it seems to involve causation without contiguity—"action at a distance"—though that was, in the seventeenth century, as in our own, a controversial idea. At least, however, the masses exerting gravitational force on each other have spatial locations. The mind, if it is truly distinct from the body and not a physical substance at all, has no spatial location. So how can it act on anything physical?

Descartes grapples with these questions and arguments in his letters to Elizabeth and, finally, in his work *The Passions of the Soul*, which he dedicated to her, but advances little beyond his response to her that the senses show us that mind and body interact.

10.2.1 Princess Elizabeth, Letter to Descartes—The Hague, May 16, 1643

Mr. Descartes:

I learned, with much joy and regret, of your intention to see me the last few days. I am touched by your charity to be willing to communicate with an ignorant and disobedient person and by the misfortune which deprived me of so advantageous a conversation. Mr. Pallotti greatly increased this last passion by repeating to me the solutions that you gave him of the obscurities contained in the physics of Mr. Rhegius. I would have been informed better from your mouth, as I would also have been on a question I proposed to the professor when I saw him, concerning which he returned me to you to receive a satisfactory answer.... I am asking you to tell me how the soul of man (being only one thinking substance) can determine the spirits of the body to produce voluntary actions. For it seems that all determination of movement is done by an impulse of a moving thing: The way in which a thing is pushed is determined by that which drives it or by the quality and appearance of surface of the latter. Contact is necessary for the first two conditions, and extension for the third. You entirely exclude the former from the concept that you have of the soul, and the latter seems to me incompatible with an immaterial thing. This is why I ask you for a definition of the soul more specific than that in your metaphysics, i.e., of its substance, separated from its action in thought. For even if we suppose them to be inseparable (which, however, is difficult to prove in the mother's womb and in seizures), like the attributes of God, we can, by considering them separately, acquire a more perfect idea of them.

Knowing you to be the best doctor for me, I am sure that you will discover the weaknesses of this speculation and hope that, observing the oath

Source: Translated by Daniel Bonevac.

of Hippocrates, you will bring remedies without publishing them, and do what I ask you to do, such as suffering these importunities from your affectionate friend, at your service,
Elizabeth

10.2.2 Princess Elizabeth, Letter to Descartes—The Hague, June 20, 1643

Mr. Descartes,

... That makes me confess, without shame, to have found in myself all the causes of error which you notice in your letter, and still to be unable to banish them entirely, since the life that I am forced to carry out does not leave me the provision of enough time to acquire a practice of meditation according to your rules. Sometimes the interests of my house, which I should not neglect, sometimes talks and kindnesses, which I cannot avoid, wear me down so extremely that this weak spirit is, for a long time afterwards, useless for anything else.

I hope to have been useful, to excuse my stupidity, not to have been able to understand the idea by which we must judge how something nonextended and immaterial can move the body—an idea such as that which you formerly had of gravity; nor why this power, that you attributed to it then under the name of a quality, falsely attributed, to carry a body towards the center of the earth, must rather persuade us that a body can be pushed by something immaterial. The demonstration contrary to the truth (that you promise in your physics) to confirm our belief in its impossibility. For, to cite the main reason, this idea (being able to claim to the same perfection and objective reality as that of God alone) must arise from ignorance of what truly moves these bodies toward the center. And since no material cause is presented to the senses, it would have been allotted to its opposite, the immaterial—which, nevertheless, I could never conceive but as a negation of matter—which cannot have any communication with it.

And I acknowledge that it would be easier to me to concede matter and extension to the soul than to concede the capacity to move the body and to be moved by it to an immaterial being. For, if the former were done by information, it would have to be the case that the spirits that produce the movement were intelligent, which you do not grant to anything corporeal. And even in your metaphysical *Meditations*, where you show the possibility of the second, however, it is very difficult to understand how a soul, as you describe it, after having had the faculty and the practice of reasoning well, can lose all that by some vapors, and that, being able to remain without the body, and not having anything in common with it, is governed to such an extent by it.

But, since you undertook to instruct me, I speak of these feelings only as of friends whom I do not wish to preserve, being assured that you will explain to me as well the nature of an immaterial substance and the manner of its actions and passions in the body, as well as all the other things you wanted to teach. I ask you to believe that you can grant this charity to nobody who is more sensitive to her obligation to you than your very affectionate friend,
Elizabeth

10.2.3 Princess Elizabeth, Letter to Descartes—The Hague, July 1, 1643

Mr. Descartes,

... I too find that the senses show me that the soul moves the body, but they do not teach me (any more than the understanding and the imagination do) the way in which it does it. And, with respect to that, I think that there are properties of the soul we do not yet know that will perhaps be able to reverse what your metaphysical *Meditations* persuaded me of, with such good reasons, namely, the inextension of the soul. And this doubt seems to be well founded on the rule that you provide in speaking about truth and falsehood: that all our error consists in forming judgments about what we do not sufficiently perceive. Though extension is not necessary to thought—though it is not incompatible with it—it may be able to belong with some other function of the soul, which is no less essential to it. At least it contradicts the Scholastics, for whom it is all in the whole body, and all in each of its parts. I do not excuse myself consequently to confuse the notion of the soul with that of the body for the same reason as the vulgar; but that does nothing to remove the first doubt, and I will despair to find certainty in a thing of the world, if you do not give me anything to prevent me from being a skeptic, to which my reasoning first carried me. Although I owe you this confession, to give you thanks, it would I believe be extremely imprudent if I did not recognize your kindness and generosity, equal to the rest of your virtues as much by the experience that I already had of them as by reputation. You can bear witness to them more kindly only by the explanations and councils you grant me, which I prize above the greatest treasures that your very affectionate friend could possess, at your service,

Elizabeth

10.2.4 Princess Elizabeth, Letter to Descartes—The Hague, April 25, 1646

Mr. Descartes,

The treaty that my brother Philippe concluded with the Republic of Venice gave me, ever since your departure, an occupation much less pleasant than the one you had left me, concerning a matter which surpasses my knowledge, for which I was called only to compensate for the impatience of the young man to which it was addressed. That has prevented me up to now from taking advantage of the permission that you gave me, to set out for you the obscurities that my stupidity makes me find in your treatise on the passions. They are small in number, since to understand only the order, definition and distinctions that you give to the passions, and finally the whole moral part of the treatise, surpasses anything ever said about this subject.

But since its physical part is not so clear to the ignorant, I do not see how one can know the various movements of blood that cause five primitive

Source: Translated by Daniel Bonevac.

passions, since they are never in isolation. For example, love is always accompanied by desire and joy, or desire and sadness, and as it is strengthened, the others also grow, and vice versa. How is it then possible to notice the difference of the beat of the pulse, the digestion of meats and other changes of the body, that are used to discover the nature of these movements? Also that which you note, of each one of these passions, is not the same for all temperaments. Mine is such that sadness always takes away my appetite, no matter whether it is mixed with hate or comes to me only from the death of a friend.

When you speak about the external signs of these passions, you say that admiration, joined with joy, makes the lungs swell with various jolts to cause laughter. I beg you to add how admiration (which, according to your description, seems to operate only on the brain) can so promptly open the openings of the heart to create this effect.

These passions, you note with a sigh, do not always seem to be there, since habit and the fullness of the stomach produce them too....

Your very affectionate friend, at your service, Elizabeth.

10.3 LOCKE ON CRITERIA OF PERSONAL IDENTITY

John Locke (1632–1704) takes Descartes's problem seriously but finds an empirical unity of mind and body in a person. For all that Descartes says, our minds could be unstructured streams of consciousness—known intimately, to be sure, known better than we know our bodies, but nevertheless unpredictable. But the mind's states are linked to one another in many ways, in particular, by memory. You think of yourself as the same person you were when you were a child because there are chains of continuity. You may not remember being a very young child, but you can remember earlier states in which you could remember still earlier states, in which you could remember being a very young child.

Locke asks quite generally for criteria of identity: What makes an *F* the same *F*? Locke is a *relative identity* theorist: The answer varies, he says, depending on what *F* is. For lumps of matter, the criterion is continuity of substance. For machines, it is continuity of structure. (Replacing the tires on a car does not make it a different car.) For animals as well as human beings, it is bodily continuity. If Socrates were reincarnated as Caesar Borgia, we would still count two different human beings. We individuate humans by bodies. Locke is not denying that there could be lines of continuity beyond the grave; his point is that to be the same human being is to be the same living body, one that is born and that dies.

But what about *me*? As Descartes stresses, I am essentially a thing that thinks. My mind is essential to me in a way my body is not. So my identity as a person should not be tied to my body.

Being the same human being is being the same life in the same body. But being the same person is essentially mental. We find it intelligible to imagine a prince being turned into a frog, for example, or Smith waking up to find herself in Jones's body, or Socrates being reincarnated as Caesar Borgia, and so on. Whether or not these things are physically possible, they are conceptually possible; they are not incoherent. So Locke distinguishes being the same human being from being the same person. A human being is an animal, so being the same human being is just a matter of being the same animal—the same life in the same body. But a person is essentially rational, a "thing that thinks." So being the same person is being the same conscious mind.

The identity of a person thus consists in continuity of consciousness. What makes a person is the network of memories, hopes, expectations, fantasies, convictions, and other thoughts and awarenesses that constitute a single consciousness. To ask whether Smith and Gomez are the same person is to ask whether they have the same consciousness, whether there is one interwoven chain of memories, hopes, expectations, etc. If so, they are the same person; if not, not.

Plainly one can be the same person, or even the same human being, without being the same lump of matter. Every time Smith breathes, her body takes in some molecules (of oxygen, for example) and expels others. Jones might be in an accident and lose a finger and yet be the same human being and the same person. A more interesting question is whether different human beings can count as the same person or different people count as the same human being. In other words, can one person inhabit two different bodies? Can two people inhabit the same body? Conceptually, the answer seems to be yes.

Locke is nevertheless highly skeptical of claims of reincarnation. A reincarnated person has no memory of prior lives; there is no continuity of consciousness. There is no reason why there could not be such continuity, however, without a body or with a very different kind of body. So Locke has no objection to thinking that we might have a life after death. In any case, the term *person* has great moral significance, for we may hold *A* responsible for what *B* has done only if *A* and *B* are the same person.

In all these matters, Locke speaks of what is conceptually possible. There is no contradiction in thinking of two people inhabiting the same body—indeed, men or women with multiple personalities may be an instance of this phenomenon—nor of one person inhabiting different bodies. There is no contradiction in thinking of consciousness surviving death. But whether these things are really possible depends on facts about the mind and consciousness that we do not know.

10.3.1 John Locke, from *An Essay Concerning Human Understanding*

Book II, Chapter 27: Of Identity and Diversity

1. *Wherein identity consists.* Another occasion the mind often takes of comparing is the very being of things, when, considering anything as existing at any determined time and place, we compare it with itself existing at another time, and thereon form the ideas of identity and diversity. When we see anything to be in any place in any instant of time, we are sure (be it what it will) that it is that very thing, and not another which at that

Source: John Locke, *An Essay Concerning Human Understanding*. London: William Tegg, 1689.

same time exists in another place, how like and undistinguishable soever it may be in all other respects: and in this consists identity, when the ideas it is attributed to vary not at all from what they were that moment wherein we consider their former existence, and to which we compare the present.

6. *Identity of animals.* The case is not so much different in brutes but that any one may hence see what makes an animal and continues it the same. Something we have like this in machines, and may serve to illustrate it. For example, what is a watch? It is plain it is nothing but a fit organization or construction of parts to a certain end, which, when a sufficient force is added to it, it is capable to attain. If we would suppose this machine one continued body, all whose organized parts were repaired, increased, or diminished by a constant addition or separation of insensible parts, with one common life, we should have something very much like the body of an animal, with this difference, that, in an animal the fitness of the organization, and the motion wherein life consists, begin together, the motion coming from within; but in machines the force, coming sensibly from without, is often away when the organ is in order, and well fitted to receive it.

7. *The identity of man.* This also shows wherein the identity of the same man consists; viz., in nothing but a participation of the same continued life, by constantly fleeting particles of matter, in succession vitally united to the same organized body. He that shall place the identity of man in anything else but, like that of other animals, in one fitly organized body, taken in any one instant, and from thence continued, under one organization of life, in several successively fleeting particles of matter united to it, will find it hard to make an embryo, one of years, mad and sober, the same man, by any supposition that will not make it possible for Seth, Ismael, Socrates, Pilate, St. Augustine, and Caesar Borgia to be the same man. For if the identity of soul alone makes the same man, and there be nothing in the nature of matter why the same individual spirit may not be united to different bodies, it will be possible that those men, living in distant ages, and of different tempers, may have been the same man: which way of speaking must be from a very strange use of the word *man*, applied to an idea out of which body and shape are excluded. And that way of speaking would agree yet worse with the notions of those philosophers who allow of transmigration, and are of opinion that the souls of men may, for their miscarriages, be detruded into the bodies of beasts, as fit habitations, with organs suited to the satisfaction of their brutal inclinations. But yet I think nobody, could he be sure that the soul of Heliogabalus were in one of his hogs, would yet say that hog were a man or Heliogabalus.

8. *Idea of identity suited to the idea it is applied to.* It is not therefore unity of substance that comprehends all sorts of identity, or will determine it in every case; but to conceive and judge of it aright, we must consider what idea the word it is applied to stands for: it being one thing to be the same substance, another the same man, and a third the same person, if *person, man*, and *substance*, are three names standing for three different ideas;—for such as is the idea belonging to that name, such must be the identity; which, if it had been a little more carefully attended to, would possibly have prevented a great deal of that confusion which often occurs about this matter, with no small seeming difficulties, especially concerning personal identity, which therefore we shall in the next place a little consider.

9. *Same man.* An animal is a living organized body; and consequently the same animal, as we have observed, is the same continued life communicated to different particles of matter, as they happen successively to be united to that organized living body. And whatever is talked of other definitions, ingenious observation puts it past doubt that the idea in our minds, of which the sound man in our mouths is the sign, is nothing else but of an animal of such a certain form. Since I think I may be confident, that whoever should see a creature of his own shape or make, though it had no more reason all its life than a cat or a parrot, would call him still a man; or whoever should hear a cat or a parrot discourse, reason, and philosophize, would

call or think it nothing but a cat or a parrot; and say the one was a dull irrational man and the other a very intelligent rational parrot.

For I presume it is not the idea of a thinking or rational being alone that makes the idea of a man in most people's sense: but of a body so and so shaped, joined to it: and if that be the idea of a man, the same successive body not shifted all at once must, as well as the same immaterial spirit, go to the making of the same man.

11. *Personal identity.* This being premised, to find wherein personal identity consists, we must consider what person stands for;—which, I think, is a thinking, intelligent being, that has reason and reflection and can consider itself as itself, the same thinking thing, in different times and places; which it does only by that consciousness which is inseparable from thinking and, as it seems to me, essential to it: it being impossible for any one to perceive without perceiving that he does perceive. When we see, hear, smell, taste, feel, meditate, or will anything, we know that we do so. Thus it is always as to our present sensations and perceptions: and by this everyone is to himself that which he calls self:—it not being considered, in this case, whether the same self be continued in the same or diverse substances. For, since consciousness always accompanies thinking, and it is that which makes everyone to be what he calls self, and thereby distinguishes himself from all other thinking things, in this alone consists personal identity, i.e., the sameness of a rational being: and as far as this consciousness can be extended backwards to any past action or thought, so far reaches the identity of that person; it is the same self now it was then; and it is by the same self with this present one that now reflects on it that that action was done.

12. *Consciousness makes personal identity.* But it is further inquired whether it be the same identical substance. This few would think they had reason to doubt of, if these perceptions, with their consciousness, always remained present in the mind, whereby the same thinking thing would be always consciously present and, as would be thought, evidently the same to itself. But that which seems to make the difficulty is this, that this consciousness being interrupted always by forgetfulness, there being no moment of our lives wherein we have the whole train of all our past actions before our eyes in one view, but even the best memories losing the sight of one part whilst they are viewing another; and we sometimes, and that the greatest part of our lives, not reflecting on our past selves, being intent on our present thoughts, and in sound sleep having no thoughts at all, or at least none with that consciousness which remarks our waking thoughts,—I say, in all these cases, our consciousness being interrupted, and we losing the sight of our past selves, doubts are raised whether we are the same thinking thing, i.e., the same substance or no. Which, however reasonable or unreasonable, concerns not personal identity at all. The question being what makes the same person; and not whether it be the same identical substance, which always thinks in the same person, which, in this case, matters not at all: different substances, by the same consciousness (where they do partake in it) being united into one person, as well as different bodies by the same life are united into one animal, whose identity is preserved in that change of substances by the unity of one continued life. For, it being the same consciousness that makes a man be himself to himself, personal identity depends on that only, whether it be annexed solely to one individual substance, or can be continued in a succession of several substances. For as far as any intelligent being can repeat the idea of any past action with the same consciousness it had of it at first, and with the same consciousness it has of any present action, so far it is the same personal self. For it is by the consciousness it has of its present thoughts and actions that it is self to itself now, and so will be the same self as far as the same consciousness can extend to actions past or to come, and would be by distance of time, or change of substance, no more two persons, than a man be two men by wearing other clothes today than he did yesterday, with a long or a short sleep between: the same consciousness uniting those distant actions into the same person, whatever substances contributed to their production.

13. *Whether in change of thinking substances there can be one person.* But next, as to the first part of the question, whether, if the same thinking substance (supposing immaterial substances only to think) be changed, it can be the same person? I answer, that cannot be resolved but by those who know what kind of substances they are that do think; and whether the consciousness of past actions can be transferred from one thinking substance to another. I grant were the same consciousness the same individual action it could not: but it being a present representation of a past action, why it may not be possible that that may be represented to the mind to have been which really never was, will remain to be shown. And therefore how far the consciousness of past actions is annexed to any individual agent, so that another cannot possibly have it, will be hard for us to determine till we know what kind of action it is that cannot be done without a reflex act of perception accompanying it, and how performed by thinking substances, who cannot think without being conscious of it. But that which we call the same consciousness, not being the same individual act, why one intellectual substance may not have represented to it, as done by itself, what it never did, and was perhaps done by some other agent—why, I say, such a representation may not possibly be without reality of matter of fact, as well as several representations in dreams are, which yet whilst dreaming we take for true—will be difficult to conclude from the nature of things. And that it never is so will by us, till we have clearer views of the nature of thinking substances, be best resolved into the goodness of God; who, as far as the happiness or misery of any of his sensible creatures is concerned in it, will not, by a fatal error of theirs, transfer from one to another that consciousness which draws reward or punishment with it. How far this may be an argument against those who would place thinking in a system of fleeting animal spirits, I leave to be considered. But yet, to return to the question before us, it must be allowed that, if the same consciousness (which, as has been shown, is quite a different thing from the same numerical figure or motion in body) can be transferred from one thinking substance to another, it will be possible that two thinking substances may make but one person. For the same consciousness being preserved, whether in the same or different substances, the personal identity is preserved.

14. *Whether, the same immaterial substance remaining, there can be two persons.* As to the second part of the question, whether, the same immaterial substance remaining, there may be two distinct persons; which question seems to me to be built on this,—whether the same immaterial being, being conscious of the action of its past duration, may be wholly stripped of all the consciousness of its past existence and lose it beyond the power of ever retrieving it again: and so as it were beginning a new account from a new period, have a consciousness that cannot reach beyond this new state. All those who hold preexistence are evidently of this mind; since they allow the soul to have no remaining consciousness of what it did in that pre-existent state, either wholly separate from body, or informing any other body; and if they should not, it is plain experience would be against them. So that personal identity, reaching no further than consciousness reaches, a pre-existent spirit not having continued so many ages in a state of silence, must needs make different persons. Suppose a Christian Platonist or a Pythagorean should, upon God's having ended all his works of creation the seventh day, think his soul hath existed ever since; and should imagine it has revolved in several human bodies; as I once met with one, who was persuaded his had been the soul of Socrates (how reasonably I will not dispute; this I know, that in the post he filled, which was no inconsiderable one, he passed for a very rational man, and the press has shown that he wanted not parts or learning)—would anyone say, that he, being not conscious of any of Socrates's actions or thoughts, could be the same person with Socrates? Let anyone reflect upon himself and conclude that he has in himself an immaterial spirit, which is that which thinks in him and, in the constant change of his body keeps him the

same: and is that which he calls himself: let him also suppose it to be the same soul that was in Nestor or Thersites, at the siege of Troy, (for souls being, as far as we know anything of them, in their nature indifferent to any parcel of matter, the supposition has no apparent absurdity in it), which it may have been, as well as it is now the soul of any other man: but he now having no consciousness of any of the actions either of Nestor or Thersites, does or can he conceive himself the same person with either of them? Can he be concerned in either of their actions? attribute them to himself, or think them his own, more than the actions of any other men that ever existed? So that this consciousness, not reaching to any of the actions of either of those men, he is no more one self with either of them than if the soul or immaterial spirit that now informs him had been created, and began to exist, when it began to inform his present body; though it were never so true, that the same spirit that informed Nestor's or Thersites' body were numerically the same that now informs his. For this would no more make him the same person with Nestor, than if some of the particles of matter that were once a part of Nestor were now a part of this man; the same immaterial substance, without the same consciousness, no more making the same person, by being united to any body, than the same particle of matter, without consciousness, united to any body, makes the same person. But let him once find himself conscious of any of the actions of Nestor, he then finds himself the same person with Nestor.

15. *The body, as well as the soul, goes to the making of a man.* And thus may we be able, without any difficulty, to conceive the same person at the resurrection, though in a body not exactly in make or parts the same which he had here,—the same consciousness going along with the soul that inhabits it. But yet the soul alone, in the change of bodies, would scarce to anyone but to him that makes the soul the man, be enough to make the same man. For should the soul of a prince, carrying with it the consciousness of the prince's past life, enter and inform the body of a cobbler as soon as deserted by his own soul, everyone sees he would be the same person with the prince, accountable only for the prince's actions: but who would say it was the same man? The body too goes to the making of the man, and would, I guess, to everybody determine the man in this case, wherein the soul, with all its princely thoughts about it, would not make another man: but he would be the same cobbler to everyone besides himself. I know that, in the ordinary way of speaking, the same person, and the same man, stand for one and the same thing. And indeed everyone will always have a liberty to speak as he pleases, and to apply what articulate sounds to what ideas he thinks fit, and change them as often as he pleases. But yet, when we will inquire what makes the same spirit, man, or person, we must fix the ideas of spirit, man, or person in our minds; and having resolved with ourselves what we mean by them, it will not be hard to determine, in either of them, or the like, when it is the same, and when not.

16. *Consciousness alone unites actions into the same person.* But though the same immaterial substance or soul does not alone, wherever it be, and in whatsoever state, make the same man; yet it is plain, consciousness, as far as ever it can be extended—should it be to ages past—unites existences and actions very remote in time into the same person, as well as it does the existences and actions of the immediately preceding moment: so that whatever has the consciousness of present and past actions is the same person to whom they both belong. Had I the same consciousness that I saw the ark and Noah's flood as that I saw an overflowing of the Thames last winter, or as that I write now I could no more doubt that I who write this now, that saw the Thames overflowed last winter, and that viewed the flood at the general deluge, was the same self,—place that self in what substance you please—than that I who write this am the same myself now whilst I write (whether I consist of all the same substance, material or immaterial, or no) that I was yesterday. For as to this point of being the same self, it matters not whether this present self be made up of the same or other substances—I being as much concerned, and as justly accountable for any action that was

done a thousand years since, appropriated to me now by this self-consciousness, as I am for what I did the last moment.

17. *Self depends on consciousness, not on substance.* Self is that conscious thinking thing,—whatever substance be made up of, (whether spiritual or material, simple or compounded, it matters not)—which is sensible or conscious of pleasure and pain, capable of happiness or misery, and so is concerned for itself, as far as that consciousness extends. Thus everyone finds that, whilst comprehended under that consciousness, the little finger is as much a part of himself as what is most so. Upon separation of this little finger, should this consciousness go along with the little finger, and leave the rest of the body, it is evident the little finger would be the person, the same person; and self then would have nothing to do with the rest of the body. As in this case it is the consciousness that goes along with the substance, when one part is separate from another which makes the same person and constitutes this inseparable self: so it is in reference to substances remote in time. That with which the consciousness of this present thinking thing can join itself makes the same person, and is one self with it, and with nothing else; and so attributes to itself, and owns all the actions of that thing, as its own, as far as that consciousness reaches, and no further; as everyone who reflects will perceive.

18. *Persons, not substances, the objects of reward and punishment.* In this personal identity is founded all the right and justice of reward and punishment; happiness and misery being that for which everyone is concerned for himself, and not mattering what becomes of any substance not joined to or affected with that consciousness. For, as it is evident in the instance I gave but now, if the consciousness went along with the little finger when it was cut off, that would be the same self which was concerned for the whole body yesterday, as making part of itself, whose actions then it cannot but admit as its own now. Though, if the same body should still live, and immediately from the separation of the little finger have its own peculiar consciousness, whereof the little finger knew nothing, it would not at all be concerned for it, as a part of itself, or could own any of its actions, or have any of them imputed to him.

19. *Which shows wherein personal identity consists.* This may show us wherein personal identity consists: not in the identity of substance, but, as I have said, in the identity of consciousness, wherein if Socrates and the present mayor of Queinborough agree, they are the same person: if the same Socrates waking and sleeping do not partake of the same consciousness, Socrates waking and sleeping is not the same person. And to punish Socrates waking for what sleeping Socrates thought, and waking Socrates was never conscious of, would be no more of right, than to punish one twin for what his brother-twin did, whereof he knew nothing, because their outsides were so like, that they could not be distinguished; for such twins have been seen.

20. *Absolute oblivion separates what is thus forgotten from the person, but not from the man.* But yet possibly it will still be objected,—Suppose I wholly lose the memory of some parts of my life, beyond a possibility of retrieving them, so that perhaps I shall never be conscious of them again; yet am I not the same person that did those actions, had those thoughts that I once was conscious of, though I have now forgot them? To which I answer, that we must here take notice what the word *I* is applied to; which, in this case, is the man only. And the same man being presumed to be the same person, *I* is easily here supposed to stand also for the same person. But if it be possible for the same man to have distinct incommunicable consciousness at different times, it is past doubt the same man would at different times make different persons; which, we see, is the sense of mankind in the solemnest declaration of their opinions, human laws not punishing the mad man for the sober man's actions, nor the sober man for what the mad man did,—thereby making them two persons: which is somewhat explained by our way of speaking in English when we say such an one is "not himself," or is "beside himself"; in which phrases it is insinuated, as if those who now, or at least first used them, thought that self was

changed; the selfsame person was no longer in that man.

21. *Difference between identity of man and of person.* But yet it is hard to conceive that Socrates, the same individual man, should be two persons. To help us a little in this, we must consider what is meant by *Socrates*, or *the same individual man.*

> First, it must be either the same individual, immaterial, thinking substance; in short, the same numerical soul, and nothing else.
>
> Secondly, or the same animal, without any regard to an immaterial soul.
>
> Thirdly, or the same immaterial spirit united to the same animal.

Now, take which of these suppositions you please, it is impossible to make personal identity to consist in anything but consciousness; or reach any further than that does.

For, by the first of them, it must be allowed possible that a man born of different women, and in distant times, may be the same man. A way of speaking which, whoever admits, must allow it possible for the same man to be two distinct persons, as any two that have lived in different ages without the knowledge of one another's thoughts.

By the second and third, Socrates, in this life and after it, cannot be the same man anyway but by the same consciousness; and so making human identity to consist in the same thing wherein we place personal identity, there will be no difficulty to allow the same man to be the same person. But then they who place human identity in consciousness only, and not in something else, must consider how they will make the infant Socrates the same man with Socrates after the resurrection. But whatsoever to some men makes a man, and consequently the same individual man, wherein perhaps few are agreed, personal identity can by us be placed in nothing but consciousness, (which is that alone which makes what we call self) without involving us in great absurdities.

22. *But is not a man drunk and sober the same person?* Why else is he punished for the fact he commits when drunk, though he be never afterwards conscious of it? Just as much the same person as a man that walks, and does other things in his sleep, is the same person, and is answerable for any mischief he shall do in it. Human laws punish both, with a justice suitable to their way of knowledge;—because, in these cases, they cannot distinguish certainly what is real, what counterfeit: and so the ignorance in drunkenness or sleep is not admitted as a plea. For, though punishment be annexed to personality, and personality to consciousness, and the drunkard perhaps be not conscious of what he did, yet human judicatures justly punish him; because the fact is proved against him, but want of consciousness cannot be proved for him. But in the Great Day, wherein the secrets of all hearts shall be laid open, it may be reasonable to think, no one shall be made to answer for what he knows nothing of, but shall receive his doom, his conscience accusing or excusing him.

23. *Consciousness alone unites remote existences into one person.* Nothing but consciousness can unite remote existences into the same person: the identity of substance will not do it; for whatever substance there is, however framed, without consciousness there is no person: and a carcass may be a person, as well as any sort of substance be so, without consciousness.

Could we suppose two distinct incommunicable consciousnesses acting the same body, the one constantly by day, the other by night; and, on the other side, the same consciousness, acting by intervals, two distinct bodies: I ask, in the first case, whether the day and the night man would not be two as distinct persons as Socrates and Plato? And whether, in the second case, there would not be one person in two distinct bodies, as much as one man is the same in two distinct clothings? Nor is it at all material to say that this same, and this distinct consciousness, in the cases above mentioned, is owing to the same and distinct immaterial substances, bringing it with them to those bodies; which, whether true or no, alters not the case: since it is evident the personal identity would equally be determined by the consciousness, whether that consciousness were annexed to some individual immaterial substance or no. For, granting that the thinking substance in man must be necessarily supposed immaterial, it is evident that immaterial thinking thing may sometimes part with its past consciousness, and be restored to it again: as appears in the forgetfulness men often have of their past actions; and the mind many times recovers the memory of a past consciousness, which it had lost for twenty years together. Make these intervals of memory and forgetfulness to take their turns regularly by day and night, and you have two persons with the same immaterial spirit, as much as in the former instance two persons with the same body. So that self is not determined by identity or diversity of substance, which it cannot be sure of, but only by identity of consciousness.

26. *"Person" a forensic term. Person*, as I take it, is the name for this self. Wherever a man finds what he calls himself, there, I think, another may say is the same person. It is a forensic term, appropriating actions and their merit; and so belongs only to intelligent agents, capable of a law, and happiness, and misery. This personality extends itself beyond present existence to what is past only by consciousness,—whereby it becomes concerned and accountable; owns and imputes to itself past actions, just upon the same ground and for the same reason as it does the present. All which is founded in a concern for happiness, the unavoidable concomitant of consciousness; that which is conscious of pleasure and pain, desiring that that self that is conscious should be happy. And therefore whatever past actions it cannot reconcile or appropriate to that present self by consciousness, it can be no more concerned in than if they had never been done: and to receive pleasure or pain, i.e., reward or punishment, on the account of any such action is all one as to be made happy or miserable in its first being, without any demerit at all. For, supposing a man punished now for what he had done in another life, whereof he could be made to have no consciousness at all, what difference is there between that punishment and being created miserable? And therefore, conformable to this, the apostle tells us, that, at the Great Day, when everyone shall "receive according to his doings, the secrets of all hearts shall be laid open." The sentence shall be justified by the consciousness all persons shall have, that they themselves, in what bodies soever they appear, or what substances soever that consciousness adheres to, are the same that committed those actions, and deserve that punishment for them.

10.4 HUME: THE CONSTRUCTED SELF

In the West, the British empiricist David Hume (1711–1776) puts forth views similar to those of Buddhist philosophers. First, the "self" is continually changing. There is no unchanging soul. Second, Hume says that all ideas originate in experience (in "impressions," in Hume's terminology). He cannot find a self in experience. He thus takes a Western "no-self" stance. Hume introspects and finds only a progression of one thought, perception, desire, etc., after another. Nowhere in all this does the same consciousness appear twice. Reflection yields nothing but flux. There is no separate self.

Like Buddhists, Hume argues that all sense of identity through change is imposed by the mind through associative memory. Physical objects are mental constructions. So is the self. Buddhists typically view change as universal and continuous; they too say that the world is mind-constructed.

Aristotle puts forth, against this, a commonsense view like that of the Indian realist schools. In his view, a thing can change while remaining the same object. For example, a river continually changes in the sense that new waters are always passing. (Aristotle takes this image from the pre-Socratic philosopher Heraclitus.) We nevertheless think of ourselves as putting our foot into the same river from one day to the next. It doesn't matter that the water flowing past is completely different from yesterday's. Solid objects are, less dramatically, also changing all the time, losing some particles and gaining others. But it seems ridiculous to count the stone today and the stone yesterday as different objects.

A famous puzzle mentioned by Aristotle is called the Ship of Theseus. Imagine a wooden sailboat whose boards, sails, ropes, rudder, etc., are replaced one by one over the course of several years. Also imagine that the replaced parts are collected one by one and then reassembled, duplicating, down to the nails, the boat that originally set sail. Which then of the two boats is properly called Theseus's ship? Which is "the same" as the one that was launched and dubbed "the Ship of Theseus"?

Hume studies how we decide cases like this. Criteria of identity vary, he says. The stone that breaks is no longer the same stone—consider New Hampshire's "Old Man in the Mountain," which collapsed in 2003—but its gradual erosion would not tempt us to say that it was now a different rock. Hume takes this to show that identity is not in the world. It is something we impose on the world.

We do this, constructing objects in the process, based on our own feelings of expectation. The ship with the new planks deserves the appellation "The Ship of Theseus," Hume tells us, for it is continuous with the original in purpose if not in matter. But this too shows that identity is a human construction, for we impose purposes on the world; they are not part of the world itself.

Hume is thus a projectivist. Is this the same as that? There is no fact of the matter. Nothing objective decides the question. The answer is subjective, depending on our goals and purposes. We project a structure onto the world. We divide it into objects for our own reasons. We do not merely discover an objective structure that is already there independent of us.

Sometimes, as with animals and plants, we attribute identity on the basis of causal continuity. We say that the acorn and the oak are the same plant and the baby and the adult are the same person because of their causal relations to one another. But it is important to note that according to Hume causation is itself something we impose on the world. All we find in experience are events following other events. Necessity and causation are our mental inventions. So this kind of identity too is something we impose on the world, not something found in things as they really are.

These arguments apply to the mind as well as to external objects. Indeed, they apply more effectively, for the only thing that could lead us to think that the mind is a unity is a causal connection among the various perceptions, thoughts, and desires we have. But Hume's general thesis about causation now applies with a vengeance. Just as we never experience a causal link between things, we never experience such a connection between mental events. We introspect and find only a sequence of impressions and ideas. Hume concludes, "The identity, which we ascribe to the mind of man, is only a fictitious one."

Hume finds the source of the ideas of mind, person, and self-identity in memory. Some of our mental states are memories of other mental states. That gives us a sense of continuity. Other mental states seem to be causes or effects of others. We find that some states resemble others or are constantly conjoined with them. That leads us to form the idea of a self. But this is our construction. It has no justification in experience itself.

Hume draws two conclusions. First, the self is not a unified thing or substance; it is a complex system, best compared to a commonwealth. Second, questions of identity are not questions about the world, but rather questions about what we ought to impose on the world. They are verbal questions about how we should use language, not real questions about things.

This strain of Hume's thought leads through twentieth-century philosophers such as Ludwig Wittgenstein and P. F. Strawson, who are similarly dismissive of metaphysical problems concerning the self. Like Hume's contention that "nice and subtile questions concerning personal identity can never possibly be decided and are to be regarded rather as grammatical than as philosophical difficulties," Wittgenstein and other "ordinary-language philosophers" see the philosophical task as simply to get clear about the criteria for use of certain words, such as *I*. Another attractive feature of Hume's position is its flexible account of causal relationships with respect to membership in causal sequences. A mental event can cause a physical event, and a physical event can cause a mental occurrence. We observe sequences and pick the useful conceptions in framing laws.

10.4.1 David Hume, from *A Treatise of Human Nature*

Books I, IV, VI
Of Personal Identity

There are some philosophers who imagine we are every moment intimately conscious of what we call our self; that we feel its existence and its continuance in existence; and are certain, beyond the evidence of a demonstration, both of its perfect identity and simplicity. The strongest sensation, the most violent passion, say they, instead of distracting us from this view, only fix it the more intensely, and make us consider their influence on self either by their pain or pleasure. To attempt a farther proof of this were to weaken its evidence; since no proof can be deriv'd from any fact, of which we are so intimately conscious; nor is there any thing, of which we can be certain, if we doubt of this.

Unluckily all these positive assertions are contrary to that very experience, which is pleaded for them, nor have we any idea of self after the manner it is here explain'd. For from what impression cou'd this idea be deriv'd? This question 'tis impossible to answer without a manifest contradiction and absurdity; and yet 'tis a question, which must necessarily be answer'd, if we wou'd have the idea of self pass for clear and intelligible. It must be some one impression that gives rise to every real idea. But self or person is not any one impression, but that to which our several impressions and ideas are suppos'd to have a reference. If any impression gives rise to the idea of self, that impression must continue invariably the same, thro' the whole course of our lives, since self is suppos'd to exist after that manner. But there is no impression constant and invariable. Pain and pleasure, grief and joy, passions and sensations succeed each other, and never all exist at the same time. It cannot, therefore, be from any of these impressions, or from any other, that the idea of

Source: David Hume, *A Treatise of Human Nature*, 1739.

self is deriv'd; and consequently there is no such idea. But farther, what must become of all our particular perceptions upon this hypothesis? All these are different, and distinguishable, and separable from each other, and may be separately consider'd, and may exist separately, and have no deed of tiny thing to support their existence. After what manner, therefore, do they belong to self; and how are they connected with it? For my part, when I enter most intimately into what I call myself, I always stumble on some particular perception or other, of heat or cold, light or shade, love or hatred, pain or pleasure. I never can catch myself at any time without a perception, and never can observe anything but the perception. When my perceptions are remov'd for any time, as by sound sleep, so long am I insensible of myself, and may truly be said not to exist. And were all my perceptions remov'd by death, and cou'd I neither think, nor feel, nor see, nor love, nor hate after the dissolution of my body, I shou'd be entirely annihilated, nor do I conceive what is farther requisite to make me a perfect non-entity. If anyone, upon serious and unprejudic'd reflection thinks he has a different notion of himself, I must confess I call reason no longer with him. All I can allow him is, that he may be in the right as well as I, and that we are essentially different in this particular. He may, perhaps, perceive something simple and continu'd, which he calls himself; tho' I am certain there is no such principle in me.

But setting aside some metaphysicians of this kind, I may venture to affirm of the rest of mankind that they are nothing but a bundle or collection of different perceptions, which succeed each other with an inconceivable rapidity, and are in a perpetual flux and movement. Our eyes cannot turn in their sockets without varying our perceptions. Our thought is still more variable than our sight; and all our other senses and faculties contribute to this change; nor is there any single power of the soul, which remains unalterably the same, perhaps for one moment. The mind is a kind of theatre, where several perceptions successively make their appearance; pass, re-pass, glide away, and mingle in an infinite variety of postures and situations. There is properly no simplicity in it at one time, nor identity in different, whatever natural propension we may have to imagine that simplicity and identity. The comparison of the theatre must not mislead us. They are the successive perceptions only, that constitute the mind; nor have we the most distant notion of the place, where these scenes are represented, or of the materials, of which it is compos'd.

What then gives us so great a propension to ascribe an identity to these successive perceptions, and to suppose ourselves possest of an invariable and uninterrupted existence thro' the whole course of our lives? In order to answer this question, we must distinguish betwixt personal identity, as it regards our thought or imagination, and as it regards our passions or the concern we take in ourselves. The first is our present subject; and to explain it perfectly we must take the matter pretty deep, and account for that identity, which we attribute to plants and animals, there being a great analogy betwixt it and the identity of a self or person.

We have a distinct idea of an object that remains invariable and uninterrupted thro' a suppos'd variation of time; and this idea we call that of identity or sameness. We have also a distinct idea of several different objects existing in succession and connected together by a close relation; and this to an accurate view affords as perfect a notion of diversity as if there was no manner of relation among the objects. But tho' these two ideas of identity and a succession of related objects be in themselves perfectly distinct, and even contrary, yet 'tis certain that in our common way of thinking they are generally confounded with each other. That action of the imagination, by which we consider the uninterrupted and invariable object, and that by which we reflect on the succession of related objects, are almost the same to the feeling, nor is there much more effort of thought requir'd in the latter case than in the former. The relation facilitates the transition of the mind from one object to another, and renders its passage as smooth as if it contemplated one continu'd object. This resemblance is the cause of the confusion and mistake, and makes us substitute the notion of identity, instead of that of related objects. However at one instant we may consider the related succession as variable or interrupted, we are sure the next to ascribe to it a perfect identity, and regard it as enviable and uninterrupted. Our propensity to this mistake is so great from the resemblance above-mention'd that we fall into it before we are aware; and tho' we incessantly correct ourselves by reflection, and return to a more accurate method of thinking, yet we cannot long sustain our philosophy, or take off this bias from the imagination. Our last resource is to yield to it and boldly assert that these different related objects are in effect the same, however interrupted and variable. In order to justify to ourselves this absurdity, we often feign some new and unintelligible principle that connects the objects together and prevents their interruption or variation. Thus we feign the continu'd existence of the perceptions of our senses, to remove the interruption: and run into the notion of a soul, and self, and substance, to disguise the variation. But we may farther observe that where we do not give rise to such a fiction, our propension to confound identity with relation is so great that we are apt to imagine something unknown and mysterious, connecting the parts, beside their relation; and this I take to be the case with regard to the identity we ascribe to plants and vegetables. And even when this does not take place, we still feel a propensity to confound these ideas, tho' we are not able fully to satisfy ourselves in that particular, nor find anything invariable and uninterrupted to justify our notion of identity.

Thus the controversy concerning identity is not merely a dispute of words. For when we attribute identity in an improper sense to variable or interrupted objects, our mistake is not confin'd to the expression but is commonly attended with a fiction, either of something invariable and uninterrupted, or of something mysterious and inexplicable, or at least with a propensity to such fictions. What will suffice to prove this hypothesis to the satisfaction of every fair enquirer is to shew from daily experience and observation that the objects, which are variable or interrupted, and yet are suppos'd to continue the same, are such only as consist of a succession of parts, connected together by resemblance, contiguity, or causation. For as such a succession answers evidently to our notion of diversity, it can only be by mistake we ascribe to it an identity; and as the relation of parts, which leads us into this mistake, is really nothing but a quality, which produces an association of ideas and an easy transition of the imagination from one to another, it can only be from the resemblance, which this act of the mind bears to that, by which we contemplate one continu'd object, that the error arises. Our chief business, then, must be to prove, that all objects, to which we ascribe identity without observing their invariableness and uninterruptedness are such as consist of a succession of related objects.

In order to this, suppose any mass of matter, of which the parts are contiguous and connected, to be plac'd before us; 'tis plain we must attribute a perfect identity to this mass, provided all the parts continue uninterruptedly and invariably the same, whatever motion or change of place we may observe either in the whole or in any of the parts. But supposing some very small or inconsiderable part to be added to the mass, or subtracted from it; tho' this absolutely destroys the identity of the whole, strictly speaking; yet as we seldom think so accurately, we scruple not to pronounce a mass of matter the same, where we find so trivial an alteration. The passage of the thought from the object before the change to the object after it, is so smooth and easy that we scarce perceive the transition, and are apt to imagine that 'tis nothing but a continu'd survey of the same object.

There is a very remarkable circumstance that attends this experiment; which is, that tho' the change of any considerable part in a mass of matter destroys the identity of the whole, lest we must measure the greatness of the part not absolutely but by its proportion to the whole. The addition or diminution of a mountain wou'd not be sufficient to produce a diversity in a planet: tho' the change of a very few inches wou'd be able to destroy the identity of some bodies. 'Twill be impossible to account for this but by reflecting that objects operate upon the mind, and break or interrupt the continuity of its actions not according to their real greatness but according to their proportion to each other: And therefore, since this interruption makes an object cease to appear the same, it must be the uninterrupted progress o'the thought, which constitutes the imperfect identity.

This may be confirm'd by another phenomenon. A change in any considerable part of a body destroys its identity; but 'tis remarkable, that where the change is produc'd gradually and insensibly we are less apt to ascribe to it the same effect. The reason can plainly be no other, than that the mind, in following the successive changes of the body, feels an easy passage from the surveying its condition in one moment to the viewing of it in another, and at no particular time perceives any interruption in its actions. From which continu'd perception, it ascribes a continu'd existence and identity to the object. But whatever precaution we may use in introducing the changes gradually, and making them proportionable to the whole, 'tis certain, that where the changes are at last observ'd to become considerable, we make a scruple of ascribing identity to such different objects. There is, however, another artifice, by which we may induce the imagination to advance a step farther; and that is, by producing a reference of the parts to each other, and a combination to some common end or purpose. A ship, of which a considerable part has been chang'd by frequent reparations, is still considered as the same; nor does the difference of the materials hinder us from ascribing an identity to it. The common end, in which the parts conspire, is the same under all their variations, and affords an easy transition of the imagination from one situation of the body to another.

But this is still more remarkable when we add a sympathy of parts to their common end and suppose that they bear to each other the reciprocal relation of cause and effect in all their actions and operations. This is the case with all animals and vegetables; where not only the several parts have a reference to some general purpose, but also a mutual dependence on and connexion with each other. The effect of so strong a relation is that tho' everyone must allow that in a very few years both vegetables and animals endure a total change, yet we still attribute identity to them while their form, size, and substance are entirely alter'd. An oak, that grows from a small plant to a large tree, is still the same oak; tho' there be not one particle of matter or figure of its parts the same. An infant becomes a man, and is sometimes fat, sometimes lean, without any change in his identity.

We may also consider the two following phaenomena, which are remarkable in their kind. The first is, that tho' we commonly be able to distinguish pretty exactly betwixt numerical and specific identity, yet it sometimes happens that we confound them, and in our thinking and reasoning employ the one for the other. Thus a man, who hears a noise, that is frequently interrupted and renew'd, says, it is still the same noise, tho' 'tis evident the sounds have only a specific identity or resemblance, and there is nothing numerically the same but the cause which produc'd them. In like manner it may be said without breach of the propriety of language that such a church, which was formerly of brick, fell to ruin, and that the parish rebuilt the same church of free-stone and according to modern architecture. Here neither the form nor materials are the same, nor is there anything common to the two objects, but their relation to the inhabitants of the parish; and yet this alone is sufficient to make us denominate them the same. But we must observe, that in these cases the first object is in a manner annihilated before the second comes into existence; by which means we are never presented in any one point of time with the idea of difference and multiplicity: and for that reason are less scrupulous in calling them the same.

Secondly, we may remark that tho' in a succession of related objects it be in a manner requisite that the change of parts be not sudden nor entire, in order to preserve the identity, yet where the objects are in their nature changeable and inconstant, we admit of a more sudden transition than wou'd otherwise be consistent with that relation. Thus as the nature of a river consists in the motion and change of parts, tho' in less than four and twenty hours these be totally alter'd, this hinders not the river from continuing the same during several ages. What is natural and essential to anything is, in a manner, expected; and what is expected makes less impression, and appears of less moment, than what is unusual and extraordinary. A considerable change of the former kind seems really less to the imagination than the most trivial alteration of the latter, and by breaking less the continuity of the thought has less influence in destroying the identity.

We now proceed to explain the nature of personal identity, which has become so great a question in philosophy, especially of late years in England, where all the abstruser sciences are study'd with a peculiar ardour and application. And here 'tis evident the same method of reasoning must be continu'd which has so successfully explain'd the identity of plants, and animals, and ships, and houses, and of all the compounded and changeable productions either of art or nature. The identity, which we ascribe to the mind of man, is only a fictitious one, and of a like kind with that which we ascribe to vegetables and animal bodies. It cannot, therefore, have a different origin, but must proceed from a like operation of the imagination upon like objects.

But lest this argument shou'd not convince the reader, tho' in my opinion perfectly decisive, let him weigh the following reasoning, which is still closer and more immediate. 'Tis evident that the identity which we attribute to the human mind, however perfect we may imagine it to be, is not able to run the several different perceptions into one, and make them lose their characters of distinction and difference, which are essential to them. 'Tis still true that every distinct perception which enters into the composition of the mind is a distinct existence, and is different, and distinguishable, and separable from every other perception, either contemporary or successive. But, as, notwithstanding this distinction and separability, we suppose the whole train of perceptions to be united by identity, a question naturally arises concerning this relation of identity; whether it be something that really binds our several perceptions together, or only associates their ideas in the imagination. That is, in other words, whether in pronouncing concerning the identity of a person, we observe some real bond among his perceptions, or only feel one among the ideas we form of them. This question we might easily decide if we wou'd recollect what has been already prov'd at large, that the understanding never observes any real connexion among objects, and that even the union of cause and effect, when strictly examin'd, resolves itself into a customary association of ideas. For from thence it evidently follows that identity is nothing really belonging to these different perceptions and uniting them together; but is merely a quality, which we attribute to them, because of the union of their ideas in the imagination, when we reflect upon them. Now the only qualities which can give ideas a union in the imagination are these three relations above-mention'd. These are the uniting principles in the ideal world, and without them every distinct object is separable by the mind, and may be separately considered, and appears not to have any more connexion with any other object than if disjoin'd by the greatest difference and remoteness. 'Tis, therefore, on some of these three relations of resemblance, contiguity and causation that identity depends; and as the very essence of these relations consists in their producing an easy transition of ideas, it follows that our notions of personal identity proceed entirely from the smooth and uninterrupted progress of the thought along a train of connected ideas, according to the principles above-explain'd. The only question, therefore, which remains, is, by what relations this uninterrupted progress of our thought is produc'd when we consider the successive existence of a mind or thinking person. And here 'tis evident we must confine ourselves to resemblance and causation, and must drop contiguity, which has little or no influence in the present case.

To begin with resemblance; suppose we cou'd see clearly into the breast of another and observe that succession of perceptions which constitutes his mind or thinking principle, and suppose that he always preserves the memory of a considerable part of past perceptions; 'tis evident that nothing cou'd more contribute to the bestowing a relation on this succession amidst all its variations. For what is the memory but a faculty by which we raise up the images of past perceptions? And as an image necessarily resembles its object, must not the frequent placing of these resembling perceptions in the chain of thought convey the imagination more easily from one link to another, and make the whole seem like the continuance of one object? In this particular, then, the memory not only discovers the identity but also contributes to its production by producing the relation of resemblance among the perceptions. The case is the same whether we consider ourselves or others.

As to causation; we may observe that the true idea of the human mind is to consider it as a system of different perceptions or different existences which are link'd together by the relation of cause and effect, and mutually produce, destroy, influence, and modify each other. Our impressions give rise to their correspondent ideas; these ideas in their turn produce other impressions. One thought chases another, and draws after it a third by which it is expell'd in its turn. In this respect, I cannot compare the soul more properly to anything than to a republic or commonwealth, in which the several members are united by the reciprocal ties of government and subordination, and give rise to other persons, who propagate the same republic in the incessant changes of its parts. And as the same individual republic may not only change its members, but also its laws and constitutions; in like manner the same person may vary his character and disposition, as well as his impressions and ideas, without losing his identity. Whatever changes he endures, his several parts are still connected by the relation of causation. And in this view our identity with regard to the passions serves to corroborate that with regard to the imagination, by the making our distant perceptions influence each other and by giving us a present concern for our past or future pains or pleasures.

As a memory alone acquaints us with the continuance and extent of this succession of perceptions, 'tis to be considered, upon that account chiefly, as the source of personal identity. Had we no memory, we never shou'd have any notion of causation, nor consequently of that chain of causes and effects which constitute our self or person. But having once acquir'd this notion of causation from the memory, we can extend the same chain of causes, and consequently the identity of our persons beyond our memory, and can comprehend times, and circumstances, and actions, which we have entirely forgot but suppose in general to have existed. For how few of our past actions are there of which we have any memory? Who can tell me, for instance, what were his thoughts and actions on the 1st of January 1715, the 11th of March 1719, and the 3rd of August 1733? Or will he affirm, because he has entirely forgot the incidents of these days, that the present self is not the same person with the self of that time; and by that means overturn all the most established notions of personal identity? In this view, therefore, memory does not so much produce as discover personal identity, by shewing us the relation of cause and effect among our different perceptions. 'Twill be incumbent on those, who affirm that memory produces entirely our personal identity to give a reason why we can thus extend our identity beyond our memory.

The whole of this doctrine leads us to a conclusion, which is of great importance in the present affair, viz. that all the nice and subtile questions concerning personal identity can never possibly be decided, and are to be regarded rather as grammatical than as philosophical difficulties. Identity depends on the relations of ideas; and these relations produce identity, by means of that easy transition they occasion. But as the relations and the easiness of the transition may diminish by insensible degrees, we have no just standard by which we can decide any dispute concerning the time when they acquire or lose a title to the name of identity. All the disputes concerning the identity of connected objects are merely verbal, except so far as the relation of parts gives rise to some fiction or imaginary principle of union, as we have already observed.

What I have said concerning the first origin and uncertainty of our notion of identity, as apply'd to the human mind may be extended with little or no variation to that of simplicity. An object, whose different co-existent parts are bound together by a close relation, operates upon the imagination after much the same manner as one perfectly simple and indivisible, and requires not a much greater stretch of thought in order to its conception. From this similarity of operation we attribute a simplicity to it, and feign a principle of union as the support of this simplicity and the center of all the different parts and qualities of the object.

CHAPTER 11

African Philosophy of Mind

"The peculiarity of the human mind"

"The proper study of mankind is man," wrote Alexander Pope. And indeed our curiosity about our own nature, our desire to understand ourselves, has gripped people who have reflected on the human condition throughout the history of the world. Africa is no exception. African philosophers today grapple with questions concerning the nature of mind and self. African languages and cultures offer perspectives informed by a conceptual framework and set of intuitions different in various ways from those that have dominated Western philosophy. This is not new. Three centuries ago, a thinker from West Africa became a philosophy professor in Germany, writing a critique of Descartes that, Kwasi Wiredu has speculated, reflects his native Akan framework for thinking about the relation between mind and body.

11.1 AMO'S CRITIQUE OF DESCARTES

Anton Wilhelm Amo (1703–1759?) was born in a small village near Axim in western Ghana to a family of the Nzema, an Akan people. When he was 3 or 4, he evidently impressed a missionary working for the Dutch West Indies Company, who, with his parents' approval, took him to Europe. German Duke Anton Ulrich Brunswick-Wolfenbüttel of Lower Saxony took him in and raised him, giving him a nobleman's education. In addition to his native language, he became fluent in German, Dutch, English, Latin, Greek, French, and Hebrew. After graduating from the University of Helmstedt, he studied law at the University of Halle—the first African student ever to attend that university—but soon found himself drawn to philosophy, receiving his doctorate in 1730 for a dissertation, now lost, criticizing slavery and defending the rights of Africans in Europe. He then entered medical school at the University of Wittenberg and became a Doctor of Medicine and Science in 1733. Amo, who usually appended the title *Afer* (*African*) to his name, became the first black professor in Germany, teaching at Halle, Wittenberg, and Jena. In 1747 or 1748, he returned to Ghana to search for his family, and he managed to find them. Little is known about his life after that. A Swiss-Dutch doctor who visited him in 1753 found him in the village where he was born, where "he lived like a hermit, and acquired the reputation of a soothsayer."

Amo's *Habilitazion* (second dissertation, required of those seeking German professorships), published in 1734, was *The Apatheia of the Human Mind*, a critique of Descartes's dualism. *Apatheia*, from which we derive the word *apathy*, means nonreactiveness, passionlessness, imperturbability, or unresponsiveness. The Stoics thought of *apatheia* as an ideal state in which the mind is free of *pathe*, things affecting it, primarily emotions and passions. But Amo uses it more broadly.

Amo focuses on a distinction that underlies much Western thought about the mind. Emotions are called "passions" because the mind is thought to be passive in receiving them. Anger, love, desire, pleasure, pain—all are thought to be active in affecting the mind, which is passive in being affected by their causal power. Sensation, traditionally, is similar. The mind passively receives sensory impressions from the world. (Notice the imagery: The world makes impressions on the mind much as a seal might make an impression on hot wax.) The mind is active, on this picture, only when it exercises reason.

Sensation, Amo argues, is essentially bodily. Say that Jones sees a table. That requires a complex physical interaction between the table, a physical object, and Jones's body, in which the body may or may not be passive. But how does that interaction have any effect on the mind? Amo grants the Cartesian assumption that the mind is a spiritual substance. But a spiritual substance, he insists, is "purely active, immaterial, always gains understanding through itself (i.e., directly), and acts from self-motion and with intention in regard to an end and goal of which it is conscious to itself." The human mind differs from, say, the mind of God, in being incarnate, a spiritual substance in a physical body. Somehow, it is supposed to receive sensations from the body. (The mind of God, Amo argues, could not have sensations, for God has no body. Moreover, God's mind knows everything directly; it cannot know things by means of representations, as the human mind does, for "representation presupposes the absence of what must be represented," and everything is directly present to God.)

But now Amo points out a paradox. The mind as spiritual substance is purely active; anything receiving sensations is in so doing purely passive. For Descartes, the gap between sensation and reason is filled with ideas; indeed, Descartes's contribution to early modern philosophy is often summarized as "the new way of ideas." But Descartes is assigning ideas to different and, in Amo's eyes, incompatible roles. Amo refers to Descartes's correspondence, where he writes of "two factors in the human soul": "the part that thinks" and "that which, united to the body, moves and feels with it." The second part, which includes sensation, must itself be material, Amo argues, if it is to move the body and sense the world: "Man has sensation of material objects not as regards his mind but as regards his organic and living body." There is a difference between Jones's thinking "There's a table" and seeing the table. There is a difference between Jones's thinking "The table feels solid" and feeling the solidity of the table. Amo argues that a spiritual substance could do only the former. The actual seeing and feeling must be material. The faculty of sensation is not mental but physical.

If so, Amo contends, we are not essentially things that think, as Descartes declares, and only inessentially bodies. We are essentially both. A person is essentially a thinking being, but also essentially a sensing being, and therefore essentially embodied.

11.1.1 Anton Wilhelm Amo, from *The Apatheia of the Human Mind*

1.1 The State of the Argument

Man has sensation of material objects not as regards his mind but as regards his organic and living body. These statements are here asserted and defended against Descartes and his expressed opinion in his *Correspondence*, part I, letter XXIX, where the passage reads: "For since there are two factors in the human soul on which depends the whole cognition which we can have concerning its nature, of which one is the part that thinks and the other that which united to the body moves it and feels with it."

To this statement we give the following warning and dissent: that the mind acts with the body with which it is in mutual union, we concede; but that it suffers with the body, we deny.

NOTE. Among living things, to suffer and to feel are synonymous. But among things destitute of life, to feel is to admit in oneself changes coming from elsewhere as far as quantity and quality are concerned. In other words it is for them to be modified and determined from outside.

First Caution. But he openly contradicts himself, *loc. cit.* part I, *Epistola* 99, in the preceding programmatic investigation where he lays it down that the nature of the soul consists solely in the faculty of thinking; and yet thinking is an activity of the mind, not a passion....

Second Caution. But he stands in contradiction to himself (p. 563) with the words, "To receive sensible forms is the function of an organ. To judge it when received is the function of the soul." To receive the sensible forms is to feel; but this is appropriate to organs, and in consequence to body, for organs are appropriate not to minds but to body. Again he himself distinguishes between feeling and judging, attributing the former to organs and the latter to minds....

Third Caution. He contradicts himself further subsequently where he says that three things are to be distinguished: (1) the action of an object on an organ; (2) the passion of the organ, (3) says he: "When an organ is affected, the mind is upset, and the mind feels the sensation of its body being affected." Now if the mind should really have this feeling he should have expressed it in this way: "and the mind feels its body to be affected, it feels, or rather it understands itself not to have been affected." But he confuses the act of understanding with the business of feeling: it is the same as if he should have said, "and the mind understands its body to have been affected."

2.1 First Negative Thesis

The human mind is not affected by sensible things.

EXPOSITION. The thesis means the same as if you said: The human mind is not affected by sensible things however much they are immediately

Source: Anton Wilhelm Amo, *On the Apatheia of the Human Mind*, from *Antonius Gvilielmus Amo Afer in Axim in Ghana: Translation of His Works*, by Anton Wilhelm Amo. Halle (Saale, Germany): Martin Luther University, Halle-Wittenberg, 1968.

present to the body in which the mind is. But it has knowledge of the sensations arising in the body and employs them when possessed in its operations....

NOTE. When man is considered logically, mind, operation of mind, idea and immediate sensation must not be confused; mind and its operation are immaterial. For as is the nature of a substance so is the nature of the property of the substance, and yet that mind is immaterial has been shown in what we have already said and therefore its property too is immaterial. Idea is a composite entity; for there is an idea when the mind makes present to itself a sensation preexisting in the body, and thereby brings the feeling before the mind....

First Proof of Thesis. Whatever feels, lives; whatever lives, depends on nourishment; whatever lives and depends on nourishment grows; whatever is of this nature is in the end resolved into its basic principles; whatever comes to be resolved into its basic principles is complex; every complex has its constituent parts; whatever this is true of is a divisible body. If therefore the human mind feels, it follows that it is a divisible body.

Second Proof of Thesis. No spirit has sensation of material objects. Since the human mind is spirit, it has no sensation of material objects.

The major premise has been proved under the first exposition with notes and applications supplied. The minor premise is incapable of contradiction.

NOTE I. To live and to have sensation are two inseparable predicates. The proof is in the following inversion: everything which lives necessarily feels; and everything which feels necessarily lives. The result is that the presence of one feature imports of necessity the presence of the other.

NOTE II. *To live* and *to exist* are not synonyms. Whatever lives exists, but not everything that exists lives, for both spirit and stones exist, but can hardly be said to live. For spirit exists and operates with knowledge; matter exists and suffers the action of another agent. On the other hand both men and animals exist, act, live, and feel.

Third Proof of Thesis. "Fear not," our Saviour says, "those who kill the body yet cannot kill the soul." Matthew X 28. From that we gather that whatever is killed or can be killed, necessarily lives. (For to be killed is to be deprived of life by violence from some other quarter.) If therefore the body is slain or can be slain, it follows that it lives; and if it lives, feels; and if it feels, it follows that it enjoys the faculty of sensation. For living and feeling are always and right from the beginning conjoined in the same subject.

NOTE. There is agreement between us and the whole assembly of medical men and others whose opinion is that sensation occurs in fluid of the kind in the nerves, and this nervous fluid was by the ancients called animal spirits....

EXAMPLE. Exceptionally appropriate here is the solemn pronouncement of Frederick the Wise, Elector, of the most glorious memory, most beneficent founder of our University which flourishes here, Wittenberg. In his last breath of life he was asked how he felt. He answered that his body was in mortal pain but his mind was at peace....

2.2 Thesis II

And there is no faculty of sensation in the mind.

PROOF. Anything to which circulation of blood is appropriate is that also to which the principle of life is. Whatever the latter pertains to, to that also does the faculty of sense. Yet circulation of the blood and the principle of life pertain to the body.... Since these things are so, it follows that the principle of life with the faculty of sense is not appropriate to mind. Rather, they belong to the body.

2.3 Thesis III

Hence sensation and the faculty of sense belong to the body.

PROOF. Sensation and the faculty of sense belong either to the mind or to the body, not both. That they do not pertain to the mind has been shown by our broad conclusions. Therefore they belong to the body.

11.2 THE AKAN CONCEPTION OF MIND AND SELF

The Akan tribe, from Ghana, in west Africa, has a distinctive analysis of the nature of mind and self. Kwasi Wiredu (1931–) addresses the question What is the mind? He observes that Amo's insistence that sensation is a physical rather than mental phenomenon has a parallel in the Akan language, which treats mind (*adwene*) as intellectual, as a faculty of thinking rather than sensing or feeling. In Western thought, identity theorists hold that the mind and brain are identical. For the Akan, such an identification is impossible. The mind is a "permanent possibility of thought," which is not an object at all. The mind consists of thoughts, but it is not simply a bundle of thoughts; it is a certain kind of capacity, a capacity to have thoughts. For the Akan, the brain is the basis of the mind; it is by having a brain that I have the capacity for thought. A person consists of body, life force, and personality. The mind is not a constituent of a person for the simple reason that it is not a thing. The mind is not a component of a person for the same reason that moving is not a part of a car. Since the mind is not a thing, the question of how it can relate to a material thing, the body, does not arise.

What is a human being? Western philosophers often split the self into mind and body, or spirit and flesh, or reason and desire, or some other pair of elements. The Akan conception, N. K. Dzobo explains, recognizes that we tend to think of people in terms of dualities such as these, and takes duality itself as the most important feature of what it is to be human. The dual elements, however we might identify them, are complementary but also conflicting. Reconciling and unifying them is the central human task.

The distinction between male and female provides a model for this kind of duality. The union of male and female brings about creation. So, too, is the union of dual elements a fundamentally creative process. Human beings are thus essentially creative. Our central obligation is to create. This includes having children, but it involves much more than that. We create things; we create a personality through our actions. Together we create a social order. In each case, we must reconcile and unite conflicting elements, synthesizing them into an organic whole.

Our creative essence rests on our freedom. The conflicting forces we must unite do not control or determine us. We are self-determining; we are free to reconcile conflicting elements as we please, creating, in the process, our own distinctive personalities and lives. Our creative essence also rests on our choosing among possibilities. Possibilities, potentialities, are thus central to who we are. Finally, our creative essence implies that we are also essentially agents. We make choices and act, changing the world and ourselves as we do. Descartes writes, "What am I? A thing that thinks." For the Akan, it would be more accurate to say, "What am I? A thing that acts." I am a thing that confronts and realizes possibilities, makes choices, reconciles conflicts, and creates things, including myself.

11.2.1 Kwasi Wiredu, from "The Concept of Mind"

The Akan Conception of Mind

The preceding remarks permit us now to begin to answer the question whether there is any exact equivalent in Akan of the English word "mind." A simple yes or no answer is not available. It matters little, I think, whether we answer: "Yes, with a qualification" or "No, with a qualification." In either case it is the qualification that is crucial for our purposes here. The only conceivable translation of "mind" into Akan is "*adwene*." However, while the word "mind," as we have seen, is susceptible of either a substance or a nonsubstance interpretation, "*adwene*" is susceptible of only a nonsubstance one. The same word, "*adwene*" also translates the English word "thought;" and "*adwene*" is simply the noun form of the verb "*dwen*," which means "to think." In the English language, in which "mind" does not have the same sort of relationship with "thought," it is natural, though not unavoidable, to think of mind as that which produces thought. In Akan there is little temptation to think in this way.

It might be insisted that the Akans ought to have a conception of what it is that thinks. If there is thinking, it might be argued, there must be something that does the thinking. The Akan answer would be simple: What does the thinking is the person, *onipa*. Our interlocutor is unlikely to be satisfied with this. He might urge the following consideration to try to show that the answer is inadequate. Although it is correct—so might go the reasoning—to say in the case of thinking, as in regard to any human activity, that it is the person who does what is done, it might still be necessary to indicate which part or aspect of a person is actually involved in the execution of a particular type of activity. Thus it is true that walking is done by a person, but it is appropriate to note that a person walks with his legs rather than, say, his tongue. So the question remains open as to the part or aspect of a person that is most directly involved in the thinking process. Alternatively, it might he suggested that even if it be accepted without any qualms that the agent of thought is the person, it may still be that a person, as a thinking being, is something more rarefied than the moving object that is visibly encountered in the external world.

As regards the first point, it should be noted that what it shows is only that some part or aspect of a person may be the instrument of thought—it does not show that any such part could appropriately be called the agent of thought. As to the instrument or mechanism of thought, it is clear from the speech of the Akans that they believe that it is the brain, *amene*, that has this status. They know that thinking cannot go on in a human being without the brain, that certain injuries to the brain will impair thought and that generally there is a correlation between brain activity and thinking. This is responsible, by the way, for the figure of speech by which, wishing to intimate that a fellow is thoughtless, an Akan might say that he has no *adwene* in his head. And while on figures of speech, it might be of interest to note one parity and a couple of disparities of usage between Akan and English. Locating thought figuratively in the head is admissible in both languages, for in English too one can speak of a thought entering one's head. On the other hand, in English one cannot speak of the "mind" in a person's head, while it is no breach of linguistic propriety in Akan to decry a person's mental habits by remarking that the *adwene* inside his head is no good. Furthermore, though it is accredited idiom in English to mention brain while meaning mind, as when it

Source: Kwasi Wiredu, "The Concept of Mind," *Ibadan Journal of Humanistic Studies* 3, October 1983. Reprinted by permission of the Faculty of Arts, University of Ibadan, Nigeria.

is said that somebody has good brains, it would be absurdly unidiomatic to say with the same purport in Akan that somebody has a good *amene*. One only talks of a good *adwene* in such a context.

These points of linguistic usage do not teach us much philosophy of mind beyond the fact that the speakers of both English and Akan recognize the instrumentality of the brain in thinking. This recognition does not, of course, necessarily imply the identity of mind and brain. In fact an interesting contrast between the two languages in this connection is that, whereas in English the notion of the identity of mind and brain can appear to make sense, no such appearance is possible in Akan. Mind (*adwene*) being conceived of in an exclusively nonsubstance way in Akan, the slightest temptation to suggest such an identity would betray a radical mixing-up of categories, specifically, of the categories of concept and object at one level and of the categories of potentiality and actuality at another. This is because, as might be inferred from earlier remarks, particularly, about the relationship between the words *adwene* (mind) and *dwen* (to think), mind is, from the Akan point of view, a logical construction out of actual and potential thoughts. To adapt a phrase of John Stuart Mill, mind, at any rate in its aspect of potentiality, is the relatively permanent possibility of thought. Now, neither a thought (i.e., a combination of concepts) nor the mere possibility of thought could, as a matter of logical impossibility, be any kind of object. A concept is, by definition, a non-object, and, as will be pointed out more at length below, an object is, by definition, a non-concept. Therefore, since the brain is a species of object, it is evident that to identify the mind with the brain would be to commit the multiple error of confusing not only a class of concepts but also their possibility with an object—a particularly full-blooded example of what Ryle calls a category mistake.

Using a terminology introduced earlier on, we may now characterize the Akan concept of mind as both ideational and dispositional. That it is ideational is immediately clear from the fact that mind is, as we have seen, conceived in one aspect as consisting of thoughts. On this conception, mind is not that which thinks, but the thought which is thought when there is thinking. What distinguishes mind in this sense from a fortuitous aggregation of isolated thoughts is the unity arising from possession by an individual. On this showing, thoughts are not in the mind but of the mind; that is to say, thoughts are what mind is made of; and if we talk, as we often do in both Akan and English, of thoughts in our minds, we must, in Akan at least, mean the "in" genetively rather than locatively.

That the Akan conception of mind is also dispositional would be clear on a little reflection. When, for example, an Akan says of a person in deep slumber that "he has a good mind" (*owo adwene paa*) he does not mean that any sequence of brilliant thoughts is taking place in him at the material time; what he means is that the person concerned has the capacity for thoughts of that quality. In other words, a certain kind of disposition is being attributed to the individual. This dispositional attribution implies that if and when the circumstances are ripe, he will display suitably impressive thinking. But its whole meaning cannot be thus hypothetical. The potentiality must have a categorical basis; there must be a present condition in the make-up of the person which accounts for it. If, as we have suggested already, the brain (*amene*) is recognized in Akan thought as the instrument of thought, then this categorical basis can be nothing other than the condition of the brain.

This last remark touches, of course, on the problem of the relation between the mind and the brain, which is one of the principal problems of the philosophy of mind. It is perhaps necessary to stress that the suggestion is not that the brian is identical with the mind but only that the brain is the basis of the mind. This in itself is not a particularly controversial thesis. It is recognized on all hands, even among the most "spiritual" of idealists, that the brain is a necessary condition for human thinking. The question is whether it is also a sufficient condition. In Western philosophy the contention of idealists and dualists has been that it is not. Their view is that it is necessary to postulate an immaterial entity which works on, or alongside, the brain to produce thoughts. This entity is said to be the mind. If this were true, it would presumably be taken to bear out the view, noted in the second paragraph of the present section, that, although the agent of human thought is a person, yet, as a thinking being, a person may be in essence a spirit or something of that sort. I will argue below that this is a conceptually faulty hypothesis. But what I want immediately to point out is that it is a hypothesis which does not have a place in Akan thought on account of its nonsubstance conception of mind.

11.2.2 N. K. Dzobo, from "The Image of Man in Africa"

The African View of Man: Synthesis Model of Human Nature

Unity in Duality

The African view of man is derived from the African view of reality which is found in the indigenous religion, creation myths, personal names, symbols and proverbs. This view is expressed simply by a Tanzanian proverb: "In the world all things are two and two." This is a basic ontological statement of the African perception of reality. The two which form the nature of everything in the universe are made up of opposites which become one while remaining two. The Mende of Sierra Leone express the dual origin of all things by saying that the High God, *Mangala*, created the twin varieties of eleusine seed conceived as twins of opposite sex in the "egg of God" which is also called the "egg of the world." The Ewe cosmogony expresses this same view of reality in more detail. It says that in the beginning there was only one androgynous High God called *Nana Buluku* (*Bruku, Briku*) who gave birth to Siamese twins called *Mawu-Lisa*, whose union has become the basis of the organization of the world. In this divine duality *Mawu*, the female, is envisaged as a Janus-like figure. One side of its body being female, with its eyes forming the moon and bearing the name *Mawu*. The other portion is male, whose eyes are the sun, and whose name is *Lisa*. P. Mercier pointed out that "their dual and conflicting nature expresses, even before the world of men was organized, the complementary forces which were to be active in it." He went on to report from his study of the Fon of Benin (Dahomey) that *Mawu*, the female principle, is fertility, motherhood, life, creativity, gentleness, forgiveness, night, freshness, rest and joy, while *Lisa*, the male principle, is power, warlikeness, death, strength, toughness, destructivity, day, heat, labor, and all hard things.

Those two references express very well not just a fundamental theory of man, but a theory of reality that conceives the basic structure of reality as unity in duality. The primordial unity referred to either as the Egg of God or the Androgynous High God called *Nana Buluku* is the one in which all the opposites are contained. But, as June Singer pointed out, one pair is basic, i.e., the female and male pair which serves as the symbolic expression of the power behind all the other polarities and forms the creating principle.

The opposites in any duality and their relationship are therefore modeled on the paradigm of

Source: N. K. Dzobo, "The Image of Man in Africa," in Kwasi Wiredu and Kwame Gyekye (ed.), *Person and Community*, Ghanian Philosophical Studies, I. Washington, DC: The Council of Research for Values and Philosophy, 1992.

the female and male relationship paradigm, i.e., on the principle of creativity, complementarity, tension, balance and otherness. The female–male polarity as seen in the indigenous cultures of the Wolof (Gambia), Mendes (Sierra Leone), Ewe (Ghana, Togo and Benin), Akan and Tallensi (Ghana), Herero (Namibia), Burundi (Central Africa), Lango (Uganda) and in the religion of ancient Egypt, to mention a few, is a primordial image of reality. It is an archetype which the whole human race has inherited, and so is a universal collective image of reality and of man. It appears in us as an innate sense of a primordial cosmic unity, having existed in oneness or wholeness before any separation was made and still remaining one. W. J. Argyle commenting on the polar view of reality as found in the religious tradition of the Fon of Benin said, "*Mawu-Lisa* (the Dual High God) expresses together the unity of the world conceived in terms of duality." The Akan of Ghana express this by giving Siamese personal names to people, one half of the name being female and the other half male. An example is *Dua-Agyeman*, in which the dual name *Dua*, meaning "tree," is the female principle and *Agyeman*, meaning "warrior," is the male principle. In the religious tradition of the Akan the Sky God, *Nyame*, and the Earth God, *Asase Yaa*, are paired together: *Nyame* is the male principle and *Asase Yaa* is the female principle in the pair. The Ga of Ghana have such a dual name for their High God called *Ataa-Naa Nyonmo* which literally means "Father-Mother Sky God."

In sum, Africans see reality, including the reality of man and society, structured as unity in duality comprising two conflicting elements. Polarity and unity are, therefore, basic categories of being. Since the female and male pair is basic to all polarities, creativity becomes the essence of polarity as is the case in the union of woman and man. Leopold S. Senghor was right therefore when he observed that, while Western and Middle Eastern view of reality is founded on separation and opposition, on analysis and conflict, the African conceives the world, beyond the diversity of its forms, as a fundamentally mobile, yet unique, reality that seeks synthesis.

Creativity is thus the goal of human striving, and the polar elements find their unity in creativity. Paul Tillich stated a similar idea thus: "A polar relation is a relation of interdependent elements, each of which is necessary for the other one and for the whole, although it is in tension with the opposite element. The tension drives both to conflicts and beyond the conflicts to possible unions of polar elements."

Man as Possibility

The whole of life therefore is perceived in Africa as oriented toward creativity and is symbolized by woman; Man, used generically, is seen as an integral part of this creative process of life. Thus, the drive to create is the basic and ultimate force behind all human behaviour; the goal of human creation is to realize a synthesis of being.

The creative principle in man is given different names by the different ethnic groups, but its essential oneness with the High God is always maintained. The following are some of its names: *se* or *kra* (Ewe), *okra* (Akan), *kla* (Ga), *ori* (Yoruba), *Chi* (Igbo), *dya* (Mende), and *we* (Kassem of Ghana). Some of these names for the creative principle, which is the principle of life in man, are fragments of the names for the High Gods. Thus *se* comes from *Segbo*, meaning "The Source of the Creative Principle of Life," *Ori* from *Orise* meaning, "The Source from which Beings Spring," and *Chi* from Chukwu meaning "The Great, Immense, Undimensional Source of Being."

Man's ultimate goal as an individual and as a member of his clan therefore is to multiply and increase because he is the repository of the creative power, the right use of which is his chief responsibility. Likewise, when a woman marries the most important thing that she takes to her husband's house is her productive powers because this is the essential part of her nature.

The creative process is not limited to bringing forth children, but is seen as embracing the whole of man's life and his relationships. The individual therefore is to grow in the development of a creative personality and to develop the capacity to maintain creative relationship. He is to see his individual life and that of his society as fields that are sown with life's experiences and which should yield fruit. This understanding of life is expressed in such personal names as *Agbefanu* (Ewe) "Life sows seeds," *Agbefovi* (Ewe) "Life hatches things." The person who has achieved a creative personality and productive life and is able to maintain a productive relationship with others is said "to have become a person" (*Ezu ame*—Ewe; *Oye onipa pa*—Akan). The persons who are considered models of creative life are the chief, the elders and the ancestors. Such a life is counted as the greatest value in the indigenous culture.

Man as an Agent

The conception that creativity is the essence of true human personality implies that man is not just a being who thinks but also a being who acts to change his world. This implies that man is free and self-determining and has a say in shaping his own history and destiny. Through his free action he releases forces which shape the world and society, and because of his dual nature he also can release forces which will destroy society and the world. These two forces are basic to his nature and he does not evolve from one into the other. Since this capacity for action is essential to being a man it follows that, where freedom to act is denied there is a diminution in the fullest sense of humanity; one's dignity is taken away and one's capacity for creativity is destroyed.

The most devastating effect of Western colonization and missionary proselytization on Africa is the removal of a genuine capacity for free action from Africans who have been made into objects of history instead of being its subjects. To a considerable extent Africans have lost their capacity for creativity; instead of assuming the active role of self-creators and makers of culture, they have adopted the passive role of acquiescence before alleged immutable cosmic laws imposed on them by foreign religion and education.

Man as a Communal Being

One important deduction from the fact that polarity has been woven into the fabric of the universe and of society is that community belongs to the very being of man. The origin of all being is existence in a polar relation. The individual's being arises from a prior social whole which is truly other; it comes into being for the sake of him and exists for his development and growth. Hence, an individual who is cut off from the communal organism is nothing. In Africa it is true then to say, "As the glow of a coal depends on its remaining in the fire, so the vitality, the psychic security, the very humanity of man, depends on his integration into the family."

By living creatively the individual is also contributing to the life and quality of his community, and so we can say "We are, therefore I am, and since I am, therefore we are."

The Meaning of Life

Let us return again to the seed concept of the origin of life. As seeds sprout into living plants by breaking the bonds of their beginning seed life, so also human life springs up and out by breaking the bonds of death. Life has to be freed from its own sleeping enabling power to realize the fullness of its splendor through the cultivation of its potential.

Life, then, has no *a priori* meaning. It starts as a sleeping enabling power and acquires meaning through existence, where existence is used in its original Latin sense of *ex-sistere*: going forth or coming into being through a process. The Ewe refer to human existence conceived as a process of releasing and developing the imprisoned enabling power of life as *amenyenye*, which means "to realize being in space and time through the process of struggle." As a pregnant woman has to labor to bring out her new baby, so human life has to struggle to acquire meaning. To the Ewe then to be is to be engaged in the process of becoming.

One Ewe proverb puts it this way, "There is no resting place on the journey of life" (*Dzudzo mele alifo o*).

Meaning, then, is given to life in the process of living, which is characterized by making choices. Life's decisions, however, are made in the light of life's master purpose, called in Ewe *du*. This is given to both individuals and nations in a dispensation from God, called *Fa*. The main content of the individual's *du* may be summarized as the realization of creative humanity. Where life is seen as possibility it always has unlimited meaning and its success depends upon the individual's ability to see "the sign" of life that is coiled in the heart of death.

Finally, to the Ewe physical death is neither a threat nor an annihilation, but a transformation and communion of the individualized and personalized *se* with what the Ewe call *Segbo*, i.e., the Big and Supreme *Se*, for the sake of rejuvenation and rebirth of a new being. This cycle continues *ad infinitum*.

11.3 AFRICAN PERSPECTIVES ON PERSONAL IDENTITY

Philosophers of mind ask not only "What am I?" and "What makes me human?" but also "What makes me *me*?" What makes me the person I am? Am I really the same person I was as a baby or a small child? Will I be the same person when I am old? If so, what explains that? What makes me the same person throughout the entire course of my life?

These questions are closely related. If I am essentially mind or consciousness, I will tend to look to mind or consciousness to explain my continuing identity. If I am essentially a physical being, I will tend to look for physical explanations of my continuity. Conversely, if I can explain my identity in certain terms, that will suggest that my essence can be understood in those same terms.

Leke Adeofe, from Nigeria, outlines the Yoruba conception of a person. Just as Plato divides the soul into three, the Yoruba, like many west African tribes, divide the self into three components: the body, the mind (or soul, or consciousness), and the *ori*, the "inner head" or personality. Western philosophers tend to explain the essence of human beings either in mental terms, seeing us as essentially things that think and explaining our identity in terms of continuity of consciousness, or in physical terms, seeing us as essentially material beings and explaining our identity in terms of physical continuity. Faced with various thought experiments—if Jones's brain (or mind) is transplanted into Smith's body, is the resulting person Smith or Jones?—this leaves us with two options. But many people, in Africa and outside it, see a third option. They want to know how the resulting being acts. Does it act like Jones or like Smith? The Yoruba see this as a question about *ori*. Does this person have Smith's *ori* or Jones's? I am a being consisting of body and mind and personality, the Yoruba affirm, but what is essential to my identity is my *ori*, my personality. That is what makes me *me*. Anything that radically changed my personality would disrupt my identity, even if it did not disrupt body or consciousness.

11.3.1 Leke Adeofe, from "Personal Identity in African Metaphysics"

Pre-theoretic concerns about personal identity challenge us to provide a coherent and unified response to the following questions: What is a person? What is it for a person to be the same persisting entity across time (or at a time)? How many ontologically distinct entities constitute a person? What relationship, if any, exists between an individual's first-person, subjective experiences and our objective, third person's perspective? African philosophy takes the challenge much more seriously than Western philosophy. In the former, unlike in the latter, plausible responses to one question are routinely informed by plausible responses to others. In this essay, I explore the extent to which an African theory of reality has provided integrated responses to the personal identity questions and build on those responses. My approach, partly descriptive and partly imaginative, ought to be familiar; it has been borrowed from a tradition that dates back at least to John Locke. What emerges is a tested conception of human existence that is formidable enough to be explanatorily useful vis-à-vis personal identity questions.

The Ontological Distinction

A tripartite conception of a person characterizes the African thought system. A person is conceived to be the union of his or her *ara* (body), *emi* (mind/soul), and *ori* ("inner head"). Unlike *ara*, which is physical, both the *emi* and *ori* are mental (or spiritual). This dichotomy might induce us to think of the African view as dualistic. But it would be a mistake to do so, since *ori* is conceived ontologically independent of the other two elements. Thus, the African view is properly thought of as triadic. It is philosophically interesting that a person is a creation of different deities. *Ara*, the body, is constructed by Orisa-nla, the arch deity; Olodumare (God or "Supreme Deity") brings forth the *emi*; while another deity, Ajala, is responsible for creating *ori*. *Ara* is the corporeal entity from head to toe, including internal and external organs, and it becomes conscious with *emi*, which, apart from its life-giving capacity, is conceived as immortal and transmigratory. The inner or metaphysical head, *ori*, the other noncorporeal entity, is the bearer of destiny and, hence, constitutive of personality.

Understanding the Distinction

Thus, within the purview of African metaphysics, a person is made up three elements, *ara, emi*, and *ori*. Since their ontologies are logically independent of each other, the three elements are ontologically distinct and properly conceived as a triadic view of persons. *Ara* refers not only to the whole body, but also its various parts. However, the metaphysics does not make clear how much of a body is minimally needed for sameness (or continuity) of body. Presumably, our nontheoretical assumptions about what sameness or continuity of body amounts to will suffice for our discussions. However, those nontheoretical assumptions may include those that are peculiarly African, for example, the *abiku* or *ogbanje* syndrome, in which some children are believed to continuously repeat life cycles. As evidence for this syndrome, Africans point to similarities of bodies involved to posit bodily continuity between them. What is not clear

Source: Leke Adeofe, "Personal Identity in African Metaphysics," in Lee M. Brown (ed.), *African Philosophy: New and Traditional Perspectives*. Oxford: Oxford University Press, 2004.

is whether in these special cases, similarities in bodies are constitutive of, not merely evidence for, bodily continuity. *Emi* is the mind/soul. Its presence is indicated by phenomenal consciousness, an effect of divine breath that manifests (sort of) in breathing. We may note parenthetically that nonhuman creatures and plants have *emi*. Injunctions are usually made not to maltreat *nnkanelemi*, things "inhabited" by *emi*. This attitude, however, has not led to Jainism. *Emi* is taken to be essential to having ratiocinative activities, but it is not endowed with person-like characteristics as in certain Western traditions, for example, Descartes's. Indeed, the Western view that where the soul goes, there goes the person is not African, not at first blush anyway. Some African philosophers, however, have described *emi* as "the most enduring and most important characteristic of a person," but there is no support within the African system of thoughts to understand this in a Platonic or Cartesian sense. That *emi* is considered most enduring might tempt us to think that for Africans ensoulment embodies personhood much like in Western thought systems. But this temptation should be resisted for they also contend that *emi* has no variable qualities, that is, *emi* has no distinguishing characteristics. What *emi* does, it seems, is help ground consciousness. Thus, while *emi* is most enduring and perhaps the most important element of a person, it is arguable that it encapsulates personhood. *Ori* refers to both the physical head and the inner/metaphysical head, and the latter is sometimes referred to as *ori-inu* to avoid ambiguity. Notice that Africans seem to think that there are metaphysical components of several body parts, most notably, the head, the heart, and the intestines. But the metaphysical components of the latter two serve largely the semantic function of conveying the roles of the relevant body parts in the proper bodily and psychic functioning of a person. One philosophically interesting question then is why only *ori* has been elevated into an ontologically constitutive element of a person. A plausible response is that *ori*, unlike other metaphysical components, is a deity in that, among other things, it is considered worthy of worship and appeasement. But this response is not satisfying: Why has *ori*, and not any other metaphysical body part, been deified? Why is deification of *ori* not due to its ontological status rather than the other way around? ...

The Thought Experiment

What is a person in the African view? This question is ambiguous between two different but related questions: What are the constitutive elements of a person? What makes a person the same persisting entity across time? In response to the first question, the constitutive elements are *ara, emi*, and *ori*. The task is to determine the extent to which this response would help with the second but interrelated question about persistence. Suppose we become Cartesian, and conceive of the soul of one person, Adler's, transferred to the soulless body of another. If ensoulment embodies personhood, Adler now has a different body. (Locke, who does not think that the soul is immortal, would want Adler's brain transferred instead.) But do we have any reason to think of the issue this way rather than as a case of mental derangement or clairvoyance? This is the personal identity issue in Western metaphysics. In reidentifying a person, do we trace the body or the mind? Generally, the mental (or psychological) continuity theorists think that we are to trace the mind because the mind encapsulates all that is really important: our hopes, fears, beliefs, and values. And if our mental life were to cease, we would have ceased to live. For them, we are defined by the mental. Bodily continuity theorists, on the other hand, think that we are to trace the body. That way, they reason, we respect the biological fact that we are basically organic beings, no matter what else we happen to be. Underlying the issue here is the distinction between a person and a human being. "Person" refers to the fact that we are social entities, "human being" to the fact that we are organic entities. The mental theorist emphasizes the first fact, the bodily theorist, the second. Thus, John

Locke, a mental theorist, assumes that if we successfully transfer, say, Adler's brain into John's brainless body, the John-bodied person is now Adler. For the John-bodied person now exhibits the mental life of Adler. (Of course, there are serious difficulties in imagining this kind of exchange, but let us put them aside till much later.) Lockean followers, for example, Derek Parfit, have gone further by claiming that transfer of the brain is not necessary: what is important is securing Adler's mental life in John's body no matter how that comes about. What is important in these transactions, they argue, is that relevant mental lives continue irrespective of how this is done.

Applying the Concept of *Ori*

My concern with personal identity is concern with my psychic unity, not my soul—unless I am worried about the possibility of life after death. Concern with psychic unity is concern with the extent to which activities in my life fulfill a purpose. The purpose in turn provides meaning to my life, and it is that meaning that evidences to me psychic unity, that my life is on track. Now, we do impose purpose on ourselves. For example, I may decide to spend the rest of my life feeding the homeless, but this kind of purpose and attendant psychic unity are second best. Notice that I could have made my purpose the harassment or killing of the elderly, and my psychic unity could have been derived from this. Thus, self-imposed purpose and psychic unity may help to calm the nerves, but what is needed is the purpose that emerges from a quasi-historical self-actualization. Self-actualization here depends on our state of being and on the state of being we are yet to become, albeit with a *ceteris paribus* become. A life lived consciously or otherwise in conformity with this state of becoming is a life on course, and the purpose that emerges from it provides genuine psychic unity to the individual. *Ori*, understood as destiny, embodies the quasi-historical self-actualization. Trees do not have *ori*, and neither do cats, dogs, and dolphins. My concern with my identity is with whether my life is on track. It helps if my physical and psychological lives are not radically discontinuous, but this requirement is neither necessary nor sufficient for my identity.

For greater perspicuity of issues involved, imagine a transfer of Adler's *ori* to John's physical head—without his *ori*, of course. Since *ori* embodies personality, the moderating characteristics underlying an individual's social relations, John's new life should now resemble Adler's former life. But what does "resemble" mean in this context? Two pictures suggest themselves. First is the Lockean picture: John is now capable of fulfilling the social roles of Adler, for he now exhibits Adler's former mental life. Second is what I will call Abel's picture: John now has the characteristic fortunes (or misfortunes) defining Adler's former life. The second picture is closer to the African view; the first would make *ori* functionally isomorphic with the brain (or soul) in Western metaphysics, thereby undermining the philosophical basis for *ori*.

To sharpen the example, assume the following: Adler's former life had been enviable. His desires were nicely moderated. He was successful in friendships, business, health, and in his communal relations. He could hardly do anything wrong. John's former life was the exact opposite. He failed consistently in his endeavors. His sincere and worthy efforts to succeed and be perceived differently came to naught. Indeed, John was not doing anything substantially different from what Adler was doing, but the outcome for John had been consistently bad, and for Adler consistently good. Africans would ascribe the disparities in results to their choices to *ori*. If we now suppose an exchange of *ori* between Adler and John, we would expect John's life to be consistently worthwhile and admirable, and Adler's life consistently the opposite. The supposed exchange between Adler and John exemplifies what we might call, broadly speaking, an exchange of personalities. With changes in a person's personality, there are likely to be corresponding changes in the person's social roles; and with new social roles come new social identities. This explains the motivation of the mental theorist in Western metaphysics in assuming there had been an exchange of persons in cases involving an exchange of social roles. Notice that the main objection to the mental theorist is that his or her solution violates our organic nature. The African solution appears not to have done this. Human identity is preserved in the union of the body and the soul (*emi*). In *ori* resides personality. A tripartite conception of a person allows for transferring the latter without violating "human beingness," at least not in the way the bodily theorist finds objectionable.

A possible objection might be that an exchange of *ori* might not lead to an exchange of social roles, and that there would be no basis then for thinking people have exchanged anything. To illustrate the objection, consider again the Lockean mentalist approach. In transferring a brain from one body to another, our intuition that personhood is transferred in the exchange of brains is based partly on the assumption that such a transfer would lead to exchange of social roles. But with an exchange of *ori*, we need not assume an exchange of social roles. What an exchange of *ori* secures is a change of fortunes and self-realization. A change in fortunes might lead to a change in social roles, but this need not be so. Thus, with the exchange of *ori* a person may be suitable to perform only his or her former roles and tasks. The question then is why we must think personhood has been transferred with the exchange of *ori* when there is no noticeable change in social roles.

The objector here incorrectly assumes that our concern with specific social roles underlies our concern with personal identity. To be sure, our view of ourselves is to some extent manifested in the social roles we perform. This explains why social roles may help to flesh out our intuitions about personal identity. Social roles help to make clear what is personal about personal identity. However, our concern is not with specific social roles but with whatever roles we are involved in to be as enhanced as possible. No specific social roles are constitutive of anyone's identity. Mental theorists are confused about this. They correctly notice that we care about the continuity of our intentions, beliefs, and memories. They correctly assume that the reason for this is because we care about the success of our projects. And since our intentions, beliefs, and memories are particularly suited for our projects, they wrongly elevate the projects into the criterion of personal identity. They reason that our projects define us and we are whatever can fulfill the projects under consideration. But if, as African metaphysics suggests, our concern with personal identity is that whatever projects we are engaged in are to be fulfilled as well as possible, then it is a mistake to elevate these projects into a criterion of personal identity as the mental theorists have done. The concern with the continuity of our intentions, beliefs, and memories is a concern not with specific projects but with the successful completion of whatever projects there are, as long as they contribute to our self-actualization. Thus, the mentalist intuition about the defining role of projects in a person's identity cannot be used to undermine the view of *ori* as a constitutive element of a person.

PART III

Epistemology

CHAPTER 12

Indian Theories of Knowledge

"The light of a lamp"

Knowledge, according to most philosophers East and West, is a kind of belief. And knowledge implies truth; we can't know what isn't so. But knowledge is more than true belief. People can make lucky guesses; they can form beliefs on the basis of little or no evidence and stumble onto the truth. What more does a true belief need to count as knowledge? Whatever that property is, let's agree to call it *warrant*. By definition, then, knowledge is warranted true belief.

But what is warrant? Is it something internal to the mind of the knower, like belief? Or is it something external to the mind of the knower, like truth, which relates the knower's mind to the world? *Internalists* adopt the first option: A belief is warranted if it stands in the right sort of relation to other beliefs. That relation is *justification*. So, for an internalist, knowledge is justified true belief. *Externalists* adopt the second option: A belief is warranted if it stands in the right sort of relation to the world. Truth relates the belief to the world *now*; warrant must have to do with how the belief came about. So, for an externalist, knowledge is true belief that arises in the right way. Usually, externalists say, knowledge is true belief arising from a reliable process.

Western philosophy, for most of its history, has been predominantly internalist; knowledge has been defined as justified true belief. In classical India, the predominant approach is externalist: Knowledge is the result of a process external to ourselves that connects us with the known. Perception, for example, is a process that depends on a connection between objects and our sense organs. Each sense organ works through its own type of connection. Other, nonperceptual ways of knowing, such as inference and testimony, do not depend on a direct connection with the object or objects known. These processes involve indirect connections. Nevertheless, all knowledge-generating processes are parts of the world—as we are as knowers—and must be examined from an external or impersonal point of view.

12.1 INDIAN REALISM: NYAYA AND VAISHESHIKA

Two long-running schools of Indian philosophy with a realist attitude toward the objects of experience are Vaisheshika (Particularism) and Nyaya (Logic). For centuries, Indian philosophers considered the two distinct, and each could claim its own self-defining literature. But with Udayana, who lived around 1000 CE, the schools merged, and proponents afterwards are called simply Nyaya philosophers. Here we refer to them as *Realists*.

Before 1000 CE, Vaisheshika tends to focus more on the metaphysical question "What is there?" Nyaya, in contrast, is more concerned with the epistemological questions "How do we know what we know?" and "What are the right methods of inquiry and debate?" The earliest Nyaya work, the *Nyaya Sutra*, by the Indian philosopher Gautama (c. 200 CE), and a commentary by Vatsyayana (c. 400) characterize four *pramanas*, or sources of knowledge: perception, inference, analogy (restricted to acquisition of vocabulary), and testimony. Knowledge, according to the *Nyaya Sutra*, is true belief produced by a source of knowledge.

Those who have internalist views—in India, for instance, the Buddhists—should note right away that we do not necessarily, by Realism's lights, know whether an awareness is a genuine perception or an illusion. An illusion may be indistinguishable from a veridical cognition, from a first-person point of view. An illusion, that is, may seem to be a genuine perception. Nevertheless, it does not, according to Realism, deserve the label "perception," because it is false. A central thesis of Realism is that any false awareness must involve deviation from the workings of genuine knowledge generating processes. Illusion, wrong inference, false belief generated by another's words, etc., are never produced by genuine perception, inference, or testimony. Part of the Realist project is to spell out the conditions for recognizing knowledge generators so that, when we do have doubt or dispute, we know how to resolve it.

Doubt, however, is an abnormal condition. We do not have to doubt or examine our beliefs in order to know. Consider driving a car or riding a horse. We act immediately on our perceptual knowledge without giving a thought to skeptical possibilities. We normally do not wonder, for example, whether the appearance of oncoming traffic is true or an illusion. Nevertheless, some conditions do call for doubt and inquiry. When we find ourselves in those conditions, knowing about the ways knowledge is generated tells us how to proceed. Identifying a belief's source in a reliable knowledge generator provides warrant, which does indeed present a barrier to further doubt—at least a higher barrier than we have with bits of knowledge that are not certified. Knowledge does not require justification; it requires only the right connection with the known.

The *Nyaya Sutra* defines perceptual awareness in terms of external links to the world:

- *A genuine perception must be veridical.* An illusion may seem veridical from a subject's own perspective, but we do not say it is a genuine perception once we know that it does not present things the way they are.
- *Perceptual awareness arises from sense-organ connection with the object known.* The nature of the connection varies according to sensory modality, vision, hearing, touching, and so on. But all perceptual awareness involves a direct sensory relationship to the object known.

- *It is not mediated by language.* Thus it differs from knowledge resulting from testimony ("It is not due to words"), although previously learned classifications of things (cows, horses, etc.) as preserved in memory may inform a perceptual presentation ("That's a cow").
- *A vaguely perceived object is not known; the vaguely perceiving awareness is not a genuine perception.* We know only what is definite. In the distance, say, there is something that we cannot quite make out: Is it a person or a post? We have no genuine perception of a person in that case, even if it is a person, since the object of a perception produced by a knowledge generator has to be known distinctly. In such a case, we may know that there is something that *looks* like a person in the distance, but we do not perceive a person.

Realists and practically all other classical Indian philosophers view perception as our principal cognitive link with things in the world. All other knowledge sources depend on perception. Inference starts with information from perception, for example, but it does not reduce to it since it produces knowledge about things we do not immediately perceive.

The *Nyaya Sutra* distinguishes three kinds of inference:

1. *Inferring the effect from the cause.* We see the dark, threatening clouds, and infer that it will rain. We see the lightning and brace ourselves for the thunder.
2. *Inferring the cause from the effect.* We see the wet ground and the swollen creek and infer that it rained. Or we hear thunder and infer that there was lightning.
3. *Inferring a general rule from its instances.* We see dark clouds and then rain; we see lightning and then hear thunder. We infer that, in general, dark clouds cause rain and lightning causes thunder. Or we hear Smith say things that turn out to be true. We infer that Smith's word is reliable. This category is broad enough to include analogies. Vatsyayana gives an intriguing example: proving that pleasure and other feelings belong to a spiritual substance, namely, a self, which then shows that selves are substances: "Pleasure and the like have a substratum, since they are qualities, like color."

The final two knowledge sources on Realism's list are analogy and testimony. We learn most of what we know from the testimony of others—from what they say and write. Their telling us what they do *causes* us to know it. You tell me the Astros won yesterday and (presuming it is true) I am made to know it by your words. Analogy is restricted to acquisition of vocabulary, i.e., learning a word through someone's drawing an analogy. The standard example is learning the meaning of water buffalo by being told that the creature looks like a cow except for its color and wider horns.

What about the skeptic's challenge? How do we know whether our source of knowledge gives us the truth? For that matter, how do we know what our sources of knowledge are? Realism dismisses these worries. We start our investigation knowing that we have knowledge and examining precisely how. If, for whatever reason, we become concerned to certify, not just that a particular belief is true but that a particular process is a knowledge generator ("Why do you believe the cat is on the mat?" "I see her right there. She's in plain sight." "Why do you believe that referring to your sight is a good answer to the previous question?" etc.). Realists answer that, like anything else, there are ways that we can know and certify knowledge. For example, we know inference to be a knowledge generator because we base successful actions on it. Similarly, we know that perception is a knowledge generator. Results (bits of knowledge) and causes (knowledge-generating processes) stand, in a sense, in balance, each reinforcing our confidence in the other.

This is the meaning of a passage from the *Nyaya Sutra* about a scale and a nugget. The nugget's weight is determined by the scale under normal conditions. But if we have reason to wonder about the accuracy of the scale, we use a nugget whose weight has been determined by other scales to calibrate the scale we are worried about. A scale is a source of knowledge (*pramana*) when the weight of a piece of gold, for example, is in question. But the same scale would be the object of knowledge (*prameya*), what is to be known—and the piece of gold the means of knowledge—when the question is calibration. If we wish to judge the accuracy of scales, we do not seek some further "scale of scales"—we take something whose weight is known independently, from another source, and see what the scale in question says about it.

There are two levels to the Nyaya theory, raw animal knowledge so to say and knowledge self-consciously certified. We'll take up the certified first. The view put forward with the gold-nugget example is a form of *coherentism*: There are no self-evident reasons; our beliefs form a coherent system of mutual support. This holds for any investigation we might undertake as we turn away from animal knowledge to the enterprises of inquiry. In the nugget case, we have doubt about a scale. In resolving doubt, the same thing may be justifier or justified, depending on the circumstances. No mental state in itself reveals a knowledge generator with certainty. Disagreement is to be resolved by argument, and no premises are sacrosanct.

The Nyaya view is not only a coherentism but also a *foundationalism* in the following sense: The direct results of perception, inference, and testimony count as basic, potentially resolving disagreement without requiring further justification. As the direct effects of the knowledge sources, these bits of information enjoy a default status of not normally being subject to doubt: "Innocent until proven guilty." Normally we assume the scale is accurate.

Nevertheless, in any particular case of doubt it is always a matter of coherence with other beliefs that decides a question. Or, we might say, certification is always a matter of inference. "That object in the distance is a person, not a post, since it has fingers. Whatever has fingers is a person."

When we are not investigating and worrying about justification, we have knowledge if and when perception and the other sources are working. Thus we have, along with reflective knowledge, prereflective animal knowledge. We share at least perceptual knowledge with animals, who like us act on sensory information. According to Nyaya, what we are told is also generally accepted prereflectively. Inference completes the list of fundamental knowledge sources concerning the world. Inference cannot be reduced to perception or testimony.

The *Nyaya Sutra* uses another analogy to support the commitment to basic sources of knowledge against the skeptic: Perception is like "the light of a lamp." Sources of knowledge are self-revealing. Light shows itself as it shows us the objects we see. Light is a knowledge generator when it lets us see other objects; it is an object of knowledge when we direct our attention to the light itself. The light is the source of knowledge in one context and object of knowledge in another. To be a source of knowledge is simply to play a certain role in an epistemic context.

12.1.1 From the *Nyaya Sutra*, with Commentary by Vatsyayana

Sutra 4: Perception is the cognition resulting from sense-object contact [which is] "not due to words," "invariably related" [to the object] and is "of a definite character."

Commentary: The cognition which results from the contact of the sense with the object is called perception. ... [Take a mirage, for example:] During the summer the flickering rays of the sun intermingled with the heat radiating from the surface of the earth come in contact with the eyes of a person at a distance. Due to this sense-object contact, there arises, in the rays of the sun, the cognition: this is water. Even such a knowledge may be taken for valid perceptual knowledge. Hence Gautama says, "invariably connected with the object." An erroneous perception is the perception of an object as something which it is not. A right perception is the perception of an object as it actually is.

Sutra 5: Next [is discussed] inference, which is preceded by it [i.e., by perception], and is of three kinds, namely, inferring the effect (i.e., having the antecedent as the probans), inferring the cause (i.e., having the consequent as the probans) and inferring the rule (i.e., where the general law is ascertained by general observation).

Commentary: Perception has for its object things present. Inference has for its object things both present and absent. Why? Because of its capacity for knowing objects belonging to the three times (i.e., past, present, and future). By inference one knows objects belonging to the three times. We infer: it will be, it is, and it was.

Sutra 6: Comparison is the instrument of the valid knowledge of an object derived through its similarity with another well-known object.

Sutra 7: Verbal testimony is the communication from a "trustworthy person."

Commentary: A trustworthy person is the speaker who has the direct knowledge of an object and is motivated by the desire of communicating the object as directly known by him.

Critical Examination of the Instruments of Knowledge in General

The terms *pramana* (source of knowledge) and *prameya* (object of knowledge) may coexist (i.e., may be interchangeable) in the same object, if there is adequate ground for using the terms (interchangeably). And the grounds for using the terms are (as follows): *pramana* is that which produces knowledge and *prameya* is that which becomes the object of knowledge. In the event of an object of knowledge becoming instrumental in producing the knowledge of something else, the same object is termed both a *pramana* and a *prameya*. To convey this implication is said the following—

Sutra 16: Just as the "measuring instrument" (which usually has the status of a *pramana*) can be a *prameya* as well (i.e., when its own accuracy is subject to investigation).

Commentary: The measuring instrument is a *pramana* when it gives the knowledge of correct weight. The objects of knowledge, in this case, are gold etc. which have weight. If however the accuracy of another measuring instrument is determined by gold etc., then for the knowledge of the other measuring instrument, gold etc. are *pramanas*. And the other measuring instrument is a *prameya*. ... Thus the self is mentioned in the list of *prameyas*, because of its being the object

Source: *Nyaya Philosophy: Gautama's Nyaya-sutra and Vatsyayana's Bhashya*. Translated by Mrinalkanti Gangopadhyay. Calcutta: Indian Studies, 1967.

of knowledge. It is (also) considered *pramatr* (knower), because of its independent role in producing knowledge. Knowledge is considered to be a *pramana* when it leads to another knowledge, it is itself a *prameya* when it is itself the object of another knowledge, it is *pramiti* (right knowledge) when it is neither of the two....

Sutra 19: ... these (i.e., perception etc.) are apprehended in the same way as the light of a lamp.

Commentary: As, for example, the light of the lamp, which is an auxiliary cause of perception, is itself an instrument of knowledge in the perception of the visible objects and it is apprehended over again by another instrument of valid perceptual knowledge, viz. its contact with the eyes. (The lamp) is inferred to be a cause of visual perception, because the presence and absence of the lamp are followed by the presence and absence of visual perception.

12.2 NAGARJUNA'S SKEPTICAL REGRESS

One of the greatest debates in the long history of epistemology in India centers not on skepticism per se—though it is often misinterpreted as an argument about skepticism—but rather on the concept of a "knowledge source." Is it important and useful to examine the nature of perception, inference, and so on? Should we argue by citing further knowledge sources? At the center of the controversy stands the great Buddhist reasoner, Nagarjuna, who rejects the projects of epistemology.

Nagarjuna (150 CE) was born in south India but taught at Nalanda, a Buddhist university in north India. According to tradition, he was born into a Hindu Brahmin family and was trained in Hindu thought but converted to Buddhism. A Mahayana Buddhist and the founder of Madhyamika Buddhism, Nagarjuna believes that focusing on sources of knowledge leads away from the practical message of the Buddha and his opposition to metaphysics. Nagarjuna tries to keep people from speculating airily but does not try to alter conventional meanings.

> For we do not speak without accepting, for practical purposes, the work-a-day world.

Nagarjuna, who is among the earliest of the classical Indian philosophers writing in Sanskrit, is commonly interpreted as a skeptic. And indeed he is about metaphysics and the theory of knowledge. He is an insistent critic of Nyaya and Vaisheshika. But Nagarjuna accepts the language and claims of everyday life and seems intent only to show that there is room for the truth of the Buddhist message:

- *Interdependent origination*: Everything is interconnected.
- *Emptiness*: Everything is "without a reality of its own."

The truth of "interdependent origination" and "emptiness" is not backed up by any of Realism's "knowledge sources" and is no worse off for that.

Nagarjuna's identification of impossibilities is also part of a strategy that he claims the Buddha uses. Thinking of anything as having an independent existence leads to absurdity. Applying this to oneself, one comes to see the truth of the Buddha's teaching of *anatman*, "no-self." Understanding this is a step toward the goal of eliminating selfish desire and thus toward enlightenment and perfection.

Nagarjuna mounts an onslaught on the Nyaya notion of a source of knowledge. Realists deny Buddhist teachings in asserting, among other things, that some things are self-existent (e.g., God, individual selves, universals). Nagarjuna states his opponents' objections to the Buddhist theses of interdependent origination and emptiness—which entail that nothing is self-existent—and then proceeds to disarm them by showing the faultiness of suppositions on which they rely.'

Which side of the Realist/Buddhist dispute is backed up by veritable "knowledge sources"? This is the heart of the issue from the Realist perspective. The Realists purport to show that Nagarjuna's position is self-contradictory and self-defeating. The objections stated in verses 5 and 6 and the replies in verse 30 and following bring out the controversy. The passage is difficult since much is left to context, some of which we try to provide in the following reconstruction.

> *Realists*: How can you say that nothing has self-existence? What is the basis, the knowledge source (*pramana*) for your claim?
>
> *Nagarjuna*: There is none. Your thinking like that is what's wrong.
>
> *Realists*: Since you cite no knowledge source, you have no right to say what you say.
>
> *Nagarjuna*: Only according to you do I need a "knowledge source." Your views block appreciation of the Buddhist message, but through seeing the untoward ramifications of your positions, your mind may be opened. For example, tell me, once you identify a "knowledge source" for a claim, what is the "source" for the identification? You fall into an infinite regress, looking for the sources of your sources.
>
> *Realists*: A source of knowledge is like a self-illumining lamp, justifying both its result (e.g., perception showing things) and itself (perception showing itself as a knowledge source). Or the situation is like a scale that can be calibrated. Identification of sources of knowledge depends on the objects to be made known.
>
> *Nagarjuna*: The analogies are inapt. First of all, a lamp does not illumine itself, for it does not stand in need of illumination. Second, something to be proved cannot be a prover; a father cannot be the son of his own son.

Nagarjuna continues, at once upholding the logic of everyday speech and showing impossibilities in the mental constructions of the realists. To gain knowledge, we must acquire it from the appropriate source, say the Realists. Jones cannot sense that $2+2 = 4$ or infer that the page looks gray to him at the moment. In any given case, therefore, we must appeal to the appropriate source of knowledge. We need a source of knowledge for determining when we are using the appropriate source of knowledge, retorts Nagarjuna.

If we are to avoid a circle or an infinite regress, there must be some sources of knowledge that are self-supporting, for which it is self-evident that they are sources of knowledge. But first, we need some explanation for why those things, and they alone, have this special status. And second, if there is more than one, as the standard account has it, how do we know which applies to which cases?

Nagarjuna is aware that skepticism can be taken to be a self-refuting doctrine. If knowledge is impossible, how can we know the truth of skepticism? If all assertions are unreliable or unjustified, isn't skepticism itself unreliable or unjustified? But Nagarjuna's skepticism has a point: To prepare us for the new outlook consonant with taking up a Buddhist path. All his followers, known as Madhyamikas (the School of the Middle), accept the religious direction of Nagarjuna's refutations. There are, however, two main subschools or interpretations of his philosophy: Prasangika (Refutational) and

Svatantrika (Doctrinal). The latter holds that Nagarjuna does advance his own views, though these are few and restricted to religious content. The Refutational interpretation says he advances no views of his own but only refutes other views to help people become fit for a Buddhist path. On this reading, Nagarjuna attempts to undermine any claims to knowledge; he does not advance any view of his own. He does not, in other words, put forth the doctrine that knowledge, justification, reliability, and so on, are impossible; he undercuts any attempt to establish them. It appears that this makes his position coherent, but at the cost of making it unstatable. As B. K. Matilal observes,

> The upshot is that a radical scepticism of this kind is not, or does not seem to be, a statable position. For if it is statable, it becomes incoherent or paradoxical. In other words such a position could be coherent only at the risk of being unstatable! It seems to me that both radical scepticism and Nagarjunian Buddhism would welcome this situation, for here we may find the significance of the doctrine of silence in Madhyamika.

Nagarjuna's followers become greatly adept in finding difficulties in the positions of others. They see the ability to knock down others' views as a manifestation of wisdom or insight, the most important of the "perfections" that are the mark of a bodhisattva.

12.2.1 Nagarjuna, from *Averting the Arguments*

22. The "being dependent nature" of existing things: that is called "emptiness." That which has a nature of "being dependent"—of that there is a non-self-existent nature.

23. Just as a magically formed phantom could deny a phantom created by its own magic, just so would be that negation....

28. Or else the grounds are that which is to be proved; certainly sound does not exist as real. For we do not speak without accepting, for practical purposes, the work-a-day world.

29. If I would make any proposition whatever, then by that I would have a logical error; but I do not make a proposition, therefore I am not in error....

31. And if, for you, there is a source [of knowledge] of each and every object of proof, then tell how, in turn, for you there is proof of those sources. If by other sources [of knowledge] there would be the proof of a source—that would be an "infinite regress"; in that case neither a beginning, middle, or an end is proved.

32. Or if there is proof of those [objects] without sources, your argument is refuted. There is a [logical] inconsistency in this, and you ought to explain the cause of the difference [between the principles of validity in your statement and others]....

34. That reconciliation of difficulty is not [realized in the claim:] "Fire illumines itself." Certainly it is not like the non-manifest appearance of a pot in the dark.

35. And if, according to your statement, fire illumines its own self, then is this not like a fire which would illumine its own self and something else?

36. If, according to your statement, fire would illumine both "its own self" and an "other self,"

Source: Nagarjuna, *Averting the Arguments* (*Vigrahavyavartani*). From Frederick J. Streng (trans.), *Emptiness: A Study in Religious Meaning*. New York: Abingdon Press, 1967.

then also darkness, like fire, would darken itself and an "other self."...

40. If your sources [of knowledge] are proved by their own strength, then, for you, the sources are proved without respect to "that which is to be proved"; then you have a proof of a source, [but] no sources are proved without relation to something else.

41. If, according to you, the sources [of knowledge] are proved without being related to the objects of "that which is to be proved," then these sources will not prove anything.

42. Or if [you say]: What error is there in thinking, "The relationship of these [sources of knowledge to their objects] is [already] proved"? [The answer is:] This would be the proving of what is proved. Indeed "that which is not proved" is not related to something else.

43. Or if the sources [of knowledge] in every case are proved in relation to "what is to be proved," then "what is to be proved" is proved without relation to the sources.

44. And if "what is to be proved" is proved without relation to the sources [of knowledge], what [purpose] is the proof of the sources for you—since that for the purpose of which those [sources] exist is already proved?

45. Or if, for you, the sources [of knowledge] are proved in relation to "what is to be proved," then, for you, there exists an interchange between the sources and "what is to be proved."

46. Or if, for you, there are the sources [of knowledge] being proved when there is proof of "what is to be proved," and if "what is to be proved" exists when the source is proved, then, for you, the proof of them both does not exist.

47. If those things which are to be proved are proved by these sources [of knowledge], and those things which are proved by "what is to be proved," how will they prove [anything]?

48. And if those sources [of knowledge] are proved by what is to be proved, and those things which are to be proved by the sources, how will they prove [anything]?

49. If a son is produced by a father, and if that [father] is produced by that very son [when he is born], then tell me, in this case, who produces whom?

50. You tell me! Which of the two becomes the father, and which the son—since they both carry characteristics of "father" and "son"? In that case there is doubt.

51. The proof of the sources [of knowledge] is not [established] by itself, nor by each other, or not by other sources. It does not exist by that which is to be proved and not from nothing at all....

70. All things prevail for him for whom emptiness prevails; nothing whatever prevails for him for whom emptiness prevails.

12.3 NEW LOGIC RESPONSES TO SKEPTICISM

The "New Logician," Gangesha (fl. around 1325 CE), founder of the New Logic (*Navya-Nyaya*), and contemporary of Geoffrey Chaucer and such later medieval European philosophers as John Buridan and William of Ockham, advances another argument against skepticism. He insists that a skeptic's argument is self-defeating—employing the very logical patterns it denounces—and pragmatically inconsistent as well. The skeptic expects to be understood. Why? If it is impossible to know anything, how can we know what the skeptic is talking about? How can we understand anything the skeptic says? The skeptic uses inference to guide action—including speech—just like everyone else. So why can't we use it to back up our views?

Skeptics, in other words, rely on an abnormal conception of doubt; their thresholds for suspicion are far too low. They doubt in the seminar room what they accept perfectly well outside it. Their doubt is only theoretical. In Gangesa's view, that makes it hypocritical or worse. A purely theoretical doubt is not the genuine item, the real McCoy, but a false extension of it. A real skeptic would be like the poor fool who fails to get out of the way of stampeding elephants, wondering whether it's all a dream.

Recall the *Nyaya Sutra* passage about a scale and a nugget. If we worry about the accuracy of the scale, we use a nugget whose weight has been determined by other scales to calibrate it. When we seek to know whether a scale is giving the correct weight, we use it to weigh objects whose weights we already know—whose weights, in other words, we have already established by using other scales. We ask, in effect, whether the results from that scale match the results from other scales.

This example illustrates both the strength and the weakness of the Nyaya response. Doubting the accuracy of an apparent source of knowledge in a particular case—a scale, our eyes, a bit of testimony, etc.—we consider how that source applies to other cases and how well its results cohere with those from other sources of knowledge. Doubting what you say, I consider the reliability of other things you say. I may also try to confirm your testimony with additional evidence. Doubting my eyes, I see whether they are giving me accurate information about other things of similar size, shape, color, and so on, ask others what they see, try to touch the object, and so on, to confirm or disconfirm the evidence my eyes give me. The strength of this coherentism, then, is that it accords well with our practices when we have legitimate doubt. But the weakness is that, at best, we get coherence with other knowledge generators and pieces of information rather than correspondence with reality. Even if all our "sources of knowledge" agree, it remains possible that none give us knowledge of the world as it exists. Perhaps all the scales are wrong. Perhaps everyone we talk to gives false testimony. Perhaps our eyes are deceiving us, and everyone else's eyes are deceiving them too.

Gangesha dismisses this concern. There is no reason to engage in skeptical doubt of this kind. We have no reason to think that our faculties systematically mislead us.

We engage in *local* doubt when we wonder whether a given scale is accurate or worry whether our eyes are deceiving us in a particular case. Those local doubts we resolve in coherentist fashion, as the *Nyaya Sutra* explicates, checking to see if our belief-generator in a particular case is a true source of knowledge. We compare the scale to other scales; we ask others whether they see what we see.

Admittedly, this does not assure us that our sensations or thoughts correspond to reality, for the other scales and the other people's eyes might be wrong too. But that would be a *global* doubt that we have no reason to entertain. We doubt a scale or our eyes when something anomalous happens—when, in short, we get a result we did not expect. But there is no global equivalent. We can say, at a certain time, that we don't see what we expected. But it makes no sense to say that, in general, nothing is what we expected.

Skeptics may claim to have such global doubts. In fact, however, skeptics live like everyone else; they put aside their doubts outside specifically philosophical contexts and behave as if they had no doubts at all.

Nagarjuna would not deny this. He distinguishes our everyday attitude, which is fine from a pragmatic point of view but leads to paradoxes when analyzed carefully; from an absolute perspective we gain when we reflect on our everyday attitudes or engage in meditation. We can live like everyone else outside the study, the seminar room, or the monastery. But in those contexts we can recognize the incoherence of the everyday point of view.

Gangesha charges that this twofold attitude involves a kind of pragmatic inconsistency. It gives us evidence that even skeptics do not take their own doubts seriously. They try to use a type of "indirect proof" against the dogmatist, showing that a belief in anything leads to a contradiction. But their behavior leaves them open to exactly the same sort of argument. If the beliefs of dogmatists are incoherent, so are the actions of skeptics.

12.3.1 Gangesha, from *The Jewel of Thought about Epistemology*

Indirect proof is appropriately pursued as long as there is doubt. Where there would be pragmatic contradiction (i.e., speech or other behavior contradicting the negation of the thesis to be established)—and indeed no doubt occurring—one can grasp the pervasion [causal law] without resorting to indirect proof.

As an example, consider the particular doubt (against the indirect proof I earlier said demolishes doubt about concomitance of smoke with fire). If smoke is not produced from a set of causes excluding fire, then (in conformity with the doubt about the concomitance) *smoke*—if it were not produced from a causal complex including fire—*would not be produced* (a conclusion in contradiction, presumably, with the doubter's belief that smoke is produced). Now the doubt (against this indirect proof): Could the smoke come to be from something that is not fire? Or could it arise, just in some instances without fire? Or could it come to be simply by chance (without a cause)?

Were a person *P*, who has ascertained thoroughgoing positive correlations (*x* wherever *y*) and negative correlations (wherever no *y*, no *x*), to doubt that an effect might arise without a cause then—to take up the example of smoke and fire—why should *P* regularly, as he does, resort to fire for smoke (in the case, say, of a desire to get rid of mosquitoes)? (Similarly,) to food to allay hunger, and to speech to communicate to another person?

For (there would be a presupposition to *P*'s doubt, namely) that without the one the other is possible. Therefore, just the resorting to this and that (i.e., the causes of the desired effects) blocks and terminates such a doubt.

When there is doubt, there is no regular pattern of behavior (with respect to using *x* to bring about *y*). When there is (such) a regular pattern, doubt does not occur.

Thus it has been said (by Udayana): "That is doubted concerning which as doubted there occurs no contradiction with the doubter's action."

For it is not possible at once to resort regularly to fire and the like for smoke and the like and to doubt that fire causes it (it would be meaningless behavior). This is how we should understand (Udayana's) saying.

Thus we may reject the argument that contradiction—understood as natural opposition, governing precisely which *x* cannot occur along with precisely which *y* (as horsehood and cowhood in the same individual)—cannot block a vicious infinite regress. It is the doubter's own behavior that proves the lie to the doubt, i.e., that blocks it.

Source: Gangesha, *The Jewel of Thought about Epistemology (Tattvacintamani)*. Translated by Stephen H. Phillips.

CHAPTER 13

Chinese Theories of Knowledge

"In subjective relation with all things"

Plato defines knowledge as justified true belief. Internally, knowers can know whether they have knowledge by examining the reasons for their beliefs. In the Realism school in India, in contrast, knowledge is veridical cognition that has arisen from a knowledge-generator, a process connecting objects with knowers. Internalists such as Plato and externalists such as the Realists disagree about the nature of warrant and thus about the nature of knowledge. But they agree that knowledge is possible. Skeptics form a third group. They hold that beliefs or cognitions of certain kinds are unjustified or ungenerated by any genuine knowledge source. *Academic* skeptics assert that knowledge is impossible; *Pyrrhonian* skeptics decline to assert anything, instead suspending judgment.

Skeptics typically take particular targets for their doubt. One might, for example, be skeptical of people's claims to have been abducted by aliens. How did they come to believe such a thing? Does the process in general confer justification? Is it generally reliable? For similar reasons, one might be skeptical of religious claims that go beyond all possible human experience, of scientific claims about the origins of the universe, or of parapsychology. Philosophic skeptics have systematic reasons why certain purported areas of knowledge are not really within our grasp.

In its most extreme form, skepticism maintains that there is no knowledge whatsoever. But many skeptical philosophers and schools in China have maintained slightly more moderate forms, targeting an area or type of claim that they consider unknowable—especially claims about the objective nature of the world. Furthermore, they conform to the Confucian or Socratic model of inquiry, themselves presenting reasons why certain other reasons are no good.

13.1 DAOIST SKEPTICISM

Zhuangzi (also called Chuang Tzu, c. 350 BCE), roughly a contemporary of Plato and early Greek skeptics such as Pyrrho, is one of the two great thinkers of Daoism. He gives skepticism a mystical turn. Laozi wrote of the One, which is indescribable but nevertheless the fount of the entire universe. The One, for Zhuangzi, amounts to the Dao's universal spontaneousness. Wisdom consists in seeking unity with Dao. To achieve such unity, you need to abandon thoughts of yourself and attune yourself to the flow of nature. Zhuangzi goes beyond Laozi in recommending self-development as part of becoming attuned to Dao. The Daoist master learns to use paradox to communicate; only paradox can express the true understanding that comes from overcoming the distinctions and divisions inherent in thinking.

Zhuangzi's skepticism thus seems sweeping, excluding only the paradoxical language that would express a master's true understanding. Distinctions in thought correspond to no distinctions in reality. We cannot trust thinking or even sense experience. In consequence, there is no point in trying to accomplish anything—anything, at least, that depends on the distinctions of an everyday mindset. Effort is pointless (except, perhaps, effort at becoming a Daoist master).

Zhuangzi offers five basic arguments for his conclusion that knowledge (as generally understood) is impossible:

- interdependence of the objective and subjective
- the unity of everything
- universal variability
- the problem of the criterion
- the possibility of dreaming

The interdependence of the objective and subjective. We can frame the question of the possibility of knowledge in terms of objectivity: Is it possible to become completely objective? Zhuangzi answers no, because subjectivity and objectivity are inevitably interlocked. The objective and subjective depend on each other. You can attain objective knowledge, if at all, only by beginning with your own subjective mental states and making them match reality. But if you are in a certain subjective mental state, then (a) it is objectively true that you are in that state, and (b) you are in it by virtue of certain objective truths about you. So objectivity and subjectivity go together. They depend on one another. But they are ordinarily supposed to be contraries: The subjective is that which is not objective. Zhuangzi concludes that the distinction between the subjective and the objective is incoherent. But then out the window too goes all pretense to objectivity and thus to knowledge.

How good is this argument? It seems to turn on an equivocation with the word *subjective*. We might call something subjective if it is or relates essentially to a mental state, and objective if it pertains to reality, i.e., our common world. In this way, the subjective and objective need not be contraries at all. Smith's feeling of heat on touching a radiator is subjective and objective at the same time if the radiator really is hot. Alternatively, we might call something subjective if it merely relates to a mental state, that is, relates to a mental state without reflecting reality. Then the subjective and objective are indeed contraries, but there is no longer any reason to think that knowledge is at all subjective. In fact, if it were, it would not be knowledge of the objective world.

The unity of everything. Distinctions should be rejected, Zhuangzi insists, because all things are at root identical. Oddly, this argument begins with what makes individual objects distinct. Each thing has its own nature (*de*), which determines what it is, what it can be, and what it tends to be. But the argument concludes with the statement that individual objects are not distinct after all. The contradiction disappears when we realize that the identity is only from the "perspective of Dao," not from our untransformed perspective. That is the real opposition. Thus we see that Zhuangzi's skepticism is really a recommendation for a certain kind of perspective.

Thus the Daoist not only argues that knowledge is impossible but also advises us about how to think about the world and how to live. The recommendation is threefold: Reject distinctions, take refuge in Dao, and place yourself in subjective relations to things—that is, give up claims to objectivity. Knowledge being impossible, stop pretending to know. This seems reasonable. But the connection between the thesis and the recommendation, easy as it is to understand, is not easy to defend. Does the thesis (knowledge is impossible) justify the recommendation? If so, do we know it? Wouldn't that undermine the claim that knowledge is impossible? But if the recommendation is unreliable or unjustified, why should we accept it? Skepticism tied to a recommendation like this seems self-defeating.

Zhuangzi does not spell his argument out very explicitly, but he gives an important and entertaining illustration of what he has in mind in the story of the monkeys and the chestnuts. The idea is this. Things seem to have their own individual natures. But at root they are one. We make distinctions between them, dividing one from another by distinguishing one nature from another. Just as the monkeys distinguish the three-in-the-morning arrangement from the three-at-night arrangement even though the number of chestnuts is the same, so we distinguish beams from pillars, beauty from ugliness, and so on, even though the underlying reality is the same. "Beauty is in the eye of the beholder," people sometimes say. Zhuangzi is claiming that *everything* is in the eye of the beholder. Everything is merely subjective; there is no such thing as objectivity. So there is no such thing as knowledge.

Universal variability. A third argument relies on a premise of universal variability along with a premise of undecidability. Thus:

- *Variability*: Things are perceived differently (by different subjects or at different times).
- *Undecidability*: There is no way to decide which perceptions ought to be trusted.
- *Skeptical conclusion*: Therefore, knowledge is impossible.

Zhuangzi puts this in terms of the different subjectivities belonging to different species: humans versus eels, humans versus monkeys, and so on.

Variability we may admit. But is the undecidability thesis true? Zhuangzi claims that there is no way to decide which way of seeing things is correct. One might try then to defuse the argument by seeking a criterion for distinguishing correct from incorrect perceptions. But where could we get such a touchstone, a measuring rod to put to the task?

The problem of the criterion. In support of undecidability Zhuangzi has another argument. If two people, Smith and Jones, argue and Jones concedes defeat, is Smith necessarily right and Jones wrong? Or if Jones "beats" Smith, in Jones's judgment, is Jones necessarily the one who knows? Couldn't there be error in how they decide the argument? If Jones says, "By this criterion, I am right," Smith can say, "By that other one, you are wrong." The debate jumps a level—focusing now on criteria—and appears unresolvable. Any criterion proposed may itself be disputed.

Can't a neutral party decide? If Jones employs an arbiter who takes Jones's view, couldn't Smith do the same? We have no way to decide who would count as neutral. Arbitration is thus impossible.

It might seem, then, that we could find a criterion for deciding which perceptions are accurate. But the eel will have its criterion; the monkey, another criterion; the owl, yet another; and so on. How can we decide which criterion to choose? That too is undecidable.

Versions of this argument have driven much Western epistemology, and there are responses to it in classical India, too. So let us come back to it and move on to a final argument.

The Possibility of Dreaming. This argument is contained in a passage from Zhuangzi that expresses what is probably his most famous image: Zhuangzi dreaming he is a butterfly—or is it a butterfly dreaming he is Zhuangzi?

Many of Zhuangzi's arguments concern questions of value: standards of beauty or virtue, for example. But here the issue is broader. Given that there is no mark by which we can determine whether a given experience is a dream or reflective of reality, we cannot tell from our own point of view whether we are justified in believing anything. We might be dreaming it. There is no objective point of view from which we can distinguish a genuine means of knowledge, such as perception, from an apparent one—one that presents only fabrications of our own consciousness, such as dreaming.

This argument is used to draw idealist conclusions in early modern Western philosophy and by Buddhists in India. The Buddhist concurrence with the Daoist idea may help to explain Chinese receptivity for Buddhism centuries after Zhuangzi. Zhuangzi himself recommends skepticism and disengagement from ordinary life.

13.1.1 From *Zhuangzi*

"Great knowledge embraces the whole: small knowledge, a part only. Great speech is universal: small speech is particular.

"For whether the mind is locked in sleep or whether in waking hours the body is released, we are subject to daily mental perturbations,

Source: Chuang Tzu. Translated from the Chinese by Herbert A. Giles. First edition, 1889; second edition, 1923. We have made minor editorial changes.

indecision, want of penetration, concealment, fretting fear, and trembling terror. Now like a javelin the mind flies forth, the arbiter of right and wrong. Now like a solemn covenanter it remains firm, the guardian of rights secured. Then, as under autumn and winter's blight, comes gradual decay, a passing away, like the flow of water, never to return. Finally, the block when all is choked up like an old drain the failing mind which shall not see light again.

"Joy and anger, sorrow and happiness, caution and remorse, come upon us by turns, with everchanging mood. They come like music from hollowness, like mushrooms from damp. Daily and nightly they alternate within us, but we cannot tell whence they spring. Can we then hope in a moment to lay our finger upon their very cause?

"But for these emotions I should not be. But for me, they would have no scope. So far we can go; but we do not know what it is that brings them into play. 'Twould seem to be a soul; but the clue as to its existence is wanting. That such a power operates is credible enough, though we cannot see its form. Perhaps it has functions without form.

"Take the human body with all its manifold divisions. Which part of it does a man love best? Does he not cherish all equally, or has he a preference? Do not all equally serve him? And do these servitors then govern themselves, or are they subdivided into rulers and subjects? Surely there is some soul which sways them all.

"But whether or not we ascertain what are the functions of this soul, it matters but little to the soul itself. For coming into existence with this mortal coil of mine, with the exhaustion of this mortal coil its mandate will also be exhausted. To be harassed by the wear and tear of life, and to pass rapidly through it without possibility of arresting one's course, is not this pitiful indeed? To labour without ceasing, and then, without living to enjoy the fruit, worn out, to depart, suddenly, one knows not whither, is not that a just cause for grief?

"What advantage is there in what men call not dying? The body decomposes, and the mind goes with it. This is our real cause for sorrow. Can the world be so dull as not to see this? Or is it I alone who am dull, and others not so?

"If we are to be guided by the criteria of our own minds, who shall be without a guide? What need to know of the alternations of passion, when the mind thus affords scope to itself? verily even the minds of fools! Whereas, for a mind without criteria to admit the idea of contraries, is like saying, I went to Yueh today, and got there yesterday. Or, like placing nowhere somewhere, topography which even the Great Yu would fail to understand; how much more I?

"Speech is not mere breath. It is differentiated by meaning. Take away that, and you cannot say whether it is speech or not. Can you even distinguish it from the chirping of young birds?

"But how can Dao be so obscured that we speak of it as true and false? And how can speech be so obscured that it admits the idea of contraries? How can Dao go away and yet remain? How can speech exist and yet be impossible?

"Dao is obscured by our want of grasp. Speech is obscured by the gloss of this world. Hence the affirmatives and negatives of the Confucian and Mohist schools, each denying what the other affirmed and affirming what the other denied. But he who would reconcile affirmative with negative and negative with affirmative must do so by the light of nature.

"There is nothing which is not objective: there is nothing which is not subjective. But it is impossible to start from the objective. Only from subjective knowledge is it possible to proceed to objective knowledge. Hence it has been said, 'The objective emanates from the subjective; the subjective is consequent upon the objective. This is the Alternation Theory.' Nevertheless, when one is born, the other dies. When one is possible, the other is impossible. When one is affirmative, the other is negative. Which being the case, the true sage rejects all distinctions of this and that. He takes his refuge in Dao, and places himself in subjective relation with all things.

"And inasmuch as the subjective is also objective, and the objective also subjective, and as the contraries under each are indistinguishably blended, does it not become impossible for us to say whether subjective and objective really exist at all?

"When subjective and objective are both without their correlates, that is the very axis of Dao. And when that axis passes through the centre at which all infinities converge, positive and negative alike blend into an infinite one. Hence it has been said that there is nothing like the light of nature.

"To take a finger in illustration of a finger not being a finger is not so good as to take something which is not a finger. To take a horse in illustration of a horse not being a horse is not so good as to take something which is not a horse.

"So with the universe and all that in it is. These things are but fingers and horses in this sense. The possible is possible; the impossible is impossible. Dao operates, and given results follow. Things receive names and are what they are. They achieve this by their natural affinity for what they are and their natural antagonism to what they are not. For all things have their own particular constitutions and potentialitites. Nothing can exist without these.

"Therefore it is that, viewed from the standpoint of Dao, a beam and a pillar are identical. So are ugliness and beauty, greatness, wickedness, perverseness, and strangeness. Separation is the same as construction; construction is the same as destruction. Nothing is subject either to construction or to destruction, for these conditions are brought together into one.

"Only the truly intelligent understand this principle of the identity of all things. They do not view things as apprehended by themselves, subjectively, but transfer themselves into the position of the things viewed. And viewing them thus they are able to comprehend them, nay, to master them; and he who can master them is near. So it is that to place oneself in subjective relation with externals, without consciousness of their objectivity, this is Dao. But to wear out one's intellect in an obstinate adherence to the individuality of things, not recognizing the fact that all things are one, this is called Three in the Morning."

"What is Three in the Morning?" asked Zi Yu.

"A keeper of monkeys," replied Zi Qi, "said with regard to their rations of chestnuts that each monkey was to have three in the morning and four at night. But at this the monkeys were very angry, so the keeper said they might have four in the morning and three at night, with which arrangement they were all well pleased. The actual number of the chestnuts remained the same, but there was an adaptation to the likes and dislikes of those concerned. Such is the principle of putting onself into subjective relation with externals.

"Wherefore the true sage, while regarding contraries as identical, adapts himself to the laws of Heaven. This is called following two courses at once....

"Therefore what the true sage aims at is the light which comes out of darkness. He does not view things as apprehended by himself, subjectively, but transfers himself into the position of the things viewed. This is called using the light.

"There remains, however, speech. Is that to be enrolled under either category of contraries, or not? Whether it is so enrolled or not, it will in any case belong to one or the other, and thus be as though it had an objective existence. At any rate, I should like to hear some speech which belongs to neither category....

"If then all things are one, what room is there for speech? On the other hand, since I can utter these words, how can speech not exist?

"If it does exist, we have one and speech = two; and two and one = three. From which point onwards even the best mathematicians will fail to reach: How much more then will ordinary people fail?

"Hence, if from nothing you can proceed to something, and subsequently reach three, it follows that it would be still more easy if you were to start from something. To avoid such progression, you must put yourself into subjective relation with the external.

"Before conditions existed, Dao was. Before definitions existed, speech was. Subjectively, we are conscious of certain delimitations which are,

- Right and Left
- Relationship and Obligation
- Division and Discrimination
- Emulation and Contention.

"These are called the Eight Predicables.

"For the true sage, beyond the limits of an external world, they exist, but are not recognized. By the true sage, within the limits of an external world, they are recognized, but are not assigned. And so, with regard to the wisdom of the ancients, as embodied in the Canon of Spring and Autumn, the true Sage assigns, but does not justify by argument. And thus, classifying he does not classify; arguing, he does not argue."

"How can that be?" asked Zi Yu.

"The true sage," answered Zi Qi, "keeps his knowledge within him, while men in general set forth theirs in argument, in order to convince each other. And therefore it is said that in argument he does not manifest himself.

"Perfect Dao does not declare itself. Nor does perfect argument express itself in words. Nor does perfect charity show itself in act. Nor is perfect honesty absolutely incorruptible. Nor is perfect courage absolutely unyielding.

"For the Dao which shines forth is not Dao. Speech which argues falls short of its aim. Charity which has fixed points loses its scope. Honesty which is absolute is wanting in credit. Courage which is absolute misses its object. These five are, as it were, round, with a strong bias towards squareness. Therefore that knowledge which stops at what it does not know is the highest knowledge.

"Who knows the argument which can be argued without words? the Dao which does not declare itself as Dao? He who knows this may be said to be of Dao. To be able to pour in without making full, and pour out without making empty, in ignorance of the power by which such results are accomplished, this is accounted Light."

Of old, the Emperor Yao said to Shun, "I would smite the Zongs, and the Guis, and the Xuaos. Ever since I have been on the throne I have had this desire. What do you think?"

"These three states," replied Shun, "are paltry out-of-the-way places. Why can you not shake off this desire? Once upon a time, ten suns came out together, and all things were illuminated thereby. How much more then should virtue excel suns?"

Ye Que asked Wang Yi, saying, "Do you know for certain that all things are subjectively the same?"

"How can I know?" answered Wang Yi. "Do you know what you do not know?"

"How can I know?" replied Ye Que. "But can then nothing be known?"

"How can I know?" said Wang Yi. "Nevertheless, I will try to tell you. How can it be known that what I call knowing is not really not knowing and that what I call not knowing is not really knowing? Now I would ask you this. If a man sleeps in a damp place, he gets lumbago and dies. But how about an eel? And living up in a tree is precarious and trying to the nerves: but how about monkeys? Of the man, the eel, and the monkey, whose habitat is the right one, absolutely? Human beings feed on flesh, deer on grass, centipedes on snakes' brains, owls and crows on mice. Of these four, whose is the right taste, absolutely? Monkey mates with monkey, the buck with the doe; eels consort with fishes, while men admire Mao Ch'iang and Liji, at the sight of whom fishes plunge deep down in the water, birds soar high in the air, and deer hurry away. Yet who shall say which is the correct standard of beauty? In my opinion, the standard of human virtue, and of positive and negative, is so obscured that it is impossible to actually know it as such."

"If you then," asked Ye Que, "do not know what is bad for you, is the perfect man equally without this knowledge?"

"The perfect man," answered Wang Yi, "is a spiritual being. Were the ocean itself scorched up, he would not feel hot. Were the Milky Way frozen hard, he would not feel cold. Were the mountains to be riven with thunder, and the great deep to be thrown up by storm, he would not tremble. In such case, he would mount upon the clouds of heaven, and driving the sun and the moon before him, would pass beyond the limits of this external world, where death and life have no more victory over man; how much less what is bad for him?"

Zhu Qiao addressed Zhang Wuzi as follows: "I heard Confucius say, 'The true sage pays no heed to mundane affairs. He neither seeks gain nor avoids injury. He asks nothing at the hands of man. He adheres, without questioning, to Dao. Without speaking, he can speak; and he can speak and yet say nothing. And so he roams beyond the limits of this dusty world. These,' added Confucius, 'are wild words.' Now to me they are the skilful embodiment of Dao. What, sir, is your opinion?"

"Points upon which the Yellow Emperor doubted," replied Zhang Wuzi, "how should Confucius know? You are going too fast. You see your egg, and expect to hear it crow. You look at your cross-bow, and expect to have broiled pigeon before you. I will say a few words to you at random, and do you listen at random.

"How does the sage seat himself by the sun and moon, and hold the universe in his grasp? He blends everything into one harmonious whole, rejecting the confusion of this and that. Rank and precedence, which the vulgar prize, the sage stolidly ignores. The revolutions of ten thousand years leave his unity unscathed. The universe itself may pass away, but he will flourish still.

"How do I know that love of life is not a delusion after all? How do I know but that he who dreads to die is not as a child who has lost the way and cannot find his home?

"The Lady Liji was the daughter of Ai Feng. When the Duke of Jin first got her, she wept until the bosom of her dress was drenched with tears. But when she came to the royal residence, and lived with the Duke, and ate rich food, she repented of having wept. How then do I know that the dead repent of having previously clung to life?

"Those who dream of the banquet wake to lamentation and sorrow. Those who dream of lamentation and sorrow wake to join the hunt. While they dream, they do not know that they dream. Some will even interpret the very dream they are dreaming; and only when they awake do they know it was a dream.

"By and by comes the Great Awakening, and then we find out that this life is really a great dream. Fools think they are awake now, and flatter themselves they know if they are really princes or peasants. Confucius and you are both dreams; and I who say you are dreams, I am but a dream myself. This is a paradox. Tomorrow a sage may arise to explain it; but that tomorrow will not be until ten thousand generations have gone by.

"Granting that you and I argue. If you beat me, and not I you, are you necessarily right and I wrong? Or if I beat you and not you me, am I necessarily right and you wrong? Or are we both partly right and partly wrong? Or are we both wholly right and wholly wrong? You and I cannot know this, and consequently the world will be in ignorance of the truth.

"Who shall I employ as arbiter between us? If I employ someone who takes your view, he will side with you. How can such a one arbitrate between us? If I employ someone who takes my view, he will side with me. How can such a one arbitrate between us? And if I employ someone who either differs from, or agrees with, both of us, he will be equally unable to decide between us. Since then you, and I, and man, cannot decide, must we not depend upon another? Such dependence is as though it were not dependence. We are embraced in the obliterating unity of Dao. There is perfect adaption to whatever may eventuate; and so we complete our allotted span.

"But what is it to be embraced in the obliterating unity of Dao? It is this. With reference to positive and negative, to that which is so and that which is not so, if the positive is really positive, it must necessarily be different from its negative: there is no room for argument. And if that which is so really is so, it must necessarily be different from that which is not so: there is no room for argument.

"Take no heed of time, nor of right and wrong. But passing into the realm of the Infinite, take your final rest therein."

The Penumbra said to the Umbra. "At one moment you move; at another you are at rest. At one moment you sit down; at another you get up. Why this instability of purpose?" "I depend," replied the Umbra, "upon something which causes me to do as I do; and that something depends in turn upon something else which causes it to do as it does. My dependence is like that of a snake's scales or of a cicada's wings. How can I tell why I do one thing, or why I do not do another?"

Once upon a time, I, Zhuangzi, dreamt I was a butterfly, fluttering hither and thither, to all intents and purposes a butterfly. I was conscious only of following my fancies as a butterfly, and was unconscious of my individuality as a man. Suddenly, I awaked, and there I lay, myself again. Now I do not know whether I was then a man dreaming I was a butterfly, or whether I am now a butterfly dreaming I am a man.

13.2 THE EMPIRICISM OF WANG CHONG

Chinese philosopher Wang Chong (Wang Ch'ung, 27–97 CE) articulated the central doctrine of empiricism. Wang, an orphan, lived in poverty for most of his life. He read books at a bookstore, studied at the national university, and returned to his hometown to teach. He earned a reputation as a genius. He was awarded a job as district secretary but promptly lost it due to his rather difficult personality.

By Wang Chong's time, during the Han Dynasty, both Confucianism and Daoism had accumulated a thick layer of superstition. Confucianism was China's leading philosophical school, rapidly developing into a religion and attracting a set of superstitions. Daoism was becoming a mystical religion with an elaborate set of rituals. Confucius and Laozi were worshipped as gods. People believed in divination and destiny. They thought gods routinely interfered in human affairs to reward the good, punish the bad, and enforce a variety of seemingly pointless rules. People arranged their houses and lives according to the principles of *feng shui*.

Wang Chong believed that all this violated the basic principles of Confucius and Laozi—and, for that matter, common sense. He advanced skeptical arguments, especially against the Confucians. Wang, a thoroughgoing naturalist, argued that nature is spontaneous, acting according to its own laws without divine intervention or interference. Natural events have no religious meaning. Nature has no discernible purpose; we can understand things only by understanding their causes. And we can gain knowledge of those only through experience. That is the key thesis of any empiricist: Everything we know about the world comes from experience. Though the science of Wang's time remained primitive, he stressed the importance of scientific method. His writings received little attention during his lifetime but influenced Confucianism and Daoism profoundly after his death, stripping away much of the superstition that surrounded them and returning them to their roots in the works of Confucius and Laozi.

13.2.1 Wang Chong, from *Balanced Enquiries*

Spontaneous Action

Why must we assume that the heavens act spontaneously? Because they have neither mouth nor eyes. Intentional activity is associated with a mouth and with eyes: the mouth wishes to eat, and the eyes to see. These desires manifested outside come from inside. When the mouth and the eyes are craving for something considered advantageous, it is due to those desires. Now, when the mouth and the eyes are not activated by desire, there is nothing for them to seek. Why should there be activity then?

How do we know that heaven possesses neither mouth nor eyes? From the earth. The body of the earth is formed of rocks and soil, and rocks and soil have neither mouth nor eyes. The heavens and earth are like husband and wife. Since the body of the earth is not provided with a mouth or eyes, we know that the heavens also have no mouth or eyes. Supposing that the heavens have a body, then it must be like that of the earth. As a vital force, it should be air alone, and this air would be like clouds and fog. How can a cloudy or nebular substance have a mouth or an eye?

Someone might argue that every movement originates from inaction. There is desire provoking movement and, as soon as there is motion, there is action. The changes in the heavens are similar to those of man; how could they be spontaneous without intention or purpose? I reply that, when the heavens move, they bring forth matter and energy. The mass of the heavens move, matter and energy come forth, and things are produced.

When the heavens are changing, they do not desire to produce things thereby; things are produced of their own accord. That is spontaneity. Releasing matter and energy, the heavens do not desire to create things, but things are created of themselves. That is spontaneous action without intention or desire.

The Purposeless Heavens

By the fusion of the matter and energy of the heavens and earth, all things of the world are produced spontaneously, just as by the mixture of matter and energy of husband and wife children are born spontaneously. Among the things thus produced, creatures with blood in their veins are sensitive to hunger and cold. Seeing that the five grains can be eaten, they use them as food; and discovering that silk and hemp can be worn, they take them and wear them. Some people are of the opinion that the heavens produce grain for the purpose of feeding mankind, and silk and hemp to clothe them. That would be tantamount to making the heavens the farmer of man, or his mulberry girl; it would not be in accordance with spontaneity, therefore this opinion is very questionable and unacceptable.

Reasoning on Daoist principles we find that nature imbues all things with matter and energy. Among the many things of this world, grain dispels hunger, and silk and hemp protect from cold. For that reason man eats grain, and wears silk and hemp. The heavens do not produce grain, silk, and hemp purposely, in order to feed and clothe mankind, just as by calamitous changes they do not intend to reprove man. Things are produced spontaneously, and man wears and eats them; natural forces change spontaneously, and man is frightened by them. The usual theory is disheartening. Where would spontaneity be,

Source: Wang Chong, *Lung-Heng (Balanced Enquiries)*, Part I, *Philosophical Essays of Wang Chung*. Translated by Alfred Forke. London: Luzac and Company, 1907.

if changes in the heavens were intentional, and where would be spontaneous action without aim or purpose?

The Indifferent Heavens

King Xiang of Chin sent a sword to Po Chi, who thereupon was going to commit suicide, falling on the sword. "How have I offended Heaven?" he asked. After a long while he answered, "I see why I must die. At the battle of Chang-ping, the army of Chao—several hundred thousand men—surrendered, but I deceived them, and caused them to be buried alive. Therefore I deserve to die." Afterwards he killed himself.

Po Chi was well aware of his former crime, and acquiesced in the punishment consequent upon it. He knew how he himself had failed, but not why the soldiers of Chao were buried alive. If heaven really had punished the guilty, what offence against heaven had the soldiers of Chao committed, those who surrendered? If, instead, there had been wounding and killing on the battlefield by the random blows of weapons, many of the four hundred thousand would certainly have survived. Why were these also buried in spite of their goodness and innocence? Those soldiers being unable to obtain heaven's protection through their virtue, why did Po Chi alone suffer the condign punishment for his crime from heaven? We see from this that Po Chi was mistaken in what he concluded.

If the heavens had produced creatures on purpose, they ought to have taught them to love each other, and not to prey upon and destroy one another. One might object that such is the nature of the five elements, that when the heavens create all things, they are imbued with the matter and energies of the five elements, and that these fight together, and destroy one another. But then the heavens ought to have filled creatures with the matter and energy of one element alone, and taught them mutual love, not permitting the forces of the five elements to resort to strife and mutual destruction.

Destiny

It is said that three different kinds of destiny can be distinguished: the natural, the acquired, and the adverse. One speaks of natural destiny if somebody's luck is the simple consequence of his original organization. His constitution being well ordered, and his bones good, he need not toil in order to obtain happiness, since his luck comes of itself. This is what is meant by natural destiny. Acquired destiny comes into play when a man becomes happy only by dint of hard work, but is pursued by misfortune as soon as he yields to his evil propensities, and gives rein to his desires. This is what is understood by acquired destiny. As for adverse destiny, a man may, contrary to his expectations, reap bad fruits from all his good deeds; he will rush into misfortune and misery, which will strike him from afar. In this case, therefore, one can speak of adverse destiny.

Natural Destiny

Every mortal receives his own natural destiny; already at the time of his conception, he obtains a lucky or an unlucky future. Man's nature does not correspond to his destiny: his disposition may be good, but his destiny unlucky, or his disposition bad, and his fate lucky. Good and bad actions are the result of natural disposition, happiness and misfortune, good and bad luck are destiny.... A favorite of fate, though not doing well, is not, of necessity, deprived of happiness for that reason, whereas an ill-fated man does not get rid of his misfortune, though trying his best.

Acquired Destiny

In acquired destiny, bad deeds are followed by misfortune. Yet the robbers Che and Chuang Chiao were scourges to the whole empire. With some thousands of other bandits whom they had collected, they assaulted and robbed people of their property, and cut them to pieces. As outlaws they were unequalled. They ought to have been disgraced; far from it, they finished their lives as old men. In the face of this, how can the idea of an acquired destiny be upheld?

Adverse Destiny

Men with an adverse destiny do well in their hearts, but meet with disasters abroad.... Chu Ping and Wu Yuan were the most loyal ministers of their sovereigns, and scrupulously fulfilled their duties as servants to the king. In spite of this, the corpse of Chu Ping was left unburied in Chu, and in Wu Yuan's body was cooked. For their good works they should have obtained the happiness of acquired destiny, but they fell in with the misfortune of adverse fate. How is such a thing possible?

Consequently, there is no guarantee whatever that men of high endowments and excellent conduct will in any case attain to wealth and honor, and we must not imagine that others whose knowledge is very limited, and whose virtue is but small, are therefore doomed to poverty and misery. Sometimes, men of great talents and excellent conduct have a bad fate, which cripples them, and keeps them down, and people with scanty knowledge and small virtue may have such a propitious fate that they soar up and take a brilliant flight.

Ghosts

People say that the dead become spirit beings, or ghosts, that they are conscious, and can hurt men. Let us examine this by comparing men with other beings.

The dead do not become ghosts, have no consciousness, and cannot injure others. How do we know this? We know it from other beings. Man is a being, and other creatures are likewise beings. When a creature dies, it does not become a ghost, for what reason then must man alone become a ghost when he expires? In this world you can separate man from other creatures, but not on the ground that he becomes a ghost. The faculty to become a ghost cannot be a distinctive mark. If, on the other hand, there is no difference between man and other creatures, we have no reason either to suppose that man may become a ghost.

Man lives by virtue of his vital force. When he dies, this vital force is exhausted. It resides in the arteries. At death the pulse stops, and the vital force ceases to work; then the body decays, and turns into earth and clay. By what could it become a ghost?

Without ears or eyes men have no perceptions. In this respect the deaf and the blind resemble plants and trees. But are men, whose vital force is gone, merely as if they had no eyes, or no ears? No, their decay means complete dissolution.

When men see ghosts, they appear like living men. Just from the fact that they have the shape of living men we can infer that they cannot be the spirits of the dead, as will be seen from the following.

Fill a bag with rice, and a sack with millet. The rice in the bag is like the millet in the sack. Full, they look strong, stand upright, and can be seen. Looking at them from afar, people know that they are a bag of rice, and a sack of millet, because their forms correspond to their contents, and thus become perceptible. If the bag has a hole, the rice runs out, and if the sack is damaged, the millet is spilt. Then the bag and the sack collapse, and are no more visible, when looked at from afar.

Man's vital force resides in the body, as the millet and rice do in the bag and the sack. At death the body decays, and the vital force disperses, just as the millet and the rice escape from the pierced or damaged bag, or sack. When the millet or the rice are gone, the bag and the sack do not take a form again. How then could there be a visible body again, after the vital force has been scattered and lost?

The nature of heaven and earth is such that a new fire can be lighted, but a burnt-out fire cannot be set ablaze again. A new man can be born, but a dead one cannot be resurrected. If burnt-out ashes could be kindled again into a blazing fire,

I would be very much of opinion that the dead might take a bodily form again. Since, however, a burnt-out fire cannot burn again, we are led to the conclusion that the dead cannot become ghosts.

The Dead

Since the dead cannot become ghosts, they cannot have any consciousness either. We infer this from the fact that before their birth men have no consciousness. Before they are born, they form part of the primigenial force, and when they die, they revert to it. This primigenial force is vague and diffuse, and the human spirit, a part of it. Anterior to his birth, man is devoid of consciousness, and at his death he returns to this original state of unconsciousness, for how could he be conscious?

Man is intelligent and sagacious, because he has in him the forces of the five virtues. These are in him because the five organs are in his body. As long as the five parts are uninjured, man is bright and clever, but, when they become diseased, his intellect is dimmed and confused, which is tantamount to stupidity and dullness. After death the five inward parts putrefy, and, when they do so, the five virtues lose their substratum. That which harbors intelligence is destroyed, and that which is called intelligence disappears. The body requires the vital force for its maintenance; and with this, the body becomes conscious. There is no fire in the world burning quite of itself, how could there be an essence without a body, but conscious of itself?

Man's death is like sleep, and sleep comes next to a trance, which resembles death. If a man does not wake up again from a trance, he dies. If he awakes, he returns from death, as though he had been asleep. Thus sleep, a trance, and death are essentially the same. A sleeper cannot know what he did, when he was awake, as a dead man is unaware of his doings during his lifetime. People may talk or do anything by the side of a sleeping man, he does not know, and similarly the dead man has no consciousness of the good or bad actions performed in front of his coffin. When a man is asleep, his vital force is still there, and his body intact, and yet he is unconscious. How much more must this be the case with a dead man, whose vital force is scattered and gone, and whose body is in a state of decay?

No Messages from Beyond

Nowadays, living persons in a trance will sometimes act as mediums to speak for those who have died; and diviners, striking black chords, will call down the dead, whose souls then will talk through the diviner's mouth. All that is bragging and wild talk. If it were not mere gossip, then we would have a manifestation of the vital force of some being.

Some say that the spirit cannot speak. If it cannot speak, it cannot have any knowledge either. Knowledge requires a vital force, just as speech does.

Human death is like the extinction of fire. When a fire is extinguished, its light does not shine any more, and when man dies, his intellect does not perceive any more. The nature of both is the same. If people nevertheless pretend that the dead have knowledge, they are mistaken. What is the difference between a sick man about to die and a light about to go out? When a light is extinguished, its radiation is dispersed, and only the candle remains. When man has died, his vital force is gone, and the body alone remains. To assert that a person after death is still conscious is like saying that an extinguished light shines again.

Fictitious Influences

We learn from historical books that the wife of Chi Liang turned towards the city wall, which collapsed in consequence. This implies that when Chi Liang did not come back from a military expedition, his wife cried out in despair in the direction of the city wall; so heart-felt were her sorrow and her laments that her feelings affected the wall, which tumbled down in consequence.

That the woman cried, turned towards the wall, may be true, but the subsequent collapse of the city-wall is an invention.... The city-wall is of earth. As earth, like cloth, is devoid of a heart and intestines, how could it be moved by sobs and tears and fall down? Should the sounds of genuine grief be apt to affect the earth of a wall, then complaints uttered among the trees of a forest would tear apart plants and snap trunks.

If somebody should weep, when turned towards a water or a fire, would the water boil up, or the fire go out? As plants, water, and fire do not differ from earth, it is plain that the wife of Chi Liang should not have to answer for the dissolution of the wall.

Perhaps the wall was just going to tumble down of itself when the wife of Chi Liang happened to cry below. The world is partial to fictions and does not investigate the true cause of things; consequently this story of the downfall of the city-wall has, up till now, not faded from memory....

Neither ancient nor modern history affords any instances of men knowing spontaneously without study or being enlightened without inquiry.... When a man of great natural intelligence and remarkable parts is confined to his own thoughts and has no experience, neither beholding signs and omens nor observing the working of various sorts of beings, he may imagine that after many generations a horse will give birth to an ox, and an ox to a donkey, or that from a peach-tree plums may grow, or cherries from a plum-tree.... Let us suppose that somebody standing at that east side of a wall raises his voice, and that a sage hears him from the west side, would he know whether he was of a dark or a pale complexion, whether he was tall or short, and which was his native place, his surname, his designation, and his origin?... Not that a sage is devoid of knowledge, but this cannot be known through his knowledge. Something unknowable by knowledge may only be learned by inquiry.

CHAPTER 14

Ancient Greek Theories of Knowledge

"Rational explanation"

The three great epistemological traditions of Western philosophy are the rationalist, the empiricist, and the skeptical. All three stem from ancient Greek philosophy. The rationalist tradition begins with Plato, who first defines knowledge as justified true belief and then argues that our knowledge of the material world depends on our prior acquaintance with forms. The empiricist tradition begins with Aristotle, who sees the intellect as depending on sensation for its contents. And a long sequence of skeptics developed arguments against the possibility of knowing anything at all—arguments masterfully presented by Sextus Empiricus.

14.1 PLATO'S INTERNALISM

What is knowledge? This is the question Plato examines in the *Meno.* Socrates and his friend Meno easily agree that knowledge involves a relation to the truth. But what relation? Plato advocates internalism. Knowledge is justified true belief. To know something is to believe it, have reasons for believing it, and have it be true. We can examine our reasons for believing something; we can reflect on why we believe what we believe. If we know something, therefore we can reflect on our reasons and be in a position to know that we know. Or, at least, we can be in a position to know that we have warrant for our belief.

Plato, following Socrates (who asks questions of the form "Please tell me why you think that *p*, since you claim to know"), thinks that a person who cannot justify a belief, say, that Paris is the capital of France, does not know it. Of course, if Paris were not the capital of France, then no one could know that Paris is the capital. Truth is presupposed by knowledge. No one can know that Lincoln was the first American president, since that statement is false. But in order really to know, do we have to be aware, as Plato thinks, of our reasons for believing Washington was the first president, not Lincoln? Could we bring another person to know it, too? This is the heart of the internalist/externalist dispute that arises throughout this chapter. Plato and Socrates assume that you can talk to others and show them the truth by explaining your reasons in a clear and convincing fashion.

Plato formulates the classic internalist definition of knowledge both in the *Meno* and in the later dialogue, the *Theaetetus*. In the *Meno*, Socrates says that recollection constitutes justification. It distinguishes genuine knowledge from mere true belief. True belief is useful, but it might be the result of luck. It is thus not as useful as the true belief tied down to the facts by a reason—that is, by justification. In Greek, the word used for "reason" is *logos*, more precisely an "explanation" of the belief, an "account" of it. Thus we see what philosophers, following Peter Geach, have come to call Socratic intellectualism or even the Socratic fallacy: One is justified in believing something only if one can give an account of it. In Socrates' view, this requires stating a definition. You can know something about *X*s only if you can define *X*.

According to the *Meno*, an account of *X* must meet at least three conditions:

1. It must be applicable to all instances of *X* (that is, it must not be too narrow: A list, such as Meno gives when asked to define virtue, would always be too narrow unless it manages to list every possible instance).
2. It must not be applicable to things that are not *X* (i.e., it must not be too broad).
3. It must not be circular: It must not contain in the account itself any mention of that which is to be defined or explained.

In the *Meno*, Socrates gives the following account of shape: "That which alone of existing things always follows [i.e., accompanies] color." In later works by Plato, an acceptable account or explanation must identify the criterion (or form) whereby all the many things called *X* are rightly called *X*. This could be a characteristic, or property, common to all the members of a set or class, in virtue of which they belong to the class. As an explanation of knowledge, a common characteristic is proposed: being-belief-tied-to-the-truth-in-virtue-of-a-reason; that is to say, knowledge is "justified true belief."

In the *Theaetetus*, after rejecting a definition of knowledge as perception—which is too narrow and which seems unsatisfactory also because people sometimes disagree about what they perceive (shouldn't knowledge be objective?)—Plato backtracks to the view that knowledge is simply true belief. That definition is, however, too wide, as a little reflection can help us see. Presented with evidence in court, a jury concludes that the defendant is guilty. Suppose that the defendant really is guilty. The jurors have a belief, and it is true. But do they really know that the defendant is guilty? What if they cite as the reason for their conclusion the false testimony of a jilted lover who wanted to get revenge? (Everyone on the jury, let us also suppose, universally dislikes people with colorful hair, and the defendant sports a top dyed hot pink.) If the jury had seen the defendant commit the crime, in person or on film, then they might have knowledge. But we have described a situation in which, though they make the correct judgment, none of them really knows. A similar example comes from Indian philosophy. The Realists point to a sight of dust mistaken for smoke trailing up from a mountain in the distance leading someone to conclude that there is fire on the mountain. As it turns out, there really is fire on the mountain. But the subject does not *know* that, since a misperception led to the belief.

So Plato moves from "true belief" to "justified true belief" and thus has Socrates formulate again the classic internalist definition of knowledge. Knowledge is justified true belief, true belief "with an account." Jones can know something only if he can justify his belief, that is, explain why it is true.

That explanation, however, relies on other facts and principles that Jones must also know. So he must have in turn explanations of why those other beliefs are true in terms of still other, prior items of knowledge. Ultimately, knowledge must rest on a foundation consisting of basic items that are known directly and irreducibly, not being explainable with reference to other items. Socrates uses the analogy of words as depending on syllables, which depend on letters. Letters don't depend on anything else. They are basic and unanalyzable.

Initially, Socrates accepts the proposal that knowledge is justified true belief. But quickly he becomes dissatisfied. What about those basic items? Do we really know them? They are supposed to be perceived directly. We can give no account of them. If knowledge is justified true belief and we can't justify the basic items, it seems we can't know them. But how could knowledge rest on a foundation that is not itself known?

Socrates' objection assumes that a belief can't be justified except by other things known. We can justify what we believe only in terms of what else we know. But this can't go on forever. Eventually we must reach basic items (like the letters) that we can't justify by appealing to anything else. Since we have no justification of basic items but nevertheless know them, the definition of knowledge as justified true belief seems wrong. We need a definition of knowledge that covers our beliefs about the basic items as well as beliefs based on them. Indeed, we need a definition that shows that we know the basic items more clearly and directly than anything else.

We may reconstruct Socrates' argument:

1. If knowledge is justified true belief, there is a foundation of knowledge that justifies everything else.
2. Items in the foundation cannot themselves be justified.
3. Items in the foundation are known, in fact known more clearly and directly than anything else.
4. Therefore, knowledge is not justified true belief.

This suggests three ways an internalist can defend the conception of knowledge as justified true belief—by battling against one or another of the three premises.

Coherentists deny the first premise. There are no foundations to knowledge. Our reasons for our beliefs go around in circles. Some beliefs justify others; those justify others in turn. No beliefs are priviledged. No beliefs are immediate, justified by nothing else. Nothing is known directly. Just as the words in a dictionary are defined in terms of other words without recourse to a set of undefined words, so our beliefs are justified in terms of other bits of knowledge without any ultimate items that cannot themselves be justified. Aristotle, contemplating this possibility, objects that, if everything is to be defined, there would be an infinite regress (A justified by B, which is justified by C, and so on infinitely) or a circle (A justified by B, which is justified by C, which is justified by *D*, which is justified by *A*). But coherentists embrace the circle option, on the model of a dictionary, which is finite and does not extend indefinitely. Now, small circles seem objectionable when we are arguing, presupposing what it is at issue. ("Why do you believe *A*?" "Well, because of *B*." "And why *B*?" "Because of *A*." "Sorry! That would beg the question because we are worried about the truth of *A* in the first place!") But large circles are not in this way objectionable, coherentists allege, since the mutual support system is overwhelming. Consider, for example, the unity and overall coherence of science.

Foundationalists pursue the option of denying Plato's second premise while retaining the first. They argue that we do know basic truths directly. But how, if we can't justify them? Foundationalists answer that they justify themselves. Items in the foundation are self-justified or *self-evident*. Knowledge is based on items that are self-explanatory. Descartes, perhaps the most famous foundationalist, looks out of a second-story window at night. He sees a cold street where passersby are bundled up in coats and hats. Descartes cannot see their faces. There are many shadows. He reflects that he may be wrong that there are people down there; his perceptual evidence is inconclusive. But he cannot be wrong that it *seems* to him as if he is seeing people on the street. The belief about what seems to him true is self-evident. It is about something subjective, his own perception, which he knows in a self-illumining way (as some Indian philosophers would put it). His knowledge does not depend on any other belief. Most foundationalists hold that at least some truths of logic and mathematics are also self-evident: "2 plus 2 equals 4," for example, or "If *p*, then *p*," as Augustine argues. The Declaration of Independence famously says that the proposition that all men are created equal is self-evident. Just what makes a truth self-evident is, however, a difficult question, one to which we shall return several times in this chapter.

Finally, an internalist may deny Plato's final premise, maintaining that things other than beliefs or items of knowledge can justify a belief. The most common version of this approach, sometimes called *direct realism*, holds that sensations justify beliefs. But they do not themselves constitute knowledge. Sensations are not beliefs, and knowledge consists of beliefs. You may claim that the sky is clear tonight, for example, and prove it by taking your friends outside to show them. They see it for themselves, and there is nothing to say or argue about. What justifies belief in such a case is not another belief but a perception—seeing how the sky looks.

14.1.1 Plato, from *Meno*

Socrates: I'm afraid, Meno, that you and I aren't good for much and that Gorgias has been as poor an educator of you as Prodicus has been of me. Certainly we'll have to look to ourselves

Source: Plato, *Meno*, from *The Dialogues of Plato*. Translated by Benjamin Jowett. Oxford: Clarendon Press, 1892. We have altered the translation for readability.

and try to find someone who will help in some way or other to improve us. This I say, because I observe that in the previous discussion none of us remarked that right and good action is possible to man under other guidance than that of knowledge;—and indeed if this is denied, there is no seeing how there can be any good men at all.

Meno: How do you mean, Socrates?

Socrates: I mean that good men are necessarily useful or profitable. Weren't we right in admitting this? It must be so.

Meno: Yes.

Socrates: And in supposing that they'll be useful only if they are true guides to us of action—there we were also right?

Meno: Yes.

Socrates: But when we said that a man cannot be a good guide unless he have knowledge, we were wrong.

Meno: What do you mean by the word "right"?

Socrates: I'll explain. If a man knew the way to Larissa, or anywhere else, and went to the place and led others there, wouldn't he be a right and good guide?

Meno: Certainly.

Socrates: And a person who had a right opinion about the way but had never been and didn't know might be a good guide also, might he not?

Meno: Certainly.

Socrates: And while he has true opinion about what the other knows, he'll be just as good a guide if he thinks the truth as he who knows the truth?

Meno: Exactly.

Socrates: Then true opinion is as good a guide to correct action as knowledge. That was the point we omitted in our speculation about the nature of virtue, when we said that knowledge alone is the guide of right action; for there is also right opinion.

Meno: True.

Socrates: Then right opinion is not less useful than knowledge?

Meno: The difference, Socrates, is only that he who has knowledge will always be right. He who has right opinion will sometimes be right, and sometimes not.

Socrates: What do you mean? Can he be wrong who has right opinion, so long as he has right opinion?

Meno: I admit the cogency of your argument, and therefore, Socrates, I wonder that knowledge should be preferred to right opinion—or why they should ever differ.

Socrates: And shall I explain this wonder to you?

Meno: Do tell me.

Socrates: You wouldn't wonder if you had ever observed the images of Daedalus; but perhaps you don't have them in your country?

Meno: What do they have to do with the question?

Socrates: Because they need to be fastened in order to keep them; if they aren't fastened, they'll play truant and run away.

Meno: Well, so what?

Socrates: I mean to say that they're not very valuable possessions if they're at liberty, for they'll walk off like runaway slaves; but when fastened, they're of great value, for they're really beautiful works of art. Now, this is an illustration of the nature of true opinions: While they abide with us they're beautiful and fruitful, but they run away out of the human soul and don't remain long. Therefore they're not of much value until they're fastened by the tie of the cause. This fastening of them, friend Meno, is recollection, as you and I have agreed to call it. But when they're bound, in the first place, they have the nature of knowledge; and, in the second place, they are abiding. And this is why knowledge is more honourable and excellent than true opinion, because fastened by a chain.

Meno: What you're saying, Socrates, seems to be very like the truth.

14.1.2 Plato, from *Theaetetus*

Theaetetus: Knowledge was said by us to be true opinion; and true opinion is surely unerring. The results that follow from it are all noble and good.

Socrates: He who led the way into the river, Theaetetus, said, "The experiment will show"; and perhaps if we go forward in the search, we may stumble upon the thing we're looking for. But if we stay where we are, nothing will come to light.

Theaetetus: Very true; let's go forward and try.

Socrates: The trail soon comes to an end, for a whole profession is against us.

Theaetetus: How is that, and what profession do you mean?

Socrates: The profession of the great wise ones who are called orators and lawyers; for they persuade men by their art and make them think whatever they like, but they don't teach them. Do you imagine that there are any teachers in the world so clever as to be able to convince others of the truth about acts of robbery or violence of which they were not eyewitnesses, while a little water is flowing in the water clock [that is, in a very short time]?

Theaetetus: Certainly not; they can only persuade them.

Socrates: And wouldn't you say that persuading them is making them have an opinion?

Theaetetus: To be sure.

Socrates: When, therefore, judges are justly persuaded about matters you can know only by seeing them and not in any other way, and when thus judging of them from report they attain a true opinion about them, they judge without knowledge and yet are rightly persuaded, if they have judged well.

Theaetetus: Certainly.

Socrates: And yet, my friend, if true opinion in law courts and knowledge are the same, the perfect judge could not have judged rightly without knowledge. Therefore I must infer that they're not the same.

Theaetetus: That's a distinction, Socrates, that I've heard made by someone else, but I had forgotten it. He said that true opinion, combined with reason, was knowledge, but that the opinion that had no reason was out of the sphere of knowledge; and that things of which there is no rational account are not knowable—such was the singular expression he used—and that things that have a reason or explanation are knowable.

Socrates: Excellent; but then, how did he distinguish between things that are and are not "knowable"? I wish that you'd repeat to me what he said. Then I'll know whether you and I have heard the same tale.

Theaetetus: I don't know whether I can recall it; but if another person would tell me, I think that I could follow him.

Socrates: Let me give you, then, a dream in return for a dream:— I thought that I too had a dream, and I heard in my dream that the primeval letters or elements out of which you and I and all other things are compounded have no reason or explanation. You can only name them, but no predicate can be either affirmed or denied of them. For in the one case existence, in the other nonexistence, is already implied, neither of which must be added, if you mean to speak of this or that thing by itself alone. It shouldn't be called itself, that, each, alone, this, or the like; for these go about everywhere and are applied to all things but are distinct from them. But if the first elements could

---

Source: Plato, *Theaetetus*, from *The Dialogues of Plato*. Translated by Benjamin Jowett. Oxford: Clarendon Press, 1892. We have altered the translation for readability.

be described and had a definition of their own, they would be spoken of apart from all else. But none of these primeval elements can be defined. They can only be named, for they have nothing but a name, and the things compounded of them, as they are complex, are expressed by a combination of names, for the combination of names is the essence of a definition. Thus, then, the elements or letters are only objects of perception, and can't be defined or known. But the syllables or combinations of them are known and expressed and are apprehended by true opinion. When, therefore, anyone forms the true opinion of anything without rational explanation, you may say that his mind is truly exercised but has no knowledge. For he who can't give and receive a reason for a thing has no knowledge of it. But when he adds rational explanation, then he is perfected in knowledge and may be all that I've been denying of him. Was that the form in which the dream appeared to you?

Theaetetus: Precisely.

Socrates: And you allow and maintain that true opinion, combined with definition or rational explanation, is knowledge?

Theaetetus: Exactly.

Socrates: Then may we assume, Theaetetus, that today, and in this casual manner, we've found a truth that in former times many wise men have grown old and have not found?

Theaetetus: At any rate, Socrates, I'm satisfied with the present statement.

Socrates: Well, but won't you be equally inclined to disagree with him when you remember your own experience in learning to read?

Theaetetus: What experience?

Socrates: Why, that in learning you kept trying to distinguish the separate letters both by the eye and by the ear, in order that, when you heard them spoken or saw them written, you might not be confused by their position.

Theaetetus: Very true.

Socrates: And is the education of the harp player complete unless he can tell what string answers to a particular note; the notes, as everyone would allow, are the elements or letters of music?

Theaetetus: Exactly.

Socrates: Then, if we argue from the letters and syllables we know to other simples and compounds, we'll say that the letters or simple elements as a class are much more certainly known than the syllables and much more indispensable to a perfect knowledge of any subject; and if someone says that the syllable is known and the letter unknown, we shall consider that either intentionally or unintentionally he is talking nonsense?

Theaetetus: Exactly.

Socrates: And there might be given other proofs of this belief, if I'm not mistaken. But in looking for them let's not lose sight of the question before us, which is the meaning of the statement that right opinion with rational definition or explanation is the most perfect form of knowledge.

Theaetetus: We must not.

Socrates: Well, and what is the meaning of the term "explanation"? I think that we have a choice of three meanings.

Theaetetus: What are they?

Socrates: In the first place, the meaning may be manifesting one's thought by the voice with verbs and nouns, imaging an opinion in the stream which flows from the lips, as in a mirror or water. Does not explanation appear to be of this nature?

Theaetetus: Certainly; he who so manifests his thought is said to explain himself.

Socrates: And everyone who is not born deaf or dumb is able sooner or later to manifest what he thinks of anything; and if so, all those who have a right opinion about anything will also have right explanation. Right opinion won't be found to exist apart from knowledge anywhere.

Theaetetus: True.

Socrates: Let's not, therefore, hastily charge him who gave this account of knowledge with uttering an unmeaning word. Perhaps he only intended to say that when a person was asked what was the nature of anything, he should be able to answer his questioner by giving the elements of the thing.

Theaetetus: Can you give me an example, Socrates?

Socrates: As, for example, when Hesiod says that a wagon is made up of a hundred planks. Now, neither you nor I could describe all of them individually. But if anyone asked what a wagon is, we'd be content to answer that a wagon consists of wheels, axle, body, rims, yoke.

Theaetetus: Certainly.

Socrates: And our opponent will probably laugh at us, just as he would if we professed to be grammarians and to give a grammatical account of the name of Theaetetus and yet could only tell the syllables and not the letters of your name. That would be true opinion and not knowledge; for knowledge, as has been already remarked, is not attained until, combined with true opinion, there is an enumeration of the elements out of which anything is composed.

Theaetetus: Yes.

Socrates: In the same general way, we might also have true opinion about a wagon. But he who can describe its essence by an enumeration of the hundred planks adds rational explanation to true opinion, and instead of opinion has art and knowledge of the nature of a wagon, in that he attains to the whole through the elements.

Theaetetus: And don't you agree in that view, Socrates?

Socrates: If you do, my friend; but I want to know first whether you admit the resolution of all things into their elements to be a rational explanation of them, and the consideration of them in syllables or larger combinations of them to be irrational—is this your view?

Theaetetus: Precisely.

Socrates: Well, and do you conceive that a man has knowledge of any element who at one time affirms and at another time denies that element of something or thinks that the same thing is composed of different elements at different times?

Theaetetus: Assuredly not.

Socrates: And don't you remember that in your case and in that of others this often occurred in the process of learning to read?

Theaetetus: You mean that I mistook the letters and misspelled the syllables?

Socrates: Yes.

Theaetetus: To be sure; I perfectly remember, and I'm very far from supposing that they who are in this condition have knowledge.

Socrates: When a person at the time of learning writes the name of Theaetetus and thinks that he ought to write and does write Th and e; but, again, meaning to write the name of Theodorus, thinks that he ought to write and does write T and e—can we suppose that he knows the first syllables of your two names?

Theaetetus: We've already admitted that such a one has not yet attained knowledge.

Socrates: And in like manner he may enumerate the second and third and fourth syllables of your name without knowing them?

Theaetetus: He may.

Socrates: And in that case, when he knows the order of the letters and can write them out correctly, he has right opinion?

Theaetetus: Clearly.

Socrates: But although we admit that he has right opinion, he will still be without knowledge?

Theaetetus: Yes.

Socrates: And yet he'll have explanation as well as right opinion, for he knew the order of the letters when he wrote; and this we admit to be explanation.

Theaetetus: True.

Socrates: Then, my friend, there is such a thing as right opinion united with definition or explanation, which doesn't yet attain to the exactness of knowledge.

Theaetetus: It would seem so.

Socrates: And what we fancied to be a perfect definition of knowledge is a dream only. But perhaps we'd better not say so just yet, for were there not three explanations of knowledge, one of which must, as we said, be adopted by him who maintains knowledge to be true opinion combined with rational explanation? And very likely there may be found someone who will not prefer this but the third.

Theaetetus: You're quite right. There's still one remaining. The first was the image or expression of the mind in speech; the second, just mentioned, is a way of reaching the whole by an enumeration of the elements. But what's the third definition?

Socrates: There is, further, the popular notion of telling the mark or sign of difference which distinguishes the thing in question from all others.

Theaetetus: Can you give me any example of such a definition?

Socrates: As, for example, in the case of the sun, I think that you would be contented with the statement that the sun is the brightest of the heavenly bodies which revolve about the earth.

Theaetetus: Certainly.

Socrates: Understand why: The reason is, as I was just now saying, that if you get at the difference and distinguishing characteristic of each thing, then, as many persons affirm, you'll get at the definition or explanation of it. But while you lay hold only of the common and not of the characteristic notion, you will only have the definition of those things to which this common quality belongs.

Theaetetus: I understand you, and your account of definition is in my judgment correct.

Socrates: But he who having right opinion about anything can find out the difference which distinguishes it from other things will know that of which before he had only an opinion.

Theaetetus: Yes; that's what we're maintaining.

Socrates: Nevertheless, Theaetetus, on a nearer view, I find myself quite disappointed; the picture, which at a distance was not so bad, has now become altogether unintelligible.

Theaetetus: What do you mean?

Socrates: I'll endeavour to explain: I'll suppose myself to have true opinion of you, and if to this I add your definition, then I have knowledge, but if not, opinion only.

Theaetetus: Yes.

Socrates: The definition was assumed to be the interpretation of your difference.

Theaetetus: True.

Socrates: But when I had only opinion, I had no conception of your distinguishing characteristics.

Theaetetus: I suppose not.

Socrates: Then I must have conceived of some general or common nature which no more belonged to you than to another.

Theaetetus: True.

Socrates: Tell me, now—How in that case could I have formed a judgment of you any more than of anyone else? Suppose that I imagine Theaetetus to be a man who has nose, eyes, and mouth, and every other member complete; how would that enable me to distinguish Theaetetus from Theodorus or from some outer barbarian?

Theaetetus: How could it?

Socrates: Or if I had further conceived of you, not only as having nose and eyes, but as having a snub nose and prominent eyes, should I have any more notion of you than of myself and others who resemble me?

Theaetetus: Certainly not.

Socrates: Surely I can have no conception of Theaetetus until your snub-nosedness has left an impression on my mind different from the snub-nosedness of all others I've ever seen, and until your other peculiarities have a like distinctness; and so when I meet you tomorrow the right opinion will be recalled?

Theaetetus: Most true.

Socrates: Then right opinion implies the perception of differences?

Theaetetus: Clearly.

Socrates: What, then, shall we say of adding reason or explanation to right opinion? If the meaning is that we should form an opinion of the way in which something differs from another thing, the proposal is ridiculous.

Theaetetus: How so?

Socrates: We are supposed to acquire a right opinion of the differences which distinguish one thing from another when we've already a right opinion of them, and so we go round and round: The revolution of the scytal, or pestle, or any other rotary machine, in the same circles, is as nothing compared with such a requirement. We may be truly described as the blind leading the blind. For to add to what we already have to learn what we already think is like a soul utterly benighted.

Theaetetus: Tell me: What were you going to say just now, when you asked the question?

Socrates: If, my boy, the argument, in speaking of adding the definition, had used the word to "know," and not merely "have an opinion" of the difference, this which is the most promising of all the definitions of knowledge would have come to a pretty end, for to know is surely to acquire knowledge.

Theaetetus: True.

Socrates: And so, when the question is asked, What is knowledge? this fair argument will answer "Right opinion with knowledge,"—knowledge, that is, of difference, for this, as the said argument maintains, is adding the definition.

Theaetetus: That seems to be true.

Socrates: But how utterly foolish, when we are asking what is knowledge, that the reply should only be right opinion with knowledge of difference or of anything! And so, Theaetetus, knowledge is neither sensation nor true opinion, nor yet definition and explanation accompanying and added to true opinion?

Theaetetus: I suppose not.

14.2 ARISTOTLE ON THOUGHT AND INFERENCE

On the internalist approach, knowledge requires an ability to produce a justifying argument except perhaps in the foundational cases. Even direct realists hold that, for an enormous number of beliefs—for all nonbasic beliefs—justifying arguments are crucial. What, then, is an argument? We turn to Plato's student Aristotle (384–322 BCE), the founder of logic in the West, for an overview and a few definitions of crucial logical terms.

Aristotle's foundationalism about knowledge is expressed in a passage in his *Posterior Analytics* where he lays bare the general structure of knowledge by examining deductive knowledge. An argument is composed of statements. One or more statements serve as premises, another statement as conclusion. The conclusion is demonstrated and thereby known. (Think of a proof in geometry.) Aristotle says that a good argument requires not only that the conclusion follow logically from the truth of the premises (the premises could not be true without the conclusion being true as well) but also that the premises must themselves be known. The premises have to be true and known to be true to function as generating new knowledge through deductive inference.

Indeed, Aristotle says that the premises have to be known better than the conclusion. But then how are they known? Say that *C* follows from *A* and *B*; they are *C*'s justifiers. But what justifies *A* and *B*? Suppose *Z* justifies *A*. What justifies *Z*? An infinite regress looms, and Aristotle says that we know basic items in an absolutely immediate and nondeductive manner.

Aristotle talks about ***deductive*** (in his language, *syllogistic*) arguments, which are defined as arguments the truth of whose premises guarantee the conclusion's truth. But there are of course also ***inductive*** arguments, which are defined as arguments with premises that support a conclusion but may not guarantee it. Geometric proofs are perhaps the best-known examples of deductive arguments, and generalizations made from finite samplings ("All rubies are red, since this ruby is red, and that one, and that one, and so on.") are paradigm cases of inductive arguments.

Aristotle develops a broader epistemological theory as part of his philosophy of mind. He draws an analogy between the mind and "a writing tablet upon which as yet nothing actually stands written," an analogy that exerts a powerful influence on later empiricists, such as John Locke and David Hume. Knowledge, Aristotle says, is identical with its object. The mind in some sense takes on the form of the object. The soul is the form of forms; sense is the form of sensible things. We think in terms of images. We get those images from the faculty of sense. Thus, all the materials of thought come ultimately from sensation.

14.2.1 Aristotle, from *On the Soul*

Book III

4. Turning now to the part of the soul with which the soul knows and thinks (whether this is separable from the others in definition only, or spatially as well) we have to inquire (1) what differentiates this part, and (2) how thinking can take place.

If thinking is like perceiving, it must be either a process in which the soul is acted upon by what is capable of being thought, or a process different from but analogous to that. The thinking part of the soul must therefore be, while impassible, capable of receiving the form of an object; that is, must be potentially identical in character with its object without being the object. Mind must be related to what is thinkable, as sense is to what is sensible.

Therefore, since everything is a possible object of thought, mind in order, as Anaxagoras says, to dominate, that is, to know, must be pure from all admixture; for the co-presence of what is alien to its nature is a hindrance and a block: It follows that it too, like the sensitive part, can have no nature of its own, other than that of having a certain capacity. Thus that in the soul which is called *mind* (by *mind* I mean that whereby the soul thinks and judges) is, before it thinks, not actually any real thing. For this reason it cannot reasonably be regarded as blended with the body: if so, it would acquire some quality, e.g., warmth or cold, or even have an organ like the sensitive faculty: as it is, it has none. It was a good idea to call the soul "the place of forms," though (1) this description holds only of the intellective soul, and (2) even this is the forms only potentially, not actually.

Observation of the sense-organs and their employment reveals a distinction between the impassibility of the sensitive and that of the intellective faculty. After strong stimulation of a sense we are less able to exercise it than before, as, e.g., in the case of a loud sound we cannot hear easily immediately after, or in the case of a bright colour or a powerful odour we cannot see or smell, but in the case of mind thought about an object that is highly intelligible renders it more and not less able afterwards to think about objects that are less intelligible: the reason is that while the faculty of sensation is dependent upon the body, mind is separable from it.

Once the mind has become each set of its possible objects, as a man of science has, when this phrase is used of one who is actually a man of

Source: Aristotle, *On the Soul*. From *De Anima*, Book III. Translated by J. A. Smith. Oxford: Oxford University Press, 1931.

science (this happens when he is now able to exercise the power on his own initiative), its condition is still one of potentiality, but in a different sense from the potentiality which preceded the acquisition of knowledge by learning or discovery: the mind too is then able to think itself.

Since we can distinguish between a spatial magnitude and what it is to be such, and between water and what it is to be water, and so in many other cases (though not in all, for in certain cases the thing and its form are identical), flesh and what it is to be flesh are discriminated either by different faculties, or by the same faculty in two different states: for flesh necessarily involves matter and is like what is snub-nosed, a this in a this. Now it is by means of the sensitive faculty that we discriminate the hot and the cold, i.e., the factors which combined in a certain ratio constitute flesh: the essential character of flesh is apprehended by something different either wholly separate from the sensitive faculty or related to it as a bent line to the same line when it has been straightened out.

Again in the case of abstract objects what is straight is analogous to what is snub-nosed; for it necessarily implies a continuum as its matter: its constitutive essence is different, if we may distinguish between straightness and what is straight: let us take it to be two-ness. It must be apprehended, therefore, by a different power or by the same power in a different state. To sum up, insofar as the realities it knows are capable of being separated from their matter, so it is also with the powers of mind.

The problem might be suggested: if thinking is a passive affection, then if mind is simple and impassible and has nothing in common with anything else, as Anaxagoras says, how can it come to think at all? For interaction between two factors is held to require a precedent community of nature between the factors. Again it might be asked, is mind a possible object of thought to itself? For if mind is thinkable per se and what is thinkable is in kind one and the same, then either (a) mind will belong to everything, or (b) mind will contain some element common to it with all other realities which makes them all thinkable.

(1) Have not we already disposed of the difficulty about interaction involving a common element, when we said that mind is in a sense potentially whatever is thinkable, though actually it is nothing until it has thought? What it thinks must be in it just as characters may be said to be on a writing tablet on which as yet nothing actually stands written: this is exactly what happens with mind.

Mind is itself thinkable in exactly the same way as its objects are. For (a) in the case of objects which involve no matter, what thinks and what is thought are identical; for speculative knowledge and its object are identical. (Why mind is not always thinking we must consider later.) (b) In the case of those which contain matter each of the objects of thought is only potentially present. It follows that while they will not have mind in them (for mind is a potentiality of them only insofar as they are capable of being disengaged from matter) mind may yet be thinkable.

5. Since in every class of things, as in nature as a whole, we find two factors involved, (1) a matter which is potentially all the particulars included in the class, (2) a cause which is productive in the sense that it makes them all (the latter standing to the former, as, e.g., an art to its material), these distinct elements must likewise be found within the soul.

And in fact mind as we have described it is what it is by virtue of becoming all things, while there is another which is what it is by virtue of making all things: this is a sort of positive state like light; for in a sense light makes potential colours into actual colours.

Mind in this sense of it is separable, impassible, unmixed, since it is in its essential nature activity (for always the active is superior to the passive factor, the originating force to the matter which it forms).

Actual knowledge is identical with its object: in the individual, potential knowledge is in time prior to actual knowledge, but in the universe as a whole it is not prior even in time. Mind is not at one time knowing and at another not. When mind is set free from its present conditions it appears as just what it is and nothing more: this alone is immortal and eternal (we do not, however, remember its former activity because, while mind in this sense is impassible, mind as passive is destructible), and without it nothing thinks.

6. The thinking then of the simple objects of thought is found in those cases where falsehood is impossible: where the alternative of true or false applies, there we always find a putting together of objects of thought in a quasi-unity. As Empedocles said that "where heads of many a creature sprouted without necks" they afterwards by Love's power were combined, so here too objects of thought which were given separate are combined, e.g., "incommensurate" and "diagonal": if the combination be of objects past or future the combination of thought includes in its content the date. For falsehood always involves a synthesis; for even if you assert that what is white is not white you have included not white in a synthesis. It is possible also to call all these cases division as well as combination. However that may be, there is not only the true or false assertion that Cleon is white but also the true or false assertion that he was or will be white. In each and every case that which unifies is mind.

Since the word "simple" has two senses, i.e., may mean either (a) "not capable of being divided" or (b) "not actually divided," there is nothing to prevent mind from knowing what is undivided, e.g., when it apprehends a length (which is actually undivided) and that in an undivided time; for the time is divided or undivided in the same manner as the line. It is not possible, then, to tell what part of the line it was apprehending in each half of the time: the object has no actual parts until it has been divided: if in thought you think each half separately, then by the same act you divide the time also, the half-lines becoming as it were new wholes of length. But if you think it as a whole consisting of these two possible parts, then also you think it in a time which corresponds to both parts together. (But what is not quantitatively but qualitatively simple is thought in a simple time and by a simple act of the soul.)

But that which mind thinks and the time in which it thinks are in this case divisible only incidentally and not as such. For in them too there is something indivisible (though, it may be, not isolable) which gives unity to the time and the whole of length; and this is found equally in every continuum whether temporal or spatial.

Points and similar instances of things that divide, themselves being indivisible, are realized in consciousness in the same manner as privations.

A similar account may be given of all other cases, e.g., how evil or black is cognized; they are cognized, in a sense, by means of their contraries. That which cognizes must have an element of potentiality in its being, and one of the contraries must be in it. But if there is anything that has no contrary, then it knows itself and is actually and possesses independent existence.

Assertion is the saying of something concerning something, e.g., affirmation, and is in every case either true or false: this is not always the case with mind: the thinking of the definition in the sense of the constitutive essence is never in error nor is it the assertion of something concerning something, but, just as while the seeing of the special object of sight can never be in error, the belief that the white object seen is a man may be mistaken, so too in the case of objects which are without matter.

7. Actual knowledge is identical with its object: potential knowledge in the individual is in time prior to actual knowledge but in the universe it has no priority even in time; for all things that come into being arise from what actually is. In the case of sense clearly the sensitive faculty already was potentially what the object makes it to be actually; the faculty is not affected or altered. This must therefore be a different kind from movement; for movement is, as we saw, an activity of what is imperfect; activity in the unqualified sense, i.e., that of what has been perfected, is different from movement.

To perceive then is like bare asserting or knowing; but when the object is pleasant or painful, the soul makes a quasi-affirmation or negation, and pursues or avoids the object. To feel pleasure or pain is to act with the sensitive mean towards what is good or bad as such. Both avoidance and appetite when actual are identical with this: the faculty of appetite and avoidance are not different, either from one another or from the faculty of sense-perception; but their being is different.

To the thinking soul images serve as if they were contents of perception (and when it asserts or denies them to be good or bad it avoids or pursues them). That is why the soul never thinks without an image. The process is like that in which the air modifies the pupil in this or that way and the pupil transmits the modification to some third thing (and similarly in hearing), while the ultimate point of arrival is one, a single mean, with different manners of being.

With what part of itself the soul discriminates sweet from hot I have explained before and must now describe again as follows: That with which it does so is a sort of unity, but in the way just mentioned, i.e., as a connecting term. And the two faculties it connects, being one by analogy and numerically, are each to each as the qualities discerned are to one another (for what difference does it make whether we raise the problem of discrimination between disparates or between contraries, e.g., white and black?). Let then C be to D as A is to B: it follows *alternando* that $C : A :: D : B$. If then C and D belong to one subject, the case will be the same with them as with A and B; A and B form a single identity with different modes of being; so too will the former pair. The same reasoning holds if A be sweet and B white.

The faculty of thinking then thinks the forms in the images, and as in the former case what is to be pursued or avoided is marked out for it, so where there is no sensation and it is engaged upon the images it is moved to pursuit or avoidance. E.g., perceiving by sense that the beacon is fire, it recognizes in virtue of the general faculty of sense that it signifies an enemy, because it sees it moving; but sometimes by means of the images or thoughts which are within the soul, just as if it were seeing, it calculates and deliberates what is to come by reference to what is present; and when it makes a pronouncement, as in the case of sensation, it pronounces the object to be pleasant or painful, in this case it avoids or pursues and so generally in cases of action.

That too which involves no action, i.e., that which is true or false, is in the same province with what is good or bad: yet they differ in this, that the one set imply and the other do not a reference to a particular person.

The so-called abstract objects the mind thinks just as, if one had thought of the snub-nosed not as snub-nosed but as hollow, one would have thought of an actuality without the flesh in which it is embodied: it is thus that the mind when it is thinking the objects of mathematics thinks as separate elements which do not exist as separate. In every case the mind which is actively thinking is the objects which it thinks. Whether it is possible for it while not existing separately from spatial conditions to think anything that is separate, or not, we must consider later.

8. Let us now summarize our results about soul, and repeat that the soul is in a way all existing things; for existing things are either sensible or thinkable, and knowledge is in a way what is knowable, and sensation is in a way what is sensible: in what way we must inquire.

Knowledge and sensation are divided to correspond with realities, potential knowledge and sensation answering to potentialities, actual knowledge and sensation to actualities. Within the soul the faculties of knowledge and sensation are potentially these objects, the one what is knowable, the other what is sensible. They must be either the things themselves or their forms. The former alternative is of course impossible: it is not the stone which is present in the soul but its form.

It follows that the soul is analogous to the hand; for as the hand is a tool of tools, so the mind is the form of forms and sense the form of sensible things.

Since according to common agreement there is nothing outside and separate in existence from sensible spatial magnitudes, the objects of thought are in the sensible forms, viz. both the abstract objects and all the states and affections of sensible things. Hence (1) no one can learn or understand anything in the absence of sense, and when the mind is actively aware of anything it is necessarily aware of it along with an image; for images are like sensuous contents except in that they contain no matter.

Imagination is different from assertion and denial; for what is true or false involves a synthesis of concepts. In what will the primary concepts differ from images? Must we not say that neither these nor even our other concepts are images, though they necessarily involve them?

14.3 SEXTUS EMPIRICUS'S SKEPTICISM

Roughly contemporaneous with the flowering of Indian epistemology several centuries after Aristotle is a Greek physician, Sextus Empiricus (c. 200 CE), who, like Zhuangzi much earlier in China, was a skeptic—about philosophy and, more broadly, about claims to knowledge of any sort. Given his views, it is perhaps fitting that we do not know where he lived or taught, though we do have his texts, in a masterful Greek that displays acquaintance with Athens, Rome, and Alexandria. Sextus offers ten arguments, called *modes* or *tropes*, for skeptical conclusions. The first seven appear in the next selection. The first mode is based on the differing sensory systems of different species of animals. It is thus a version of the argument from variability. Sextus draws the conclusion explicitly. We cannot tell what is really in the object and what contributed by our own cognitive faculties.

Sextus's thesis is that knowledge is impossible. His recommendation is that we should suspend judgment, neither affirming nor denying anything as reflecting the true nature of the world, the "external underlying objects." Anyone who makes a claim about a thing's true nature Sextus would consider a dogmatist. In addition to the argument from variability, he offers an infinite regress argument as a version of the problem of the criterion. Many people claim to know the truth. Is there any criterion to distinguish those who know from those who don't? This is probably the question for which Sextus is most renowned.

Is there a criterion of truth? To settle the matter, we need a criterion—but that is precisely what's at issue! The dogmatist either argues in a circle, using a criterion to support itself, or falls into an infinite regress, trying to support the first criterion by appealing to a second, the second by appealing to a third, and so on. Sextus argues that we should suspend judgment, not only because we cannot justify our claims to know, but because suspension of judgment leads to quietude and peace of mind.

It is important that Sextus does not assert that suspension of judgment causes peace of mind. That would be a claim to know the nature of things and would appear unjustified by his own lights. Instead, he tells a story and observes that the skeptic lives skeptically, suspending judgment, and simply finds peace of mind to arrive.

But how can the skeptic live skeptically? To stay alive, we need to make judgments. It is said that the extreme skeptic Carneades, doubting all appearances, refused to believe anything; his students had to lead him around to prevent him from being run over by chariots (the appearance of which, of course, he insisted gave no reason whatever to believe that they were really there). But Sextus advocates no such policy. Indeed, he invokes a practical criterion, namely, to accept appearances, and to suspend judgment only on the question of whether appearances truly reflect reality.

14.3.1 Sextus Empiricus, from *Outlines of Pyrrhonism*

Book I

Chapter I.—Of the main difference between philosophic systems. The natural result of any investigation is that the investigators either discover the object of search or deny that it is discoverable and confess it to be inapprehensible or persist in their search. So, too, with regard to the objects investigated by philosophy, this is probably why some have claimed to have discovered the truth, others have asserted that it cannot be apprehended, while others again go on inquiring. Those who believe they have discovered it are the "Dogmatists," specially so called—Aristotle, for example, and Epicurus and the Stoics and certain others; Cleitomachus and Carneades and other Academics treat it as inapprehensible: the Sceptics keep on searching. Hence it seems reasonable to hold that the main types of philosophy are three—the Dogmatic, the Academic, and the Sceptic. Of the other systems it will best become others to speak: our task at present is to describe in outline the Sceptic doctrines first premising that of none of our future statements do we positively affirm that the fact is exactly as we state it, but we simply record each fact, like a chronicler, as it appears to us at the moment.

Chapter VI.—Of the principles of scepticism. The originating cause of Scepticism is, we say, the hope of attaining quietude. Men of talent, who were perturbed by the contradictions in things and in doubt as to which of the alternatives they ought to accept, were led on to inquire what is true in things and what false, hoping by the settlement of this question to attain quietude. The main basic principle of the Sceptic system is that of opposing to every proposition an equal proposition; for we believe that as a consequence of this we end by ceasing to dogmatize.

Chapter XI.—Of the criterion of scepticism. That we adhere to appearances is plain from what we say about the criterion of the Sceptic School. The word "criterion" is used in two senses: in the one it means "the standard regulating belief in reality or unreality" (and this we shall discuss in our refutation); in the other it denotes the standard of action by conforming to which in the conduct of life we perform some actions and abstain from others; and it is of the latter that we are now speaking. The criterion, then, of the Sceptic School is, we say, the appearance, giving this name to what is virtually the sense-presentation. For since this lies in feeling and involuntary affection, it is not open to question. Consequently, no one, I suppose, disputes that the underlying object has this or that appearance; the point in dispute is whether the object is in reality such as it appears to be.

Adhering, then, to appearances we live in accordance with the normal rules of life, undogmatically, seeing that we cannot remain wholly inactive. And it would seem that this regulation of life is fourfold, and that one part of it lies in the guidance of nature, another in the constraint of the passions, another in the tradition of laws and customs, another in the instruction of the arts. Nature's guidance is that by which we are naturally capable of sensation and thought; constraint of the passions is that whereby hunger drives us to food and thirst to drink; tradition of customs and laws, that whereby we regard piety in the conduct of life as good, but impiety as evil; instruction of the arts, that whereby we are not inactive in such arts as we adopt. But we make all these statements undogmatically.

Source: Sextus Empiricus, *Outlines of Pyrrhonism*. Translated by R. G. Bury. The Loeb Classical Library. London: William Heinemann, 1933.

Chapter XII.—What is the end of scepticism? Our next subject will be the end of the Sceptic system. Now an "end" is "that for which all actions or reasonings are undertaken, while it exists for the sake of none"; or, otherwise, "the ultimate object of appentency." We assert still that the Sceptic's end is quietude in respect of matters of opinion and moderate feeling in respect of things unavoidable. For the skeptic, having set out to philosophize with the object of passing judgment on the sense impressions and ascertaining which of them are true and which false, so as to attain quietude thereby, found himself involved in contradictions of equal weight, and being unable to decide between them suspended judgment; and as he was thus in suspense there followed, as it happened, the state of quietude in respect of matters of opinion. For the man who opines that anything is by nature good or bad is forever being disquieted: when he is without the things which he deems good he believes himself to be tormented by things naturally bad and he pursues after the things which are, as he thinks, good; which when he has obtained he keeps falling into still more perturbations because of his irrational and immoderate elation, and in his dread of a change of fortune he uses every endeavor to avoid losing the things which he deems good. On the other hand, the man who determines nothing as to what is naturally good or bad neither shuns nor pursues anything eagerly; and, in consequence, he is unperturbed.

The Sceptic, in fact, had the same experience which is said to have befallen the painter Apelles. Once, they say, when he was painting a horse and wished to represent in the painting the horse's foam, he was so unsuccessful that he gave up the attempt and flung at the picture the sponge on which he used to wipe the paints off his brush, and the mark of the sponge produced the effect of a horse's foam. So, too, the Sceptics were in hopes of gaining quietude by means of a decision regarding the disparity of the objects of sense and of thought, and being unable to effect this they suspended judgment; and they found that quietude, as if by chance, followed upon their suspense, even as a shadow follows its substance. We do not, however, suppose that the Sceptic is wholly untroubled; but we say that he is troubled by things unavoidable; for we grant that he is cold at times and thirsty, and suffers various affections of that kind. But even in these cases, whereas ordinary people are afflicted by two circumstances,—namely, by the affections themselves and, in no less a degree, by the belief that these conditions are evil by nature,—the Sceptic, by his rejection of the added belief in the natural badness of all these conditions, escapes here too with less discomfort. Hence we say that, while in regard to matters of opinion the Sceptic's end is quietude, in regard to things unavoidable it is "moderate affection." But some notable Sceptics have added the further definition "suspension of judgment in investigations."

Chapter XIII.—Of the general modes leading to the suspension of judgement. Now that we have been saying that tranquillity follows on suspension of judgment, it will be our next task to explain how we arrive at this suspension. Speaking generally, one may say that it is the result of setting things in opposition. We oppose either appearances to appearances or objects of thought to objects of thought or alternando. For instance, we oppose appearances to appearances when we say, "The same tower appears round from a distance, but square from close at hand"; and thoughts to thoughts, when in answer to him who argues the existence of providence from the order of the heavenly bodies we oppose the fact that often the good fare ill and the bad fare well, and draw from this the inference that providence does not exist. And thoughts we oppose to appearances, as when Anaxagoras countered the notion that snow is white with the argument "Snow is frozen water, and water is black; therefore snow also is black." With a different idea we oppose things present sometimes to things present, as in the foregoing examples, and sometimes to things past or future, as, for instance, when someone propounds to us a theory which we are unable to refute, we say to him in reply, "Just as, before the birth of the founder of the school to which you belong, the theory it holds was not as yet apparent as a sound theory, although it was really in existence, so likewise it is possible that the opposite theory to that which you now propound is already existent, though not yet apparent to us, so that we ought not as yet to yield assent to this theory which at the moment seems to be valid."

But in order that we may have a more exact understanding of these antitheses I will describe the modes by which suspension of judgment is brought about, but without making any positive assertion regarding either their number or their validity; for it is possible that they may be unsound or there may be more of them than I shall enumerate.

Chapter XIV.—Concerning the ten modes. The usual tradition amongst the older skeptics is that the "modes" by which "suspension" is supposed to be brought about are ten in number; and they also give them the synonymous names of "arguments" and "positions." They are these: the first, based on the variety in animals; the second, on the differences in human beings; the third, on the different structures of the organs of sense; the fourth, on the circumstantial conditions; the fifth, on positions and intervals and locations; the sixth, on intermixtures; the seventh, on the quantities and formations of the underlying objects; the eighth, on the fact of relativity; the ninth, on the frequency or rarity of occurrence; the tenth, on the disciplines and customs and laws, the legendary beliefs and the dogmatic convictions. This order, however, we adopt without prejudice....

The **First Argument** (or Trope), as we said, is that which shows that the same impressions are not produced by the same objects owing to the differences in animals. This we infer both from the differences in their origins and from the variety of their bodily structures....

Moreover, the differences found in the most important parts of the body, and especially in those of which the natural function is judging and perceiving, are capable of producing a vast deal of divergence in the sense-impressions [owing to the variety in the animals]. Thus, sufferers from jaundice declare that objects which seem to us white are yellow, while those whose eyes are bloodshot call them blood-red....

Of the other sense organs also the same account holds good... so likewise is it probable that the external objects appear different owing to differences in the structure of the animals which experience the sense-impressions.

But one may learn this more clearly from the preferences and aversions of animals. Thus, sweet oil seems very agreeable to men, but intolerable to beetles and bees; and olive oil is beneficial to men, but when poured on wasps and bees it destroys them; and seawater is a disagreeable and poisonous potion for men, but fish drink and enjoy it. Pigs, too, enjoy wallowing in the stinking mire rather than in clear and clean water. And whereas some animals eat grass, others eat shrubs, others feed in the woods, others live on seeds or flesh or milk; some of them, too, prefer their food high, others like it fresh, and while some prefer it raw, others like it cooked. And so generally, the things which are agreeable to some are to others disagreeable, distasteful, and deadly.... [I]f the same things are displeasing to some but pleasing to others, and pleasure and displeasure depend upon sense impression, then animals receive different impressions from the underlying objects.

But if the same things appear different owing to the variety in animals, we shall, indeed, be able to state our own impressions of the real object, but as to its essential nature we shall suspend judgment. For we cannot ourselves judge between our own impressions and those of other animals, since we ourselves are involved in the dispute and are, therefore, rather in need of a judge than competent to pass judgment ourselves....

Such, then, is the first of the modes which induce suspense. The **Second Mode** is, as we said, that based on the differences in men; for even if we grant for the sake of argument that men are more worthy of credence than irrational animals, we shall find that even our own differences of themselves lead to suspense. For man, you know, is said to be compounded of two things, soul and body, and in both these we differ one from another.

Thus, as regards the body, we differ in our figures and "idiosyncrasies," or constitutional peculiarities.... Owing to this difference in the predominant humors the sense impressions also come to differ, as we indicated in our first argument. So too in respect of choice and avoidance of external objects men exhibit great differences: thus Indians enjoy some things, our people other things, and the enjoyment of different things is an indication that we receive varying impressions from the underlying objects....

But the greatest proof of the vast and endless differences in men's intelligence is the discrepancy in the statements of the Dogmatists concerning the right objects of choice and avoidance, as well as other things. Regarding this the poets, too, have expressed themselves fittingly. Thus Pindar says:

The crowns and trophies of his storm-foot steeds
Give joy to one; yet others find it joy
To dwell in gorgeous chambers gold-bedeckt;
Some even take delight in voyaging
O'er ocean's billows in a speeding barque.

And the poet [Homer] says: "One thing is pleasing to one man, another thing to another." Tragedy, too, is full of such sayings; for example:

Were fair and wise the same thing unto all,
There had been no contentious quarrelling.

And again:

Tis strange that the same thing abhorr'd by some
Should give delight to others.

Seeing, then, that choice and avoidance depend on pleasure and displeasure, while pleasure and displeasure depend on sensation and sense-impression, whenever some men choose the very things which are avoided by others, it is logical for us to conclude that they are also differently affected by the same things, since otherwise they would all alike have chosen or avoided the same things. But if the same objects affect men differently owing to the differences in the men, then, on this ground also, we shall reasonably be led to suspension of judgment. For while we are, no doubt, able to state what each of the underlying objects appears to be, relatively to each difference, we are incapable of explaining what it is in reality. For we shall have to believe either all men or some. But if we believe all, we shall be attempting the impossible and accepting contradictories; and if some, let us be told whose opinions we are to endorse. For the Platonist will say "Plato's," the Epicurean, "Epicurus's"—and so on with the rest; and thus by their unsettled disputations they will bring us round again to a state of suspense. Moreover, he who maintains that we ought to assent to the majority is making a childish proposal, since no one is able to visit the whole of mankind and determine what pleases the majority of them—for there may possibly be races of whom we know nothing amongst whom conditions rare with us are common, and conditions common with us rare,—possibly, for instance, most of them feel no pain from the bites of spiders, though a few on rare occasions feel such pain; and so likewise with the rest of the "idiosyncrasies" mentioned above. Necessarily, therefore, the differences in men afford a further reason for bringing in suspension of judgment....

This **Third Mode** is, we say, based on differences in the senses. That the senses differ from one another is obvious. Thus, to the eye paintings seem to have recesses and projections, but not so to the touch. Honey, too, seems to some pleasant to the tongue but unpleasant to the eyes; so that it is impossible to say whether it is absolutely pleasant or unpleasant.... Consequently we are unable to say what is the real nature of each of these things, although it is possible to say what each thing at the moment appears to be.

A longer list of examples might be given, but to avoid prolixity, in view of the plan of our treatise, we will say just this. Each of the phenomena perceived by the senses seems to be a complex: the apple, for example, seems smooth, odorous, sweet, and yellow. But it is non-evident whether it really possesses these qualities only; or whether it has but one quality but appears varied owing to the varying structure of the sense organs; or whether, again, it has more qualities than are apparent, some of which elude our perception. That the apple has but one quality might be argued from what we said above regarding the food absorbed by bodies, and the water sucked up by trees, and the breath in flutes and pipes and similar instruments; for the apple likewise may be all of one sort but appear different owing to differences in the sense organs in which perception takes place. And that the apple may possibly possess more qualities than those apparent to us we argue in this way. Let us imagine a man who possesses from birth the senses of touch, taste, and smell, but can neither hear nor see. This man, then, will assume that nothing visual or audible has any existence, but only those three kinds of qualities which he is able to apprehend. Possibly, then, we also, having only our five senses, perceive only such of the apple's qualities as we are capable of apprehending; and possibly it may possess other underlying qualities which affect other sense organs, though we, not being endowed with those organs, fail to apprehend the sense objects which come through them.

"But," it may be objected, "Nature made the senses commensurate with the objects of sense." What kind of "nature"? we ask, seeing that there exists so much unresolved controversy amongst the Dogmatists concerning the reality which belongs to nature. For he who decides the question as to the existence of nature will be discredited by them if he is an ordinary person, while if he is a philosopher he will be a party to the controversy and therefore himself subject to judgment and not a judge. If, however, it is possible that only those qualities which we seem to perceive subsist in the apple, or that a greater number subsist, or, again, that not even the qualities which affect us subsist, then it will be non-evident to us what the nature of the apple really is. And the same argument applies to all the other objects of sense. But if the senses do not apprehend external objects, neither can the mind apprehend them; hence, because of this argument also, we shall be driven, it seems, to suspend judgment regarding the external underlying objects.

In order that we may finally reach suspension by basing our argument on each sense singly, or even by disregarding the senses, we further adopt the **Fourth Mode** of suspension. This is the mode based, as we say, on the "circumstances," meaning by "circumstances" conditions or dispositions. And this mode, we say, deals with states that are natural or unnatural, with waking or sleeping, with conditions due to age, motion or rest, hatred or love, emptiness or fullness, drunkenness or soberness, predispositions, confidence or fear, grief or joy. Thus, according as the mental state is natural or unnatural, objects produce dissimilar impressions, as when men in a frenzy or in a state of ecstasy believe they hear demons' voices, while we do not. Similarly they often say that they perceive an odor of storax or frankincense, or some such scent, and many other things, though we fail to perceive them. Also, the same water which feels very hot when poured on inflamed spots seems lukewarm to us.... [J]ust as healthy men are in a state that is natural for the healthy but unnatural for the sick, so also sick men are in a state that is unnatural for the healthy but natural for the sick, so that to these last also we must give credence as being, relatively speaking, in a natural state.

Sleeping and waking, too, give rise to different impressions, since we do not imagine when awake what we imagine in sleep, nor when asleep what we imagine when awake; so that the existence or non-existence of our impressions is not absolute but relative, being in relation to our sleeping or waking condition. Probably, then, in dreams we see things which to our waking state are unreal, although not wholly unreal; for they exist in our dreams, just as waking realities exist although non-existent in dreams....

Another cause why the real objects appear different lies in motion and rest. For those objects which, when we are standing still, we see to be motionless, we imagine to be in motion when we are sailing past them....

Drunkenness and soberness are a cause; since actions which we think shameful when sober do not seem shameful to us when drunk.

Predispositions are a cause; for the same wine which seems sour to those who have previously eaten dates or figs seems sweet to those who have just consumed nuts or chickpeas; and the vestibule of the bathhouse, which warms those entering from outside, chills those coming out of the bathroom if they stop long in it.

Fear and boldness are a cause; as what seems to the coward fearful and formidable does not seem so in the least to the bold man.

Grief and joy are a cause; since the same affairs are burdensome to those in grief but delightful to those who rejoice.

Seeing then that the dispositions also are the cause of so much disagreement, and that men are differently disposed at different times, although, no doubt, it is easy to say what nature each of the underlying objects appears to each man to possess, we cannot go on to say what its real nature is, since the disagreement admits in itself of no settlement. For the person who tries to settle it is either in one of the aforementioned dispositions or in no disposition whatsoever. But to declare that he is in no disposition at all—as, for instance, neither in health nor sickness, neither in motion nor at rest, of no definite age, and devoid of all the other dispositions as well—is the height of absurdity. And if he is to judge the sense-impressions while he is in some one disposition, he will be a party to the disagreement, and, moreover, he will not be an impartial judge of the external underlying objects owing to his being confused by the dispositions in which he is placed. The waking person, for instance, cannot compare the impressions of sleepers with those of men awake, nor the sound person those of the sick with those of the sound; for we assent more readily to things present, which affect us in the present, than to things not present.

In another way, too, the disagreement of such impressions is incapable of settlement. For he who prefers one impression to another, or one "circumstance" to another, does so either uncritically and without proof or critically and with proof; but he can do this neither without these means (for then he would be discredited) nor with them. For if he is to pass judgment on the impressions he must certainly judge them by a criterion; this criterion, then, he will declare to be true, or else false. But if false, he will be discredited; whereas, if he shall declare it to be true, he will be stating that the criterion is true either without proof or with proof. But if without proof, he will be discredited; and if with proof, it will certainly be necessary for the proof also to be true, to avoid being discredited. Shall he, then, affirm the truth of the proof adopted to establish the criterion after having judged it or without judging it? If without judging, he will be discredited; but if after judging, plainly he will say that he has judged it by a criterion; and of that criterion we shall ask for a proof, and of that proof again a criterion. For the proof always requires a criterion to confirm it, and the criterion also a proof to demonstrate its truth; and neither can a proof be sound without the previous existence of a true criterion nor can the criterion be true without the previous confirmation of the proof. So in this way both the criterion and the proof are involved in the circular process of reasoning, and thereby both are found to be untrustworthy; for since each of them is dependent on the credibility of the other, the one is lacking in credibility just as much as the other. Consequently, if a man can prefer one impression to another neither without a proof and a criterion nor with them, then the different impressions due to the differing conditions will admit of no settlement; so that as a result of this mode also we are brought to suspend judgment regarding the nature of external realities.

The **Fifth Argument** (or Trope) is that based on positions, distances, and locations; for owing to each of these the same objects appear different; for example, the same porch when viewed from one of its corners appears curtailed, but viewed from the middle symmetrical on all sides; and the same ship seems at a distance to be small and stationary, but from close at hand large and in motion; and the same tower from a distance appears round but from a near point quadrangular.

These effects are due to distances. Among effects due to locations are the following: the light of a lamp appears dim in the sun but bright in the dark; and the same oar bent when in the water but straight when out of the water; and the egg soft when inside the fowl but hard when in the air; and the jacinth fluid when in the lynx but hard when in the air; and the coral soft when in the sea but hard when in the air; and sound seems to differ in quality according as it is produced in a pipe, or in a flute, or simply in the air....

Since, then, all apparent objects are viewed in a certain place, and from a certain distance, or in a certain position, and each of these conditions produces a great divergency in the sense-impressions, as we mentioned above, we shall be compelled by this mode also to end up in suspension of judgment. For in fact anyone who purposes to give the preference to any of these impressions will be attempting the impossible. For if he shall deliver his judgment simply and without proof, he will be discredited; and should he, on the other hand, desire to adduce proof, he will confute himself if he says that the proof is false, while if he asserts that the proof is true he will be asked for a proof of its truth, and again for a proof of this latter proof, since it also must be true, and so on ad infinitum. But to produce proofs to infinity is impossible; so that neither by the use of proofs will he be able to prefer one sense impression to another. If, then, one cannot hope to pass judgment on the aforementioned impressions either with or without proof, the conclusion we are driven to is suspension; for while we can, no doubt, state the nature which each object appears to possess as viewed in a certain position or at a certain distance or in a certain place, what its real nature is we are, for the foregoing reasons, unable to declare.

The **Sixth Mode** is that based on admixtures, by which we conclude that, because none of the real objects affects our senses by itself but always in conjunction with something else, though we may possibly be able to state the nature of the resultant mixture formed by the external object and that along with which it is perceived, we shall not be able to say what is the exact nature of the external reality in itself. That none of the external objects affects our senses by itself but always in conjunction with something else, and that, in consequence, it assumes a different appearance is, I imagine, quite obvious. Thus, our own complexion is of one hue in warm air, of another in cold, and we should not be able to say what our complexion really is, but only what it looks like in conjunction with each of these conditions. And the same sound appears of one sort in conjunction with rare air and of another sort with dense air; and odors are more pungent in a hot bathroom or in the sun than in chilly air; and a body is light when immersed in water but heavy when surrounded by air.

The **Seventh Mode** is that based, as we said, on the quantity and constitution of the underlying objects, meaning generally by "constitution" the manner of composition. And it is evident that by this mode also we are compelled to suspend judgment concerning the real nature of the objects. Thus, for example, the filings of a goat's horns appear white when viewed simply by themselves and without combination, but when combined in the substance of the horn they look black. And silver filings appear black when they are by themselves, but when united to the whole mass they are sensed as white....

As a general rule, it seems that wholesome things become harmful when used in immoderate quantities, and things that seem hurtful when taken to excess cause no harm when in minute quantities. What we observe in regard to the effects of medicines is the best evidence in support of our statement; for there the exact blending of the simple drugs makes the compound wholesome, but when the slightest oversight is made in the measuring, as sometimes happens, the compound is not only unwholesome but frequently even most harmful and deleterious. Thus the argument from quantities and compositions causes confusion as to the real nature of the external substances. Probably, therefore, this mode also will bring us round to a suspension of judgment, as we are unable to make any absolute statement concerning the real nature of external objects.

Chapter XVI. Of the two modes. They hand down also two other modes leading to suspension of judgment. Since every object of apprehension seems to be apprehended either through itself or through another object, by showing that nothing is apprehended either through itself or through another thing, they introduce doubt, as they suppose, about everything. That nothing is apprehended through itself is plain, they say, from the controversy which exists amongst the physicists regarding, I imagine, all things, both sensibles and intelligibles: which controversy admits of no settlement because we can neither employ a sensible nor an intelligible criterion, since every criterion we may adopt is controverted and therefore discredited. And the reason why they do not allow that anything is apprehended through something else is this: If that through which an object is apprehended must always itself be apprehended through some other thing, one is involved in a process of circular reasoning or in regress ad infinitum. And if, on the other hand, one should choose to assume that the thing through which another object is apprehended is itself apprehended through itself, this is refuted by the fact that, for the reasons already stated, nothing is apprehended through itself.

CHAPTER 15

Jewish, Christian, and Islamic Theories of Knowledge

"Infinite changes and variations"

Deeply influenced by ancient Greek philosophy, Jewish, Christian, and Islamic philosophers have developed skeptical, rationalist, and empiricist theories of knowledge based on ancient paradigms. All three approaches to theory of knowledge appear in each religious tradition. This chapter surveys only a few representatives. Philo, in one of his works, reviews skeptical arguments, giving long-standing tropes some new twists. Augustine takes on the skeptic, strategically retreating in certain respects, the better to defend the possibility of knowledge in others—particularly, to defend the possibility of self-knowledge. Finally, Avicenna sees in self-knowledge an argument for rationalism, proposing a thought experiment that has inspired both rationalists and empiricists.

15.1 THE SKEPTICISM OF PHILO OF ALEXANDRIA

Skepticism, as a school of Greek philosophy, began with Pyrrho (c. 365–270 BCE)—who, intriguingly, is said to have admired the "naked philosophers" he met in India while traveling with Alexander the Great—and extended, more or less continuously, through the thought of many Greek, Roman, and Alexandrian philosophers for the next thousand years. We will look here at an important figure in this development. Philo, often called Philo Judaeus or Philo of Alexandria (20 BCE–40 CE), was born into a wealthy Jewish family in Alexandria, Egypt. By his time, North Africa, a part of the Roman Empire, had become an important intellectual center, and it would remain one during the first several centuries of the Common Era. Alexandria was the site of a Platonic school and a world-famous library. Because of the school, Plato's influence was especially strong in Alexandria, and most important philosophers of the region were platonists. They wrote in Greek and saw themselves as part of the Hellenistic tradition. Their work often concentrates on the problems of reconciling Judaism or Christianity with the intellectual framework of Greek thought. Well educated in both Judaism and Greek thought, Philo sought to reconcile Jewish religious convictions with Greek philosophy. His central strategy was to interpret the Jewish scriptures allegorically, treating the stories of the Books of Moses as illustrating general aspects of the human condition.

Just as Adam and Eve were tempted in the Garden of Eden, Philo argues, we are tempted to think that we can know the true nature of the world. But that, Philo argues, is a vain conceit. He advances three primary arguments. First, he develops the argument from variability in several forms. There is great variation in perception between animals of different species, different people, and even the same person at different times or in different circumstances. We have no way of telling which perceptions accurately portray reality. Philo concludes that we must suspend judgement.

Second, Philo advances an argument from illusion. We are often mistaken. How do we know that any given occasion is not one of those?

The argument, to formulate it more precisely, is

- We often misperceive things.
- There is no way to tell when we are misperceiving things.
- Therefore, on any given occasion, we might be misperceiving things.

Finally, Philo advances an argument from comparison that foreshadows Immanuel Kant's Copernican Revolution. We know, not things in themselves, but things as they are in relation to other things—especially, to give the argument a Kantian twist, to ourselves.

The crucial premise of this argument, is "Now, whatever is incapable of attesting itself and needs to be vouched for by something else gives no sure ground for belief." Philo gives no argument for it—though, in the hands of Kant, it takes on real power. There is no reason why the relational character of truths should imply skepticism; "Chicago is north of Des Moines" seems no less knowable than "Chicago is windy." But if we can know things only as they relate to us, then (Kant argues) we cannot distinguish what is really in the object from what is being contributed by our own faculties of perception and knowledge.

Philo extends these arguments to morality. Different groups of people have different ways of life. Philosophy does not provide any way of deciding which is best, for philosophers disagree as much as anyone about the nature of the good life. His recommendation: to seek not knowledge but a mystical vision of God.

15.1.1 Philo, from *On Drunkenness*

XLI. On which account it is said, "They made their father drink wine" (Genesis 19:33). That is to say, they brought complete insensibility on the mind, so that it fancied itself competent by its own abilities to judge what was expedient, and to assent to all sorts of apparent facts, as if they really had solid truth in them; human nature being by no means and under no circumstances competent either to ascertain the truth by consideration, or to choose real truth and advantage, or to reject what is false and the cause of injury; for the great darkness which is spread over all existing bodies and things does not permit one to see the real nature of each thing, but even if anyone, under the influence of immoderate curiosity or of real love of learning, wishes to emerge from ignorance and to obtain a closer view, he, like people wholly deprived of sight, stumbling over what is before his feet, will fall, and not be able to lay hold of anything; or else, snatching at something with his hands, he will make uncertain guesses, having only conjecture in the place of truth. For even if education, holding a torch to the mind, conducts it on his way, kindling its own peculiar light, it would still, with reference to the perception of existing things, do harm rather than good; for a slight light is naturally liable to be extinguished by dense darkness, and when the light is extinguished all power of seeing is useless. Accordingly we must, on these accounts, remind the man who gives himself airs by reason of his power of deliberating, or of wisely choosing one kind of objects and avoiding others, that if the same unalterable perceptions of the same things always occurred to us, it might perhaps be requisite to admire the two faculties of judging which are implanted in us by nature, namely, the outward senses and the intellect, as unerring and incorruptible, and never to doubt or hesitate about anything, but trusting in every first appearance to choose one kind of thing and to reject the contrary kind. But since we are found to be influenced in different manners by the same things at different times, we should have nothing positive to assert about anything, inasmuch as what appears has no settled or stationary existence, but is subject to various, and multiform, and ever-recurring changes.

XLII. For it follows of necessity, since the imagination is unstable, that the judgment formed by it must be unstable likewise; and there are many reasons for this. In the first place, the differences which exist in animals are not in one particular only, but are unspeakable in point of number, extending through every part, having reference both to their creation and to the way in which they are furnished with their different faculties, and to their way of being supported and their habits, and to the manner in which they choose and avoid different things, and to the energies and motions of the outward senses, and to the peculiar properties of the endless passions affecting both the soul and body. For without mentioning those animals which have the faculty of judgment, consider also some of those which are the objects of judgment, such as the chameleon and the polypus; for they say that the former of these animals changes his complexion so as to resemble the soils over which he is accustomed to creep, and that the other is like the rocks of the sea-shore to which it clings, nature herself, perhaps, being their saviour, and endowing them with a quality to protect them from being caught, namely, with that of changing to all kinds of complexions, as a defence against evil. Again, have you never perceived the neck of the dove changing colour so as to assume a countless variety of hues in the rays of the sun? Is it not

---

Source: Philo of Alexandria, *On Drunkenness*, from *The Works of Philo Judaeus*. Translated from the Greek by Charles Duke Yonge. London: H. G. Bohn, 1854–1890. We have made a few alterations for readability.

by turns red, and purple and fiery coloured, and cinereous, and again pale, and ruddy, and every other variety of colour, the very names of which it is not easy to enumerate? They say indeed that among the Scythians, among that tribe which is called the Geloni, most marvellous things happen, rarely indeed, but nevertheless it does happen; namely that there is a beast seen which is called the tarandus, not much less than an ox in size, and exceedingly like a stag in the character of his face. The story goes that this animal continually changes his coat according to the place in which he is, or the trees which he is near, and that in short he always resembles whatever he is near, so that through the similarity of his colour he escapes the notice of those who fall in with him, and that it is owing to this, rather than to any vigour of body, that he is hard to catch. Now these facts and others which resemble them are visible proofs of our inability to comprehend everything.

XLIII. In the next place, not only are there all these variations with respect to animals, but there are also innumerable changes and varieties in men, and great differences between one man and another. For not only do they form different opinions respecting the same things at different times, but different men also judge in different manners, some looking on things as pleasures which others on the contrary regard as annoyances. For the things with which some persons are sometimes vexed, others delight in, and on the contrary the things which some persons are eager to acquire and look upon as pleasant and suitable, those very same things others reject and drive to a distance as unsuitable and ill-omened. At all events I have before now often seen in the theatre, when I have been there, some persons influenced by a melody of those who were exhibiting on the stage, whether dramatists or musicians, as to be excited and to join in the music, uttering encomiums without intending it; and I have seen others at the same time so unmoved that you would think there was not the least difference between them and the inanimate seats on which they were sitting; and others again so disgusted that they have even gone away and quitted the spectacle, stopping their ears with their hands, lest some atom of a sound being left behind and still sounding in them should inflict annoyance on their morose and unpleasable souls. And yet why do I say this? Every single individual among us (which is the most surprising thing of all) is subject to infinite changes and variations both in body and soul, and sometimes chooses and sometimes rejects things which are subject to no changes themselves, but which by their intrinsic nature do always remain in the same condition. For the same fancies do not strike the same men when they are well and when they are ill, nor when they are awake and when they are asleep, nor when they are young and when they are old. And a man who is standing still often conceives different ideas from those which he entertains when he is in motion; and also when he is courageous, or when he is alarmed; again when he is grieved, or when he is delighted, and when he is in love, he feels differently from what he does when he is full of hatred. And why need I be prolix and deep dwelling on these points? For in short every motion of both body and soul, whether in accordance with nature or in opposition to nature, is the cause of a great variation and change respecting the appearances which present themselves to us; from which all sorts of inconsistent and opposite dreams arise to occupy our minds.

XLIV. And that is not the least influential cause of the instability of one's perceptions which arises from the position of the objects, from their distance, and from the places by which they are each of them surrounded. Do we not see that the fishes in the sea, when they stretch out their fins and swim about, do always appear larger than their real natural size? And oars too, even though they are very straight, look as if they were broken when they are under water; and things at a great distance display false appearances to our eyes, and in this way do frequently deceive the mind. For at times inanimate objects have been imagined to be alive, and on the contrary living animals have been considered to be lifeless; sometimes again stationary things appear to be in motion, and things in motion appear to be standing still: even things which are approaching towards us do sometimes appear to be retreating from us, and things which are going away do on the other hand appear to be approaching. At times very short things seem to be exceedingly long, and things which have many angles appear to be circular. There is also an infinite number of other things of which a false impression is given though they are open to the sight, which however no man in his senses would subscribe to as certain.

XLV. What again are we to say of the quantities occurring in things compounded? For it is through the admixture of a greater or a lesser quantity that great injury or good is often done, as in many other instances, so most especially in the case of medicines compounded by medical science. For quantity in such compounds is measured by fixed limits and rules, and it is not safe either to stop short before one has reached them, nor to advance beyond them. For if too little be applied, it relaxes, and if too much, it strains the natural powers; and each extremity is mischievous, the one from its impotence being capable of producing any effect at all, and the other by reason of its exceeding strength being necessarily hurtful. Again it is very plain with reference to smoothness and roughness, and thickness and close compression, or on the other hand leanness and slackness, how very much influence all these differences have in respect of doing good or harm. Nor indeed is anyone ignorant that scarcely anything whatever of existing things, if you consider it in itself and by itself, is accurately understood; but by comparing it with its opposite, then we arrive at a knowledge of its true nature. As for instance, we comprehend what is meant by little by placing it in juxtaposition with what is great; we understand what dry is by comparing it with wet, cold by comparing it with heat, light by comparing it with heavy, black by contrasting it with white, weak by contrasting it with strong, and few by comparing it with many. In the same way also, in whatever is named to virtue or to vice, what is advantageous is recognised by a comparison with what is injurious, what is beautiful by a comparison with what is unseemly, what is just and generally good, by placing it in juxtaposition with what is unjust and bad. And, indeed, if anyone considers everything that there is in the world, he will be able to arrive at a proper estimate of its character by taking it in the same manner; for each separate thing is by itself incomprehensible, but by a comparison with another thing, it is easy to understand it. Now, that which is unable to bear witness to itself, but which stands in need of the advocacy of something else, is not to be trusted or thought steady. So that in this way those men are convicted who say that they have no difficulty in assenting to or denying propositions about anything. And why need we wonder? For anyone who advances far into matters and who contemplates them in an unmixed state will know this, that nothing is ever presented to our view according to its real plain nature, but that everything has the most various possible mixtures and combinations.

XLVI. Someone will say, We at once comprehend colours. How so? Do we not do so by means of the external things, air and light, and also by the moisture which exists in our eyes themselves? And in what way are sweet and bitter comprehended? Is it apart from the moisture in our mouths? And as to all the flavours which are in accordance with, or at variance with, nature, are not they in the same case? What, again, are we to say of the smells arising from perfumes which are burnt? Do they exhibit plain unmixed simple natures, or rather qualities compounded of themselves and of the air, and sometimes also of the fire which consumes their bodies, and also of the faculty existing in our own nostrils? From all this we collect the inference that we have neither any proper comprehension of colours, not only of the combination which consists of the objects submitted to our view and of light; nor of smells, but only of the mixture which consists of that which flows from substances and the all-receiving air; nor of tastes, but only of the union which arises from the tasteable object presented to us and the moist substance in our mouths.

XLVII. Since, then, this is the state of affairs with respect to these matters, it is worthwhile to appreciate correctly the simplicity, or rashness, or impudence of those who pretend to be able with ease to form an opinion, so as to assent to or deny what is stated with respect to anything whatever. For if the simple faculties are wanting, but the mingled powers and those which are formed by contributions from many sources are within sight, and if it is impossible for those which are invisible to be seen, and if we are unable to comprehend separately the character of all the component parts which are united to make up each faculty, then what remains except that we must think it necessary to suspend our judgment? And then, too, do not those facts which are diffused over nearly the whole world, and which have caused both to Greeks and barbarians such erroneous judgments, exhort us not to be too ready in giving our credence to what is not seen? And what are these facts? Surely they are the instructions which we have received from our childhood, and our national customs and ancient laws, of which it is admitted that there is not a single one which is of equal force among all people; but it is notorious that they vary according to the different countries, and nations, and cities, aye, and even still more, in every village and private house, and even with respect to men, and women, and infant children, in almost every point. At all events, what are accounted disgraceful actions among us, are by others looked upon as honourable; what we think becoming, others call unseemly; what we pronounce just, others renounce as iniquitous; others think our holy actions impious, our lawful deeds lawless: and further, what we think praiseworthy, they find fault with; what we think worthy of all honour, is, in the eyes of others, deserving of punishment; and, in fact, they think most things to be of a contrary character to what we think. And why need I be prolix and dwell further on this subject, when I am called off by other, more important points? If then, anyone, leaving out of the question all other more remarkable subjects of speculation, were to choose to devote his time to an investigation of the subject here proposed, namely, to examine the education, and customs, and laws of every different nation, and country, and place, and city, of all subjects and rulers, of all men, whether renowned or inglorious, whether free or slaves, whether ignorant or endowed with knowledge, he would spend not one day or two, nor a month, nor even a year, but his whole life, even though he were to reach a great age, in the investigation; and he would nevertheless still leave a vast number of subjects unexamined, uninvestigated, and unmentioned without perceiving it. Therefore, since there are some persons and things removed from other persons and things, not by a short distance only, but since they are utterly different, it then follows of necessity that the perceptions which occur to men of different things must also differ, and that their opinions must be at variance with one another.

XLVIII. And since this is the case, who is so foolish and ridiculous as to affirm positively that such and such a thing is just, or wise, or honourable, or expedient? For whatever this man defines as such, someone else, who from his childhood has learnt a contrary lesson, will be sure to deny. But I am not surprised if a confused and mixed multitude, being the inglorious slave of customs and laws, however introduced and established, accustomed from its very cradle to obey them as if they were masters and tyrants, having their souls beaten and buffeted, as it were, and utterly unable to conceive any lofty or magnanimous thoughts, believes at once every tradition which is represented to it, and leaving its mind without any proper training, assents to and denies propositions without examination and without deliberation. But even if the multitude of those who are called philosophers, pretending that they are really seeking for certainty and accuracy in things, being divided into ranks and companies, come to discordant, and often even to diametrically opposite decisions, and that too, not about some one accidental matter, but about almost everything, whether great or small, with respect to which any discussion can arise. For when some persons affirm that the world is infinite, while others pronounce it to be confined within limits; or while some look upon the world as uncreated, and others assert that it is created; or when some persons look upon it as destitute of any ruler and superintendent, attributing to it a motion, deprived of reason, and proceeding on some independent internal impulse, while others think that there is a care of and providence, which looks over the whole and its parts of marvellous power and wisdom, God ruling and governing the whole, in a manner free from all stumbling and full of protection. How is it possible for anyone to affirm that the comprehension of such objects as are brought before them is the same in all men? And again, the imaginations which are occupied with the consideration of what is good, are not they compelled to suspend their judgment rather than to agree? While some think that it is only what is good that is beautiful, and treasure that up in the soul, others divide it into numbers of minute particles, and extend it as far as the body and external circumstances. These men affirm that such pieces of prosperity as are granted by fortune are the body-guards of the body, namely strength and good health, and that the integrity and sound condition of the organs of the external senses, and all things of that kind, are the guards of that princess, the soul; for since the nature of good is divided according to three divisions, the third and outermost is the champion and defender of the second and yielding one, and the second in its turn is a great bulwark and protection to the first; and about these very things, and about the different ways of life, and about the ends to which all actions ought to be referred, and about ten thousand other things which logical, and moral, and natural philosophy comprehends, there have been an unspeakable number of discussions, as to which, up to the present time, there is no agreement whatever among all these philosophers who have examined into such subject.

XLIX. Is it not then strictly in accordance with nature that while its two daughters, Counsel and Assent, were agreed together, and sleeping together, the mind is introduced as embarrassed by an ignorance of all knowledge? For we read in the scripture, "They knew not when they lay down, or when they rose up." (Genesis 19:35) For it was not likely that in his state he could clearly and distinctly comprehend either sleep or waking, or a stationary position or motion; but when he appears to have come to an opinion in the best manner, then above all other times is he found to be most foolish, since his affairs then come to an end, by no means resembling that which was expected; and whenever he has decided on assenting to some things as true, then he incurs a reproach and condemnation for his facility in adopting opinions, those things which he previously believed as most certain now appearing untrustworthy and uncertain; so that, as matters are in the habit of turning out contrary to what was expected, the safest course appears to be to suspend one's judgment.

15.2 AUGUSTINE'S FOUNDATIONALISM

The best-known answers to skepticism in Western philosophy have been internalist and specifically foundationalist. Saint Augustine (354–430 CE), a Christian platonist, argued vigorously against skepticism, which was popular in late antiquity. This was partly because of the influence of the Roman orator, statesman, and philosopher Cicero (106–43 BCE), partly because of the influence of Sextus and his followers, partly because Plato's Academy was now under the leadership of the skeptic Carneades—to whom Augustine responds in the next selection—and perhaps mostly because of the plethora of philosophical, religious, and political worldviews that competed for people's attention and allegiance in the declining Roman Empire. Augustine tackles skepticism head-on, arguing that logical truths, for example, can be known even if skeptical contentions are justified. Suppose, for example, that the argument from variability is sound and that there is no way to know which of several views about something is correct. We may nevertheless know that any proposed view is either correct or incorrect. No skeptical argument, Augustine maintains, should lead us to doubt truths of logic and mathematics.

What about perceptual knowledge, knowledge attained through sense perception? Augustine is not convinced by arguments from illusion, dreaming, or madness. He presents the essential foundationalist point, long before Descartes, that beliefs about our own subjective states are self-evident, immune to both doubt and the enterprises of justification. You may doubt that there is really a book on the table, though you seem to see one. But you cannot doubt that it looks as though you see a book. So you may be justified in doubting something external to yourself, but you know your own state of mind. Even if we do not know things in the world, at least we know appearances. This shows that we have one sort of knowledge even if we grant the argument from variability, since that is restricted to knowledge of something that transcends appearances—that appears different from different points of view. Concerning how things appear from our own first-person perspective, there is only the one point of view and thus no possibility of variation.

There is also knowledge of ourselves. No skeptical argument can touch our assurance that we exist. As we shall see, this is a linchpin of Cartesian theory of knowledge.

Augustine is a platonist. To put it perhaps too simply, Augustine adopts the *Republic*'s solution to the problem of how we know the Forms, but replaces the idea or form of the Good with God. Plato's successors were skeptics largely because they could not see how we could know the Forms. Plato's solution seems inadequate: If we do not understand how we could interact with the Forms, how can we understand how we can interact with the Form of the Good? Interaction with God is not a problem, however, for God can do anything.

Augustine follows Philo in identifying the Forms with ideas in the mind of God. He describes the process by which we apprehend the Forms as illumination, an act of revelation. God reveals a portion of the divine mind to us. In that way God makes our minds resemble the divine mind to some degree. We have innate cognitive abilities that reflect the principles according to which God created the world.

15.2.1 Augustine, from *Answer to Skeptics*

Chapter 10

You say that in philosophy nothing can be understood. And, in order to spread your utterance far and wide, you ridicule the quarrels and dissensions of philosophers. And you think that those quarrels and dissensions supply you with arms against the philosophers themselves. How, for

Source: *Answer to Skeptics*, translated by Denis J. Kavanagh. *Writings of Saint Augustine*, Volume I. New York: Cima Publishing Company, 1948.

instance, are we going to adjudicate the contest between Democritus and the earlier cosmologists as to the oneness or incalculable multiplicity of the world, inasmuch as it was impossible to preserve agreement between Democritus himself and his heir, Epicurus? That voluptuary was glad to grasp atoms in the darkness and to make those little bodies his handmaids, but he dissipated his entire patrimony through litigation when he allowed them to deviate from their respective proper courses and to diverge capriciously into one another's paths.... Nevertheless, I know something about these matters of cosmology, for I am certain that either there is only one world or there are more worlds than one. I am likewise certain that if there are more worlds than one, their number is either finite or infinite. Carneades would teach that this notion resembles a false one. Furthermore, I know for certain that this world of ours has its present arrangement either from the nature of bodies or from a foresight of some kind. I am also certain that either it always was and always will be, or it had a beginning and will never end, or it existed before time and will have an end, or it had a beginning and will not last forever. And I have the same kind of knowledge with regard to countless cosmological problems, for those disjunctives are true, and no one can confuse them with any likeness to falsity....

Chapter 11

"But," says he, "if the senses are deceptive, how do you know that this world exists?" Your reasons will never be able to refute the testimony of the senses to such extent as to convince us that nothing is perceived by us. In fact, you have never ventured to try that, but you have strenuously exerted yourself to convince us that a thing can be something other than what it seems to be. So, by the term *world*, I mean this totality which surrounds us and sustains us. Whatever its nature may be, I apply the term *world* to that which is present to my eyes, and which I see to be holding the earth and the heavens, or the *quasi* earth and the *quasi* heavens. If you say that nothing appears to me, I shall never be in error: the man that is in error is the man who rashly accepts as true whatever appears to him. Indeed, you yourselves say that to sentient beings a false thing can appear to be true, but you do not say that nothing can so appear to them. You are anxious to gain a victory in this dispute. But, if we know nothing, and if nothing even appears to us as true, then the entire reason for our dispute will vanish. And if you maintain that what appears to me is not a world, then you are disputing about words only, for I have said that I call it a world.

But, you will ask me: "Is it the very same world that you are seeing, even if you are asleep?" I have already said that I am using the term *world* to designate whatever appears as such to me. But, if you think that the term ought to be restricted to that which appears to those who are awake and of sound mind, then contend—if you can—that sleeping men and deranged men are not in this world while they are asleep or deranged. My only assertion is that this entire mass and frame of bodies in which we exist is either a unit or not a unit; and that it is what it is, whether we be asleep or awake, deranged or of sound mind.... In any case, it must be true that the world is what it is. Of course, I am not saying that I perceived [in sleep] the same thing I would perceive if I were awake, but you can say that what I perceive when I am awake could appear to me also when I am asleep. Therefore, it can be very similar to something false. However, if there are one world and six worlds, it is clear that there are seven worlds, no matter how I may be affected. And, with all due modesty, I maintain that I know this.... I regard it as already sufficiently plain that the things which are seen awry through sleep or derangement are things that pertain to the bodily senses, for, even if the whole human race were fast asleep, it would still be necessarily true that three times three are nine, and that this is the square of intelligible numbers. Furthermore, I see that, on behalf of the senses, one could urge many arguments which we do not find reprehended by the Academics. In fact, I believe that the senses are not untrustworthy either because deranged persons suffer illusions, or because we see things wrongly when we are asleep. If the senses correctly intimate things to the vigilant and the sane, it is no affair of theirs what the mind of a sleeping or insane person may fancy for itself.

Inquiry is still to be made as to whether the senses report the truth whenever they report anything. Well, suppose that some Epicurean would say: "I have no complaint to make about the senses, for it would be unfair to demand of them anything beyond their power. And, whatever the eyes can see, they see that which is true." Therefore, as to what they see with regard to an oar in the water—is that true? It is absolutely true. In fact, since there is a special reason for the oar's appearing that way, I should rather accuse my eyes of deception if it appeared to be straight when dipped into the water, for, in that case, they would not be seeing what ought to be seen. But what is the need of many examples? The same can be said about the motion of towers, the wings of birds, and countless other things. "Nevertheless," says someone or other, "I am deceived if I give assent." Restrict your assent to the mere fact of your being convinced that it appears thus to you. Then there is no deception, for I do not see how even an Academic can refute a man who says: "I know that this appears white to me. I know that I am delighted by what I am hearing. I know that this smells pleasant to me. I know that this tastes sweet to me. I know that this feels cold to me." Tell me, rather, whether the oleaster leaves—for which a goat has a persistent appetite—are bitter per se. O, shameless man! Is not the goat more moderate? I know not how the oleaster leaves may be for flocks and herds; as to myself, they are bitter. What more do you wish to know? Perhaps there is even some man for whom they are not bitter. Are you contending for the sake of annoyance? Have I said that they are bitter for everybody? I have said that they are bitter for me, but I do not say that they will always be so. What, if at different times and for diverse reasons, something be found to taste sweet at one time and bitter on some other occasion? This is what I say: that when a man tastes something, he can in good faith swear that it is sweet to his palate or that it is not, and that by no Greek sophistry can he be beguiled out of this knowledge. If I am relishing the taste of something, who would be so brazen as to say to me: "Perhaps you are not tasting it: it may be only a dream"? Would I discontinue? Why, that would afford me pleasure even in a dream. Wherefore, no resemblance to falsity can confuse what I said that I know.

15.2.2 Augustine, *The City of God*

Book XI

Chapter 26. Of the Image of the Supreme Trinity, Which We Find in Some Sort in Human Nature Even in Its Present State

And we indeed recognize in ourselves the image of God, that is, of the supreme Trinity, an image which, though it be not equal to God, or rather, though it be very far removed from Him,—being neither co-eternal, nor, to say all in a word, consubstantial with Him,—is yet nearer to Him in nature than any other of His works, and is destined to be yet restored, that it may bear a still closer resemblance. For we both are, and know

Source: *St. Augustine's City of God and Christian Doctrine*, edited by Philip Schaff. New York: Christian Literature 1890.

that we are, and delight in our being, and our knowledge of it. Moreover, in these three things no true-seeming illusion disturbs us; for we do not come into contact with these by some bodily sense, as we perceive the things outside of us,—colors, e.g., by seeing, sounds by hearing, smells by smelling, tastes by tasting, hard and soft objects by touching,—of all which sensible objects it is the images resembling them, but not themselves which we perceive in the mind and hold in the memory, and which excite us to desire the objects. But, without any delusive representation of images or phantasms, I am most certain that I am, and that I know and delight in this. In respect of these truths, I am not at all afraid of the arguments of the Academicians, who say, What if you are deceived? For if I am deceived, I am. For he who is not, cannot be deceived; and if I am deceived, by this same token I am. And since I am if I am deceived, how am I deceived in believing that I am? For it is certain that I am if I am deceived. Since, therefore, I, the person deceived, should be, even if I were deceived, certainly I am not deceived in this knowledge that I am. And, consequently, neither am I deceived in knowing that I know. For, as I know that I am, so I know this also, that I know. And when I love these two things, I add to them a certain third thing, namely, my love, which is of equal moment. For neither am I deceived in this, that I love, since in those things which I love I am not deceived; though even if these were false, it would still be true that I loved false things. For how could I justly be blamed and prohibited from loving false things, if it were false that I loved them? But, since they are true and real, who doubts that when they are loved, the love of them is itself true and real? Further, as there is no one who does not wish to be happy, so there is no one who does not wish to be. For how can he be happy, if he is nothing?

Chapter 27. Of Existence, and Knowledge of It, and the Love of Both

And truly the very fact of existing is by some natural spell so pleasant that even the wretched are, for no other reason, unwilling to perish; and, when they feel that they are wretched, wish not that they themselves be annihilated but that their misery be so. Take even those who, both in their own esteem and in point of fact, are utterly wretched, and who are reckoned so, not only by wise men on account of their folly, but by those who count themselves blessed, and who think them wretched because they are poor and destitute,—if anyone should give these men an immortality, in which their misery should be deathless, and should offer the alternative, that if they shrank from existing eternally in the same misery they might be annihilated and exist nowhere at all, nor in any condition, on the instant they would joyfully, nay exultantly, make election to exist always, even in such a condition, rather than not exist at all. The well-known feeling of such men witnesses to this. For when we see that they fear to die, and will rather live in such misfortune than end it by death, is it not obvious enough how nature shrinks from annihilation? And, accordingly, when they know that they must die, they seek, as a great boon, that this mercy be shown them, that they may a little longer live in the same misery and delay to end it by death. And so they indubitably prove with what glad alacrity they would accept immortality, even though it secured to them endless destruction. What! do not even all irrational animals, to whom such calculations are unknown, from the huge dragons down to the least worms, all testify that they wish to exist, and therefore shun death by every movement in their power? Nay, the very plants and shrubs, which have no such life as enables them to shun destruction by movements we can see, do not they all seek in their own fashion to conserve their existence, by rooting themselves more and more deeply in the earth, that so they may draw nourishment and throw out healthy branches towards the sky? *In fine*, even the lifeless bodies, which want not only sensation but seminal life, yet either seek the upper air or sink deep, or are balanced in an intermediate position, so that they may protect their existence in that situation where they can exist in most accordance with their nature.

And how much human nature loves the knowledge of its existence, and how it shrinks from being deceived, will be sufficiently understood from this fact, that every man prefers to grieve in a sane mind rather than to be glad in madness. And this grand and wonderful instinct belongs to men alone of all animals; for, though some of them have keener eyesight than ourselves for this world's light, they cannot attain to that spiritual light with which our mind is somehow irradiated so that we can form right judgments of all things. For our power to judge is proportioned to our acceptance of this light. Nevertheless, the irrational animals, though they have not knowledge, have certainly something resembling knowledge; whereas the other material things are said to be sensible, not because they have senses, but because they are the objects of our senses. Yet among plants, their nourishment and generation have some resemblance to sensible life. However, both these and all material things have their causes hidden in their nature; but their outward forms, which lend beauty to this visible structure of the world, are perceived by our senses, so that they seem to wish to compensate for their own want of knowledge by providing us with knowledge. But we perceive them by our bodily senses in such a way that we do not judge of them by these senses. For we have another and far superior sense, belonging to the inner man, by which we perceive what things are just, and what unjust,—just by means of an intelligible idea, unjust by the want of it. This sense is aided in its functions neither by the eyesight, nor by the orifice of the ear, nor by the airholes of the nostrils, nor by the palate's taste, nor by any bodily touch. By it I am assured both that I am and that I know this; and these two I love, and in the same manner I am assured that I love them.

15.3 AVICENNA (IBN SINA) ON LOGIC AND SCIENCE

Avicenna (ibn-Sina, 980–1037) makes some of his most important contributions to philosophy by clarifying the structure of knowledge. Working from a careful reading of Aristotle, he distinguishes, notably, propositions "that may be known through intellect" from those requiring added information gotten from experience or another source. The former he calls "intuitional" or "apprehensive" and the latter "judgmental." Propositions that may be known through intellect require knowledge of the meanings of their terms, reasoning, and reflection alone, whereas the other type requires information from perception or another source.

Avicenna's distinction has a deep influence on later thought, but in different terms. Western philosophers employ Avicenna's distinction between intuitional and judgmental truths by distinguishing *a priori* from *a posteriori* truths. A priori truths can be known independent of experience, through reflection and reasoning alone. A posteriori truths can be known only on the basis of experience.

Some truths can be known through reasoning, Avicenna argues, while other things require "intuition," by which he probably means, more broadly than the empiricists' "experience," any additional information. This could take the form of sensation, to be sure, but also testimony, common opinion, and so on. Avicenna calls those propositions we can know through reasoning alone First Principles. Everything else we know through intuition: by inference from perception, testimony, or experiment (that is, causal reasoning).

Avicenna holds that four kinds of premise can be used to infer knowledge of the world: First Principle, Perceptual, Experiential, and Testimonial premises are used in syllogistic reasoning. This kind of reasoning gives certainty and guarantees truth. First Principle premises are independent of experience, while the others depend on experience. It is easy to see that Avicenna's distinctions lie at the heart of much theory of knowledge.

Avicenna says that First Principle premises, which are known by the First Intellect, cannot be doubted. If a person imagines that he came into the world knowing nothing except the meaning of two parts of a First Principle premise and he were asked to doubt the truth of the premise, he would not be able to perform the task. For example, if a person knows by intuition the meaning of "whole" and "part," "greater" and "lesser," then he cannot help knowing that "the whole is greater than its parts," and that "things which are equal to the same thing are equal to one another." Avicenna's stress on knowing meanings suggests that these are analytic truths. And some there surely are. But his general theory of knowledge suggests that some a priori truths are synthetic, too.

He offers a dramatic and influential argument to that effect. Imagine a "flying man," who is in effect in a condition of sensory deprivation and has been his entire life. No information arrives from any of the five senses. Is there anything he could know? Is there anything of which he could be aware? Yes. He could be aware of his own existence and of his own awareness.

15.3.1 Avicenna, from *A Treatise on Logic*

The Purpose and Use of Logic

There are two kinds of cognition: One is called intuitive or perceptive or apprehensive. For example, if someone says, "Man," or "Fairy," or "Angel," or the like, you will understand, conceive and grasp what he means by the expression. The other kind of cognition is judgment. As for example when you acknowledge that angels exist or human beings are under surveillance and the like.

Cognition can again be analyzed into two kinds. One is the kind that may be known through intellect; it is known necessarily by reasoning through itself. For example, there are the intuitive cognitions of the whatness of the soul, and judgments about what is grasped by intuitive cognition, such as, the soul is eternal.

The other kind of cognition is one that is known by intuition. Judgments about these intuitions, however, are made, not by intellect, or by reason but by the First Principle. For example, it is known that if two things are equal to the same thing then those things are equal to each other. Then there is the kind of cognition known by the senses, such as the knowledge that the sun is bright. Also, there is the knowledge that is received from authority, such as those received from sages and prophets. And the kind that is obtained from the general opinion and those we are brought by it, for example, that it is wrong to

Source: *Avicenna's Treatise on Logic: Part One of Danesh-Name Alai.* Translated from the Persian by Farhang Zabeeh. The Hague: Martinus Nijhoff, 1971. Reprinted by permission of Springer Publishers.

lie and injustice ought not to be done. And still other kinds—which may be named later.

Whatever is known by intellect, whether it is simple intuitive cognition, or judgment about intuitive cognition, or cognitive judgment, should be based on something which is known prior to the thing (a posteriori).

An example of an intuitive or perceptual cognition is this: If we don't know what "man" means, and someone tells us that a man is an animal who talks, we first have to know the meaning of "animal" and "talking," and we must have intuitive cognition of these things before we can leam something we didn't know before about man.

An example of a judgment acquired by intellect is this: If we don't know the meaning of "the world was created," and someone tells us that the world possesses color, and whatever possesses color is created; then, and only then, can we know what we didn't know before about the world.

Thus, whatever is not known but desired to be known can be known through what is known before. But it is not the case that whatever is known can be a ground for knowing what is unknown. Because for everything that is unknown there is a proper class of known things that can be used for knowing the unknown.

There is a method by which one can discover the unknown from what is known. It is the science of logic. Through it one may know how to obtain the unknown from the known. This science is also concerned with the different kinds of valid, invalid, and near-valid inferences.

The science of logic is the science of scales. Other sciences are practical, they can give direction in life. The salvation of men lies in their purity of soul. This purity of soul is attainable by contemplating the pure form and avoiding this-worldly inclinations. And the way to these two are through science. And no science which cannot be examined by the balance of logic is certain and exact. Thus, without the acquisition of logic, nothing can be truly called science. Therefore, there is no way except learning the science of logic. It is characteristic of the ancient sciences that the student, at the beginning of his study, is unable to see the use or application of the sciences. This is so because only after a thorough study of the whole body of science will the real value of his endeavor become apparent. Thus I pray that the reader of this book will not grow impatient in reading things which do not appear of use upon first sight.

A Discussion of Essential and Accidental Universals

The universal contains its particulars either (a) essentially or (b) accidentally. The Essential Universal and its Particulars are apprehended if, at least, three conditions are fulfilled: 1. The particular has meaning. Thus, if you know the meaning of "animal," "man," "number," and "number four," you cannot help knowing the meaning of the expressions "man is an animal" and "four is a number." But if you add "exists" or "is white" to the words "animal" and "number," you will not understand the meaning of the resulting expressions "man exists," "number four exists," or "man is not white" or "man is white." 2. The existence of the Essential Universal is prerequisite for the existence of its Particular. For example, there should first be animal in order that animal be man, and first there should be number in order that number be four, and first there should be human being in order that human being be Zid. 3. Nothing gives meaning to a particular, rather its meaning is derived from its essence. For example, nothing makes human being animal, and nothing makes four number, except its essence. For if it were otherwise, if the essence of a thing did not exist, there could be a man which is not animal, and there could be four, but no number; but this is impossible.

To further elaborate what has been said, take the saying "something may make some other thing." Its meaning is this: a thing cannot be in its essence another thing, but only could be that other thing by means of something else which is accidental to it. If it is impossible for a thing to be what another thing is, nothing could make it that thing. That thing which makes man, man, makes animal, animal. But it does not make man animal, since man in itself is animal, and four in itself is number. But this relation does not exist between whiteness and man. Hence, there should be something which makes man white.

Thus, when every meaning has the above three characteristics it is essential. Whatever does not have all these characteristics is accidental. Accidental qualities are those which can never arise from the essence of a thing, not even by imagination. Therefore, they are unlike kinds of deduction that are made in the case of the number thousand which is an even number or in the case of a triangle, the sum total of whose angles is equal to two right angles. An example of an accidental quality is laughter, an attribute of men. This problem will be discussed later on.

And I should have mentioned also that a human being has two characteristics: essential and accidental. His essential characteristic may be exemplified by his ability to speak, because this property is the essence of his soul. An accidental quality of his is laughter, because it is the character of man, on seeing or hearing a strange and unfamiliar thing (unless hindered by instinct or habit) to perchance laugh. But before there be wonder and laughter there must be a soul for a man, in order that this soul be united with a body and man becomes a man. First, there should be a soul in order that there be a man; not first there should be laughter in order that there be a soul. Thus, the characteristic which comes first is essential, and whatever does not come from a man is not essential, but accidental. When you say, "Zid is seated," "Zid slept," "Zid is old," and "Zid is young," these characteristics, without doubt, are accidental, no matter what their temporal sequence be.

15.3.2 Avicenna, from *The Book of Healing*

Medicine considers the human body as to the means by which it is cured and by which it is driven away from health. The knowledge of anything, since all things have causes, is not acquired or complete unless it is known by its causes. Therefore in medicine we ought to know the causes of sickness and health. And because health and sickness and their causes are sometimes manifest, and sometimes hidden and not to be comprehended except by the study of symptoms, we must also study the symptoms of health and disease. Now it is established in the sciences that no knowledge is acquired save through the study of its causes and beginnings, if it has had causes and beginnings; nor completed except by knowledge of its accidents and accompanying essentials. Of these causes there are four kinds: material, efficient, formal, and final.

Material causes, on which health and sickness depend, are—the affected member, which is the immediate subject, and the humors; and in these are the elements. And these two are subjects that, according to their mixing together, alter. In the composition and alteration of the substance which is thus composed, a certain unity is attained.

Efficient causes are the causes changing and preserving the conditions of the human body; as airs and what are united with them; and evacuation and retention; and districts and cities, and habitable places, and what are united with them; and changes in age and diversities in it, and in races and arts and manners, and bodily and animate

Source: Charles F. Horne (ed.), *The Sacred Books and Early Literature of the East.* Vol. VI: Medieval Arabia. New York: Parke, Austin, and Lipscomb, 1917.

movings and restings, and sleepings and wakings on account of them; and in things which befall the human body when they touch it, and are either in accordance or at variance with nature.

Formal causes are physical constitutions and combinations and virtues which result from them. Final causes are operations. And in the science of operations lies the science of virtues, as we have set forth. These are the subjects of the doctrine of medicine, whence one inquires concerning the disease and curing of the human body. One ought to attain perfection in this research, namely, how health may be preserved and sickness cured. And the causes of this kind are rules in eating and drinking, and the choice of air, and the measure of exercise and rest; and doctoring with medicines and doctoring with the hands. All this with physicians is according to three species: the well, the sick, and the medium of whom we have spoken.

15.3.3 Avicenna, from *On the Soul*

We shall say, therefore, that someone from among us ought to be thought of as if he were created all at once and full grown, but with his eyes covered so that he would not see external things. And he would be so created as if he were moving in the air—or in a void, in such a way that the density of the air would not touch him that he might sense it. And his limbs would be, as it were, spread out in such a way that they would not come together or touch one another.

Now let him see if he affirms the being of his essence. For he will have no doubt about affirming that he exists. Yet he will not affirm outward things about his limbs, or interior things about what is inside him, neither his mind nor his brain, nor anything else outside him. But he, whose length or breadth or depth he will not affirm, will affirm that he exists. If, however, it were possible for him at that time to imagine a hand or another limb, still he would not imagine it to be a part of him, or necessary to his essence.

Now you know that what is affirmed is other than what is not affirmed, and what is granted is other than what is not granted. And, because the essence that he affirms to exist is proper to him, insofar as he is that very essence, and is something besides his body and his limbs, which he does not affirm, therefore, once he has been awakened, he has a pathway to proceed in full wakefulness to knowing that the being of his soul is other than the being of his body. Indeed, he does not need the body in order to know the soul and perceive it. But if he is a dullard, he will have to turn to that way [and rely on the body to gain a knowledge of the soul].

Source: S. van Riet (ed.), *Avicenna Latinus: Liber de anima seu sextus de naturalibus*, Volume 1. Louvain, Belgium: E. Peeters, and Leiden, The Netherlands: E. J. Brill, 1972.

CHAPTER 16

Modern Theories of Knowledge

"Sublime thoughts which tower above the clouds"

The Renaissance acquainted European philosophers with the works of ancient Greek skeptics for the first time in a thousand years. Philosophers of the seventeenth and eighteenth centuries saw it as the greatest threat to philosophy—and to the scientific revolution and the age of Enlightenment that accompanied it. They sought out ancient weapons with which to combat skepticism. Rationalists turned to Plato, whose theory of forms underwrote the possibility of objective knowledge, and to Augustine, whose insistence that some knowledge is self-evident inspired them. Empiricists turned to Aristotle, inspired by his image of the mind as a writing tablet on which nothing but sensation was capable of writing.

16.1 DESCARTES' FOUNDATIONALISM

René Descartes (1596–1650), French philosopher, scientist, and mathematician, was a contemporary of Thomas Hobbes, Galileo, John Milton, and Rembrandt. He is often considered the father of modern philosophy. Certainly he changed the course of Western philosophy by bringing the theory of knowledge to its center. Descartes puts skeptical arguments in their strongest form, and uses a new skeptical argument of his own in order to show that there is a foundation of certain beliefs on which all other knowledge rests.

Descartes seeks to stop the infinite regress of justification the skeptic alleges by finding foundational truths that cannot be doubted. His method is doubt itself. Descartes promises to doubt everything he can, to see whether anything emerges as an irrefutable foundation for knowledge.

Thus Descartes' method is to doubt everything he can, to discover truths that are certain. He says that illusion shows that we can doubt the evidence of our senses and that dreaming shows that we might be deceived not only about what our senses attest but about the body, the very existence and nature of our own physical frames. These arguments, Descartes believes, give us reason to doubt everything we have learned from our senses and, by extension, all the scientific knowledge we think we have of the world.

As Augustine argued, these arguments leave mathematics and logic untouched. Perhaps a person could be deceived about whether she has a body, but surely she knows that either she has a body or she does not.

A new skeptical argument, however, shows that even these beliefs might be incorrect. This argument is Descartes' famous thought experiment about an evil demon or "genius." Imagine that God has crafted us so that we are wrong not only about what we glean from our senses but also about what results from thought itself. Perhaps God has made our minds so that we go wrong every time we try to do a calculation or draw a conclusion. Now, God, Descartes will eventually argue, would not do that. But an evil genius might. We can imagine an evil genius who controls our every avenue of information, even our thought, and leads us astray. This possibility shows that we can be certain of nothing.

Or does it? Descartes finds one thing he can know even if an evil genius is deceiving him about everything else: "I am," "I exist" (in Latin, *sum*), is true every time it is thought. It is not necessarily true; the person thinking could be obliterated. But it is automatically true in the sense that it is true in every context in which it is thought or asserted. The same is true of "I think" (in Latin, *cogito*). In the *Principles of Philosophy*, Descartes connects the two in his famous *cogito, ergo sum* ("I think, therefore I am"). In the *Meditations*, however, they appear to be on a par; both are true whenever they are thought. They cannot be doubted. If you doubt that you exist, who is doing the doubting?

Descartes thus finds a secure foundation for knowledge. He cannot doubt that he exists; no skeptical arguments make any headway against "I think" or "I am."

Those two propositions, however, are a very narrow basis for science. Can we know anything about the world outside ourselves? Descartes's way of securing our knowledge of the world outside us depends on a proof of the existence of God. His line of reasoning proceeds from "I exist" to "God exists" because "I" (i.e., each of us, here, Descartes) have an idea of God that could not have been produced by an evil genius. The right idea of God is that God is good, indeed morally perfect, such that God would not allow it to come about that I am systematically deceived; therefore, what I think I know about the external world must, on the whole, be right.

Descartes thinks we can draw three conclusions even before saying anything about God. First, what am I? I can doubt the evidence of my senses or even my thought processes; I can doubt whether I have a body. What I cannot doubt is that I think. So I am essentially a thing that thinks. Everything else about me I can doubt. I cannot be sure that I have a body or that, if I do, it looks anything like I conceive it to look. But I cannot doubt that I doubt, understand, affirm, deny, will, feel, etc. The properties that are essential to me—without which I would not be what I am—are mental properties, not physical properties.

Second, I can know my own mind more directly and securely than I can know anything about my surroundings. It may be that I am deceived about everything around me, but I cannot be deceived about my own thoughts. As Descartes concludes, "I see clearly that there is nothing which is easier for me to know than my mind." This surprising conclusion sets the stage for much of the philosophical drama that transpired in Europe and the Americas over the subsequent several centuries.

Third, Descartes concludes that anything that I perceive clearly and distinctly must be true. He finds, in other words, an answer to the problem of the criterion. What allows me to distinguish the "I think" and "I am" from other things I can doubt? I know them clearly and distinctly. They are self-evident; they need no other justification. As we shall see in subsequent chapters, Descartes uses this criterion to prove God's existence and distinguish the aspects of our thoughts that correspond to reality from the aspects that do not.

Here we present most of the First Meditation of the six within Descartes' *Meditations on First Philosophy*. Please look also at the excerpts from the Second Meditation, in this book in Chapter 10.

16.1.1 René Descartes, from *Meditations on First Philosophy*

Meditation I: Of the Things Which May Be Brought within the Sphere of the Doubtful

It is now some years since I detected how many were the false beliefs that I had from my earliest youth admitted as true, and how doubtful was everything I had since constructed on this basis; and from that time I was convinced that I must once for all seriously undertake to rid myself of all the opinions which I had formerly accepted, and commence to build anew from the foundation, if I wanted to establish any firm and permanent structure in the sciences. But as this enterprise appeared to be a very great one, I waited until I had attained an age so mature that I could not hope that at any later date I should be better fitted to execute my design. This reason caused me to delay so long that I should feel that I was doing wrong were I to occupy in deliberation the time that yet remains to me for action. Today, then, since very opportunely for the plan I have in view I have delivered my mind from every care [and am happily agitated by no passions] and since I have procured for myself an assured leisure in a peaceable retirement, I shall at last seriously and freely address myself to the general upheaval of all my former opinions....

All that up to the present time I have accepted as most true and certain I have learned either from the senses or through the senses; but it is sometimes proved to me that these senses are deceptive, and it is wiser not to trust entirely to anything by which we have once been deceived.

But it may be that although the senses sometimes deceive us concerning things which are hardly perceptible, or very far away, there are yet many others to be met with as to which we cannot reasonably have any doubt, although we recognise them by their means. For example, there is the fact that I am here, seated by the fire, attired in a dressing gown, having this paper in my hands and

Source: René Descartes, *The Philosophical Works of Descartes*. Translated by Elizabeth S. Haldane. Cambridge: Cambridge University Press, 1911.

other similar matters. And how could I deny that these hands and this body are mine, were it not perhaps that I compare myself to certain persons, devoid of sense, whose cerebella are so troubled and clouded by the violent vapours of black bile that they constantly assure us that they think they are kings when they are really quite poor, or that they are clothed in purple when they are really without covering, or who imagine that they have an earthenware head or are nothing but pumpkins or are made of glass. But they are mad, and I should not be any the less insane were I to follow instances so extravagant.

At the same time I must remember that I am a man, and that consequently I am in the habit of sleeping, and in my dreams representing to myself the same things or sometimes even less probable things than do those who are insane in their waking moments. How often has it happened to me that in the night I dreamt that I found myself in this particular place, that I was dressed and seated near the fire, whilst in reality I was lying undressed in bed! At this moment it does indeed seem to me that it is with eyes awake that I am looking at this paper; that this head which I move is not asleep, that it is deliberately and of set purpose that I extend my hand and perceive it; what happens in sleep does not appear so clear nor so distinct as does all this. But in thinking over this I remind myself that on many occasions I have in sleep been deceived by similar illusions, and in dwelling carefully on this reflection I see so manifestly that there are no certain indications by which we may clearly distinguish wakefulness from sleep that I am lost in astonishment. And my astonishment is such that it is almost capable of persuading me that I now dream....

That is possibly why our reasoning is not unjust when we conclude from this that Physics, Astronomy, Medicine and all other sciences which have as their end the consideration of composite things are very dubious and uncertain; but that Arithmetic, Geometry and other sciences of that kind which only treat of things that are very simple and very general, without taking great trouble to ascertain whether they are actually existent or not, contain some measure of certainty and an element of the indubitable. For whether I am awake or asleep, two and three together always form five, and the square can never have more than four sides, and it does not seem possible that truths so clear and apparent can be suspected of any falsity [or uncertainty].

Nevertheless I have long had fixed in my mind the belief that an all-powerful God existed by whom I have been created such as I am. But how do I know that He has not brought it to pass that there is no earth, no heaven, no extended body, no magnitude, no place, and that nevertheless [I possess the perceptions of all these things and that] they seem to me to exist just exactly as I now see them? And, besides, as I sometimes imagine that others deceive themselves in the things which they think they know best, how do I know that I am not deceived every time that I add two and three, or count the sides of a square, or judge of things yet simpler, if anything simpler can be imagined? But possibly God has not desired that I should be thus deceived, for He is said to be supremely good. If, however, it is contrary to His goodness to have made me such that I constantly deceive myself, it would also appear to be contrary to His goodness to permit me to be sometimes deceived, and nevertheless I cannot doubt that He does permit this....

I shall then suppose, not that God who is supremely good and the fountain of truth, but some evil genius not less powerful than deceitful has employed his whole energies in deceiving me; I shall consider that the heavens, the earth, colours, figures, sound, and all other external things are nought but the illusions and dreams of which this genius has availed himself in order to lay traps for my credulity; I shall consider myself as having no hands, no eyes, no flesh, no blood, nor any senses, yet falsely believing myself to possess all these things; I shall remain obstinately attached to this idea, and if by this means it is not in my power to happen at the knowledge of any truth, I may at least do what is in my power [i.e., suspend my judgment], and with firm purpose avoid giving credence to any false thing, or being imposed upon by this arch deceiver, however powerful and deceptive he may be. But this task is a laborious one, and insensibly a certain lassitude leads me into the course of my ordinary life. And just as a captive who in sleep enjoys an imaginary liberty, when he begins to suspect that his liberty is but a dream, fears to awaken, and conspires with these agreeable illusions that the deception may be prolonged, so insensibly of my own accord I fall back into my former opinions, and I dread awakening from this slumber, lest the laborious wakefulness which would follow the tranquillity of this repose should have to be spent not in daylight, but in the excessive darkness of the difficulties which have just been discussed.

16.2 JOHN LOCKE'S EMPIRICISM

What can we know? What are the sources of knowledge? What are its limits? Philosophers addressing these questions in the early modern period in Europe split into two camps. Both have precursors in Aristotelian traditions of logic and science. *Empiricists* maintain that all knowledge of the world comes from experience. *Rationalists* maintain that it does not—that we can attain some knowledge of things independent of experience. Rationalists stress our innate, or inborn, capacities; empiricists treat our knowledge and concepts as acquired. Descartes (1596–1650), Spinoza (1632–1637), and Leibniz (1646–1716) are probably the three best-known rationalists. Empiricists have a whole sky of luminaries in the early modern period, from Francis Bacon (1561–1626), who stressed observation in scientific procedure and learning from nature, to Thomas Reid (1710–1796), the founder of commonsense philosophy. Two of the brightest stars are John Locke (1632–1704) and David Hume (1711–1776).

John Locke, a contemporary of Boyle, Leibniz, and Newton, is the first Western philosopher to distinguish truths of meaning from truths of fact. He is also the first Western philosopher to center his philosophy on empiricism. He was born in Wrington, England, into a liberal Puritan family. He earned a BA and an MA from Oxford and joined the faculty there as censor in moral philosophy. When he was 29, his father died, and he received a small inheritance. He studied medicine and became personal physician to the Earl of Shaftesbury. His scientific achievements earned him appointment to the Royal Society. Political turmoil in England led Locke to spend several years in France and Holland, where he became an advisor to William of Orange. The Glorious Revolution of 1688 enabled him to return to England in the company of the future queen, Mary. Locke finally published the *Essay Concerning Human Understanding* and the *Two Treatises of Government*, the philosophical works that made him famous, and served as Commissioner of the Board of Trade and Plantations with great distinction until failing health forced him to retire.

Locke says that what he calls "trifling propositions" have no real content about the world and thus "bring no increase to our knowledge." A trifling proposition has a predicate that is the same as its subject ("A soul is a soul") or part of the subject ("Lead is a metal"). Such propositions give us no real knowledge since they are true in virtue of meanings, or, as Locke says, mere ideas. The empiricist, insisting that all knowledge of fact comes from experience, sets them aside. It takes no experience to know that a soul is a soul, but it gives no knowledge of fact either. The currently employed technical terms, due to Kant, for truths of meaning and truths about things are *analytic* and *synthetic*. Locke claims that only the latter are the stuff of knowledge.

Locke also famously denies that we have innate ideas or concepts; the mind of a newborn child is a *tabula rasa*, a "blank slate" to be written on by experience. This position has come to be known as *concept empiricism*. Locke acknowledges that the mind has innate higher-order abilities, to manipulate concepts once we have them. The mind works on the raw material of experience and derives abstract ideas from impressions by separating, combining, negating, etc., the basic ideas so formed. Abstraction, negation, combination, and so on are cognitive abilities, but they are of higher order in that they operate on other concepts. No empiricist, in fact, should be interpreted as demeaning these abilities of the mind, which make it possible for us to learn. The chief issue between rationalists and empiricists concerns concepts that apply directly to things in the world.

16.2.1 John Locke, from *An Essay Concerning Human Understanding*

Introduction

3. *Method.* It is therefore worth while to search out the bounds between opinion and knowledge, and examine by what measures, in things whereof we have no certain knowledge, we ought to regulate our assent and moderate our persuasion. In order whereunto I shall pursue this following method:

First, I shall inquire into the original of those ideas, notions, or whatever else you please to call them, which a man observes, and is conscious to himself he has in his mind, and the ways whereby the understanding comes to be furnished with them.

Secondly, I shall endeavour to show what knowledge the understanding hath by those ideas, and the certainty, evidence, and extent of it.

Thirdly, I shall make some inquiry into the nature and [grounds] of faith or opinion: whereby I mean that assent which we give to any proposition as true, of whose truth yet we have no certain knowledge. And here we shall have occasion to examine the reasons and degrees of assent.

8. *What "idea" stands for.* Thus much I thought necessary to say concerning the occasion of this inquiry into human understanding. But, before I proceed on to what I have thought on this subject, I must here in the entrance beg pardon of my reader for the frequent use of the word *idea*, which he will find in the following treatise. It being that term which, I think, serves best to stand for whatsoever is the object of the understanding when a man thinks, I have used it to express whatever is meant by phantasm, notion, species, or whatever it is which the mind can be employed about in thinking; and I could not avoid frequently using it.

I presume it will be easily granted me that there are such ideas in men's minds: everyone is conscious of them in himself, and men's words and actions will satisfy him that they are in others.

Our first inquiry then shall be,—how they come into the mind.

Source: John Locke, *An Essay Concerning Human Understanding*. London: William Tegg, 1689.

Book I: Neither Principles nor Ideas Are Innate

Chapter I: No Innate Speculative Principles

1. *The way shown how we come by any knowledge, sufficient to prove it not innate.* It is an established opinion amongst some men, that there are in the understanding certain innate principles, some primary notions, *koinai ennoiai*, characters, as it were stamped upon the mind of man, which the soul receives in its very first being and brings into the world with it. It would be sufficient to convince unprejudiced readers of the falseness of this supposition, if I should only show (as I hope I shall in the following parts of this Discourse) how men, barely by the use of their natural faculties, may attain to all the knowledge they have without the help of any innate impressions; and may happen at certainty, without any such original notions or principles. For I imagine anyone will easily grant that it would be impertinent to suppose the ideas of colours innate in a creature to whom God hath given sight and a power to receive them by the eyes from external objects: and no less unreasonable would it be to attribute several truths to the impressions of nature, and innate characters, when we may observe in ourselves faculties fit to attain as easy and certain knowledge of them as if they were originally imprinted on the mind.

Book II: Of Ideas

Chapter I: Of Ideas in General, and Their Original

1. *Idea is the object of thinking.* Every man being conscious to himself that he thinks, and that which his mind is applied about whilst thinking being the ideas that are there, it is past doubt that men have in their minds several ideas, such as are those expressed by the words *whiteness, hardness, sweetness, thinking, motion, man, elephant, army, drunkenness,* and others: It is in the first place then to be inquired how he comes by them?

I know it is a received doctrine that men have native ideas, and original characters, stamped upon their minds in their very first being. This opinion I have at large examined already; and I suppose what I have said in the foregoing Book will be much more easily admitted when I have shown whence the understanding may get all the ideas it has, and by what ways and degrees they may come into the mind; for which I shall appeal to everyone's own observation and experience.

2. *All ideas come from sensation or reflection.* Let us then suppose the mind to be, as we say, white paper, void of all characters, without any ideas: How comes it to be furnished? Whence comes it by that vast store which the busy and boundless fancy of man has painted on it with an almost endless variety? Whence has it all the materials of reason and knowledge? To this I answer, in one word, from EXPERIENCE. In that all our knowledge is founded, and from that it ultimately derives itself. Our observation employed either about external sensible objects or about the internal operations of our minds perceived and reflected on by ourselves is that which supplies our understandings with all the materials of thinking. These two are the fountains of knowledge, from whence all the ideas we have, or can naturally have, do spring.

3. *The objects of sensation one source of ideas.* First, our senses, conversant about particular sensible objects, do convey into the mind several distinct perceptions of things, according to those various ways wherein those objects do affect them. And thus we come by those ideas we have of yellow, white, heat, cold, soft, hard, bitter, sweet, and all those which we call sensible qualities; which when I say the senses convey into the mind, I mean, they from external objects convey into the mind what produces there those perceptions. This great source of most of the ideas we have, depending wholly upon our senses, and derived by them to the understanding, I call SENSATION.

4. *The operations of our minds, the other source of them.* Secondly, the other fountain from which

experience furnisheth the understanding with ideas is the perception of the operations of our own mind within us, as it is employed about the ideas it has got; which operations, when the soul comes to reflect on and consider, do furnish the understanding with another set of ideas, which could not be had from things without. And such are perception, thinking, doubting, believing, reasoning, knowing, willing, and all the different actings of our own minds; which we being conscious of, and observing in ourselves, do from these receive into our understandings as distinct ideas as we do from bodies affecting our senses. This source of ideas every man has wholly in himself; and though it be not sense, as having nothing to do with external objects, yet it is very like it, and might properly enough be called internal sense. But as I call the other SENSATION, so I call this REFLECTION, the ideas it affords being such only as the mind gets by reflecting on its own operations within itself. By *reflection* then, in the following part of this discourse, I would be understood to mean that notice which the mind takes of its own operations, and the manner of them, by reason whereof there come to be ideas of these operations in the understanding. These two, I say, viz. external material things, as the objects of SENSATION, and the operations of our own minds within, as the objects of REFLECTION, are to me the only originals from whence all our ideas take their beginnings. The term *operations* here I use in a large sense, as comprehending not barely the actions of the mind about its ideas, but some sort of passions arising sometimes from them, such as is the satisfaction or uneasiness arising from any thought.

5. *All our ideas are of the one or the other of these.* The understanding seems to me not to have the least glimmering of any ideas which it doth not receive from one of these two. External objects furnish the mind with the ideas of sensible qualities, which are all those different perceptions they produce in us; and the mind furnishes the understanding with ideas of its own operations.

These, when we have taken a full survey of them, and their several modes, combinations, and relations, we shall find to contain all our whole stock of ideas, and that we have nothing in our minds which did not come in one of these two ways. Let anyone examine his own thoughts and thoroughly search into his understanding, and then let him tell me whether all the original ideas he has there are any other than of the objects of his senses, or of the operations of his mind, considered as objects of his reflection. And how great a mass of knowledge soever he imagines to be lodged there, he will, upon taking a strict view, see that he has not any idea in his mind but what one of these two have imprinted, though perhaps, with infinite variety compounded and enlarged by the understanding, as we shall see hereafter.

24. *The original of all our knowledge.* In time the mind comes to reflect on its own operations about the ideas got by sensation, and thereby stores itself with a new set of ideas, which I call ideas of reflection. These are the impressions that are made on our senses by outward objects that are extrinsical to the mind; and its own operations, proceeding from powers intrinsical and proper to itself, which, when reflected on by itself, become also objects of its contemplation, are, as I have said, the original of all knowledge. Thus the first capacity of human intellect is that the mind is fitted to receive the impressions made on it, either through the senses by outward objects or by its own operations when it reflects on them. This is the first step a man makes towards the discovery of anything and the earthwork whereon to build all those notions whichever he shall have naturally in this world. All those sublime thoughts which tower above the clouds, and reach as high as heaven itself, take their rise and footing here: in all that great extent wherein the mind wanders, in those remote speculations it may seem to be elevated with, it stirs not one jot beyond those ideas which sense or reflection have offered for its contemplation.

25. *In the reception of simple ideas, the understanding is for the most part passive.* In this part

the understanding is merely passive; and whether or no it will have these beginnings, and as it were materials of knowledge, is not in its own power. For the objects of our senses do, many of them, obtrude their particular ideas upon our minds whether we will or not; and the operations of our minds will not let us be without, at least, some obscure notions of them. No man can be wholly ignorant of what he does when he thinks. These simple ideas, when offered to the mind, the understanding can no more refuse to have, nor alter when they are imprinted, nor blot them out and make new ones itself, than a mirror can refuse, alter, or obliterate the images or ideas which the objects set before it do therein produce. As the bodies that surround us do diversely affect our organs, the mind is forced to receive the impressions, and cannot avoid the perception of those ideas that are annexed to them.

Chapter II: Of Simple Ideas

1. *Uncompounded appearances.* The better to understand the nature, manner, and extent of our knowledge, one thing is carefully to be observed concerning the ideas we have; and that is that some of them are simple and some complex.

Though the qualities that affect our senses are, in the things themselves, so united and blended that there is no separation, no distance between them, yet it is plain, the ideas they produce in the mind enter by the senses simple and unmixed. For, though the sight and touch often take in from the same object, at the same time, different ideas;—as a man sees at once motion and colour; the hand feels softness and warmth in the same piece of wax: yet the simple ideas thus united in the same subject are as perfectly distinct as those that come in by different senses. The coldness and hardness which a man feels in a piece of ice being as distinct ideas in the mind as the smell and whiteness of a lily; or as the taste of sugar, and smell of a rose. And there is nothing can be plainer to a man than the clear and distinct perception he has of those simple ideas, which, being each in itself uncompounded, contains in it nothing but one uniform appearance, or conception in the mind, and is not distinguishable into different ideas.

Chapter XXXI: Of Adequate and Inadequate Ideas

1. *Adequate ideas are such as perfectly represent their archetypes.* Of our real ideas, some are adequate, and some are inadequate. Those I call adequate, which perfectly represent those archetypes which the mind supposes them taken from: which it intends them to stand for, and to which it refers them. Inadequate ideas are such, which are but a partial or incomplete representation of those archetypes to which they are referred. Upon which account it is plain—

2. *Simple ideas all adequate.* First, that all our simple ideas are adequate. Because, being nothing but the effects of certain powers in things, fitted and ordained by God to produce such sensations in us, they cannot but be correspondent and adequate to those powers: and we are sure they agree to the reality of things. For, if sugar produce in us the ideas which we call whiteness and sweetness, we are sure there is a power in sugar to produce those ideas in our minds, or else they could not have been produced by it. And so each sensation answering the power that operates on any of our senses, the idea so produced is a real idea (and not a fiction of the mind, which has no power to produce any simple idea); and cannot but be adequate, since it ought only to answer that power: and so all simple ideas are adequate. It is true, the things producing in us these simple ideas are but few of them denominated by us, as if they were only the causes of them; but [they are denominated by us] as if those ideas were real beings in them.

For, though fire be called painful to the touch, whereby is signified the power of producing in us the idea of pain, yet it is denominated also light and hot; as if light and heat were really something in the fire, more than a power to excite these ideas in us; and therefore are called qualities in or of the fire. But these being nothing, in truth, but powers to excite such ideas in us, I must in that sense be understood when I speak of secondary qualities as being in things; or of their ideas as being the objects that excite them in us. Such ways of speaking, though accommodated to the vulgar notions without which one cannot be well understood, yet truly signify nothing but those powers which are in things to excite certain sensations or ideas in us. Since were there no fit organs to receive the impressions fire makes on the sight and touch, nor a mind joined to those organs to receive the ideas of light and heat by those impressions from the fire or sun, there would yet be no more light or heat in the world than there would be pain if there were no sensible creature to feel it, though the sun should continue just as it is now, and Mount Etna flame higher than ever it did. Solidity and extension, and the termination of it, figure, with motion and rest, whereof we have the ideas, would be really in the world as they are, whether there were any sensible being to perceive them or no: and therefore we have reason to look on those as the real modifications of matter, and such as are the exciting causes of all our various sensations from bodies. But this being an inquiry not belonging to this place, I shall enter no further into it, but proceed to show what complex ideas are adequate, and what not.

16.3 LEIBNIZ'S RATIONALISM

Gottfried Wilhelm Leibniz (1646–1716), a polymath and European diplomat writing in Latin, French, and German, and a contemporary of Locke and Newton, presents a sustained argument for rationalism. Leibniz argues that we have innate concepts and innate knowledge of synthetic necessary truths. Leibniz calls a proposition ***necessary*** if it cannot be false, if it is true, to use his phrase, in every possible world. A proposition is ***impossible*** if it cannot be true—if it is true in no possible world—and ***contingent*** if it is neither necessary nor impossible, that is, if it is true in some possible worlds and false in others. "Every effect has a cause" is necessary, true by virtue of the meanings of its terms. "Every event has a cause" is also true in every possible world, by the necessity of causal relations in any world that could be created by God. "Caesar crossed the Rubicon" is contingent; it could be true or false, depending on what else is true.

Leibniz is a concept rationalist who believes that the mind has not only certain structures independent of experience but also a certain conceptual content. Not all concepts derive from experience; some shape experience. The subtlety of the shaping accounts for confusions on the part of empiricists such as Locke. Leibniz also holds, with Descartes and against Locke, that by deductive methods beginning from innate ideas we come to know not just "trifling propositions" but also real facts about the world. He is then, to boot, a judgment rationalist, holding that some of our knowledge of the world is deducible from innate concepts in a priori fashion.

Leibniz views himself as working within a Platonic tradition. So let us review a line of thought broached in the *Meno* and developed in the *Republic* and Plato's later dialogues: knowledge by recollection of innate ideas or forms.

Consider a judgment of perception, for example, "This is a triangle" (spoken as the speaker points to a figure on a blackboard). According to Plato, the mind making this judgment is Janus-faced. It is turned toward a perceptual object, a triangle, if it judges correctly. It is also turned toward the abstract form of a triangle. Both the object and the form have real explanatory power. The object is causally responsible for our perception of it; we are able to perceive it as a triangle only because we apprehend the general form of triangularity. The form of a triangle is exemplified in the triangle itself, which in turn is an instance of, or, in Plato's technical language, *participates* in the form.

How can an empiricist, Leibniz asks, account for the regularities in our experience? Locke's *Essay* relies on generalities. Regularities and general principles account for repeated experience and our ability to identify a thing from one occasion to the next. They explain how different people can think the same thought. Moreover, they explain how thoughts can be veridical, that is, accurate in representing the world. Locke's notion of "abstraction," says Leibniz, is insufficient to do all this work. We do not abstract the idea of a pure triangle from triangular objects we perceive; indeed, we never encounter a pure triangle in experience. Instead, we recognize objects as triangular because we apprehend the form of pure triangularity and recognize that the objects approximate that pure form. In this sense, the forms have causal power; we are able to think of things as triangular by apprehending the form.

Now, medieval rationalists claimed to know many a priori truths, not only truths of metaphysics ("The world consists of substances and their attributes," "Every substance has an essence," "The will is free," etc.), but also truths of theology ("God exists," "The soul is immortal," etc.) and morality ("One ought to seek the good," "Happiness is good for its own sake," "Courage is a virtue," etc.). Some of these may seem questionable, and surely all are worthy of debate. But giving up all of them would seem to bankrupt philosophy. Are we able to do philosophy without any synthetic a priori truths?

Rationalists argue that experience is far too poor to yield the knowledge we have. Throw out a priori truths about the world, Leibniz contends, and you throw out more than metaphysics, theology, and morality; you throw out all knowledge of universal truths that are necessary in any other way than as mere definitions.

We may put Leibniz's argument in the following form:

1. Experience is always of particular instances.
2. Knowledge immediately justified by experience is always of particular instances.
3. Universal truths do not follow from their instances.
4. Therefore: Universal truths cannot be justified by experience.

Consider, for example, Newton's law, $F = ma$ (force is equal to mass times acceleration). This holds for all bodies, in all places, at all times. It is moreover necessary; we can use it to make predictions and draw conclusions not only about circumstances that do exist but also about circumstances that might exist. (In contemporary philosophical language, laws such as $F = ma$ support counterfactual reasoning—reasoning about what would happen if such and such were to happen—as well as reasoning about actual courses of events.) Now, this law is well confirmed scientifically. Still, it has been tested only finitely many times; our experience falls far short of supporting it for all objects in all places and times. The rationalist argument, then, is this. Much of our knowledge of the world—especially our knowledge of basic mathematical and scientific laws—we hold to be necessary and universal, applying to all objects in all places at all times. Nothing in experience can justify those claims to universality and necessity. We thus face a dilemma: Admit innate concepts and a priori knowledge about things, or abandon mathematics and science as unjustified. One cannot be a principled, empiricist skeptic about metaphysics and theology without also being a skeptic about mathematics and science.

If there are innate concepts and a priori truths that reveal the necessary nature of the world, what are they? Leibniz gives some examples of innate concepts—"being, unity, substance, duration, change, activity, perception, pleasure"—and he attempts to derive all truths about the world known a priori from truths of logic, mathematics, and meaning plus one further principle that he derives, like Descartes, from the idea of God: the principle of sufficient reason. The truths of mathematics, logic, and meaning themselves follow from a single principle, the principle of contradiction (for any proposition p, not both p and not-p), and all truths about the world from those together with the principle of sufficient reason.

16.3.1 G. W. Leibniz, from *New Essays Concerning Human Understanding*

Preface

Although the author of the *Essay* says a thousand beautiful things that I applaud, our systems differ greatly. His has more in common with Aristotle, and mine with Plato, though we depart from the doctrines from these two ancient philosophers on many issues....

Our disagreements are on subjects of some importance. It is a question of knowing whether the soul in itself is empty entirely like a page on which one has not written anything (*tabula rasa*), as Aristotle and Locke maintain, and all that is traced there comes only from the senses and experience; or whether the soul contains originally the principles of several concepts and doctrines which external objects only awaken on certain occasions, as I believe, along with Plato and even the Schoolmen, as well as all those who understand the significance of the passage of St. Paul (Romans 2:15) that declares that the law of God is written in our hearts. The Stoics called these first principles, i.e., fundamental assumptions, or what one takes for granted in advance. The mathematicians call them Common Notions. The modern philosophers give them other beautiful names, and Jules Scaliger in particular named them *Semina aeternitatis*, "eternal seeds," "living fires or flashes of light" hidden inside us but made visible by the stimulation of the senses as sparks struck on steel. And it is not without reason that we believe that these flashes mark something divine and eternal that appears especially in necessary truths.

This raises another question, whether knowledge of all truths depends on experience, i.e., on induction from particular cases, or if there are some which have another foundation. For if some events can be foreseen before any test is made of them, it is manifest that we contribute something of our own. The senses, though *necessary* for all

Source: G. W. Leibniz, *New Essays Concerning Human Understanding*. Translated by Daniel Bonevac.

our current knowledge, are not *sufficient* to provide them all, since the senses never give anything but *instances*, i.e., particular or individual truths. All the instances that confirm a general truth, however, no matter how numerous they are, are not enough to establish the universal necessity of this same truth, because it does not follow that what has happened will always happen in the same way. For example, the Greeks, Romans, and all the other peoples of the earth always noticed that after 24 hours passed, day changes into night and night into day. But they would have been mistaken if they had believed that the same rule is observed everywhere, since we observe the opposite in the region of the North Pole. And anyone who believes that it is a necessary and eternal truth in our climate, at least, would still be mistaken, since the earth and the sun do not even exist necessarily. There may come a time, perhaps, when this beautiful star will not be there any more, at least in its present form, and the solar system will perish with it.

From this it appears that necessary truths, such as those found in pure mathematics, and particularly in arithmetic and in geometry, must have principles the proof of which does not depend on their instances, nor, consequently, on the testimony of the senses; though without the senses it would never have occurred to us to think of them. It is necessary to distinguish what Euclid understood so well, what is demonstrated on the basis of reason, from what is seen on the basis of experience and sensory images. Logic, along with metaphysics and morals—one of which comprises theology, and the other jurisprudence—are full of such truths, and consequently their proof can come only from internal principles that are innate. It is true that it should not be thought that we can read these eternal laws of reason in the heart as in an opened book, as the edict of the herald is read from his scroll, without toil and research. But it is enough that one can discover them through attention to occasions provided by the senses. The success of experiments confirms reason, just as checks are useful in arithmetic to avoid errors of calculation when the reasoning is long.

This is how our knowledge differs from that of animals: animals are purely empirical, and do nothing but be ruled by instances. As far as we can judge, they never manage to form necessary propositions. Human beings are capable of deductive sciences. The faculty of reasoning in animals forms consecutions [progressions of thought] of a lower order than those characteristic of human reason. Consecutions of animals are purely like those of a simple empiric who claims that what happened sometimes will happen again in a case that strikes him as similar, without being able to judge whether the same reasons remain operative. This is why it is so easy for men to catch animals, and why it is so easy for a simple empiric to make mistakes.... Consecutions of animals are only a shadow of reasoning—that is, they are only connections in imagination, the passage from one image to another. In a new case that appears similar to a previous one, an animal expects just what happened before, as if the things were connected in fact because their images are connected in memory. It is true that reason ordinarily leads us to expect to find in the future what conforms with our long experience of the past, but it is not for all a necessary and infallible truth, and it can fail when one least expects it—when the factors that maintained the pattern change. This is why the wisest do not trust it; they try to probe (if it is possible) the reason for a fact to judge when exceptions will have to be made. For reason is only able

- to lay down steadfast rules,
- to compensate for what it misses by making exceptions, and, finally,
- to find logical connections certain due to the force of necessary consequences.

This often gives us a way to foresee an event without needing to observe the connections between images, as animals are reduced to doing. So, what justifies the internal principles of necessary truths also distinguishes man from animal.

Perhaps Locke will not reject my view entirely. For, after having employed all his first book to reject innate illumination, understood in a certain way, he acknowledges at the beginning of the second book and from there on that ideas that do not have their origin in sensation come from reflection. However, reflection is just attention to what is *in* us, and sensation does not give us what we already carry with us. That being the case, can one deny that much is innate in our minds, since we are innate, so to speak, to ourselves, and that there is in us, to wit:

- Unit,
- Substance,
- Duration,
- Change,
- Action,
- Perception,
- Pleasure,

and a thousand other objects of our intellectual ideas? These objects being immediate and always present in our understanding—though they can't always be seen because of our distractions and our needs—why be astonished that we say that these ideas are innate in us, with all that follows from it? I have also made use of the analogy of a veined slab of marble rather than a smooth marble slab, or an empty page, i.e., what philosophers call a *tabula rasa*. For if the soul resembled an empty page, truths would be in us as the figure of Hercules is in a slab of marble when the marble is completely indifferent to receive this or that figure. But if there were veins in the stone which marked the figure of Hercules in preference to other figures, Hercules would be innate there in some fashion, though we would need to work to discover these veins, and to clean them by polishing, while cutting off what obscures them. Thus ideas and truths are innate in us, like inclinations, natural dispositions, tendencies, or potentialities, and not like actions, though these potentialities are always accompanied by certain often insensitive mental acts that answer to them.

It seems that Locke claims that there is nothing potential in us and even nothing that we do not always realize; but he cannot maintain that rigorously. Otherwise, his view would be too paradoxical. We are not always aware of the dispositions and tendencies we have. Our memories are not always before us; they don't always come to our help when we need them, even though we often easily call them to mind on some light occasion that makes us remember, just as it is not necessary for us to hear the beginning of a song to recall the remainder. Locke limits his thesis in other places by saying that there is nothing in us that we weren't aware of at some earlier time. But nobody can guarantee by reason alone how far our forgotten apperceptions might extend. The Platonic doctrine of reminiscence, fabulous as it is, does not contain anything nakedly incompatible with reason. In addition, say I, why is it necessary that we acquire everything by apperceptions of external things? Why can we unearth nothing in ourselves? Is our soul by itself a vacuum, which without borrowed images from outside would be nothing? That (I am sure) is not a view that Locke would approve. And where can we find pages that do not vary in any respect? Do we ever see a perfectly smooth and uniform surface? Why, therefore, couldn't we provide ourselves with some object of thought from our own depths, if we decide to dig there? Thus I am brought to believe that in its content his view on this point is not so different from common sense—the more so as it recognizes two sources of our knowledge, sensation and reflection....

16.4 HUME'S EMPIRICISM

David Hume (1711–1776), a contemporary of Voltaire, Rousseau, Handel, Bach, and fellow Scotsman Adam Smith, develops empiricism in rigorous fashion. He entered the

University of Edinburgh at age 12. After dabbling at careers in law and business, he went to France and wrote *A Treatise of Human Nature*, his greatest philosophical work, when still in his 20s. He argued for a skeptical empiricism, maintaining that all knowledge comes from sense experience and that, therefore, we can have no knowledge of anything beyond experience. Hume never held an academic position. But he achieved fame in his own lifetime as a writer, more for his economic and historical works than for his philosophical ones.

Hume admitted the problems pointed out by Leibniz concerning the limitations of experience. His solutions, however, are in line with the tradition of British empiricism. Someone deaf from birth has no notion of sound; someone blind from birth no idea of color. People who have not tasted wine have no "notion of the relish of wine." They do not know what the words mean. People who talk beyond their experience talk nonsense. Thus when we hear the high-sounding philosophies of the rationalists, we should ask ourselves, what are the experiences from which such ideas could arise? If there are no such experiences, so much the worse for the theories.

As philosophers and scientists, we must recognize the limitations of experience. Induction, for example, is a scandal, Hume says. Having affirmed experience as the only source of evidence for questions of fact, he argues that "even after we have experience of the operations of cause and effect, our conclusions from that experience are not founded on reasoning, or any process of the understanding." We do draw universal conclusions from finite evidence, but we have no reason to do so. We have no justification. This is the celebrated scandal. Inductive inferences have no rational justification.

Consider a few inductive inferences from lists of cases to universal conclusions or further instances:

- All ravens that have been observed are black. So all ravens are black.
- Whenever Jane has eaten bread, she has found it nourishing. So she'll find this bread nourishing.
- When the sun has set, it has always risen the next morning. So the sun will rise tomorrow.

Hume points out that such reasoning cannot be a priori. The conclusions are certainly not necessary. The next raven we encounter might be albino. The bread might make Jane sick. Before dawn the sun could go nova. Support for these inferences must come from experience.

But how can experience justify them? The issue is precisely how experience, by its nature finite and limited, can support universal conclusions. So to appeal to experience would be to beg the question. In short, there is no rational justification for inductive generalization and the assumption that the future will resemble the past. We make such assumptions as a matter of custom or habit, not as a matter of reason. Of course, we do make inductive leaps launched from experience. But we should recognize that in the end we rely only on custom or convention. Necessity is not in the world but in us.

16.4.1 David Hume, from *An Enquiry Concerning Human Understanding*

Of the Origin of Ideas

Everyone will readily allow that there is a considerable difference between the perceptions of the mind, when a man feels the pain of excessive heat, or the pleasure of moderate warmth, and when he afterwards recalls to his memory this sensation or anticipates it by his imagination. These faculties may mimic or copy the perceptions of the senses; but they never can entirely reach the force and vivacity of the original sentiment. The utmost we say of them, even when they operate with greatest vigour, is that they represent their object in so lively a manner that we could almost say we feel or see it: But, except the mind be disordered by disease or madness, they never can arrive at such a pitch of vivacity as to render these perceptions altogether undistinguishable. All the colours of poetry, however splendid, can never paint natural objects in such a manner as to make the description be taken for a real landskip. The most lively thought is still inferior to the dullest sensation.

We may observe a like distinction to run through all the other perceptions of the mind. A man in a fit of anger is actuated in a very different manner from one who only thinks of that emotion. If you tell me that any person is in love, I easily understand your meaning, and form a just conception of his situation; but never can mistake that conception for the real disorders and agitations of the passion. When we reflect on our past sentiments and affections, our thought is a faithful mirror and copies its objects truly; but the colours which it employs are faint and dull, in comparison of those in which our original perceptions were clothed. It requires no nice discernment or metaphysical head to mark the distinction between them.

Here therefore we may divide all the perceptions of the mind into two classes or species, which are distinguished by their different degrees of force and vivacity. The less forcible and lively are commonly denominated *Thoughts* or *Ideas.* The other species want a name in our language, and in most others, I suppose, because it was not requisite for any but philosophical purposes to rank them under a general term or appellation. Let us, therefore, use a little freedom, and call them *Impressions*, employing that word in a sense somewhat different from the usual. By the term *impression*, then, I mean all our more lively perceptions, when we hear, or see, or feel, or love, or hate, or desire, or will. And impressions are distinguished from ideas, which are the less lively perceptions of which we are conscious when we reflect on any of those sensations or movements above mentioned.

Nothing, at first view, may seem more unbounded than the thought of man, which not only escapes all human power and authority, but is not even restrained within the limits of nature and reality. To form monsters, and join incongruous shapes and appearances, costs the imagination no more trouble than to conceive the most natural and familiar objects. And while the body is confined to one planet, along which it creeps with pain and difficulty; the thought can in an instant transport us into the most distant regions of the universe; or even beyond the universe, into the unbounded chaos, where nature is supposed to lie in total confusion. What never was seen, or heard of, may yet be conceived; nor is anything beyond the power of thought except what implies an absolute contradiction.

But though our thought seems to possess this unbounded liberty, we shall find, upon a nearer

Source: David Hume, *An Enquiry Concerning Human Understanding*. London, 1748.

examination, that it is really confined within very narrow limits, and that all this creative power of the mind amounts to no more than the faculty of compounding, transposing, augmenting, or diminishing the materials afforded us by the senses and experience. When we think of a golden mountain, we only join two consistent ideas, gold, and mountain, with which we were formerly acquainted. A virtuous horse we can conceive; because, from our own feeling, we can conceive virtue; and this we may unite to the figure and shape of a horse, which is an animal familiar to us. In short, all the materials of thinking are derived either from our outward or inward sentiment: the mixture and composition of these belong alone to the mind and will. Or, to express myself in philosophical language, all our ideas or more feeble perceptions are copies of our impressions or more lively ones. To prove this, the two following arguments will, I hope, be sufficient. First, when we analyze our thoughts or ideas, however compounded or sublime, we always find that they resolve themselves into such simple ideas as were copied from a precedent feeling or sentiment. Even those ideas, which, at first view, seem the most wide of this origin, are found, upon a nearer scrutiny, to be derived from it. The idea of God, as meaning an infinitely intelligent, wise, and good Being, arises from reflecting on the operations of our own mind, and augmenting, without limit, those qualities of goodness and wisdom. We may prosecute this enquiry to what length we please; where we shall always find that every idea which we examine is copied from a similar impression. Those who would assert that this position is not universally true nor without exception have only one, and that an easy method of refuting it; by producing that idea, which, in their opinion, is not derived from this source. It will then be incumbent on us, if we would maintain our doctrine, to produce the impression, or lively perception, which corresponds to it....

There is, however, one contradictory phenomenon, which may prove that it is not absolutely impossible for ideas to arise independent of their correspondent impressions. I believe it will readily be allowed that the several distinct ideas of colour, which enter by the eye, or those of sound, which are conveyed by the ear, are really different from each other, though, at the same time, resembling. Now if this be true of different colours, it must be no less so of the different shades of the same colour; and each shade produces a distinct idea, independent of the rest. For if this should be denied, it is possible, by the continual gradation of shades, to run a colour insensibly into what is most remote from it; and if you will not allow any of the means to be different, you cannot, without absurdity, deny the extremes to be the same. Suppose, therefore, a person to have enjoyed his sight for thirty years, and to have become perfectly acquainted with colours of all kinds except one particular shade of blue, for instance, which it never has been his fortune to meet with. Let all the different shades of that colour, except that single one, be placed before him, descending gradually from the deepest to the lightest; it is plain that he will perceive a blank, where that shade is wanting, and will be sensible that there is a greater distance in that place between the contiguous colour than in any other. Now I ask, whether it be possible for him, from his own imagination, to supply this deficiency, and raise up to himself the idea of that particular shade, though it had never been conveyed to him by his senses? I believe there are few but will be of opinion that he can: and this may serve as a proof that the simple ideas are not always, in every instance, derived from the correspondent impressions, though this instance is so singular that it is scarcely worth our observing, and does not merit that for it alone we should alter our general maxim.

Here, therefore, is a proposition, which not only seems, in itself, simple and intelligible, but, if a proper use were made of it, might render every dispute equally intelligible, and banish all that jargon which has so long taken possession of metaphysical reasonings and drawn disgrace upon them. All ideas, especially abstract ones, are naturally faint and obscure: the mind has but a slender hold of them: they are apt to be confounded with other resembling ideas; and when we have often employed any term, though without a distinct meaning, we are apt to imagine it has a determinate idea annexed to it. On the contrary, all impressions, that is, all sensations, either outward or inward, are strong and vivid: the limits between them are more exactly determined; nor is it easy to fall into any error or mistake with regard to them. When we entertain therefore, any suspicion that a philosophical term is employed without any meaning or idea (as is but too frequent), we need but enquire from what impression is that supposed idea derived? And if it be impossible to assign any, this will serve to confirm our suspicion. By bringing ideas into so clear a light we may reasonably hope to remove all dispute which may arise concerning their nature and reality.

Sceptical Doubts concerning the Operations of the Understanding

Part I

All the objects of human reason or enquiry may naturally be divided into two kinds, to wit, *Relations of Ideas* and *Matters of Fact*. Of the first kind are the sciences of Geometry, Algebra, and Arithmetic; and in short, every affirmation which is either intuitively or demonstratively certain. That the square of the hypothenuse is equal to the square of the two sides is a proposition which expresses a relation between these figures. That three times five is equal to the half of thirty expresses a relation between these numbers. Propositions of this kind are discoverable by the mere operation of thought, without dependence on what is anywhere existent in the universe. Though there never were a circle or triangle in nature, the truths demonstrated by Euclid would forever retain their certainty and evidence.

Matters of fact, which are the second objects of human reason, are not ascertained in the same manner; nor is our evidence of their truth, however great, of a like nature with the foregoing. The contrary of every matter of fact is still possible; because it can never imply a contradiction and is conceived by the mind with the same facility and distinctness as if ever so conformable to reality. That the sun will not rise tomorrow is no less intelligible a proposition, and implies no more contradiction than the affirmation, that it will rise. We should in vain, therefore, attempt to demonstrate its falsehood. Were it demonstratively false, it would imply a contradiction, and could never be distinctly conceived by the mind.

It may, therefore, be a subject worthy of curiosity, to enquire what is the nature of that evidence which assures us of any real existence and matter of fact, beyond the present testimony of our senses or the records of our memory....

All reasonings concerning matter of fact seem to be founded on the relation of Cause and Effect. By means of that relation alone we can go beyond the evidence of our memory and senses. If you were to ask a man why he believes any matter of fact, which is absent; for instance, that his friend is in the country, or in France; he would give you a reason; and this reason would be some other fact; as a letter received from him, or the knowledge of his former resolutions and promises. A man finding a watch or any other machine in a desert island would conclude that there had once been men in that island. All our reasonings concerning fact are of the same nature. And here it is constantly supposed that there is a connexion between the present fact and that which is inferred from it. Were there nothing to bind them together, the inference would be entirely precarious. The hearing of an articulate voice and rational discourse in the dark assures us of the presence of some person: Why? because these are the effects of the human make and fabric and closely connected with it. If we anatomize all the other reasonings of this nature, we shall find that they are founded on the relation of cause and effect and that this relation is either near or remote, direct or collateral. Heat and light are collateral effects of fire, and the one effect may justly be inferred from the other.

If we would satisfy ourselves, therefore, concerning the nature of that evidence which assures us of matters of fact, we must enquire how we arrive at the knowledge of cause and effect.

I shall venture to affirm, as a general proposition which admits of no exception, that the knowledge of this relation is not, in any instance, attained by reasonings a priori, but arises entirely from experience, when we find that any particular objects are constantly conjoined with each other. Let an object be presented to a man of ever so strong natural reason and abilities, if that object be entirely new to him, he will not be able, by the most accurate examination of its sensible qualities, to discover any of its causes or effects. Adam, though his rational faculties be supposed, at the very first, entirely perfect, could not have inferred from the fluidity and transparency of water that it would suffocate him, or from the light and warmth of fire that it would consume him. No object ever discovers, by the qualities which appear to the senses, either the causes which produced it, or the effects which will arise from it; nor can our reason, unassisted by experience, ever draw any inference concerning real existence and matter of fact.

This proposition, that causes and effects are discoverable not by reason but by experience, will readily be admitted with regard to such objects as we remember to have once been altogether unknown to us, since we must be conscious of the utter inability, which we then lay under, of foretelling what would arise from them. Present two smooth pieces of marble to a man who has no tincture of natural philosophy; he will never discover that they will adhere together in such a manner as to require great force to separate them in a direct line while they make so small a resistance to a lateral pressure. Such events as bear little analogy to the common course of nature are also readily confessed to be known only by experience; nor does any man imagine that the explosion of gunpowder, or the attraction of a loadstone, could ever be discovered by arguments a priori. In like manner, when an effect is supposed to depend upon an intricate machinery or secret structure of parts, we make no difficulty in attributing all our knowledge of it to experience. Who will assert that he can give the ultimate reason why milk or bread is proper nourishment for a man, not for a lion or a tiger?

But the same truth may not appear, at first sight, to have the same evidence with regard to events which have become familiar to us from our first appearance in the world, which bear a close analogy to the whole course of nature, and which are supposed to depend on the simple qualities of objects without any secret structure of parts. We are apt to imagine that we could discover these effects by the mere operation of our reason, without experience. We fancy that were we brought of a sudden into this world, we could at first have inferred that one billiard-ball would communicate motion to another upon impulse, and that we needed not to have waited for the event, in order to pronounce with certainty concerning it. Such is the influence of custom that, where it is strongest, it not only covers our natural ignorance, but even conceals itself, and seems not to take place, merely because it is found in the highest degree.

But to convince us that all the laws of nature, and all the operations of bodies without exception, are known only by experience, the following reflections may, perhaps, suffice. Were any object presented to us, and were we required to pronounce concerning the effect which will result from it without consulting past observation, after what manner, I beseech you, must the mind proceed in this operation? It must invent or imagine some event, which it ascribes to the object as its effect; and it is plain that this invention must be entirely arbitrary. The mind can never possibly find the effect in the supposed cause by the most accurate scrutiny and examination. For the effect is totally different from the cause, and consequently can never be discovered in it. Motion in the second billiard-ball is a quite distinct event from motion in the first; nor is there anything in the one to suggest the smallest hint of the other. A stone or piece of metal raised into the air, and left without any support, immediately falls: but to consider the matter a priori, is there anything we discover in this situation which can beget the idea of a downward, rather than an upward, or any other motion in the stone or metal?

And as the first imagination or invention of a particular effect, in all natural operations, is arbitrary where we consult not experience, so must we also esteem the supposed tie or connexion between the cause and effect, which binds them together and renders it impossible that any other effect could result from the operation of that cause. When I see, for instance, a billiard-ball moving in a straight line towards another, even suppose motion in the second ball should by accident be suggested to me as the result of their contact or impulse, may I not conceive that a hundred different events might as well follow from that cause? May not both these balls remain at absolute rest? May not the first ball return in a straight line, or leap off from the second in any line or direction? All these suppositions are consistent and conceivable. Why then should we give the preference to one which is no more consistent or conceivable than the rest? All our reasonings a priori will never be able to show us any foundation for this preference.

In a word, then, every effect is a distinct event from its cause. It could not, therefore, be discovered in the cause, and the first invention or conception of it, a priori, must be entirely arbitrary. And even after it is suggested, the conjunction of it with the cause must appear equally arbitrary, since there are always many other effects which to reason must seem fully as consistent and natural. In vain, therefore, should we pretend to determine any single event, or infer any cause or effect, without the assistance of observation and experience.

Sceptical Doubts concerning the Operations of the Understanding

Part II

But we have not yet attained any tolerable satisfaction with regard to the question first proposed. Each solution still gives rise to a new question as difficult as the foregoing and leads us on to farther enquiries. When it is asked, What is the nature of all our reasonings concerning matter of fact? the proper answer seems to be, that they are founded on the relation of cause and effect. When again it is asked, What is the foundation of all our reasonings and conclusions concerning that relation? it may be replied in one word, Experience. But if we still carry on our sifting humour and ask, What is the foundation of all conclusions from experience? this implies a new question, which may be of more difficult solution and explication. Philosophers, that give themselves airs of superior wisdom and sufficiency, have a hard task when they encounter persons of inquisitive dispositions, who push them from every corner to which they retreat, and who are sure at last to bring them to some dangerous dilemma. The best expedient to prevent this confusion is to be modest in our pretensions, and even to discover the difficulty ourselves before it is objected to us. By this means, we may make a kind of merit of our very ignorance.

I shall content myself, in this section, with an easy task, and shall pretend only to give a negative answer to the question here proposed. I say then, that, even after we have experience of the operations of cause and effect, our conclusions from that experience are not founded on reasoning, or any process of the understanding. This answer we must endeavour both to explain and to defend.

All reasonings may be divided into two kinds, namely, demonstrative reasoning, or that concerning relations of ideas, and moral reasoning, or that concerning matter of fact and existence. That there are no demonstrative arguments in the case seems evident, since it implies no contradiction that the course of nature may change, and that an object, seemingly like those which we have experienced, may be attended with different or contrary effects. May I not clearly and distinctly conceive that a body, falling from the clouds, and which, in all other respects, resembles snow, has yet the taste of salt or feeling of fire? Is there any more intelligible proposition than to affirm that all the trees will flourish in December and January and decay in May and June? Now whatever is intelligible, and can be distinctly conceived, implies no contradiction, and can never be proved false by any demonstrative argument or abstract reasoning a priori.

If we be, therefore, engaged by arguments to put trust in past experience, and make it the standard of our future judgment, these arguments must be probable only, or such as regard matter of fact and real existence according to the division above mentioned. But that there is no argument of this kind must appear, if our explication of that species of reasoning be admitted as solid and satisfactory. We have said that all arguments concerning existence are founded on the relation of cause and effect; that our knowledge of that relation is derived entirely from experience; and that all our experimental conclusions proceed upon the supposition that the future will be conformable to the past. To endeavour, therefore, the proof of this last supposition by probable arguments, or arguments regarding existence, must be evidently going in a circle and taking that for granted which is the very point in question....

It is certain that the most ignorant and stupid peasants—nay infants, nay even brute beasts—improve by experience, and learn the qualities of natural objects, by observing the effects which result from them. When a child has felt the sensation of pain from touching the flame of a candle, he will be careful not to put his hand near any candle, but will expect a similar effect from a cause which is similar in its sensible qualities and appearance. If you assert, therefore, that the understanding of the child is led into this conclusion by any process of argument or ratiocination, I may justly require you to produce that argument; nor have you any pretence to refuse so equitable a demand. You cannot say that the argument is abstruse, and may possibly escape your enquiry, since you confess that it is obvious to the capacity of a mere infant. If you hesitate, therefore, a moment, or if, after reflection, you produce any intricate or profound argument, you, in a manner, give up the question, and confess that it is not reasoning which engages us to suppose the past resembling the future and to expect similar effects from causes which are, to appearance, similar. This is the proposition which I intended to enforce in the present section. If I be right, I pretend not to have made any mighty discovery. And if I be wrong, I must acknowledge myself to be indeed a very backward scholar, since I cannot now discover an argument which, it seems, was perfectly familiar to me long before I was out of my cradle.

Sceptical Solution of These Doubts

Part I

... Suppose a person, though endowed with the strongest faculties of reason and reflection, to be brought of a sudden into this world; he would, indeed, immediately observe a continual succession of objects, and one event following another; but he would not be able to discover anything farther. He would not, at first, by any reasoning, be able to reach the idea of cause and effect, since the particular powers by which all natural operations are performed never appear to the senses; nor is it reasonable to conclude merely because one event, in one instance, precedes another, that therefore the one is the cause, the other the effect. Their conjunction may be arbitrary and casual. There may be no reason to infer the existence of one from the appearance of the other. And in a word, such a person, without more experience, could never employ his conjecture or reasoning concerning any matter of fact, or be assured of anything beyond what was immediately present to his memory and senses.

Suppose, again, that he has acquired more experience, and has lived so long in the world as to have observed familiar objects or events to be constantly conjoined together, what is the consequence of this experience? He immediately infers the existence of one object from the appearance of the other. Yet he has not, by all his experience, acquired any idea or knowledge of the secret power by which the one object produces the other; nor is it by any process of reasoning he is engaged to draw this inference. But still he finds himself determined to draw it: and though he should be convinced that his understanding has no part in the operation, he would nevertheless continue in the same course of thinking. There is some other principle which determines him to form such a conclusion.

This principle is Custom or Habit. For wherever the repetition of any particular act or operation produces a propensity to renew the same act or operation, without being impelled by any reasoning or process of the understanding, we always say that this propensity is the effect of Custom. By employing that word, we pretend not to have given the ultimate reason of such a propensity. We only point out a principle of human nature, which is universally acknowledged, and which is well known by its effects. Perhaps we can push our enquiries no farther, or pretend to give the cause of this cause, but must rest contented with it as the ultimate principle which we can assign of all our conclusions from experience. It is sufficient satisfaction that we can go so far without repining at the narrowness of our faculties because they will carry us no farther. And it is certain we here advance a very intelligible proposition at least, if not a true one, when we assert that, after the constant conjunction of two objects, heat and flame, for instance, weight and solidity, we are determined by custom alone to expect the one from the appearance of the other. This hypothesis seems even the only one which explains the difficulty, why we draw, from a thousand instances, an inference which we are not able to draw from one instance, that is, in no respect, different from them. Reason is incapable of any such variation. The conclusions which it draws from considering one circle are the same which it would form upon surveying all the circles in the universe. But no man, having seen only one body move after being impelled by another, could infer that every other body will move after a like impulse. All inferences from experience, therefore, are effects of custom, not of reasoning.

Custom, then, is the great guide of human life. It is that principle alone which renders our experience useful to us, and makes us expect, for the future, a similar train of events with those which have appeared in the past. Without the influence of custom, we should be entirely ignorant of every matter of fact beyond what is immediately present to the memory and senses. We should never know how to adjust means to ends, or to employ our natural powers in the production of any effect. There would be an end at once of all action, as well as of the chief part of speculation.

Of the Idea of Necessary Connexion

Part I

... There are no ideas, which occur in metaphysics, more obscure and uncertain than those of power, force, energy or necessary connexion, of which it is every moment necessary for us to treat in all our disquisitions. We shall, therefore, endeavour, in this section, to fix, if possible, the precise meaning of these terms, and thereby remove some part of that obscurity which is so much complained of in this species of philosophy.

It seems a proposition, which will not admit of much dispute, that all our ideas are nothing but copies of our impressions, or, in other words, that it is impossible for us to think of anything which we have not antecedently felt either by our external or internal senses. I have endeavoured to explain and prove this proposition, and have expressed my hopes that by a proper application of it men may reach a greater clearness and precision in philosophical reasonings than what they have hitherto been able to attain. Complex ideas may, perhaps, be well known by definition, which is nothing but an enumeration of those parts or simple ideas that compose them. But when we have pushed up definitions to the most simple ideas, and find still more ambiguity and obscurity, what resource are we then possessed of? By what invention can we throw light upon these ideas and render them altogether precise and determinate to our intellectual view? Produce the impressions or original sentiments from which the ideas are copied. These impressions are all strong and sensible. They admit not of ambiguity. They are not only placed in a full light themselves, but may throw light on their correspondent ideas, which lie in obscurity. And by this means, we may, perhaps, attain a new microscope or species of optics by which, in the moral sciences, the most minute and most simple ideas may be so enlarged as to fall readily under our apprehension and be equally known with the grossest and most sensible ideas that can be the object of our enquiry.

To be fully acquainted, therefore, with the idea of power or necessary connexion, let us examine its impression; and in order to find the impression with greater certainty, let us search for it in all the sources from which it may possibly be derived.

When we look about us towards external objects, and consider the operation of causes, we are never able, in a single instance, to discover any power or necessary connexion, any quality which binds the effect to the cause and renders the one an infallible consequence of the other. We only find that the one does actually, in fact, follow the other. The impulse of one billiard-ball is attended with motion in the second. This is the whole that appears to the outward senses. The mind feels no sentiment or inward impression from this succession of objects: consequently, there is not, in any single, particular instance of cause and effect anything which can suggest the idea of power or necessary connexion.

From the first appearance of an object, we never can conjecture what effect will result from it. But were the power or energy of any cause discoverable by the mind, we could foresee the effect, even without experience; and might, at first, pronounce with certainty concerning it by mere dint of thought and reasoning....

Of the Idea of Necessary Connexion

Part II

But to hasten to a conclusion of this argument, which is already drawn out to too great a length: we have sought in vain for an idea of power or necessary connexion in all the sources from which we could suppose it to be derived. It appears that, in single instances of the operation of bodies, we never can, by our utmost scrutiny, discover anything but one event following another, without being able to comprehend any force or power by which the cause operates, or any connexion between it and its supposed effect. The same difficulty occurs in contemplating the operations of mind on body—where we observe the motion of the latter to follow upon the volition of the former but are not able to observe or conceive the tie which binds together the motion and volition or the energy by which the mind produces this effect. The authority of the will over its own faculties and ideas is not a whit more comprehensible; so that, upon the whole, there appears not, throughout all nature, any one instance of connexion which is conceivable by us. All events seem entirely loose and separate. One event follows another, but we never can observe any tie between them. They seem conjoined, but never connected. And as we can have no idea of anything which never appeared to our outward sense or inward sentiment, the necessary conclusion seems to be that we have no idea of connexion or power at all, and that these words are absolutely without any meaning when employed either in philosophical reasonings or common life.

But there still remains one method of avoiding this conclusion, and one source which we have not yet examined. When any natural object or event is presented, it is impossible for us, by any sagacity or penetration, to discover, or even conjecture, without experience, what event will result from it, or to carry our foresight beyond that object which is immediately present to the memory and senses. Even after one instance or experiment where we have observed a particular event to follow upon another, we are not entitled to form a general rule, or foretell what will happen in like cases, it being justly esteemed an unpardonable temerity to judge of the whole course of nature from one single experiment, however accurate or certain. But when one particular species of event has always, in all instances, been conjoined with another, we make no longer any scruple of foretelling one upon the appearance of the other, and of employing that reasoning which can alone assure us of any matter of fact or existence. We then call the one object, Cause, the other, Effect. We suppose that there is some connexion between them, some power in the one, by which it infallibly produces the other and operates with the greatest certainty and strongest necessity.

It appears, then, that this idea of a necessary connexion among events arises from a number of similar instances which occur of the constant conjunction of these events; nor can that idea ever be suggested by any one of these instances, surveyed in all possible lights and positions. But there is nothing in a number of instances, different from every single instance, which is supposed to be exactly similar, except only, that after a repetition of similar instances, the mind is carried by habit, upon the appearance of one event, to expect its usual attendant, and to believe that it will exist. This connexion, therefore, which we feel in the mind, this customary transition of the imagination from one object to its usual attendant, is the sentiment or impression from which we form the idea of power or necessary connexion. Nothing farther is in the case. Contemplate the subject on all sides, you will never find any other origin of that idea. This is the sole difference between one instance, from which we can never receive the idea of connexion, and a number of similar instances, by which it is suggested. The first time a man saw the communication of motion by impulse, as by the shock of two billiard-balls, he could not pronounce that the one event was connected: but only that it was conjoined with the other. After he has observed several instances of this nature, he then pronounces them to be connected. What alteration has happened to give rise to this new idea of connexion? Nothing but that he now feels these events to be connected in his imagination, and can readily foretell the existence of one from the appearance of the other. When we say, therefore, that one object is connected with another, we mean only that they have acquired a connexion in our thought, and give rise to this inference, by which they become proofs of each other's existence: A conclusion which is somewhat extraordinary, but which seems founded on sufficient evidence. Nor will its evidence be weakened by any general diffidence of the understanding, or sceptical suspicion concerning every conclusion which is new and extraordinary. No conclusions can be more agreeable to scepticism than such as make discoveries concerning the weakness and narrow limits of human reason and capacity.

And what stronger instance can be produced of the surprising ignorance and weakness of the understanding than the present. For surely, if there be any relation among objects which it imports to us to know perfectly, it is that of cause and effect. On this are founded all our reasonings concerning matter of fact or existence. By means of it alone we attain any assurance concerning objects which are removed from the present testimony of our memory and senses. The only immediate utility of all sciences is to teach us how to control and regulate future events by their causes. Our thoughts and enquiries are, therefore, every moment employed about this relation: yet so imperfect are the ideas which we form concerning it that it is impossible to give any just definition of cause except what is drawn from something extraneous and foreign to it. Similar objects are always conjoined with similar. Of this we have experience. Suitably to this experience, therefore, we may define a cause to be an object followed by another and where all the objects similar to the first are followed by objects similar to the second. Or in other words where, if the first object had not been, the second never had existed. The appearance of a cause always conveys the mind, by a customary transition, to the idea of the effect. Of this also we have experience. We may, therefore, suitably to this experience, form another definition of cause, and call it an object followed by another and whose appearance always conveys the thought of that other. But though both these definitions be drawn from circumstances foreign to the cause, we cannot remedy this inconvenience, or attain any more perfect definition, which may point out that circumstance in the cause which gives it a connexion with its effect. We have no idea of this connexion, nor even any distant notion what it is we desire to know when we endeavour at a conception of it. We say, for instance, that the vibration of this string is the cause of this particular sound. But what do we mean by that affirmation? We either mean that this vibration is followed by this sound, and that all similar vibrations have been followed by similar sounds; or, that this vibration is followed by this sound, and that upon the appearance of one the mind anticipates the senses and forms immediately an idea of the other. We may consider the relation of cause and effect in either of these two lights; but beyond these, we have no idea of it.

To recapitulate, therefore, the reasonings of this section: Every idea is copied from some preceding impression or sentiment; and where we cannot find any impression, we may be certain that there is no idea. In all single instances of the operation of bodies or minds, there is nothing that produces any impression, nor consequently can suggest any idea of power or necessary connexion. But when many uniform instances appear, and the same object is always followed by the same event, we then begin to entertain the notion of cause and connexion. We then feel a new sentiment or impression, to wit, a customary connexion in the thought or imagination between one object and its usual attendant; and this sentiment is the original of that idea which we seek for. For as this idea arises from a number of similar instances, and not from any single instance, it must arise from that circumstance in which the number of instances differ from every individual instance. But this customary connexion or transition of the imagination is the only circumstance in which they differ. In every other particular they are alike. The first instance which we saw of motion communicated by the shock of two billiard-balls (to return to this obvious illustration) is exactly similar to any instance that may, at present, occur to us; except only that we could not, at first, infer one event from the other; which we are enabled to do at present, after so long a course of uniform experience. I know not whether the reader will readily apprehend this reasoning. I am afraid that, should I multiply words about it, or throw it into a greater variety of lights, it would only become more obscure and intricate. In all abstract reasonings there is one point of view which, if we can happily hit, we shall go farther towards illustrating the subject than by all the eloquence and copious expression in the world. This point of view we should endeavour to reach, and reserve the flowers of rhetoric for subjects which are more adapted to them.

Of the Academical or Sceptical Philosophy

Part III

... Those who have a propensity to philosophy will still continue their researches, because they reflect that, besides the immediate pleasure attending such an occupation, philosophical decisions are nothing but the reflections of common life methodized and corrected. But they will never be tempted to go beyond common life so long as they consider the imperfection of those faculties which they employ, their narrow reach and their inaccurate operations. While we cannot give a satisfactory reason why we believe, after a thousand experiments, that a stone will fall, or fire burn; can we ever satisfy ourselves concerning any determination which we may form, with regard to the origin of worlds and the situation of nature from and to eternity?

This narrow limitation, indeed, of our enquiries is, in every respect, so reasonable that it suffices to make the slightest examination into the natural powers of the human mind and to compare them with their objects in order to recommend it to us. We shall then find what are the proper subjects of science and enquiry.

It seems to me that the only objects of the abstract science or of demonstration are quantity and number, and that all attempts to extend this more perfect species of knowledge beyond these bounds are mere sophistry and illusion....

All other enquiries of men regard only matter of fact and existence; and these are evidently incapable of demonstration. Whatever is may not be.

No negation of a fact can involve a contradiction. The non-existence of any being, without exception, is as clear and distinct an idea as its existence. The proposition which affirms it not to be, however false, is no less conceivable and intelligible than that which affirms it to be. The case is different with the sciences, properly so called. Every proposition which is not true is there confused and unintelligible. That the cube root of 64 is equal to the half of 10, is a false proposition and can never be distinctly conceived. But that Csar, or the angel Gabriel, or any being never existed, may be a false proposition, but still is perfectly conceivable and implies no contradiction.

The existence, therefore, of any being can only be proved by arguments from its cause or its effect; and these arguments are founded entirely on experience. If we reason a priori, anything may appear able to produce anything. The falling of a pebble may, for aught we know, extinguish the sun; or the wish of a man control the planets in their orbits. It is only experience which teaches us the nature and bounds of cause and effect and enables us to infer the existence of one object from that of another. Such is the foundation of moral reasoning, which forms the greater part of human knowledge and is the source of all human action and behaviour.

Moral reasonings are either concerning particular or general facts. All deliberations in life regard the former; as also all disquisitions in history, chronology, geography, and astronomy.

The sciences, which treat of general facts, are politics, natural philosophy, physics, chemistry, etc. where the qualities, causes and effects of a whole species of objects are enquired into.

Divinity or Theology, as it proves the existence of a Deity, and the immortality of souls, is composed partly of reasonings concerning particular, partly concerning general facts. It has a foundation in reason so far as it is supported by experience. But its best and most solid foundation is faith and divine revelation.

Morals and criticism are not so properly objects of the understanding as of taste and sentiment. Beauty, whether moral or natural, is felt, more properly than perceived. Or if we reason concerning it, and endeavour to fix its standard, we regard a new fact, to wit, the general tastes of mankind, or some such fact, which may be the object of reasoning and enquiry.

When we run over libraries, persuaded of these principles, what havoc must we make? If we take in our hand any volume, of divinity or school metaphysics, for instance, let us ask, *Does it contain any abstract reasoning concerning quantity or number?* No. *Does it contain any experimental reasoning concerning matter of fact and existence?* No. Commit it then to the flames: for it can contain nothing but sophistry and illusion.

CHAPTER 17

Spanish, Portuguese, and Latin American Theories of Knowledge

"To join in wedlock life and reason!"

The theory of knowledge has been a major concern of Spanish, Portuguese, and Latin American philosophers. For centuries, most remained within the bounds set by Aristotle and St. Thomas Aquinas. In the sixteenth century, however, Spanish thinkers led the attack against that paradigm. Some became skeptics, setting the stage for Descartes and other early modern philosophers. Some tried to provide a theory of knowledge adequate to the new science, based on probabilistic reasoning from experience. More recently, some have sought to recognize that living, breathing people facing particular practical problems are knowers, and they have tried to understand how the contexts of our lives shape how we think and reason.

17.1 THE SKEPTICISM OF FRANCISCO SANCHES

Francisco Sanches (1551–1623) was born into a Portuguese family from Braga that had converted to Christianity. In the face of the Inquisition, the family moved to southwestern France when Sanches was 11. Son of a prominent physician, Sanches studied medicine in Rome and Montpellier and for thirty years served as doctor at the Hotel Dieu in Toulouse. He also studied scholastic philosophy, and became Regius Professor of Philosophy and Medicine at the University of Toulouse. He wrote his only surviving philosophical work, *That Nothing Is Known*, in 1576, when he was only 25 years old, and published it five years later. Appearing in six editions throughout the next two centuries, it earned Sanches a reputation as "Sanches the skeptic." He was listed among the most dangerous enemies of Christianity. German theologian Gabriel Wedderkopff called him "the most ruinous of the skeptics." But Coralnik praises him as "the only skeptic who was at the same time a positive thinker." Sanches helped to bring epistemology to center stage in philosophy—a development that had a deep impact on Descartes, Hume, and other early modern philosophers in Europe. Socrates famously said that he knew only that he knew nothing. Sanches denies that he knows even that.

Sanches attacks the common medieval practice, stemming from Aristotle, of defining a thing in terms of a *genus* (plural, *genera*)—the kind of thing it is—and *differentiae*, differences between it and other things of that kind. Thus Aristotle defines a human being as a rational animal. *Animal* marks the genus, the kind, and *rational* marks the difference between humans and other animals. Sanches uses an infinite regress argument. By this means, we cannot understand anything. We define *A* in terms of *B* and *C*—but how do we understand them? In terms of *D*, *E*, *F*, and *G*? We can ask for definitions of them.

Sanches attacks deductive reasoning in the same way. Knowledge, since Plato, has generally been thought to be justified true belief—that is, true belief with an account, with an argument. So, to know that *p*, we must be able to justify it. Say that we argue for *p* from premises *q* and *r*. What justifies them? Maybe we can argue for them from premises *s* and *t*. Clearly this cannot go on forever; if it did, *p* would never be justified. But resting *p* ultimately on things that are not justified, and therefore not known, cannot justify *p* either.

17.1.1 Francisco Sanches, from *That Nothing Is Known*

"Everyone by nature desires to know." [Aristotle, *Metaphysics* I, 1] To few has it been granted to know what to desire; to even fewer, to know. My own luck has been no different from that of others. From a young age I was led to the contemplation of nature; I inquired into all the minute details. And at first my mind, starving for knowledge, was satisfied with any food it could find. After some time, nevertheless, gripped by indigestion, it began to regurgitate everything. Even then I was trying to find something that would satisfy me completely and absolutely, but nothing could fulfill my desire. I read the sayings of prior generations, and put my contemporaries to the test; they gave the same response. Nevertheless, nothing was able to satisfy me. Some reflected a shadow of truth, but I found not even one who offered judgment of things

Source: Francisco Sanches, *That Nothing Is Known (Quod Nihil Scitur)*. Translated by Daniel Bonevac.

sincerely and completely. So, I withdrew into myself; I called everything into doubt, and began to examine the things themselves as if no one had ever said anything about them—which is the true method of science. I broke everything down to first principles. Beginning my contemplation in this way, the more I thought, the more I doubted. I could understand nothing completely. I despaired. Nevertheless, I persisted. More, I went to the Doctors, hoping avidly to learn the truth from them. What then? Each construes his science partly out of the imaginings of others, partly out of his own. From these they infer other things, and then from those still others, without looking at the facts, producing a labyrinth of words without any basis in truth. In the end, you understanding nothing of nature, but you learn new things, a fictional texture that no mind suffices to understand. For who could understand what doesn't even exist? From this proceed Democritus's atoms, Plato's forms, Pythagoras's numbers, and Aristotle's universals, agent intellect, and intelligences....

I do not know even this one thing, that I know nothing. I nevertheless conjecture that neither I nor anyone else knows anything. Let this proposition be my banner, and come to be followed: Nothing is known. If I come to know how to prove this, I will be justified in concluding that nothing is known; if not, even more so; for I asserted just that. But you will say: If you know how to prove it, the contrary will follow, for you then know something. But I anticipated your objection and arrived at the opposite conclusion. I already begin to upset the matter: it already follows from this very thing that nothing is known. Perhaps you have not understood, and call me ignorant or a sophist. You have told the truth. But I can say the same of you even more so, for you have not understood. We are both ignorant. Therefore, you have unknowingly reached the conclusion I was seeking. If you have understood the ambiguity of the inference, you have seen clearly that nothing is known; if not, then think, draw some distinctions, and untangle this knot for me. Sharpen your wits. I am on your trail.

Let us reckon the thing by its name. For from my point of view every definition and every question is about names. I will explain. We cannot recognize the natures of things; I at least cannot. If you say you can, then fine; I won't argue with you. Nevertheless, it is false: for why are you more capable than I? And hence we know nothing. If we do not comprehend, how can we demonstrate anything? We can't. You nevertheless say that there is a definition that demonstrates the nature of the thing. Give me one. You don't have one. I therefore draw my conclusion. Moreover, how can we give names to things we do not understand? I don't see how. Nevertheless, there they are. Hence, surrounding names there is perpetual doubt, and there is much confusion and fallacy about words—even, maybe, in what I have just put forward.

Draw the conclusion. You say that you can define a thing, man—not just a word—with this definition: a mortal, rational animal. I deny it. For I in turn doubt the word *animal*, and *rational*, and the rest. You will go on to define these in terms of higher genera and differentiae, as you call them, until you reach Being. I will ask the same question about each of these. Finally, the last, Being: for you know nothing about what it signifies. You cannot define it, for it has no higher genus, you will say. I don't understand this. Neither do you. You don't know what Being is. Even less do I. You will nonetheless say that questions should finally be put to rest. This neither resolves doubt nor satisfies the mind. You are forced to display your ignorance. I rejoice. So am I....

Listen. Prove that a man is a being. You say this: A man is a substance; a substance is a being; therefore a man is a being. I doubt the first and second premises. Say you argue for the first: A man is a body; a body is a substance; therefore a man is a substance. Again I doubt both premises. You say: A man is a living thing; a living thing is a body; so, a man is a body. I say the same.

You argue: A man is an animal; an animal is a living thing; therefore a man is a living thing. Highest God! What a series, what a hodge-podge, all to prove that a man is a being! The answer is more obscure than the question....

We know nothing. Suppose that the explication of knowledge I have laid down is correct, for the purposes of discussion. From this let us infer that nothing is known. For to suppose is not to know but to pretend; that is why from suppositions we get fictions, not knowledge. See where the argument has led us: All knowledge is fiction. It is clear. Knowledge is obtained by demonstration. This presupposes a definition. Definitions cannot be proved; they must be believed. Therefore, a demonstration from what is supposed produces only supposed knowledge, not firm and certain knowledge. All these things follow from your own premises. As you say, first principles must be supposed in every field of knowledge, and these must not be disputed. Hence what follows from these will be supposed, not known. What could be more miserable? To know, we must be ignorant. For what is "supposing" but admitting that we do not know? Wouldn't it be better to know the first principles? I deny your first principles: prove them. You don't have to argue against people who deny your first principles? You don't know how to prove them. You are ignorant, not knowledgeable. A higher or more general science can establish the first principles of other sciences? Maybe, then, the person who knows this higher and more general science has knowledge; you don't. For anyone who is ignorant of first principles is ignorant of the thing. What is that more general science, anyway?...

But aren't these fables for children? For in a public place—a courtyard, a marketplace, a field—they construct little gardens, mark their boundaries with tiles, and prohibit others from entering their little spaces. I see what this is about. Since no one can embrace everything, each chooses a part for himself while others tear the rest to pieces. Hence nothing is known. For since all the things in the world constitute a single whole, some cannot exist without others; some cannot persist with others. Each fulfills it own function, different from the rest. But all contribute to the whole. Some cause others; some are caused by others. The concatenation of all of them is indescribably complex. It is therefore not surprising that, if we are ignorant of one, we are ignorant of the rest....

17.2 THE CONTEXTUALISM OF UNAMUNO

Miguel de Unamuno y Jugo (1864–1936), born in Bilbao, Spain, forged a version of existentialism long before Jean-Paul Sartre made the view famous. Inspired by *Don Quixote*, he insists that life is essentially quixotic. We strive for immortality but cannot achieve it. We want our ideas, families, and institutions to be permanent, but they are bound to perish. Life is inevitably tragic.

Unamuno expresses deep suspicion of the rationalism of Descartes, which had influenced him as a student. Descartes, employing the method of doubt, realizes that *I think, I am* are true every time they are thought or uttered. He concludes that we are essentially things that think. Sensation, emotion, and other aspects of the self are inessential. Unamuno worries that this imparts a rationalist bias. We are things that think, but we are also things that sense and feel, that want and fear, that laugh and cry, that live and die.

17.2.1 Miguel de Unamuno, from *The Tragic Sense of Life*

I. The Man of Flesh and Bone

"*Homo sum; nihil humani a me alienum puto*," said the Latin playwright. And I would rather say, "*Nullum hominem a me alienum puto*": I am a man; no other man do I deem a stranger. For to me the adjective "humanus" is no less suspect than its abstract substantive "humanitas," humanity. Neither "the human" nor "humanity," neither the simple adjective nor the substantivized adjective, but the concrete substantive—man. The man of flesh and bone; the man who is born, suffers, and dies—above all, who dies; the man who eats and drinks and plays and sleeps and thinks and wills; the man who is seen and heard; the brother, the real brother.

For there is another thing which is also called man, and he is the subject of not a few lucubrations, more or less scientific. He is the legendary featherless biped, the *zon politikhon* [political animal] of Aristotle, the social contractor of Rousseau, the *homo economicus* [economic man] of the Manchester school, the *homo sapiens* of Linnaeus, or, if you like, the vertical mammal. A man neither of here nor there, neither of this age nor of another, who has neither sex nor country, who is, in brief, merely an idea. That is to say, a no-man.

The man we have to do with is the man of flesh and bone—I, you, reader of mine, the other man yonder, all of us who walk solidly on the earth.

And this concrete man, this man of flesh and bone, is at once the subject and the supreme object of all philosophy, whether certain self-styled philosophers like it or not.

In most of the histories of philosophy that I know, philosophic systems are presented to us as if growing out of one another spontaneously, and their authors, the philosophers, appear only as mere pretexts. The inner biography of the philosophers, of the men who philosophized, occupies a secondary place. And yet it is precisely this inner biography that explains for us most things....

Philosophy answers to our need of forming a complete and unitary conception of the world and of life, and as a result of this conception, a feeling which gives birth to an inward attitude and even to outward action. But the fact is that this feeling, instead of being a consequence of this conception, is the cause of it. Our philosophy—that is, our mode of understanding or not understanding the world and life—springs from our feeling towards life itself. And life, like everything affective, has roots in subconsciousness, perhaps in unconsciousness.

It is not usually our ideas that make us optimists or pessimists, but it is our optimism or our pessimism, of physiological or perhaps pathological origin, as much the one as the other, that makes our ideas.

Man is said to be a reasoning animal. I do not know why he has not been defined as an affective or feeling animal. Perhaps that which differentiates him from other animals is feeling rather than reason. More often I have seen a cat reason than laugh or weep. Perhaps it weeps or laughs inwardly—but then perhaps, also inwardly, the crab resolves equations of the second degree.

And thus, in a philosopher, what must needs most concern us is the man.

II. The Starting Point

The defect of Descartes' *Discourse of Method* lies not in the antecedent methodical doubt; not in his beginning by resolving to doubt everything, a merely intellectual device; but in his resolution to begin by emptying himself of himself, of Descartes, of the real man, the man of flesh and bone, the man who does not want to die, in

Source: Miguel de Unamuno, *The Tragic Sense of Life*. Translated by J. E. Crawford Flitch. London: Macmillan, 1921.

order that he might be a mere thinker—that is, an abstraction. But the real man returned and thrust himself into the philosophy.

"Le bon sens est la chose du monde la mieux partagée." ["Good sense is of all the things of the world the most evenly distributed."] Thus begins the *Discourse of Method*, and this good sense saved him. He continues talking about himself, about the man Descartes, telling us among other things that he greatly esteemed eloquence and loved poetry; that he delighted above all in mathematics because of the evidence and certainty of its reasons, and that he revered our theology and claimed as much as any to attain to heaven—*et prétendais autant qu'aucun autre à gagner le ciel.* And this pretension—a very laudable one, I think, and above all very natural—was what prevented him from deducing all the consequences of his methodical doubt. The man Descartes claimed, as much as any other, to attain to heaven, "but having learned as a thing very sure that the way to it is not less open to the most ignorant than to the most learned, and that the revealed truths which lead thither are beyond our intelligence, I did not dare submit them to my feeble reasonings, and I thought that to undertake to examine them and to succeed therein, I should want some extraordinary help from heaven and need to be more than man." And here we have the man. Here we have the man who "did not feel obliged, thank God, to make a profession (*métier*) of science in order to increase his means, and who did not pretend to play the cynic and despise glory." And afterwards he tells us how he was compelled to make a sojourn in Germany, and there, shut up in a stove (*poêle*) he began to philosophize his method. But in Germany, shut up in a stove! And such his discourse is, a stove-discourse, and the stove a German one, although the philosopher shut up in it was a Frenchman who proposed to himself to attain to heaven.

And he arrives at the *cogito ergo sum*, which St. Augustine had already anticipated; but the *ego* implicit in this enthymeme, *ego cogito, ergo ego sum* [I think, therefore I am], is an unreal—that is, an ideal—*ego* or I, and its *sum*, its existence, something unreal also. "I think, therefore I am" can only mean "I think, therefore I am a thinker"; this being of the "I am," which is deduced from "I think," is merely a knowing; this being is knowledge, but not life. And the primary reality is not that I think, but that I live, for those also live who do not think. Although this living may not be a real living. God! what contradictions when we seek to join in wedlock life and reason!

The truth is *sum, ergo cogito*—I am, therefore I think, although not everything that is thinks. Is not consciousness of thinking above all consciousness of being? Is pure thought possible, without consciousness of self, without personality? Can there exist pure knowledge without feeling, without that species of materiality which feeling lends to it? Do we not perhaps feel thought, and do we not feel ourselves in the act of knowing and willing? Could not the man in the stove have said: "I feel, therefore I am"? or "I will, therefore I am"? And to feel oneself, is it not perhaps to feel oneself imperishable? To will oneself, is it not to wish oneself eternal—that is to say, not to wish to die? What the sorrowful Jew of Amsterdam called the essence of the thing, the effort that it makes to persist indefinitely in its own being, self-love, the longing for immortality, is it not perhaps the primal and fundamental condition of all reflective or human knowledge? And is it not therefore the true base, the real starting point, of all philosophy, although the philosophers, perverted by intellectualism, may not recognize it?

And, moreover, it was the *cogito* that introduced a distinction which, although fruitful of truths, has been fruitful also of confusions, and this distinction is that between object, *cogito*, and subject, *sum*. There is scarcely any distinction that does not also lead to confusion. But we will return to this later.

For the present let us remain keenly suspecting that the longing not to die, the hunger for personal immortality, the effort whereby we tend to persist indefinitely in our own being, which is, according to the tragic Jew, our very essence, that this is the affective basis of all knowledge and the personal inward starting point of all human philosophy, wrought by a man and for men. And we shall see how the solution of this inward affective problem, a solution which may be but the despairing renunciation of the attempt at a solution, is that which colours all the rest of philosophy. Underlying even the so-called problem of knowledge there is simply this human feeling, just as underlying the enquiry into the "why," the cause, there is simply the search for the "wherefore," the end. All the rest is either to deceive oneself or to wish to deceive others; and to wish to deceive others in order to deceive oneself.

And this personal and affective starting point of all philosophy and all religion is the tragic sense of life. Let us now proceed to consider this....

VI. In the Depths of the Abyss

Parce unic spes totius orbis. [Spare the one hope of the whole world.]—Tertullian, *Adversus Marcionem*, 5.

We have seen that the vital longing for human immortality finds no consolation in reason and that reason leaves us without incentive or consolation in life and life itself without real finality. But here, in the depths of the abyss, the despair of the heart and of the will and the scepticism of reason meet face to face and embrace like brothers. And we shall see it is from this embrace, a tragic—that is to say, an intimately loving—embrace, that the wellspring of life will flow, a life serious and terrible. Scepticism, uncertainty—the position to which reason, by practising its analysis upon itself, upon its own validity, at last arrives—is the foundation upon which the heart's despair must build up its hope.

Disillusioned, we had to abandon the position of those who seek to give consolation the force of rational and logical truth, pretending to prove the rationality, or at any rate the nonirrationality, of consolation; and we had to abandon likewise the position of those who seek to give rational truth the force of consolation and of a motive for life. Neither the one nor the other of these positions satisfied us. The one is at variance with our reason, the other with our feeling. These two powers can never conclude peace and we must needs live by their war. We must make of this war, of war itself, the very condition of our spiritual life.

Neither does this high debate admit of that indecent and repugnant expedient which the more or less parliamentary type of politician has devised and dubbed "a formula of agreement," the property of which is to render it impossible for either side to claim to be victorious. There is no place here for a time-serving compromise. Perhaps a degenerate and cowardly reason might bring itself to propose some such formula of agreement, for in truth reason lives by formulas; but life, which cannot be formulated, life which lives and seeks to live forever, does not submit to formulas. Its sole formula is: all or nothing. Feeling does not compound its differences with middle terms.

Initium sapienti timor Domini [The beginning of wisdom is the fear of the Lord], it is said, meaning perhaps *timor mortis* [fear of death], or it may be, *timor vit* [fear of life], which is the same thing. Always it comes about that the beginning of wisdom is a fear.

Is it true to say of this saving scepticism which I am now going to discuss, that it is doubt? It is doubt, yes, but it is much more than doubt. Doubt is commonly something very cold, of very little vitalizing force, and above all something rather artificial, especially since Descartes degraded it to the function of a method. The conflict between reason and life is something more than a doubt. For doubt is easily resolved into a comic element.

The methodical doubt of Descartes is a comic doubt, a doubt purely theoretical and provisional—that is to say, the doubt of a man who acts as if he doubted without really doubting. And because it was a stove-excogitated doubt, the man who deduced that he existed from the fact that he thought did not approve of "those turbulent (*brouillonnes*) and restless persons who, being called neither by birth nor by fortune to the management of public affairs, are perpetually devising some new reformation," and he was pained by the suspicion that there might be something of this kind in his own writings. No, he, Descartes, proposed only to "reform his own thoughts and to build upon ground that was wholly his." And he resolved not to accept anything as true when he did not recognize it clearly to be so, and to make a clean sweep of all prejudices and received ideas, to the end that he might construct his intellectual habitation anew. But "as it is not enough, before beginning to rebuild one's dwelling-house, to pull it down and to furnish materials and architects, or to study architecture oneself... but it is also necessary to be provided with some other wherein to lodge conveniently while the work is in progress," he framed for himself a provisional ethic—*une morale de provision*—the first law of which was to observe the customs of his country and to keep always to the religion in which, by the grace of God, he had been instructed from his infancy, governing himself in all things according to the most moderate opinions. Yes, exactly, a provisional religion and even a provisional God! And he chose the most moderate opinions "because these are always the most convenient for practice." But it is best to proceed no further.

This methodical or theoretical Cartesian doubt, this philosophical doubt excogitated in a stove, is not the doubt, is not the scepticism, is not the incertitude, that I am talking about here. No! This other doubt is a passionate doubt, it is the eternal conflict between reason and feeling, science and life, logic and biotic. For science destroys the concept of personality by reducing it to a complex in continual flux from moment to moment—that is to say, it destroys the very foundation of the spiritual and emotional life, which ranges itself unyieldingly against reason.

And this doubt cannot avail itself of any provisional ethic, but has to found its ethic, as we shall see, on the conflict itself, an ethic of battle, and itself has to serve as the foundation of religion. And it inhabits a house which is continually being demolished and which continually it has to rebuild. Without ceasing the will, I mean the will never to die, the spirit of unsubmissiveness to death labours to build up the house of life, and without ceasing the keen blasts and stormy assaults of reason beat it down.

PART IV

Metaphysics

CHAPTER 18

Classical Indian Metaphysics

"Just like the double moon"

The Indian philosophical tradition includes more than two and a half millennia of metaphysical debate. Classical Indian metaphysics centers on the contrast between realism and idealism. Buddhism and the most popular school of Hinduism, Advaita Vedanta, are thoroughly idealist. They insist that everything is mind dependent. What appear to be independent objects—rocks, stones, and trees as well as pots, animals, and people, even ourselves—are mental constructions. Objects do not really endure over time; they exist for no more than a moment. What we take to be objects are really bundles of momentary entities that we group together for our own purposes. Hindu philosophers of the Logic and Particularist schools, in contrast, are realists. They outline the perspective on the world that they view as implicit in our language and our commonsense understanding of the world. They hold that objects such as rocks, stones, and trees are truly "out there" in the world. These objects in no sense depend on our minds. They endure over time. The Taj Mahal is the same structure as the one that stood on that spot in 1653, the year of its completion, whether anyone happens to think so or not.

18.1 CLASSICAL REALIST ONTOLOGY

Among the traditional schools of Indian philosophy are *Vaisheshika* (*Particularism*) and *Nyaya* (Logic). These long-running, realist schools of Indian philosophy developed independently but merged around the year 1000 CE in the work of Udayana. Especially before that date, Particularist philosophers focused primarily on ontology: the study of what there is. What is there? What in general do we experience and talk about? Ontologists try to answer these questions. They try to classify the most fundamental constituents of the world. Particularist philosophers hammer out a system of categories (*padartha*, literally, "types of things to which words refer"). Their concerns parallel Aristotle's. They seek to classify everything into one of the categories.

To the question "What is there?" the early Particularists (those roughly contemporary with Aristotle) answer that, most generally, there are three types of things:

1. Substances, such as a pot or a cloth
2. Qualities (or attributes), such as shapes and colors
3. Actions, such as moving up or shrinking

Some substances are basic—simple, not made up of other substances—such as atoms of fire, earth, water, and so on. Others are composite substances, such as rocks, trees, houses, and people. The Particularist category of substance includes space and time, which Aristotle lists separately. It also includes minds and selves. The category of qualities includes relations and probably states and positions as well. And the category of actions combines, we might think, Aristotle's categories of action and affection. Though motions are like qualities in that they dwell in individual substances, they have causal effects that qualities by themselves do not have, bringing about conjunctions and disjunctions of substances, for example. So the Particularist scheme manages to include everything in Aristotle's categories. It divides them up differently, however, and in some cases would require combinations of things where Aristotle finds one thing—a relation (category: quality) to a place (category: substance), for example, rather than a location.

Some scholars, pointing to the similarity of this list to the list compiled by Aristotle, suspect Greek influence on the Indian system. Since Aristotle was tutor to Alexander the Great, who conquered everything between Greece and India and brought Greek philosophers with him to talk to their Indian counterparts, this is not completely implausible. However, a more likely source of the resemblance is the fact that Greek and Sanskrit have similar grammatical structures, with adjectives (representing qualities) qualifying (inhering in) nouns (representing substances), and so on. Both languages belong to the Indo-European language family.

The Particularist tradition adds other categories, which allow us to make meaningful statements and which have no parallel in Aristotle's scheme. Three occur in some texts as old as those of Aristotle, while the last is a later innovation.

Inherence is the relationship between substances and qualities. In the case of a blue pot, inherence is the relationship between the pot and the color blue. Inherence includes things like the pot's being blue or Socrates's being a man. This category seems more system-driven than the first three. "What ties the blue to the blue pot?" The answer the Realists give is that it is inherence, a special ontic glue that binds qualities to substances and motions. We may even say that substances inhere in other substances. A piece of cloth inheres in its threads, and the threads in what make them up, all the way down to the atoms. So substances inhere in substances (except for atoms, which have no inherent causes). The pile of rice inheres in the individual grains. Inherence, by the way, is said to be known in the same way the things it relates are known. This might be by perception, as in the case of blue inhering in a blue pot. It might also be by inference, as in the case of earthhood inhering in an earthen atom, since atoms are known by inference.

Universality, such as potness and cowness, includes abstract properties and kinds, such as being blue or being a man. We must include universals, things that can have multiple instances; otherwise we would not even be able to identify the three basic categories. When we talk about substances as a category, we are talking about substances in general, not just a collection of pots, pieces of cloth, and so on. Also, when we say, "Bessie is a cow," "Flossie is a cow," and so on, we draw on a recurrent experience of cowness, the factor common to Bessie and Flossie. Indeed, "Bessie is a cow" is equivalent in meaning to "Bessie has cowness" (that is, has the property of being a cow). Universals inhere in substances, qualities, and motions but not in inherence itself, nor in other universals; otherwise, the Particularists argue, there would be an infinite regress. There is thus no such universal as "being a universal." But then what are we saying when we call cowhood a universal? For this and other reasons, the topic of universals is much debated, particularly with Buddhists. The Realists are not platonists—there are no uninstanced universals dwelling apart from the individuals that are their instances—but universals are a separate category and thus a separate kind of thing. They are directly given in perception insofar as we perceive their instances. Indeed, we come to know individuals only through the general, repeatable characteristics they present. We get to know Bessie by recognizing her as a cow, as brown, and so on.

Individualizers differentiate ultimate particulars such as atoms. The earliest Particularist texts correlate individualizers with universals. Bessie is *this* cow; Flossie is *that* one. Later, the reason for positing individualizers as a separate type of thing appears to be that otherwise individual atoms all of the same type (water, for example) would be identical. In general, individualizers distinguish objects that are otherwise similar, having exactly the same qualities. How can we distinguish one drop of water or one electron from another, for example? We appear to have the same kind of substance, the same qualities, and the same universals. Something must distinguish one from the other.

Absences, such as of an elephant in this room, is a category that is not made explicit in the *Vaisheshika-sutra* but is defended in all later Vaisheshika texts. Absences, or lacks, allow us to make sense of language that seems to refer to nothing ("the elephant in the room," "my glasses on the table," etc.).

These additional categories are controversial. The original three categories spark debate, especially concerning whether some are more fundamental than others: Can we think of substances as just bundles of qualities? As collections of events? Can we think of events as objects gaining or losing qualities? But everyone more or less agrees that there are in some sense pots, colors, and actions. In contrast, the added categories are far more peculiar. What is inherence? Do we have to think of it as an object? That is, in addition to the pot and the color blue, do we have to recognize separately the pot's being blue? But if we do not, how do we account for sentences such as "The pot's being blue surprised me"? Moreover, if we count inherences as objects, we seem to face an argument Plato dubbed "The Third Man." Suppose that, in addition to Socrates and the quality of being a man, we have the inherence relation between them—Socrates's being a man. Don't we need yet another relation to link Socrates, the quality, and the inherence relation? But then don't we need yet another relation to link it to those three things? We appear to face an infinite regress. Late Logic philosophers, faced with a similar problem voiced by their idealist adversaries, proclaimed inherence to be self-linking. Like a rope tied around a goat's neck that can be tied to a tree without requiring another rope, inherence self-links with its relata.

Individualizers are odd entities—sometimes called "bare particulars" in the West—that are over and above a thing's properties and relations and thus seem to be unobservable and unknowable. But without them, how can one distinguish two qualitatively identical things? Contemporary American philosopher Max Black devises a puzzle of a universe consisting of nothing but two qualitatively identical black iron spheres. They have the same properties, and their relations to each other are completely symmetrical. So how can they differ? (A universe with one uniform sphere does as well—the two halves are qualitatively identical and symmetrically related.) Finally, Buddhists and Exegetes argue that absences or lacks are especially peculiar things to count among the things in the world. If we are counting the basic constituents of the world, surely we don't have to count the holes in the wall or the siblings we never had. Yet we can sensibly talk about the dog that did not bark in the nighttime or the questions the professor did not ask on the exam.

In all these cases, we get a puzzle like that facing platonism in ancient Greek philosophy. If we accept entities like inherences, universals, individualizers, and absences as inhabiting the world, how do we have knowledge of them? We evidently do not experience them directly. On the other hand, if we do not accept such entities, how do we make sense of sentences that seem to refer to them? This dilemma confronts any categorical framework. Particularists say we know them by a form of inference.

The Particularists are realists. The substances, qualities, actions, and so on that make up the world are in general mind independent. That puts them at odds with Buddhist philosophers, who are idealists. From their perspective, everything is dependent on mind. The Buddhists argue that there are no enduring substances. Instead, they contend, there are processes of momentary objects strung together causally. Their argument, as we shall see, depends crucially on recognizing only sufficient causes as deserving the name. In the ensuing metaphysical battle, it is crucial that Particularism reject this understanding and defend a division of causes into necessary factors and sufficient factors. Most causes are necessary; what suffices to bring about an effect is a complex bundle of factors. This distinction is vital. Unless a cause can exist as a potential factor at a time prior to its inclusion in the bundle, then, if "to be a causal factor" is what it is to exist, as the Buddhist Dharmakirti argues, nothing could last longer than a moment, and the Buddhist idealists would achieve a significant victory.

Realism's differentiation of types of cause is also similar to Aristotle's, although there are no formal or final causes and there is an "emergent" cause not recognized in Aristotelian theory. Causes fall into three groups:

1. *Instrumental.* Agents, a potter, for instance, and tools, for instance, a stick used by a potter to turn the wheel, are viewed as instrumental causes. But time and space are also included as instruments for any effect, and the late conception is of any factor that is necessary to bring about an effect of a certain type.
2. *Inherent.* An inherent cause is a substratum of a superstratum related to it by inherence. In the case of a blue pot, the pot is the inherent cause of the blue color. A cow is an inherent cause of cowhood. The inherent causes of a cloth are the threads in which it is nested. And so on. Instances are inherent causes of the universals they instantiate; parts are inherent causes of wholes. Note that substances are not the only inherent causes; universals inhere in qualities and in motions as well as in substances. Thus, a cognition, itself a quality whose inherent

cause is an individual self, is an inherent cause of the universal, cognitionhood, which has multiple inherent causes—all the cognitions in the universe.

3. *Emergent.* An emergent cause is always a quality or a motion. Recall that a whole is said to inhere in its parts. A quality that inheres in the inherent causes of a whole can emerge as, or cause, a quality of the whole. For example, the blue color of the threads of a blue piece of cloth is the emergent cause of the blue of the cloth.

In general, a cause is a factor that is necessary to the arising of an effect. Instrumental factors can be quite numerous. There can also be alternative bundles of factors that bring about an effect, such as the tinderbox and straw as distinct from sunlight, jewel, and camphor, to make fire. The test of a factor's being a cause is that it must invariably precede the effect without being counted "irrelevant."

The stock example of precedence that is irrelevant is a donkey that just happens always to be used to bring the clay out of which a particular kind of pot is made. The donkey plays a role in the production of the pot, but it can hardly be said to be the cause of the pot. A modern example would be a barometric change that invariably precedes a storm.

The presence of a truly necessary factor—a factor not instrumentally irrelevant—does not entail the occurrence of the effect. Other factors typically are necessary also. For example, the presence of smoke entails the occurrence of fire, a necessary factor, though fires can be smokeless (for instance, the fire in molten metal). Fire itself is insufficient to bring about smoke. Damp fuel is also necessary. Sufficient causality amounts to a set of causal conditions whose being in place unfailingly brings about an effect of a particular type. But normally the causal principles formulated in Logic involve only necessary factors.

Within a set of necessary conditions that together are sufficient for an effect, the instrumental cause called the *trigger* gets special attention. The trigger is the unique condition which, on being added to a heap of enabling conditions already in place, necessitates the effect. The trigger is sometimes the called the "proximate instrumental cause," but perhaps "chief instrumental cause" would be a better rendering. (An early example is an axe used to fell a tree. Later Logic philosophers say that the action of the woodsman with his last swing was the trigger.)

18.1.1 From the *Vaisheshika Sutras of Kanada*

Book I, Chapter 1

1. Now, therefore, we shall explain *dharma* (righteousness).

2. *Dharma* (is) that from which (results) the accomplishment of exaltation and of the supreme good.

Source: Translated by Nandalal Sinha. *The Sacred Books of the Hindus*, Volume VI. Allahabad, India: Panini Office, 1923. For purposes of clarity, we have translated certain terms that the translator left in the original Sanskrit, and in some instances we have altered the translations of key terms to make them consistent with other readings in this book.

3. The authoritativeness of the Veda (arises from its) being the word of God.

4. The supreme good (results) from the knowledge, produced by a particular *dharma*, of the essence of the [categories] substance, attribute, action, genus, species, and combination [inherence] by means of their resemblances and differences.

5. Earth, water, fire, air, ether, time, space, self (or soul), and mind (are) the only substances.

6. Attributes are color, taste, smell, and touch, numbers, measures, separateness, conjunction and disjunction, priority and posteriority, understandings, pleasure and pain, desire and aversion, and volitions.

7. Throwing upwards, throwing downwards, contraction, expansion, and motion are actions.

8. The resemblance of substance, attribute, and action lies in this that they are existent and nonetemal, have substance as their combinative cause [inherent cause], are effect as well as cause, and are both genus and species.

9. The resemblance of substance and attribute is the characteristic of being the originators of their class concepts [universals].

10. Substances originate another substance, and attributes another attribute.

15. It possesses action and attribute, it is a combinative cause—such (is) the mark of substance.

16. Inhering in substance, not possessing attribute, not an independent cause in conjunctions and disjunctions—such is the mark of attribute.

17. Residing in one substance only, not possessing attribute, an independent cause of conjunctions and disjunctions—such is the mark of action.

20. Action is the common cause of conjunction, disjunction, and impetus.

21. Action is not the cause of substances.

22. (Action is not the cause of substance) because of its cessation.

Book I, Chapter 2

1. Nonexistence of effect (follows) from the nonexistence of cause.

2. But nonexistence of cause (does) not (follow) from the nonexistence of the effect.

3. The notions *genus* and *species* [particular] are relative to the understanding.

4. Existence, being the cause of assimilation only, is only a genus.

5. Substantiality, and attribute-ness and action-ness are both genera and species.

6. (The statement of genus and species has been made) with the exception of the final species.

7. Existence is that to which are due the belief and usage, namely "(it is) existent," in respect of substance, attribute, and action.

Book II, Chapter 1

1. Earth possesses color, taste, smell, and touch.

2. Waters possess color, taste, and touch and are fluid and viscid.

3. Fire possesses color and touch.

4. Air possesses touch.

5. These (characteristics) are not in ether.

27. By the method of elimination (sound) is the mark of ether.

29. The unity (of ether is explained) by (the explanation of the unity of) existence.

30. (Ether is one), because there is no difference in sound which is its mark, and because there exists no other distinguishing mark.

31. And individuality also belongs to ether, since individuality follows unity.

Book III, Chapter 1

1. The objects of the senses are universally known.

2. The universal experience of the objects of the senses is the mark of (the existence of an) object different from the senses and their [phenomenal] objects.

4. (The body or the senses cannot be the seat of perception), because there is no consciousness in the causes [i.e., the component parts, of the body].

19. And activity and inactivity, observed in one's own self, are the marks of (the existence of) other selves.

Book III, Chapter 2

1. The appearance and nonappearance of knowledge, on contact of the self with the senses and the objects, are the marks (of the existence) of the mind.

3. From the nonsimultaneity of volitions, and from the nonsimultaneity of cognitions, (it follows that there is only) one (mind) (in each organism).

4. The ascending life-breath, the descending life-breath, the closing of the eyelids, the opening of the eyelids, life, the movement of the mind, and the affections of the other senses, and also pleasure, pain, desire, aversion, and volition are marks (of the existence) of the self.

6. [Objection:] There is no visible mark (of the existence of the self), because there being contact (of the senses with the body of Yajnadatta), perception does not arise (that this self is Yajnadatta).

7. And from a commonly observed mark (there is) no (inference of anything in) particular.

8. Therefore (the self is) proved by revelation.

9. [Answer:] (The proof of the existence of the self is not solely) from revelation, because ot the nonapplication of the word "I" (to other designates or objects).

10. If (there are) such sensuous observations (or perceptions) as "I am Devadatta," "I am Yajnadatta," (then there is no need of inference).

11. As in the case of other percepts, so, if the self, which is grasped by perception, is also accompanied with, or comes at the top of, marks (from which it can be inferred), then by means of confirmation the intuition becomes fastened to one and only one object.

14. Because the intuition "I" exists in one's own self, and because it does not exist otherwhere, therefore the intuition has the individual self as the object of perception.

18. (The self is) not proved (only) by revelation, since (as ether is proved by sound as its medium, so) (the self is) proved in particular by the innate as well as the sensible cognition in the form of "I," accompanied by the invariable divergence (of such cognition from all other things), as is the case with sound.

Book IV, Chapter 1

1. The eternal is that which is existent and uncaused.

2. The effect is the mark (of the existence) of the ultimate atom.

5. (It is) an error (to suppose that the ultimate atom is not eternal).

21. Space, time, and also ether are inactive, because of their difference from that which possesses activity.

23. (The relation) of the inactive [i.e., attribute and action] (to substance) is combination [inherence], (which is) independent of actions.

Book VII, Chapter 1

2. The color, taste, smell, and touch of earth, water, fire, and air are also nonetemal, on account of the nonetemality of their substrata.

22. Ether, in consequence of its vast expansion, is infinitely large. So also is the self.

23. In consequence of nonexistence of universal expansion, mind is atomic or infinitely small.

24. By attributes, space is explained (to be all-pervading).

25. Time (is the name given) to (a specific, or a universal) cause. (Hence, in either case it is all-pervading.)

Book VII, Chapter 2

9. Conjunction is produced by action of any one of two things, is produced by action of both, and is produced by conjunction, also.

10. By this disjunction is explained.

21. The prior and the posterior (are produced by two objects) lying in the same direction, existing at the same time, and being near and remote.

22. (Temporal priority and temporal posteriority are said, by suggestion, to arise respectively) from priority of the cause and from posteriority of the effect.

26. That is combination [inherence] by virtue of which (arises the intuition) in the form of "This is here," with regard to [subject and attribute].

Book VIII, Chapter 1

2. Among substances, the self, the mind and others are not objects of perception.

4. Substance is the cause of the production of cognition, where attributes and actions are in contact (with the senses).

6. (Cognition which is produced) in respect of substance, attributes and action (is) dependent upon genus and species.

Book VIII, Chapter 2

5. By reason of (its) predominance and of possession of smell, earth is the material cause of the olfactory sense.

6. In like manner, water, fire and air (are the material causes of the sense organs of taste, color and touch), inasmuch as there is no difference in the taste, color and touch (which they respectively possess, from what they respectively apprehend).

Book IX, Chapter 1

1. In consequence of the nonapplication of action and attribute (to it), (an effect is) nonexistent prior (to its production).

3. (The existent is) a different object (from the nonexistent), inasmuch as action and attribute cannot be predicated of the nonexistent.

5. And that which is a different nonexistent from these is (absolutely) nonexistent.

9. That which has not been produced does not exist;—this is a [tautological] proposition.

11. Perceptual cognition of the self (results) from a particular conjunction of the self and the mind in the self.

Book IX, Chapter 2

6. Reminiscence (results) from a particular conjunction between the soul and the mind and also from impression or latency.

10. False knowledge (arises) from imperfection of the senses and from imperfection of impression.

11. That is imperfect knowledge.

12. (Cognition) free from imperfection is (called) scientific knowledge.

13. Cognition of advanced sages, as also vision of the perfected ones, (results) from *dharma* or merits.

18.2 HINDU IDEALISM

Vedanta is an Indian philosophical school with its roots in the Upanishads, which are among the oldest texts in Sanskrit. The Upanishads center on metaphysics: What is ultimate reality? How does it relate to the world? How can it be known? The ultimate reality is Brahman. All Vedanta is Brahman-centered. Some Vedantins take Brahman to be God; others see it as an impersonal ground of Being. But the crucial division is between those who identify the self (*atman*) with Brahman and those who do not. *Dualists* maintain that the self and Brahman are distinct—the knower is not identical with God, or the ground of all being—and that the self's ability to know Brahman is limited. *Nondualists*, called *Advaita Vedantins*, hold that the self and Brahman are one and the same. In their view, by mystical knowledge of Brahman one knows the One, the Sole True Existent, whose nature is perfect being, consciousness, and bliss—and "Thou art that!" The nondualist view, plainly, is idealist. Everything is mind dependent, for the ground of all being is the self, mind. All the objects of experience are said to exist only as a kind of dream and have no reality to the one who knows Brahman.

Throughout the history of philosophy East and West, there appear many different stripes of idealism. But most idealists embrace a kind of monism. That is, they contend that ultimately the world consists of one thing or kind of thing. Idealists are always monists if they hold that there is ultimately only one kind of thing, everything being mental. They sometimes take the further step of holding not only that there is only one *kind* of thing but that there is only one thing. Shankara and subsequent Advaita Vedantins do exactly that. Brahman is that one thing—the one ultimate reality of which everything else is merely appearance. Everything is ultimately Brahman. Although there does seem to be a second thing, namely, dreams, in that our experiences are Brahman's dreams, the One is the universal subject. Nothing appears except as an object (a dream object) to its consciousness. So, on this view, everything worldly is mental in a sense, though not a product of the minds of you and me. We shall see later Bishop Berkeley in Britain—perhaps the West's most famous idealist—maintaining similarly that everything is an idea in the mind of God and would not exist except for His, and our, perceptions. According to Advaita, to be is either to be Brahman or, it would seem, in a secondary kind of reality or nonreality ("appearance," *maya*) to be part of Brahman's dreams.

The most famous Advaita Vedantin is its founder, the South Indian philosopher Shankara (788–820). Shankara at first appears to be a realist. He defends the dualism between mind and body, the existence of many minds, the thesis that physical objects are mind independent, and the thesis that there is one God, distinct from the self—all at the level of our commonsense view of the world. "It is a matter not requiring any proof that the object and the subject, ...which are opposed to each other as much as darkness and light are, cannot be identified. All the less can their respective attributes be identified," he writes.

But he then rejects this commonsense view as incompatible with scripture and with enlightenment experience. Our commonsense view of the world is thoroughly dualist and realist, he maintains, but it is inaccurate; it does not reflect the true nature of reality. In truth, there is only one thing—the ultimate reality, Brahman—and everything else is illusion, appearance, a dream. "In their literal, superficial meaning, 'Brahman' and 'Atman' have opposite attributes, like the sun and the glowworm, and king and his servant, the ocean and the well, or Mount Meru and the atom. Their identity is established only when they are understood in their true significance, and not in a superficial sense.... [t]his apparent opposition is caused by *maya* and her effects. It is not real, therefore, but superimposed." The process of meditation reveals to us that the distinction between subject and object, between perceiver and perceived, between knower and known, is unreal. It confirms that thesis of the Upanishads that all things are ultimately one. Shankara concludes: "The wise men of true discrimination understand that the essence of both Brahman and Atman is Pure Consciousness, and thus realize their absolute identity."

Shankara's key concept is ***superimposition***, which he defines as "The apparent presentation, in the form of remembrance, to consciousness of something previously observed, in some other things....[In other words,] the apparent presentation of the attributes of one thing in another thing." This is what we do routinely, and even reasonably, in our ordinary lives. We attribute properties of ourselves to the world, and properties of the world to ourselves. We see a cow and take it to be distinct from the barn. We look at ourselves in the mirror and think we are different from both. We describe the cow as brown, the barn as red, and ourselves as human. But everything we observe is a manifestation of Brahman. We attribute properties of Brahman to a wide variety of things, including ourselves. Thus we become trapped in ignorance. Through study, yoga, and meditation, we can learn to escape ignorance and see the true reality.

18.2.1 Shankara, from the *Brahmasutra Commentary*

It is a matter not requiring any proof that the object and the subject whose respective spheres are the notion of the "thou" (the non-ego) and the "ego," and which are opposed to each other as much as darkness and light are, cannot be identified. All the less can their respective attributes be identified. Hence it follows that it is wrong to superimpose upon the subject—whose self is intelligence, and which has for its sphere the notion of the ego—the object whose sphere is the notion of the non-ego, and the attributes of the object, and vice versa to superimpose the subject and the attributes of the subject on the object. In spite of this it is on the part of man a natural procedure—which has its cause in wrong knowledge—not to distinguish the two entities (object and subject) and their respective attributes, although they are absolutely distinct, but to superimpose upon each the characteristic nature and the attributes of the other, and thus, coupling the real and the unreal, to make use of expressions such as "That am I," "That is mine."

But what have we to understand by the term "superimposition"?—The apparent presentation, in the form of remembrance, to consciousness of something previously observed, in some other thing.

Some indeed define the term "superimposition" as the superimposition of the attributes of one thing on another thing. Others, again, define superimposition as the error founded on the non-apprehension of the difference of that which is superimposed from that on which it is superimposed. Others, again, define it as the fictitious assumption of attributes contrary to the nature of that thing on which something else is superimposed. But all these definitions agree insofar as they represent superimposition as the apparent presentation of the attributes of one thing in another thing. And therewith agrees also the popular view which is exemplified by expressions such as the following: "Mother-of-pearl appears like silver," "The moon although one only appears as if she were double." But how is it possible that

Source: Shankara, *Brahmasutrabhasya (the Brahmasutra Commentary)*, in *The Vedanta Sutras of Badarayana*, translated by Georg Thibaut. *Sacred Books of the East*, 1890.

on the interior self which itself is not an object there should be superimposed objects and their attributes? For everyone superimposes an object only on such other objects as are placed before him (i.e., in contact with his sense-organs), and you have said before that the interior self which is entirely disconnected from the idea of the thou (the non-ego) is never an object. It is not, we reply, non-object in the absolute sense. For it is the object of the notion of the ego, and the interior self is well known to exist on account of its immediate (intuitive) presentation. Nor is it an exceptionless rule that objects can be superimposed only on such other objects as are before us, i.e., in contact with our sense-organs; for non-discerning men superimpose on the ether, which is not the object of sensuous perception, dark-blue colour.

Hence it follows that the assumption of the non-self being superimposed on the interior self is not unreasonable.

This superimposition thus defined, learned men consider to be nescience (*avidya*), and the ascertainment of the true nature of that which is (the self) by means of the discrimination of that (which is superimposed on the self), they call knowledge (*vidya*). There being such knowledge (neither the self nor the non-self) are affected in the least by any blemish or (good) quality produced by their mutual superimposition. The mutual superimposition of the self and the non-self, which is termed nescience, is the presupposition on which there base all the practical distinctions—those made in ordinary life as well as those laid down by the Veda—between means of knowledge, objects of knowledge (and knowing persons), and all scriptural texts, whether they are concerned with injunctions and prohibitions (of meritorious and non-meritorious actions), or with final release.—But how can the means of right knowledge such as perception, inference, etc., and scriptural texts have for their object that which is dependent on nescience?—Because, we reply, the means of right knowledge cannot operate unless there be a knowing personality, and because the existence of the latter depends on the erroneous notion that the body, the senses, and so on, are identical with, or belong to, the self of the knowing person. For without the employment of the senses, perception and the other means of right knowledge cannot operate. And without a basis (i.e., the body) the senses cannot act. Nor does anybody act by means of a body on which the nature of the self is not superimposed. Nor can, in the absence of all that, the self which, in its own nature is free from all contact, become a knowing agent. And if there is no knowing agent, the means of right knowledge cannot operate (as said above). Hence perception and the other means of right knowledge, and the Vedic texts have for their object that which is dependent on nescience.

(That human cognitional activity has for its presupposition the superimposition described above), follows also from the non-difference in that respect of men from animals. Animals, when sounds or other sensible qualities affect their sense of hearing or other senses, recede or advance according as the idea derived from the sensation is a comforting or disquieting one. A cow, for instance, when she sees a man approaching with a raised stick in his hand, thinks that he wants to beat her, and therefore moves away, while she walks up to a man who advances with some fresh grass in his hand. Thus men also—who possess a higher intelligence—run away when they see strong fierce-looking fellows drawing near with shouts and brandishing swords, while they confidently approach persons of contrary appearance and behaviour. We thus see that men and animals follow the same course of procedure with reference to the means and objects of knowledge. Now it is well known that the procedure of animals bases on the non-distinction (of self and non-self); we therefore conclude that, as they present the same appearances, men also—although distinguished by superior intelligence—proceed with regard to perception and so on, in the same way as animals do; as long, that is to say, as the mutual superimposition of self and non-self lasts.

18.3 BUDDHIST IDEALISM

Schools of Indian Buddhism have made several exciting contributions to our understanding of the distinction between appearance and reality. The possibility that our ordinary waking experience is a dream, an illusion, from the perspective of an "awakened" state, is the core Buddhist message. Nirvana reveals what is real. Ordinary consciousness shows only appearance, which is dependent on our state of mind. Buddhist idealism insists that Nirvana is related to everything. The Buddha mind is all-encompassing.

Central to Buddhism is a *causal* analysis of the human predicament: desire, attachment, a mental way of grasping reality lies at the root of our suffering. Uproot the cause and the effect disappears. Causal relations serve Buddhist metaphysicians, furthermore, the way enduring substances serve their Hindu realist counterparts (in the Logic school, for instance) to explain the ways we speak of things in everyday language. The common touchstone for all philosophies, we should keep in mind, is being able to illumine the beliefs we live by in everyday life. These are expressed in such commonly employed expressions as "The pot is blue" and "This is the same person I saw yesterday." The Buddhist Idealist contends that you are the person you were yesterday—and we call you by the same name—because there are causal streams connecting the you of yesterday with today's you. Similarly, a river—or the flame of a candle, to use the preferred example in India—is continually different, but the thing now and the thing a moment earlier are related causally—as is everything, say the schools of Indian Buddhism practically in unison. Indeed, Dharmakirti holds that "causal efficacy" or "having causal power" is the best definition of being. To be is to cause.

Buddhists also emphasize unique particulars. These ultimate particulars are, on some Buddhist views, a kind of "phenomenal atom": a basic, indivisible unit of consciousness. Their groupings stand as the ultimate subjects of predication. This is sometimes called the Buddhist nominalist position.

A clear expression of the central Buddhist argument for idealism occurs in the works of the Indian Buddhist philosopher Dignaga (c. 450), who argues that everything is mind dependent. He argues that things are not as they appear. Like Nagarjuna (and indeed Socrates!), he tests opponents' views by drawing out untoward ramifications. Against the Logic and Particularist schools, Dignaga points out that though atoms serve, they say, as causes of sensory consciousness, we have no sensory awareness of atoms. The actual objects of sensory consciousness are not atoms but everyday objects. We never see atoms one by one. Thus, according to the opponent's view, sensory consciousness does not arise from what is presented in it. The opponent is distinguishing two kinds of objects: internal objects (*artha*), the everyday objects of our consciousness, and what Dignaga calls "supportive objects": the atoms. He does so sarcastically; his term, *alambana*, in Sanskrit means "substratum," and there is no external substratum in Dignaga's view. The only substratum is consciousness itself. Supportive objects are purported to cause our perceptions; internal objects are what they are (or appear to be) perceptions of. But we do not see atoms. What we see is an effect of perception, not its cause. So, on the opponent's view, what we see does not exist in reality. Thus, it is "just like the double moon," an illusion.

Clearly, however, our everyday perceptions are, by and large, not illusions. Our beliefs about the objects we encounter in everyday life are acceptable on their own terms, on Dignaga's view. The idealist/realist dispute in metaphysics is not relevant to logical principles, which he works out in the context of a theory of everyday knowledge. Dignaga has a pragmatic view of concept formation and a coherentist view of truth. Everyday beliefs are okay insofar as they guide us to get what we want and avoid what we want to avoid.

Logic and Particularism go wrong in thinking that ordinary beliefs are more than this. Realist philosophers take our everyday beliefs to be about the real constituents of the world. Taking that seriously in light of the atomic theory of matter, however, implies that our everyday beliefs are radically mistaken. We think there is really a table in the room, but there is not; there are just atoms. Everyday reality is an illusion. Dignaga's idealism disagrees. It does not see our everyday reality as illusory. True objects are the ones presented to us in such a way that we can act successfully. We know the world only through our sense organs. Thus, we can know an object only insofar as it becomes an object of consciousness. The presented pot, not a heap of atoms, is real—at least from our everyday perspective. Dignaga belongs to the Yogacara school. Yogacara philosophers try to uphold a systematic understanding of everyday appearance.

Idealists face a difficulty in the apparent intersubjectivity of the world. We seem to see the same trees, flowers, and people. Yogacara philosophers account for this by a common "storehouse" of ideas and *karma*; on some deep level we project the same things in consciousness because we have common *karma* and desires. This subjectivism seems tied to the religious commitment of Mahayanism: Everyone and everything is interconnected, and someday we shall all pass together into the final Bliss that is our common consciousness's core.

18.3.1 Dignaga, from the *Investigation of the Object of Awareness*

A Treatise on the Examination of the Object [Cause] of Consciousness

1. Though atoms serve as causes of the consciousness (*vijnapti*) of the sense-organs, they are not its actual objects like the sense-organs; because the consciousness does not represent the image of the atoms.

[As regards the nature of] the object, [declares the author,] consciousness grasps only the form of its own; because it arises in that form. Though the atoms are causes of consciousness, they do not possess the form reflected in consciousness just like the sense-organs. Therefore they cannot become its actual objects (*alambana*).

Though aggregates of atoms are alike the image of consciousness, [they cannot become its actual objects;] because

2a. The consciousness does not arise from what is represented in it.

Source: Dignaga, *The Investigation of the Object of Awareness (Alambanapariksha)*, with extracts from Vinitadeva's Commentary. Translated by N. Aiyaswami Sastri. Adyar, Chennai, India: The Adyar Library and Research Centre, the Theosophical Society, 1942. Reprinted with permission from AL & RC, Theosophical Society.

What object produces the consciousness endowed with the image of the object is properly said to be the actual object (*alambana*) of the consciousness....

2b. Because they do not exist in substance just like the double moon.

The double moon is perceived [by a man] on account of defects of his sense-organs. But [this perception is not produced by the double moon, as] there exists no object like the double moon. Similarly the aggregates of atoms do not exist in substance and cannot act as causes of consciousness. Hence they are not its actual objects.

2c–d. Thus both the external things are unfit to be real objects of consciousness.

The external things, atoms and their aggregates, cannot serve as the actual objects of consciousness, as both of them are defective in one or other respect.

3a–b. Some hold that the combined form of atoms is the cause of consciousness....

3c–d. The atomic form does not become the object of consciousness just like the attributes such as solidity, etc.

Just as the attributes, solidity and others, though existent in atoms, are not perceived by the visual consciousness, so also the atomic form.

4a–b. In that case, the [different] perceptions of a pot, cup, etc. will be identical.

Though the atoms of a pot are greater in number and that of a cup [less], there exists no distinction whatever amongst the atoms.

4c. If [the opponent says that] the perception differs in accordance with differences in the forms of the pot and others;...

4d–5a. But it never exists in the atoms which exist in substance, because the atoms are absolutely identical in their dimensions.

Though the atoms are different in substance, there exists absolutely no distinction in their atomic size.

5b. Therefore the differentiation goes along with things substantially non-existent....

5c–d. For, if you remove one by one the atoms [of the pot, etc.] the perception illuminating the image of the pot, etc. will immediately vanish away....

... It is, therefore, rationally deduced that the objects of different sensual cognitions do not exist externally.

6a–c. It is the object (*artha*) which exists internally in knowledge itself as a knowable aspect and which appears to us as if it exists externally.

Though the external things are denied, what exists internally in knowledge itself [i.e., its knowable aspect] and appears to us as though it is existent externally, serves as a condition of the actual object (*alambana-pratyaya*) [to consciousness].

6c–d. Because consciousness is the essence [of the external object] and that [object essence of which is consciousness] acts as the condition [to consciousness].

The internal consciousness appears as [manifold external] object (*artha*) and also arises from that [objective aspect of its own]. Thus the internal consciousness is endowed with two parts (i.e., image and cause) and therefore what exists internally in the consciousness (i.e., the objective aspect) is the object-condition (*alambana-pratyaya*) to the consciousness.

If only the objective appearance of consciousness is experienced, [it will be a part of the consciousness and appearing simultaneously with it]. How can a part of consciousness and appearing simultaneously be a condition to the consciousness [itself]?

7a. [Though the external object] is only a part [of the internal consciousness], it is a condition [to the consciousness], because it is invariably associated with the consciousness.

[The objective aspect of consciousness,] though arising simultaneously with it, becomes condition to [the consciousness] which is produced by other [conditions]....

Or,

7b. It becomes condition also in succession by transmitting the force.

It is also possible successively that the objective appearance of consciousness, in order to give rise to a result homogeneous with itself, makes the force seated in the [storehouse] consciousness, and it is not contradictory [to the reasoning].

[The opponent says:] If only the self of consciousness constitutes the object-condition, how should we explain [the saying that] the visual consciousness arises depending upon the eye and [form]?

[The author replies:]

7c–d. What is the sense-organ is [nothing but] the force itself [in consciousness] by virtue of its acting simultaneously [with the object] as an auxiliary cause [for raising up of consciousness]....

8a. That force is not contradictory to the consciousness.

8b–d. Thus the objective aspect (of consciousness] and the force [called sense-organ] go mutually conditioned from immemorial time.

Depending upon the force called eye and the interior form arises the consciousness which appears as though it is the external object, but it arises undifferentiated from the perceivable object. These two act mutually conditioned without beginning in time. Sometime when the force gets matured, consciousness is transformed into a form of object and sometime the force arises from [the consciousness] endowed with the form of object. The consciousness and force, both may be said to be either different from or identical with one another as one may like. Thus the interior object [which is not different from consciousness] is endowed with two factors [image and cause], and therefore it is logically concluded that consciousness [alone] is transformed into [external] object.

18.4 JAINIST PERSPECTIVISM

Jainism, a religion and philosophy tracing from Mahavira (599–527 BCE), is best known for its emphasis on nonviolence. Jains base their ethical views on five great vows: noninjury, truthfulness, respect for property, chastity, and nonattachment. They believe that these vows can be fulfilled only from a certain metaphysical standpoint. A conviction that one has the absolute truth, for example, is likely to lead one to be willing to injure others for its sake and to become attached to it. So Jainist philosophers have developed a metaphysics resting on a principle of nonabsolutism (*anekantavada*, non-one-sidedness), holding that no statement captures the truth absolutely. Everything we say is true, at best, *in some respect*; nothing is true *simpliciter*. The same is true of falsehood. Every statement approaches its topic from one point of view. To understand the topic, however, we must see it from many points of view. We should respect people no matter what they believe or say, therefore, because every statement contains some element of truth. Everything is true in some respect or from some point of view.

Jains traditionally illustrate the point with the story of the blind men and the elephant, nicely presented in a poem by John Godfrey Saxe (1816–1887):

It was six men of Hindustan
To learning much inclined,
Who went to see the Elephant
(Though all of them were blind)
That each by observation
Might satisfy the mind.

The first approached the Elephant
And happening to fall
Against his broad and sturdy side
At once began to bawl:
"Bless me, it seems the Elephant
Is very like a wall."

The second, feeling of his tusk,
Cried, "Ho! What have we here
So very round and smooth and sharp?
To me 'tis mighty clear
This wonder of an Elephant
Is very like a spear."

The third approached the animal,
And happening to take
The squirming trunk within his hands,
Then boldly up and spake:
"I see," quoth he, "the Elephant
Is very like a snake."

The Fourth reached out an eager hand,
And felt about the knee.
"What most this wondrous beast is like
Is mighty plain," quoth he;
"'Tis clear enough the Elephant
Is very like a tree!"

The Fifth, who chanced to touch the ear,
Said: "E'en the blindest man
Can tell what this resembles most;
Deny the fact who can,
This marvel of an Elephant
Is very like a fan!"

The Sixth no sooner had begun
About the beast to grope,
Than, seizing on the swinging tail
That fell within his scope,

"I see," quoth he, "the Elephant
Is very like a rope!"

And so these men of Hindustan
Disputed loud and long,
Each in his own opinion
Exceeding stiff and strong,
Though each was partly in the right
And all were in the wrong.

Of course, they are all correct, in a way; the elephant really does have all those aspects. Just so, our beliefs may capture some aspects of reality. But, like the statements of the blind men, they are true only of some aspects of reality, from a certain point of view.

Jainist metaphysics maintains that reality is like the elephant in the poem. It is many-sided; indeed, it has infinitely many facets, some of which are opposites. Whatever we say is true *syat*, maybe, perhaps, in some respect; it is also false in some respect. We never capture the whole truth. Everything we say comes from a limited perspective that gives us a view of only some facets of reality.

Accompanying nonabsolutism is a view of language as expressing the truth only from some point of view. This doctrine of postulation, "maybeism," or relativism (*syadvada*), becomes one of the tenets of Jainism. Vadi Devasuri (twelfth century) develops this into a theory of language based on the Law of Sevenfold Predication, which identifies seven modes of predication:

1. It is.
2. It is not.
3. It is and is not.
4. It is indeterminate.
5. It is and is indeterminate.
6. It is not and is indeterminate.
7. It is and is not and is indeterminate.

All should be modified by *syat*. All are true in some respect, but none captures the entire truth.

Thus nonabsolutism—a positive pluralism of perspectives—is the position that reality is so rich that it makes true, with qualifications, every intellectual stance. The Jain metaphysics is not a form of skepticism but rather a bold promise of reconciliation of apparently opposed points of view, unlike the perspectivism of Nietzsche, for example, which emphasizes the opposite, the limitations of perspectives. The Jain position targets only the absolutism that partisans propose for their preferred views, blind to the truth in their opponents' theories. In other words, Jains do not set out to challenge even the most general positive claims about the nature of everything or an underlying reality. The point is not to deny but to affirm, to affirm seemingly incompatible perspectives. The special sevenfold logic—the seven styles (seven combinations of three truth values: truth, falsity, and indeterminacy), the "maybeism"—was developed to facilitate the disarming of controversy. Here are the weapons of intellectual nonviolence (*ahimsa*).

There is a similar metaphilosophical position in Buddhism, the avoiding of extremes, advocated by Nagarjuna and his "school of the Middle," Madhyamika. What distinguishes the Buddhist skeptic from the Jain perspectivalist is that the Buddhist rejects opposing positions as departing from the middle, while the Jain accepts them as complementary and incomplete without each other. All truths are truths only from a perspective. Some are true to us and, so far as we know, to everyone. Even if we are not aware of controversy concerning a claim, it is still only from a perspective, and there may be a perspective in which it is not true. We may accept that claim but we do so recognizing that we might be wrong. No claim is immune from the possibility of error.

Nevertheless, some claims, or cognitions, are false from our own point of view and every point of view that we know of. Some are indeterminate; it is impossible to say whether they are true or false. On the classical Indian scene, Advaita Vedanta is famous for proposing such a third truth value, the inexplicable, which holds for statements about the relationship of Brahman to the world as it appears to us. We as finite individual knowers cannot know what the world looks like from Brahman's viewpoint. Jains use the category of the indeterminate similarly to classify apparently unanswerable questions.

In recognizing that a claim can be simultaneously true and false, or true and indeterminate, or indeterminate and false, or all three together, the Jain view again relativizes to standpoints. From some standpoints a claim is true while in others it is false. From our own standpoint, it is true in some standpoints and false in others, and so on. Reality is so incredibly rich that it can underlie and give rise to opposed pictures.

The Jain position is not self-defeating. Contrary to what the Vedantin Shankara alleged, it is not meant to be an absolute claim. That would be like practicing *ahimsa* toward everyone except oneself. Nonharmfulness requires humility.

18.4.1 Vadi Devasuri, from *Ornament Illuminating the Means and Principles of Awareness*

SUTRA: In all cases a word in expressing its object follows the Law of Sevenfold Predication by its affirmation and negation.

COMMENTARY: According to the principle of the Jaina philosophy, a thing is not confined to one aspect only but has many aspects (*anekanta*). Thus in some sense, it is existent; in some sense, again, it is non-existent. Similarly, viewed from one standpoint, a thing is eternal, but viewed from another, it is impermanent. As a matter of fact seven such aspects may be found out in a thing from seven viewpoints. Now, word is but a counterpart of the thing and like those in the thing, a word also has seven

Source: From Vadi Devasuri's *Pramana-naya-tattvalokalankara*. Translated by Hari Satya Bhattacharya. Mumbai, India: Jain Sahitya Vikas Mandal, 1967.

aspects, so far as its manners of expressing it are concerned.

SUTRA: The Law of Sevenfold Predication consists in using seven sorts of expression, regarding one and the same thing with reference to its particular aspects, one by one, without any inconsistency, by means of affirmation and negation, made either separately or together, all these seven expressions being marked with "in some respects" (*syat*).

COMMENTARY: This is a description of the celebrated doctrine of the *Sapta-Bhangi* or Law of Sevenfold Predication. Analysing the description given above, we can thus find out the nature and conditions of the *Sapta-Bhangi*.

1. The Seven Predications are to be made regarding one and the same thing, e.g., *jiva* or animal. The words "one and the same thing" prevent the predications being a "hundred-fold" (i.e., many-fold) one, things in the world being so many, hundreds and hundreds in number.
2. The Seven Predications are to be made not only with regard to one and the same thing but with reference to "one" only of its various attributes, e.g., existence. Seven propositions, indicating seven different attributes of a thing, do not constitute the *Sapta Bhanga*. Attributes, as aspects of a thing, are infinite in number. If one of such attributes or aspects be taken into consideration, we shall see that seven predications or statements can be made with reference to it. It is thus that a predication is said to be seven-fold and not infinite-fold. Of course, if it is contended that the attributes or aspects of a thing are infinite in number and that with reference to each one of these attributes and aspects, seven predications can be made and that, consequently, predication may be infinitely-seven-fold, well, the Jaina philosophers have no objection to that position.
3. Each of these Predications must be based on principles of "affirmation" and "negation."
4. That Seven Predications must be made in such a way that none of them be inconsistent with the facts of perception, etc.
5. Each of these statements must be marked with the expression, "in some respects" (*syat*).

...

That which was non-existent comes into existence; that which is existent vanishes into non-existence; the substratum persists; well, these are the three peculiar characteristics of the phenomena of origination, etc., well-known to all. Then again the three phenomena, although different from each other in some respects, are not absolutely so. They are all connected with each other. There is no origination without decay and persistence; there is no decay without origination and persistence; and there is no persistence without origination and decay. The facts of origination, persistence and decay are thus dependent on each other and inhere in the thing. Why then can a thing not have a triple nature? The following poetic lines are also interesting in this connection:

"When the pitcher on her head was destroyed, the daughter was sorry, the son was glad, and the king was indifferent." In the same light the truth is to be understood that a thing has a triple nature; one of its forms is destroyed; another is generated; the substratum underlying both the forms persists. Thus it is that a thing is both permanent and impermanent and as such many-sided.

Similarly it may be shown that a thing is many-sided inasmuch as it is both existent and non-existent. One may of course contend: Well, that is a contradiction; how can one and the same thing, e.g., a pitcher, be both existent and non-existent? Existence and non-existence repudiate each other; otherwise, they would have been identical phenomena; hence if a fact is existent, how can it be non-existent? And if it is non-existent, how can it be existent? The Jaina philosophers point out that the contention is unsound. The objection might have force, if it were held that a thing is existent in those very respects in which it is non-existent and that it is non-existent in those very respects in which it is existent. A thing may be said to be existent with respect to its (1) own form, e.g., that of a pitcher, (2) own substance, e.g., gold, (3) own place, e.g., a city and (4) own time, e.g., spring-season. There would be no inconsistency or contradiction, if it is said that the thing, e.g., the pitcher, does not exist (1) as a cloth, (2) as made up of threads, (3) as a thing made in a village and (4) as a thing of the summer-season....

A thing which is a mode, e.g., a pitcher or a cloth, has thus an aspect of existence and an aspect of non-existence or negation. It is not rightly conceived or described, if it is said to be simply existent. From the view-point of its own substance, a thing is certainly existent; but so far as the substance of other things is concerned, it has also an element of non-existence or negation in itself; the result is that a thing which is thus a negation of things other than itself has no chance of identifying itself with these other things.

It is clear that a thing has many aspects (*anekanta*), viz., the existent and the non-existent. In the same manner, an intelligent man should understand the manifold character of other similar aspects of a thing, should see, that is, how a thing is, for example, different from another thing (in some respects) as also not different from it (in some respects)....

The *arhatas*, or the thinkers of the Jaina School, hold that all things, e.g., the soul etc., are *anekanta* in nature, i.e., that all reals have various aspects. Hence they are prepared to admit every well-reasoned truth. It is redundant accordingly to argue or urge the matter of such truths as that the soul exists etc., before the Jainas, the truths being well-known to them.

CHAPTER 19

Ancient Greek Metaphysics

"The things that are"

Austin is a city in Texas. There is only one of it. It is a unique *particular*, to use the technical term of philosophers. Nothing other than itself, not New York, not Dallas, not even San Antonio, is identical with Austin. If a replica were built in Oklahoma, the new city would be a replica of Austin, not Austin itself. We would say that Austin continues to be in Texas, not that the city was now both there and in Oklahoma.

Universals are multiply instanced. The property *sprawling*, for example, and the kind *city* are true of numerous individuals. Many things can be sprawling, all at the same time, in different places, and not just cities (consider handwriting all over a page). There are cities, simultaneously, in different countries, on different continents. Austin is sprawling; it instantiates both sprawling and city. But so do Los Angeles and Caracas and Lagos and Dacca.

To talk of properties and kinds seems a strange way of looking at things, at least compared with good old particulars—such as Socrates and Abraham Lincoln, tables and chairs, and all the other things we count. Are features and types real, or are they just the way we see things? Is red, for instance, a real component of the red truck in the garage? Is red something other than the paint that is red? Is it more than the pigment? Red is, we might say, a feature of the truck, one for which we might be willing to pay (preferring the red truck on the lot to the one with green and yellow stripes, for instance). But the color does seem to depend on its being perceived in a way that the truck does not; the truck could, after all, be painted blue. Are kinds and properties really parts of reality?

There are several approaches to this question, the most prominent being realism, conceptualism, and nominalism. In broader perspective, the question connects with the distinction between appearance and reality. That, in turn, is inseparable from our sense of illusion (e.g., seeing two moons) as different from seeing things as they really are (seeing the one moon). When we perceive things as they are, we perceive veridically. In this chapter we shall be occupied with the large theme of appearance and reality. We start with the question about reality of universals or properties and kinds, but we shall also have to learn about substances, primary and secondary properties, and arguments why we should regard things as real outside the mind. Furthermore, we shall take a hard look at causality.

19.1 PLATO'S FORMS (UNIVERSALS)

Realists, or platonists (so-called after the most famous Western advocate of the position), hold that universals are real and independent of human cognition. Conceptualists hold that universals exist but in some way depend on the mind. Nominalists hold that universals do not exist; everything is particular. The properties and kinds that others take to be real nominalists see as mere mental projections.

In the West, the question of the reality of universals springs from Plato, who reasons that there is a realm of abstract entities called forms (or, in an alternative translation, ideas) that exist independent of us as thinkers. Plato sometimes speaks of them as ideal *F*s and *G*s and *H*s: the perfect square, ideal beauty, the archetypal horse. He sometimes speaks of them as qualities or properties. Plato's universals make things the way they are. Having horsehood, the property of being a horse—which every horse has—makes Trigger a horse. By grasping these ideals apart from their instances (the pure square apart from all actual squares), we gain true knowledge. Furthermore, by knowing the abstract *F* or *G* or *H* it becomes possible to know some things that are *F* or *G* or *H*—a square computer screen, for instance, a beautiful painting, or a beautiful song.

In his most famous contribution to the history of thought, Plato distinguishes the perceptible or visible world from the intellectual or intelligible world, the realm of forms. Then he divides each realm into two. (1) The visible world is populated by (a) shadows and reflections, which are different from (b) directly perceivable objects. (2) The intelligible world is populated by (c) mathematical forms or shapes and (d) higher, more abstract forms, such as justice. Corresponding to this fourfold schema are cognitive relations that we as subjects have to these things: (1a) perceptions of shadows, etc., (1b) opinions deriving from fallible perception of visible things, (2a) understanding through knowing forms that are instanced in visible things, and (2b) reason that contemplates, for example, the ideal of justice.

Plato says that shadows and reflections, while real in the sense that such things occur, are nevertheless less real than true objects of perception, such as people, trees, and rocks. Reflections are derivative; they are mere copies, images, of the originals. His next move is to say that the relation of shadows to the things that cast them, as well as of reflections to things reflected, is the same as the relation between the visible world and the intelligible world, the world of forms. A geometer, for example, trying to prove a theorem about squares and circles, draws diagrams. Those diagrams are visible, concrete objects, lines in pencil or chalk. But the geometer has an interest, not in the lines' unique actuality, but in their representing general forms of squares and circles—that which all particular squares and circles have in common. The square drawn with chalk is to the general form of a square as the shadow of a pole is to the pole itself. Furthermore, just as the shadow of a pole moves while the pole remains stationary, so objects in the visible world move and change while the forms remain unchanging. The forms about which the geometer reasons are the general forms, the abstract forms, shapes and colors, and so on, of things we perceive. They are not located in their entirety in any particular place, though they have instances that exist at particular places, dwelling in particulars that are directly perceived. But not all universals are properties of things perceived. Not all kinds are perceptual kinds. Plato seeks to understand other universals with the art of dialectic. These are the most abstract universals, but also, for that reason, potentially the most real.

Plato illustrates the fourfold schema (called the ***divided line***) with a famous allegory, the allegory of the cave. Socrates imagines people inhabiting a cave, watching a play of shadows on the wall, believing they are seeing the world as it is. Plato suggests that philosophy is able to turn people away from shadows. Philosophy can make people see the true nature of things, shot through as they are with forms that are truer, unchanging realities. All particulars are limited in place and time. Universals are unlimited in these ways. To know them is akin to a cave dweller coming up and out into the sunlight, realizing then that mere shadows were all he had previously perceived.

Released from the cave, the prisoner sees first reflections, then objects, then the moon and stars, and finally the sun. The progression is that of a philosopher moving in contemplation to the mathematical forms of perceivable things and then, finally, to abstract forms themselves, such as Justice, Beauty, and, in the ***Republic***, the idea of the Good. Socrates explains the significance of the allegory: The sun, which gives light to everything else, corresponds to the form of the Good.

Why, according to Plato, should we assume that forms exist? Why think there is anything beyond the cave we inhabit, that is, the sensible world? The forms, Plato would answer, are necessary for knowledge even of sensible things. They solve two problems with which earlier Greek philosophers had wrestled.

First, the forms explain how change is possible. People, for example, sleep and then wake up. Parmenides had argued that such change is an illusion, for no one thing can have contrary properties such as sleeping and waking. Heraclitus had argued that change is constant—that you cannot step into the same river twice—for, since no one thing could have contrary properties, the person sleeping cannot be the same as the person waking. Every change must change the identity of the object undergoing it. Plato uses the forms to explain how one object can change while retaining its identity—while remaining the same thing. The object can stop participating in one form and start participating in another while remaining the same object. You can fall asleep and then wake up the same person as before.

Second, and more importantly, the forms explain how we can have objective knowledge of the world. Plato's chief opponents were the Sophists—thinkers who argued that all truth is relative. Protagoras famously proclaimed that "man is the measure of all things." He meant that each individual person is the measure of truth and falsehood. The day might be cool for me and hot for you. The theft might be right for me and wrong for you. There is no saying what is true or false, right or wrong, period; there is only what seems true or false, right or wrong, to me or to you. Indeed, there is only what seems true or false, right or wrong, to me or to you, *now or at another time*, for I have no way of knowing whether how things seem to me, or the content of my own thoughts, remains stable over time. Plato affirms, in contrast, that some things are true, full stop. They are true for you and for me, at any time, from any point of view. Thus, $1 + 1 = 2$, for me and for you, on every day of the week, whether you're feeling well or ill, etc. Things participate in forms independent of our perceptions of them. When we think about them, we are capable of grasping the very forms in which they participate. When we do, we grasp objective truth.

Socrates, in questioning Athenians about justice, courage, piety, friendship, and so on, is typically given a single example instead of a definition in general form. He asks what courage is, and someone says, "A soldier's fighting at his post and not running away." Socrates points out that people display courage in situations other than soldiering, concluding, "There must be something that all these instances of courage have in common—something that makes them all instances of courage." In Plato's theory, that something is the form of courage.

Plato sees mathematics, science, and philosophy as reasoning, not about particulars—the cities of Austin, Los Angeles, Dacca, and so on—but about forms, about what in general it is to be, in our examples, a city. Plato's theory of forms, however, creates puzzles as well as answers. How do we know anything about forms? How can the same form be known by two different reasoners? How can it be present at the same time to both of their minds? On Plato's view, forms have causal power; we are able to think of the abstract form of a circle by having some kind of mental contact with circularity. But how is this possible? A chief motivation for the rival theories of conceptualism and nominalism is the suspicion that the platonist cannot explain how we know the forms. Human beings seem to be limited to the evidence of their senses. Through our senses we have cognitive contact with the world. But according to Plato the forms lie beyond the senses.

In the *Meno*, Plato speaks of recollection. By recollection, Plato means that we had knowledge of forms in previous births (sounding like an Indian philosopher in invoking a doctrine of reincarnation). But how did we have access to them then? You cannot explain a mystery with an enigma.

In the *Republic*, the form of the Good, like the sun, sheds light that makes the rest of the forms visible to our mind's eye. But if it is unclear how the forms can do anything, how can the form of the Good illumine the others?

Within the confines of Plato's theory, then, the problem of our knowledge of the forms is hard to overcome. Indeed, within a generation, the teachers and students at Plato's Academy had become skeptics. They could not see how knowledge of the forms is possible. But they still agreed with Plato that, if we cannot know the forms, we cannot know anything.

Modern analogues to Plato's metaphors seem more promising. Perhaps we are born with access to forms, in the sense that an ability to think abstractly is hard-wired genetically. Perhaps we can account for our ability to reason in pragmatic terms by the fact that abstract reasoning is highly successful and thus selected and justified by the results it yields for concrete situations in life. Contemporary neuroscience and evolutionary biology thus breathe new life into Plato's responses.

19.1.1 Plato, from *Republic*

You have to imagine, then, that there are two ruling powers and that one of them is set over the intellectual world, the other over the visible. I don't say heaven, lest you should fancy that I'm playing upon the name (*ourhanoz, orhatoz*). May I suppose that you have this distinction of the visible and intelligible fixed in your mind?

I have.

Now take a line that's been cut into two unequal parts and divide each of them again in the same proportion. Suppose the two main divisions to answer, one to the visible and the other to the intelligible. Then compare the subdivisions in respect of their clearness and want of clearness. You'll find that the first section in the sphere of the visible consists of images. And by images I mean, in the first place, shadows, and in the second place, reflections in water and in solid, smooth and polished bodies and the like: Do you understand?

Yes, I understand.

Imagine, now, the other section, of which this is only the resemblance, to include the animals we see and everything that grows or is made.

Very good.

Wouldn't you admit that both the sections of this division have different degrees of truth and that the copy is to the original as the sphere of opinion is to the sphere of knowledge?

Most undoubtedly.

Next proceed to consider the manner in which the sphere of the intellectual is to be divided.

In what manner?

Thus:—There are two subdivisions, in the lower of which the soul uses the figures given by the former division as images. The enquiry can only be hypothetical. Instead of going upwards to a principle it descends to the other end. In the higher of the two, the soul passes out of hypotheses and goes up to a principle, which is above hypotheses, making no use of images as in the former case but proceeding only in and through the ideas themselves.

I don't quite understand your meaning, he said.

Then I'll try again; you'll understand me better when I've made some preliminary remarks. You're aware that students of geometry, arithmetic, and the kindred sciences assume the odd and the even and the figures and three kinds of angles and the like in their several branches of science. These are their hypotheses, which they and everybody are supposed to know. Therefore they do not deign to give any account of them either to themselves or to others. They begin with them and go on until they arrive at last, and in a consistent manner, at their conclusion?

Yes, he said, I know.

And don't you also know that although they make use of the visible forms and reason about them, they're thinking not of these, but of the ideals they resemble; not of the figures which they draw, but of the absolute square and the absolute diameter, and so on—the forms they draw or make, and which have shadows and reflections in water of their own, are converted by them into images. But they're really seeking to behold the things themselves, which can only be seen with the eye of the mind?

That's true.

In the search after the intelligible the soul is compelled to use hypotheses—not ascending to a first principle—because she's unable to rise above the region of hypothesis. But employing the objects of which the shadows below are resemblances in their turn as images, they have in relation to their shadows and reflections a greater distinctness and therefore a higher value.

I understand, he said, that you're speaking of the province of geometry and the sister arts.

Source: Plato, *Republic*. Translated by Benjamin Jowett. New York: Charles Scribner's Sons, 1871. We have revised the translation for readability.

And when I speak of the other division of the intelligible, you'll understand me to speak of that other sort of knowledge that reason herself attains by the power of dialectic, using the hypotheses not as first principles, but only as hypotheses—that is to say, as steps and points of departure into a world above hypotheses, in order that she may soar beyond them to the first principle of the whole. Clinging to this and then to what depends on it, by successive steps she descends again without the aid of any sensible object. From ideas, through ideas, and in ideas she ends.

I understand you, he replied; not perfectly, for you seem to me to be describing a task that's really tremendous. But, at any rate, I understand you to say that knowledge and being, which the science of dialectic contemplates, are clearer than the notions of the arts, as they are termed, which proceed from hypotheses only. These are also contemplated by the understanding and not by the senses. Yet, because they start from hypotheses and don't ascend to a principle, those who contemplate them appear to you not to exercise the higher reason upon them, although when a first principle is added to them they are cognizable by the higher reason. And the habit concerned with geometry and the cognate sciences I suppose that you would term understanding and not reason, as being intermediate between opinion and reason.

You have quite conceived my meaning, I said; and now, corresponding to these four divisions, let there be four faculties in the soul—reason answering to the highest, understanding to the second, faith (or conviction) to the third, and perception of shadows to the last—and let there be a scale of them, and let us suppose that the several faculties have clearness in the same degree that their objects have truth.

I understand, he replied, and give my assent, and accept your arrangement....

And now, I said, let me show in a figure how far our nature is enlightened or unenlightened:—Behold! Human beings living in an underground den, which has a mouth open towards the light and reaching all along the den. Here they have been from their childhood, and have their legs and necks chained so that they can't move, and can only see before them, being prevented by the chains from turning round their heads. Above and behind them a fire is blazing at a distance, and between the fire and the prisoners there is a raised way. You will see, if you look, a low wall built along the way, like the screen which marionette players have in front of them, over which they show the puppets.

I see.

And do you see, I said, men passing along the wall carrying all sorts of vessels, and statues and figures of animals made of wood and stone and various materials, which appear over the wall? Some of them are talking, others silent.

You've shown me a strange image, and they're strange prisoners.

Like ourselves, I replied; and they see only their own shadows or the shadows of one another, which the fire throws on the opposite wall of the cave?

True, he said; how could they see anything but the shadows if they were never allowed to move their heads?

And of the objects which are being carried in like manner they would only see the shadows?

Yes, he said.

And if they were able to converse with one another, wouldn't they suppose that they were naming what was actually before them?

Very true.

And suppose further that the prison had an echo that came from the other side. Wouldn't they be sure to fancy when one of the passersby spoke that the voice which they heard came from the passing shadow?

No question, he replied.

To them, I said, the truth would be literally nothing but the shadows of the images.

That's certain.

And now look again, and see what will naturally follow if the prisoners are released and disabused of their error. At first, when any of them is liberated and compelled suddenly to stand up and turn his neck round and walk and look towards the light, he'll suffer sharp pains. The glare will distress him. He'll be unable to see the realities of which in his former state he had seen the shadows. Then imagine someone saying to him that what he saw before was an illusion, but that now, when he's approaching nearer to being and his eye is turned towards more real existence, he has a clearer vision,—what will be his reply? And you may further imagine that his instructor is pointing to the objects as they pass and requiring him to name them,—won't he be perplexed? Won't he fancy that the shadows he formerly saw are truer than the objects now shown to him?

Far truer.

And if he's compelled to look straight at the light, won't he have a pain in his eyes that will make him turn away to take refuge in the objects of vision he can see, and which he will conceive to be in reality clearer than the things which are now being shown to him?

True, he said.

And suppose, once more, that he's reluctantly dragged up a steep and rugged ascent and held fast until he's forced into the presence of the sun itself. Isn't he likely to be pained and irritated? When he approaches the light his eyes will be dazzled, and he won't be able to see anything at all of what are now called realities.

Not all in a moment, he said.

He'll need to grow accustomed to the sight of the upper world. And first he'll see the shadows best, next the reflections of men and other objects in the water, and then the objects themselves. Then he'll gaze upon the light of the moon and the stars and the spangled heaven; and he'll see the sky and the stars by night better than the sun or the light of the sun by day?

Certainly.

Last of all he'll be able to see the sun and not mere reflections of it in the water, but he'll see it in its own proper place and not in another; and he'll contemplate it as it is.

Certainly.

He'll then proceed to argue that this is what gives the season and the years, and is the guardian of all that's in the visible world, and in a certain way the cause of all things he and his fellows have been accustomed to behold?

Clearly, he said, he'd first see the sun and then reason about him.

And when he remembered his old habitation and the wisdom of the den and his fellow prisoners, don't you suppose that he'd congratulate himself on the change and pity them?

Certainly, he would.

And if they were in the habit of conferring honors among themselves on those who were quickest to observe the passing shadows and to remark which of them went before, and which followed after, and which were together; and who were therefore best able to draw conclusions as to the future, do you think that he would care for such honors and glories, or envy the possessors of them? Wouldn't he say with Homer, "Better to be the poor servant of a poor master," and to endure anything, rather than think as they do and live after their manner?

Yes, he said, I think that he'd rather suffer anything than entertain these false notions and live in this miserable manner.

Imagine once more, I said, such a one coming suddenly out of the sun to be replaced in his old situation; wouldn't he be certain to have his eyes full of darkness?

To be sure, he said.

And if there were a contest, and he had to compete in measuring the shadows with the prisoners who had never moved out of the den, while his sight was still weak, and before his eyes had become steady (and the time which would be needed to acquire this new habit of sight might be very considerable), wouldn't he be ridiculous? Men would say of him that up he went and down he came without his eyes; and that it was better not even to think of ascending. If anyone tried to loose another and lead him up to the light, let them only catch the offender, and they would put him to death.

No question, he said.

This entire allegory, I said, you may now append, dear Glaucon, to the previous argument. The prison house is the world of sight, the light of the fire is the sun, and you won't misapprehend me if you interpret the journey upwards to be the ascent of the soul into the intellectual world, according to my poor belief, which, at your desire, I have expressed—whether rightly or wrongly God knows. But, whether true or false, my opinion is that in the world of knowledge the idea of Good appears last of all and is seen only with an effort. When seen, it's also inferred to be the universal author of all things beautiful and right, parent of light and of the lord of light in this visible world, and the immediate source of reason and truth in the intellectual. This is the power upon which he who would act rationally, in either public or private life, must have his eye fixed.

19.2 ARISTOTLE: CATEGORIES AND CAUSES

Plato's student Aristotle addressed the access problem. Universals are real, he reasoned, and in some cases mind independent, but we need no special faculty to know them. We learn everything from sense experience, including what we know about the forms. That is, we know them by perceiving objects in which they dwell. We know something about circles in general from experiencing circles. By reasoning from our experience, we find the general features of circularity. Aristotle's contribution is to present a view of particulars that would avoid Plato's problem of how we know general features.

But what, then, is a particular, and how do particulars connect with universals? Aristotle's answer centers on a theory of substance. Substances are the things we ordinarily talk about when we say anything. *Primary* substances are individual physical things, such as tables and chairs, people and penguins, "cabbages and kings," as well as their physical parts. *Secondary* substances are kinds. Substances are the ultimate particulars, the subjects of predication. They are the objects of our perception; we see them and touch them. A substance can be primary, like Socrates, who as a human being is more than the sum of his parts. A substance can also be composite, for example, a heap of rocks.

There are of course other categories of things we refer to. The Greek language has various parts of speech. Accordingly, there are—in addition to substances, which are picked out by nouns—other things meant and experienced. Aristotle lists ten categories and provides examples (we add a few in parentheses):

Category	Examples
substance	the horse, Socrates (Austin, tables and chairs)
quantity	two cubits long (a kilogram in weight, fifty miles an hour in velocity)
quality	white, grammatical (sprawling, wise, wooden)
relation	double, half, greater than (loves, is angry at)
place	in the marketplace, in the Lyceum (west of San Antonio)
time	yesterday, last year (at noon, for a month)
position	lying, sitting (standing)
state	shod, armed (puzzled, impressed)
action	to lance, to cauterize (to do, to make, to go)
affection	to be lanced, to be cauterized (to be eaten, to be addressed)

Aristotle considers the basic building blocks from which sentences are formed. His ten categories are the fundamental types of things that basic verbal elements pick out. The central task of metaphysics is to investigate how these kinds of things relate to each other.

What is a substance? Aristotle gives various criteria. Most importantly, a substance is a "This." We can refer to a substance to answer the question "What is that?" If we ask what a thing is, we do not expect to be told, "It's white" or "It's sitting down" or "It's in Texas" but "It's a cat" or "It's Socrates." But now a substance such as Socrates is always a substance of a certain kind, belonging to a *genus* or kind, which we can also designate by a noun: "Socrates is a man (a human being)." Human beings belong to a still wider category: animals. There are characteristics—*differentia*—that distinguish Socrates from other human beings; there are also differentia that distinguish human beings from other kinds of animals. A proper Aristotelian definition states a thing's genus—the kind of thing it is—and its differentia—its distinguishing features.

All things of other categories depend on substance. Qualities, quantities, actions, affections, relations, and so on, are always qualities, quantities, etc., of substances. We can speak of Socrates as six feet tall, wise, in Athens, lying down yesterday, puzzled at a proposed definition, questioning and being questioned. But to talk of combinations of other categories (for example, "wise in Athens puzzled") apart from substance would make no sense.

Substances have other characteristic features. There are no degrees of substance in the way there are degrees of quantity, quality, relation, and so on. A cat may be more or less white or old or more or less far away, but a cat cannot be more or less a cat. Socrates may be a little angry or very wise, a little puzzled or very impressed, but he cannot be a little bit man or very Socrates. Also, substances admit contrary qualities, while things of other categories do not. Socrates may be sitting one moment and lying down the next. He may go from being angry to being puzzled to being impressed. In short, substances can change in quality, relation, position, and so on. Things of other categories cannot change in these ways.

Primary substances thus change over time while remaining the same substance. A river remains the same though composed of different water at different times. Not only can it be cold at one moment and warm the next, calm in one spot and turbulent elsewhere, full after rain and low after drought; it can consist of different parts at different times. It is nevertheless the same river.

This shows the centrality of Aristotle's concept of *essence*. Certain properties are essential to the river; it cannot lose them without losing its identity. Other properties are accidental. The river can lose them and remain the same river.

In general, a property is essential to a thing, or kind of thing, when it is necessary to it; without the property, it would not be that thing (or kind of thing). A thing has a property essentially if it has it by its own nature—that is, by virtue of itself, by virtue of being the thing it is. Aristotle's phrase for essence is "what it is to be (a thing)." What is essential to Socrates? That is to ask what it is to be Socrates. Most Western philosophers have assumed that "being human" is essential to Socrates; if something were not human, that something could not be Socrates. Hindu and Buddhist philosophers, in contrast, insist on the possibility of reincarnation and the transmigration of souls and hold that humanity is not essential to being a self; a humanly embodied self could be a cow or a god in another lifetime. But selfhood, or being-a-self, might be an Aristotelian essence on some of these views. Some modern philosophers have suggested that having the particular parents Socrates had was essential to Socrates' being Socrates; the man could not have been the son of Jean-Paul Sartre and Simone de Beauvoir. But clearly many of Socrates's properties are accidental to him. He might have failed to be the teacher of Plato, for example, if Plato had studied with Protagoras. But he would still have been Socrates.

If we could give a definition of what it is to be Socrates, that would express Socrates' essence. Aristotle doubts, however, that we can do this. There may not be essences of individual, primary substances, such as Socrates. (Medieval philosophers would later refer to such individual essences as *haecceities*, "this-nesses.") There are essences of secondary substances, expressed in definitions. By giving a definition of "river" we express what is essential to being a river. Aristotle defines a human being as a rational animal. Being an animal and being capable of rationality are essential to being human, he contends. Everything else is accidental.

A river can contain different (or fewer or more) water molecules without becoming a different river. Aristotle would say that something's matter can be different so long as its form remains. Socrates can lose or gain weight without becoming a different person. So, in one sense, a substance is matter made particular by certain essential properties, by its "form." But, in another sense, a substance is not to be identified with either its matter or the combination of form and matter it comprises. Instead, we identify it with its "form," that is to say, its essence, what it is to be that particular individual.

Aristotle lists four types of cause. He is interested in causes because he believes that explanations are causal. A cause explains its effect. Smoke rising from a mountain is explained by the fire there. In fact, we know there is fire because it explains the smoke in this sense.

Medieval commentators understood Aristotle as saying that there are four kinds of causal explanation: *formal, material, efficient,* and *final.*

Suppose we ask why Socrates is human. A formal explanation relies on an essence or definition: Socrates is human because he is a rational animal. A material explanation relies on matter: Socrates is human because he has a certain biochemical composition. An efficient explanation relies on a causal chain of events: Socrates is human because his parents were human and produced him in the usual way. And a final explanation relies on some goal, purpose, or function that Socrates serves. Thus we might say, "Socrates is human in order to..." What is the purpose of a human being? That becomes the key question of Aristotle's ethics.

19.2.1 Aristotle, from *Categories*

Expressions which are in no way composite signify substance, quantity, quality, relation, place, time, position, state, action, or affection. To sketch my meaning roughly, examples of substance are

Source: Aristotle, *Categories.* Translated by E. M. Edgehill, in *The Works of Aristotle.* Oxford: Clarendon Press, 1924.

"man" or "the horse," of quantity, such terms as "two cubits long" or "three cubits long," of quality, such attributes as "white," "grammatical." "Double," "half," "greater," fall under the category of relation; "in the marketplace," "in the Lyceum," under that of place; "yesterday," "last year," under that of time. "Lying," "sitting," are terms indicating position; "shod," "armed," state; "to lance," "to cauterize," action; "to be lanced," "to be cauterized," affection.

No one of these terms in and by itself involves an affirmation; it is by the combination of such terms that positive or negative statements arise. For every assertion must, as is admitted, be either true or false, whereas expressions which are not in any way composite, such as "man," "white," "runs," "wins," cannot be either true or false.

5 Substance, in the truest and primary and most definite sense of the word, is that which is neither predicable of a subject nor present in a subject; for instance, the individual man or horse. But in a secondary sense those things are called substances within which, as species, the primary substances are included; also those which, as genera, include the species. For instance, the individual man is included in the species "man," and the genus to which the species belongs is "animal"; these, therefore—that is to say, the species "man" and the genus "animal,"—are termed secondary substances.

It is plain from what has been said that both the name and the definition of the predicate must be predicable of the subject. For instance, "man" is predicated of the individual man. Now in this case the name of the species "man" is applied to the individual, for we use the term "man" in describing the individual; and the definition of "man" will also be predicated of the individual man, for the individual man is both man and animal. Thus, both the name and the definition of the species are predicable of the individual.

With regard, on the other hand, to those things which are present in a subject, it is generally the case that neither their name nor their definition is predicable of that in which they are present. Though, however, the definition is never predicable, there is nothing in certain cases to prevent the name being used. For instance, "white" being present in a body is predicated of that in which it is present, for a body is called white: the definition, however, of the colour "white" is never predicable of the body.

Everything except primary substances is either predicable of a primary substance or present in a primary substance. This becomes evident by reference to particular instances which occur. "Animal" is predicated of the species "man," therefore of the individual man, for if there were no individual man of whom it could be predicated, it could not be predicated of the species "man" at all. Again, colour is present in body, therefore in individual bodies, for if there were no individual body in which it was present, it could not be present in body at all. Thus everything except primary substances is either predicated of primary substances, or is present in them, and if these last did not exist, it would be impossible for anything else to exist.

Of secondary substances, the species is more truly substance than the genus, being more nearly related to primary substance. For if anyone should render an account of what a primary substance is, he would render a more instructive account, and one more proper to the subject, by stating the species than by stating the genus. Thus, he would give a more instructive account of an individual man by stating that he was man than by stating that he was animal, for the former description is peculiar to the individual in a greater degree, while the latter is too general. Again, the man who gives an account of the nature of an individual tree will give a more instructive account by mentioning the species "tree" than by mentioning the genus "plant."

Moreover, primary substances are most properly called substances in virtue of the fact that they are the entities which underlie everything else, and that everything else is either predicated of them or present in them. Now the same relation which subsists between primary substance and everything else subsists also between the species and the genus: for the species is to the genus as subject is to predicate, since the genus is predicated of the species, whereas the species cannot be predicated of the genus. Thus we have a second ground for asserting that the species is more truly substance than the genus.

Of species themselves, except in the case of such as are genera, no one is more truly substance than another. We should not give a more appropriate account of the individual man by stating the species to which he belonged, than we should of an individual horse by adopting the same method of definition. In the same way, of primary substances, no one is more truly substance than another; an individual man is not more truly substance than an individual ox.

It is, then, with good reason that of all that remains, when we exclude primary substances, we concede to species and genera alone the name "secondary substance," for these alone of all the predicates convey a knowledge of primary substance. For it is by stating the species or the genus that we appropriately define any individual man; and we shall make our definition more exact by stating the former than by stating the latter. All other things that we state, such as that he is white, that he runs, and so on, are irrelevant to the definition. Thus it is just that these alone, apart from primary substances, should be called substances.

Further, primary substances are most properly so called, because they underlie and are the subjects of everything else. Now the same relation that subsists between primary substance and everything else subsists also between the species and the genus to which the primary substance belongs, on the one hand, and every attribute which is not included within these, on the other. For these are the subjects of all such. If we call an individual man "skilled in grammar," the predicate is applicable also to the species and to the genus to which he belongs. This law holds good in all cases....

All substance appears to signify that which is individual. In the case of primary substance this is indisputably true, for the thing is a unit. In the case of secondary substances, when we speak, for instance, of "man" or "animal," our form of speech gives the impression that we are here also indicating that which is individual, but the impression is not strictly true; for a secondary substance is not an individual, but a class with a certain qualification; for it is not one and single as a primary substance is; the words "man," "animal," are predicable of more than one subject....

Substance, again, does not appear to admit of variation of degree. I do not mean by this that one substance cannot be more or less truly substance than another, for it has already been stated that this is the case; but that no single substance admits of varying degrees within itself. For instance, one particular substance, "man," cannot be more or less man either than himself at some other time or than some other man. One man cannot be more man than another, as that which is white may be more or less white than some other white object, or as that which is beautiful may be more or less beautiful than some other beautiful object. The same quality, moreover, is said to subsist in a thing in varying degrees at different times. A body, being white, is said to be whiter at one time than it was before, or, being warm, is said to be warmer or less warm than at some other time. But substance is not said to be more or less that which it is: a man is not more truly a man at one time than he was before, nor is anything, if it is substance, more or less what it is. Substance, then, does not admit of variation of degree.

The most distinctive mark of substance appears to be that, while remaining numerically one and the same, it is capable of admitting contrary qualities. From among things other than substance, we should find ourselves unable to bring forward any which possessed this mark. Thus, one and the same colour cannot be white and black. Nor can the same one action be good and bad: this law holds good with everything that is not substance. But one and the selfsame substance, while retaining its identity, is yet capable of admitting contrary qualities. The same individual person is at one time white, at another black, at one time warm, at another cold, at one time good, at another bad. This capacity is found nowhere else, though it might be maintained that a statement or opinion was an exception to the rule. The same statement, it is agreed, can be both true and false. For if the statement "he is sitting" is true, yet, when the person in question has risen, the same statement will be false. The same applies to opinions. For if anyone thinks truly that a person is sitting, yet, when that person has risen, this same opinion, if still held, will be false. Yet although this exception may be allowed, there is, nevertheless, a difference in the manner in which the thing takes place. It is by themselves changing that substances admit contrary qualities. It is thus that that which was hot becomes cold, for it has entered into a different state. Similarly that which was white becomes black, and that which was bad good, by a process of change; and in the same way in all other cases it is by changing that substances are capable of admitting contrary qualities. But statements and opinions themselves remain unaltered in all respects: it is by the alteration in the facts of the case that the contrary quality comes to be theirs. The statement "he is sitting" remains unaltered, but it is at one time true, at another false, according to circumstances. What has been said of statements applies also to opinions. Thus, in respect of the manner in which the thing takes place, it is the peculiar mark of substance that it should be capable of admitting contrary qualities; for it is by itself changing that it does so....

To sum up, it is a distinctive mark of substance that, while remaining numerically one and the same, it is capable of admitting contrary qualities, the modification taking place through a change in the substance itself.

19.2.2 Aristotle, from *Metaphysics*

Book IV

1 There is a science which investigates being as being and the attributes which belong to this in virtue of its own nature. Now this is not the same as any of the so-called special sciences; for none of these others treats universally of being as being. They cut off a part of being and investigate the attribute of this part; this is what the mathematical sciences, for instance, do. Now since we are seeking the first principles and the highest causes, clearly there must be something to which these belong in virtue of its own nature. If then those who sought the elements of existing things were seeking these same principles, it is necessary that the elements must be elements of being not by accident but just because it is being. Therefore it is of being as being that we also must grasp the first causes.

2 There are many senses in which a thing may be said to "be," but all that "is" is related to one central point, one definite kind of thing, and is not said to "be" by a mere ambiguity. Everything which is healthy is related to health, one thing in the sense that it preserves health, another in the sense that it produces it, another in the sense that it is a symptom of health, another because it is capable of it. And that which is medical is relative to the medical art, one thing being called medical because it possesses it, another because it is naturally adapted to it, another because it is a function of the medical art. And we shall find other words

Source: Aristotle, *Metaphysics*, in *The Works of Aristotle*. Translated by W. D. Ross. Oxford: Clarendon Press, 1924.

used similarly to these. So, too, there are many senses in which a thing is said to be, but all refer to one starting-point; some things are said to be because they are substances, others because they are affections of substance, others because they are a process towards substance, or destructions or privations or qualities of substance, or productive or generative of substance, or of things which are relative to substance, or negations of one of these things of substance itself. It is for this reason that we say even of nonbeing that it is nonbeing. As, then, there is one science which deals with all healthy things, the same applies in the other cases also. For not only in the case of things which have one common notion does the investigation belong to one science, but also in the case of things which are related to one common nature; for even these in a sense have one common notion. It is clear then that it is the work of one science also to study the things that are, qua being.—But everywhere science deals chiefly with that which is primary, and on which the other things depend, and in virtue of which they get their names. If, then, this is substance, it will be of substances that the philosopher must grasp the principles and the causes.

Now for each one class of things, as there is one perception, so there is one science, as for instance grammar, being one science, investigates all articulate sounds. Hence to investigate all the species of being qua being is the work of a science which is generically one, and to investigate the several species is the work of the specific parts of the science.

If, now, being and unity are the same and are one thing in the sense that they are implied in one another as principle and cause, not in the sense that they are explained by the same definition (though it makes no difference even if we suppose them to be like that—in fact this would even strengthen our case); for "one man" and "man" are the same thing, and so are "existent man" and "man," and the doubling of the words in "one man and one existent man" does not express anything different (it is clear that the two things are not separated either in coming to be or in ceasing to be); and similarly "one existent man" adds nothing to "existent man," and it is obvious that the addition in these cases means the same thing, and unity is nothing apart from being; and if, further, the substance of each thing is one in no merely accidental way, and similarly is from its very nature something that is:—all this being so, there must be exactly as many species of being as of unity. And to investigate the essence of these is the work of a science which is generically one—I mean, for instance, the discussion of the same and the similar and the other concepts of this sort; and nearly all contraries may be referred to this origin; let us take them as having been investigated in the "Selection of Contraries."

And there are as many parts of philosophy as there are kinds of substance, so that there must necessarily be among them a first philosophy and one which follows this. For being falls immediately into genera; for which reason the sciences too will correspond to these genera. For the philosopher is like the mathematician, as that word is used; for mathematics also has parts, and there is a first and a second science and other successive ones within the sphere of mathematics....

It is evident, then, that it belongs to one science to be able to give an account of these concepts as well as of substance (this was one of the questions in our book of problems), and that it is the function of the philosopher to be able to investigate all things. For if it is not the function of the philosopher, who is it who will inquire whether Socrates and Socrates seated are the same thing, or whether one thing has one contrary, or what contrariety is, or how many meanings it has? And similarly with all other such questions. Since, then, these are essential modifications of unity qua unity and of being qua being, not qua numbers or lines or fire, it is clear that it belongs to this science to investigate both the essence of these concepts and their properties. And those who study these properties err not by leaving the sphere of philosophy, but by forgetting that substance, of which they have no correct idea, is prior to these other things. For number qua number has peculiar attributes, such as oddness and evenness, commensurability and equality, excess and defect, and these belong to numbers either in themselves or in relation to one another. And similarly the solid and the motionless and that which is in motion and the weightless and that which has weight have other peculiar properties. So too there are certain properties peculiar to being as such, and it is about these that the philosopher has to investigate the truth.—An indication of this may be mentioned: dialecticians and sophists assume the same guise as the philosopher, for sophistic is wisdom which exists only in semblance, and dialecticians embrace all things in their dialectic, and being is common to all things; but evidently their dialectic embraces these subjects because these are proper to philosophy.—For sophistic and dialectic turn on the same class of things as philosophy, but this differs from dialectic in the nature of the faculty required and from sophistic in respect of the purpose of the philosophic life. Dialectic is merely critical where philosophy claims to know, and sophistic is what appears to be philosophy but is not....

Obviously then it is the work of one science to examine being qua being, and the attributes which belong to it qua being, and the same science will examine not only substances but also their attributes, both those above named and the concepts "prior" and "posterior," "genus" and "species," "whole" and "part," and the others of this sort.

Book VII

1 There are several senses in which a thing may be said to "be," as we pointed out previously in our book on the various senses of words; for in one sense the "being" meant is "what a thing is" or a "this," and in another sense it means a quality or quantity or one of the other things that are predicated as these are. While "being" has all these senses, obviously that which "is" primarily is the "what," which indicates the substance of the thing. For when we say of what quality a thing is, we say that it is good or bad, not that it is three cubits long or that it is a man; but when we say what it is, we do not say "white" or "hot" or "three cubits long," but "a man" or "a god." And all other things are said to be because they are, some of them, quantities of that which is in this primary sense, others qualities of it, others affections of it, and others some other determination of it. And so one might even raise the question whether the words "to walk," "to be healthy," "to sit" imply that each of these things is existent, and similarly in any other case of this sort; for none of them is either self-subsistent or capable of being separated from substance, but rather, if anything, it is that which walks or sits or is healthy that is an existent thing. Now these are seen to be more real because there is something definite which underlies them (i.e., the substance or individual), which is implied in such a predicate; for we never use the word "good" or "sitting" without implying this. Clearly then it is in virtue of this category that each of the others also is. Therefore that which is primarily, i.e., not in a qualified sense but without qualification, must be substance.

Now there are several senses in which a thing is said to be first; yet substance is first in every sense—(1) in definition, (2) in order of knowledge, (3) in time. For (3) of the other categories none can exist independently, but only substance. And (1) in definition also this is first; for in the definition of each term the definition of its substance must be present. And (2) we think we know each thing most fully, when we know what it is, e.g., what man is or what fire is, rather than when we know its quality, its quantity, or its place; since we know each of these predicates also only when we know what the quantity or the quality is.

And indeed the question which was raised of old and is raised now and always, and is always the subject of doubt, viz. what being is, is just the question, what is substance? For it is this that some assert to be one, others more than one, and that some assert to be limited in number, others unlimited. And so we also must consider chiefly and primarily and almost exclusively what that is which is in this sense.

3 The word "substance" is applied, if not in more senses, still at least to four main objects; for both the essence and the universal and the genus are thought to be the substance of each thing, and fourthly the substratum. Now the substratum is that of which everything else is predicated, while it is itself not predicated of anything else. And so we must first determine the nature of this; for that which underlies a thing primarily is thought to be in the truest sense its substance. And in one sense matter is said to be of the nature of substratum, in another, shape, and in a third, the compound of these. (By the matter I mean, for instance, the bronze, by the shape the pattern of its form, and by the compound of these the statue, the concrete whole.) Therefore if the form is prior to the matter and more real, it will be prior also to the compound of both, for the same reason.

We have now outlined the nature of substance, showing that it is that which is not predicated of a stratum, but of which all else is predicated. But we must not merely state the matter thus; for this is not enough. The statement itself is obscure, and further, on this view, matter becomes substance. For if this is not substance, it baffles us to say what else is. When all else is stripped off evidently nothing but matter remains. For while the rest are affections, products, and potencies of bodies, length, breadth, and depth are quantities and not substances (for a quantity is not a substance), but the substance is rather that to which these belong primarily. But when length and breadth and depth are taken away we see nothing left unless there is something that is bounded by these; so that to those who consider the question thus matter alone must seem to be substance. By matter I mean that which in itself is neither a particular thing nor of a certain quantity nor assigned to any other of the categories by which being is determined. For there is something of which each of these is predicated, whose being is different from that of each of the predicates (for the predicates other than substance are predicated of substance, while substance is predicated of matter). Therefore the ultimate substratum is of itself neither a particular thing nor of a particular quantity nor otherwise positively characterized; nor yet is it the negations of these, for negations also will belong to it only by accident.

If we adopt this point of view, then, it follows that matter is substance. But this is impossible; for both separability and "thisness" are thought to belong chiefly to substance. And so form and the compound of form and matter would be thought to be substance, rather than matter. The substance compounded of both, i.e., of matter and shape, may be dismissed; for it is posterior and its nature is obvious. And matter also is in a sense manifest. But we must inquire into the third kind of substance; for this is the most perplexing.

Some of the sensible substances are generally admitted to be substances, so that we must look first among these. For it is an advantage to advance to that which is more knowable. For learning proceeds for all in this way—through that which is less knowable by nature to that which is more knowable; and just as in conduct our task is to start from what is good for each and make what is without qualification good good for each, so it is our task to start from what is more knowable to oneself and make what is knowable by nature knowable to oneself. Now what is knowable and primary for particular sets of people is often knowable to a very small extent, and has little or nothing of reality. But yet one must start from that which is barely knowable but knowable to oneself, and try to know what is knowable without qualification, passing, as has been said, by way of those very things which one does know.

4 Since at the start we distinguished the various marks by which we determine substance, and one of these was thought to be the essence, we must investigate this. And first let us make some linguistic remarks about it. The essence of each thing is what it is said to be *propter se* [on account of being itself]. For being you is not being musical, since you are not by your very nature musical. What, then, you are by your very nature is your essence.

Nor yet is the whole of this the essence of a thing; not that which is *propter se* as white is to a surface, because being a surface is not identical with being white. But again the combination of both—"being a white surface"—is not the essence of surface, because "surface" itself is added. The formula, therefore, in which the term itself is not present but its meaning is expressed, this is the formula of the essence of each thing. Therefore if to be a white surface is to be a smooth surface, to be white and to be smooth are one and the same.

But since there are also compounds answering to the other categories (for there is a substratum for each category, e.g., for quality, quantity, time, place, and motion), we must inquire whether there is a formula of the essence of each of them, i.e., whether to these compounds also there belongs an essence, e.g., "white man." Let the compound be denoted by "cloak." What is the essence of cloak? But, it may be said, this also is not a *propter se* expression. We reply that there are just two ways in which a predicate may fail to be true of a subject *propter se*, and one of these results from the addition, and the other from the omission, of a determinant. One kind of predicate is not *propter se* because the term that is being defined is combined with another determinant, e.g., if in defining the essence of white one were to state the formula of white man; the other because in the subject another determinant is combined with that which is expressed in the formula, e.g., if "cloak" meant "white man," and one were to define cloak as white; white man is white indeed, but its essence is not to be white.

But is being-a-cloak an essence at all? Probably not. For the essence is precisely what something is; but when an attribute is asserted of a subject other than itself, the complex is not precisely what some "this" is, e.g., white man is not precisely what some "this" is, since thisness belongs only to substances. Therefore there is an essence only of those things whose formula is a definition. But we have a definition not where we have a word and a formula identical in meaning (for in that case all formulae or sets of words would be definitions; for there will be some name for any set of words whatever, so that even the *Iliad* will be a definition), but where there is a formula of something primary; and primary things are those which do not imply the predication of one element in them of another element. Nothing, then, which is not a species of a genus will have an essence—only species will have it, for these are thought to imply not merely that the subject participates in the attribute and has it as an affection, or has it by accident, but for every thing else as well, if it has a name, there be a formula of its meaning—viz. that this attribute belongs to this subject; or instead of a simple formula we shall be able to give a more accurate one; but there will be no definition nor essence.

Or has "definition," like "what a thing is," several meanings? "What a thing is" in one sense means substance and the "this," in another one or other of the predicates, quantity, quality, and the like. For as "is" belongs to all things, not, however, in the same sense, but to one sort of thing primarily and to others in a secondary way, so too "what a thing is" belongs in the simple sense to substance, but in a limited sense to the other categories. For even of a quality we might ask what it is, so that quality also is a "what a thing is,"—not in the simple sense, however, but just as, in the case of that which is not, some say, emphasizing the linguistic form, that that which is not—not *is* simply—but is non-existent; so too with quality.

We must no doubt inquire how we should express ourselves on each point, but certainly not more than how the facts actually stand. And so now also, since it is evident what language we use, essence will belong, just as "what a thing is" does, primarily and in the simple sense to substance, and in a secondary way to the other categories also,—not essence in the simple sense, but the essence of a quality or of a quantity. For it must be either by an equivocation that we say these are, or by adding to and taking from the meaning of "are" (in the way in which that which is not known may be said to be known),—the truth being that we use the word neither ambiguously nor in the same sense, but just as we apply the word "medical" by virtue of a reference to one and the same thing, not meaning one and the same thing, nor yet speaking ambiguously; for a patient and an operation and an instrument are called medical neither by an ambiguity nor with a single meaning, but with reference to a common end. But it does not matter at all in which of the two ways one likes to describe the facts; this is evident, that definition and essence in the primary and simple sense belong to substances. Still they belong to other things as well, only not in the primary sense. For if we suppose this it does not follow that there is a definition of every word which means the same as any formula; it must mean the same as a particular kind of formula; and this condition is satisfied if it is a formula of something which is one, not by continuity like the *Iliad* or the things that are one by being bound together, but in one of the main senses of "one," which answer to the senses of "is"; now "that which is" in one sense denotes a "this," in another a quantity, in another a quality. And so there can be a formula or definition even of white man, but not in the sense in which there is a definition either of white or of a substance.

19.2.3 Aristotle, from *Physics*

Book I

3 Now that we have established these distinctions, we must proceed to consider causes, their character and number. Knowledge is the object of our inquiry, and men do not think they know a thing till they have grasped the "why" of it (which is to grasp its primary cause). So clearly we too must do this as regards both coming to be and passing away and every kind of physical change, in order that, knowing their principles, we may try to refer to these principles each of our problems.

In one sense, then, (1) that out of which a thing comes to be and which persists is called "cause," e.g., the bronze of the statue, the silver of the bowl, and the genera of which the bronze and the silver are species.

In another sense (2) the form or the archetype, i.e., the statement of the essence, and its genera are called "causes" (e.g., of the octave, the relation of 2:1, and generally number), and the parts in the definition.

Again (3) the primary source of the change or coming to rest; e.g., the man who gave advice is a cause, the father is cause of the child, and generally what makes of what is made and what causes change of what is changed.

Again (4) in the sense of end or "that for the sake of which" a thing is done, e.g., health is the cause of walking about. ("Why is he walking about?" we say. "To be healthy," and, having said that, we think we have assigned the cause.) The same is true also of all the intermediate steps which are brought about through the action of something else as means towards the end, e.g., reduction of flesh, purging, drugs, or surgical instruments are means towards health. All these things are "for the sake of" the end, though they differ from one another in that some are activities, others instruments.

This then perhaps exhausts the number of ways in which the term "cause" is used.

As the word has several senses, it follows that there are several causes of the same thing not merely in virtue of a concomitant attribute, e.g., both the art of the sculptor and the bronze are causes of the statue. These are causes of the statue qua statue, not in virtue of anything else that it

Source: Aristotle, *Physics*. Translated by R. P. Hardie and R. K. Gaye, in *The Works of Aristotle*. Oxford: Clarendon Press, 1930.

may be—only not in the same way, the one being the material cause, the other the cause whence the motion comes. Some things cause each other reciprocally, e.g., hard work causes fitness and vice versa, but again not in the same way, but the one as end, the other as the origin of change. Further the same thing is the cause of contrary results. For that which by its presence brings about one result is sometimes blamed for bringing about the contrary by its absence. Thus we ascribe the wreck of a ship to the absence of the pilot whose presence was the cause of its safety.

All the causes now mentioned fall into four familiar divisions. The letters are the causes of syllables, the material of artificial products, fire, etc., of bodies, the parts of the whole, and the premises of the conclusion, in the sense of "that from which." Of these pairs the one set are causes in the sense of substratum, e.g., the parts, the other set in the sense of essence—the whole and the combination and the form. But the seed and the doctor and the adviser, and generally the maker, are all sources whence the change or stationariness originates, while the others are causes in the sense of the end or the good of the rest; for "that for the sake of which" means what is best and the end of the things that lead up to it. (Whether we say the "good itself" or the "apparent good" makes no difference.) Such then is the number and nature of the kinds of cause.

Now the modes of causation are many, though when brought under heads they too can be reduced in number. For "cause" is used in many senses and even within the same kind one may be prior to another (e.g., the doctor and the expert are causes of health, the relation 2:1 and number of the octave), and always what is inclusive to what is particular. Another mode of causation is the incidental and its genera, e.g., in one way "Polyclitus," in another "sculptor" is the cause of a statue, because "being Polyclitus" and "sculptor" are incidentally conjoined. Also the classes in which the incidental attribute is included; thus "a man" could be said to be the cause of a statue or, generally, "a living creature." An incidental attribute too may be more or less remote, e.g., suppose that "a pale man" or "a musical man" were said to be the cause of the statue.

All causes, both proper and incidental, may be spoken of either as potential or as actual; e.g., the cause of a house being built is either "house-builder" or "house-builder building." Similar distinctions can be made in the things of which the causes are causes, e.g., of "this statue" or of "statue" or of "image" generally, of "this bronze" or of "bronze" or of "material" generally. So too with the incidental attributes. Again we may use a complex expression for either and say, e.g., neither "Polyclitus" nor "sculptor" but "Polyclitus, sculptor."

All these various uses, however, come to six in number, under each of which again the usage is twofold. Cause means either what is particular or a genus, or an incidental attribute or a genus of that, and these either as a complex or each by itself; and all six either as actual or as potential. The difference is this much, that causes which are actually at work and particular exist and cease to exist simultaneously with their effect, e.g., this healing person with this being-healed person and that house-building man with that being-built house; but this is not always true of potential causes—the house and the housebuilder do not pass away simultaneously.

In investigating the cause of each thing it is always necessary to seek what is most precise (as also in other things): thus man builds because he is a builder, and a builder builds in virtue of his art of building. This last cause then is prior: and so generally.

Further, generic effects should be assigned to generic causes, particular effects to particular causes, e.g., statue to sculptor, this statue to this sculptor; and powers are relative to possible effects, actually operating causes to things which are actually being effected.

CHAPTER 20

Metaphysics in Early Modern Philosophy

"The workmanship of the understanding"

Aristotle's theory of substance dominated metaphysics for centuries, becoming known, in the form in which Aquinas and other medieval philosophers developed it, as the perennial philosophy. But gradually the progress of science disrupted its view of objects. By the seventeenth century, the atomic theory of matter became generally accepted by the scientific community. The theory was still in a relatively primitive form, little advanced from where Democritus and other ancient atomists had left it. But it nonetheless forced a rethinking of the nature of objects.

20.1 PRIMARY AND SECONDARY QUALITIES

René Descartes (1596–1650) begins with a commonsense, Aristotelian picture of how we think of external objects. We naturally assume that the objects causing our experiences are as they seem to be; we assume that they are similar to the ideas and sensations they cause in us. But we cannot hold that assumption for very long. We are prone to too many illusions and mistakes.

Illusions might tempt us to conclude that we know nothing about how the outside world might be in reality. How can we trust our senses when we know they sometimes deceive us? How can we distinguish aspects of our perceptions that reflect the way the world really is from those that arise solely from our own nervous system?

We can deduce that external objects exist from the fact that God is good and would not systematically deceive us. But we can trust as reflecting the way things really are only what we perceive clearly and distinctly. Descartes maintains that we can perceive clearly and distinctly only the mathematical properties of objects, such as extension (size, shape) and motion. Only they can be trusted as reflecting the true nature of things.

Other characteristics of objects, however, are untrustworthy. It is not that colors, sounds, scents, taste, heat, texture, etc., are random; our perceptions are systematic and regular enough that we can infer that we are responding to something in the object. But we have no reason to believe that the object itself is in these respects as we perceive it to be.

Descartes thus refines a standard idealist argument. We have reason to believe that the objects of our perception really do exist and really do serve as the causes of our perceptions. But we also have reason to believe that they differ in important ways from our perceptions of them. In some respects—corresponding to the mathematical properties of the objects—we perceive objects as they really are. In other respects, we respond to features of the objects in ways that are not similar to those features at all.

A venerable tradition of British empiricism contributes much to developing Descartes' argument. John Locke (1632–1704) is famous for the statement that the mind is a *tabula rasa*, a "blank slate" to be written on by experience. There are no innate ideas. But how can we be sure that the ideas experience creates correspond to things in the world? Snowballs, grains of wheat, and so forth may cause our perceptions, giving rise to our ideas of snowballs, our "impressions" of grains of wheat, etc. But do our ideas correspond to the snowball the way it really is? By Locke's time science and the atomic theory were becoming parameters for serious inquiry. But clearly we do not see atoms. Are the qualities we perceive in the snowball really there in the thing materially? And if not, why do we have the perceptions we do?

It is to Locke's credit that he puts this question in the terms that philosophers use today. The qualities we perceive, the white of a snowball and its feeling cold, for instance, Locke calls its *secondary qualities.* The properties of the thing as it is in itself unperceived are, in Locke's locution, its *primary qualities.* How do the snowball's primary qualities give rise to its secondary qualities, the properties we perceive? Locke says that primary qualities are inseparable from material bodies; very small particles of air, water, etc., have them. They are the qualities matter has according to the atomic theory. Secondary qualities are effects of primary qualities on our sense organs and nervous systems; they are "response-dependent" or "perceiver-relative." They do not resemble the ideas they produce in us. Indeed, if our sense organs were more powerful than they are—or if we artificially supplement them, by looking through a microscope, for example—we would see something very different from what we see now. Things would still have extension, figure, and motion, and we could still count them, but their colors, textures, etc., would be very different. Among primary qualities are powers to cause other objects to produce sensations in us (such as the power of fire to produce a new color in clay); to cause other objects to cause other objects to produce sensations in us (such as the power of a spark to produce fire), and so on. How do qualities in objects produce our sensations? The answer, Locke would say today, is given by biology, chemistry, and physics. Locke says our ideas are produced by qualities of objects by way of impulses. With better science, we might say that tiny particles (or waves) from the object strike our sense organs, which respond by sending neural impulses to the brain. Locke's story makes reference only to the primary qualities of the object (and of our bodies), and so his view seems in accord with most versions of contemporary materialism.

In keeping with the distinction between two kinds of qualities, Locke distinguishes two kinds of essences: real and nominal. Thomas Aquinas and other Aristotelians held the following three concepts to be equivalent:

- The *essence* of x = the properties necessary to x, without which x would not be what it is.
- The *nominal essence* of x = what x's definition expresses.
- The *nature* of x = what makes x what it is.

This makes good sense as long as we hold that objects are as they appear. The atomic theory, however, breaks apart the concept of essence into at least two notions. The essence of a thing or kind expressed in a definition—which Locke therefore dubs a *nominal essence*—would typically be defined in terms of secondary qualities. We might define water, for example, as a tasteless, odorless, clear liquid occupying over two-thirds of the earth's surface. Or we might define gold as a shiny, malleable yellow or white metal of great value. These definitions focus on secondary qualities: tasteless, odorless, clear, shiny, malleable, yellow or white, of great value. But, on the atomic theory, these statements do not express the real nature of water or gold; the properties they mention do not make water or gold what they are. Water is what it is because it is H_2O. It may have relational properties that depend on the natures of other things. But all the explanatory value, according to a reductionist materialism that is a direct heir of Locke, comes from our conceptions of the thing as it is. Other views emphasize emergence of properties not explained by an underlying structure. Locke's position is that the nature of a thing or kind—what Locke dubs its *real essence*—is given by its material structure. It comprises the internal constitution of the thing.

A nominal essence would be an abstraction, something for which a general term stood. As creatures of the mind, nominal essences are crafted according to pragmatic desiderata taking into account our human point of view. But real essences are different. We are not free to craft them. They stem from the real internal constitutions of things. They correspond to natural kinds, kinds that are in nature, not in our understanding alone. (Plato's realism about universals would be in this respect correct: There are natural kinds. And the philosopher is right, too, that what we try to do intellectually is, in his phrase, "cut nature at the joints.") The real essence is that on which the other properties of objects of a certain kind depend. Now, Locke doubts whether we can know this. Little wonder; the state of material science in his day was still crude. But, at least this much is uncontroversial: recent scientific theories show that understanding such real essences as Locke's (atoms, molecules, DNA, etc.) has explanatory power of which Locke could not have dreamed.

20.1.1 René Descartes, from *Meditations on First Philosophy*

Meditation VI: Of the Existence of Material Things, and of the Real Distinction between the Soul and Body of Man

Nothing further now remains but to inquire whether material things exist. And certainly I at least know that these may exist insofar as they are considered as the objects of pure mathematics, since in this aspect I perceive them clearly and distinctly. For there is no doubt that God possesses the power to produce everything that I am capable of perceiving with distinctness, and I have never deemed that anything was impossible for Him, unless I found a contradiction in attempting to conceive it clearly. Further, the faculty of imagination which I possess, and of which, experience tells me, I make use when I apply myself to the consideration of material things, is capable of persuading me of their existence; for when I attentively consider what imagination is, I find that it is nothing but a certain application of the faculty of knowledge to the body which is immediately present to it and which therefore exists.

And to render this quite clear, I remark in the first place the difference that exists between the imagination and pure intellection [or conception]. For example, when I imagine a triangle, I do not conceive it only as a figure comprehended by three lines, but I also apprehend these three lines as present by the power and inward vision of my mind, and this is what I call imagining. But if I desire to think of a chiliagon, I certainly conceive truly that it is a figure composed of a thousand sides, just as easily as I conceive of a triangle that it is a figure of three sides only; but I cannot in any way imagine the thousand sides of a chiliagon [as I do the three sides of a triangle], nor do I, so to speak, regard them as present [with the eyes of my mind]. And although in accordance with the habit I have formed of always employing the aid of my imagination when I think of corporeal things, it may happen that in imagining a chiliagon I confusedly represent to myself some figure, yet it is very evident that this figure is not a chiliagon, since it in no way differs from that which I represent to myself when I think of a myriagon or any other many-sided figure; nor does it serve my purpose in discovering the properties which go to form the distinction between a chiliagon and other polygons. But if the question turns upon a pentagon, it is quite true that I can conceive its figure as well as that of a chiliagon without the help of my imagination; but I can also imagine it by applying the attention of my mind to each of its five sides, and at the same time to the space which they enclose. And thus I clearly recognise that I have need of a particular effort of mind in order to effect the act of imagination, such as I do not require in order to understand, and this particular effort of mind clearly manifests the difference which exists between imagination and pure intellection.

I remark besides that this power of imagination which is in one, inasmuch as it differs from the power of understanding, is in no wise a necessary element in my nature, or in [my essence, that is to say, in] the essence of my mind; for although I did not possess it I should doubtless ever remain the same as I now am, from which it appears that we might conclude that it depends on something which differs from me. And I easily conceive that if some body exists with which my mind is conjoined and united in such a way that it can apply itself to consider it when it pleases, it may be that by this means it can imagine corporeal objects; so that this mode of thinking differs from pure intellection

Source: René Descartes, *Meditations*, in *The Philosophical Works of Descartes*. Translated by Elizabeth S. Haldane. Cambridge: Cambridge University Press, 1911.

only inasmuch as mind in its intellectual activity in some manner turns on itself, and considers some of the ideas which it possesses in itself; while in imagining it turns towards the body, and there beholds in it something conformable to the idea which it has either conceived of itself or perceived by the senses. I easily understand, I say, that the imagination could be thus constituted if it is true that body exists; and because I can discover no other convenient mode of explaining it, I conjecture with probability that body does exist; but this is only with probability, and although I examine all things with care, I nevertheless do not find that from this distinct idea of corporeal nature, which I have in my imagination, I can derive any argument from which there will necessarily be deduced the existence of body.

But I am in the habit of imagining many other things besides this corporeal nature which is the object of pure mathematics, to wit, the colours, sounds, scents, pain, and other such things, although less distinctly. And inasmuch as I perceive these things much better through the senses, by the medium of which, and by the memory, they seem to have reached my imagination, I believe that, in order to examine them more conveniently, it is right that I should at the same time investigate the nature of sense perception, and that I should see if from the ideas which I apprehend by this mode of thought, which I call feeling, I cannot derive some certain proof of the existence of corporeal objects.

And first of all I shall recall to my memory those matters which I hitherto held to be true, as having perceived them through the senses, and the foundations on which my belief has rested; in the next place I shall examine the reasons which have since obliged me to place them in doubt; in the last place I shall consider which of them I must now believe.

First of all, then, I perceived that I had a head, hands, feet, and all other members of which this body—which I considered as a part, or possibly even as the whole, of myself—is composed. Further I was sensible that this body was placed amidst many others, from which it was capable of being affected in many different ways, beneficial and hurtful, and I remarked that a certain feeling of pleasure accompanied those that were beneficial, and pain those which were harmful. And in addition to this pleasure and pain, I also experienced hunger, thirst, and other similar appetites, as also certain corporeal inclinations towards joy, sadness, anger, and other similar passions. And outside myself, in addition to extension, figure, and motions of bodies, I remarked in them hardness, heat, and all other tactile qualities, and, further, light and colour, and scents and sounds, the variety of which gave me the means of distinguishing the sky, the earth, the sea, and generally all the other bodies, one from the other. And certainly, considering the ideas of all these qualities which presented themselves to my mind, and which alone I perceived properly or immediately, it was not without reason that I believed myself to perceive objects quite different from my thought, to wit, bodies from which those ideas proceeded; for I found by experience that these ideas presented themselves to me without my consent being requisite, so that I could not perceive any object, however desirous I might be, unless it were present to the organs of sense; and it was not in my power not to perceive it when it was present. And because the ideas which I received through the senses were much more lively, more clear, and even, in their own way, more distinct than any of those which I could of myself frame in meditation, or than those I found impressed on my memory, it appeared as though they could not have proceeded from my mind, so that they must necessarily have been produced in me by some other things. And having no knowledge of those objects excepting the knowledge which the ideas themselves gave me, nothing was more likely to occur to my mind than that the objects were similar to the ideas which were caused. And because I likewise remembered that I had formerly made use of my senses rather than my reason, and recognised that the ideas which I formed of myself were not so distinct as those which I perceived through the senses, and that they were most frequently even composed of portions of these last, I persuaded myself easily that I had no idea in my mind which had not formerly come to me through the senses. Nor was it without some reason that I believed that this body (which by a certain special right I call my own) belonged to me more properly and more strictly than any other; for in fact I could never be separated from it as from other bodies; I experienced in it and on account of it all my appetites and affections, and finally I was touched by the feeling of pain and the titillation of pleasure in its parts, and not in the parts of other bodies which were separated from it. But when I inquired why from some, I know not what, painful sensation there follows sadness of mind, and from the pleasurable sensation there arises joy, or why this mysterious pinching of the stomach which I call hunger causes me to desire to eat, and dryness of throat causes a desire to drink, and so on, I could give no reason excepting that nature taught me so; for there is certainly no affinity (that I at least can understand) between the craving of the stomach and the desire to eat, any more than between the perception of whatever causes pain and the thought of sadness which arises from this perception. And in the same way it appeared to me that I had learned from nature all the other judgments which I formed regarding the objects of my senses, since I remarked that these judgments were formed in me before I had the leisure to weigh and consider any reasons which might oblige me to make them.

But afterwards many experiences little by little destroyed all the faith which I had rested in my senses; for I from time to time observed that those towers which from afar appeared to me to be round, more closely observed seemed square, and that colossal statues raised on the summit of these towers, appeared as quite tiny statues when viewed from the bottom; and so in an infinitude of other cases I found error in judgments founded on the external senses. And not only in those founded on the external senses, but even in those founded on the internal as well; for is there anything more intimate or more internal than pain? And yet I have learned from some persons whose arms or legs have been cut off, that they sometimes seemed to feel pain in the part which had been amputated, which made me think that I could not be quite certain that it was a certain member which pained me, even although I felt pain in it. And to those grounds of doubt I have lately added two others, which are very general; the first is that I never have believed myself to feel anything in waking moments which I cannot also sometimes believe myself to feel when I sleep, and as I do not think that these things which I seem to feel in sleep proceed from objects outside of me, I do not see any reason why I should have this belief regarding objects which I seem to perceive while awake. The other was that being still ignorant, or rather supposing myself to be ignorant, of the author of my being, I saw nothing to prevent me from having been so constituted by nature that I might be deceived even in matters which seemed to me to be most certain. And as to the grounds on which I was formerly persuaded of the truth of sensible objects, I had not much trouble in replying to them. For since nature seemed to cause me to lean towards many things from which reason repelled me, I did not believe that I should trust much to the teachings of nature. And although the ideas which I receive by the senses do not depend on my will, I did not think that one should for that reason conclude that they proceeded from things different from myself, since possibly some faculty might be discovered in me—though hitherto unknown to me—which produced them.

But now that I begin to know myself better, and to discover more clearly the author of my being, I do not in truth think that I should rashly admit all the matters which the senses seem to teach us, but, on the other hand, I do not think that I should doubt them all universally.

And first of all, because I know that all things which I apprehend clearly and distinctly can be created by God as I apprehend them, it suffices that I am able to apprehend one thing apart from another clearly and distinctly in order to be certain that the one is different from the other, since they may be made to exist in separation at least by the omnipotence of God; and it does not signify by what power this separation is made in order to compel me to judge them to be different: and, therefore, just because I know certainly that I exist, and that meanwhile I do not remark that any other thing necessarily pertains to my nature or essence, excepting that I am a thinking thing, I rightly conclude that my essence consists solely in the fact that I am a thinking thing. And although possibly (or rather certainly, as I shall say in a moment) I possess a body with which I am very intimately conjoined, yet because, on the one side, I have a clear and distinct idea of myself inasmuch as I am only a thinking and unextended thing, and as, on the other, I possess a distinct idea of body, inasmuch as it is only an extended and unthinking thing, it is certain that this I is entirely and absolutely distinct from my body, and can exist without it.

I further find in myself faculties employing modes of thinking peculiar to themselves, to wit, the faculties of imagination and feeling, without which I can easily conceive myself clearly and distinctly as a complete being; while, on the other hand, they cannot be so conceived apart from me, that is, without an intelligent substance in which they reside, for [in the notion we have of these faculties, or, to use the language of the Schools] in their formal concept, some kind of intellection is comprised, from which I infer that they are distinct from me as its modes are from a thing. I observe also in me some other faculties such as that of change of position, the assumption of different figures and such like, which cannot be conceived, any more than can the preceding, apart from some substance to which they are attached, and consequently cannot exist without it; but it is very clear that these faculties, if it be true that they exist, must be attached to some corporeal or extended substance, and not to an intelligent substance, since in the clear and distinct conception of these there is some sort of extension found to be present but no intellection at all. There is certainly further in me a certain passive faculty of perception, that is, of receiving and recognising the ideas of sensible things, but this would be useless to me [and I could in no way avail myself of it], if there were not either in me or in some other thing another active faculty capable of forming and producing these ideas. But this active faculty cannot exist in me [inasmuch as I am a thing that thinks] seeing that it does not presuppose thought, and also that those ideas are often produced in me without my contributing in any way to the same, and often even against my will; it is thus necessarily the case that the faculty resides in some substance different from me in which all the reality which is objectively in the ideas that are produced by this faculty is formally or eminently contained, as I remarked before. And this substance is either a body, that is, a corporeal nature in which there is contained formally [and really] all that which is objectively [and by representation] in those ideas, or it is God Himself, or some other creature more noble than body in which that same is contained eminently. But, since God is no deceiver, it is very manifest that He does not communicate to me these ideas immediately and by Himself, nor yet by the intervention of some creature in which their reality is not formally, but only eminently, contained. For since He has given me no faculty to recognise that this is the case, but, on the other hand, a very great inclination to believe [that they are sent to me or] that they are conveyed to me by corporeal objects, I do not see how He could be defended from the accusation of deceit if these ideas were produced by causes other than corporeal objects. Hence we must allow that corporeal things exist. However, they are perhaps not exactly what we perceive by the senses, since this comprehension by the senses is in many instances very obscure and confused; but we must at least admit that all things which I conceive in them clearly and distinctly, that is to say, all things which, speaking generally, are comprehended in the object of pure mathematics, are truly to be recognised as external objects.

As to other things, however, which are either particular only, as, for example, that the sun is of such and such a figure, etc., or which are less clearly and distinctly conceived, such as light, sound, pain and the like, it is certain that although they are very dubious and uncertain, yet on the sole ground that God is not a deceiver, and that consequently He has not permitted any falsity to exist in my opinion which He has not likewise given me the faculty of correcting, I may assuredly hope to conclude that I have within me the means of arriving at the truth even here. And first of all there is no doubt that in all things which nature teaches me there is some truth contained; for by nature, considered in general, I now understand no other thing than either God Himself or else the order and disposition which God has established in created things; and by my nature in particular I understand no other thing than the complexus of all the things which God has given me.

But there is nothing which this nature teaches me more expressly [nor more sensibly] than that I have a body which is adversely affected when I feel pain, which has need of food or drink when I experience the feelings of hunger and thirst, and so on; nor can I doubt there being some truth in all this.

Nature also teaches me by these sensations of pain, hunger, thirst, etc., that I am not only lodged in my body as a pilot in a vessel, but that I am very closely united to it, and so to speak so intermingled with it that I seem to compose with it one whole. For if that were not the case, when my body is hurt, I, who am merely a thinking thing, should not feel pain, for I should perceive this wound by the understanding only, just as the sailor perceives by sight when something is damaged in his vessel; and when my body has need of drink or food, I should clearly understand the fact without being warned of it by confused feelings of hunger and thirst. For all these sensations of hunger, thirst, pain, etc. are in truth none other than certain confused modes of thought which are produced by the union and apparent intermingling of mind and body.

Moreover, nature teaches me that many other bodies exist around mine, of which some are to be avoided and others sought after. And certainly from the fact that I am sensible of different sorts of colours, sounds, scents, tastes, heat, hardness, etc., I very easily conclude that there are in the bodies from which all these diverse sense-perceptions proceed certain variations which answer to them, although possibly these are not really at all similar to them. And also from the fact that amongst these different sense-perceptions some are very agreeable to me and others disagreeable, it is quite certain that my body (or rather myself in my entirety, inasmuch as I am formed of body and soul) may receive different impressions agreeable and disagreeable from the other bodies which surround it.

But there are many other things which nature seems to have taught me, but which at the same time I have never really received from her, but which have been brought about in my mind by a certain habit which I have of forming inconsiderate judgments on things; and thus it may easily happen that these judgments contain some error. Take, for example, the opinion which I hold that all space in which there is nothing that affects [or makes an impression on] my senses is void; that in a body which is warm there is something entirely similar to the idea of heat which is in me; that in a white or green body there is the same whiteness or greenness that I perceive; that in a bitter or sweet body there is the same taste, and so on in other instances; that the stars, the towers, and all other distant bodies are of the same figure and size as they appear from far off to our eyes, etc. But in order that in this there should be nothing which I do not conceive distinctly, I should define exactly what I really understand when I say that I am taught somewhat by nature. For here I take nature in a more limited signification than when I term it the sum of all the things given me by God, since in this sum many things are comprehended which only pertain to mind (and to these I do not refer in speaking of nature) such as the notion which I have of the fact that what has once been done cannot ever be undone and an infinitude of such things which I know by the light of nature [without the help of the body]; and seeing that it comprehends many other matters besides which only pertain to body, and are no longer here contained under the name of nature, such as the quality of weight which it possesses and the like, with which I also do not deal; for in talking of nature I only treat of those things given by God to me as a being composed of mind and body.

But the nature here described truly teaches me to flee from things which cause the sensation of pain, and seek after the things which communicate to me the sentiment of pleasure and so forth; but I do not see that beyond this it teaches me that from those diverse sense-perceptions we should ever form any conclusion regarding things outside of us, without having [carefully and maturely] mentally examined them beforehand. For it seems to me that it is mind alone, and not mind and body in conjunction, that is requisite to a knowledge of the truth in regard to such things. Thus, although a star makes no larger an impression on my eye than the flame of a little candle there is yet in me no real or positive propensity impelling me to believe that it is not greater than that flame; but I have judged it to be so from my earliest years, without any rational foundation. And although in approaching fire I feel heat, and in approaching it a little too near I even feel pain, there is at the same time no reason in this which could persuade me that there is in the fire something resembling this heat any more than there is in it something resembling the pain; all that I have any reason to believe from this is that there is something in it, whatever it may be, which excites in me these sensations of heat or of pain. So also, although there are spaces in which I find nothing which excites my senses, I must not from that conclude that these spaces contain no body; for I see in this, as in other similar things, that I have been in the habit of perverting the order of nature, because these perceptions of sense having been placed within me by nature merely for the purpose of signifying to my mind what things are beneficial or hurtful to the composite whole of which it forms a part, and being up to that point sufficiently clear and distinct, I yet avail myself of them as though they were absolute rules by which I might immediately determine the essence of the bodies which are outside me, as to which, in fact, they can teach me nothing but what is most obscure and confused.

20.1.2 John Locke, from *An Essay Concerning Human Understanding*

Book II: Of Ideas

Chapter VIII: Some Further Considerations concerning Our Simple Ideas of Sensation

7. *Ideas in the mind, qualities in bodies.* To discover the nature of our ideas the better, and to discourse of them intelligibly, it will be convenient to distinguish them as they are ideas or perceptions in our minds; and as they are modifications of matter in the bodies that cause such perceptions in us: that so we may not think (as perhaps usually is done) that they are exactly the images and resemblances of something inherent in the subject; most of those of sensation being inthe mind no more the likeness of something existing without us than the names that stand for them are the likeness of our ideas, which yet upon hearing they are apt to excite in us.

8. *Our ideas and the qualities of bodies.* Whatsoever the mind perceives in itself, or is the immediate object of perception, thought, or understanding, that I call idea; and the power to produce any idea in our mind, I call quality of the subject wherein that power is. Thus a snowball having the power to produce in us the ideas of white, cold, and round, the power to produce those ideas in us as they are in the snowball, I call qualities;

Source: John Locke, *An Essay Concerning Human Understanding*. London: William Tegg, 1689.

and as they are sensations or perceptions in our understandings, I call them ideas; which ideas, if I speak of sometimes as in the things themselves, I would be understood to mean those qualities in the objects which produce them in us.

9. *Primary qualities of bodies.* Qualities thus considered in bodies are, first, such as are utterly inseparable from the body, in what state soever it be, and such as in all the alterations and changes it suffers—all the force can be used upon it—it constantly keeps; and such as sense constantly finds in every particle of matter which has bulk enough to be perceived; and the mind finds inseparable from every particle of matter, though less than to make itself singly be perceived by our senses: e.g. take a grain of wheat, divide it into two parts; each part has still solidity, extension, figure, and mobility: divide it again, and it retains still the same qualities; and so divide it on, till the parts become insensible; they must retain still each of them all those qualities. For division (which is all that a mill, or pestle, or any other body, does upon another, in reducing it to insensible parts) can never take away either solidity, extension, figure, or mobility from any body, but only makes two or more distinct separate masses of matter of that which was but one before; all which distinct masses, reckoned as so many distinct bodies, after division, make a certain number. These I call original or primary qualities of body, which I think we may observe to produce simple ideas in us, viz. solidity, extension, figure, motion or rest, and number.

10. *Secondary qualities of bodies.* Secondly, such qualities which in truth are nothing in the objects themselves but power to produce various sensations in us by their primary qualities, i.e., by the bulk, figure, texture, and motion of their insensible parts, as colours, sounds, tastes, etc. These I call secondary qualities. To these might be added a third sort, which are allowed to be barely powers, though they are as much real qualities in the subject as those which I, to comply with the common way of speaking, call qualities, but for distinction, secondary qualities. For the power in fire to produce a new colour, or consistency, in wax or clay, by its primary qualities is as much a quality in fire as the power it has to produce in me a new idea or sensation of warmth or burning, which I felt not before, by the same primary qualities, viz. the bulk, texture, and motion of its insensible parts.

11. *How bodies produce ideas in us.* The next thing to be considered is how bodies produce ideas in us; and that is manifestly by impulse, the only way which we can conceive bodies to operate in.

12. *By motions, external and in our organism.* If then external objects be not united to our minds when they produce ideas therein, and yet we perceive these original qualities in such of them as singly fall under our senses, it is evident that some motion must be thence continued by our nerves, or animal spirits, by some parts of our bodies, to the brains or the seat of sensation, there to produce in our minds the particular ideas we have of them. And since the extension, figure, number, and motion of bodies of an observable bigness may be perceived at a distance by the sight, it is evident some singly imperceptible bodies must come from them to the eyes and thereby convey to the brain some motion, which produces these ideas which we have of them in us.

13. *How secondary qualities produce their ideas.* After the same manner that the ideas of these original qualities are produced in us, we may conceive that the ideas of secondary qualities are also produced, viz. by the operation of insensible particles on our senses. For, it being manifest that there are bodies and good store of bodies, each whereof are so small that we cannot by any of our senses discover either their bulk, figure, or motion, as is evident in the particles of the air and water and others extremely smaller than those; perhaps as much smaller than the particles of air and water, as the particles of air and water are smaller than peas or hail-stones;—let us suppose at present that the different motions and figures, bulk and number, of such particles, affecting the several organs of our senses, produce in us those different sensations which we have from the colours and smells of bodies; e.g. that a violet, by the impulse of such insensible particles of matter, of peculiar

figures and bulks, and in different degrees and modifications of their motions, causes the ideas of the blue colour and sweet scent of that flower to be produced in our minds. It being no more impossible to conceive that God should annex such ideas to such motions, with which they have no similitude, than that he should annex the idea of pain to the motion of a piece of steel dividing our flesh, with which that idea hath no resemblance.

14. *They depend on the primary qualities.* What I have said concerning colours and smells may be understood also of tastes and sounds and other the like sensible qualities, which, whatever reality we by mistake attribute to them, are in truth nothing in the objects themselves but powers to produce various sensations in us; and depend on those primary qualities, viz. bulk, figure, texture, and motion of parts as I have said.

15. *Ideas of primary qualities are resemblances; of secondary, not.* From whence I think it easy to draw this observation, that the ideas of primary qualities of bodies are resemblances of them, and their patterns do really exist in the bodies themselves, but the ideas produced in us by these secondary qualities have no resemblance of them at all. There is nothing like our ideas existing in the bodies themselves. They are, in the bodies we denominate from them, only a power to produce those sensations in us: and what is sweet, blue, or warm in idea, is but the certain bulk, figure, and motion of the insensible parts in the bodies themselves which we call so.

16. *Examples.* Flame is denominated hot and light; snow, white and cold; and manna, white and sweet, from the ideas they produce in us. Which qualities are commonly thought to be the same in those bodies that those ideas are in us, the one the perfect resemblance of the other, as they are in a mirror, and it would by most men be judged very extravagant if one should say otherwise. And yet he that will consider that the same fire that, at one distance produces in us the sensation of warmth, does, at a nearer approach, produce in us the far different sensation of pain, ought to bethink himself what reason he has to say—that this idea of warmth, which was produced in him by the fire, is actually in the fire; and his idea of pain, which the same fire produced in him the same way, is not in the fire. Why are whiteness and coldness in snow, and pain not, when it produces the one and the other idea in us; and can do neither but by the bulk, figure, number, and motion of its solid parts?

17. *The ideas of the primary alone really exist.* The particular bulk, number, figure, and motion of the parts of fire or snow are really in them, whether anyone's senses perceive them or no: and therefore they may be called real qualities, because they really exist in those bodies. But light, heat, whiteness, or coldness are no more really in them than sickness or pain is in manna. Take away the sensation of them, let not the eyes see light or colours, nor the ears hear sounds, let the palate not taste, nor the nose smell, and all colours, tastes, odours, and sounds, as they are such particular ideas, vanish and cease, and are reduced to their causes, i.e., bulk, figure, and motion of parts.

18. *The secondary exist in things only as modes of the primary.* A piece of manna of a sensible bulk is able to produce in us the idea of a round or square figure; and by being removed from one place to another, the idea of motion. This idea of motion represents it as it really is in manna moving: a circle or square are the same, whether in idea or existence, in the mind or in the manna. And this, both motion and figure, are really in the manna, whether we take notice of them or no: this everybody is ready to agree to. Besides, manna, by the bulk, figure, texture, and motion of its parts, has a power to produce the sensations of sickness, and sometimes of acute pains or gripings in us. That these ideas of sickness and pain are not in the manna, but effects of its operations on us, and are nowhere when we feel them not; this also everyone readily agrees to. And yet men are hardly to be brought to think that sweetness and whiteness are not really in manna, which are but the effects of the operations of manna, by the motion, size, and figure of its particles on the eyes and palate: as the pain and sickness caused by manna are confessedly nothing but the effects of its operations on the stomach and guts, by the size, motion, and figure of its insensible parts (for

by nothing else can a body operate, as has been proved): as if it could not operate on the eyes and palate and thereby produce in the mind particular distinct ideas, which in itself it has not, as well as we allow it can operate on the guts and stomach, and thereby produce distinct ideas, which in itself it has not. These ideas, being all effects of the operations of manna on several parts of our bodies, by the size, figure number, and motion of its parts; why those produced by the eyes and palate should rather be thought to be really in the manna than those produced by the stomach and guts; or why the pain and sickness, ideas that are the effect of manna, should be thought to be nowhere when they are not felt; and yet the sweetness and whiteness, effects of the same manna on other parts of the body, by ways equally as unknown should be thought to exist in the manna when they are not seen or tasted, would need some reason to explain.

19. *Examples.* Let us consider the red and white colours in porphyry. Hinder light from striking on it, and its colours vanish; it no longer produces any such ideas in us: upon the return of light it produces these appearances on us again. Can any one think any real alterations are made in the porphyry by the presence or absence of light, and that those ideas of whiteness and redness are really in porphyry in the light, when it is plain it has no colour in the dark? It has, indeed, such a configuration of particles, both night and day, as are apt, by the rays of light rebounding from some parts of that hard stone, to produce in us the idea of redness, and from others the idea of whiteness; but whiteness or redness are not in it at any time, but such a texture that hath the power to produce such a sensation in us.

20. Pound an almond, and the clear white colour will be altered into a dirty one, and the sweet taste into an oily one. What real alteration can the beating of the pestle make in any body, but an alteration of the texture of it?

21. *Explains how water felt as cold by one hand may be warm to the other.* Ideas being thus distinguished and understood, we may be able to give an account how the same water, at the same time, may produce the idea of cold by one hand and of heat by the other: whereas it is impossible that the same water, if those ideas were really in it, should at the same time be both hot and cold. For, if we imagine warmth, as it is in our hands, to be nothing but a certain sort and degree of motion in the minute particles of our nerves or animal spirits, we may understand how it is possible that the same water may, at the same time, produce the sensations of heat in one hand and cold in the other; which yet figure never does, that never producing the idea of a square by one hand which has produced the idea of a globe by another. But if the sensation of heat and cold be nothing but the increase or diminution of the motion of the minute parts of our bodies, caused by the corpuscles of any other body, it is easy to be understood that if that motion be greater in one hand than in the other, if a body be applied to the two hands which has in its minute particles a greater motion than in those of one of the hands, and a less than in those of the other, it will increase the motion of the one hand and lessen it in the other; and so cause the different sensations of heat and cold that depend thereon.

22. *An excursion into natural philosophy.* I have in what just goes before been engaged in physical inquiries a little further than perhaps I intended. But, it being necessary to make the nature of sensation a little understood, and to make the difference between the qualities in bodies, and the ideas produced by them in the mind, to be distinctly conceived, without which it were impossible to discourse intelligibly of them—I hope I shall be pardoned this little excursion into natural philosophy; it being necessary in our present inquiry to distinguish the primary and real qualities of bodies, which are always in them (viz. solidity, extension, figure, number, and motion or rest, and are sometimes perceived by us, viz. when the bodies they are in are big enough singly to be discerned), from those secondary and imputed qualities which are but the powers of several combinations of those primary ones when they operate without being distinctly discerned;—whereby we may also come to know what ideas are, and what

are not, resemblances of something really existing in the bodies we denominate from them.

23. *Three sorts of qualities in bodies.* The qualities, then, that are in bodies, rightly considered, are of three sorts: First, the bulk, figure, number, situation, and motion or rest of their solid parts. Those are in them, whether we perceive them or not; and when they are of that size that we can discover them, we have by these an idea of the thing as it is in itself, as is plain in artificial things. These I call primary qualities.

Secondly, the power that is in any body, by reason of its insensible primary qualities, to operate after a peculiar manner on any of our senses, and thereby produce in us the different ideas of several colours, sounds, smells, tastes, etc. These are usually called sensible qualities.

Thirdly, the power that is in any body, by reason of the particular constitution of its primary qualities, to make such a change in the bulk, figure, texture, and motion of another body as to make it operate on our senses differently from what it did before. Thus the sun has a power to make wax white, and fire to make lead fluid. These are usually called powers.

The first of these, as has been said, I think may be properly called real, original, or primary qualities; because they are in the things themselves, whether they are perceived or not: and upon their different modifications it is that the secondary qualities depend.

The other two are only powers to act differently upon other things: which powers result from the different modifications of those primary qualities.

Chapter XXIII: Of Our Complex Ideas of Substances

2. So that if anyone will examine himself concerning his notion of pure substance in general, he will find he has no other idea of it at all, but only a supposition of he knows not what support of such qualities which are capable of producing simple ideas in us; which qualities are commonly called accidents. If anyone should be asked, what is the subject wherein colour or weight inheres, he would have nothing to say but the solid extended parts; and if he were demanded, what is it that solidity and extension adhere in, he would not be in a much better case than the Indian before mentioned who, saying that the world was supported by a great elephant, was asked what the elephant rested on; to which his answer was—a great tortoise: but being again pressed to know what gave support to the broad-backed tortoise, replied—something, he knew not what. And thus here, as in all other cases where we use words without having clear and distinct ideas, we talk like children: who, being questioned what such a thing is, which they know not, readily give this satisfactory answer, that it is something: which in truth signifies no more, when so used either by children or men, but that they know not what; and that the thing they pretend to know, and talk of, is what they have no distinct idea of at all, and so are perfectly ignorant of it and in the dark. The idea then we have to which we give the general name substance being nothing but the supposed, but unknown, support of those qualities we find existing, which we imagine cannot subsist *sine re substante*, without something to support them, we call that support *substantia*, which, according to the true import of the word, is, in plain English, standing under or upholding.

9. *Three sorts of ideas make our complex ones of corporeal substances.* The ideas that make our complex ones of corporeal substances are of these three sorts. First, the ideas of the primary qualities of things, which are discovered by our senses and are in them even when we perceive them not; such are the bulk, figure, number, situation, and motion of the parts of bodies; which are really in them whether we take notice of them or not. Secondly, the sensible secondary qualities, which, depending on these, are nothing but the powers those substances have to produce several ideas in us by our senses; which ideas are not in the things themselves otherwise than as anything is in its cause. Thirdly, the aptness we consider in any substance to give or receive such alterations of primary qualities as that the substance so altered should produce in us different ideas from what it

did before; these are called active and passive powers: all which powers, as far as we have any notice or notion of them, terminate only in sensible simple ideas. For whatever alteration a loadstone has the power to make in the minute particles of iron, we should have no notion of any power it had at all to operate on iron, did not its sensible motion discover it: and I doubt not but there are a thousand changes that bodies we daily handle have a power to use in one another, which we never suspect because they never appear in sensible effects.

10. *Powers thus make a great part of our complex ideas of particular substances.* Powers therefore justly make a great part of our complex ideas of substances. He that will examine his complex idea of gold will find several of its ideas that make it up to be only powers, as the power of being melted but of not spending itself in the fire, of being dissolved in *aqua regia*, are ideas as necessary to make up our complex idea of gold as its colour and weight: which, if duly considered, are also nothing but different powers. For, to speak truly, yellowness is not actually in gold, but is a power in gold to produce that idea in us by our eyes when placed in a due light: and the heat, which we cannot leave out of our ideas of the sun, is no more really in the sun than the white colour it introduces into wax. These are both equally powers in the sun, operating by the motion and figure of its sensible parts so on a man as to make him have the idea of heat; and so on wax as to make it capable to produce in a man the idea of white.

11. *The now secondary qualities of bodies would disappear, if we could discover the primary ones of their minute parts.* Had we senses acute enough to discern the minute particles of bodies, and the real constitution on which their sensible qualities depend, I doubt not but they would produce quite different ideas in us: and that which is now the yellow colour of gold would then disappear, and instead of it we should see an admirable texture of parts of a certain size and figure. This microscopes plainly discover to us; for what to our naked eyes produces a certain colour is, by thus augmenting the acuteness of our senses, discovered to be quite a different thing; and the thus altering, as it were, the proportion of the bulk of the minute parts of a coloured object to our usual sight produces different ideas from what it did before. Thus, sand or pounded glass, which is opaque and white to the naked eye, is pellucid in a microscope; and a hair seen in this way loses its former colour and is, in a great measure, pellucid, with a mixture of some bright sparkling colours, such as appear from the refraction of diamonds and other pellucid bodies. Blood, to the naked eye, appears all red; but by a good microscope, wherein its lesser parts appear, shows only some few globules of red, swimming in a pellucid liquor, and how these red globules would appear if glasses could be found that could yet magnify them a thousand or ten thousand times more is uncertain.

12. *Our faculties for discovery of the qualities and powers of substances suited to our state.* The infinite wise Contriver of us, and all things about us, hath fitted our senses, faculties, and organs, to the conveniences of life and the business we have to do here. We are able, by our senses, to know and distinguish things: and to examine them so far as to apply them to our uses and several ways to accommodate the exigencies of this life. We have insight enough into their admirable contrivances and wonderful effects to admire and magnify the wisdom, power, and goodness of their Author. Such a knowledge as this, which is suited to our present condition, we want not faculties to attain. But it appears not that God intended we should have a perfect, clear, and adequate knowledge of them: that perhaps is not in the comprehension of any finite being. We are furnished with faculties (dull and weak as they are) to discover enough in the creatures to lead us to the knowledge of the Creator and the knowledge of our duty; and we are fitted well enough with abilities to provide for the conveniences of living: these are our business in this world. But were our senses altered, and made much quicker and acuter, the appearance and outward scheme of things would have quite another face to us; and, I am apt to think, would be inconsistent with our being, or at least well-being, in this part of the universe which we

inhabit. He that considers how little our constitution is able to bear a remove into parts of this air, not much higher than that we commonly breath in, will have reason to be satisfied that in this globe of earth allotted for our mansion the all-wise Architect has suited our organs, and the bodies that are to affect them, one to another. If our sense of hearing were but a thousand times quicker than it is, how would a perpetual noise distract us. And we should in the quietest retirement be less able to sleep or meditate than in the middle of a sea-fight. Nay, if that most instructive of our senses, seeing, were in any man a thousand or a hundred thousand times more acute than it is by the best microscope, things several millions of times less than the smallest object of his sight now would then be visible to his naked eyes, and so he would come nearer to the discovery of the texture and motion of the minute parts of corporeal things; and in many of them, probably get ideas of their internal constitutions: but then he would be in a quite different world from other people: nothing would appear the same to him and others: the visible ideas of everything would be different. So that I doubt whether he and the rest of men could discourse concerning the objects of sight, or have any communication about colours, their appearances being so wholly different. And perhaps such a quickness and tenderness of sight could not endure bright sunshine, or so much as open daylight; nor take in but a very small part of any object at once, and that too only at a very near distance. And if by the help of such microscopical eyes (if I may so call them) a man could penetrate further than ordinary into the secret composition and radical texture of bodies, he would not make any great advantage by the change if such an acute sight would not serve to conduct him to the market and exchange, if he could not see things he was to avoid, at a convenient distance, nor distinguish things he had to do with by those sensible qualities others do. He that was sharp-sighted enough to see the configuration of the minute particles of the spring of a clock, and observe upon what peculiar structure and impulse its elastic motion depends, would no doubt discover something very admirable: but if eyes so framed could not view at once the hand and the characters of the hour-plate, and thereby at a distance see what o'clock it was, their owner could not be much benefited by that acuteness; which, whilst it discovered the secret contrivance of the parts of the machine, made him lose its use.

Book III: Of Words

Chapter III: Of General Terms

6. *How general words are made.* The next thing to be considered is how general words come to be made. For, since all things that exist are only particulars, how come we by general terms; or where find we those general natures they are supposed to stand for? Words become general by being made the signs of general ideas: and ideas become general by separating from them the circumstances of time and place and any other ideas that may determine them to this or that particular existence. By this way of abstraction they are made capable of representing more individuals than one; each of which having in it a conformity to that abstract idea is (as we call it) of that sort.

7. *Shown by the way we enlarge our complex ideas from infancy.* But, to deduce this a little more distinctly, it will not perhaps be amiss to trace our notions and names from their beginning, and observe by what degrees we proceed and by what steps we enlarge our ideas from our first infancy. There is nothing more evident than that the ideas of the persons children converse with (to instance in them alone) are, like the persons themselves, only particular. The ideas of the nurse and the mother are well framed in their minds; and, like pictures of them there, represent only those individuals. The names they first gave to them are confined to these individuals; and the names of nurse and mamma the child uses determine themselves to those persons. Afterwards, when time and a larger acquaintance have made them observe that there are a great many other things in the world, that in some common agreements of shape,

and several other qualities, resemble their father and mother and those persons they have been used to, they frame an idea which they find those many particulars do partake in; and to that they give, with others, the name *man*, for example. And thus they come to have a general name and a general idea. Wherein they make nothing new; but only leave out of the complex idea they had of Peter and James, Mary and Jane, that which is peculiar to each, and retain only what is common to them all.

8. *And further enlarge our complex ideas by still leaving out properties contained in them.* By the same way that they come by the general name and idea of man, they easily advance to more general names and notions. For, observing that several things that differ from their idea of man, and cannot therefore be comprehended under that name, have yet certain qualities wherein they agree with man, by retaining only those qualities, and uniting them into one idea, they have again another and more general idea; to which having given a name they make a term of a more comprehensive extension: which new idea is made, not by any new addition, but only as before, by leaving out the shape and some other properties signified by the name *man*, and retaining only a body, with life, sense, and spontaneous motion, comprehended under the name *animal.*

9. *General natures are nothing but abstract and partial ideas of more complex ones.* That this is the way whereby men first formed general ideas, and general names to them, I think is so evident that there needs no other proof of it but the considering of a man's self, or others, and the ordinary proceedings of their minds in knowledge. And he that thinks general natures or notions are anything else but such abstract and partial ideas of more complex ones, taken at first from particular existences, will, I fear, be at a loss where to find them. For let anyone effect, and then tell me, wherein does his idea of man differ from that of Peter and Paul, or his idea of horse from that of Bucephalus, but in the leaving out something that is peculiar to each individual and retaining so much of those particular complex ideas of several particular existences as they are found to agree in? Of the complex ideas signified by the names *man* and *horse*, leaving out but those particulars wherein they differ, and retaining only those wherein they agree, and of those making a new distinct complex idea, and giving the name *animal* to it, one has a more general term that comprehends with man several other creatures. Leave out of the idea of animal, sense and spontaneous motion, and the remaining complex idea, made up of the remaining simple ones of body, life, and nourishment, becomes a more general one, under the more comprehensive term, *vivens.* And, not to dwell longer upon this particular, so evident in itself, by the same way the mind proceeds to body, substance, and at last to being, thing, and such universal terms, which stand for any of our ideas whatsoever. To conclude: this whole mystery of genera and species, which make such a noise in the schools, and are with justice so little regarded out of them, is nothing else but abstract ideas, more or less comprehensive, with names annexed to them. In all which this is constant and unvariable, that every more general term stands for such an idea, and is but a part of any of those contained under it....

11. *General and universal are creatures of the understanding, and belong not to the real existence of things.* To return to general words: it is plain, by what has been said, that general and universal belong not to the real existence of things, but are the inventions and creatures of the understanding, made by it for its own use, and concern only signs, whether words or ideas. Words are general, as has been said, when used for signs of general ideas, and so are applicable indifferently to many particular things; and ideas are general when they are set up as the representatives of many particular things: but universality belongs not to things themselves, which are all of them particular in their existence, even those words and ideas which in their signification are general. When therefore we quit particulars, the generals that rest are only creatures of our own making; their general nature being nothing but the capacity they are put into, by the understanding, of signifying or representing many

particulars. For the signification they have is nothing but a relation that, by the mind of man, is added to them.

12. *Abstract ideas are the essences of genera and species.* The next thing therefore to be considered is, what kind of signification it is that general words have. For, as it is evident that they do not signify barely one particular thing; for then they would not be general terms, but proper names, so, on the other side, it is as evident they do not signify a plurality; for *man* and *men* would then signify the same; and the distinction of numbers (as the grammarians call them) would be superfluous and useless. That then which general words signify is a sort of things; and each of them does that by being a sign of an abstract idea in the mind; to which idea, as things existing are found to agree, so they come to be ranked under that name, or, which is all one, be of that sort. Whereby it is evident that the essences of the sorts, or, if the Latin word pleases better, species of things, are nothing else but these abstract ideas. For the having the essence of any species being that which makes anything to be of that species; and the conformity to the idea to which the name is annexed being that which gives a right to that name; the having the essence, and the having that conformity, must needs be the same thing: since to be of any species, and to have a right to the name of that species, is all one. As, for example, to be a man, or of the species man, and to have right to the name *man*, is the same thing. Again, to be a man, or of the species man, and have the essence of a man, is the same thing. Now, since nothing can be a man, or have a right to the name *man*, but what has a conformity to the abstract idea the name *man* stands for, nor anything be a man, or have a right to the species man, but what has the essence of that species; it follows that the abstract idea for which the name stands, and the essence of the species, is one and the same. From whence it is easy to observe that the essences of the sorts of things, and, consequently, the sorting of things, is the workmanship of the understanding that abstracts and makes those general ideas.

13. *They are the workmanship of the understanding, but have their foundation in the similitude of things.* I would not here be thought to forget, much less to deny, that nature, in the production of things, makes several of them alike: there is nothing more obvious, especially in the race of animals and all things propagated by seed. But yet I think we may say the sorting of them under names is the workmanship of the understanding, taking occasion, from the similitude it observes amongst them, to make abstract general ideas and set them up in the mind, with names annexed to them, as patterns or forms (for, in that sense, the word *form* has a very proper signification) to which as particular things existing are found to agree, so they come to be of that species, have that denomination, or are put into that class. For when we say this is a man, that a horse; this justice, that cruelty; this a watch, that a jack; what do we else but rank things under different specific names, as agreeing to those abstract ideas of which we have made those names the signs? And what are the essences of those species set out and marked by names, but those abstract ideas in the mind, which are, as it were, the bonds between particular things that exist and the names they are to be ranked under? And when general names have any connexion with particular beings, these abstract ideas are the medium that unites them: so that the essences of species, as distinguished and denominated by us, neither are nor can be anything but those precise abstract ideas we have in our minds. And therefore the supposed real essences of substances, if different from our abstract ideas, cannot be the essences of the species we rank things into. For two species may be one, as rationally as two different essences be the essence of one species: and I demand what are the alterations [which] may or may not be made in a horse or lead without making either of them to be of another species? In determining the species of things by our abstract ideas, this is easy to resolve: but if anyone will regulate himself herein by supposed real essences, he will, I suppose, be at a loss: and he will never be able to know when anything precisely ceases to be of the species of a horse or lead....

15. *Several significations of the word "essence."* But since the essences of things are thought by

some (and not without reason) to be wholly unknown, it may not be amiss to consider the several significations of the word *essence*. Real essences. First, essence may be taken for the very being of anything, whereby it is what it is. And thus the real internal, but generally (in substances) unknown constitution of things, whereon their discoverable qualities depend, may be called their essence. This is the proper original signification of the word, as is evident from the formation of it; *essentia*, in its primary notation, signifying properly, being. And in this sense it is still used, when we speak of the essence of particular things without giving them any name. Nominal essences. Secondly, the learning and disputes of the schools having been much busied about genus and species, the word *essence* has almost lost its primary signification: and, instead of the real constitution of things, has been almost wholly applied to the artificial constitution of genus and species. It is true, there is ordinarily supposed a real constitution of the sorts of things; and it is past doubt there must be some real constitution on which any collection of simple ideas co-existing must depend. But, it being evident that things are ranked under names into sorts or species only as they agree to certain abstract ideas to which we have annexed those names, the essence of each genus, or sort, comes to be nothing but that abstract idea which the general, or sortal (if I may have leave so to call it from *sort*, as I do general from *genus*), name stands for. And this we shall find to be that which the word *essence* imports in its most familiar use. These two sorts of essences, I suppose, may not unfitly be termed, the one the real, the other nominal essence.

16. *Constant connexion between the name and nominal essence*. Between the nominal essence and the name there is so near a connexion that the name of any sort of things cannot be attributed to any particular being but what has this essence, whereby it answers that abstract idea whereof that name is the sign.

20.2 THE IDEALISM OF BERKELEY AND HUME

Historically Locke hardly had the last word. In the tradition of empiricism, Bishop George Berkeley (1685–1753) is often counted as having refuted Locke's best arguments. Berkeley, an anglicized Irishman, graduated from Trinity College, Dublin, at 19; he was appointed Fellow of the College the same year. He wrote most of his important works of philosophy by the age of 28.

Berkeley sees idealism as the best defense of common sense against skepticism. A follower of Descartes who accepted Descartes' conclusion that a person knows best his or her own consciousness, Berkeley reasoned that the French philosopher had not gone far enough. He had not been true to his own insights: Through experience our own minds are not just what we know best, but *all* that we know. How could we know things that by definition transcend experience? Berkeley argues that Locke's notion of an object makes no sense.

Moreover, the distinction between primary and secondary qualities is ill grounded. In effect, he says, every quality is a secondary quality. We have no basis for thinking that any of our ideas corresponds to a mind-independent reality. Further, our ideas of primary qualities are supposed to resemble the qualities themselves. But we have no access to the qualities apart from our ideas of them, and we have no way to recognize resemblance.

Thus Berkeley has two chief arguments for idealism: (1) an attack on the idea of primary qualities and (2) an attack on the idea of matter as independent of mind. Berkeley rejects primary qualities on the grounds that our perceptions of length, width, height, etc., vary, while objects remain unchanged. He rejects mind-independent matter because there could be no evidence for such a thing (defined as it is as "beyond evidence").

Berkeley wrote a series of dialogues whose characters are Hylas, who defends Locke, and Philonous, who speaks for Berkeley himself. Philonous says that the reasons for regarding certain qualities as secondary apply to primary qualities, too. The underlying principle, as David Hume notes, is that "when different impressions of the same sense arise from any object, every one of these impressions has not a resembling quality existent in the object." Moreover, we have access to nothing but our own ideas. So we have no good reason for thinking external objects exist at all or are anything but our own ideas. And we have no way of comparing our ideas to the actual qualities in things to see whether there is a resemblance.

Berkeley also attacks Locke's idea of substance. Locke himself admits that there is little content to the idea. His concept is not Aristotle's, which is, as we have seen, basically the concept of an object like a chair. Substance, for Locke, is a substratum in which the qualities of objects inhere. Berkeley's argument against this idea of substance relies on Locke's admission that the idea is virtually content-free: "something, I know not what."

Locke's position, Berkeley insists, leads inevitably to skepticism. David Hume (1711–1776) agrees with Berkeley in this, maintaining that our commonsense picture of the world, when analyzed, leads directly to skepticism. He also pushes forward the attack on substance with reasoning exactly parallel to his attack on the self. How could we obtain an idea of substance? How could we have an impression in experience of a container in which qualities of objects outside of us inhere? Is there an experience of "inherence"? Our ideas correspond to the qualities we perceive, and no one perceives inherence.

Hume also purchases the tenet fundamental to all idealism that, as Berkeley puts it, "to be is to be perceived": *esse est percipi*. We have no access to anything except that which is before the mind. A thing can exist, therefore, only if it can be perceived. Indeed, Hume goes further: A thing can exist only if it is perceived. He finds the idea of an unperceived object absurd.

But if to be is to be perceived, what happens to the books in my room when I walk out of it and am no longer there to perceive them? when I fall asleep and neither perceive nor even think of them? Do they go out of existence, as my perceptions and thoughts do? No, Berkeley says—but only because God perceives them.

20.2.1 George Berkeley, from *Three Dialogues Between Hylas and Philonous*

Hylas. I frankly own, Philonous, that it is in vain to stand out any longer. Colours, sounds, tastes, in a word all those termed secondary qualities, have certainly no existence without the mind.

Source: George Berkeley, *Three Dialogues Between Hylas and Philonous*, 1713.

But by this acknowledgment I must not be supposed to derogate the reality of matter, or external objects; seeing it is no more than several philosophers maintain, who nevertheless are the farthest imaginable from denying matter. For the clearer understanding of this, you must know sensible qualities are by philosophers divided into Primary and Secondary. The former are Extension, Figure, Solidity, Gravity, Motion, and Rest; and these they hold exist really in bodies. The latter are those above enumerated; or, briefly, all sensible qualities beside the Primary, which they assert are only so many sensations or ideas existing nowhere but in the mind. But all this, I doubt not, you are apprised of. For my part, I have been a long time sensible there was such an opinion current among philosophers, but was never thoroughly convinced of its truth until now.

Philonous. You are still then of opinion that extension and figures are inherent in external unthinking substances?

Hylas. I am.

Philonous. But what if the same arguments which are brought against Secondary Qualities will hold good against these also?

Hylas. Why then I shall be obliged to think, they too exist only in the mind.

Philonous. Is it your opinion the very figure and extension which you perceive by sense exist in the outward object or material substance?

Hylas. It is.

Philonous. Have all other animals as good grounds to think the same of the figure and extension which they see and feel?

Hylas. Without doubt, if they have any thought at all.

Philonous. Answer me, Hylas. Think you the senses were bestowed upon all animals for their preservation and well-being in life? or were they given to men alone for this end?

Hylas. I make no question but they have the same use in all other animals.

Philonous. If so, is it not necessary they should be enabled by them to perceive their own limbs, and those bodies which are capable of harming them?

Hylas. Certainly.

Philonous. A mite therefore must be supposed to see his own foot, and things equal or even less than it, as bodies of some considerable dimension, though at the same time they appear to you scarce discernible, or at best as so many visible points?

Hylas. I cannot deny it.

Philonous. And to creatures less than the mite they will seem yet larger?

Hylas. They will.

Philonous. Insomuch that what you can hardly discern will to another extremely minute animal appear as some huge mountain?

Hylas. All this I grant.

Philonous. Can one and the same thing be at the same time in itself of different dimensions?

Hylas. That were absurd to imagine.

Philonous. But, from what you have laid down it follows that both the extension by you perceived, and that perceived by the mite itself, as likewise all those perceived by lesser animals, are each of them the true extension of the mite's foot; that is to say, by your own principles you are led into an absurdity.

Hylas. There seems to be some difficulty in the point.

Philonous. Again, have you not acknowledged that no real inherent property of any object can be changed without some change in the thing itself?

Hylas. I have.

Philonous. But, as we approach to or recede from an object, the visible extension varies, being at one distance ten or a hundred times greater than another. Doth it not therefore follow from hence likewise that it is not really inherent in the object?

Hylas. I own I am at a loss what to think.

Philonous. Your judgment will soon be determined, if you will venture to think as freely concerning this quality as you have done concerning the rest. Was it not admitted as a good argument that neither heat nor cold was in the water because it seemed warm to one hand and cold to the other?

Hylas. It was.

Philonous. Is it not the very same reasoning to conclude there is no extension or figure in an object because to one eye it shall seem little, smooth, and round, when at the same time it appears to the other, great, uneven, and regular?

Hylas. The very same. But does this latter fact ever happen?

Philonous. You may at any time make the experiment by looking with one eye bare and with the other through a microscope.

Hylas. I know not how to maintain it; and yet I am loath to give up extension, I see so many odd consequences following upon such a concession.

Philonous. Odd, say you? After the concessions already made, I hope you will stick at nothing for its oddness. But, on the other hand, should it not seem very odd, if the general reasoning which includes all other sensible qualities did not also include extension? If it be allowed that no idea, nor anything like an idea, can exist in an unperceiving substance, then surely it follows that no figure, or mode of extension, which we can either perceive, or imagine, or have any idea of, can be really inherent in matter; not to mention the peculiar difficulty there must be in conceiving a material substance prior to and distinct from extension to be the substratum of extension. Be the sensible quality what it will—figure, or sound, or colour, it seems alike impossible it should subsist in that which doth not perceive it....

Hylas. One great oversight I take to be this—that I did not sufficiently distinguish the object from the sensation. Now, though this latter may not exist without the mind, yet it will not thence follow that the former cannot.

Philonous. What object do you mean? the object of the senses?

Hylas. The same.

Philonous. It is then immediately perceived?

Hylas. Right.

Philonous. Make me to understand the difference between what is immediately perceived and a sensation.

Hylas. The sensation I take to be an act of the mind perceiving; besides which, there is something perceived; and this I call the object. For example, there is red and yellow on that tulip. But then the act of perceiving those colours is in me only, and not in the tulip.

Philonous. What tulip do you speak of? Is it that which you see?

Hylas. The same.

Philonous. And what do you see beside colour, figure, and extension?

Hylas. Nothing.

Philonous. What you would say then is that the red and yellow are coexistent with the extension; is it not?

Hylas. That is not all; I would say they have a real existence without the mind, in some unthinking substance.

Philonous. That the colours are really in the tulip which I see is manifest. Neither can it be denied that this tulip may exist independent of your mind or mine; but, that any immediate object of the senses—that is, any idea, or combination of ideas—should exist in an unthinking substance, or exterior to all minds, is in itself an evident contradiction. Nor can I imagine how this follows from what you said just now, to wit, that the red and yellow were on the tulip you saw, since you do not pretend to see that unthinking substance....

Hylas. If it comes to that the point will soon be decided. What more easy than to conceive a tree or house existing by itself, independent of, and unperceived by, any mind whatsoever? I do at this present time conceive them existing after that manner.

Philonous. How say you, Hylas, can you see a thing which is at the same time unseen?

Hylas. No, that were a contradiction.

Philonous. Is it not as great a contradiction to talk of conceiving a thing which is unconceived?

Hylas. It is.

Philonous. The tree or house therefore which you think of is conceived by you?

Hylas. How should it be otherwise?

Philonous. And what is conceived is surely in the mind?

Hylas. Without question, that which is conceived is in the mind.

Philonous. How then came you to say you conceived a house or tree existing independent and out of all minds whatsoever?

Hylas. That was I own an oversight; but stay, let me consider what led me into it.—It is a pleasant mistake enough. As I was thinking of a tree in a solitary place, where no one was present to see it, methought that was to conceive a tree as existing unperceived or unthought of; not considering that I myself conceived it all the while. But now I plainly see that all I can do is to frame ideas in my own mind. I may indeed conceive in my own thoughts the idea of a tree, or a house, or a mountain, but that is all. And this is far from proving that I can conceive them existing out of the minds of all Spirits.

Philonous. You acknowledge then that you cannot possibly conceive how any one corporeal sensible thing should exist otherwise than in the mind?

Hylas. I do.

Philonous. And yet you will earnestly contend for the truth of that which you cannot so much as conceive?...

Hylas. To speak the truth, Philonous, I think there are two kinds of objects:—the one perceived immediately, which are likewise called ideas; the other are real things or external objects, perceived by the mediation of ideas, which are their images and representations. Now, I own ideas do not exist without the mind; but the latter sort of objects do. I am sorry I did not think of this distinction sooner; it would probably have cut short your discourse.

Philonous. Are those external objects perceived by sense or by some other faculty?

Hylas. They are perceived by sense.

Philonous. Is there anything perceived by sense which is not immediately perceived?

Hylas. Yes, Philonous, in some sort there is. For example, when I look on a picture or statue of Julius Caesar, I may be said after a manner to perceive him (though not immediately) by my senses.

Philonous. It seems then you will have our ideas, which alone are immediately perceived, to be pictures of external things: and that these also are perceived by sense, inasmuch as they have a conformity or resemblance to our ideas?

Hylas. That is my meaning.

Philonous. And, in the same way that Julius Caesar, in himself invisible, is nevertheless perceived by sight; real things, in themselves imperceptible, are perceived by sense.

Hylas. In the very same.

Philonous. Tell me, Hylas, when you behold the picture of Julius Caesar, do you see with your eyes any more than some colours and figures, with a certain symmetry and composition of the whole?

Hylas. Nothing else.

Philonous. And would not a man who had never known anything of Julius Caesar see as much?

Hylas. He would.

Philonous. Consequently he hath his sight, and the use of it, in as perfect a degree as you?

Hylas. I agree with you.

Philonous. Whence comes it then that your thoughts are directed to the Roman emperor, and his are not? This cannot proceed from the sensations or ideas of sense by you then perceived, since you acknowledge you have no advantage over him in that respect. It should seem therefore to proceed from reason and memory: should it not?

Hylas. It should.

Philonous. Consequently, it will not follow from that instance that anything is perceived by sense which is not immediately perceived. Though I grant we may, in one [accepted usage], be said to perceive sensible things mediately by sense: that is, when, from a frequently perceived connexion, the immediate perception of ideas by one sense suggests to the mind others, perhaps belonging to another sense, which are wont to be connected with them. For instance, when I hear a coach drive along the streets, immediately I perceive only the sound; but, from the experience I have had that such a sound is connected with a coach, I am said to hear the coach. It is nevertheless evident that, in truth and strictness, nothing can be heard but sound; and the coach is not then properly perceived by sense, but suggested from experience. So likewise when we are said to see a red-hot bar of iron; the solidity and heat of the iron are not the objects of sight, but suggested to the imagination by the colour and figure which are properly perceived by that sense. In short, those things alone are actually and strictly perceived by any sense which would have been perceived in case that same sense had then been first conferred on us. As for other things, it is plain they are only suggested to the mind by experience, grounded on former perceptions. But, to return to your comparison of Caesar's picture, it is plain, if you keep to that, you must hold the real things, or archetypes of our ideas, are not perceived by sense, but by some internal faculty of the soul, as reason or memory. I would therefore fain know what arguments you can draw from reason for the existence of what you call real things or material objects. Or, whether you remember to have seen them formerly as they are in themselves; or, if you have heard or read of any one that did.

Hylas. I see, Philonous, you are disposed to raillery; but that will never convince me.

Philonous. My aim is only to learn from you the way to come at the knowledge of material beings. Whatever we perceive is perceived immediately or mediately: by sense, or by reason and reflexion. But, as you have excluded sense, pray shew me what reason you have to believe their existence; or what medium you can possibly make use of to prove it, either to mine or your own understanding.

Hylas. To deal ingenuously, Philonous, now I consider the point, I do not find I can give you any good reason for it. But, thus much seems pretty plain, that it is at least possible such things may really exist. And, as long as there is no absurdity in supposing them, I am resolved to believe as I did, till you bring good reasons to the contrary.

Philonous. What! Is it come to this, that you only believe the existence of material objects, and that your belief is founded barely on the possibility of its being true? Then you will have me bring reasons against it: though another would think it reasonable the proof should lie on him who holds the affirmative. And, after all, this very point which you are now resolved to maintain, without any reason, is in effect what you have more than once during this discourse seen good reason to give up. But, to pass over all this; if I understand you rightly, you say our ideas do not exist without the mind, but that they are copies, images, or representations, of certain originals that do?

Hylas. You take me right.

Philonous. They are then like external things?

Hylas. They are.

Philonous. Have those things a stable and permanent nature, independent of our senses; or are they in a perpetual change, upon our producing any motions in our bodies—suspending, exerting, or altering, our faculties or organs of sense?

Hylas. Real things, it is plain, have a fixed and real nature, which remains the same notwithstanding any change in our senses, or in the posture and motion of our bodies, which indeed may affect the ideas in our minds, but it were absurd to think they had the same effect on things existing without the mind.

Philonous. How then is it possible that things perpetually fleeting and variable as our ideas should be copies or images of anything fixed and constant? Or, in other words, since all sensible qualities, as size, figure, colour, etc., that is, our ideas, are continually changing upon every alteration in the distance, medium, or instruments of sensation, how can any determinate material objects be properly represented or painted forth by several distinct things, each of which is so different from and unlike the rest? Or, if you say it resembles some one only of our ideas, how shall we be able to distinguish the true copy from all the false ones?

Hylas. I profess, Philonous, I am at a loss. I know not what to say to this.

Philonous. But neither is this all. Which are material objects in themselves—perceptible or imperceptible?

Hylas. Properly and immediately nothing can be perceived but ideas. All material things, therefore, are in themselves insensible, and to be perceived only by our ideas.

Philonous. Ideas then are sensible, and their archetypes or originals insensible?

Hylas. Right.

Philonous. But how can that which is sensible be like that which is insensible? Can a real thing, in itself invisible, be like a colour; or a real thing, which is not audible, be like a sound? In a word, can anything be like a sensation or idea, but another sensation or idea?

Hylas. I must own, I think not.

Philonous. Is it possible there should be any doubt on the point? Do you not perfectly know your own ideas?

Hylas. I know them perfectly; since what I do not perceive or know can be no part of my idea.

Philonous. Consider, therefore, and examine them, and then tell me if there be anything in them which can exist without the mind: or if you can conceive anything like them existing without the mind.

Hylas. Upon inquiry, I find it is impossible for me to conceive or understand how anything but an idea can be like an idea. And it is most evident that no idea can exist without the mind.

Philonous. You are therefore, by your principles, forced to deny the reality of sensible things; since you made it to consist in an absolute existence exterior to the mind. That is to say, you are a downright sceptic. So I have gained my point, which was to shew your principles led to Scepticism.

20.2.2 George Berkeley, from *Principles of Human Knowledge*

9. Some there are who make a distinction betwixt primary and secondary qualities. By the former they mean extension, figure, motion, rest, solidity, impenetrability, and number; by the latter they denote all other sensible qualities, as colours, sounds, tastes, and so forth. The ideas we have of these last they acknowledge not to be the resemblances of anything existing without the mind, or unperceived, but they will have our ideas of the primary qualities to be patterns or images of things which exist without the mind, in an unthinking substance which they call matter. By matter, therefore, we are to understand an inert, senseless substance, in which extension, figure, and motion do actually subsist. But it is evident, from what we have already shewn, that extension, figure, and motion are only ideas existing in the mind, and that an idea can be like nothing but another idea, and that consequently neither they nor their archetypes can exist in an unperceiving substance. Hence, it is plain that the very notion of what is called matter or corporeal substance involves a contradiction in it.

10. They who assert that figure, motion, and the rest of the primary or original qualities do exist without the mind, in unthinking substances, do at the same time acknowledge that colours, sounds, heat, cold, and suchlike secondary qualities do not—which they tell us are sensations existing in the mind alone, that depend on and are occasioned by the different size, texture, and motion of the minute particles of matter. This they take for an undoubted truth, which they can demonstrate beyond all exception. Now, if it be certain that those original qualities are inseparably united with the other sensible qualities, and not, even in thought, capable of being abstracted from them, it plainly follows that they exist only in the mind. But I desire anyone to reflect and try whether he can, by any abstraction of thought, conceive the extension and motion of a body without all other sensible qualities. For my own part, I see evidently that it is not in my power to frame an idea of a

Source: George Berkeley, *Principles of Human Knowledge*, 1710.

body extended and moving, but I must withal give it some colour or other sensible quality which is acknowledged to exist only in the mind. In short, extension, figure, and motion, abstracted from all other qualities, are inconceivable. Where therefore the other sensible qualities are, there must these be also, to wit, in the mind and nowhere else....

14. I shall further add that, after the same manner as modern philosophers prove certain sensible qualities to have no existence in matter, or without the mind, the same thing may be likewise proved of all other sensible qualities whatsoever. Thus, for instance, it is said that heat and cold are affections only of the mind, and not at all patterns of real beings existing in the corporeal substances which excite them, for that the same body which appears cold to one hand seems warm to another. Now, why may we not as well argue that figure and extension are not patterns or resemblances of qualities existing in matter, because to the same eye at different stations, or eyes of a different texture at the same station, they appear various, and cannot therefore be the images of anything settled and determinate without the mind? Again, it is proved that sweetness is not really in the sapid thing, because the thing remaining unaltered the sweetness is changed into bitter, as in case of a fever or otherwise vitiated palate. Is it not as reasonable to say that motion is not without the mind, since if the succession of ideas in the mind become swifter, the motion, it is acknowledged, shall appear slower without any alteration in any external object.

15. In short, let anyone consider those arguments which are thought manifestly to prove that colours and tastes exist only in the mind, and he shall find they may with equal force be brought to prove the same thing of extension, figure, and motion—Though it must be confessed this method of arguing does not so much prove that there is no extension or colour in an outward object, as that we do not know by sense which is the true extension or colour of the object. But the arguments foregoing plainly shew it to be impossible that any colour or extension at all, or other sensible quality whatsoever, should exist in an unthinking subject without the mind, or in truth, that there should be any such thing as an outward object.

16. But let us examine a little the received opinion. It is said extension is a mode or accident [or attribute] of matter, and that matter is the substratum that supports it. Now I desire that you would explain to me what is meant by matter's supporting extension. Say you, I have no idea of matter and therefore cannot explain it. I answer, though you have no positive, yet, if you have any meaning at all, you must at least have a relative idea of matter; though you know not what it is, yet you must be supposed to know what relation it bears to accidents, and what is meant by its supporting them. It is evident "support" cannot here be taken in its usual or literal sense—as when we say that pillars support a building; in what sense therefore must it be taken?

17. If we inquire into what the most accurate philosophers declare themselves to mean by material substance, we shall find them acknowledge they have no other meaning annexed to those sounds but the idea of being in general, together with the relative notion of its supporting accidents. The general idea of Being appeareth to me the most abstract and incomprehensible of all others; and as for its supporting accidents, thus, as we have just now observed, cannot be understood in the common sense of those words; it must therefore be taken in some other sense, but what that is they do not explain. So that when I consider the two parts or branches which make the signification of the words "material substance," I am convinced there is no distinct meaning annexed to them. But why should we trouble ourselves any farther, in discussing this material substratum or "support" of figure, and motion, and other sensible qualities? Does it not suppose they have an existence without the mind? And is not this a direct repugnancy, and altogether inconceivable?

18. But, though it were possible that solid, figured, moveable substances may exist without the mind, corresponding to the ideas we have of

bodies, yet how is it possible for us to know this? Either we must know it by sense or by reason. As for our senses, by them we have the knowledge only of our sensations, ideas, or those things that are immediately perceived by sense, call them what you will: but they do not inform us that things exist without the mind, or unperceived, like to those which are perceived. This the materialists themselves acknowledge. It remains therefore that if we have any knowledge at all of external things, it must be by reason inferring their existence from what is immediately perceived by sense. But what reason can induce us to believe the existence of bodies without the mind, from what we perceive, since the very patrons of matter themselves do not pretend there is any necessary connection betwixt them and our ideas? I say it is granted on all hands—and what appears in dreams, frenzies, and the like puts it beyond dispute—that it is possible we might be affected with all the ideas we have now, though there were no bodies existing without resembling them. Hence, it is evident the supposition of external bodies is not necessary for producing our ideas, since it is granted they are produced sometimes, and might possibly be produced always in the same order we see them in at present, without their concurrence....

23. But, say you, surely there is nothing easier than for me to imagine trees, for instance, in a park, or books existing in a closet, and nobody by to perceive them. I answer, you may so, there is no difficulty in it; but what is all this, I beseech you, more than framing in your mind certain ideas which you call books and trees, and at the same time omitting to frame the idea of anyone that may perceive them? But do not you yourself perceive or think of them all the while? This therefore is nothing to the purpose; it only shews you have the power of imagining or forming ideas in your mind; but it does not shew that you can conceive it possible the objects of your thought may exist without the mind. To make out this, it is necessary that you conceive them existing unconceived or unthought of, which is a manifest repugnancy. When we do our utmost to conceive the existence of external bodies, we are all the while only contemplating our own ideas. But the mind, taking no notice of itself, is deluded to think it can and does conceive bodies existing unthought of or without the mind, though at the same time they are apprehended by or exist in itself. A little attention will discover to anyone the truth and evidence of what is here said, and make it unnecessary to insist on any other proofs against the existence of material substance.

20.2.3 David Hume, from *A Treatise of Human Nature*

Part 1. Of Ideas, Their Origin, Composition, Connexion, Abstraction, etc.

Sect. VI.—Of Modes and Substance

I wou'd fain ask those philosophers, who found so much of their reasonings on the distinction of substance and accident, and imagine we have clear ideas of each, whether the idea of substance be deriv'd from the impressions of sensation or of reflection? If it be convey'd to us by our senses, I ask, which of them, and after what manner? If it be perceiv'd by the eyes, it must be a colour; if by the ears, a sound; if by the palate, a taste; and so of the other senses. But I believe none will assert that

Source: David Hume, *A Treatise of Human Nature*. London, 1739.

substance is either a colour, or sound, or a taste. The idea of substance must therefore be deriv'd from an impression of reflection, if it really exist. But the impressions of reflection resolve themselves into our passions and emotions: none of which can possibly represent a substance. We have therefore no idea of substance distinct from that of a collection of particular qualities, nor have we any other meaning when we either talk or reason concerning it.

The idea of a substance as well as that of a mode is nothing but a collection of simple ideas that are united by the imagination, and have a particular name assigned them, by which we are able to recall, either to ourselves or others, that collection. But the difference betwixt these ideas consists in this, that the particular qualities, which form a substance, are commonly refer'd to an unknown something in which they are supposed to inhere; or granting this fiction should not take place, are at least supposed to be closely and inseparably connected by the relations of contiguity and causation. The effect of this is that whatever new simple quality we discover to have the same connexion with the rest, we immediately comprehend it among them, even tho' it did not enter into the first conception of the substance. Thus our idea of gold may at first be a yellow colour, weight, malleableness, fusibility; but upon the discovery of its dissolubility in *aqua regia*, we join that to the other qualities, and suppose it to belong to the substance as much as if its idea had from the beginning made a part of the compound one. The principal of union being regarded as the chief part of the complex idea, gives entrance to whatever quality afterwards occurs, and is equally comprehended by it as are the others which first presented themselves.

That this cannot take place in modes is evident from considering their nature. The simple ideas of which modes are formed either represent qualities, which are not united by contiguity and causation, but are dispers'd in different subjects, or if they be all united together, the uniting principle is not regarded as the foundation of the complex idea. The idea of a dance is an instance of the first kind of modes; that of beauty of the second. The reason is obvious why such complex ideas cannot receive any new idea without changing the name which distinguishes the mode.

Part IV. Of the Sceptical and Other Systems of Philosophy

Sect. IV.—Of the Modern Philosophy

But here it may be objected that the imagination, according to my own confession, being the ultimate judge of all systems of philosophy, I am unjust in blaming the ancient philosophers for making use of that faculty, and allowing themselves to be entirely guided by it in their reasonings. In order to justify myself, I must distinguish in the imagination betwixt the principles which are permanent, irresistible, and universal; such as the customary transition from causes to effects and from effects to causes: And the principles, which are changeable, weak, and irregular, such as those I have just now taken notice of. The former are the foundation of all our thoughts and actions, so that upon their removal human nature must immediately perish and go to ruin. The latter are neither unavoidable to mankind, nor necessary, or so much as useful in the conduct of life; but on the contrary are observ'd only to take place in weak minds, and, being opposite to the other principles of custom and reasoning, may easily be subverted by a due contrast and opposition. For this reason the former are received by philosophy, and the latter rejected. One who concludes somebody to be near him, when he hears an articulate voice in the dark, reasons justly and naturally, tho' that conclusion be deriv'd from nothing but custom, which infixes and enlivens the idea of a human creature on account of his usual conjunction with the present impression. But one who is tormented he knows not why with the apprehension of spectres in the dark may, perhaps, be said to reason, and to reason naturally too: But then it must be in the same sense that a malady is said to be natural; as arising from natural causes, tho' it be contrary to health, the most agreeable and most natural situation of man.

The opinions of the ancient philosophers, their fictions of substance and accident, and their reasonings concerning substantial forms and occult qualities are like the spectres in the dark, and are deriv'd from principles which, however common, are neither universal nor unavoidable in human nature. The modern philosophy pretends to be entirely free from this defect, and to arise only from the solid, permanent, and consistent principles of the imagination. Upon what grounds this pretension is founded must now be the subject of our enquiry.

The fundamental principle of that philosophy is the opinion concerning colours, sounds, tastes, smells, heat and cold; which it asserts to be nothing but impressions in the mind, deriv'd from the operation of external objects and without any resemblance to the qualities of the objects. Upon examination, I find only one of the reasons commonly produc'd for this opinion to be satisfactory, viz. that deriv'd from the variations of those impressions, even while the external object, to all appearance, continues the same. These variations depend upon several circumstances. Upon the different situations of our health: A man in a malady feels a disagreeable taste in meats, which before pleas'd him the most. Upon the different complexions and constitutions of men that seems bitter to one which is sweet to another. Upon the difference of their external situation and position: Colours reflected from the clouds change according to the distance of the clouds, and according to the angle they make with the eye and luminous body. Fire also communicates the sensation of pleasure at one distance and that of pain at another. Instances of this kind are very numerous and frequent.

The conclusion drawn from them is likewise as satisfactory as can possibly be imagin'd. 'Tis certain that when different impressions of the same sense arise from any object, everyone of these impressions has not a resembling quality existent in the object. For as the same object cannot, at the same time, be endow'd with different qualities of the same sense, and as the same quality cannot resemble impressions entirely different, it evidently follows, that many of our impressions have no external model or archetype. Now from like effects we presume like causes. Many of the impressions of colour, sound, etc. are confest to be nothing but internal existences, and to arise from causes which no ways resemble them. These impressions are in appearance nothing different from the other impressions of colour, sound, etc. We conclude, therefore, that they are, all of them, deriv'd from a like origin.

This principle being once admitted, all the other doctrines of that philosophy seem to follow by an easy consequence. For upon the removal of sounds, colours, heat, cold, and other sensible qualities from the rank of continu'd independent existences, we are reduc'd merely to what are called primary qualities as the only real ones of which we have any adequate notion. These primary qualities are extension and solidity, with their different mixtures and modifications; figure, motion, gravity, and cohesion. The generation, increase, decay, and corruption of animals and vegetables are nothing but changes of figure and motion; as also the operations of all bodies on each other; of fire, of light, water, air, earth, and of all the elements and powers of nature. One figure and motion produces another figure and motion; nor does there remain in the material universe any other principle, either active or passive, of which we can form the most distant idea.

CHAPTER 21

Metaphysics in Kant and Post-Kantian Philosophy

"Truth crushed to earth shall rise again"

The seventeenth and eighteenth centuries were times of great system-building in philosophy. The new science, developed by Galileo, Kepler, and Newton, rested not only on a new spirit of empirical observation and on new mathematical theories but also on the discovery of physical laws. Every philosopher of the early modern period thought that the new science demanded a new philosophy. Descartes, Spinoza, and Leibniz constructed rationalist systems designed to explain a law-governed nature and establish important metaphysical theses as synthetic a priori truths. Locke, Berkeley, and Hume offered empiricist reconstructions of our knowledge of the world in keeping with the new scientific method.

Universality and necessity became primary battlegrounds in the conflicts among these systems. Scientific laws such as Newton's laws of motion exhibit both features. They apply to all objects, in all places and times, in all circumstances. Rationalists charged that empiricists could not explain that, since we experience only particular objects in particular circumstances. Experience is not enough to justify universal and necessary conclusions. Empiricists saw no reason to think that the structure of our thought, as revealed through reflection, matches the necessary structure of the world. So they denied that rational reflection could justify universal and necessary conclusions.

Prussian philosopher Immanuel Kant (1724–1804) devises an ingenious resolution of the rationalist/empiricist conflict. He argues that the regularity and law-governed character of nature have their source, not in nature itself, but in us. In Kant's view, Hume is right to think that we project a law-governed pattern on experience. But Hume is wrong to think of this as strictly a matter of custom, habit, or passion. The very structure of our thought, Kant contends, forces nature into a law-governed mold. We can understand that mold by uncovering the laws of the understanding on which our thought rests.

Kant thinks of the laws of the understanding as universal and unchanging, holding for all people at all places and times. His nineteenth-century successors, however, questioned that assumption, seeing the world as shaped by ways of thinking that change and develop in both rational and nonrational ways.

21.1 KANT'S COPERNICAN REVOLUTION

Immanuel Kant's *Critique of Pure Reason* established a new paradigm that dominated philosophy for at least a century. The *Critique's* central character is human reason. Reason develops principles to deal with experience; within the realm of experience, those principles are well justified. Reason finds itself driven, however, to ask questions extending beyond that realm. The very principles it has developed and on which it properly continues to rely in dealing with experience there lead it "into confusion and contradictions."

Kant claims that he uses the *transcendental method* and establishes the truth of *transcendental idealism.* What is the transcendental method? To understand it, we must understand what Kant called his Copernican revolution in philosophy. Copernicus explained the motions of the heavenly bodies as resulting, not just from their own motion, but also from the motion of the observers on earth. Kant seeks the laws governing the realm of experience not in the objects themselves but in us.

Kant is a rationalist, but a rationalist of a peculiar kind. He argues that we have innate concepts—he calls them *pure concepts of the understanding*, or the *categories.* We can deduce what they are a priori, independent of experience, from the mere *possibility* of experience. They are revealed by logic, specifically by the logical forms of judgments, and include universality, necessity, and causation. He also holds that there are synthetic a priori truths: truths about the world that we can know independent of experience. But these truths hold only of things as we perceive and think about them, not as they are in themselves.

Kant distinguishes the world of appearance, things as they are known to us—the *phenomenal* world—from the world of things-in-themselves—the *noumenal* world. We can know appearances by using our senses. Things-in-themselves, in contrast, lie beyond our cognitive capacities. We can know something about the world independent of experience, but our knowledge cannot extend beyond experience. We cannot know the world as it really is.

Just as the Buddhist idealist Dignaga distinguishes actual objects, the causes of perception, from the internal objects of our perceptions, so Kant distinguishes things-in-themselves, *noumena*—things as they actually exist, unconditioned by our perceiving or thinking about them—from objects of experience, also called *appearances* or *phenomena*, which are objects as they appear to us. Kant denies that we can have knowledge of noumena. Indeed, we never encounter things-in-themselves; everything we perceive or conceive has been conditioned by our faculties of perception and thought. Sensibility, our faculty of perception, imposes the form of space and time on objects perceived. The understanding, the faculty of thought, imposes the categories, which give our thoughts logical form. We can speak of objects or events causing other objects or events; we can speak of things existing or failing to exist. But we thereby speak solely of appearances. The categories apply only to things as conditioned by sensibility and understanding. We cannot legitimately apply them to things-in-themselves. So we cannot even officially say that that there are things-in-themselves. Much less can we say that they cause us to perceive what we perceive. Like Dignaga, then, Kant begins with the distinction between actual objects (things-in-themselves) as causes of our perceptions and internal objects (appearances) that those perceptions are about. But, like Dignaga, he finds that he can say nothing about actual objects; we have access only to things as conditioned by our modes of knowledge. Kant's philosophy is thus a large-scale application of Philo's argument from relation.

Both rationalists and empiricists misunderstand the status of objects of experience, in Kant's view. They think that the things we see, hear, etc., are in themselves as they appear to us. But we have no reason to assume that. The phenomenal world can be sensed and known; the noumenal world cannot. With respect to appearances, therefore, the skeptic is wrong; we can have knowledge of objects of experience. In fact, some of this knowledge is independent of experience. With respect to things-in-themselves, however, the skeptic triumphs. We can have no knowledge of things as they are, independent of us.

Kant reverses the traditional conception of the relation between thought and its object, or, as he puts it, between object and concept. Philosophers traditionally hold objects causally responsible for our perceptions of them. We see a circle because a circle is there. We think of some events as causing others because they do. Kant turns this around. He holds that thought is causally responsible for constituting the object. A circle is there because we see it. Some events cause others because we think they do. Our minds construct the world, but in a universal and rule-governed way. That is what makes knowledge of objects possible. Indeed, it makes a priori knowledge of them possible, for we can understand the rules according to which we constitute them.

Necessary connections, Hume observed, cannot be found in experience. We are aware of a succession of things but not of the connections between them. Our concept of necessity, Hume concludes, must come from us, not from what we experience. Hume attributes the source of our concept of necessity to the passionate side of our nature, to a feeling of expectation. Kant, in contrast, finds necessity's source in the unity of objects. We experience objects, not just a whirling mass of sensations. And it is a necessary truth that all objects are unified. The source of the unity of objects, moreover, is also the source of the concept of an object in general. It underlies our experience of any object.

It also underlies universality, necessity, and our concept of substance. Finding no experience from which the ideas of universality and necessary connection can be derived, Kant postulates them as a priori necessary conditions of experience. We do not abstract them from experience; they are an inborn part of our mental toolbox. The same is true of substance as the ground in which the qualities of objects inhere. We have experience only of the qualities; we do not perceive anything underlying them. Still, we organize our perceptions and thoughts around objects. That must then reflect a basic organizing principle of our thinking. Hume would agree, to an extent; the concepts of causality and substance, he would say, are not in the world but in us. Kant turns this around: They are in the world because they are in us. All rest on the unity of the self.

The transcendental ground of the unity Kant terms *transcendental apperception.* When we reflect on the contents of our own consciousness, as Hume stresses, we are aware only of a succession of mental states; we do not confront a unified self. The contents of consciousness are always changing. Thus, we find no unity in what Kant calls *empirical apperception* or *inner sense.* But, for me to be conscious of things, there must be a *me.* There must be a ground of unity in us. Consciousness itself is unified; each of us is a single self. Hume's view leads him to the conclusion that there is no self. But that, Kant thinks, is absurd. There is a single, unified self. It comes with the concepts that organize our experience into objects. We can know certain truths about objects independent of experience, therefore, for we can uncover the pure concepts of the understanding relating to the form of an object in general. These concepts do not arise from experience; they underlie its possibility. So we can know a priori that any experience will conform to them.

Kant concludes that "appearances have a necessary relation to the understanding." We can experience something as an object only if it meets certain conditions. Those conditions are specified by the categories. Kant therefore characterizes the understanding as the faculty of rules. We can know objects because we construct them according to those rules: "Thus the order and regularity in the appearances, which we entitle nature, we ourselves introduce. We could never find them in appearances, had not we ourselves, or the nature of our mind, originally set them there." The understanding, consequently, is nothing less than "the lawgiver of nature."

21.1.1 Immanuel Kant, from *Critique of Pure Reason*

Preface to the Second Edition, 1787

Metaphysics is a completely isolated speculative science of reason, which soars far above the teachings of experience, and in which reason is indeed meant to be its own pupil. Metaphysics rests on concepts alone—not, like mathematics, on their application to intuition. But though it is older than all other sciences and would survive even if all the rest were swallowed up in the abyss of an all-destroying barbarism, it has not yet had the good fortune to enter upon the secure path of a science. For in it reason is perpetually being brought to a stand, even when the laws into which it is seeking to have, as it professes, an a priori insight are those that are confirmed by our most common experiences. Ever and again we have to retrace our steps, as not leading us in the direction in which we desire to go. So far, too, are the students of metaphysics from exhibiting any kind of unanimity in their contentions that metaphysics has rather to be regarded as a battleground quite

Source: Immanuel Kant, *Critique of Pure Reason*. Translated by Norman Kemp Smith. New York: Macmillan, 1929. Reprinted by permission of Palgrave Macmillan.

peculiarly suited for those who desire to exercise themselves in mock combats. No participant has ever yet succeeded in gaining even so much as an inch of territory, not at least in such manner as to secure him in its permanent possession. This shows, beyond all questioning, that the procedure of metaphysics has hitherto been a merely random groping and, what is worst of all, a groping among mere concepts. What, then, is the reason why, in this field, the sure road to science has not hitherto been found? Is it, perhaps, impossible to discover? Why, in that case, should nature have visited our reason with the restless endeavour whereby it is ever searching for such a path, as if this were one of its most important concerns? Nay, more, how little cause have we to place trust in our reason, if, in one of the most important domains of which we would fain have knowledge, it does not merely fail us, but lures us on by deceitful promises and in the end betrays us! Or if it is only that we have thus far failed to find the true path, are there any indications to justify the hope that by renewed efforts we may have better fortune than has fallen to our predecessors?

The examples of mathematics and natural science, which by a single and sudden revolution have become what they now are, seem to me sufficiently remarkable to suggest our considering what may have been the essential features in the changed point of view by which they have so greatly benefited. Their success should incline us, at least by way of experiment, to imitate their procedure, so far as the analogy which, as species of rational knowledge, they bear to metaphysics may permit. Hitherto it has been assumed that all our knowledge must conform to objects. But all attempts to extend our knowledge of objects by establishing something in regard to them a priori, by means of concepts, have, on this assumption, ended in failure. We must therefore make trial whether we may not have more success in the tasks of metaphysics if we suppose that objects must conform to our knowledge. This would agree better with what is desired, namely, that it should be possible to have knowledge of objects a priori, determining something in regard to them prior to their being given. We should then be proceeding precisely on the lines of Copernicus' primary hypothesis. Failing of satisfactory progress in explaining the movements of the heavenly bodies on the supposition that they all revolved round the spectator, he tried whether he might not have better success if he made the spectator to revolve and the stars to remain at rest. A similar experiment can be tried in metaphysics, as regards the intuition of objects. If intuition must conform to the constitution of the objects, I do not see how we could know anything of the latter a priori; but if the object (as object of the senses) must conform to the constitution of our faculty of intuition, I have no difficulty in conceiving such a possibility. Since I cannot rest in these intuitions if they are to become known, but must relate them as representations to something as their object, and determine this latter through them, either I must assume that the concepts, by means of which I obtain this determination, conform to the object, or else I assume that the objects, or what is the same thing, that the experience in which alone, as given objects, they can be known, conform to the concepts. In the former case, I am again in the same perplexity as to how I can know anything a priori in regard to the objects. In the latter case the outlook is more hopeful. For experience is itself a species of knowledge which involves understanding; and understanding has rules which I must presuppose as being in me prior to objects being given to me, and therefore as being a priori. They find expression in a priori concepts to which all objects of experience necessarily conform and with which they must agree. As regards objects which are thought solely through reason, and indeed as necessary, but which can never—at least not in the manner in which reason thinks them—be given in experience, the attempts at thinking them (for they must admit of being thought) will furnish an excellent touchstone of what we are adopting as our new method of thought, namely, that we can know a priori of things only what we ourselves put into them.

This method, modelled on that of the student of nature, consists in looking for the elements of pure reason in what admits of confirmation or refutation by experiment. Now the propositions of pure reason, especially if they venture out beyond all limits of possible experience, cannot be brought to the test through any experiment with their objects, as in natural science. In dealing with those concepts and principles which we adopt a priori, all that we can do is to contrive that they be used for viewing objects from two different points of view—on the one hand, in connection with experience, as objects of the senses and of the understanding, and on the other hand, for the isolated reason that strives to transcend all limits of experience, as objects which are thought merely. If, when things are viewed from this twofold standpoint, we find that there is agreement with the principle of pure reason but that when we regard them only from a single point of view reason is involved in unavoidable self-conflict, the experiment decides in favour of the correctness of this distinction.

This experiment succeeds as well as could be desired and promises to metaphysics, in its first part—the part that is occupied with those concepts a priori to which the corresponding objects, commensurate with them, can be given in experience—the secure path of a science. For the new point of view enables us to explain how there can be knowledge a priori; and, in addition, to furnish satisfactory proofs of the laws which form the a priori basis of nature, regarded as the sum of the objects of experience—neither achievement being possible on the procedure hitherto followed.

But this deduction of our power of knowing a priori, in the first part of metaphysics, has a consequence which is startling and which has the appearance of being highly prejudicial to the whole purpose of metaphysics, as dealt with in the second part. For we are brought to the conclusion that we can never transcend the limits of possible experience, though that is precisely what this science is concerned, above all else, to achieve. This situation yields, however, just the very experiment by which, indirectly, we are enabled to prove the truth of this first estimate of our a priori knowledge of reason, namely, that such knowledge has to do only with appearances and must leave the thing in itself as indeed real per se but as not known by us. For what necessarily forces us to transcend the limits of experience and of all appearances is the unconditioned, which reason, by necessity and by right, demands in things in themselves, as required to complete the series of conditions. If, then, on the supposition that our empirical knowledge conforms to objects as things in themselves, we find that the unconditioned cannot be thought without contradiction and that when, on the other hand, we suppose that our representation of things, as they are given to us, does not conform to these things as they are in themselves but that these objects, as appearances, conform to our mode of representation, the contradiction vanishes; and if, therefore, we thus find that the unconditioned is not to be met with in things so far as we know them, that is, so far as they are given to us, but only so far as we do not know them, that is, so far as they are things in themselves, we are justified in concluding that what we at first assumed for the purposes of experiment is now definitely confirmed....

Book I: Transcendental Analytic of Concepts

Chapter II: The Deduction of the Pure Concepts of Understanding

Section 2... The A Priori Grounds of the Possibility of Experience At this point we must make clear to ourselves what we mean by the expression "an object of representations." We have stated above that appearances are themselves nothing but sensible representations. As such and in themselves, they must not be taken as objects capable of existing outside our power of representation. What, then, is to be understood when we speak of an object corresponding to, and consequently also distinct from, our knowledge? It is easily seen that this object must be thought only as something in general = x. For outside our knowledge we have nothing we could set over against this knowledge as corresponding to it. Now we find that our thought of the relation of all knowledge to its object carries with it an element of necessity. The object is viewed as something that prevents our modes of knowledge from being haphazard or arbitrary and determines them a priori in some definite fashion. For insofar as our thoughts are to relate to an object, they must necessarily agree with one another. That is, they must possess that unity which constitutes the concept of an object.

But it is clear that, since we have to deal only with the manifold of our representations, and since that x (the object) that corresponds to them is nothing to us—being, as it is, something that has to be distinct from all our representations—the unity the object makes necessary can be nothing other than the formal unity of consciousness in the synthesis of the manifold of representations. It is only when we have thus produced synthetic unity in the manifold of intuition that we are in a position to say that we know the object. But this unity is impossible if the intuition cannot be generated in accordance with a rule by means of a function of synthesis that makes the reproduction of the manifold a priori necessary and renders possible a concept in which it is united. Thus we think a triangle as an object, in that we are conscious of the combination of three straight lines according to a rule by which such an intuition can always be represented. This unity of rule determines all the manifold and limits it to conditions which make unity of apperception possible. The concept of this unity is the representation of the object = x, which I think through the predicates, above mentioned, of a triangle.

All knowledge demands a concept. That concept may, indeed, be quite imperfect or obscure. But a concept is always, in form, something universal that serves as a rule. The concept of *body*, for instance, is the unity of the manifold which is thought through it. It serves as a rule in our knowledge of outer appearances. But it can be a rule for intuitions only insofar as it represents in any given appearances the necessary reproduction of their manifold and thereby the synthetic unity in our consciousness of them. The concept of *body*, in the perception of something outside us, necessitates the representation of extension and therewith representations of impenetrability, shape, etc.

All necessity, without exception, is grounded in a transcendental condition. There must, therefore, be a transcendental ground of the unity of consciousness in the synthesis of the manifold of all our intuitions. This must consequently also be a transcendental ground of the concepts of objects in general and so of all objects of experience—a ground without which it would be impossible to think any object for our intuitions. For this object is no more than that something the concept of which expresses such a necessity of synthesis.

This original and transcendental condition is no other than transcendental apperception. Consciousness of self according to the determinations of our state in inner perception is merely empirical and always changing. No fixed and abiding self can present itself in this flux of inner appearances. Such consciousness is usually named *inner sense* or *empirical apperception*. What has necessarily to be represented as numerically identical cannot be thought as such through empirical data. To render such a transcendental presupposition valid, there must be a condition which precedes all experience and makes experience itself possible.

There can be in us no modes of knowledge, no connection or unity of one mode of knowledge with another, without the unity of consciousness that precedes all data of intuitions. By relation to it representation of objects is alone possible. This pure original unchangeable consciousness I name *transcendental apperception*. That it deserves this name is clear from the fact that even the purest objective unity, namely, that of the a priori concepts—space and time—is only possible through relation of the intuitions to such unity of consciousness. The numerical unity of this apperception is thus the a priori ground of all concepts, just as the manifoldness of space and time is the a priori ground of the intuitions of sensibility.

This transcendental unity of apperception forms, out of all the possible appearances that can stand alongside one another in one experience, a connection of all these representations according to laws. For this unity of consciousness would be impossible if the mind in knowledge of the manifold could not become conscious of the identity of function whereby it synthetically combines it into one knowledge.

The original and necessary consciousness of the identity of the self is thus at the same time a consciousness of an equally necessary unity of the synthesis of all appearances according to concepts, that is, according to rules. This not only makes them necessarily reproducible but also in so doing determines an object for their intuition—that is, the concept of something in which they are necessarily interconnected. For the mind could never think its identity in the manifoldness of its representations, and indeed think this identity a priori, if it did not have before its eyes the identity of its act whereby it subordinates all synthesis of apprehension (which is empirical) to a transcendental unity, thereby rendering possible their interconnection according to a priori rules.

Now, also, we are in a position to determine more adequately our concept of an object in general. All representations have, as representations, their object and can themselves in turn become objects of other representations. Appearances are the sole objects which can be given to us immediately, and that in them which relates immediately to the object is called *intuition*. But these appearances are not things in themselves; they are only representations, which in turn have their object—an object which cannot itself be intuited by us and which may, therefore, be named the nonempirical, that is, transcendental object = x.

The pure concept of this transcendental object, which in reality throughout all our knowledge is always one and the same, is what can alone confer upon all our empirical concepts in general relation to an object, that is, objective reality. This concept cannot contain any determinate intuition and therefore refers only to the unity which must be found in any manifold of knowledge that stands in relation to an object. This relation is nothing but the necessary unity of consciousness, and therefore also of the synthesis of the manifold, through a common function of the mind that combines it in one representation. This unity must be regarded as necessary a priori—otherwise knowledge would be without an object. So the relation to a transcendental object, that is, the objective reality of our empirical knowledge, rests on the transcendental law that all appearances, insofar as through them objects are to be given to us, must stand under a priori rules—those of synthetic unity whereby the interrelating of these appearances in empirical intuition is alone possible. In other words, appearances in experience must stand under the conditions of the necessary unity of apperception, just as in mere intuition they must be subject to the formal conditions of space and of time. Only thus can any knowledge become possible at all....

But the possibility, indeed the necessity, of these categories rests on the relation our entire sensibility, and with it all possible appearances, bear to original apperception. In original apperception everything must necessarily conform to the conditions of the thoroughgoing unity of self-consciousness—that is, to the universal functions of synthesis. This synthesis is one according to concepts in which alone apperception can demonstrate a priori its complete and necessary identity.

Thus the concept of a cause is nothing but a synthesis (of that which follows in the time series, with other appearances) according to concepts. Without such unity—which has its a priori rule and which subjects the appearances to itself—no thoroughgoing, universal, and therefore necessary unity of consciousness would be met with in the manifold of perceptions. These perceptions would not then belong to any experience. Consequently they would be without an object, merely a blind play of representations, even less than a dream.

All attempts to derive these pure concepts of understanding from experience and so to ascribe to them a merely empirical origin are entirely vain and useless. I need not insist upon the fact that, for instance, the concept of a cause involves the character of necessity, which no experience can yield. Experience does indeed show that one appearance customarily follows upon another, but not that this sequence is necessary, nor that we can argue a priori and with complete universality from the antecedent, viewed as a condition, to the consequent. Consider the empirical rule of association, which we must postulate throughout when we assert that everything in the series of events is so subject to rule that nothing ever happens save insofar as something precedes it on which it universally follows. Upon what, I ask, does this rule, as a law of nature, rest? How is this association itself possible? The ground of the possibility of the association of the manifold, so far as it lies in the object, is named the *affinity* of the manifold. I therefore ask, how are we to make comprehensible to ourselves the thoroughgoing affinity of appearances, whereby they stand and must stand under unchanging laws?

On my principles it is easy to explain. All possible appearances, as representations, belong to the totality of a possible self-consciousness. But as self-consciousness is a transcendental representation, numerical identity is inseparable from it and is a priori certain. For nothing can come to our knowledge save in terms of this original apperception. This identity must necessarily enter into the synthesis of all the manifold of appearances, so far as the synthesis is to yield empirical knowledge. So the appearances are subject to a priori conditions. The synthesis of their apprehension must be in complete accordance with them. The representation of a universal condition according to which a certain manifold can be posited in uniform fashion is called a rule, and—when it must be so posited—a law. Thus all appearances stand in thoroughgoing connection according to necessary laws. They stand therefore in a transcendental affinity, of which the empirical is a mere consequence.

That nature should direct itself according to our subjective ground of apperception, and should indeed depend upon it in respect of its conformity to law, sounds very strange and absurd. But when we consider that this nature is not a thing in itself but is merely an aggregate of appearances—so many representations of the mind—we shall not be surprised that we can discover it only in the radical faculty of all our knowledge, namely, in transcendental apperception. In that unity alone it can be entitled the object of all possible experience, that is, nature. Nor shall we be surprised that just for this very reason this unity can be known a priori and therefore as necessary. Were the unity given in itself, independent of the first sources of our thought, this would never be possible. We would not then know of any source from which we could obtain the synthetic propositions asserting such a universal unity of nature. For they would then have to be derived from the objects of nature themselves. As this could take place only empirically, none but a merely accidental unity could be obtained. That would fall far short of the necessary interconnection that we have in mind when we speak of nature....

Thus the order and regularity in the appearances, which we entitle *nature*, we ourselves introduce. We could never find them in appearances had not we ourselves, or the nature of our mind, originally set them there. For this unity of nature has to be a necessary one, that is, has to be an a priori certain unity of the connection of appearances. Such synthetic unity could not be established a priori if there were not subjective grounds of such unity contained a priori in the original cognitive powers of our mind, and if these subjective conditions—inasmuch as they are the grounds of the possibility of knowing any object whatsoever in experience—were not at the same time objectively valid.

We have already defined the understanding in various different ways: as a spontaneity of knowledge (in distinction from the receptivity of sensibility), as a power of thought, as a faculty of concepts, or again of judgments. All these definitions, when they are adequately understood, are identical. We may now characterize it as the faculty of rules. This distinguishing mark is more fruitful and approximates more closely its essential nature. Sensibility gives us forms (of intuition), but understanding gives us rules. The latter is always occupied in investigating appearances, in order to detect some rule in them. Rules, so far as they are objective and therefore necessarily depend upon the knowledge of the object, are called *laws*. Although we learn many laws through experience, they are only special determinations of still higher laws. The highest of these, under which the others all stand, issue a priori from the understanding itself. They are not borrowed from experience. On the contrary, they have to confer upon appearances their conformity to law. They thus make experience possible. Hence the understanding is something more than a power of formulating rules through comparison of appearances. It is itself the lawgiver of nature....

21.2 HEGEL'S HISTORICISM

Georg Wilhelm Friedrich Hegel (1770–1831) was perhaps the last great philosophical system builder. His distinctively dynamic form of idealism set the stage for other nineteenth-century Western philosophers. Hegel was born in Stuttgart, Germany, and studied at Tübingen, where he formed friendships with two other students who would shape nineteenth-century German thought: the poet Friedrich Hölderlin and the philosopher Friedrich von Schelling. He spent most of his career teaching, first as a private tutor and then at the universities of Jena, Heidelberg, and Berlin.

Hegel, like Kant, is an idealist: Everything depends on mind. The world as we know it is something we construct. But Hegel differs from Kant in important ways. One of the most obvious is his rejection of Kant's realm of noumena—things-in-themselves. Kant distinguishes himself from Berkeley by insisting on the role of things-in-themselves. But in fact, as Hegel sees it, they play no role in his system. The pure concepts of the understanding do not apply to them. So they do not fall under the categories. We cannot say that things-in-themselves, in combination with our cognitive faculties, cause things to appear as they do, for causation is one of the categories. We cannot even officially say that things-in-themselves exist! Hegel speaks of the Absolute—that which is not relative to us or to anything else—initially as Kant's thing-in-itself but, finally, as the ultimate goal of human thought.

Hegel differs from Kant in several other important ways. First, Hegel's thought is historicist. Kant maintained that we could have universal and necessary knowledge of the world by uncovering the laws of the understanding. To give us universal and necessary knowledge, those laws must be constant; they must be the same for each person, in all times and circumstances. Why, however, should we expect human beings to construct the world in the same way, at all times and places, in all circumstances, in all cultures? Hegel contends that the way in which we construct the world develops systematically over time. Philosophy, like other aspects of human thought, thus varies with historical circumstances: "Philosophy is its own time raised to the level of thought." Hegel tells the story of Spirit or Mind (in German, *Geist*), which progresses through a variety of stages to reach Absolute Knowledge.

This is not to say that philosophy cannot express any universal or necessary truths. But they are not the kinds of truths sought by Kant or other previous rationalists. What stays constant across historical circumstances are not a priori propositions or innate concepts but the set of dynamic principles governing the development of our ways of constructing the world. Second, then, Hegel finds some universal and necessary truths, but they are high-level, dynamic principles governing the development of thought. The best known is the thesis–antithesis–synthesis pattern. People adopt a certain way of looking at and thinking about the world (the thesis). Because it is only partially correct, over time people encounter contrary evidence, counterexamples, anomalies, and contradictions. Inspired by these, they shift to a new and contrary way of looking at and thinking about things (the antithesis). That too is only a partial truth, however, so it also gradually confronts contrary evidence, counterexamples, anomalies, and contradictions. The conflict between thesis and antithesis is eventually transcended in a synthesis that draws elements from both while transforming the way people see and think. That becomes a new thesis, and the process begins again.

Third, Hegel sees human thought as essentially social. Kant's theoretical philosophy reverses the traditional relationship between concept and object, between knower and thing known. The laws of the understanding that provide the basis for synthetic a priori knowledge are those governing the individual knower and are the same for each knower. The social and historical context of the knowing makes no difference. For Hegel, however, both dimensions of context are crucial. We learn our language, which provides our basic categories of thought, from other people, at a particular time, in the context of a particular society. What Kant and other rationalists take as stemming from our nature as knowers Hegel sees as reflecting a specific social background.

Fourth, Hegel stresses the dynamics of the self. Kant sees the realm of appearance as rule-governed because it is one realm. My experiences are all *mine*. They all relate the same underlying self, transcendental apperception—a thing-in-itself that exists beyond experience. Hegel, rejecting things-in-themselves, sees the unity of the self not as a given but as an *achievement*. His *Phenomenology of Spirit* (phenomenology = study of phenomena, that is, appearances) traces the development of the self through a variety of stages, including one he famously terms "unhappy consciousness." In that stage, the self is divided, alienated from itself. We overcome that alienation socially, achieving self-consciousness by recognizing other people as self-conscious agents, by being recognized as selves by them, and recognizing that recognition ourselves. We become integrated selves by being seen as such by others we recognize as selves.

Fifth, Hegel rejects what he refers to as *immediacy*, the sharp divide in Kant and other (especially empiricist) philosophers between sensibility and understanding—that is, between perception and conceptual knowledge. Traditionally, philosophers have thought of experience as supplying data—"the given"—which is preconceptual. We then sort the data, using concepts, logic, and perhaps other cognitive means, and obtain knowledge. Hegel denies that we can distinguish any given, preconceptual portion of our experience. The concepts we have shape the way we perceive the world.

21.2.1 G. W. F. Hegel, from *Phenomenology of Mind*

Introduction

73. It is natural to suppose that, before philosophy enters upon its subject proper—namely, the actual knowledge of what truly is—it is necessary to come first to an understanding concerning knowledge, which is looked upon as the instrument by which to take possession of the Absolute, or as the means through which to get a sight of it. The apprehension seems legitimate, on the one hand, that there may be various kinds of knowledge, among which one might be better adapted than another for the attainment of our purpose—and thus a wrong choice is possible: on the other hand, again that, since knowing is a faculty of a definite kind and with a determinate range, without the more precise determination of its nature and limits we might take hold on clouds of error instead of the heaven of truth.

This apprehensiveness is sure to pass even into the conviction that the whole enterprise which sets out to secure for consciousness by means of knowledge what exists per se, is in its very nature absurd; and that between knowledge and the Absolute there lies a boundary which completely cuts off the one from the other. For if knowledge is the instrument by which to get possession of absolute Reality, the suggestion immediately occurs that the application of an instrument to anything does not leave it as it is for itself, but rather entails in the process, and has in view, a moulding and alteration of it. Or, again, if knowledge is not an instrument which we actively employ, but a kind of passive medium through which the light of the truth reaches us, then here, too, we do not receive it as it is in itself, but as it is through and in this medium. In either case we employ a means which immediately brings about the very opposite of its own end; or, rather, the absurdity lies in making use of any means at all. It seems indeed open to us to find in the knowledge of the way in which the instrument operates, a remedy for this parlous state; for thereby it becomes possible to remove from the result the part which, in our idea of the Absolute received through that instrument, belongs to the instrument, and thus to get the truth in its purity. But this improvement would, as a matter of fact, only bring us back to the point where we were before. If we take away again from a definitely formed thing that which the instrument has done in the shaping of it, then the thing (in this case the Absolute) stands before us once more just as it was previous to all this trouble, which, as we now see, was superfluous. If the Absolute were only to be brought on the whole nearer to us by this agency, without any change being wrought in it, like a bird caught by a limestick, it would certainly scorn a trick of that sort, if it were not in its very nature, and did it not wish to be, beside us from the start. For a trick is what knowledge in such a case would be, since by all its busy toil and trouble it gives itself the air of doing something quite different from bringing about a relation that is merely immediate, and so a waste of time to establish. Or, again, if the examination of knowledge, which we represent as a medium, makes us acquainted with the law of its refraction, it is likewise useless to eliminate this refraction from the result. For knowledge is not the divergence of the ray, but the ray itself by which the truth comes in contact with us; and if this be removed, the bare direction or the empty place would alone be indicated.

74. Meanwhile, if the fear of falling into error introduces an element of distrust into science, which without any scruples of that sort goes to work and actually does know, it is not easy to understand why, conversely, a distrust should not be placed in this very distrust, and why we should not take care lest the fear of error is not just the

Source: G. W. F. Hegel, *Phenomenology of Mind*. Translated by J. B. Baillie. London: George Allen & Unwin, 1910.

initial error. As a matter of fact, this fear presupposes something, indeed a great deal, as truth, and supports its scruples and consequences on what should itself be examined beforehand to see whether it is truth. It starts with ideas of knowledge as an instrument and as a medium; and presupposes a distinction of ourselves from this knowledge. More especially it takes for granted that the Absolute stands on one side, and that knowledge, on the other side, by itself and cut off from the Absolute, is still something real; in other words, that knowledge, which, by being outside the Absolute, is certainly also outside truth, is nevertheless true—a position which, while calling itself fear of error, makes itself known rather as fear of the truth.

75. This conclusion comes from the fact that the Absolute alone is true or that the True is alone absolute. It may be set aside by making the distinction that a knowledge which does not indeed know the Absolute as science wants to do is nonetheless true too; and that knowledge in general, though it may possibly be incapable of grasping the Absolute, can still be capable of truth of another kind. But we shall see as we proceed that random talk like this leads in the long run to a confused distinction between the absolute truth and a truth of some other sort, and that "absolute," "knowledge," and so on, are words which presuppose a meaning that has first to be got at.

76. With suchlike useless ideas and expressions about knowledge as an instrument to take hold of the Absolute, or as a medium through which we have a glimpse of truth, and so on (relations to which all these ideas of a knowledge which is divided from the Absolute and an Absolute divided from knowledge in the last resort lead), we need not concern ourselves. Nor need we trouble about the evasive pretexts which create the incapacity of science out of the presupposition of such relations in order at once to be rid of the toil of science and to assume the air of serious and zealous effort about it. Instead of being troubled with giving answers to all these, they may be straightway rejected as adventitious and arbitrary ideas; and the use which is here made of words like "absolute," "knowledge," as also "objective" and "subjective," and innumerable others, whose meaning is assumed to be familiar to everyone, might well be regarded as so much deception. For to give out that their significance is universally familiar and that everyone indeed possesses their notion rather looks like an attempt to dispense with the only important matter which is just to give this notion. With better right, on the contrary, we might spare ourselves the trouble of taking any notice at all of such ideas and ways of talking which would have the effect of warding off science altogether; for they make a mere empty show of knowledge which at once vanishes when science comes on the scene.

But science, in the very fact that it comes on the scene, is itself a phenomenon; its "coming on the scene" is not yet itself carried out in all the length and breadth of its truth. In this regard, it is a matter of indifference whether we consider that it (science) is a phenomenon because it makes its appearance alongside another kind of knowledge, or call that other untrue knowledge its process of appearing. Science, however, must liberate itself from this phenomenality, and it can only do so by turning against it. For science cannot simply reject a form of knowledge which is not true, and treat this as a common view of things, and then assure us that it itself is an entirely different kind of knowledge, and holds the other to be of no account at all; nor can it appeal to the fact that in this other there are presages of a better. By giving that assurance it would declare its force and value to lie in its bare existence; but the untrue knowledge appeals likewise to the fact that it is, and assures us that to it science is nothing. One barren assurance, however, is of just as much value as another. Still less can science appeal to the presages of a better, which are to be found present in untrue knowledge and are there pointing the way towards science; for it would, on the one hand, be appealing again in the same way to a merely existent fact, and, on the other, it would be appealing to itself, to the way in which it exists in untrue knowledge, i.e., to a bad form of its own existence, to its appearance rather than to its real and true nature (*in und für sich*). For this reason we shall here undertake the exposition of knowledge as a phenomenon.

77. Now because this exposition has for its object only phenomenal knowledge, the exposition itself seems not to be science, free, self-moving in the shape proper to itself, but may, from this point of view, be taken as the pathway of the natural consciousness which is pressing forward to true knowledge. Or it can be regarded as the path of the soul, which is traversing the series of its own forms of embodiment, like stages appointed for it by its own nature, that it may possess the clearness of spiritual life when, through the complete experience of its own self, it arrives at the knowledge of what it is in itself.

78. Natural consciousness will prove itself to be only knowledge in principle or not real knowledge. Since, however, it immediately takes itself to be the real and genuine knowledge, this pathway has a negative significance for it; what is a realization of the notion of knowledge means for it rather the ruin and overthrow of itself; for on this road it loses its own truth. Because of that, the road can be looked on as the path of doubt, or more properly a highway of despair. For what happens there is not what is usually understood by doubting, a jostling against this or that supposed truth, the outcome of which is again a disappearance in due course of the doubt and a return to the former truth, so that at the end the matter is taken as it was before. On the contrary, that pathway is the conscious insight into the untruth of the phenomenal knowledge, for which that is the most real which is after all only the unrealized notion. On that account, too, this thoroughgoing scepticism is not what doubtless earnest zeal for truth and science fancies it has equipped itself with in order to be ready to deal with them—viz. the resolve, in science, not to deliver itself over to the thoughts of others on their mere authority, but to examine everything for itself, and only follow its own conviction, or, still better, to produce everything itself and hold only its own act for true.

79. The series of shapes, which consciousness traverses on this road, is rather the detailed history of the process of training and educating consciousness itself up to the level of science. That resolve presents this mental development in the simple form of an intended purpose, as immediately finished and complete, as having taken place; this pathway, on the other hand, is, as opposed to this abstract intention, or untruth, the actual carrying out of that process of development. To follow one's own conviction is certainly more than to hand oneself over to authority; but by the conversion of opinion held on authority into opinion held out of personal conviction, the content of what is held is not necessarily altered, and truth has not thereby taken the place of error. If we stick to a system of opinion and prejudice resting on the authority of others, or upon personal conviction, the one differs from the other merely in the conceit which animates the latter. Scepticism, directed to the whole compass of phenomenal consciousness, on the contrary, makes mind for the first time qualified to test what truth is; since it brings about a despair regarding what are called natural views, thoughts, and opinions, which it is a matter of indifference to call personal or belonging to others, and with which the consciousness that proceeds straight away to criticize and test is still filled and hampered, thus being, as a matter of fact, incapable of what it wants to undertake.

The completeness of the forms of unreal consciousness will be brought about precisely through the necessity of the advance and the necessity of their connection with one another. To make this comprehensible we may remark, by way of preliminary, that the exposition of untrue consciousness in its untruth is not a merely negative process. Such a one-sided view of it is what the natural consciousness generally adopts; and a knowledge, which makes this one-sidedness its essence, is one of those shapes assumed by incomplete consciousness which falls into the course of the inquiry itself and will come before us there. For this view is scepticism—which always sees in the result only pure nothingness and abstracts from the fact that this nothing is determinate, is the nothing of that out of which it comes as a result. Nothing, however, is only, in fact, the true result, when taken as the nothing of what it comes from; it is thus itself a determinate nothing and has a content. The scepticism which ends with the abstraction "nothing" or "emptiness" can advance from this not a step farther, but must wait and see whether there is possibly anything new offered and what that is—in order to cast it into the same abysmal void. When once, on the other hand, the result is apprehended as it truly is, as determinate negation, a new form has thereby immediately arisen; and in the negation the transition is made by which the progress through the complete succession of forms comes about of itself.

80. The goal, however, is fixed for knowledge just as necessarily as the succession in the process. The terminus is at that point where knowledge is no longer compelled to go beyond itself, where it finds its own self, and the notion corresponds to the object and the object to the notion. The progress towards this goal consequently is without a halt, and at no earlier stage is satisfaction to be found. That which is confined to a life of nature is unable of itself to go beyond its immediate existence; but by something other than itself it is forced beyond that; and to be thus wrenched out of its setting is its death. Consciousness, however, is to itself its own notion; thereby it immediately transcends what is limited, and, since this latter belongs to it, consciousness transcends its own self. Along with the particular there is at the same time set up the "beyond," were this only, as in spatial intuition, beside what is limited. Consciousness, therefore, suffers this violence at its own hands; it destroys its own limited satisfaction. When feeling of violence, anxiety for the truth may well withdraw, and struggle to preserve for itself that which is in danger of being lost. But it can find no rest. Should that anxious fearfulness wish to remain always in unthinking indolence, thought will agitate the thoughtlessness, its restlessness will disturb that indolence. Or let it take its stand as a form of sentimentality which assures us it finds everything good in its kind, and this assurance likewise will suffer violence at the hands of reason, which finds something not good just because and insofar as it is a kind. Or, again, fear of the truth may conceal itself from itself and others behind the pretext that precisely burning zeal for the very truth makes it so difficult, nay impossible, to find any other truth except that of which alone vanity is capable—that of being ever so much cleverer than any ideas, which one gets from oneself or others, could make possible. This sort of conceit which understands how to belittle every truth and turn away from it back into itself, and gloats over this its own private understanding, which always knows how to dissipate every possible thought, and to find, instead of all the content, merely the barren Ego—this is a satisfaction which must be left to itself; for it flees the universal and seeks only an isolated existence on its own account.

81. As the foregoing has been stated, provisionally and in general, concerning the manner and the necessity of the process of the inquiry, it may also be of further service to make some observations regarding the method of carrying this out. This exposition, viewed as a process of relating science to phenomenal knowledge, and as an inquiry and critical examination into the reality of knowing, does not seem able to be effected without some presupposition which is laid down as an ultimate criterion. For an examination consists in applying an accepted standard, and, on the final agreement or disagreement therewith of what is tested, deciding whether the latter is right or wrong; and the standard in general, and so science, were this the criterion, is thereby accepted as the essence or inherently real. But here, where science first appears on the scene, neither science nor any sort of standard has justified itself as the essence or ultimate reality; and without this no examination seems able to be instituted.

82. This contradiction and the removal of it will become more definite if, to begin with, we call to mind the abstract determinations of knowledge and of truth as they are found in consciousness. Consciousness, we find, distinguishes from itself something to which at the same time it relates itself; or, to use the current expression, there is something for consciousness; and the determinate

form of this process of relating, or of there being something for a consciousness, is knowledge. But from this being for another we distinguish being in itself or per se; what is related to knowledge is likewise distinguished from it, and posited as also existing outside this relation; the aspect of being per se or in itself is called Truth. What really lies in these determinations does not further concern us here; for since the object of our inquiry is phenomenal knowledge, its determinations are also taken up, in the first instance, as they are immediately offered to us. And they are offered to us very much in the way we have just stated.

83. If now our inquiry deals with the truth of knowledge, it appears that we are inquiring what knowledge is in itself. But in this inquiry knowledge is our object, it is for us; and the essential nature of knowledge, were this to come to light, would be rather its being for us: what we should assert to be its essence would rather be, not the truth of knowledge, but only our knowledge of it. The essence or the criterion would lie in us; and that which was to be compared with this standard, and on which a decision was to be passed as a result of this comparison, would not necessarily have to recognize that criterion.

84. But the nature of the object which we are examining surmounts this separation, or semblance of separation, and presupposition. Consciousness furnishes its own criterion in itself, and the inquiry will thereby be a comparison of itself with its own self; for the distinction, just made, falls inside itself. In consciousness there is one element for another, or, in general, consciousness implicates the specific character of the moment of knowledge. At the same time this "other" is to consciousness not merely for it, but also outside this relation, or has a being in itself, i.e., there is the moment of truth. Thus in what consciousness inside itself declares to be the essence or truth we have the standard which itself sets up and by which we are to measure its knowledge. Suppose we call knowledge the notion, and the essence or truth "being" or the object, then the examination consists in seeing whether the notion corresponds with the object. But if we call the inner nature of the object, or what it is in itself, the notion, and, on the other side, understand by object the notion qua object, i.e., the way the notion is for another, then the examination consists in our seeing whether the object corresponds to its own notion. It is clear, of course, that both of these processes are the same. The essential fact, however, to be borne in mind throughout the whole inquiry is that both these moments, notion and object, "being for another" and "being in itself," themselves fall within that knowledge which we are examining. Consequently we do not require to bring standards with us, nor to apply our fancies and thoughts in the inquiry; and just by our leaving these aside we are enabled to treat and discuss the subject as it actually is in itself and for itself, as it is in its complete reality.

21.3 PEIRCE'S PRAGMATISM

American philosopher Charles Sanders Peirce (1839–1914) founded a uniquely American version of idealism known as *pragmatism*. He was born in Cambridge, Massachusetts, son of a Harvard mathematician. He attended Harvard and, at 24, earned a degree in chemistry. He worked for thirty years for the U.S. Coast and Geodetic Survey, occasionally teaching at various universities, though he was never able to secure a permanent academic position. But he worked on philosophical and mathematical questions, developing modern logic (independently from German mathematician Gottlob Frege, who developed his theory of quantification around the same time) and outlining the principles of pragmatism. At 48 he moved to Milford, Pennsylvania, to write philosophy. Over the next twenty-seven years he earned a little money by lecturing and writing but lived most of the time in poverty and ill health.

Peirce became interested in Hegel at a young age. But his scientific and mathematical training gave him a novel perspective on Hegel's idealism. Peirce stresses the importance of *action*. We can understand what we are thinking and, in general, account for meaning by understanding how our thoughts systematically relate to action. There is no difference in meaning without a difference in practice. Meaning, in short, depends entirely on practice. So, to get clear about the meanings of our terms and thoughts, we need to be clear about their practical antecedents and effects.

This is what Peirce calls "the Principle of Pragmatism," which defines his pragmatist philosophical method:

> In order to ascertain the meaning of an intellectual conception we should consider what practical consequences might conceivably result by necessity from the truth of that conception; and the sum of these consequences will constitute the entire meaning of the conception.

What about truth? Thought aims at truth. Not all practice does. Much of what we do is directed purely at practical ends—getting food, seeing friends, and so on. But inquiry—*scientific* activity—aims at truth. It aims in particular at stable belief, beliefs that will not have to be given up in the face of further information. Most philosophers take this as defining scientific activity; it is that activity that aims at the truth. Peirce turns this on its head. The truth is that at which scientific activity aims. The truth is "the opinion which is fated to be agreed to by all who investigate." Scientific practice is not arbitrary; the scientist collects evidence, conducts experiments, and evaluates hypotheses. Many hypotheses are proposed only to be rejected or revised as investigation proceeds. But eventually science will lead us to hypotheses that no further investigation will subvert. Those hypotheses will constitute the truth.

Peirce in effect adopts Hegel's idea that philosophy should look for universal and necessary truths not in a priori concepts and propositions, as rationalists traditionally did, but in higher-level principles governing the dynamics of thought. In his view, however, those higher-level principles are simply the norms of scientific method. Hegel's Absolute Knowledge thus becomes the ideal limit of scientific inquiry.

Peirce defines reality as that which is independent of what people think about it. But he also defines the truth in terms of what the ideal limit of scientific inquiry will lead us to accept. Scientific practice is not arbitrary. No matter who is inquiring or the order in which hypotheses occur to them, they will eventually reach the same conclusions. Truth is a kind of coherence, or, as Peirce puts it, concordance with the ideal limit of scientific inquiry:

> Truth is that concordance of an abstract statement with the ideal limit towards which endless investigation would tend to bring scientific belief, which concordance the abstract statement may possess by virtue of the confession of its inaccuracy and one-sidedness, and this confession is an essential ingredient of truth. A further explanation of what this concordance consists in will be given below. Reality is that mode of being by virtue of which the real thing is as it is, irrespectively of what any mind or any definite collection of minds may represent it to be. The truth of the proposition that Caesar crossed the Rubicon consists in the fact that the further we push our archaeological and other studies, the more strongly will

that conclusion force itself on our minds forever—or would do so, if study were to go on forever.

For Peirce, in short, the truth is what we all eventually are bound to agree on.

Science is a process of belief revision. We adopt certain beliefs in response to our experience, as a way of adapting to our experience and making us better fit for future experiences. We encounter new information and update our beliefs, keeping some, rejecting others, and adding new ones. Truth is what ultimately survives belief revision. Truth, in other words, is that on which our process of belief revision stabilizes. A sentence is true, on this conception, if we can assert it and keep on asserting it in the face of all future evidence. Think of finding points of equilibrium in our search for knowledge. It is always possible that further evidence could disrupt the equilibrium, forcing us to give up our assertion. But sometimes it never does. Those points of stable equilibrium are truths.

21.3.1 Charles Sanders Peirce, from "How to Make Our Ideas Clear"

IV

Let us now approach the subject of logic, and consider a conception which particularly concerns it, that of reality. Taking clearness in the sense of familiarity, no idea could be clearer than this. Every child uses it with perfect confidence, never dreaming that he does not understand it. As for clearness in its second grade, however, it would probably puzzle most men, even among those of a reflective turn of mind, to give an abstract definition of the real. Yet such a definition may perhaps be reached by considering the points of difference between reality and its opposite, fiction. A figment is a product of somebody's imagination; it has such characters as his thought impresses upon it. That those characters are independent of how you or I think is an external reality. There are, however, phenomena within our own minds, dependent upon our thought, which are at the same time real in the sense that we really think them. But though their characters depend on how we think, they do not depend on what we think those characters to be. Thus, a dream has a real existence as a mental phenomenon, if somebody has really dreamt it; that he dreamt so and so, does not depend on what anybody thinks was dreamt, but is completely independent of all opinion on the subject. On the other hand, considering, not the fact of dreaming, but the thing dreamt, it retains its peculiarities by virtue of no other fact than that it was dreamt to possess them. Thus we may define the real as that whose characters are independent of what anybody may think them to be.

But, however satisfactory such a definition may be found, it would be a great mistake to suppose that it makes the idea of reality perfectly clear. Here, then, let us apply our rules. According to them, reality, like every other quality, consists in the peculiar sensible effects which things

Source: Charles Sanders Peirce, "How to Make Our Ideas Clear," *Popular Science Monthly* 12 (January 1878), 286–302.

partaking of it produce. The only effect which real things have is to cause belief, for all the sensations which they excite emerge into consciousness in the form of beliefs. The question therefore is, how is true belief (or belief in the real) distinguished from false belief (or belief in fiction). Now, as we have seen in the former paper, the ideas of truth and falsehood, in their full development, appertain exclusively to the experiential method of settling opinion. A person who arbitrarily chooses the propositions which he will adopt can use the word *truth* only to emphasize the expression of his determination to hold on to his choice. Of course, the method of tenacity never prevailed exclusively; reason is too natural to men for that. But in the literature of the dark ages we find some fine examples of it. When Scotus Erigena is commenting upon a poetical passage in which hellebore is spoken of as having caused the death of Socrates, he does not hesitate to inform the inquiring reader that Helleborus and Socrates were two eminent Greek philosophers, and that the latter, having been overcome in argument by the former, took the matter to heart and died of it! What sort of an idea of truth could a man have who could adopt and teach, without the qualification of a "perhaps," an opinion taken so entirely at random? The real spirit of Socrates, who I hope would have been delighted to have been "overcome in argument," because he would have learned something by it, is in curious contrast with the naive idea of the glossist, for whom (as for "the born missionary" of today) discussion would seem to have been simply a struggle. When philosophy began to awake from its long slumber, and before theology completely dominated it, the practice seems to have been for each professor to seize upon any philosophical position he found unoccupied and which seemed a strong one, to intrench himself in it, and to sally forth from time to time to give battle to the others. Thus, even the scanty records we possess of those disputes enable us to make out a dozen or more opinions held by different teachers at one time concerning the question of nominalism and realism. Read the opening part of the *Historia Calamitatum* of Abelard, who was certainly as philosophical as any of his contemporaries, and see the spirit of combat which it breathes. For him, the truth is simply his particular stronghold. When the method of authority prevailed, the truth meant little more than the Catholic faith. All the efforts of the scholastic doctors are directed toward harmonizing their faith in Aristotle and their faith in the Church, and one may search their ponderous folios through without finding an argument which goes any further. It is noticeable that where different faiths flourish side by side, renegades are looked upon with contempt even by the party whose belief they adopt; so completely has the idea of loyalty replaced that of truth-seeking. Since the time of Descartes, the defect in the conception of truth has been less apparent. Still, it will sometimes strike a scientific man that the philosophers have been less intent on finding out what the facts are, than on inquiring what belief is most in harmony with their system. It is hard to convince a follower of the a priori method by adducing facts; but show him that an opinion he is defending is inconsistent with what he has laid down elsewhere, and he will be very apt to retract it. These minds do not seem to believe that disputation is ever to cease; they seem to think that the opinion which is natural for one man is not so for another, and that belief will, consequently, never be settled. In contenting themselves with fixing their own opinions by a method which would lead another man to a different result, they betray their feeble hold of the conception of what truth is.

On the other hand, all the followers of science are animated by a cheerful hope that the processes of investigation, if only pushed far enough, will give one certain solution to each question to which they apply it. One man may investigate the velocity of light by studying the transits of Venus and the aberration of the stars; another by the oppositions of Mars and the eclipses of Jupiter's satellites; a third by the method of Fizeau; a fourth by that of Foucault; a fifth by the motions of the curves of Lissajoux; a sixth, a seventh, an eighth, and a ninth may follow the different methods of comparing the measures of statical and dynamical electricity. They may at first obtain different results, but, as each perfects his method and his processes, the results are found to move steadily together toward a destined centre. So with all scientific research. Different minds may set out with the most antagonistic views, but the progress of investigation carries them by a force outside of themselves to one and the same conclusion. This activity of thought by which we are carried, not where we wish, but to a fore-ordained goal, is like the operation of destiny. No modification of the point of view taken, no selection of other facts for study, no natural bent of mind even, can enable a man to escape the predestinate opinion. This great hope is embodied in the conception of truth and reality. The opinion which is fated to be ultimately agreed to by all who investigate is what we mean by the truth, and the object represented in this opinion is the real. That is the way I would explain reality.

But it may be said that this view is directly opposed to the abstract definition which we have given of reality, inasmuch as it makes the characters of the real depend on what is ultimately thought about them. But the answer to this is that, on the one hand, reality is independent, not necessarily of thought in general, but only of what you or I or any finite number of men may think about it; and that, on the other hand, though the object of the final opinion depends on what that opinion is, yet what that opinion is does not depend on what you or I or any man thinks. Our perversity and that of others may indefinitely postpone the settlement of opinion; it might even conceivably cause an arbitrary proposition to be universally accepted as long as the human race should last. Yet even that would not change the nature of the belief, which alone could be the result of investigation carried sufficiently far; and if, after the extinction of our race, another should arise with faculties and disposition for investigation, that true opinion must be the one which they would ultimately come to. "Truth crushed to earth shall rise again," and the opinion which would finally result from investigation does not depend on how anybody may actually think. But the reality of that which is real does depend on the real fact that investigation is destined to lead, at last, if continued long enough, to a belief in it.

But I may be asked what I have to say to all the minute facts of history, forgotten never to be recovered, to the lost books of the ancients, to the buried secrets.

"Full many a gem of purest ray serene
The dark, unfathomed caves of ocean bear;
Full many a flower is born to blush unseen,
And waste its sweetness on the desert air."

Do these things not really exist because they are hopelessly beyond the reach of our knowledge? And then, after the universe is dead (according to the prediction of some scientists), and all life has ceased forever, will not the shock of atoms continue though there will be no mind to know it? To this I reply that, though in no possible state of knowledge can any number be great enough to express the relation between the amount of what rests unknown to the amount of the known, yet it is unphilosophical to suppose that, with regard to any given question (which has any clear meaning), investigation would not bring forth a solution of it, if it were carried far enough. Who would have said, a few years ago, that we could ever know of what substances stars are made whose light may have been longer in reaching us than the human race has existed? Who can be sure of what we shall not know in a few hundred years? Who can guess what would be the result of continuing the pursuit of science for ten thousand years, with the activity of the last hundred? And if it were to go on for a million, or a billion, or any number of years you please, how is it possible to say that there is any question which might not ultimately be solved?

But it may be objected, "Why make so much of these remote considerations, especially when it is your principle that only practical distinctions have a meaning?" Well, I must confess that it makes very little difference whether we say that a stone on the bottom of the ocean, in complete darkness, is brilliant or not—that is to say, that it probably makes no difference, remembering always that that stone may be fished up tomorrow. But that there are gems at the bottom of the sea, flowers in the untraveled desert, etc., are propositions which, like that about a diamond being hard when it is not pressed, concern much more the arrangement of our language than they do the meaning of our ideas.

It seems to me, however, that we have, by the application of our rule, reached so clear an apprehension of what we mean by reality, and of the fact which the idea rests on, that we should not, perhaps, be making a pretension so presumptuous as it would be singular if we were to offer a metaphysical theory of existence for universal acceptance among those who employ the scientific method of fixing belief. However, as metaphysics is a subject much more curious than useful, the knowledge of which, like that of a sunken reef, serves chiefly to enable us to keep clear of it, I will not trouble the reader with any more ontology at this moment. I have already been led much further into that path than I should have desired; and I have given the reader such a dose of mathematics, psychology, and all that is most abstruse, that I fear he may already have left me, and that what I am now writing is for the compositor and proofreader exclusively. I trusted to the importance of the subject. There is no royal road to logic, and really valuable ideas can only be had at the price of close attention. But I know that in the matter of ideas the public prefer the cheap and nasty; and in my next paper I am going to return to the easily intelligible and not wander from it again. The reader who has been at the pains of wading through this paper shall be rewarded in the next one by seeing how beautifully what has been developed in this tedious way can be applied to the ascertainment of the rules of scientific reasoning.

We have, hitherto, not crossed the threshold of scientific logic. It is certainly important to know how to make our ideas clear, but they may be ever so clear without being true. How to make them so, we have next to study. How to give birth to those vital and procreative ideas which multiply into a thousand forms and diffuse themselves everywhere, advancing civilization and making the dignity of man, is an art not yet reduced to rules, but of the secret of which the history of science affords some hints.

21.4 NIETZSCHE'S PERSPECTIVISM

German philosopher Friedrich Nietzsche (1844–1900), a fierce critic of Christianity, also rejected much of traditional philosophy—including its style. His works are, for the most part, pastiches of aphorisms, stand-alone paragraphs, and brief essays. Arguments often emerge only over the course of a work or even several works. Nietzsche's father and grandfathers were Lutheran pastors; one grandfather was a noted scholar of Christianity. But his father and younger brother died when Nietzsche was only 4. Nietzsche himself endured ill health for much of his life, suffering migraine headaches, and stomach ailments, chest injuries from being thrown from a horse at age 23, and, just three years later, catching diphtheria and dysentery while serving as a hospital attendant during the Franco-Prussian War. He became professor of classical philology at the University of Basel in Switzerland at 24 but had to resign at 35 because of his failing health. He spent the last eleven years of his life incapacitated by mental illness.

Nietzsche's unusual style and hostility to philosophical system-building make it difficult to summarize his thought. Some of his themes—especially his attack on Kant's things-in-themselves and his version of relativism, often known as *perspectivism*—appear in a relatively early book, *Human, All Too Human*. His most characteristic theses emerge in the works of his middle period: *Beyond Good and Evil*, *Thus Spoke Zarathustra*, *The Genealogy of Morals*, and *The Cheerful Science* (usually translated *The Gay Science* or *Joyful Wisdom*). The last is famous for Nietzsche's pronouncement that God is dead.

To understand what Nietzsche meant by that startling proclamation, contrast Nietzsche's position with that of Hegel. Hegel tells the story of Spirit progressing through stages, coming to self-consciousness and ultimately realizing Absolute Knowledge. Though interpreters of Hegel differ, it is tempting to identify Hegel's Absolute with God, and the state of Absolute Knowledge as unity with the mind of God. Nietzsche rejects not only the existence of God, as defended by Christianity and other religions, but also an Absolute and the possibility of Absolute Knowledge in any sense. He embraces Hegel's historicism; our thought is indeed relative to the particular historical epoch in which we find ourselves. But he rejects Hegel's identification of constant, dynamic principles governing the unfolding of human thought. The progression of human thought, Nietzsche contends, is not reducible to principles of logic or rationality, dynamic or otherwise. Indeed, it is to a large extent irrational, driven by a will to power and other factors. There is no reason to expect that it will reach some ideal fixed point of complete knowledge. In fact, there is no reason to expect it to *progress* at all. Human thought sometimes advances, sometimes retreats, sometimes bogs down, and sometimes detours.

Hegel and Peirce have confidence in rational thought and in scientific method in particular. Nietzsche sometimes seems to view his own thought as scientific. But he urges us to think of science not as an earnest inquiry into the truth or even a process of self-criticism but rather as a cheerful, playful enterprise of developing new ways of seeing, interpreting, and understanding the world. Science is not a tool for deciding between rival perspectives; there is no way to do that but to live them.

21.4.1 Friedrich Nietzsche, from *Human, All Too Human*

Of the First and Last Things

1. *The chemistry of concepts and sensations.*—Nearly all philosophical problems once again raise the same form of question as they did two thousand years ago: How can something develop from its opposite—for example, reason from the unreasonable, feeling from the dead, logic from the illogical, disinterested gaze from covetous wanting, altruism from egoism, truth from error? Metaphysical philosophy overcame this difficulty by denying the emergence of one from the other and accepting for the more highly valued things a miraculous origin in the core and nature of the "thing in itself." Historical philosophy, in contrast, which no longer should be thought

Source: Friedrich Nietzsche, *Menschliches, Allzumenschliches*, 1878. Translated by Daniel Bonevac.

separate from the natural sciences—youngest of all philosophical methods—has discovered in individual cases (and probably will discover in all to come) that there are no opposites, except in the exaggeration of popular or metaphysical views, and that a mistake of reason underlies this confrontation. According to this explanation there is, strictly speaking, neither altruistic action nor a completely disinterested gaze. Both are only sublimations whose basic elements appear nearly to have evaporated and can be seen only with the finest observation. Everything that we need and which can be given to us only now that the individual sciences have reached their present height is a *chemistry* of the moral, religious, and aesthetic conceptions and sensations—likewise all the agitations we experience in the large and small traffic of culture and society, and even in isolation. What if this chemistry would reveal that in these areas too the most glorious colors arise from low, despised materials? How many will desire to pursue such investigations? Mankind loves to put questions of origins and beginnings out of its mind: doesn't one almost have to be inhuman to feel in oneself the opposite inclination?

2. *The hereditary error of the philosophers.*—All philosophies have the common failing that they proceed from men as they are who think that they can reach their goal by an analysis of them. They automatically think of man as an *aeterna veritas* (eternal truth), as a constant in the flux, as a safe measure of things to come. Everything that philosophers say about man is no longer fundamental, but tells us something about the men of a *very limited* period of time. Lack of historical sense is the hereditary error of all philosophers. Some even take, without being aware of it, the most recent organization of humans developed under the impress of certain religions or even political events as the fixed form from which one must proceed. They do not want to learn that humans became what they are and that their cognitive ability also became what it is. Some of them, like spiders, even spin the whole world from this cognitive ability itself. Everything *essential* to human development took place in primeval times, a long time before those four thousand years, more or less, that we know about; in these, humans may not have changed much. There, however, the philosopher sees "instinct" in man as he is and assumes that these are among the constant facts of humanity delivering the key to understanding the world in general. The whole of teleology is built on talking about man of the last four millenia as eternal, to which all things in the world have had a natural direction from the beginning. Everything, however, became what it is. There are *no eternal facts*. There are no absolute truths. Therefore what is needed from now on is historical philosophizing and with it the virtue of modesty.

3. *Estimation of inconspicuous truths.*—It is the characteristic of a higher culture to value the small inconspicuous truths found by means of a rigorous method more highly than the felicitous and dazzling errors metaphysical and artistic ages and men have handed down. At first one has scorn on his lips against the former, as if it could not equal the others. So modestly, simply, soberly, apparently dishearteningly the ones stand; so beautifully, splendidly, intoxicatingly, or even rapturously stand the others. But truths that are hard-won, certain, lasting, and fraught with consequence are nevertheless the higher; to hold to them is manly and indicates bravery, sobriety, and restraint. Not only the individual but all mankind will gradually be raised to this manliness, if finally men grow accustomed to value durable knowledge more highly and lose all faith in inspiration and seemingly miraculous communication of truths.

The admirers of *forms*, with their standard of the beautiful and the sublime, will certainly have good reason to scoff at first, as soon as esteem for the inconspicuous truths and the scientific spirit begin to rule, but only because either their eye was not yet opened to the attraction of the simplest form, or because men educated in that spirit are not completely and internally filled by it for a long time so that they still copy thoughtless old forms (and badly, like someone who no longer pays much attention). Formerly the mind did not have to think rigorously; its importance lay in the spinning of symbols and forms. That changed; the importance of the symbolic has become characteristic of low culture. As our arts become more intellectual, and our senses more spiritual, and as, for example, one now judges what sounds pleasant to the ear completely differently from one hundred years ago, thus also the forms of our life become ever more *spiritual*, to the eye of older times perhaps *uglier*, but only because it is not able to see how the realm of the internal, spiritual beauty itself continually deepens and extends and how a glance can mean more to us all now, more than the most beautiful human body and sublime building.

5. *Misinterpreting the dream.*—Humans in the ages of raw primordial culture believed that, in a dream, they got to know a second material world; here is the origin of all metaphysics. Without the dream one would have found no cause for splitting the world in two. Also the dismantling of a person into soul and body is connected with the oldest view of the dream, as is the acceptance of a life of the soul, thus the origin of all faith in spirits, and probably also faith in God. "The dead live on, for they appear to the living in dreams": thus one concluded formerly, through many thousands of years.

6. *The spirit of science is powerful in the part, not the whole.*—The separate, smallest areas of science are treated purely objectively. The general, large sciences, in contrast, taken as a whole raise a question, a quite unobjective question, certainly: For what? To what use? Because of this concern for use, they as a whole become less impersonal than their parts. Now, in philosophy, the pinnacle of the pyramid of knowledge, the question of use is automatically raised, and each philosophy has the unconscious intention to ascribe to knowledge the highest use. For this reason all philosophies embrace so much high-flying metaphysics and such a shyness at the seemingly insignificant solutions of physics. The importance of knowledge for life should appear as large as possible. Here is the antagonism between particular scientific fields and philosophy. The latter wants, like art, to give life and action depth and meaning. Science first looks for knowledge and nothing else—whatever the consequences. Up to now, there have been no philosophers under whose hands philosophy has not become an apology for knowledge. On this point, at least, each is an optimist in thinking that knowledge must be accorded the highest usefulness. They all are tyrannized by logic. And logic is by nature optimism.

7. *The troublemaker in science.*—Philosophy separated from science when it asked the question: What knowledge of the world and of life helps people lead the happiest lives? This happened in the Socratic schools. The point of view of happiness constricted the veins of scientific research—and it still does so today.

8. *Pneumatic explanation of nature.*—Metaphysics explains the writings of nature as it were pneumatically, as the church and its scholars formerly explained the Bible. It takes very much understanding of nature to use the same kind of explanatory art as the philologists created for all books: with the intention of understanding simply what the writing wants to say, but without catching a whiff of, or presupposing, a *double* sense. We have not completely overcome, however, bad explanatory art even in reference to books, and one encounters allegorical and mystical interpretation even in the best company. Thus it stands in reference to nature—in fact, even more badly.

9. *Metaphysical world.*—It is true, there could be a metaphysical world. The absolute possibility of it can hardly be resisted. We regard all things by means of the human head and cannot cut it off. The question remains, nevertheless, what of the world would still be there if one had cut it off. This is a purely scientific problem and not very likely to worry people. But everything so far that has made metaphysical assumptions *valuable, frightful, delightful* is passion, error, and self-deception—the worst methods of attaining knowledge, not the very best, have taught us to believe in them. If one uncovers these methods as the foundation of all existing religions and metaphysical systems, one disproves

them. The possibility still remains, but one can do nothing at all with it, let alone base happiness, welfare, and life on the spider-thread of such a possibility.—One could assert nothing at all about the metaphysical world, except as other—as another world, inaccessible and incomprehensible to us. It would be a thing with negative characteristics. If the existence of such a world were well proven, then knowledge of it would nevertheless stand firmly as the most useless of all realizations, more useless than knowledge of the chemical analysis of water would be to the sailor in the midst of a storm.

10. *The harmlessness of metaphysics in the future.*—As soon as the emergence of religion, art, and morality have been described so that one can explain them completely without the acceptance of *metaphysical interference* at the beginning and along the way, one no longer has the strongest interest in the purely theoretical problem of the "thing-in-itself" and "appearance." For religion, art, and morality do not reach the "nature of the world in itself." We are not in the realm of concepts; "notions" can carry us further. Fully at peace, we can leave to the physiology and ontogeny (developmental history) of organisms the question of how our conception of the world differs so dramatically from the disclosed nature of the world.

16. *Appearance and thing-in-itself.*—Philosophers put themselves before life and experience—before what they call the world of appearance—as if before a painting which once and for all unfurls and constantly shows the same event. One must interpret this event correctly, they think, to draw any conclusion about the way in which the painting was brought about. They thus maintain the thing-in-itself as sufficient reason for the world of appearance. Against this, more rigorous logicians, after defining the metaphysical world sharply as the absolute one, have unbendingly determined each connection between the absolute world (the metaphysical world) and the world of appearance: so that in appearance the thing-in-itself does not appear at all, and any conclusion from one to the other is to be rejected. Both sides, however, ignore the possibility that the painting, which we now call life and experience, has *become* and is still completely in the process of becoming, and so is not to be regarded as a fixed magnitude from which one might draw or even reject a conclusion concerning its author. Because we looked at the world for thousands of years with moral, aesthetic, religious demands, with blind inclination, passion, or fear, and abandoned ourselves to the bad habits of illogical thinking, this world has gradually become so wondrously multicolored, terrible, meaningful, soulful, that it has taken on color—but we have been the colorists. The human intellect projected its errors as appearances and its basic assumptions into things. Late, very late, does it deliberate. Now the world of experience and the thing-in-itself seem so extraordinarily different and separate that it rejects conclusions about one from the other, or, in an unearthly, secret way, asks us to *give up* our intellects, our personal wills, in order to come to the essence of things by clinging to what is essential. Others have collected all the characteristic features of our world of appearances—our inherited conception of the world spun out of intellectual errors—and instead of accusing the intellect, have blamed the nature of things for causing these hard facts, this very uncanny character of the world, and preached its release.

The constant and laborious progress of science, which will finally celebrate its highest triumph in a *history of the development of thought*, will end all these views decisively. It might conclude with this proposition: What we call now the world is the result of a number of errors and fantasies which have gradually developed throughout the whole evolution of organic nature, have intertwined with one another, and are now left to us as the cumulative treasure of the entire past—as treasure, because the value of our humanity rests on it. From this conceptual world rigorous science can actually free us only in small measure—a fact we hardly wish—to the extent that it cannot substantially break the force of age-old habits of feeling. But it can gradually, bit-by-bit, clear up the history of the emergence of that conceptual world, and advance us at least for a moment above the whole process. Perhaps we will recognize then that the thing-in-itself is actually worthy of Homeric laughter: that it seemed to be so much, everything, and is actually empty, i.e., empty of meaning.

17. *Metaphysical explanations.*—Young people appreciate metaphysical explanations because they exhibit something most significant in things found unpleasant or contemptible. If they are dissatisfied with themselves, then this feeling is facilitated if they recognize in what they so greatly disapprove the deepest riddle or misery of the world. And they feel less responsible for things which are at the same time more interesting. That is the double blessing of metaphysics. Later, certainly, they grow to distrust the whole metaphysical kind of explanation. Perhaps then they see that those effects can be attained in another way, just as well and more scientifically. Physical and historical explanations cause at least as much of that very feeling of irresponsibility, and inflame their interest in life and its problems perhaps even more.

21.4.2 Friedrich Nietzsche, from *The Cheerful Science*

108. *New struggles.*—After Buddha was dead, his shadow was still shown for centuries in a cave—a tremendous, shiver-inducing shadow. God is dead; but given humans as they are, there may be caves for thousands of years in which his shadow is shown. And we—we still have to defeat his shadow!

124. *In the horizon of the infinite.*—We have left the land and gone to sea! We have burned the bridge behind us—even more, we have destroyed the land behind us! Now, ship, look out! Look ahead! Beside you lies the ocean. To be sure, it does not always roar, and every now and then it lies there, like silk and gold and a fantasy of grace. But hours will come when you will recognize that it is infinite and that there is nothing more terrible than infinity. Oh, the poor bird that felt free and now pushes against the walls of this cage! Woe, if homesickness for the land strikes you, as if there would have been more *liberty* there—and there is no longer any "land"!

125. *The madman.*—Have you not heard of that madman who lit a lantern in the bright morning, ran to the market, and cried incessantly: "I'm looking for God! I'm looking for God!" As there were many who stood together there who did not believe in God, he excited much laughter. Is he lost? said one. Did he wander off like a child? said another. Or does he keep himself hidden? Is he afraid of us? Did he go to sea? emigrate?—in such a way they laughed and yelled in disorder. [Nietzsche here echoes Elijah taunting the priests of Ba'al, reported in 1 Kings 18:27.] The madman jumped into their midst and pierced them with his gaze. "Where is God?" he cried. "I will tell you! *We killed him*—you and I! We all are his murderers! But how did we do it? How were we able to drink up the sea? Who gave us the sponge to wipe away the whole horizon? What did we do, when we loosed this earth from its sun? Where does it move now? Where do we move? Away from all suns? Don't we continually fall? And backwards,

Source: Friedrich Nietzsche, *Die Fröhliche Wissenschaft*, 1882. Translated by Daniel Bonevac.

sideways, forward, in all directions? Is there still such a thing as up or down? Don't we wander as through an infinite nothing? Don't we feel the breath of empty space? Didn't it become colder? Doesn't night follow night? Don't lanterns have to be lit in the morning? Do we still hear nothing of the noise of the gravediggers who bury God? Do we still smell nothing from the divine decay?—for gods too decay! God is dead! God remains dead! And we killed him! How can we comfort ourselves, the murderers of all murderers? The holiest and most powerful one the world possessed bled to death under our knives—who will wipe this blood off us? With what water could we clean ourselves? What ceremonies of atonement, what holy games must we invent? Isn't the size of this deed too large for us? Don't we have to become gods just to appear worthy of it? There was never a larger deed—and whoever is born after us will belong to a higher history than all history so far!" Here the madman fell silent and gazed at his listeners again. They too were silent and looked at him in astonishment. Finally he threw his lantern on the ground. It broke into pieces and went out. "I come too early," he said then. "It is not yet time. This tremendous course of events is still on its way. It has not yet reached the ears of men. Lightning and thunder require time; the light of the stars requires time; deeds require time, even after they are done, in order to be seen and heard. This deed is more distant than the furthest stars—*and yet they have done it themselves!*" It is said that the madman that same day forced his way into different churches and therein intoned his *requiem aeternam deo* [eternal rest to God]. Led out and called to account, he answered in each case: "What are these churches, if they are not the tombs and crypts of God?"

179. *Thoughts.*—Thoughts are the shadows of our feelings—always darker, emptier, simpler.

269. *What do you believe?*—This: that the weights of all things must be determined afresh.

270. *What does your conscience say?*—"You are to become the person you are."

21.5 RUSSELL'S REJECTION OF IDEALISM

Bertrand Russell (1872–1970), godson of John Stuart Mill, became one of the twentieth century's greatest philosophers, receiving the Nobel Prize for Literature in 1950. His outspoken support of radical political causes got him fired from Cambridge University; it also led to the rescinding of an offer of a position at the City University of New York. But his reputation rests on his rejection of the idealism that dominated the nineteenth century and the development of analytic philosophy as its replacement. His 1905 essay "On Denoting" revolutionized philosophical method, putting the philosophy of language at center stage, and his logical atomism established a paradigm that shaped philosophical debate for the rest of the century.

Schooled in Kantian and post-Kantian idealism, Russell rejects it in favor of realism and scientific method. Following the lead of his colleague G. E. Moore, he found that arguments for idealism relied on equivocations, confusing objects with their mental representations. Russell developed what is now known as "classical" logic, using it to uncover the underlying logical form of what we say and think. Logical analysis shows, he maintains, that the world consists of complexes of logical simples and their properties. We know some by acquaintance, that is, by standing in direct causal relations with them. We know others by description, that is, inferentially. The objects known by description are logical constructions out of atoms; the logical simples we know directly.

21.5.1 Bertrand Russell, from *Problems of Philosophy*

Idealism

The word "idealism" is used by different philosophers in somewhat different senses. We shall understand by it the doctrine that whatever exists, or at any rate whatever can be known to exist, must be in some sense mental. This doctrine, which is very widely held among philosophers, has several forms, and is advocated on several different grounds. The doctrine is so widely held, and so interesting in itself, that even the briefest survey of philosophy must give some account of it.

Those who are unaccustomed to philosophical speculation may be inclined to dismiss such a doctrine as obviously absurd. There is no doubt that common sense regards tables and chairs and the sun and moon and material objects generally as something radically different from minds and the contents of minds, and as having an existence which might continue if minds ceased. We think of matter as having existed long before there were any minds, and it is hard to think of it as a mere product of mental activity. But whether true or false, idealism is not to be dismissed as obviously absurd.

We have seen that, even if physical objects do have an independent existence, they must differ very widely from sense-data, and can only have a correspondence with sense-data, in the same sort of way in which a catalogue has a correspondence with the things catalogued. Hence common sense leaves us completely in the dark as to the true intrinsic nature of physical objects, and if there were good reason to regard them as mental, we could not legitimately reject this opinion merely because it strikes us as strange. The truth about physical objects must be strange. It may be unattainable, but if any philosopher believes that he has attained it, the fact that what he offers as the truth is strange ought not to be made a ground of objection to his opinion. The grounds on which idealism is advocated are generally grounds derived from the theory of knowledge, that is to say, from a discussion of the conditions which things must satisfy in order that we may be able to know them. The first serious attempt to establish idealism on such grounds was that of Bishop Berkeley. He proved first, by arguments which were largely valid, that our sense-data cannot be supposed to have an existence independent of us, but must be, in part at least, "in" the mind, in the sense that their existence would not continue if there were no seeing or hearing or touching or smelling or tasting. So far, his contention was almost certainly valid, even if some of his arguments were not so. But he went on to argue that sense-data were the only things of whose existence our perceptions could assure us, and that to be known is to be "in" a mind, and therefore to be mental. Hence he concluded that nothing can ever be known except what is in some mind, and that whatever is known without being in my mind must be in some other mind.

In order to understand his argument, it is necessary to understand his use of the word "idea." He gives the name "idea" to anything which is immediately known, as, for example, sense-data are known. Thus a particular colour which we see is an idea; so is a voice which we hear, and so on. But the term is not wholly confined to sense-data. There will also be things remembered or imagined, for with such things also we have immediate acquaintance at the moment of remembering or imagining. All such immediate data he calls "ideas."

He then proceeds to consider common objects, such as a tree, for instance. He shows that all we know immediately when we "perceive" the tree consists of ideas in his sense of the word, and he argues that there is not the slightest ground for

Source: Bertrand Russell, *Problems of Philosophy*. New York: Oxford University Press, 1959.

supposing that there is anything real about the tree except what is perceived. Its being, he says, consists in being perceived: in the Latin of the Schoolmen its "esse" is "percipi." He fully admits that the tree must continue to exist even when we shut our eyes or when no human being is near it. But this continued existence, he says, is due to the fact that God continues to perceive it; the "real" tree, which corresponds to what we called the physical object, consists of ideas in the mind of God, ideas more or less like those we have when we see the tree, but differing in the fact that they are permanent in God's mind so long as the tree continues to exist. All our perceptions, according to him, consist in a partial participation in God's perceptions, and it is because of this participation that different people see more or less the same tree. Thus apart from minds and their ideas there is nothing in the world, nor is it possible that anything else should ever be known, since whatever is known is necessarily an idea.

There are in this argument a good many fallacies which have been important in the history of philosophy, and which it will be as well to bring to light. In the first place, there is a confusion engendered by the use of the word "idea". We think of an idea as essentially something in somebody's mind, and thus when we are told that a tree consists entirely of ideas, it is natural to suppose that, if so, the tree must be entirely in minds. But the notion of being "in" the mind is ambiguous. We speak of bearing a person in mind, not meaning that the person is in our minds, but that a thought of him is in our minds. When a man says that some business he had to arrange went clean out of his mind, he does not mean to imply that the business itself was ever in his mind, but only that a thought of the business was formerly in his mind, but afterwards ceased to be in his mind. And so when Berkeley says that the tree must be in our minds if we can know it, all that he really has a right to say is that a thought of the tree must be in our minds. To argue that the tree itself must be in our minds is like arguing that a person whom we bear in mind is himself in our minds. This confusion may seem too gross to have been really committed by any competent philosopher, but various attendant circumstances rendered it possible. In order to see how it was possible, we must go more deeply into the question as to the nature of ideas.

Before taking up the general question of the nature of ideas, we must disentangle two entirely separate questions which arise concerning sense-data and physical objects. We saw that, for various reasons of detail, Berkeley was right in treating the sense-data which constitute our perception of the tree as more or less subjective, in the sense that they depend upon us as much as upon the tree, and would not exist if the tree were not being perceived. But this is an entirely different point from the one by which Berkeley seeks to prove that whatever can be immediately known must be in a mind. For this purpose arguments of detail as to the dependence of sense-data upon us are useless. It is necessary to prove, generally, that by being known, things are shown to be mental. This is what Berkeley believes himself to have done. It is this question, and not our previous question as to the difference between sense-data and the physical object, that must now concern us.

Taking the word "idea" in Berkeley's sense, there are two quite distinct things to be considered whenever an idea is before the mind. There is on the one hand the thing of which we are aware—say the colour of my table—and on the other hand the actual awareness itself, the mental act of apprehending the thing. The mental act is undoubtedly mental, but is there any reason to suppose that the thing apprehended is in any sense mental? Our previous arguments concerning the colour did not prove it to be mental; they only proved that its existence depends upon the relation of our sense organs to the physical object—in our case, the table. That is to say, they proved that a certain colour will exist, in a certain light, if a normal eye is placed at a certain point relatively to the table. They did not prove that the colour is in the mind of the percipient.

Berkeley's view, that obviously the colour must be in the mind, seems to depend for its plausibility upon confusing the thing apprehended with the act of apprehension. Either of these might be called an "idea"; probably either would have been called an idea by Berkeley. The act is undoubtedly in the mind; hence, when we are thinking of the act, we readily assent to the view that ideas must be in the mind. Then, forgetting that this was only true when ideas were taken as acts of apprehension, we transfer the proposition that "ideas are in the mind" to ideas in the other sense, i.e., to the things apprehended by our acts of apprehension. Thus, by an unconscious equivocation, we arrive at the conclusion that whatever we can apprehend must be in our minds. This seems to be the true analysis of Berkeley's argument, and the ultimate fallacy upon which it rests.

This question of the distinction between act and object in our apprehending of things is vitally important, since our whole power of acquiring knowledge is bound up with it. The faculty of being acquainted with things other than itself is the main characteristic of a mind. Acquaintance with objects essentially consists in a relation between the mind and something other than the mind; it is this that constitutes the mind's power of knowing things. If we say that the things known must be in the mind, we are either unduly limiting the mind's power of knowing, or we are uttering a mere tautology. We are uttering a mere tautology if we mean by "in the mind" the same as by "before the mind," i.e., if we mean merely being apprehended by the mind. But if we mean this, we shall have to admit that what, in this sense, is in the mind may nevertheless be not mental. Thus when we realize the nature of knowledge, Berkeley's argument is seen to be wrong in substance as well as in form, and his grounds for supposing that "ideas"—i.e., the objects apprehended—must be mental, are found to have no validity whatever. Hence his grounds in favour of idealism may be dismissed. It remains to see whether there are any other grounds.

It is often said, as though it were a self-evident truism, that we cannot know that anything exists which we do not know. It is inferred that whatever can in any way be relevant to our experience must be at least capable of being known by us; whence it follows that if matter were essentially something with which we could not become acquainted, matter would be something which we could not know to exist, and which could have for us no importance whatever. It is generally also implied, for reasons which remain obscure, that what can have no importance for us cannot be real, and that therefore matter, if it is not composed of minds or of mental ideas, is impossible and a mere chimæra.

To go into this argument fully at our present stage would be impossible, since it raises points requiring a considerable preliminary discussion; but certain reasons for rejecting the argument may be noticed at once. To begin at the end: there is no reason why what cannot have any practical importance for us should not be real. It is true that, if theoretical importance is included, everything real is of some importance to us, since, as persons desirous of knowing the truth about the universe, we have some interest in everything that the universe contains. But if this sort of interest is included, it is not the case that matter has no importance for us, provided it exists even if we cannot know that it exists. We can, obviously, suspect that it may exist, and wonder whether it does; hence it is connected with our desire for knowledge, and has the importance of either satisfying or thwarting this desire.

Again, it is by no means a truism, and is in fact false, that we cannot know that anything exists which we do not know. The word "know" is here used in two different senses. (1) In its first use it is applicable to the sort of knowledge which is opposed to error, the sense in which what we know is true, the sense which applies to our beliefs and convictions, i.e., to what are called *judgements*. In this sense of the word we know that something is the case. This sort of knowledge may be described as knowledge of truths. (2) In the second use of the word "know" above, the word applies to our knowledge of things, which we may call *acquaintance*. This is the sense in which we know sense-data. (The distinction involved is roughly that between *savoir* and *connaître* in French, or between *wissen* and *kennen* in German.)

Thus the statement which seemed like a truism becomes, when re-stated, the following: "We can never truly judge that something with which we are not acquainted exists." This is by no means a truism, but on the contrary a palpable falsehood. I have not the honour to be acquainted with the Emperor of China, but I truly judge that he exists. It may be said, of course, that I judge this because of other people's acquaintance with him. This, however, would be an irrelevant retort, since, if the principle were true, I could not know that anyone else is acquainted with him. But further: there is no reason why I should not know of the existence of something with which nobody is acquainted. This point is important, and demands elucidation.

If I am acquainted with a thing which exists, my acquaintance gives me the knowledge that it exists. But it is not true that, conversely, whenever I can know that a thing of a certain sort exists, I or someone else must be acquainted with the thing. What happens, in cases where I have true judgement without acquaintance, is that the thing is known to me by description, and that, in virtue of some general principle, the existence of a thing answering to this description can be inferred from the existence of something with which I am acquainted.

CHAPTER 22

Spanish and Latin American Metaphysics

"A labyrinth devised by men"

Spanish and Latin American philosophers have devised various theories of the nature of the world. In the Middle Ages, Peter of Spain defined the space of metaphysical speculation for Scholastic philosophers by linking the structure of the world to the structure of language. For centuries, most Spanish-speaking philosophers worked within that Scholastic framework. More recently, they have explored alternative conceptions of reality, wondering whether there is any content to the idea of reality beyond a given point of view and whether the traditional debate between realists and idealists has truly been understood.

22.1 THE LOGIC OF PETER OF SPAIN

From the thirteenth to the seventeenth century in Europe, logic, as one of seven liberal arts, formed part of the core of every student's university education. The standard textbook taught in the universities, which went through 166 editions, was the *Tractatus*, also known as the *Summulae Logicales*, of Peter of Spain (13th century). Indeed, freshmen at the University of Paris were dubbed *Summalistae*, "Summalists," since all had to study the *Tractatus*. Peter of Spain is generally thought to be a scholar of Portuguese descent who became Pope John XXI (1210–1277) in 1276. Some historians, however, believe that he was a Dominican monk of Spanish descent. In any case he seems to have studied at the University of Paris, then at its height, probably with Albert the Great or William of Shireswood. Dante, in the *Divine Comedy*, describes Peter of Spain in heaven: "Peter of Spain, who gave Logic light, below there, with his twelve books." He wrote not only the *Tractatus*, which contains twelve tracts, but also the *Syncategoremata* sometime between 1230 and 1245.

Because of his prominent place in the curriculum, Peter of Spain became a leading emblem of Scholasticism, the method of dialectical reasoning that dominated medieval universities. The method of the Schoolmen, as the Scholastic thinkers were known, was

- to examine a question or a work by a significant author;
- to survey various approaches to the issue;
- to find points of disagreement among these sources;
- to use logic and the analysis of language to resolve the dispute, ideally by reconciling the views and revealing a deeper agreement.

Teaching methods included lectures and disputations, which were formalized, largely impromptu debates on intellectual issues. The Scholastic method inspired many great medieval philosophers but also became a popular target among early modern philosophers such as Descartes, Locke, and Hume.

Peter's *Tractatus* devotes five books to the "old logic" of Aristotle, discussing parts of speech, propositions, syllogisms, and topics of argumentation as well as philosophical matters such as Aristotle's categories and the distinction between essential and accidental properties. The remaining seven books concern the "new logic," the logic of terms and the theory of supposition that was a major innovation of the twelfth and thirteenth centuries.

The theory of supposition is complex; its details lie beyond our scope here. But underlying it is a simple and powerful metaphysical idea—the core idea of Aristotle's categories. To understand the structure of the world in its broadest outlines, we need to understand the structure of language. To analyze the structure of language, we must distinguish *complex* expressions, which have other expressions as components, from *simple* expressions, which do not. We break down complex expressions into their simple components. Some simple terms, such as *not, if, of, such, as,* and the like, are *syncategorematic*; they organize language but themselves refer to nothing in the world. Others, including proper names and common nouns, are *categorematic*; they refer to substances or things of other categories. We can understand what there must be in the world by analyzing such language and seeing what its use commits us to.

Peter starts with Aristotle's categories. Roughly, nouns stand for substances; adjectives, for qualities; active verbs, for actions; passive verbs, for passions; and so on. The theory of supposition becomes difficult when we think about complexes and try to understand what they stand for. Peter's theory is important not for its detailed answers to such questions but because, for perhaps the first time, it recognizes their importance. His central idea is that metaphysics rests on semantics, the theory of meaning. To find out what there is in the world, analyze language, understand what it means, and see what objects have to exist for what you say about the world to be true.

Peter's own metaphysical stance is fairly neutral. His theory of supposition holds that proper names stand for objects and that common nouns stand either for a kind of object or for the individual objects falling under the kind. He commits himself, in other words, to what Aristotle would call primary and secondary substances—individual objects and kinds. The status of the other categories formed the topic of one of medieval philosophy's central debates: Are universals (qualities, relations, etc.) real? If so, are they mind dependent or mind independent? Peter himself offers no opinion.

In the next reading, *therefore* appears in valid inferences, and **therefore* in invalid ones.

22.1.1 Peter of Spain, *Tractatus*

Tract VI

On Supposition

1. Of the things that are said, some are complex; some are not. Complex: *a man is running, the man is white*; simple: *man*, which is a simple term.

Each simple term refers to a substance, quality, quantity, relation, action, passion, or something of another category.

On Signification

2. The signification of a term, as taken here, is the conventional representation of a thing by something vocal. Hence, since everything is either a universal or a particular, expressions signifying nothing universal or particular signify nothing at all. So they will not count as terms, as *term* is taken here. Terms are universal or particular signs.

One kind of signification is to a substantive thing; it is accomplished with a substantive noun such as *man*. Another kind is to an adjectival thing and is accomplished with an adjective such as *white* or a verb such as *runs*. Consequently, signification is not properly substantival or adjectival. Some things are signified substantively, and some adjectivally. *Adjectival* and *substantive* are modes of things signified, not modes of signification.

Substantive nouns are said to refer; adjectives and verbs are said to join.

On Supposition and Joining

3. Supposition is the acceptance of a substantive term for something. Supposition and signification differ in that signification occurs through the imposition of the voice on the things signified, while supposition is the acceptance of the same term already signifying a thing for someone. In *a man is running*, for example, the term *man* stands for Socrates or Plato, and so on. Thus signification is prior to supposition. Nor are they the same, for signification is vocal, and supposition involves terms already, as it were, composed by the voice and signifying. Therefore supposition is not signification.

Joining is the acceptance of an adjectival term for something.

On the Division of Supposition

4. Supposition is either common or discrete. Common supposition is through a common noun such as *man*. Discrete supposition is through a proper name, such as *Socrates* or *this man*.

Again, common supposition is sometimes natural, sometimes accidental. Natural supposition is the acceptance of a common term for anything it is naturally apt to participate in, as *man*, per se, naturally, by its nature stands for all men who were or are or will be. Accidental supposition is acceptance of a common term for those things for which it demands something additional. In *there is a man*, the term *man* stands for something present; in *there was a man*, it stands for something past; in *there will be a man*, it stands for something future. And so it has different suppositions depending on what is added to it.

5. Accidental suppositions are either simple or personal. Simple supposition is the acceptance of a common term for a universal thing signified by it. For example, in *man is a species* or *animal is a genus*, the term *man* stands for the kind, man, and not for anything inferior to it [for example, a particular man], and *animal* stands for the kind, animal, and not for anything inferior to it [for example, a particular animal]. It is similar for any other common term, for example, in *risibility is a quality, rationality is a difference, white is an accident.*

6. Simple supposition is of a common term in subject position, as in *man is a species.* Another is a common term affirmed in the predicate, as in *every man is an animal*; the term *animal* in predicate position has simple supposition, as it stands solely for the nature of the genus. Another is a common term positioned after an exceptive expression, such as *every animal except man is irrational*, for the term *man* in the predicate has simple supposition. From this does not follow: *every man except man is irrational;* * *therefore every animal except this man is irrational.* This form of speech proceeds from simple to personal supposition. It is similar to this: *man is a species;* * *therefore some man is a species*; and this: *every man is an animal;* * *therefore every man is this animal.* For every one of these suppositions proceeds from the simple to the personal.

That a common term in predicate position should be taken to have simple supposition is shown by *all contraries are the same discipline.* For unless the term *discipline* has simple supposition, this is false, since no particular discipline studies all contraries. Medicine concerns not all contraries but only sickness and health. Grammar concerns the congruous and incongruous. And so on for other disciplines.

7. Personal supposition is the acceptance of a common term for its inferiors [for example, the particular objects falling under it]. Thus, in *a man is running*, the term *man* stands for its inferiors.

8. Personal supposition may be determinate or confused. Determinate supposition is ascribed when a common term is taken indefinitely or with a particular marker, as in *a man is running* or *some man is running.* These are called determinate, although the term *man* stands for every man, whether running or not, for they are true even if only one man is running. It is one thing to stand for something and another to make something true. In these cases, the term *man* stands for every man, whether running or not, but makes the statement true only for those running. It is evident that each of these is determinate: *an animal is Socrates, an animal is Plato, an animal is Cicero*, etc., *therefore an animal is every man.* This form of speech moves from many determinates to one. And so a common term taken indefinitely has determinate supposition; and similarly with a particular sign.

9. Confused supposition is the acceptance of a common term for many things by way of a universal sign. In *every man is an animal*, the term *man* through a universal sign is taken for many things—for any one of the things it stands for.

Again, confused supposition may be confused by way of the necessity of a sign or mode or confused by way of the necessity of a thing. In *every man is an animal*, the term *man* is confused by the necessity of the sign; it is distributed over any one of the things it stands for. And since each and every man has the same essence, the verb *is* is taken by the necessity of a thing for as many essences as *man* is for men. Since in each and every man dwells the same animality, moreover, the word *animal* is taken by the necessity of a thing for as many animals as *man* for men and the verb *is* for essences. Hence the term *man* is said to stand for things confusedly, flexibly, and distributively. It stands confusedly and distributively for things, however, since it is taken for every man; it stands for them flexibly, since it licenses descent to anything that falls under it, as in *every man* *[is F], therefore Socrates [is F]*, or *every man [is F], therefore Plato [is F]*. But the term *animal* is said to stand for things confusedly but inflexibly, for it does not license such descent: *every man is an animal, *therefore every man is this animal*; this proceeds from the simple to the personal. This is like: *man is the most dignified of creatures; *therefore this man is the most dignified of creatures*; *a rose is the most beautiful of flowers; *therefore this rose is the most beautiful of flowers*. But they differ in this since in them is simple supposition by part of the subject in that by part of the predicate.

22.2 THE PERSPECTIVISM OF ORTEGA Y GASSET

José Ortega y Gasset (1883–1955) was born in Madrid, educated at Málaga, Bilbao, and Madrid, and then studied at several German universities. At 27 he was named to a professorship at Complutense University of Madrid, where he had completed his doctorate and where he remained throughout his career. Ortega became internationally famous in 1930 with the publication of *The Revolt of the Masses*. His ideas exerted a significant influence on existentialists such as Martin Heidegger and Jean-Paul Sartre.

Ortega begins from the dispute between realists and idealists. Idealists contend that everything is mind dependent; the world is a mental construction. Ortega finds this view unsatisfying; there are hard realities we confront that are not of our own making. But he finds realism unappealing as well. Realists maintain that some things are independent of mind. This, Ortega believes, isolates mind from world and makes it impossible to understand how knowledge is possible. He insists that mind and world are intertwined. The world cannot be understood without appeal to our own cognitive faculties. But we cannot understand ourselves without appeal to the world. "I am myself and my circumstance," he writes, expressing not only a thoroughgoing contextualism but also an attempt to synthesize what is right in both idealism and realism. I and my circumstances together constitute life; reason can come to reliable conclusions only when it focuses on life, taking both mind and world, both subject and object, into account. This is *vital reason*, in his phrase, which is also historical, for we cannot understand ourselves or our circumstances without understanding how they have come about.

Ortega's thought is thus not only contextualist and historical but dynamic. We frequently encounter our own limitations, imposed in part by aspects of the world not of our own making. We are free to choose who we are, but that freedom is bounded. Our lives are dramas in which our freedom confronts those boundaries.

Ortega's perspectivist view of truth shows some influence from German philosopher Friedrich Nietzsche, but he puts his own distinctive stamp on Nietzsche's view, which he says threatens to collapse into relativism. Ortega thinks of describing a landscape—a farmhouse, say, surrounded by a group of trees. No one perspective on the scene captures it completely. Yet no view is arbitrary or *merely* a mental construction. We might identify the truth about the farmhouse and copse of trees with the totality of all possible perspectives on them. But that totality is not itself a perspective; there is no place to stand from which one can see the farmhouse from all possible points of view. Thus Ortega embraces a positive pluralism of perspectives—much like Jain philosophers in India.

But he does not—unlike the Jains—try to reconcile tensions among metaphysical positions. Each of us is a separate organ of appropriation of the truth.

22.2.1 José Ortega y Gasset, from *The Modern Theme*

Chapter X. The Doctrine of the Point of View

... Let us now recall the opening considerations of this discourse. Modern tradition presents us with a choice between two opposed methods of dealing with the antinomy between life and culture. One of them—rationalism—in its design to preserve culture denies all significance to life. The other—relativism—attempts the inverse operation: it gets rid of the objective value of culture altogether in order to leave room for life. Neither of these solutions, which appeared sufficient to the generations of the past, finds an echo in our own sensibility. Neither of them can live without being blind to the other's existence. Our own age, not being a prey to such obfuscations, and seeing with perfect clarity the significance of both contending powers, cannot bring itself either to accept the idea that truth, justice and beauty do not exist, or to forget that their existence requires the support of vitality.

Let us make this point clearer by concentrating upon that element in culture which is the easiest to define, viz., knowledge.

Knowledge is the acquisition of truths, and in acquiring truths we become acquainted with the transcendental or trans-subjective universe of reality. Truths are eternal, unique and invariable. How, then, can there be, in the knower, any process by which they can be identified? The reply of rationalism is narrow and arbitrary: knowledge is only possible if reality can penetrate it without the least disturbance of its own fabric. The knower, therefore, must be a transparent medium, lacking any sort of special quality or characteristic colour: he must be the same yesterday as today or tomorrow: he must therefore be ultra-vital and extra-historical. Life has essential characters of its own, it changes and develops: in a word, it is history.

The reply of relativity is equally narrow and arbitrary. Knowledge is impossible; there is no such thing as transcendent reality, for the reason that every real knower resembles an arena that has its own special formation. Reality would have to alter its own fabric in order to enter such an arena, and the particular alteration made would in each case be falsely construed as reality.

It is interesting to notice how in recent times, without any mutual collaboration or premeditation, psychology, biology and the theory of knowledge have each, in their survey of the facts which form the basis of both rationalist and relativist views, been obliged to make certain corrections, and are now unanimous in formulating the problem in a new way.

The knower is not a transparent medium, a pure Ego, possessed of fixed identity and an invariable nature, nor does his reception of reality result in disturbances of fabric in the latter. The facts impose a third view of the process of knowledge, which is a perfect synthesis of the other two. When a sieve or a net is placed in a current of liquid

Source: José Ortega y Gasset, *The Modern Theme*. Translated from the Spanish by James Cleugh. London: C. W. Daniels, 1931.

it allows certain things to permeate it and keeps others out; it might be said to make a choice, but assuredly not to alter the forms of things. This is the function of the knower, of the living being face to face with the cosmic reality of his environment. He does not allow himself, without more ado, to be permeated by reality, as would the imaginary rational entity created by rationalist definitions. Nor does he invent an illusory reality. His function is clearly selective. From the infinite number of elements which integrate reality the individual or receiving apparatus admits a certain proportion, whose form and substance coincide with the meshes of his sensitised net. The rest, whether phenomena, facts or truths, remain beyond him. He knows nothing of them and does not perceive them.

An elementary and purely physiological instance of this process may be found in the mechanism of sight and hearing. The ocular and auditive structures of the human race admit wave vibrations between fixed minimum and maximum velocities. Such colours and sounds as remain outside the two limiting points are unknown to humanity. In a similar way man's vital framework has a certain influence upon his reception of reality; but this does not mean that this influence or intervention involves alteration of the fabric of reality. A whole repertory, and a fairly large one, of perfectly real colours and sounds reaches his consciousness, and he is unquestionably aware of them.

The same process as operates in the case of colours and sounds applies also to truths. The psychic structure of each individual plays the part of a receptive organ in possession of a determinate form which admits the comprehension of certain truths and is condemned to an obstinate blindness to others. Similarly, all peoples and all epochs have their typical souls, that is to say, their nets, provided with meshes of definite sizes and shapes which enable them to achieve a strict affinity with some truths and to be incorrigibly inept for the assimilation of others. This means that all epochs and all peoples have been able to enjoy the measure of truth which suits them, and there is no sense in any people or epoch setting up in opposition to the rest, as if their particular share of truth were the respository of the whole of it. All have their fixed position in the historical series; none can legitimately aim at abandoning their posts, for such an act would be the equivalent of converting the agent into an abstract entity, and this would involve a total renunciation of existence.

Two men may look, from different view-points, at the same landscape. Yet they do not see the same thing. Their different situations make the landscape assume two distinct types of organic structure in their eyes. The part which, in the one case, occupies the foreground, and is thrown into high relief in all its details, is, in the other case, the background, and remains obscure and vague in its appearance. Further, inasmuch as things which are put one behind the other are either wholly or partially concealed, each of the two spectators will perceive portions of the landscape which elude the attention of the other. Would there be any sense in either declaring the other's view of the landscape false? Evidently not; the one is as real as the other. But it would be just as senseless if, when our spectators found that their views of the landscape did not agree, they concluded that both views were illusory. Such a conclusion would involve belief in the existence of a third landscape, an authentic one, not subject to the same conditions as the other two. Well, an archetypal landscape of this kind does not and cannot exist. Cosmic reality is such that it can only be seen in a single definite perspective. Perspective is one of the component parts of reality. Far from being a disturbance of its fabric, it is its organising element. A reality which remained the same from whatever point of view it was observed would be a ridiculous conception.

The case of corporeal vision applies equally to all our other faculties. All knowledge is knowledge from a definite point of view. Spinoza's *species aeternitatis*, or ubiquitous and absolute point of view, has no existence on its own account: it is a fictitious and abstract point of view. We have no doubt of its utility as an instrument for the fulfilment of certain requirements of knowledge, but it is essential to remember that reality cannot be perceived from such a standpoint. The abstract point of view deals only in abstractions.

This way of thinking leads to a radical reform in philosophy, and also, which is more important, to a reform in our sensuous reaction to the cosmos.

The individuality of every real subjective entity was the insurmountable obstacle encountered by recent intellectual tradition in its attempt to make knowledge justify its claim to be able to enter into possession of truth. Two different subjective entities, it was supposed, would acquire the knowledge of two divergent types of truth. We can now see that the divergence between the worlds of two subjective entities does not involve the falsity of one of them. On the contrary, precisely because what each one sees is a reality, not a fiction, its aspect must be distinct from what the other perceives. The divergence is not a contradiction, but a complement. If the universe had presented an identical appearance to the eyes of a Greek of Socrates' time and to those of a Yankee we should have to suppose that true reality, independent of subjective entities, does not reside in the universe. For the fact that it looked the same to two men placed at such diverse standpoints as those of Athens in the fifth century B.C. and New York in the twentieth A.D. would indicate that there was no question of any objective reality at all, but rather of a mere image which happened to occur, with identical features, in the minds of the two persons concerned.

Every life is a point of view directed upon the universe. Strictly speaking, what one life sees no other can. Every individual, whether person, nation or epoch, is an organ, for which there can be no substitute, constructed for the apprehension of truth. This is how the latter, which is in itself of a nature alien from historical variation, acquires a vital dimension. Without the development, the perpetual change and the inexhaustible series of adventures which constitute life, the universe, or absolutely valid truth, would remain unknown.

The persistent error that has hitherto been made is the supposition that reality possesses in itself, independent of the point of view from which it is observed, a physiognomy of its own. Such a theory clearly implies that no view of reality relative to any one particular standpoint would coincide with its absolute aspect, and consequently all such views would be false. But reality happens to be, like a landscape, possessed of an infinite number of perspectives, all equally veracious and authentic. The sole false perspective is that which claims to be the only one there is. In other words, that which is false is Utopia, non-localised truth, which "cannot be seen from any particular place." The Utopian (and such is essentially the character of the rationalist) goes further astray than anyone, since he is the spectator who loses confidence in his own point of view and deserts his post.

Up to the present time philosophy has remained consistently Utopian. Consequently, each successive system claimed to be valid for all ages and all types of mankind. Isolated beyond vital, historical and "perspectivist" dimension, it indulged from time to time in various unconvincing gestures of definition. On the other hand, the doctrine of the point of view requires a system to contain a properly articulated declaration of the vital perspective responsible for it, thus permitting its own articulation to be linked up with those of other systems, whether future or exotic. Pure reason must now give place to a vital type of reason in which its pure form may become localised and acquire mobility and power of self-transformation....

Now, the reduction of the world to a horizon, or its conversion into one, does not lessen the quantity of reality in it to the smallest degree: the process simply puts it into relation with the living observer, whose world it is, endows it with a vital dimension and localises it in the current of life which flows from species to species, from people to people, from generation to generation and from individual to individual, gradually possessing itself of more and more universal reality.

Accordingly, the peculiar property of every living being, the individual difference, far from impeding the capture of truth, is precisely the organ by which the specially corresponding portion of reality is perceived. So that each individual, each generation or each epoch may be considered as an apparatus, for which there can be no substitute, directed to the acquisition of knowledge. Integral truth is only obtained by linking up what I see with what my neighbour sees, and so on successively. Each individual is an essential point of view in the chain. By setting everyone's fragmentary visions side-by-side it would be possible to achieve a complete panorama of absolute and universally valid truth. Now, this sum of individual perspectives, this knowledge of what each and all have seen and recognised, this omniscience, this true "absolute reason," is the sublime faculty which used to be attributed to God. God is also a point of view: but not because he possesses a watch-tower beyond the confines of the human area from which he can behold universal reality directly, as if he were one of the old rationalists. God is not a rationalist. His point of view is that of each one of us: our partial truth is also truth to him. Our perspective is veracious and our reality authentic to that extent. The only point is that God, as the catechism says, is everywhere and therefore enjoys the use of every point of view, resuming and harmonising in his own unlimited vitality all our horizons. God is the symbol of the vital torrent through whose infinite nets the universe gradually passes, being thus continuously steeped in and consecrated by life, that is to say, seen, loved, hated, painfully endured and pleasurably enjoyed by life.

Malebranche used to maintain that if we know any truth at all, it is because we see phenomena through God's eyes or from God's point of view. To me the inverse seems more probable, viz., that God sees phenomena through the medium of mankind or that mankind is the visual organ of divinity.

It is therefore peculiarly incumbent upon us not to defraud the sublime requirement that depends upon our co-operation for its fufilment, and, planting ourselves firmly in the position we find allotted to us, to open our eyes wide to our environment with a profound faith in our own organism and vital nature, and accept the labour that destiny assigns us—the modern theme.

22.3 THE METAPHYSICAL LABYRINTHS OF JORGE LUIS BORGES

Argentine writer Jorge Luis Borges (1899–1986) was born in Buenos Aires. He grew up speaking both Spanish and English. At 15 his family moved to Geneva, where he learned French and German. He graduated from the College of Geneva at 19. After spending three years in Spain, Borges returned to Buenos Aires, where he immediately began writing. He worked on the editorial staff of a newspaper, then as literary advisor to a publishing house. At 38, he got a job as an assistant at a branch of the city library, which allowed him a great deal of freedom. Four years later, he published his first book of short stories, *The Garden of Forking Paths*, which made him famous. He remained at the library until 1946, when Juan Perón became dictator and fired him. Borges' eyesight was failing, but he became a public speaker and a professor of English and American literature. When Perón fell in 1955, he became head of the National Library. By that time, he was blind. He was appointed professor of literature at the University of Buenos Aires and visiting professor at many institutions, including the University of Texas at Austin.

Borges devotes several of his stories and essays to philosophical themes. He is especially interested in idealism, the thesis that everything is mind dependent. Borges finds the thesis intriguing but ultimately unacceptable. One of his most startling investigations of idealism is his story "Tlön, Uqbar, Orbus Tertius," which tells of a distant land, Uqbar, that gradually becomes dominated by the fiction of a planet in which idealism reigns supreme. Borges imagines what such a planet would be like. Idealism is a far more radical doctrine than many of its proponents acknowledge; our very language would have to change. Realism—the idea that there might be objects (in the story, nine coins) that exist independent of us and our thoughts of them—would be a shocking heresy. The heresy points up a powerful argument in favor of realism, sometimes known as the *missing explanation argument*. There are regularities in our experiences of the world. In similar circumstances you and I have similar experiences. The realist has a simple explanation: We see the same thing. The idealist has no such explanation. Why do our experiences follow similar patterns? Why are they largely continuous, internally and with one another? The realist points to a world external to all of us. The idealist, having no such world available, seems to lack an explanation.

Borges' story ends, however, not with the triumph of realism but with the opposite. The story of Tlön gradually leaks out on earth, and people become more and more fascinated with the planet on which everything is orderly, everything is mental, and nothing has any independent existence. Idealism slowly begins to dominate the thinking of this world; fiction drives out reality.

Borges imagines himself translating an obscure work, Sir Thomas Browne's (1605–1682) *Urn Burial* (1658), solely for himself, with no intention of publishing it, for the world no longer has interest in anything beyond its fantasies. That work, incidentally, is real, and begins:

> When the general pyre was out, and the last valediction over, men took a lasting adieu of their interred friends, little expecting the curiosity of future ages should comment upon their ashes; and, having no old experience of the duration of their relics, held no opinion of such after-considerations. But who knows the fate of his bones, or how often he is to be buried? Who hath the oracle of his ashes, or whither they are to be scattered?

Borges thus wonders whether he and anything he does will have any effect on the future. Browne's work continues:

> The treasures of time lie high, in urns, coins, and monuments, scarce below the roots of some vegetables. Time hath endless rarities, and shows of all varieties; which reveals old things in heaven, makes new discoveries in earth, and even earth itself a discovery.

It concludes:

> Life is a pure flame, and we live by an invisible sun within us. A small fire sufficeth for life, great flames seemed too little after death, while men vainly affected precious pyres, and to burn like Sardanapalus....
>
> To subsist in lasting monuments, to live in their productions, to exist in their names and predicament of chimeras, was large satisfaction unto old expectations, and made one part of their Elysiums. But all this is nothing in the metaphysics of true belief. To live indeed, is to be again ourselves, which being not only a hope but an evidence in noble believers 'tis all one to lie in St Innocent's church-yard as in the sands of Egypt. Ready to be anything, in the ecstasy of being ever, and as content with six foot as the moles of Adrianus.

Borges contrasts the realism of Browne's traditional Christian belief with the idealism of Tlön—an idealism that, unlike Berkeley's, finds no place for God.

22.3.1 Jorge Luis Borges, from "Tlön, Uqbar, Orbis Tertius"

Hume noted for all time that Berkeley's arguments did not admit the slightest refutation nor did they cause the slightest conviction. This dictum is entirely correct in its application to the earth, but entirely false in Tlön. The nations of this planet are congenitally idealist. Their language and the derivations of their language—religion, letters, metaphysics—all presuppose idealism. The world for them is not a concourse of objects in space; it is a heterogeneous series of independent acts. It is successive and temporal, not spatial. There are no nouns in Tlön's conjectural Ursprache, from which the "present" languages and the dialects are derived: there are impersonal verbs, modified by monosyllabic suffixes (or prefixes) with an adverbial value. For example: there is no word corresponding to the word "moon," but there is a verb which in English would be "to moon" or "to moonate." "The moon rose above the river" is *hlor u fang axaxaxas mlö*, or literally: "upward behind the onstreaming it mooned."

The preceding applies to the languages of the southern hemisphere. In those of the northern hemisphere (on whose Ursprache there is very little data in the Eleventh Volume) the prime unit is not the verb, but the monosyllabic adjective. The noun is formed by an accumulation of adjectives. They do not say "moon," but rather "round airy-light on dark" or "pale-orange-of-the-sky" or any other such combination. In the example selected the mass of adjectives refers to a real object, but this is purely fortuitous. The literature of this hemisphere (like Meinong's subsistent world) abounds in ideal objects, which are convoked and dissolved in a moment, according to poetic needs. At times they are determined by mere simultaneity. There are objects composed of two terms, one of visual and another of auditory character: the color of the rising sun and the faraway cry of a bird. There are objects of many terms: the sun and the water on a swimmer's chest, the vague tremulous rose color we see with our eyes closed, the sensation of being carried along by a river and also by sleep. These second-degree objects can be combined with others; through the use of certain abbreviations, the process is practically infinite. There are famous poems made up of one enormous word. This word forms a poetic object created by the author. The fact that no one believes in the reality of nouns paradoxically causes their number to be unending. The languages of Tlön's northern hemisphere contain all the nouns of the Indo-European languages—and many others as well.

It is no exaggeration to state that the classic culture of Tlön comprises only one discipline: psychology. All others are subordinated to it. I have said that the men of this planet conceive the universe as a series of mental processes which do not develop in space but successively in time. Spinoza ascribes to his inexhaustible divinity the attributes of extension and thought; no one in Tlön would understand the juxtaposition of the first (which is typical only of certain states) and the second—which is a perfect synonym of the cosmos. In other words, they do not conceive that the spatial persists in time. The perception of a cloud of smoke on the horizon and then of the burning field and then of the half-extinguished cigarette that produced the blaze is considered an example of association of ideas.

This monism or complete idealism invalidates all science. If we explain (or judge) a fact, we connect it with another; such linking, in Tlön, is a

---

Source: Jorge Luis Borges, from "Tlön, Uqbar, Orbis Tertius," in *Labyrinths: Selected Stories and Other Writings by Jorge Luis Borges*. Translated by James E. Irby. New York: New Directions Publishing Corp., 1962, 1964.

later state of the subject which cannot affect or illuminate the previous state. Every mental state is irreducible: there mere fact of naming it—i.e., of classifying it—implies a falsification. From which it can be deduced that there are no sciences on Tlön, not even reasoning. The paradoxical truth is that they do exist, and in almost uncountable number. The same thing happens with philosophies as happens with nouns in the northern hemisphere. The fact that every philosophy is by definition a dialectical game, a Philosophie des Als Ob [Philosophy of As-If—the title of a work by German philosopher Hans Vaihinger], has caused them to multiply. There is an abundance of incredible systems of pleasing design or sensational type. The metaphysicians of Tlön do not seek for the truth or even for verisimilitude, but rather for the astounding. They judge that metaphysics is a branch of fantastic literature. They know that a system is nothing more than the subordination of all aspects of the universe to any one such aspect. Even the phrase "all aspects" is rejectable, for it supposes the impossible addition of the present and of all past moments. Neither is it licit to use the plural "past moments," since it supposes another operation....One of the schools of Tlön goes so far as to negate time: it reasons that the present is indefinite, that the future has no reality other than as a present memory. Another school declares that all time has already transpired and that our life is only the crepuscular and no doubt falsified and mutilated memory or reflection of an irrecoverable process. Another, that the history of the universe—and in it our lives and the most tenuous detail of our lives—is the scripture produced by a subordinate god in order to communicate with a demon. Another, that the universe is comparable to those cryptographs in which not all the symbols are valid and that only what happens every three hundred nights is true. Another, that while we sleep here, we are awake elsewhere and that in this way every man is two men.

Amongst the doctrines of Tlön, none has merited the scandalous reception accorded to materialism. Some thinkers have formulated it with less clarity than fervor, as one might put forth a paradox. In order to facilitate the comprehension of this inconceivable thesis, a heresiarch of the eleventh century devised the sophism of the nine copper coins, whose scandalous renown is in Tlön equivalent to that of the Eleatic paradoxes. There are many versions of this "specious reasoning," which vary the number of coins and the number of discoveries; the following is the most common:

On Tuesday, X crosses a deserted road and loses nine copper coins. On Thursday, Y finds in the road four coins, somewhat rusted by Wednesday's rain. On Friday, Z discovers three coins in the road. On Friday morning, X finds two coins in the corridor of his house. The heresiarch would deduce from this story the reality—i.e., the continuity—of the nine coins which were recovered. It is absurd (he affirmed) to imagine that four of the coins have not existed between Tuesday and Thursday, three between Tuesday and Friday afternoon, two between Tuesday and Friday morning. It is logical to think that they have existed—at least in some secret way, hidden from the comprehension of men—at every moment of those three periods.

The language of Tlön resists the formulation of this paradox; most people did not even understand it. The defenders of common sense at first did no more than negate the veracity of the anecdote. They repeated that it was a verbal fallacy, based on the rash application of two neologisms not authorized by usage and alien to all rigorous thought: the verbs "find" and "lose," which beg the question, because they presuppose the identity of the first and of the last nine coins. They recalled that all nouns (man, coin, Thursday, Wednesday, rain) have only a metaphorical value. They denounced the treacherous circumstance "somewhat rusted by Wednesday's rain," which presupposes what is trying to be demonstrated: the persistence of the four coins from Tuesday to Thursday. They explained that equality is one thing and identity another, and formulated a kind of reductio ad absurdum: the hypothetical case of nine men who on nine nights suffer a severe pain. Would it not be ridiculous—they questioned—to pretend that this pain is one and the same? They said that the heresiarch was prompted only by the blasphemous intention of attributing the divine category of being to some simple coins and that at times he negated plurality and at other times did not. They argued: if equality implies identity, one would also have to admit that the nine coins are one.

Unbelievably, these refutations were not definitive. A hundred years after the problem was stated, a thinker no less brilliant than the heresiarch but of orthodox tradition formulated a very daring hypothesis. This happy conjecture affirmed that there is only one subject, that this indivisible subject is every being in the universe and that these beings are the organs and masks of the divinity. X is Y and is Z. Z discovers three coins because he remembers that X lost them; X finds two in the corridor because he remembers that the others have been found.... The Eleventh Volume suggests that three prime reasons determined the complete victory of this idealist pantheism. The first, its repudiation of solipsism; the second, the possibility of preserving the psychological basis of the sciences; the third, the possibility of preserving the cult of the gods. Schopenhauer (the passionate and lucid Schopenhauer) formulates a very similar doctrine in the first volume of *Parerga und Paralipomena*.

The geometry of Tlön comprises two somewhat different disciplines: the visual and the tactile. The latter corresponds to our own geometry and is subordinated to the first. The basis of visual geometry is the surface, not the point. This geometry disregards parallel lines and declares that man in his movement modifies the forms which surround him. The basis of its arithmetic is the notion of indefinite numbers. They emphasize the importance of the concepts of greater and lesser, which our mathematicians symbolize as > and <. They maintain that the operation of counting modifies the quantities and converts them from indefinite into definite sums. The fact that several individuals who count the same quantity would obtain the same result is, for the psychologists, an example of association of ideas or of a good exercise of memory. We already know that in Tlön the subject of knowledge is one and eternal.

In literary practices the idea of a single subject is also all-powerful. It is uncommon for books to be signed. The concept of plagiarism does not exist: it has been established that all works are the creation of one author, who is atemporal and anonymous. The critics often invent authors: they select two dissimilar works—the *Tao Te Ching* and the *1001 Nights*, say—attribute them to the same writer and then determine most scrupulously the psychology of this interesting homme de lettres....

Their books are also different. Works of fiction contain a single plot, with all its imaginable permutations. Those of a philosophical nature invariably include both the thesis and the antithesis, the rigorous pro and con of a doctrine. A book which does not contain its counterbook is considered incomplete.

Centuries and centuries of idealism have not failed to influence reality. In the most ancient regions of Tlön, the duplication of lost objects is not infrequent. Two persons look for a pencil; the first finds it and says nothing; the second finds a second pencil, no less real, but closer to his expectations. These secondary objects are called *hrönir* and are, though awkward in form, somewhat longer. Until recently, the *hrönir* were the accidental products of distraction and forgetfulness. It seems unbelievable that their methodical production dates back scarcely a hundred years, but this is what the Eleventh Volume tells us. The first efforts were unsuccessful. However, the modus operandi merits description. The director of one of the state prisons told his inmates that there were certain tombs in an ancient river bed and promised freedom to whoever might make an important discovery. During the months preceding the excavation the inmates were shown photographs of what they were to find. This first effort proved that expectation and anxiety can be inhibitory; a week's work with pick and shovel did not mange to unearth anything in the way of a *hrön* except a rusty wheel of a period posterior to the experiment. But this was kept in secret and the process was repeated later in four schools. In three of them failure was almost complete; in a fourth (whose director died accidentally during the first excavations) the students unearthed—or produced—a gold mask, an archaic sword, two or three clay urns and the moldy and mutilated torso of a king whose chest bore an inscription which it has not yet been possible to decipher. Thus was discovered the unreliability of witnesses who knew of the experimental nature of the search....Mass investigations produce contradictory objects; now individual and almost improvised jobs are preferred. The methodical fabrication of *hrönir* (says the Eleventh Volume) has performed prodigious services for archaeologists. It has made possible the interrogation and even the modification of the past, which is now no less plastic and docile than the future. Curiously, the *hrönir* of second and third degree—the *hrönir* derived from another *hrön*, those derived from the *hrön* of a *hrön*—exaggerate the aberrations of the initial one; those of fifth degree are almost uniform; those of ninth degree become confused with those of the second; in those of the eleventh there is a purity of line not found in the original. The process is cyclical: the *hrön* of the twelfth degree begins to fall off in quality. Stranger and more pure than any *hrön* is, at times, the *ur*: the object produced through suggestion, educed by hope. The great golden mask I have mentioned is an illustrious example.

Things became duplicated in Tlön; they also tend to become effaced and lose their details when they are forgotten. A classic example is the doorway which survived so long it was visited by a beggar and disappeared at his death. At times some birds, a horse, have saved the ruins of an amphitheater....

—*Salto Oriental, 1940*

Postscript, 1947

...Here I bring the personal part of my narrative to a close. The rest is in the memory (if not in the hopes or fears) of all my readers. Let it suffice for me to recall or mention the following facts, with a mere brevity of words which the reflective recollection of all will enrich or amplify. Around 1944, a person doing research for the newspaper *The American* (of Nashville, Tennessee) brought to light in a Memphis library the forty volumes of the *First Encyclopedia of Tlön*. Even today there is a controversy over whether this discovery was accidental or whether it was permitted by the directors of the still nebulous Orbis Tertius. The latter is most likely. Some of the incredible aspects of the Eleventh Volume (for example, the multiplication of the *hrönir*) have been eliminated or attenuated in the Memphis copies; it is reasonable to imagine that these omissions follow the plan of exhibiting a world which is not too incompatible with the real world. The dissemination of objects from Tlön over different countries would complement this plan....The fact is that the international press infinitely proclaimed the "find." Manuals, anthologies, summaries, literal versions, authorized re-editions and pirated editions of the Greatest Work of Man flooded and still flood the earth. Almost immediately, reality yielded on more than one account. The truth is that it longed to yield. Ten years ago any symmetry with a resemblance of order—dialectical materialism, anti-Semitism, Nazism—was sufficient to entrance the minds of men. How could one do other than submit to Tlön, to the minute and vast evidence of an orderly plan? It is useless to answer that reality is also orderly. Perhaps it is, but in accordance with divine laws—I translate: inhuman laws—which we never quite grasp. Tlön is surely a labyrinth, but it is a labyrinth devised by men, a labyrinth destined to be deciphered by men.

The contact and the habit of Tlön have disintegrated this world. Enchanted by its rigor, humanity forgets over and again that it is a rigor of chess masters, not of angels. Already the schools have been invaded by the (conjectural) "primitive language" of Tlön; already the teaching of its harmonious history (filled with moving episodes) has wiped out the one which governed in my childhood; already a fictitious past occupies in our memories the place of another, a past of which we know nothing with certainty—not even that it is false. Numismatology, pharmacology and archeology have been reformed. I understand that biology and mathematics also await their avatars....A scattered dynasty of solitary men has changed the face of the world. Their task continues. If our forecasts are not in error, a hundred years from now someone will discover the hundred volumes of the Second Encyclopedia of Tlön.

Then English and French and mere Spanish will disappear from the globe. The world will be Tlön. I pay no attention to all this and go on revising, in the still days at the Adrogue hotel, an uncertain Quevedian translation (which I do not intend to publish) of Browne's *Urn Burial.*

PART V

Philosophical Theology

CHAPTER 23

Classical Christian Theology

"Give understanding to faith"

Jesus of Nazareth (4 BCE?–29 CE?), the founder of Christianity, lived in a Hellenized Middle East during the height of the Roman Empire. Alexander the Great (356–323 BCE) spread Greek culture, including Greek philosophy, all the way to the borders of India, forging a civilization that became known as Hellenistic. Greek became the language of intellectual exchange as well as of commerce and law. Judaic scripture, for example, was translated into Greek by 250 BCE.

Alexander's empire fell apart quickly. But Hellenistic culture persisted for many centuries. The Roman Empire eventually included Alexander's, together with Western Europe and northern Africa. Greek culture and ideas were gradually reclothed, with Latin emerging as the cosmopolitan language in the western part of the empire, and Greek retaining that role in the east. Paul and other disciples spread Jesus' teaching throughout the Roman Empire, initially through the medium of Greek.

The Hebrew scriptures, Greek philosophy, the teachings of Jesus, and the writings of Paul have all shaped the development of Christian theology. Christian thinkers have advanced arguments for the existence of God, though many other thinkers have argued that God's existence is a matter of faith rather than reason. Others have sought to construct a *theodicy*, explaining how it is possible for evil to exist in a world created by an all-powerful, all-knowing, and entirely good God.

23.1 AUGUSTINE

Saint Augustine (354–430), a late Church Father, was learned in the scriptures and in Greek philosophy, which he, as an African-born Roman citizen, studied in Latin translation. Plato had the most influence on Augustine; Augustine is in most respects a Platonist, who sees the forms as ideas in the mind of God. Augustine makes several outstanding contributions to Christian theism.

Immanuel Kant takes the injustice of this world as evidence for God's existence and for God's justice in an afterlife. Other philosophers, however, have seen in the world's injustice, evil, and misfortune an argument against God's existence. The argument has its origins in the ancient Greek philosopher Epicurus (341–270 BCE), but it finds its clearest expression in the words of Hume's Philo:

> Epicurus' old questions are yet unanswered. Is he willing to prevent evil, but not able? then he is impotent. Is he able, but not willing? then he is malevolent. Is he both able and willing? whence then is evil?

Hume's argument purports to show that God is either unwilling or unable to prevent evil. If God were omnipotent (all-powerful), omniscient (all-knowing), and entirely good, however, then God would be both willing and able to prevent evil. So the existence of evil shows that God does not exist—or, at least, that God does not have the properties attributed by most religions.

The world's great religions, of course, have long recognized the enigma posed by the existence of evil. The reflections of the Buddha were prompted by his encounter with the three evils of sickness, old age, and death. The book of Job wrestles with the problems posed by a good person's suffering. How can God's goodness and power be reconciled with the existence of suffering?

Augustine formulates the classic Christian response. His solution to the problem of evil has three main components. All attack Hume's premise that, if God is not willing to prevent evil, he is malevolent. The first is that we must judge the universe as a whole, not part by part, for the excellence of the whole may depend on parts that, taken alone, do not seem good. A good life, for example, is not one that contains no adversity, but rather one that contains adversity overcome. A universe with some evil may be better than one without any evil at all. It must therefore be good that there is some evil. By itself, this seems hard to swallow. Why is it good that there are murders, wars, famines, and earthquakes? But theologians have developed it into the doctrine of the general providence of God. When Job challenges God, he responds:

> Where wast thou when I laid the foundations of the earth? declare, if thou hast understanding.
>
> Who hath laid the measures thereof, if thou knowest? or who hath stretched the line upon it?
>
> Whereupon are the foundations thereof fastened? or who laid the corner stone thereof;
>
> When the morning stars sang together, and all the sons of God shouted for joy? (Job 38:4–7)

God, that is, established the universe and the natural laws that govern it. Those laws make possible the stars, the moon, the earth's green fields, blue seas, and purple mountains, and everything that brings joy to human hearts. They make possible the arts of medicine, engineering, and, in short, the entire array of human achievements. But the same laws also make possible murders, wars, famines, and earthquakes. Could God have crafted laws for the universe that would have made possible the good things without also making possible the bad? Or perhaps permit frequent violations of the laws to prevent the bad without thereby disrupting the good? It is not obvious that God could have. Gottfried Leibniz, in fact, argues that God could not have. This is the best of all possible worlds, Leibniz contends, despite its obvious defects, for any attempt to improve it would produce side effects that are even worse.

The second is the doctrine that evil is the absence of good, advocated first by the Plotinus (204–270), a philosopher of Greek ancestry who was born in Egypt and educated in Alexandria and who taught for twenty-six years in Rome. This allows Augustine to say that God does not create evil, for evil is not a thing; it is simply a lack, a thing's failure to be better. God, in fact, cannot create anything perfect; there is only one perfect being, and that is God himself. So, to create anything at all, God must create things that are imperfect. God does not create evil; everything God creates is good. But the gap between the goodness of created things and the perfection of God is what we call evil.

The third is the corruptibility of things—in particular, of human beings, who can exercise free will to do evil. God, for reasons we do not understand, created human beings with the capacity to make choices. People can do good, but can also do evil. Undoubtedly, much evil can be explained as the result of free human choices. In the twentieth century, for example, over 100 million people were killed by their own governments. The litany of such horrors is overwhelming: The Armenian genocide, Stalin's forced famine in the Ukraine, Hitler's death camps, the Gulag archipelago, and Pol Pot's murder of a third of the Cambodian population are only the best-known examples. Tens of millions more have been killed in wars. These are human acts, for which human beings are responsible.

Nevertheless, free will, it appears, cannot explain everything. Some kinds of evil are not the result of human choice. Hurricanes, tornadoes, earthquakes, and diseases strike the just and the unjust independent of human acts of will. The bubonic plague, for example, killed over half the population of Europe in the sixteenth and seventeenth centuries. The Great Plague of London of 1665 killed 68,596, over a third of the city's residents, in just four months. The Lisbon earthquake of 1755 killed over 30,000 people and did much to undermine faith in God during the Enlightenment. In some works, Augustine argues that such events are products of human action, in the sense that they are part of the punishment for original sin, that is, for Adam and Eve's disobedience in the Garden of Eden. In other places, however, he holds that such natural evils can hardly be blamed on the freedom of the human will.

Augustine remains discontent with a free-will defense for a different reason as well. Even if evil results from human free choice, isn't God responsible for giving humans the ability and the will to choose evil? Adam and Eve may have eaten the fruit of the tree in the garden, but God gave them the opportunity and the propensity to eat it. Augustine feels uncomfortable assigning responsibility either to humans or to God; to seek the root of an evil choice "is as if one sought to see darkness, or hear silence." In the end, freedom is unanalyzable: "what cause of willing can there be which is prior to willing?" God did not corrupt Adam and Eve—but he made them corruptible. Even corruptible things are good. As Augustine puts it in the *Confessions*, "whatever is, is good." Evil is not a thing, something God created or chosen by free human beings in its own right.

23.1.1 Augustine, from *Confessions*

Chapter III.—That the Cause of Evil Is the Free Judgment of the Will

4. But I also, as yet, although I said and was firmly persuaded, that You our Lord, the true God, who made not only our souls but our bodies, and not our souls and bodies alone, but all creatures and all things, were uncontaminable and inconvertible, and in no part mutable: yet I did not understand readily and clearly what was the cause of evil. And yet, whatever it was, I perceived that it must be so sought out as not to constrain me by it to believe that the immutable God was mutable, lest I myself should become the thing that I was seeking out. I sought, therefore, for it free from care, certain of the untruthfulness of what these asserted, whom I shunned with my whole heart; for I perceived that through seeking after the origin of evil, they were filled with malice, in that they liked better to think that Your Substance suffered evil than that their own committed it.

5. And I directed my attention to discern what I now heard, that free will was the cause of our doing evil, and Your righteous judgment of our suffering it. But I was unable clearly to discern it. So, then, trying to draw the eye of my mind from that pit, I was plunged again therein, and trying often, was as often plunged back again. But this raised me towards Your light, that I knew as well that I had a will as that I had life: when, therefore, I was willing or unwilling to do anything, I was most certain that it was none but myself that was willing and unwilling; and immediately I perceived that there was the cause of my sin. But what I did against my will I saw that I suffered rather than did, and that I judged not to be my fault but my punishment; whereby, believing You to be most just, I quickly confessed myself to be not unjustly punished. But again I said: "Who made me? Was it not my God, who is not only good but goodness itself? Whence came I then to will to do evil, and to be unwilling to do good, that there might be cause for my just punishment? Who was it that put this in me, and implanted in me the root of bitterness, seeing I was altogether made by my most sweet God? If the devil were the author, whence is that devil? And if he also, by his own perverse will, was a good angel become a devil, whence also was the evil will in him whereby he became a devil, seeing that the angel was made altogether good by that most Good Creator?" By these reflections was I again cast down and stifled; yet not plunged into that hell of error (where no man confesses unto You) to think that You suffer evil rather than that man does it.

Chapter IV.—That God Is Not Corruptible, Who, If He Were, Would Not Be God at All

6. For I was so struggling to find out the rest, as having already found that what was incorruptible must be better than the corruptible; and You, therefore, whatsoever You were, did I acknowledge to be incorruptible. For never yet was, nor will be, a soul able to conceive of anything better than You, who are the highest and best good. But whereas most truly and certainly that which is incorruptible is to be preferred to the corruptible (just as I myself did now prefer it), then, if You were not incorruptible, I could in my thoughts have reached unto something better than my God. Where, then, I saw that the incorruptible was to be preferred to the corruptible, there ought I to seek You, and there observe "whence evil itself was,"

Source: Augustine, *Confessions.* Translated by J. G. Pilkington, in Philip B. Schaff (ed.), *Nicene and Post-Nicene Fathers*, Volume I. Edinburgh: T & T Clark, 1886. We have revised the translation for readability.

that is, whence comes the corruption by which Your substance can by no means be profaned. For corruption, truly, in no way injures our God,—by no will, by no necessity, by no unforeseen chance,—because He is God, and what He wills is good, and Himself is that good; but to be corrupted is not good. Nor are You compelled to do anything against Your will in that Your will is not greater than Your power. But greater should it be were You Yourself greater than Yourself; for the will and power of God is God Himself. And what can be unforeseen by You, who know all things? Nor is there any sort of nature You do not know. And what more should we say "why that substance which God is should not be corruptible," seeing that if it were so it could not be God?

Chapter V.—Questions Concerning the Origin of Evil in Regard to God, Who, Since He Is the Chief Good, Cannot Be the Cause of Evil.

7. And I sought "whence is evil?" And sought in an evil way; nor saw I the evil in my very search. And I set in order before the view of my spirit the whole creation, and whatever we can discern in it, such as earth, sea, air, stars, trees, living creatures; yea, and whatever in it we do not see, as the firmament of heaven, all the angels, too, and all the spiritual inhabitants thereof. But these very beings, as though they were bodies, did my fancy dispose in such and such places, and I made one huge mass of all Your creatures, distinguished according to the kinds of bodies,—some of them being real bodies, some what I myself had feigned for spirits. And this mass I made huge,—not as it was, which I could not know, but as large as I thought well, yet every way finite. But You, O Lord, I imagined on every part environing and penetrating it, though every way infinite; as if there were a sea everywhere, and on every side through immensity nothing but an infinite sea; and it contained within itself some sponge, huge, though finite, so that the sponge would in all its parts be filled from the immeasurable sea. So conceived I Your Creation to be itself finite, and filled by You, the Infinite. And I said, Behold God, and behold what God has created; and God is good, yea, most mightily and incomparably better than all these; but yet He, who is good, has created them good, and behold how He encircles and fills them. Where, then, is evil, and whence, and how crept it in hither? What is its root, and what its seed? Or has it no being at all? Why, then, do we fear and shun that which has no being? Or if we fear it needlessly, then surely is that fear evil whereby the heart is unnecessarily pricked and tormented,—and so much a greater evil, as we have nothing to fear and yet do fear. Therefore either that is evil which we fear or the act of fearing is in itself evil. Whence, therefore, is it, seeing that God, who is good, has made all these things good? He, indeed, the greatest and chiefest Good, has created these lesser goods; but both Creator and created are all good. Whence is evil? Or was there some evil matter of which He made and formed and ordered it, but left something in it which He did not convert into good? But why was this? Was He powerless to change the whole lump, so that no evil should remain in it, seeing that He is omnipotent? Lastly, why would He make anything at all of it, and not rather by the same omnipotency cause it not to be at all? Or could it indeed exist contrary to His will? Or if it were from eternity, why did He permit it so to be for infinite spaces of times in the past, and was pleased so long after to make something out of it? Or if He wished now all of a sudden to do something, this rather should the Omnipotent have accomplished, that this evil matter should not be at all, and that He only should be the whole, true, chief, and infinite Good. Or if it were not good that He, who was good, should not also be the framer and creator of what was good, then that matter which was evil being removed, and brought to nothing, He might form good matter, whereof He might create all things. For He would not be omnipotent were He not able to create something good

without being assisted by that matter which had not been created by Himself. Such like things did I revolve in my miserable breast, overwhelmed with most gnawing cares lest I should die ere I discovered the truth; yet was the faith of Your Christ, our Lord and Saviour, as held in the Catholic Church, fixed firmly in my heart, unformed, indeed, as yet upon many points, and diverging from doctrinal rules, but yet my mind did not utterly leave it, but every day rather drank in more and more of it.

Chapter XII.—Whatever Things the Good God Has Created Are Very Good

18. And it was made clear unto me that those things are good which yet are corrupted, which, neither were they supremely good, nor, unless they were good, could be corrupted; because if supremely good, they were incorruptible, and if not good at all, there was nothing in them to be corrupted. For corruption harms, but, less it could diminish goodness, it could not harm. Either, then, corruption harms not, which cannot be; or, what is most certain, all which is corrupted is deprived of good. But if they be deprived of all good, they will cease to be. For if they be, and cannot be at all corrupted, they will become better, because they shall remain incorruptibly. And what more monstrous than to assert that those things which have lost all their goodness are made better? Therefore, if they shall be deprived of all good, they shall no longer be. So long, therefore, as they are, they are good; therefore whatsoever is, is good. That evil, then, which I sought whence it was, is not any substance; for were it a substance, it would be good. For either it would be an incorruptible substance, and so a chief good, or a corruptible substance, which unless it were good it could not be corrupted. I perceived, therefore, and it was made clear to me, that You made all things good, nor is there any substance at all that was not made by You; and because all that You have made are not equal, therefore all things are; because individually they are good, and altogether very good, because our God made all things very good.

Chapter XIII.—It Is Meet to Praise the Creator for the Good Things Which Are Made in Heaven and Earth

19. And to You is there nothing at all evil, and not only to You, but to Your whole creation; because there is nothing which can break in and mar that order which You have appointed. But in the parts thereof, some things, because they harmonize not with others, are considered evil; whereas those very things harmonize with others, and are good, and in themselves are good. And all these things which do not harmonize together harmonize with the inferior part which we call earth, having its own cloudy and windy sky concordant to it. Far be it from me, then, to say, "These things should not be." For should I see nothing but these, I should indeed desire better; but yet, if only for these, ought I to praise You; for that You are to be praised is shown from the "earth, dragons, and all deeps; fire and hail; snow and vapours; stormy winds fulfilling Your word; mountains and all hills; fruitful trees and all cedars; beasts and all cattle; creeping things and flying fowl; kings of the earth and all people; princes and all judges of the earth; both young men and maidens; old men and children," praise Your name. But when, "from the heavens," these praise You, praise You, our God, "in the heights," all Your "angels," all Your "hosts," "sun and moon," all ye stars and light, "the heavens of heavens," and the "waters that be above the heavens," praise Your name. I did not now desire better things, because I was thinking of all; and with a better judgment I reflected that the things above were better than those below, but that all were better than those above alone.

23.1.2 Augustine, from *Enchiridion*

Chapter 10.—The Supremely Good Creator Made All Things Good

By the Trinity, thus supremely and equally and unchangeably good, all things were created; and these are not supremely and equally and unchangeably good, but yet they are good, even taken separately. Taken as a whole, however, they are very good, because their ensemble constitutes the universe in all its wonderful order and beauty.

Chapter 11.—What Is Called Evil in the Universe Is but the Absence of Good

And in the universe, even that which is called evil, when it is regulated and put in its own place, only enhances our admiration of the good; for we enjoy and value the good more when we compare it with the evil. For the Almighty God, who, as even the heathen acknowledge, has supreme power over all things, being Himself supremely good, would never permit the existence of anything evil among His works, if He were not so omnipotent and good that He can bring good even out of evil. For what is that which we call evil but the absence of good? In the bodies of animals, disease and wounds mean nothing but the absence of health; for when a cure is effected, that does not mean that the evils which were present—namely, the diseases and wounds—go away from the body and dwell elsewhere: they altogether cease to exist; for the wound or disease is not a substance, but a defect in the fleshly substance,—the flesh itself being a substance, and therefore something good, of which those evils—that is, privations of the good which we call health—are accidents. Just in the same way, what are called vices in the soul are nothing but privations of natural good. And when they are cured, they are not transferred elsewhere: when they cease to exist in the healthy soul, they cannot exist anywhere else.

Chapter 12.—All Beings Were Made Good, but Not Being Made Perfectly Good, Are Liable to Corruption

All things that exist, therefore, seeing that the Creator of them all is supremely good, are themselves good. But because they are not, like their Creator, supremely and unchangeably good, their good may be diminished and increased. But for good to be diminished is an evil, although, however much it may be diminished, it is necessary, if the being is to continue, that some good should remain to constitute the being. For however small or of whatever kind the being may be, the good which makes it a being cannot be destroyed without destroying the being itself. An uncorrupted nature is justly held in esteem. But if, still further, it be incorruptible, it is undoubtedly considered of still higher value. When it is corrupted, however, its corruption is an evil, because it is deprived of some sort of good. For if it be deprived of no good, it receives no injury; but it does receive injury, therefore it is deprived of good. Therefore, so long as a being is in process of corruption, there is in it some good of which it is being deprived; and if a part of the being should remain which cannot be corrupted, this will certainly be an incorruptible being, and accordingly the process of corruption will result in the manifestation of this great good. But if it do not cease to be

Source: Augustine, *Enchiridion*. Translated by J. F. Shaw, in Philip B. Schaff (ed.), *Nicene and Post-Nicene Fathers*, Volume III, *Augustine: On the Holy Trinity; Doctrinal Treatises; Moral Treatises*. Edinburgh: T & T Clark, 1873.

corrupted, neither can it cease to possess good of which corruption may deprive it. But if it should be thoroughly and completely consumed by corruption, there will then be no good left, because there will be no being. Wherefore corruption can consume the good only by consuming the being. Every being, therefore, is a good; a great good, if it cannot be corrupted; a little good, if it can: but in any case, only the foolish or ignorant will deny that it is a good. And if it be wholly consumed by corruption, then the corruption itself must cease to exist, as there is no being left in which it can dwell.

Chapter 13.—There Can Be No Evil Where There Is No Good; and an Evil Man Is an Evil Good

Accordingly, there is nothing of what we call evil, if there be nothing good. But a good which is wholly without evil is a perfect good. A good, on the other hand, which contains evil is a faulty or imperfect good; and there can be no evil where there is no good. From all this we arrive at the curious result: that since every being, so far as it is a being, is good, when we say that a faulty being is an evil being, we just seem to say that what is good is evil, and that nothing but what is good can be evil, seeing that every being is good, and that no evil can exist except in a being. Nothing, then, can be evil except something which is good. And although this, when stated, seems to be a contradiction, yet the strictness of reasoning leaves us no escape from the conclusion. We must, however, beware of incurring the prophetic condemnation: "Woe unto them that call evil good, and good evil: that put darkness for light, and light for darkness: that put bitter for sweet, and sweet for bitter." (Isa. v. 20) And yet our Lord says: "An evil man out of the evil treasure of his heart bringeth forth that which is evil." (Luke vi. 45) Now, what is an evil man but an evil being? for a man is a being. Now, if a man is a good thing because he is a being, what is an evil man but an evil good? Yet, when we accurately distinguish these two things, we find that it is not because he is a man that he is an evil, or because he is wicked that he is a good, but that he is a good because he is a man, and an evil because he is wicked. Whoever, then, says, "To be a man is an evil," or, "To be wicked is a good," falls under the prophetic denunciation: "Woe unto them that call evil good, and good evil!" For he condemns the work of God, which is the man, and praises the defect of man, which is the wickedness. Therefore every being, even if it be a defective one, insofar as it is a being is good, and insofar as it is defective is evil.

Chapter 14.—Good and Evil Are an Exception to the Rule That Contrary Attributes Cannot Be Predicated of the Same Subject. Evil Springs Up in What Is Good, and Cannot Exist Except in What Is Good

Accordingly, in the case of these contraries which we call good and evil, the rule of the logicians that two contraries cannot be predicated at the same time of the same thing does not hold. No weather is at the same time dark and bright: no food or drink is at the same time sweet and bitter: no body is at the same time and in the same place black and white: none is at the same time and in the same place deformed and beautiful. And this rule is found to hold in regard to many, indeed nearly all, contraries, that they cannot exist at the same time in any one thing. But although no one can doubt that good and evil are contraries, not only can they exist at the same time, but evil cannot exist without good, or in anything that is not good. Good, however, can exist without evil. For a man or an angel can exist without being wicked; but nothing can be wicked except a man or an angel: and so far as he is a man or an angel, he is good; so far as he is wicked, he is an evil. And these two contraries are so far co-existent, that if good did not exist in what is evil, neither could evil exist; because corruption could not have either a place to dwell in, or a source to spring from, if there were nothing that could be corrupted; and nothing can be corrupted except what is good, for corruption is nothing else but the destruction of good. From what is good, then, evils arose, and except in what is good they do not exist; nor was there any other source from which any evil nature could arise. For if there were, then, insofar as this was a being, it was certainly a good: and a being which was incorruptible would be a great good; and even one which was corruptible must be to some extent a good, for only by corrupting what was good in it could corruption do it harm.

23.2 ANSELM'S ONTOLOGICAL ARGUMENTS

Anselm (1033–1109), Archbishop of Canterbury, presents one of the most famous arguments for God's existence. Starting from a definition of God as "that, the greater than which cannot be conceived," Anselm reasons a priori, or apart from experience, that God exists. Since to exist is better than not to exist, God has to exist to conform to the definition.

1. God is that, the greater than which cannot be conceived.
2. To exist is greater (or better) than not to exist.
3. So God exists.

Imagine a God_0 that had every attribute that a God_1 has (omnipotence, omniscience, omnibenevolence, etc.) except existence. By premise 2, having existence is better than not having it. So only God_1, not God_0, could be God according to Anselm's definition.

Several philosophers, including Descartes (1596–1650), followed Anselm in putting forth a variation of the argument. A contemporary of Anselm's named Gaunilo was an early opponent, who thought the argument would allow us to prove the existence of a perfect island, a perfect valley, etc. David Hume criticized the argument on different grounds: Only experience counts as evidence concerning a question of fact or existence. Concepts in themselves articulate possibilities only. Experience tells us whether a concept is exemplified in the world. In other words, experience tells us what exists.

Immanuel Kant (1724–1804) advanced another critique, insisting that "existence is not a predicate." Existence is not an attribute like any other. The proposition "All triangles have three sides" can be true even if there are no triangles, and we can know it is true. But only experience can tell us that there are indeed triangles in the universe. Similarly, we know that a unicorn would have a single horn whether or not there are in fact any unicorns. But no concept can tell us whether unicorns exist.

Not all philosophers, however, find these criticisms conclusive against all versions of the ontological argument. Anselm puts forth a second argument, also ontological and a priori, that concerns necessary existence rather than existence. This second argument implies that the conceivability of a perfect being is the crux of the issue. A modern version of the argument makes this explicit:

It is possible that there is a God. (The concept of God is consistent.)

It is necessarily true that, if God exists, God exists necessarily.

Therefore, God exists necessarily.

23.2.1 Anselm, from *Proslogion*

Chapter 1: Exciting the Mind to the Contemplation of God

...Let me gaze upon your light, even from far away or from out of the depths. Teach me to seek you, and show yourself to the one who seeks, for I cannot seek you unless you teach me, nor can I find you unless you show yourself. Let me, desiring, seek you; let me, seeking, desire you. Let me, loving, find you; let me, finding, love you.

I recognize, Lord, and give thanks that you created in me your image so that I can remember, think about, and love you. But your image is so sanded by the abrasions of my faults and so obscured by the smoke of my sins that it cannot do what it was made for, unless you renew and reshape it. I do not try to penetrate your height, for my intellect is in no way comparable to that. But I do try to understand to some degree your truth, which my heart believes and loves. For I do not seek to understand in order to believe; I believe in order to understand. For I also believe this: "If I were not to believe, I would not understand."

Chapter 2: God Really Exists

Therefore, O Lord, you who give understanding to faith, let me understand, to the degree you know to be best, that you are—as we believe—and that you are as we believe. And we believe you to be something the greater than which cannot be conceived. Or, is there therefore no such nature, as "the fool has said in his heart that there is no God" (Psalm 13:1, 52:1). But surely that same fool, when he hears what I just said, "something the greater than which cannot be conceived," understands what he hears; and, because he understands, it is in his understanding, even if he were not to understand that it exists. For being in the understanding is one thing, and understanding a thing to exist is another. For when a painter imagines what is to be, he has a certain thing in the understanding, but he does not understand it to exist, because he has not painted it. Once he has really painted it, he both has it in the understanding and understands it to exist, because he has made it.

Even the fool therefore is forced to agree that something, the greater than which cannot be conceived, exists in the understanding, since he understands this when he hears it, and whatever is understood is in the understanding. And surely that, the greater than which cannot be conceived, cannot exist in the understanding alone. For if it exists solely in the understanding, it can be thought to exist in reality, which is greater. If, then, that, the greater than which cannot be conceived, exists in the understanding alone, this same being, than which a greater cannot be conceived, is that than which a greater *can* be thought. But surely this is impossible. Therefore, there can be absolutely no doubt that something, the greater than which cannot be conceived, exists both in the understanding and in reality.

Chapter 3: Because He Cannot Be Conceived Not to Exist

Certainly, this being so truly exists that it cannot even be thought not to exist. For something can be thought to exist that cannot be conceived not to exist, and this is greater than whatever can be thought not to exist. Hence, if that, the greater than which cannot be conceived, can be thought not to exist, then that, the greater than which cannot be conceived, is not the same as that, the greater than which cannot be conceived,

Source: Translated by Daniel Bonevac.

which is absurd. Therefore, something, the greater than which cannot be conceived, exists so truly that it cannot even be thought not to exist.

And You are this being, O Lord, our God. You exist so truly, Lord my God, that You cannot even be thought not to exist. And this is as it should be. For, if a mind could think of something better than You, the creature would rise above its creator and judge its creator, and that is completely absurd. In fact, everything else, except You alone, can be thought not to exist. You alone, then, of all things most truly exist, and therefore of all things possess existence to the highest degree; for anything else does not exist as truly, and possesses existence to a lesser degree. Why, then, is it the case that "the fool says in his heart, 'There is no God,'" when it is obvious to any rational mind that You exist to the highest degree of all? Why, except that he is stupid and a fool?

23.3 THE COSMOLOGICAL ARGUMENTS OF ST. THOMAS AQUINAS

Many philosophers—St. Thomas Aquinas (1225–1274), for example—have been skeptical of a priori arguments for the existence of God such as Anselm's ontological argument. They have agreed with Hume and Kant that existence is not merely a matter of logic and that God's existence cannot be demonstrated on the basis of thought alone. But they have found in the world and our experience of it reasons to believe that God exists. The arguments they advance on the basis of experience are a posteriori.

A posteriori arguments fall into two groups: cosmological arguments, which turn on the idea that the origin of the universe must have some ultimate explanation, and teleological arguments, or arguments from design, which find in nature's intricate design a reason to believe in God. Aquinas advances arguments of both kinds.

Aristotle drafted the first cosmological argument, contending that there must have been a "prime mover" for the universe. His argument, however, is highly complex, and it depends on showing that the "first sphere of heaven" revolves eternally in a circular path. Various early church fathers—notably Athenian philosopher Marcianus Aristides (second century)—tried to simplify the argument.

But it was in the medieval period that Muslim, Jewish, and Christian philosophers devoted serious attention to the cosmological argument as the most important and reliable way of establishing God's existence. Aquinas advances five a posteriori arguments for God's existence, three of which are versions of the cosmological argument.

Here is one version. Every change has a cause other than itself. There cannot be an infinite regress of causes, however, for, if there were, the causal conditions of subsequent changes could never have been fulfilled. So there must have been a first cause—what Aristotle calls the prime mover. And that, Aquinas asserts, is God.

Call the current state of the world *a*. It must have had a cause. That cause must have been earlier than *a* and something other than *a* itself. Call it *b*. But then *b* must have had some other cause, *c*, and so on. The chain of causes (*a*, *b*, *c*,...) cannot be infinite; so there must have been a first cause, God.

Many objections have been raised to this argument. Two are especially obvious. First, why can't the chain of causes be infinite? Aquinas provides little supporting argument: "If you eliminate a cause you also eliminate its effects. Therefore there can be neither a last nor an intermediate cause unless there is a first." But the question is why each cause cannot have some further cause (or even, as Averroes suggests, why the chain of causes cannot loop back on itself). Aquinas offers no answer. Second, why call the first cause God?

Another a posteriori argument in Aquinas relies on necessity and contingency. This argument relies on the premise that "If all things could not be, therefore, at one time there was nothing." This is ambiguous; "all things could not be" could mean either that each thing is such that it might not exist—a reasonable claim, if all things are contingent—or that it is possible for nothing to exist, that is, for everything to fail to exist all at once. That does not follow from anything Aquinas has said. So the argument may rest on a simple fallacy.

Aquinas may, however, have had in mind the following argument. Suppose each thing is contingent and, so, might at some point fail to exist. If there were an infinite series of events stretching back into the past, all possibilities would have been realized at some point in the past; and among those is the situation in which the contingent things cease to exist all at once. That, however, would have made it impossible for anything to exist now. So the existence of some things now shows that such a thing never happened and, thus, that the series of causes cannot be infinite.

Reconstructed in this way, the argument faces two problems. First, that each thing might not exist does not establish that everything might fail to exist all at once, for the existence of things might not be independent issues. Maybe *a* might fail to exist because it could be replaced by *b*, and likewise *b* might fail to exist, being replaced by *a*. Aquinas needs the assumption that one thing's nonexistence never requires the existence of something else. Second, the idea that an infinite past would have realized every possible circumstance seems to rest on an intuitive but sloppy conception of infinity. Consider the infinite series of numbers 2, 4, 6, 8,.... It is infinite, but it does not contain every number. Similarly, a sequence of events could be infinite without containing every possible event.

23.3.1 Thomas Aquinas, from *Summa Theologica*

Question 2. The existence of God: Is the proposition "God exists" self-evident? Is it demonstrable? Does God exist?

Article 1. Whether the existence of God is self-evident?

Objection 1. It seems that the existence of God is self-evident. Now those things are said to be self-evident to us the knowledge of which is naturally implanted in us, as we can see in regard to first principles. But as Damascene says (*De Fide Orth.* i, 1,3), "the knowledge of God is naturally implanted in all." Therefore the existence of God is self-evident.

Objection 2. Further, those things are said to be self-evident which are known as soon as the terms are known, which the Philosopher (1 *Poster.* iii) says is true of the first principles of demonstration. Thus, when the nature of a whole and of a part is known, it is at once recognized that every whole is greater than its part. But as soon as the signification of the word "God" is understood, it is at once seen that God exists. For by this word is signified that thing than which nothing greater can be conceived. But that which exists actually and mentally is greater than that which exists only mentally. Therefore, since as soon as the word "God" is understood it exists mentally, it also follows that it exists actually. Therefore the proposition "God exists" is self-evident.

Objection 3. Further, the existence of truth is self-evident. For whoever denies the existence of truth grants that truth does not exist: and, if truth does not exist, then the proposition "Truth does not exist" is true: and if there is anything true, there must be truth. But God is truth itself: "I am the way, the truth, and the life" (John 14:6). Therefore "God exists" is self-evident.

On the contrary, No one can mentally admit the opposite of what is self-evident; as the Philosopher (*Metaph.* iv, lect. vi) states concerning the first principles of demonstration. But the opposite of the proposition "God is" can be mentally admitted: "The fool said in his heart, There is no God" (Psalm 52:1). Therefore, that God exists is not self-evident.

I answer that, A thing can be self-evident in either of two ways: on the one hand, self-evident in itself though not to us; on the other, self-evident in itself and to us. A proposition is self-evident because the predicate is included in the essence of the subject, as "Man is an animal," for animal is contained in the essence of man. If, therefore, the essence of the predicate and subject be known to all, the proposition will be self-evident to all; as is clear with regard to the first principles of demonstration, the terms of which are common things that no one is ignorant of, such as being and non-being, whole and part, and such like. If, however, there are some to whom the essence of the predicate and subject is unknown, the proposition will be self-evident in itself, but not to those who do not know the meaning of the predicate and subject of the proposition. Therefore, it happens, as Boethius says (*Hebdom.*, the title of which is: "Whether all that is, is good"), "that there are some mental concepts self-evident only to the learned, as that incorporeal substances are not in space." Therefore I say that this proposition, "God exists," of itself is self-evident, for the predicate is the same as the subject, because God is His own existence as will be hereafter shown (3, 4). Now because we do not know the essence of God, the proposition is not self-evident to us, but needs to be demonstrated by things that are more known

Source: *The Summa Theologica of St. Thomas Aquinas.* Translated by Fathers of the English Dominican Province, 1920.

to us, though less known in their nature—namely, by effects.

Reply to Objection 1. To know that God exists in a general and confused way is implanted in us by nature, inasmuch as God is man's beatitude. For man naturally desires happiness, and what is naturally desired by man must be naturally known to him. This, however, is not to know absolutely that God exists; just as to know that someone is approaching is not the same as to know that Peter is approaching, even though it is Peter who is approaching; for many there are who imagine that man's perfect good, which is happiness, consists in riches, and others in pleasures, and others in something else.

Reply to Objection 2. Perhaps not everyone who hears this word "God" understands it to signify something than which nothing greater can be thought, seeing that some have believed God to be a body. Yet, granted that everyone understands that by this word "God" is signified something than which nothing greater can be thought, nevertheless, it does not therefore follow that he understands that what the word signifies exists actually, but only that it exists mentally. Nor can it be argued that it actually exists, unless it be admitted that there actually exists something than which nothing greater can be thought; and this precisely is not admitted by those who hold that God does not exist.

Reply to Objection 3. The existence of truth in general is self-evident but the existence of a Primal Truth is not self-evident to us.

Article 2. Whether it can be demonstrated that God exists?

Objection 1. It seems that the existence of God cannot be demonstrated. For it is an article of faith that God exists. But what is of faith cannot be demonstrated, because a demonstration produces scientific knowledge; whereas faith is of the unseen (Hebrews 11:1). Therefore it cannot be demonstrated that God exists.

Objection 2. Further, the essence is the middle term of demonstration. But we cannot know in what God's essence consists, but solely in what it does not consist; as Damascene says (*De Fide Orth.* i, 4). Therefore we cannot demonstrate that God exists.

Objection 3. Further, if the existence of God were demonstrated, this could only be from His effects. But His effects are not proportionate to Him, since He is infinite and His effects are finite; and between the finite and infinite there is no proportion. Therefore, since a cause cannot be demonstrated by an effect not proportionate to it, it seems that the existence of God cannot be demonstrated.

On the contrary, The Apostle says: "The invisible things of Him are clearly seen, being understood by the things that are made" (Romans 1:20). But this would not be unless the existence of God could be demonstrated through the things that are made; for the first thing we must know of anything is whether it exists.

I answer that, Demonstration can be made in two ways: One is through the cause, and is called "a priori," and this is to argue from what is prior absolutely. The other is through the effect, and is called a demonstration "a posteriori"; this is to argue from what is prior relative only to us. When an effect is better known to us than its cause, from the effect we proceed to the knowledge of the cause. And from every effect the existence of its proper cause can be demonstrated so long as its effects are better known to us; because since every effect depends upon its cause, if the effect exists, the cause must pre-exist. Hence the existence of God, insofar as it is not self-evident to us, can be demonstrated from those of His effects which are known to us.

Reply to Objection 1. The existence of God and other like truths about God, which can be known by natural reason, are not articles of faith, but are preambles to the articles; for faith presupposes natural knowledge, even as grace presupposes nature, and perfection supposes something that can be perfected. Nevertheless, there is nothing to prevent a man, who cannot grasp a proof, accepting, as a matter of faith, something which in itself is capable of being scientifically known and demonstrated.

Reply to Objection 2. When the existence of a cause is demonstrated from an effect, this effect takes the place of the definition of the cause in proof of the cause's existence. This is especially the case in regard to God, because, in order to prove the existence of anything, it is necessary to accept as a middle term the meaning of the word, and not its essence, for the question of its essence follows on the question of its existence. Now the names given to God are derived from His effects; consequently, in demonstrating the existence of God from His effects, we may take for the middle term the meaning of the word "God."

Reply to Objection 3. From effects not proportionate to the cause no perfect knowledge of that cause can be obtained. Yet from every effect the existence of the cause can be clearly demonstrated, and so we can demonstrate the existence of God from His effects; though from them we cannot perfectly know God as He is in His essence.

Article 3. Whether God exists?

Objection 1. It seems that God does not exist, because if one of two contraries be infinite, the other would be altogether destroyed. But the word "God" means that He is infinite goodness. If, therefore, God existed, there would be no evil discoverable; but there is evil in the world. Therefore God does not exist.

Objection 2. Further, it is superfluous to suppose that what can be accounted for by a few principles has been produced by many. But it seems that everything we see in the world can be accounted for by other principles, supposing God did not exist. For all natural things can be reduced to one principle, which is nature; and all voluntary things can be reduced to one principle, which is human reason, or will. Therefore there is no need to suppose God's existence.

On the contrary, It is said in the person of God: "I am Who am." (Exodus 3:14)

I answer that, The existence of God can be proved in five ways.

The first and more manifest way is the argument from motion. It is certain, and evident to our senses, that in the world some things are in motion. Now whatever is in motion is put in motion by another, for nothing can be in motion except it is in potentiality to that towards which it is in motion, whereas a thing moves inasmuch as it is in act[uality]. For motion is nothing else than the reduction of something from potentiality to actuality. But nothing can be reduced from potentiality to actuality except by something in a state of actuality. Thus that which is actually hot, as fire, makes wood, which is potentially hot, to be actually hot, and thereby moves and changes it. Now it is not possible that the same thing should be at once in actuality and potentiality in the same respect, but only in different respects. For what is actually hot cannot simultaneously be potentially hot, but it is simultaneously potentially cold. It is therefore impossible that in the same respect and in the same way a thing should be both mover and moved, i.e., that it should move itself. Therefore, whatever is in motion must be put in motion by another. If that by which it is put in motion be itself put in motion, then this also must needs be put in motion by another, and that by another again. But this cannot go on to infinity, because then there would be no first mover, and, consequently, no other mover; seeing that subsequent movers move only inasmuch as they are put in motion by the first mover; as the staff moves only because it is put in motion by the hand. Therefore it is necessary to arrive at a first mover put in motion by no other, and this everyone understands to be God.

The second way is from the nature of the efficient cause. In the world of sense we find there is an order of efficient causes. There is no case known (neither is it, indeed, possible) in which a thing is found to be the efficient cause of itself; for so it would be prior to itself, which is impossible.

Now in efficient causes it is not possible to go on to infinity, because in all efficient causes following in order, the first is the cause of the intermediate cause, and the intermediate is the cause of the ultimate cause, whether the intermediate cause be several or only one. Now to take away the cause is to take away the effect. Therefore, if there be no first cause among efficient causes, there will be no ultimate, nor any intermediate cause. But if in efficient causes it is possible to go on to infinity, there will be no first efficient cause, neither will there be an ultimate effect, nor any intermediate efficient causes; all of which is plainly false. Therefore it is necessary to admit a first efficient cause, to which everyone gives the name of God.

The third way is taken from possibility and necessity, and runs thus. We find in nature things that are possible to be and not to be, since they are found to be generated and to corrupt, and, consequently, they are possible to be and not to be. But it is impossible for these always to exist, for that which is possible not to be at some time is not. Therefore, if everything is possible not to be, then at one time there could have been nothing in existence. Now if this were true, even now there would be nothing in existence, because that which does not exist only begins to exist by something already existing. Therefore, if at one time nothing was in existence, it would have been impossible for anything to have begun to exist; and thus even now nothing would be in existence—which is absurd. Therefore, not all beings are merely possible, but there must exist something the existence of which is necessary. But every necessary thing either has its necessity caused by another or not. Now it is impossible to go on to infinity in necessary things which have their necessity caused by another, as has been already proved in regard to efficient causes. Therefore we cannot but postulate the existence of some being having of itself its own necessity, and not receiving it from another, but rather causing in others their necessity. This all men speak of as God.

The fourth way is taken from the gradation to be found in things. Among beings there are some more and some less good, true, noble and the like. But "more" and "less" are predicated of different things, according as they resemble in their different ways something which is the maximum, as a thing is said to be hotter according as it more nearly resembles that which is hottest; so that there is something which is truest, something best, something noblest and, consequently, something which is uttermost being; for those things that are greatest in truth are greatest in being, as it is written in *Metaph.* ii. Now the maximum in any genus is the cause of all in that genus; as fire, which is the maximum heat, is the cause of all hot things. Therefore there must also be something which is to all beings the cause of their being, goodness, and every other perfection; and this we call God.

The fifth way is taken from the governance of the world. We see that things which lack intelligence, such as natural bodies, act for an end, and this is evident from their acting always, or nearly always, in the same way, so as to obtain the best result. Hence it is plain that not fortuitously, but designedly, do they achieve their end. Now whatever lacks intelligence cannot move towards an end unless it be directed by some being endowed with knowledge and intelligence; as the arrow is shot to its mark by the archer. Therefore some intelligent being exists by whom all natural things are directed to their end; and this being we call God.

Reply to Objection 1. As Augustine says (*Enchiridion* xi): "Since God is the highest good, He would not allow any evil to exist in His works, unless His omnipotence and goodness were such as to bring good even out of evil." This is part of the infinite goodness of God, that He should allow evil to exist, and out of it produce good.

Reply to Objection 2. Since nature works for a determinate end under the direction of a higher agent, whatever is done by nature must needs be traced back to God, as to its first cause. So also whatever is done voluntarily must also be traced back to some higher cause other than human reason or will, since these can change or fail; for all things that are changeable and capable of defect must be traced back to an immovable and self-necessary first principle, as was shown in the body of the Article.

23.4 THE CHRISTIAN MYSTICISM OF JULIAN OF NORWICH

We know little about the life of Julian of Norwich (1342–1416?) except that when she was 30 she became seriously ill and had a mystical experience in which Jesus appeared to her and revealed a series of truths. She described them in two works, written in English: *Showings* and *Revelations of Divine Love*. She took up residence at a parish church, St. Julian, in Norwich, England, by 1394, and was still there in 1416. Julian's message of mystical insight, her stress on the importance of love, and her assurance that all will be well inspired an age shaken by the Black Plague, the Papal Schism, and the Hundred Years' War.

Julian feels Christ's pain intensely—not only his physical pain on the cross, which she describes in medically accurate detail, but also his mental pain at human sin—but she also feels God's overwhelming love. We are capable of forming a close relationship with God, so the soul and God become close friends, intimately connected, feeling each other's wounds but also feeling each other's love. Our soul has a dual nature: an outer nature turned toward the world, which feels desire and is prone to sin, and an inner nature in close communion with God.

Awareness of our close relationship with God reveals God's great love for the world, his plan which, in the end, will turn out for the best. It is our obligation to act in a way consistent with God's love. Julian's mystical vision of God everywhere, even in what is regarded as sin, sparks an *instrumentalist theodicy*: Pain, she reasons, including what we call sin, is an instrument that God uses for our benefit.

23.4.1 Julian of Norwich, from *Revelations of Divine Love*

Chapter XI

"Everything that is done, it is well done: for our Lord God does all." "Sin is no deed." And after this I saw God in a point, that is to say, in my understanding,—by which sight I saw that He is in all things. I beheld and considered, seeing and knowing in sight, with a soft dread, and thought: What is sin? For I saw truly that God does every-thing, be it ever so little. And I saw truly that

Source: *Revelations of Divine Love*, Recorded by Julian, Anchoress at Norwich, 1373. From the British Museum manuscript, edited by Grace Warrack. London: Methuen and Company, 1901.

nothing is done by hap nor by adventure, but all things by the foreseeing wisdom of God: if it be hap or adventure in the sight of man, our blindness and our unforesight is the cause. For the things that are in the foreseeing wisdom of God from without beginning (which rightfully and worshipfully and continually He leads to the best end) as they come about fall to us suddenly, ourselves unwitting; and thus by our blindness and our unforesight we say: these be haps and adventures. But to our Lord God they be not so.

Wherefore it behooves me to grant that everything that is done, it is well done: for our Lord God does all. For in this time the working of creatures was not shown, but [the working] of our Lord God in the creature: for He is in the midpoint of all things, and all He does. And I was certain He does no sin.

And here I saw verily that sin is no deed: for in all this was not sin shown. And I would no longer marvel in this, but beheld our Lord, what He would show.

And thus, as much as it might be for the time, the rightfulness of God's working was shown to the soul. Rightfulness has two fair properties: it is right and it is full. And so are all the works of our Lord God: thereto needs neither the working of mercy nor grace: for they be all rightful: wherein fails nought. But in another time He gave a showing for the beholding of sin nakedly, as I shall tell, where He uses working of mercy and grace. And this vision was shown to my understanding, for that our Lord would have the soul turned truly unto the beholding of Him, and generally of all His works. For they are full good; and all His doings are easy and sweet, and to great ease bringing the soul that is turned from the beholding of the blind deeming of man unto the fair sweet deeming of our Lord God. For a man beholds some deeds well done and some deeds evil, but our Lord beholds them not so: for as all that has being in nature is of Godly making, so is all that is done, in property of God's doing. For it is easy to understand that the best deed is well done: and so well as the best deed is done—the highest—so well is the least deed done; and all thing in its property and in the order that our Lord has ordained it to from without beginning. For there is no doer but He.

I saw full surely that he changes never His purpose in no manner of thing, nor never shall, without end. For there was no thing unknown to Him in His rightful ordinance from without beginning. And therefore everything was set in order ere anything was made, as it should stand without end; and no manner of thing shall fail of that point. For He made all things in fullness of goodness, and therefore the blessed Trinity is ever full pleased in all His works. And all this showed He full blissfully, signifying thus: See! I am God: see! I am in all things: see! I do all things: see! I lift never mine hands off my works, nor ever shall, without end: see! I lead all things to the end I ordained to them from without beginning, by the same Might, Wisdom and Love whereby I made it. How should anything be amiss? Thus mightily, wisely, and lovingly was the soul examined in this Vision. Then saw I soothly [truly] that it behooved me to assent, with great reverence enjoying in God.

Chapter LXV

"The Charity of God makes in us such a unity that, when it is truly seen, no man can part himself from other." And thus I understood that what man or woman with firm will chooses God in this life, for love, he may be sure that he is loved without end: which endless love works in him that grace. For He wills that we be as assured in hope of the bliss of heaven while we are here, as we shall be in sureness while we are there. And ever the more pleasance and joy that we take in this sureness, with reverence and meekness, the better please Him, as it was shown. This reverence that I mean is a holy courteous dread of our Lord, to which meekness is united: and that is, that a creature see the Lord marvellous great and itself marvellous little. For these virtues are had endlessly by the loved of God, and this may now be seen and felt in measure through the gracious presence of our Lord when it is [seen]: which presence in all things is most desired, for it works marvellous assuredness in true faith, and sure hope, by greatness of charity, in dread that is sweet and delectable. It is God's will that I see myself as much bound to Him in love as if He had done for me all that He has done; and thus should every soul think inwardly of its Lover. That is to say, the Charity of God makes in us such a unity that, when it is truly seen, no man can part himself from other. And thus ought our soul to think that God has done for it all that He has done. And this shows He to make us to love Him and nought dread but Him. For it is His will that we perceive that all the might of our enemy is taken into our friend's hand; and therefore the soul that knows assuredly this, he shall not dread but Him that he loveth. All other dread he sets among passions and bodily sickness and imaginations. And therefore though we be in so much pain, woe, and distress that it seems to us we can think [of] right nought but [of] that [which] we are in, or [of] that [which] we feel, [yet] as soon as we may, pass we lightly over, and set we it at nought. And why? For that God wills we know [Him]; and if we know Him and love Him and reverently dread Him, we shall have peace, and be in great rest, and it shall be great pleasance to us, all that He does. And this shown our Lord in these words: What should it then aggrieve thee to suffer awhile, since it is my Will and my worship?

Chapter XXVII

"Often I wondered why by the great foreseeing wisdom of God the beginning of sin was not hindered: for then, methought, all should have been well." "Sin is behovable—[plays a needful part]—; but all shall be well."

After this the Lord brought to my mind the longing that I had to Him afore. And I saw that nothing lets me but sin. And so I looked, generally, upon us all, and methought: If sin had not been, we should all have been clean and like to our Lord, as He made us.

And thus, in my folly, afore this time often I wondered why by the great foreseeing wisdom of God the beginning of sin was not letted: for then, methought, all should have been well. This stirring [of mind] was much to be forsaken, but nevertheless mourning and sorrow I made therefore, without reason and discretion. But Jesus, who in this Vision informed me of all that is needful to me, answered by this word and said: It behoved that there should be sin; but all shall be well, and all shall be well, and all manner of thing shall be well.

In this naked word sin, our Lord brought to my mind, generally, all that is not good, and the shameful despite and the utter noughting that He bare for us in this life, and His dying; and all the pains and passions of all His creatures, ghostly and bodily; (for we be all partly noughted, and we shall be noughted following our Master, Jesus, till we be full purged, that is to say, till we be fully noughted of our deadly flesh and of all our inward affections which are not very good); and the beholding of this, with all pains that ever were or ever shall be,—and with all these I understand the Passion of Christ for most pain and overpassing. All this was shown in a touch and quickly passed over into comfort: for our good Lord would not that the soul were affeared of this terrible sight.

But I saw not sin: for I believe it has no manner of substance nor no part of being, nor could it be known but by the pain it is cause of. And thus pain, it is something, as to my sight, for a time; for it purgeth, and makes us to know ourselves and to ask mercy. For the Passion of our Lord is comfort to us against all this, and so is His blessed will. And for the tender love that our good Lord has to all that shall be saved, He comforts readily and sweetly, signifying thus: It is sooth [true] that sin is cause of all this pain; but all shall be well, and all shall be well, and all manner [of] thing shall be well. These words were said full tenderly, showing no manner of blame to me nor to any that shall be saved. Then were it a great unkindness to blame or wonder on God for my sin, since He blames not me for sin.

And in these words I saw a marvellous high mystery hid in God, which mystery He shall openly make known to us in Heaven: in which knowing we shall verily see the cause why He suffered sin to come. In which sight we shall endlessly joy in our Lord God.

CHAPTER 24

Medieval Islamic Theology

"The truly living God"

Is there a God? If so, can we prove it? Can we know it? What is God like? How does God relate to the world and, in particular, to us? Muslim thinkers have wrestled with these questions for centuries. They agree that God exists and is one. But there is no such consensus about the extent to which we can know God.

24.1 IBN SINA (AVICENNA) ON THE EXISTENCE OF GOD

The Islamic theologian Ibn Sina (Avicenna; 980–1037) expresses an idea of God that draws on Greek thought as well as the Koran. He presents an argument for the existence of God known as the cosmological argument, which was first forged by Aristotle. Avicenna defines God as the necessary being. Created things are all contingent. The way God exists is thus different from the way a chair exists, for example, in that the chair, but not God, could cease to exist or could have failed to exist. Avicenna takes pains to show that God cannot be an effect in any way. God is not brought about receptively (as the effect of an active or instrumental cause, as a pot of a potter), not materially (as a pot of clay), not formally (as clay coming to possess the form of a pot), and not finally or teleologically (as a pot exists for the sake of the uses to which it can be put). As with Aristotle, argument dominates Avicenna's writing; there is little exposition of views that is not presented in the form of tight deductive reasoning.

The oldest argument within Western rational theology is based on causality, the first-cause argument. We see that an effect e_1 arises from a cause c_1, but c_1 is also an effect arising from another cause, c_2, which is, in turn, an effect, and so on. There cannot be an infinite backward series because there would be nothing to get the series started. Thus it would appear that there has to be a first cause if there are to be effects at all. This first cause, it is concluded, is God (presumably the best candidate), who is uncaused, has intrinsic existence, or is self-caused or self-sufficient.

The argument is adumbrated in Plato (*Laws* 10.884–889d). Aristotle gives it clearer expression, expanding it to include God as the ultimate final or motivating cause (the unmoved Mover) as well as the first in a series of active or efficient causes. One line of Aristotle's argument is reformulated by a neoplatonist, Proclus (410?–485 CE) and then refined into its classical formulation by a series of Islamic philosophers.

Critics have usually responded (a) by alleging there is no difficulty in admitting an infinite backward series of causes and effects and/or (b) by claiming that without another source of information about the first cause such positing is worthless.

Ibn Sina's use of necessity and contingency is meant to circumvent these objections. Anything that does not exist necessarily (i.e., that can be imagined not to exist) has to have a reason for existing. (Leibniz calls this the Principle of Sufficient Reason.) An infinite backward series would mean that there would be no reason (or cause) to originate the series of contingencies, and so there would be nothing at all. Or, if there is supposed to be an infinite causal loop or circle, that would mean that two elements would have to be both cause and effect with respect to one another—an impossibility, says Avicenna. Thus without a necessary being, there would be no reason for the first contingency to come into being; similarly, there would be no reason for an entire causal chain (itself a contingency). Thus the chain of reasons (or causes) must terminate in a necessarily existing being, God. There cannot be an infinite series of contingencies, Avicenna implies, since something exists.

Nothing that is brought about exists necessarily but, rather, contingently. The universe as a whole is an effect and thus exists contingently. Such a contingency could come about only by being caused, or created, by God, who exists necessarily. Why is there something rather than nothing? (Since the world exists contingently, there could have been nothing.) Answer: God, who exists necessarily, creates a universe that did not have to be.

Critics have responded to the arguments about contingency as they have to the first-cause argument: (a) An infinite series of contingencies presents no difficulty, and/or (b) without information from another source about the supposedly necessary being, such a supposition does not tell us very much. There may be a necessary being, but what is it like? Nothing in the argument provides an answer.

24.1.1 Avicenna, from *On the Nature of God*

That There Is a Necessary Being

Whatever has being must either have a reason for its being or have no reason for it. If it has a reason, then it is contingent, equally before it comes into being (if we make this mental hypothesis) and when it is in the state of being—for in the case of a thing whose being is contingent

Source: *Avicenna on Theology*. Translated by Arthur J. Arberry. London: John Murray, 1951.

the mere fact of its entering upon being does not remove from it the contingent nature of its being. If on the other hand it has no reason for its being in any way whatsoever, then it is necessary in its being. This rule having been confirmed, I shall now proceed to prove that there is in being a being which has no reason for its being.

Such a being is either contingent or necessary. If it is necessary, then the point we sought to prove is established. If on the other hand it is contingent, that which is contingent cannot enter upon being except for some reason which sways the scales in favour of its being and against its not-being. If the reason is also contingent, there is then a chain of contingents linked one to the other, and there is no being at all; for this being which is the subject of our hypothesis cannot enter into being so long as it is not preceded by an infinite succession of beings, which is absurd. Therefore contingent beings end in a Necessary Being.

Of the Unicity of God

It is not possible in any way that the Necessary Being should be two. Demonstration: Let us suppose that there is another necessary being: one must be distinguishable from the other, so that the terms "this" and "that" may be used with reference to them. This distinction must be either essential or accidental. If the distinction between them is accidental, this accidental element cannot but be present in each of them, or in one and not the other. If each of them has an accidental element by which it is distinguished from the other, both of them must be caused; for an accident is what is adjoined to a thing after its essence is realized. If the accidental element is regarded as adhering to its being, and is present in one of the two and not in the other, then the one which has no accidental element is a necessary being and the other is not a necessary being. If, however, the distinction is essential, the element of essentiality is that whereby the essence as such subsists; and if this element of essentiality is different in each and the two are distinguishable by virtue of it, then each of the two must be a compound; and compounds are caused; so that neither of them will be a necessary being. If the element of essentiality belongs to one only, and the other is one in every respect and there is no compounding of any kind in it, then the one which has no element of essentiality is a necessary being, and the other is not a necessary being. Since it is thus established that the Necessary Being cannot be two, but is All Truth, then by virtue of His Essential Reality, in respect of which He is a Truth, He is United and One, and no other shares with Him in that Unity: however the All-Truth attains existence, it is through Himself.

His Attributes as Interpreted According to the Foregoing Principles

Since it is established that God is a Necessary Being, that He is One in every respect, that He is exalted above all causes, and that He has no reason of any kind for His Being; since it is further established that His Attributes do not augment His Essence, and that He is qualified by the Attributes of Praise and Perfection; it follows necessarily that we must state that He is Knowing, Living, Willing, Omnipotent, Speaking, Seeing, Hearing, and Possessed of all the other Loveliest Attributes. It is also necessary to recognize that His Attributes are to be classified as negative, positive, and a compound of the two: since His Attributes are of this order, it follows that their multiplicity does not destroy His Unity or contradict the necessary nature of His Being. Pre-eternity for instance is essentially the negation of not-being in the first place, and the denial of causality and of primality in the second place; similarly the term One means that He is indivisible in every respect, both verbally and actually. When it is stated that He is a Necessary Being, this means that He is a Being without a cause, and that He is the Cause of other than Himself: this is a combination of the negative and the positive. Examples of the positive Attributes are His being Creator, Originator, Shaper, and the entire Attributes of Action. As for the compound of both, this kind is illustrated by His being Willing and Omnipotent, for these Attributes are a compound of Knowledge with the addition of Creativeness.

24.2 AL-GHAZALI'S CRITIQUE OF THEOLOGY AND AVERROES' DEFENSE

Avicenna's cosmological argument appears in European philosophy as Aquinas's third way. It prompted many debates in Islamic circles. The argument's chief critic was Abu Hamid Muhammad al-Ghazali (1058–1111), known to medieval philosophers in the West as Algazel. He was born in a village in northeastern Persia. He became a professor and rector at Nizamiya University in Baghdad but resigned to live the ascetic life of a Sufi mystic.

Most of al-Ghazali's philosophical work attacks the possibility of metaphysical knowledge and, more generally, the utility of reason. In *The Incoherence of the Philosophers*, he tries to refute many standard philosophical views and the arguments that al-Farabi, Avicenna, and other philosophers use to support them. In particular al-Ghazali argues that the philosophers have been unsuccessful in trying to show that God exists. He uses philosophical arguments to try to demonstrate that philosophical argument on religious subjects is pointless.

Al-Ghazali's assault on the cosmological argument is straightforward. The argument depends on the impossibility of an infinite regress. But that premise is not obvious; where is the argument for it?

It cannot be immediate (that is, self-evident), al-Ghazali argues, for even such defenders of the cosmological argument as Aristotle, al-Farabi, and Avicenna hold that the world or certain portions of it are eternal. In any case it is not obvious on its face. So it must be the conclusion of an argument.

Al-Ghazali imagines an argument for it, which goes like this. Suppose that there were an infinite regress of causes or reasons for being, so that *a* exists because of *b*, which exists because of *c*, etc. The whole series (*a*, *b*, *c*, ...) would have to be necessary or contingent. But it can be neither. The idea of a necessary being made up of contingent beings is absurd, while the idea of the series depending on something outside itself is also absurd, since each element of the series depends on subsequent elements and nothing else.

Al-Ghazali rejects this argument. He sees no problem with the idea of a necessary being made up of contingent beings. The cosmological argument, then, fails, because the necessary being—the being having no reason for its being—whose existence it demonstrates may just be the world and its sequence of temporal events. The principles we use to reason about temporal events, moreover, may not apply to the world as a whole.

Averroes (ibn Rushd; 1126–1198), born in Córdoba, Spain, became a judge in Seville and then Córdoba, eventually, like his father and grandfather before him, becoming chief judge. Because of the growing intolerance of Islamic fundamentalists, however, he had to flee Spain, and he lived much of his life in exile in Morocco. He was an immensely influential philosopher who wrote many commentaries on Aristotle and tried to harmonize religion and philosophy.

In *The Incoherence of the Incoherence* Averroes attacks al-Ghazali's critiques of philosophical arguments and his implicit assertion that reason cannot discover religious truth. He agrees with al-Ghazali that Avicenna's proof does not work as it stands. It runs together two notions of "cause" or "for a reason." A cause may precede its effect in time and bring it into being, as a builder constructs a house or a swing of a bat propels a baseball over a fence. But an effect may also depend on a cause in a different way. A desk, for example, may be thirty inches high because its legs are twenty-eight inches long and its top is two inches thick. But the length of the legs, the thickness of the top, and the height of the desk are not events, and their relation is not one of temporal precedence. The sense in which the height of the desk depends on the length of its legs and the thickness of its top, Averroes holds, is precisely the sense in which the world depends on God.

That means that "contingent" and "necessary" are ambiguous. We may call something contingent if it is the effect of a temporally preceding cause; the contingent, in this sense, is what has a causal explanation. The necessary, in this sense, is what cannot be explained causally. But we may also call something contingent in another sense if it depends on something else, and necessary if it does not.

Averroes sees in al-Ghazali's criticism the seeds of a successful argument. To be precise, let's restrict "contingent" and "necessary" to the first sense we delineated (that is, "having a cause" and "not having a cause") and use "dependent" and "independent" for the second. Al-Ghazali holds that a necessary being could be made up of contingent beings. So, he concludes, Avicenna's cosmological argument shows little, for the being without a reason for its own being might just be the universe, the totality of contingent beings itself. Averroes, in effect, agrees. He maintains, however, that we can apply the same form of argument to the necessary being—that is, the being having no causal explanation—but using the other sense of "contingent" and "necessary." The being having no causal explanation may be dependent or independent. There cannot be an infinite regress of dependence, or the conditions on which the necessary being depends could never be satisfied. So there must be something that is necessary in both senses—that has no causal explanation and depends on nothing else.

Could this necessary being just be the universe? No. Averroes' argument depends on a further argument, that the world must be eternal and, in particular, that the natural kinds of things in the universe (which he calls, using Aristotle's term, the genera) are eternal. Averroes uses its conclusion to argue that anything on which the eternal depends must be infinite, as only God can be. Averroes' argument relies on a principle familiar from Descartes' argument for God from thought, that the cause must contain at least as much reality as the effect. The world is in some respects infinite; thus the cause of the world must be infinite as well. It remains open to question, however, why this infinite cause must be God.

24.2.1 Averroes, from *The Incoherence of the Incoherence*; Al-Ghazali, from *The Incoherence of the Philosophers*

The Fourth Discussion Showing that They Are Unable to Prove the Existence of a Creator of the World

Ghazali says:

> We say: Mankind is divided into two categories; one, the men of truth who have acknowledged that the world has become and know by necessity that what has become does not become by itself but needs a creator, and the reasonableness of their view lies in their affirmation of a creator; the other, the materialists, believe the world, in the state in which it exists, to be eternal and do not attribute a creator to it, and their doctrine is intelligible, although their proof shows its inanity. But as to the philosophers, they believe the world to be eternal and still attribute a creator to it. This theory is self-contradictory and needs no refutation.

I say:

The theory of the philosophers is, because of the factual evidence, more intelligible than both the other theories together. There are two kinds of agent: (1) the agent to which the object which proceeds from it is only attached during the process of its becoming; once this process is finished, the object is not any more in need of it—for instance, the coming into existence of a house through the builder; (2) the agent from which nothing proceeds but an act which has no other existence than its dependence on it. The distinctive mark of this act is that it is convertible with the existence of its object, i.e., when the act does not exist the object does not exist, and when the act exists the object exists—they are inseparable. This kind of agent is superior to the former and is more truly an agent, for this agent brings its object to being and conserves it, whereas the other agent only brings its objects to being, but requires another agent for its further conservation. The mover is such a superior agent in relation to the moved and to the things whose existence consists only in their movement. The philosophers, believing that movement is the act of a mover and that the existence of the world is only perfected through motion, say that the agent of motion is the agent of the world, and if the agent refrained for only one moment from its action, the world would be annihilated. They use the following syllogism: The world is an act, or a thing whose existence is consequent upon this act. Each act by its existence implies the existence of an agent. Therefore the world has an agent existing by reason of its existence. The man who regards it as necessary that the act which proceeds from the agent of the world should have begun in time says: The world is temporal through an eternal agent. But the man for whom the act of the Eternal is eternal says: The world has come into being, from an eternal agent having an eternal act, i.e., an act without beginning or end; which does, however, not mean that the world is eternal by itself, as people who call the world eternal imagine it to be.

Ghazali says, on behalf of the philosophers:

> The philosophers might answer: When we affirm that the world has a creator, we do not understand thereby a voluntary agent who acts after not having acted, as we observe in the various kinds of agents, like tailors, weavers, and builders, but we mean the cause of the world, and we call it the First Principle, understanding by this that there is no cause for its existence, but that it is a cause of the existence of other things; and

Source: Averroes, *Tahafut al Tahafut (The Incoherence of the Incoherence)*. Translated by Simon van den Bergh. London: Luzac and Company, 1954.

> if we call this principle the Creator, it is in this sense. It is easy to establish by a strict proof an existent for the existence of which there is no cause. For we say that the world and its existents either have a cause or have not. If it has a cause, this cause itself either has or has not a cause, and the same can be said about the latter cause, and either we go on ad infinitum in this way, and this is absurd, or we arrive at a last term, and this end is the First Cause, which has no cause for its existence and which we call First Principle. And if the world existed by itself without cause, then it would be clear what the First Principle is, for we only mean by it an existent without a cause and which is necessarily eternal. However, it is not possible that the First Principle should be the heavens, for there are many of these and the proof of unity contradicts this, and its impossibility is shown on examination of the attribute of the principle. Nor can it be said that one single heaven, or one single body, the sun or any other body, can be the First Principle; for all these are bodies, and body is composed of matter and form, and the First Principle cannot be composite, as is clear on a second examination. Our intention is to show that an existent which has no cause is eternal by necessity and by universal consent, and only about its qualities is there a divergence of opinion. And this is what we mean by a first principle.

I say:

This argument carries a certain conviction, but still it is not true. For the term "cause" is attributed equivocally to the four causes, agent, form, matter, and end. Therefore if this were the answer of the philosophers, it would be defective. For if they were asked which cause they mean by their statement that the world has a first cause, and if they answered, "That agent whose act is uncreated and everlasting, and whose object is identical with its act," their answer would be true according to their doctrine; for against this conception, in the way we expounded it, there is no objection. But if they answered, "The formal cause," the objection would be raised whether they supposed the form of the world to subsist by itself in the world, and if they answered, "We mean a form separate from matter," their statement would be in harmony with their theory; but if they answered, "We mean a form in matter," this would imply that the First Principle was not something incorporeal; and this does not accord with philosophical doctrine. Further, if they said, "It is a cause which acts for an end," this again would agree with the philosophical doctrine. As you see, this statement is capable of many interpretations, and how can it be represented there as an answer of the philosophers?

And as to Ghazali's words

> We call it the First Principle, understanding by this that there is no cause for its existence, but that it is a cause for the existence of other things.

This again is a defective statement, for this might be said also of the first sphere, or of heaven in its entirety, or generally of any kind of existents which could be supposed to exist without a cause; and between this and the materialistic theory there is no difference.

And as to Ghazali's words:

> It is easy to establish by a strict proof an existent for the existence of which there is no cause.

This again is a defective statement, for the causes must be specified, and it must be shown that each kind has an initial term without cause—that is, that the agents lead upwards to a first agent, the formal causes to a first form, the material causes to a first matter, and the final causes to a first end. And then it must still be shown that these four ultimate causes lead to a first cause. This is not clear from the statement as he expresses it here.

And in the same way the statement in which he brings a proof for the existence of a first cause is defective, i.e., his statement:

> For we say that the world and its existents either have a cause or have not.

For the term "cause" is used in an equivocal way. And similarly the infinite regress of causes is according to philosophical doctrine in one way impossible, in another way necessary; impossible when this regress is essential and in a straight line and the prior cause is a condition of the existence of the posterior, not impossible when this regress is accidental and circular, when the prior is not a condition for the posterior and when there exists an essential first cause—for instance, the origin of rain from a cloud, the origin of a cloud from vapour, the origin of vapour from rain. And this is according to the philosophers an eternal circular process, which of necessity, however, presupposes a first cause. And similarly the coming into existence of one man from another is an eternal process, for in such cases the existence of the prior is not a condition for the existence of the posterior; indeed, the destruction of some of them is often a necessary condition. This kind of cause leads upwards to an eternal first cause which acts in each individual member of the series of causes at the moment of the becoming of its final effect; for instance, when Socrates engenders Plato, the ultimate mover, according to the philosophers, is the highest sphere, or the soul, or the intellect, or all together, or God the Creator. And therefore Aristotle says that a man and the sun together engender a man, and it is clear that the sun leads upwards to its mover and its mover to the First Principle. Therefore the past man is not a condition for the existence of the future man. Similarly, when an artisan produces successively a series of products of craftsmanship with different instruments, and produces these instruments through instruments and the latter again through other instruments, the becoming of these instruments one from another is something accidental, and none of these instruments is a condition for the existence of the product of craftsmanship except the first instrument which is in immediate contact with the work produced. Now the father is necessary for the coming into existence of the son in the same way as the instrument which comes into immediate contact with the product of craftsmanship is necessary for its coming into existence. And the instrument with which this instrument is produced will be necessary for the production of this instrument, but will not be necessary for the production of the product of craftsmanship unless accidentally. Therefore sometimes, when the posterior instrument is produced from the matter of the anterior, the destruction of the anterior is a condition for the existence of the posterior, for instance, when a man comes into being from a man who has perished, through the latter becoming first a plant, then sperm or menstrual blood. And we have already discussed this problem. Those, however, who regard an infinite series of essential causes as possible are materialists, and he who concedes this does not understand the efficient cause. And about the efficient cause there is no divergence of opinion among philosophers.

And as to Ghazali's words:

> And if the world existed by itself without cause, then it would be clear what the First Principle is.

He means that the materialists as well as others acknowledge a first cause which has no cause, and their difference of opinion concerns only this principle, for the materialists say that it is the highest sphere and the others that it is a principle beyond the sphere and that the sphere is an effect; but these others are divided into two parties, those who say that the sphere is an act that has a beginning and those who say that it is an eternal act. And having declared that the acknowledgement of a first cause is common to the materialists as well as to others, Ghazali says:

> However, it is not possible that the First Principle should be the heavens, for there are many of these and the proof of unity contradicts this;

Meaning that from the order of the universe it is evident that its directing principle is one, just as it appears from the order in an army that its leader is one, namely, the commander of the army. And all this is true.

And as to Ghazali's words:

> Nor can it be said that one single heaven or one single body, the sun or any other body, can be the First Principle; for all these are bodies, and body is composed of matter and form, and the first body cannot be composite.

I say:

The statement that each body is composed of matter and form does not accord with the theory of the philosophers (with the exception of Avicenna) about the heavenly body, unless one uses "matter" here equivocally. For according to the philosophers everything composed of matter and form has a beginning, like the coming into existence of a house and a cupboard; and the heavens, according to them, have not come into existence in this sense, and so they called them eternal, because their existence is coeternal with the First Principle. For since according to them the cause of corruption is matter, that which is incorruptible could not possess matter, but must be a simple entity. If generation and corruption were not found in sublunary bodies, we should not draw the conclusion that they were composed of matter and form, for the fundamental principle is that body is a single essence not less in its existence than in perception, and if there were no corruption of sublunary bodies, we should judge that they were simple and that matter was body. But the fact that the body of the heavens does not suffer corruption shows that its matter is actual corporeality. And the soul which exists in this body does not exist in it because this body requires, as the bodies of animals do, the soul for its continuance, nor because it is necessary for the existence of this body to be animated, but only because the superior must of necessity exist in the condition of the superior and the animate is superior to the inanimate. According to the philosophers there is no change in the heavenly bodies, for they do not possess a potency in their substance. They therefore need not have matter in the way the generable bodies need this, but they are either, as Themistius affirms, forms or possess matter in an equivocal sense of the word. And I say that either the matters of the heavenly bodies are identical with their souls or these matters are essentially alive, not alive through a life bestowed on them.

Ghazali says:

> To this there are two answers. The first is that it can be said: Since it follows from the tenets of your school that the bodies of the world are eternal, it must follow too that they have no cause, and your statement that on a second examination such a conclusion must be rejected will itself be rejected when we discuss God's unity and afterwards the denial of attributes to God.

I say:

Ghazali means that since they cannot prove the unity of the First Principle, and since they cannot prove either that the One cannot be body—for since they cannot deny the attributes, the First Principle must, according to them, be an essence endowed with attributes, and such an essence must be a body or a potency in a body—it follows that the First Principle which has no cause is the celestial bodies. And this conclusion is valid against those who might argue in the way he says the philosophers argue. The philosophers, however, do not argue thus, and do not say that they are unable to prove the unity and incorporeality of the First Principle. But this question will be discussed later.

Ghazali says:

> The second answer, and it is the answer proper to this question, is to say: it is established as a possibility that these existents can have a cause, but perhaps for this cause there is another cause, and so on ad infinitum. And you have no right to assert that to admit an infinite series of causes is impossible, for we ask you, "Do you know this by immediate necessary intuition or through a middle term?" Any claim to intuition is excluded, and any method of deductive proof is forbidden to you, since you admit celestial revolutions without an initial term; and if you permit a coming into existence for what is without ends it is not impossible that the series should consist of causal relations and have as a final term an effect which has no further effect, although in the other direction the series does not end in a cause which has no anterior cause, just as the past has a final term, namely the everchanging present, but no first term. If you protest that the past occurrences do not exist together at one moment or at certain moments, and that what does not exist cannot be described as finite or infinite, you are forced

> to admit this simultaneous existence for human souls in abstraction from their bodies; for they do not perish, according to you, and the number of souls in abstraction from their bodies is infinite, since the series of becoming from sperm to man and from man to sperm is infinite, and every man dies, but his soul remains and is numerically different from the soul of any man who dies before, simultaneously, or afterwards, although all these souls are one in species. Therefore at any moment there is an infinite number of souls in existence.
>
> If you object that souls are not joined to each other, and that they have no order either by nature or by position, and that you regard only those infinite existents as impossible which have order in space, like bodies which have a spatial order of higher and lower, or have a natural order like cause and effect, and that this is not the case with souls; we answer: "This theory about position does not follow any more than its contrary"; you cannot regard one of the two cases as impossible without involving the other, for where is your proof for the distinction? And you cannot deny that this infinite number of souls must have an order, as some are prior to others and the past days and nights are infinite. If we suppose the birth of only one soul every day and night, the sum of souls, born in sequence one after the other, amounts at the present moment to infinity.
>
> The utmost you can say about the cause is that its priority to the effect exists by nature, in the way that its superiority to the effect is a matter of essence and not of space. But if you do not regard an infinite sequence as impossible for real temporal priority, it cannot be impossible for natural essential priority either. But what can the philosophers mean when they deny the possibility of an infinite spatial superposition of bodies but affirm the possibility of an infinite temporal sequence? Is this theory not really an inept theory without any foundation?

I say: As to Ghazali's words:

> But perhaps for this cause there is another cause and so on ad infinitum...and any method of deductive proof is forbidden to you, since you admit celestial revolutions without an initial term: To this difficulty an answer was given above, when we said that the philosophers do not allow an infinite causal series, because this would lead to an effect without a cause, but assert that there is such a series accidentally from an eternal cause—not, however, in a straight line, nor simultaneously, nor in infinite matters, but only as a circular process.

What he says here about Avicenna, that he regarded an infinite number of souls as possible and that infinity is only impossible in what has a position, is not true, and no philosopher has said it; indeed, its impossibility is apparent from their general proof which we mentioned, and no conclusion can be drawn against them from this assumption of an actual infinity of souls. Indeed, those who believed that the souls are of a certain number through the number of bodies and that they are individually immortal profess to avoid this assumption through the doctrine of the transmigration of souls.

And as to Ghazali's words:

> But what can the philosophers mean when they deny the possibility of an infinite spatial superposition of bodies, but affirm the possibility of an infinite temporal sequence?

I say:

The difference between these two cases is very clear to the philosophers, for from the assumption of infinite bodies existing simultaneously there follows an infinite totality and an actual infinite, and this is impossible. But time has no position, and from the existence of an infinite temporal series of bodies no actual infinite follows.

Ghazali says on behalf of the philosophers:

> The philosophers might say: The strict proof of the impossibility of an infinite causal series is as follows: each single cause of a series is either possible in itself or necessary; if it is necessary, it needs no cause, and if it is possible, then the whole series needs a cause additional to its essence, a cause standing outside the series.

I say:

The first man to bring into philosophy the proof which Ghazali gives here as a philosophical one was Avicenna, who regarded this proof as superior to those given by the ancients, since he claimed it to be based on the essence of the existent, whereas the older proofs are based on accidents consequent on the First Principle! This proof Avicenna took from the theologians, who regarded the dichotomy of existence into possible and necessary as self-evident, and assumed that the possible needs an agent and that the world in its totality, as being possible, needs an agent as a necessary existence. This was a theory of the Mu'tazilites before the Ash'arites, and it is excellent, and the only flaw in it is their assumption that the world in its totality is possible, for this is not self-evident. Avicenna wanted to give a general sense to this statement, and he gave to the "possible" the meaning of "what has a cause," as Ghazali relates. And even if this designation can be conceded, it does not effect the division which he had in view. For a primary division of existence into what has a cause and what has no cause is by no means self-evident. Further, what has a cause can be divided into what is possible and what is necessary. If we understand by "possible" the truly possible we arrive at the necessary-possibles and not at the necessary which has no cause; and if we understand by "possible" that which has a cause and is also necessary, there only follows from this that what has a cause has a cause and we may assume that this cause has a cause and so on ad infinitum. We do not therefore arrive at an existent without cause—for this is the meaning of the expression "entity as a necessary existence"—unless by the possible which Avicenna assumes as the opposite of what has no cause we understand the truly possible, for in these possibles there cannot exist an infinite series of causes. But if by "possible" is meant those necessary things which have a cause, it has not yet been proved that their infinite number is impossible, in the way it is evident of the truly possible existents, and it is not yet proved that there is a necessary existent which needs a cause, so that from this assumption one can arrive at a necessary entity existing without a cause. Indeed, one has to prove that what applies to the total causal series of possible entities applies also to the total causal series of necessary existents.

Ghazali says:

> The terms "possible" and "necessary" are obscure, unless one understands by "necessary" that which has no cause for its existence and by "possible" that which has a cause for its existence; then, by applying the terms as defined to the statement, we say: Each member of a causal series is possible in this sense of "possible," namely, that it has a cause additional to its essence, but the series as a whole is not possible in this sense of "possible." And if anything else is meant by "possible," it is obscure. If it is objected that this makes the necessary existent consist of possible existents and this is impossible, we answer: By defining "necessary" and "possible" as we have done, you have all that is needed and we do not concede that it is impossible. To say that it is impossible would be like saying that it is impossible that what is eternal should be made up of what is temporal, for time according to you philosophers is eternal, but the individual circular movements are temporal and have initial terms, though collectively they have no initial term; therefore, that which has no initial term consists of entities having initial terms, and it is true of the single units that they have a beginning, but not true of them collectively. In the same way it can be said of each term of the causal series that it has a cause, but not of the series as a whole. And so not everything that is true of single units is true of their collectivity, for it is true of each single unit that it is one and a portion and a part, but not true of their collectivity; and any place on the earth which we choose is illuminated by the sun by day and is dark by night, and according to the philosophers each unit has begun, but not the whole. Through this it is proved that the man who admits temporal entities without a beginning, namely, the forms of the four elements, cannot at the same time deny an infinity of causes, and we conclude from this that because of this difficulty there is no way in which they can prove the First Principle, and their dichotomy is purely arbitrary.

I say:

The assumption of infinite possible causes implies the assumption of a possible without an agent, but the assumption of infinite necessary entities having causes implies only that what was assumed to have a cause has none, and this argument is true with the restriction that the impossibility of infinite entities which are of a possible nature does not involve the impossibility of infinite necessary entities. If one wanted to give a demonstrative form to the argument used by Avicenna one should say: Possible existents must of necessity have causes which precede them, and if these causes again are possible it follows that they have causes and that there is an infinite regress; and if there is an infinite regress there is no cause, and the possible will exist without a cause, and this is impossible. Therefore the series must end in a necessary cause, and in this case this necessary cause must be necessary through a cause or without a cause, and if through a cause, this cause must have a cause and so on infinitely; and if we have an infinite regress here, it follows that what was assumed to have a cause has no cause, and this is impossible. Therefore the series must end in a cause necessary without a cause, i.e., necessary by itself, and this necessarily is the necessary existent. And when these distinctions are indicated, the proof becomes valid. But if this argument is given in the form in which Avicenna gives it, it is invalid for many reasons, one of which is that the term "possible" used in it is an equivocal one and that in this argument the primary dichotomy of all existents into what is possible and what is not possible, i.e., this division comprising the existent qua existent, is not true.

And as to Ghazali's words in his refutation of the philosophers:

> We say: Each member of a causal series is possible in this sense of "possible," namely, that it has a cause additional to its essence, but the whole series is not possible in this sense of "possible."

I say:

Ghazali means that when the philosophers concede that they understand by "possible existent" that which has a cause and by "necessary existent" that which has no cause, it can be said to them, "According to your own principles the existence of an infinite causal series is not impossible, and the series in its totality will be a necessary existent," for according to their own principles the philosophers admit that different judgements apply to the part and to the whole collectively. This statement is erroneous for many reasons, one of which is that the philosophers, as was mentioned before, do not allow an infinite series of essential causes, whether causes and effects of a possible or of a necessary nature, as we have shown. The objection which can be directed against Avicenna is that when you divide existence into possible and necessary and identify the possible existent with that which has a cause and the necessary existent with that which has none, you can no longer prove the impossibility of the existence of an infinite causal series, for from its infinite character it follows that it is to be classed with existents which have no cause and it must therefore be of the nature of the necessary existent, especially as, according to him and his school, eternity can consist of an infinite series of causes each of which is temporal. The fault in Avicenna's argument arises only from his division of the existent into that which has a cause and that which has none. If he had made his division in the way we have done, none of these objections could be directed against him. And Ghazali's statement that the ancients, since they admit an infinite number of circular movements, make the eternal consist of an infinite number of entities, is false. For the term "eternal," when it is attributed both to this infinite series and to the one eternal being, is used equivocally.

And as to the words of Ghazali:

> If it is objected that this makes the necessary existent consist of possible existents, and this is impossible, we answer: By defining "necessary" and "possible" as we have done, you have all that is needed, and we do not concede that it is impossible.

I say:

Ghazali means that the philosophers understand by "necessary" that which has no cause and by "possible" that which has a cause, and that he, Ghazali, does not regard it as impossible that what has no cause should consist of an infinite number of causes, because, if he conceded that this was impossible, he would be denying the possibility of an infinity of causes, whereas he only wants to show that the philosophers' deduction of a necessary being is a petitio principii [fallacy of "begging the question"]....

If all this is once established, you will see that the proposition that the man who allows the existence of an infinite series of causes cannot admit a first cause is false, and that on the contrary the opposite is evident, namely, that the man who does not acknowledge infinite causes cannot prove the existence of an eternal first cause, since it is the existence of infinite effects which demands the necessity of an eternal cause from which the infinite causes acquire their existence; for if not, the *genera*, all of whose individuals are temporal, would be necessarily finite. And in this and no other way can the eternal become the cause of temporal existents, and the existence of infinite temporal existents renders the existence of a single eternal first principle necessary, and there is no God but He.

24.3 SUFI MYSTICISM

The ideal of union with God is the driving concept of much mystical thought. The Sufism of al-Ghazali and other Islamic mystics shares this idea. A Sufi believes it possible to have direct experience of God. This is the goal of mystic practices. Rabi'a al-'Adawiyya (d. 801), born in Basra in what is now Iraq, was kidnapped as a child and sold as a slave. Her master freed her, impressed by her extraordinary devotion to God and the severity of her religious austerities. Eventually she became one of the most influential of Sufis. Rabi'a teaches an intensity of commitment typical of mystics: According to her, the only acceptable motivation for any act is love of God. Concern for oneself should not count. She uses sexual imagery to report her quest for contact and indeed union with God. Like many Sufis, she stresses the importance of experience. We cannot understand things we have not experienced. The Sufi exalts a first-person point of view: My experience of God gives me insight into God's nature that I can communicate only through poetry.

Zeb-un-Nissa (1638–1702), whose name means "the glory of womankind," was born into royalty. Her father was the last Mughal ruler of India; her mother was a descendant of the Persian emperor. Among her ancestors were Genghis Khan and Tamerlane. She studied Arabic, Persian, mathematics, and astronomy under the kingdom's most illustrious scholars. Her father consulted Zeb-un-Nissa on royal appointments, trusting her judgment more than he trusted his own. She established her own royal courts in Delhi and Lahore, employing scholars, establishing libraries, and commissioning translations of Arabic works into Persian. Though her father was increasingly severe in his interpretation of Islamic law, Zeb-un-Nissa followed her aunt into Sufi mystical practice. When she was 44, her youngest brother Akbar tried to seize the kingdom from their father. He was exiled, and she was caught communicating with him. Suspected of disloyalty, she was confined to prison in Delhi. After that, there is no record of her.

Zeb-un-Nissa's poetry speaks of God as the Beloved, for whom she desperately yearns but who spurns her, only occasionally yielding glimmers of hope. God is the Hunter of her soul, the one who inspires a sort of madness unintelligible to the world but understood by all others who know the Beloved. Real religion, she maintains, is an internal matter, a matter of the heart. Knowledgeable about Hinduism, Zoroastrianism,

Christianity, and Platonism as well as Islam, she recognizes that the mystical impulse transcends Islam or any other particular religion, expressing what all religions share—an unfulfilled and unfulfillable striving for knowledge of and union with the divine. She uses the image of traditional Sufi poets, that of a moth drawn to a flame, who attains what it desires only at its own destruction. But she also uses images drawn from other traditions, including Plato's allegory of the cave, to probe the depths of mystical experience.

24.3.1 Rabi'a al-'Adawiyya, from *Readings from the Mystics of Islam*

One day Rabi'a was seen carrying fire in one hand and water in the other and she was running with speed. They asked her what was the meaning of her action and where she was going. She replied: "I am going to light a fire in Paradise and pour water onto Hell, so that both veils (i.e., hindrances to the true vision of God) may completely disappear from the pilgrims, and their purpose may be sure, and the servants of God may see Him, without any object of hope or motive of fear. What if the hope of Paradise and the fear of Hell did not exist? Not one could worship his Lord or obey Him."

The best thing for the servant, who desires to be near his Lord, is to possess nothing in this world or the next, save Him. I have not served God from fear of Hell, for I should be like a wretched hireling, if I did it from fear: nor from love of Paradise, for I should be a bad servant if I served for the sake of what was given, but I have served Him only for the love of Him and out of desire for Him.

The Neighbour first and then the house: is it not enough for me that I am given leave to worship Him? Even if Heaven and Hell were not, does it not behove us to obey Him? He is worthy of worship without any intermediate motive.

Oh my Lord, if I worship Thee from fear of Hell, burn me in Hell; and if I worship Thee from hope for Paradise, exclude me thence; but if I worship Thee for Thine own sake, then withhold not from me Thine Eternal Beauty.

The groaning and the yearning of the lover of God will not be satisfied until it is satisfied in the Beloved.

I have made Thee the Companion of my heart,
But my body is available for those who desire its company.
And my body is friendly toward its guests,
But the Beloved of my heart is the Guest of my soul.

My peace is in solitude, but my Beloved is always with me. Nothing can take the place of His love and it is the test of me among mortal beings. Whenever I contemplate His Beauty, He is my *mihrab* [niche in the wall of a mosque toward which one prays], toward Him is my *qibla* [the direction of Mecca]—O Healer of souls, the heart feeds upon its desire and it is the striving towards union with Thee that has healed my soul. Thou art my Joy and my Life to eternity. Thou wast the source of my life, from Thee came my ecstasy. I have separated myself from all created beings: my hope is for union with Thee, for that is the goal of my quest.

Source: *Readings from the Mystics of Islam.* Edited by Margaret Smith. London: Luzac and Company, 1950.

24.3.2 Zeb-un-Nissa, from *Poetry from the Hidden One*

V

Here is the path of love—how dark and long
Its winding ways, with many snares beset!
Yet crowds of eager pilgrims onward throng
And fall like doves into the fowler's net.

Now tell me what the grain that drew the dove?
The mole it was upon a cheek so fair.
Tell me of what was wove the net of love?
The wandering curls of the Beloved's hair.

The festival of love is holden here,
The goblet passes; drink thou of this wine,
Yea, drain it to the lees, and never fear
Intoxication that is all divine.

How easy 'tis to sigh and to complain!
All the world weeps to give its woe relief;
But proudly in thy heart conceal thy pain,
And silent drink the poison of thy grief.

Here is the source of light, the heavenly fount,
Here is the vision of eternal grace;
Brighter than Moses thou, when from the Mount
He came, God's radiance shining in his face.

The wine at night unto the morning lends
Its exaltation, morning to the night
Its dream bequeaths in turn: so never ends
The sequence of the happy soul's delight.

But, Makhfi, tell me where the feast is made?
Where are the merry-makers? Lo, apart,
Here in my soul the feast of God is laid,
Within the hidden chambers of my heart.

XI

Awake, arise, my soul, for it is spring;
Let the narcissus, with its scent divine,
Cast its bewitchment, let the Saki bring
His idol, for indeed he worships wine.

To the forbidden path turn not aside,
And, tyrannous Beloved, let thine eye
Look on thy victims trampled in thy pride,
Who for a glance from thee would gladly die.

Some pay their worship at the Kaaba shrine,
Some pray within the Temple courts apart,
But, Makhfi, think what secret joy is thine,
To bear thine idol ever in thy heart.

XIII

Why should I argue that on Sinai
Celestial radiance glows?
I cannot reason; though the world deny,
My heart enlightened knows.

My heart is hot within me, yea, has burst
In flames of love the while
So fierce that like a drop to slake my thirst
Were all the floods of Nile.

So deep in sin am I—I cannot wend
Where holy pilgrims fare
To Mecca, even if Abraham, God's friend,
Should come to lead me there.

I tire of wisdom's kingdom which is mine,
I tire of reason's sway:
Passion of love, O carry me to thine,
A hundred miles away.

Lo, when I come unto the water's side
The obedient waves retire,
My flaming heart exultantly shall guide
Like Moses' torch of fire.

Though evil days are mine, of joy bereft,
With pain that never ends,
Fate, do with me your worst, there still is left
The Friend beyond all friends.

Tell me, O Makhfi, is it I who sin?
Is this my sin I bear?
Is it the body's or the soul's within
That lived and sinned elsewhere?

Source: *The Diwan of Zeb-un-Nissa*. London: Hazell, Watson and Viney, 1913.

XV

(Hatim was a chief from Yemen famed for his generosity: he never refused a request. Someone asked for his head, and he gave it, and so died.)

Behold the fire renewed within my heart,
My sighs have lashed it with their breath until
 the flames outstart;
Nor may this feeble cage, my body, stay
The fluttering of this bird, my soul, that longs to
 fly away.
The rocks would melt, and into tears would flow,
Could they but hear the never-ending murmur
 of my woe;
For in the dark foreboding of my heart
There sounds the warning bell that calls the
 caravan to start:
O Love, I have bewailed for all these years
Thy tyranny, but none has heard my voice except
 my tears.
Behold how poor I am, but yet so proud,
I would not sit at Hatim's table with the eager
 crowd:
See, I have watched throughout the lonely night
Of separation, when there never came my heart's
 delight,
And in my desolation tears of blood
Gushed from my stricken, widowed heart in
 never-ending flood:
Yet to me, purged by grief, does hope arise,
My withered chaplets change to fragrant flowers
 of Paradise.
Love holds me in these cruel fetters bound,
My faithfulness to Thee: beside Thy feet, a
 beaten hound,
I crouch and fawn for crumbs of love from Thee.
O Makhfi, if thy sighs could reach the bosom of
 the sea,
Even within the cold and lightless deep
Caught from thy heart a quenchless flame should
 leap.

XVI

O Love, I am thy thrall.
As on the tulip's burning petal glows
A spot yet more intense, of deeper dye,
So in my heart a flower of passion blows;
See the dark stain of its intensity,
Deeper than all.

This is my pride—
That I the rose of all the world have sought,
And, still unwearied in the eager quest,
Fainted nor failed have I, and murmured not;
Thus is my head exalted o'er the rest,
My turban glorified.

O blessed pain,
O precious grief I keep, and sweet unrest,
Desire that dies not, longing past control!
My heart is torn to pieces in my breast,
And for the shining diamond of the soul
I pine in vain.

Behold the light
That from Thy torch of mercy comes to bless
The garden of my heart, Beloved One,
With the white radiance of its loveliness,
Till my wall's shadow shall outvie the sun,
And seem more bright.

I humbly sit apart;
The Kaaba courts the true believer's tread,
I dwell outside, nor mix my praise with theirs;
Yet every fibre of my sacred thread
More precious is to God than all their prayers—
He sees the heart.

O Makhfi sorrowing,
Look from the valley of despair and pain;
The breath of love like morning zephyr blows,
Pearls from thine eyelids fall like gentle rain
Upon the garden, summoning the rose,
Calling the spring.

XIX

(Ferhad was a lover famous in Eastern story. He loved Shirin (the sweet one), who was the wife of King Khosru. The King, fearing his rivalry, tried to divert his mind from his passion, and sought to find for him some impossible task. As Shirin had demanded a "river of milk," he was bidden to clear away the rocks obstructing the passage of the great mountain of Beysitoun, and to cause the rivers on the opposite sides of the mountain to join. Ferhad agreed on condition that, if he were successful, Shirin should be given to him. For years he laboured, and carved out wonderful caverns, which can be seen to this day; and the Joui-shir (stream of milk) still flows from the mountain between Hamadan and Hulwan. Only a few days' work remained to be done, when the King heard reports that the project was succeeding: he thereupon sent a messenger to tell Ferhad that Shirin was dead. On hearing this, Ferhad died, some say by killing himself with his axe, others say by throwing himself over a precipice.)

Desolate one, O when
Shalt thou the shining garden see again?
Keep thou within thee, holy and apart,
The garden of thy heart;

As the long-prisoned bird,
Forgetting that it ever flew, and heard
Songs of the wild, and pinions wide unfurled,
Makes of the cage its world.

No fear indeed thou hast,
O heart within the net of love held fast,
Of separation's bitter agony—
Thy love is one with thee.

Sadly we wait and tire,
And sight of the Beloved Face desire
In vain, till in our hearts the hope is born
Of Resurrection morn.

O heart, thine be no less
Than the ascetic Brahman's faithfulness,
The knotted veins his wasted body bears
As sacred thread he wears.

What is a lover's fate?
What shall befall to him unfortunate?
The world shall cry, to please its idle whim,
"Crucify him!"

Why dost thou then complain
That on thy feet there drags this heavy chain?
Nay, it befits thee well such weights to wear;
Much hast thou learned to bear.

As, far upon the hills,
Despairing Ferhad, weary of life's ills,
Welcomed kind Death, and wept, so for relief
Weep thou and salve thy grief!

And see the thorny waste
Whereon thy bruised feet their pathway traced,
This wilderness, touched by thy blood that
flows,
Blooms fragrant as the rose.

O Love, shall I repine
The noose of death around my neck to twine
At thy behest? Nay, if thy glory gain,
Proud am I in my pain.

O Makhfi, if thy fate
Be that, without the garden, desolate
Thou dwell—reck not of it; life is a dream,
And we, that seem
To live and move and love, no more at all
Than shadows on a wall.

XXIX

Impatient were my hands, and in their haste
Never could they untie the knot of fate,
So vain it is to wail my life laid waste,
My hours unfortunate.

And strange it is that even in my heart
The sweet tormenting flame of my desire
Is quenched; impatiently I pulled apart
The brands and killed the fire.

And never did the blossoms of success
Within my hope's enchanted garden bloom,
And my fair beacon-light of happiness
Is sunk in gloom.

Faithless Beloved, many friends are Thine;
So many love and have been loved by Thee,
They give their hearts, what carest Thou for
mine?
What need hast Thou of me?

XLII

O Self-Existent, give
Unto Thy faithful ones their heart's desire,
And visit not with Thy consuming fire
O'er-burdened souls, too sorrowful to live.

No longer can I bear
The separation and the bitter grief;
Afflicted am I—grant my soul relief!
Weary and broken—look on my despair!

O Thou, whose praise we tell,
Sever the tyrant bonds, give to the slave
His freedom, save him, Lord, as Thou did'st save
Yusuf, the Moon of Canaan, from the well!

My tears fail, for they must;
The spring that fed their fountains has run dry;
Give me Thy peace, O Lord; for what am I?
Only a handful of afflicted dust.

But flowers of hope return
To bloom within my garden of desire,
For God can call even from flames of fire
Tulips like torches to arise and burn.

CHAPTER 25

Modern Theology

"The heart has its reasons"

Early modern philosophers in Europe advanced several arguments for God's existence. Some had been advanced by medieval Jewish, Christian, and Muslim philosophers. Several others were new. For the first time in many centuries, however, philosophers also advanced an ancient argument against God's existence: the problem of evil. God, on the classical conception, is wholly good. But the world contains evil. Human beings do terrible things to each other. The world endangers us through disasters such as hurricanes, tornados, earthquakes, and epidemics. We face suffering, disease, and death. How could a good God create such a world?

25.1 DESCARTES' ARGUMENTS FOR GOD'S EXISTENCE

René Descartes (1596–1650) advances two arguments for the existence of God. The first centers on the concept of God. Some might deny that there is any such concept, or at any rate that they have it, or claim that it is ultimately incoherent. But even many atheists would agree to having a concept of God; they would just deny that it corresponds to anything in the world. If there is such a concept, where do we get it? Where does it come from?

The concept of God does not seem to come from experience. Religious traditions differ on whether it is possible to experience God in this lifetime. But even Moses, "whom the Lord knew face to face," according to Deuteronomy 34:10, had a concept of God before he encountered the burning bush or ascended Mt. Sinai. This is a traditional argument for rejecting concept empiricism. Since we have a concept of God and it does not come from experience, some concepts must be a priori.

Descartes' argument from thought takes this reasoning one step further. If our capacity to think of God does not come from experience, it must be innate. But where could this inborn capacity have come from? Only from God. Our concept of God is a concept of a perfect being. We never encounter perfection, but our idea must have its origin in something perfect. Just as our idea of green has its origin in green things, our idea of perfection must have its origin in something perfect—God.

Descartes' main premise is that a cause has at least as much reality as its effect. The cause of the idea of X must have at least as much reality as X. Descartes speaks of things in the world as having *actual* or *formal* reality. The contents of our ideas—their objects, what our ideas are about—have *objective* reality. Since we now call things objective when they do not depend on our own states of mind, Descartes' usage is confusing. When he attributes objective reality to something, he means to say it is an object of thought. Such objects may or may not have actual or formal reality; we can think of things that do not exist. (Famous examples include Pegasus, the golden mountain, and the round square cupola on Berkeley College.) In short, Descartes means by "objective" something very close to what we mean by "subjective."

The cause of an idea must contain at least as much formal reality as the idea contains objective reality. We do not, in other words, derive our ideas from nothing. We get the idea of fire from fire. We get the idea of red from red things. Our ideas may be imperfect copies of the originals; our idea of fire, for example, does not capture the full richness and complexity of fire itself. The key point, however, is that our idea does not contain more richness and complexity than the thing itself.

The idea of God, then, must have come from something with at least as much reality as God; since nothing has as much reality as God, our idea must have come from God.

Scottish philosopher David Hume (1711–1776) and German philosopher Ludwig Feuerbach (1804–1872), among others, have objected that we can account for the origin of our idea of the infinite without assuming an infinite cause. We encounter finite things, and we have the idea of negation. Surely, they contend, we can combine them to form the idea of the infinite. Not so, Descartes argues. He can explain our recognition of our own imperfection, expressed explicitly in our awareness of our own finite nature and implicitly in doubt and desire. Can his opponent do so as well? One might try to argue that doubt and desire are basic or that they rest on feelings of insecurity, hunger, frustration, and so on, which are basic. One might also accept that doubt and desire presuppose an idea of something better without agreeing that they presuppose the idea of something better than anything else could possibly be. We recognize that numbers like 100 are finite by recognizing that there are larger numbers, not by having the idea of an infinite number already in mind.

Perhaps the idea of God is incoherent, or confused, or corresponds to nothing in the world. Again, Descartes argues, not so. Descartes' principle of method undergirds the argument: Everything that I perceive clearly and distinctly must be true. The idea of God cannot be a human imperfection that reflects no corresponding reality; the idea is clear and distinct and must therefore reflect reality accurately.

Descartes' argument, as we saw a moment ago, relies on his principle that everything I perceive clearly and distinctly is true. But how do I know that? In the course of the *Meditations*, he first announces the principle as a generalization from the *cogito*. But it will not do to argue that everything I clearly and distinctly perceive is true on the ground that one thing, that I exist, is something I clearly and distinctly perceive that must be true.

In the end, Descartes' answer is that God is good and cannot be a deceiver. I can trust my senses in most contexts. I can trust the clear and distinct ideas that inhabit my mind innately. God, being perfect, must be good and surely would not have ordered the world so that my mind would systematically mistake its nature.

Most philosophers have found this answer deeply unsatisfying. We can trust our clear and distinct ideas because God exists, is good, and so could not be a deceiver. But the argument for God's existence depends on the premise that we can trust our clear and distinct ideas! The argument is circular. In fact, it is known as the *Cartesian circle*. Little wonder that Descartes sought another argument for God's existence, one that would not require prior trust in clear and distinct ideas.

Descartes turned to a second argument for God's existence, one that depends on God's perfection in a different way. Anselm of Canterbury (1033–1109) presented two versions of the argument. Extending Augustine's definition of God as "something than which nothing more excellent or sublime exists," Anselm defines God as "that, the greater than which cannot be thought," that is, the greatest conceivable being, the greatest thing you could possibly think of. Descartes advances the ontological argument in his fifth *Meditation* in an especially elegant form. Descartes's argument is straightforward:

> God has all perfections. Existence is a perfection. Therefore, God exists.

This argument purports to show the existence of God from nothing more than the concept of God. It is plainly valid, and the first premise is just a definition of "God." Debate thus centers on its second premise. Is existence a perfection?

25.1.1 René Descartes, from *Meditations on First Philosophy*

Meditation III. Of God: That He Exists

I shall now close my eyes, I shall stop my ears, I shall call away all my senses, I shall efface even from my thoughts all the images of corporeal things, or at least (for that is hardly possible) I shall esteem them as vain and false; and thus holding converse only with myself and considering my own nature, I shall try little by little to reach a better knowledge of and a more familiar acquaintanceship with myself. I am a thing that thinks, that is to say, that doubts, affirms, denies, that knows a few things, that is ignorant of many [that loves, that hates], that wills, that desires, that also imagines and perceives; for as I remarked before, although the things which I perceive and imagine are perhaps nothing at all apart from me and in themselves, I am nevertheless assured that these modes of thought that I call perceptions and imaginations, inasmuch only as they are modes of thought, certainly reside [and are met with] in me.

And in the little that I have just said, I think I have summed up all that I really know, or at least all that hitherto I was aware that I knew. In order to try to extend my knowledge further, I shall now look around more carefully and see whether I cannot still discover in myself some other things which I have not hitherto perceived.

Source: René Descartes, *The Philosophical Works of Descartes*. Translated by Elizabeth S. Haldane. Cambridge: Cambridge University Press, 1911.

I am certain that I am a thing which thinks; but do I not then likewise know what is requisite to render me certain of a truth? Certainly in this first knowledge there is nothing that assures me of its truth, excepting the clear and distinct perception of that which I state, which would not indeed suffice to assure me that what I say is true, if it could ever happen that a thing which I conceived so clearly and distinctly could be false; and accordingly it seems to me that already I can establish as a general rule that all things which I perceive very clearly and very distinctly are true.

At the same time I have before received and admitted many things to be very certain and manifest, which yet I afterwards recognised as being dubious. What then were these things? They were the earth, sky, stars and all other objects which I apprehended by means of the senses. But what did I clearly [and distinctly] perceive in them? Nothing more than that the ideas or thoughts of these things were presented to my mind. And not even now do I deny that these ideas are met with in me. But there was yet another thing which I affirmed, and which, owing to the habit which I had formed of believing it, I thought I perceived very clearly, although in truth I did not perceive it at all, to wit, that there were objects outside of me from which these ideas proceeded, and to which they were entirely similar. And it was in this that I erred, or, if perchance my judgment was correct, this was not due to any knowledge arising from my perception....

But there is yet another method of inquiring whether any of the objects of which I have ideas within me exist outside of me. If ideas are only taken as certain modes of thought, I recognise amongst them no difference or inequality, and all appear to proceed from me in the same manner; but when we consider them as images, one representing one thing and the other another, it is clear that they are very different one from the other. There is no doubt that those which represent to me substances are something more, and contain so to speak more objective reality within them [that is to say, by representation participate in a higher degree of being or perfection] than those that simply represent modes or accidents; and that idea again by which I understand a supreme God, eternal, infinite, [immutable], omniscient, omnipotent, and Creator of all things which are outside of Himself, has certainly more objective reality in itself than those ideas by which finite substances are represented.

Now it is manifest by the natural light that there must at least be as much reality in the efficient and total cause as in its effect. For, pray, whence can the effect derive its reality, if not from its cause? And in what way can this cause communicate this reality to it, unless it possessed it in itself? And from this it follows, not only that something cannot proceed from nothing, but likewise that what is more perfect—that is to say, which has more reality within itself—cannot proceed from the less perfect. And this is not only evidently true of those effects which possess actual or formal reality, but also of the ideas in which we consider merely what is termed objective reality. To take an example, the stone which has not yet existed not only cannot now commence to be unless it has been produced by something which possesses within itself, either formally or eminently, all that enters into the composition of the stone [i.e., it must possess the same things or other, more excellent things than those which exist in the stone] and heat can only be produced in a subject in which it did not previously exist by a cause that is of an order [degree or kind] at least as perfect as heat, and so in all other cases. But further, the idea of heat, or of a stone, cannot exist in me unless it has been placed within me by some cause which possesses within it at least as much reality as that which I conceive to exist in the heat or the stone. For although this cause does not transmit anything of its actual or formal reality to my idea, we must not for that reason imagine that it is necessarily a less real cause; we must remember that [since every idea is a work of the mind] its nature is such that it demands of itself no other formal reality than that which it borrows from my thought, of which it is only a mode [i.e., a manner or way of thinking]. But in order that an idea should contain some one certain objective reality rather than another, it must without doubt derive it from some cause in which there is at least as much formal reality as this idea contains of objective reality. For if we imagine that something is found in an idea which is not found in the cause, it must then have been derived from nought; but however imperfect may be this mode of being by which a thing is objectively [or by representation] in the understanding by its idea, we cannot certainly say that this mode of being is nothing, nor, consequently, that the idea derives its origin from nothing.

Nor must I imagine that, since the reality that I consider in these ideas is only objective, it is not essential that this reality should be formally in the causes of my ideas, but that it is sufficient that it should be found objectively. For just as this mode of objective existence pertains to ideas by their proper nature, so does the mode of formal existence pertain to the causes of those ideas (this is at least true of the first and principal) by the nature peculiar to them. And although it may be the case that one idea gives birth to another idea, that cannot continue to be so indefinitely; for in the end we must reach an idea whose cause shall be so to speak an archetype, in which the whole reality [or perfection] which is so to speak objectively [or by representation] in these ideas is contained formally [and really]. Thus the light of nature causes me to know clearly that the ideas in me are like [pictures or] images which can, in truth, easily fall short of the perfection of the objects from which they have been derived, but which can never contain anything greater or more perfect.

And the longer and the more carefully that I investigate these matters, the more clearly and distinctly do I recognise their truth. But what am I to conclude from it all in the end? It is this, that if the objective reality of any one of my ideas is of such a nature as clearly to make me recognise that it is not in me either formally or eminently, and that consequently I cannot myself be the cause of it, it follows of necessity that I am not alone in the world, but that there is another being which exists, or which is the cause of this idea. On the other hand, had no such an idea existed in me, I should have had no sufficient argument to convince me of the existence of any being beyond myself; for I have made very careful investigation everywhere and up to the present time have been able to find no other ground.

But of my ideas, beyond that which represents me to myself, as to which there can here be no difficulty, there is another which represents a God, and there are others representing corporeal and inanimate things, others angels, others animals, and others again which represent to me men similar to myself.

As regards the ideas which represent to me other men or animals, or angels, I can however easily conceive that they might be formed by an admixture of the other ideas which I have of myself, of corporeal things, and of God, even although there were apart from me neither men nor animals, nor angels, in all the world.

And in regard to the ideas of corporeal objects, I do not recognise in them anything so great or so excellent that they might not have possibly proceeded from myself; for if I consider them more closely, and examine them individually, as I yesterday examined the idea of wax, I find that there is very little in them which I perceive clearly and distinctly. Magnitude or extension in length, breadth, or depth, I do so perceive; also figure which results from a termination of this extension, the situation which bodies of different figure preserve in relation to one another, and movement or change of situation; to which we may also add substance, duration and number. As to other things such as light, colours, sounds, scents, tastes, heat, cold and the other tactile qualities, they are thought by me with so much obscurity and confusion that I do not even know if they are true or false, i.e., whether the ideas which I form of these qualities are actually the ideas of real objects or not [or whether they only represent chimeras which cannot exist in fact]. For although I have before remarked that it is only in judgments that falsity, properly speaking, or formal falsity, can be met with, a certain material falsity may nevertheless be found in ideas, i.e., when these ideas represent what is nothing as though it were something. For example, the ideas which I have of cold and heat are so far from clear and distinct that by their means I cannot tell whether cold is merely a privation of heat, or heat a privation of cold, or whether both are real qualities, or are not such. And inasmuch as [since ideas resemble images] there cannot be any ideas which do not appear to represent some things, if it is correct to say that cold is merely a privation of heat, the idea which represents it to me as something real and positive will not be improperly termed false, and the same holds good of other similar ideas.

To these it is certainly not necessary that I should attribute any author other than myself. For if they are false, i.e., if they represent things which do not exist, the light of nature shows me that they issue from nought, that is to say, that they are only in me so far as something is lacking to the perfection of my nature. But if they are true, nevertheless because they exhibit so little reality to me that I cannot even clearly distinguish the thing represented from non-being, I do not see any reason why they should not be produced by myself.

As to the clear and distinct idea which I have of corporeal things, some of them seem as though I might have derived them from the idea which I possess of myself, as those which I have of substance, duration, number, and such like. For [even] when I think that a stone is a substance, or at least a thing capable of existing of itself, and that I am a substance also, although I conceive that I am a thing that thinks and not one that is extended, and that the stone on the other hand is an extended thing which does not think, and that thus there is a notable difference between the two conceptions—they seem, nevertheless, to agree in this, that both represent substances. In the same way, when I perceive that I now exist and further recollect that I have in former times existed, and when I remember that I have various thoughts of which I can recognise the number, I acquire ideas of duration and number which I can afterwards transfer to any object that I please. But as to all the other qualities of which the ideas of corporeal things are composed, to wit, extension, figure, situation and motion, it is true that they are not formally in me, since I am only a thing that thinks; but because they are merely certain modes of substance [and so to speak the vestments under which corporeal substance appears to us] and because I myself am also a substance, it would seem that they might be contained in me eminently.

Hence there remains only the idea of God, concerning which we must consider whether it is something which cannot have proceeded from me myself. By the name God I understand a substance that is infinite [eternal, immutable], independent, all-knowing, all-powerful, and by which I myself and everything else, if anything else does exist, have been created. Now all these characteristics are such that the more diligently I attend to them, the less do they appear capable of proceeding from me alone; hence, from what has been already said, we must conclude that God necessarily exists.

For although the idea of substance is within me owing to the fact that I am substance, nevertheless I should not have the idea of an infinite substance—since I am finite—if it had not proceeded from some substance which was veritably infinite.

Nor should I imagine that I do not perceive the infinite by a true idea, but only by the negation of the finite, just as I perceive repose and darkness by the negation of movement and of light; for, on the contrary, I see that there is manifestly more reality in infinite substance than in finite, and therefore that in some way I have in me the notion of the infinite earlier then the finite—to wit, the notion of God before that of myself. For how would it be possible that I should know that I doubt and desire, that is to say, that something is lacking to me, and that I am not quite perfect, unless I had within me some idea of a Being more perfect than myself, in comparison with which I should recognise the deficiencies of my nature?

And we cannot say that this idea of God is perhaps materially false and that consequently I can derive it from nought [i.e., that possibly it exists in me because I am imperfect], as I have just said is the case with ideas of heat, cold and other such things; for, on the contrary, as this idea is very clear and distinct and contains within it more objective reality than any other, there can be none which is of itself more true, nor any in which there can be less suspicion of falsehood. The idea, I say, of this Being who is absolutely perfect and infinite, is entirely true; for although, perhaps, we can imagine that such a Being does not exist, we cannot nevertheless imagine that His idea represents nothing real to me, as I have said of the idea of cold. This idea is also very clear and distinct; since all that I conceive clearly and distinctly of the real and the true, and of what conveys some perfection, is in its entirety contained in this idea. And this does not cease to be true although I do not comprehend the infinite, or though in God there is an infinitude of things which I cannot comprehend, nor possibly even reach in any way by thought; for it is of the nature of the infinite that my nature, which is finite and limited, should not comprehend it; and it is sufficient that I should understand this, and that I should judge that all things which I clearly perceive and in which I know that there is some perfection, and possibly likewise an infinitude of properties of which I am ignorant, are in God formally or eminently, so that the idea which I have of Him may become the most true, most clear, and most distinct of all the ideas that are in my mind.

But possibly I am something more than I suppose myself to be, and perhaps all those perfections which I attribute to God are in some way potentially in me, although they do not yet disclose themselves or issue in action. As a matter of fact I am already sensible that my knowledge increases [and perfects itself] little by little, and I see nothing which can prevent it from increasing more and more into infinitude; nor do I see, after it has thus been increased [or perfected], anything to prevent my being able to acquire by its means all the other perfections of the Divine nature; nor finally why the power I have of acquiring these perfections, if it really exists in me, shall not suffice to produce the ideas of them.

At the same time I recognise that this cannot be. For, in the first place, although it were true that everyday my knowledge acquired new degrees of perfection, and that there were in my nature many things potentially which are not yet there actually, nevertheless these excellences do not pertain to [or make the smallest approach to] the idea which I have of God in whom there is nothing merely potential [but in whom all is present really and actually]; for it is an infallible token of imperfection in my knowledge that it increases little by little. And further, although my knowledge grows more and more, nevertheless I do not for that reason believe that it can ever be actually infinite, since it can never reach a point so high that it will be unable to attain to any greater increase. But I understand God to be actually infinite, so that He can add nothing to His supreme perfection. And finally I perceive that the objective being of an idea cannot be produced by a being that exists potentially only, which properly speaking is nothing, but only by a being which is formal or actual.

To speak the truth, I see nothing in all that I have just said which by the light of nature is not manifest to anyone who desires to think attentively on the subject; but when I slightly relax my attention, my mind, finding its vision somewhat obscured and so to speak blinded by the images of sensible objects, I do not easily recollect the reason why the idea that I possess of a being more perfect than I must necessarily have been placed in me by a being which is really more perfect; and this is why I wish here to go on to inquire whether I, who have this idea, can exist if no such being exists.

And I ask, from whom do I then derive my existence? Perhaps from myself or from my parents, or from some other source less perfect than God; for we can imagine nothing more perfect than God, or even as perfect as He is.

But [were I independent of every other and] were I myself the author of my being, I should doubt nothing and I should desire nothing, and finally no perfection would be lacking to me; for I should have bestowed on myself every perfection of which I possessed any idea and should thus be God. And it must not be imagined that those things that are lacking to me are perhaps more difficult of attainment than those which I already possess; for, on the contrary, it is quite evident that it was a matter of much greater difficulty to bring to pass that I, that is to say, a thing or a substance that thinks, should emerge out of nothing, than it would be to attain to the knowledge of many things of which I am ignorant and which are only the accidents of this thinking substance. But it is clear that if I had of myself possessed this greater perfection of which I have just spoken [that is to say, if I had been the author of my own existence], I should not at least have denied myself the things which are the more easy to acquire [to wit, many branches of knowledge of which my nature is destitute]; nor should I have deprived myself of any of the things contained in the idea which I form of God, because there are none of them which seem to me specially difficult to acquire: and if there were any that were more difficult to acquire, they would certainly appear to me to be such (supposing I myself were the origin of the other things which I possess) since I should discover in them that my powers were limited.

But though I assume that perhaps I have always existed just as I am at present, neither can I escape the force of this reasoning and imagine that the conclusion to be drawn from this is that I need not seek for any author of my existence. For all the course of my life may be divided into an infinite number of parts, none of which is in any way dependent on the other; and thus from the fact that I was in existence a short time ago it does not follow that I must be in existence now, unless some cause at this instant, so to speak, produces me anew, that is to say, conserves me. It is as a matter of fact perfectly clear and evident to all those who consider with attention the nature of time that, in order to be conserved in each moment in which it endures, a substance has need of the same power and action as would be necessary to produce and create it anew, supposing it did not yet exist, so that the light of nature shows us clearly that the distinction between creation and conservation is solely a distinction of the reason.

All that I thus require here is that I should interrogate myself, if I wish to know whether I possess a power which is capable of bringing it to pass that I who now am shall still be in the future; for since I am nothing but a thinking thing, or at least since thus far it is only this portion of myself which is precisely in question at present, if such a power did reside in me, I should certainly be conscious of it. But I am conscious of nothing of the kind, and by this I know clearly that I depend on some being different from myself.

Possibly, however, this being on which I depend is not that which I call God, and I am created either by my parents or by some other cause less perfect than God. This cannot be, because, as I have just said, it is perfectly evident that there must be at least as much reality in the cause as in the effect; and thus since I am a thinking thing, and possess an idea of God within me, whatever in the end be the cause assigned to my existence, it must be allowed that it is likewise a thinking thing and that it possesses in itself the idea of all the perfections which I attribute to God. We may again inquire whether this cause derives its origin from itself or from some other thing. For if from itself, it follows by the reasons before brought forward that this cause must itself be God; for since it possesses the virtue of self-existence, it must also without doubt have the power of actually possessing all the perfections of which it has the idea, that is, all those which I conceive as existing in God. But if it derives its existence from some other cause than itself, we shall again ask, for the same reason, whether this second cause exists by itself or through another, until from one step to another, we finally arrive at an ultimate cause, which will be God.

And it is perfectly manifest that in this there can be no regression into infinity, since what is in question is not so much the cause which formerly created me, as that which conserves me at the present time.

Nor can we suppose that several causes may have concurred in my production, and that from one I have received the idea of one of the perfections which I attribute to God, and from another the idea of some other, so that all these perfections indeed exist somewhere in the universe, but not as complete in one unity which is God. On the contrary, the unity, the simplicity or the inseparability of all things which are in God is one of the principal perfections which I conceive to be in Him. And certainly the idea of this unity of all Divine perfections cannot have been placed in me by any cause from which I have not likewise received the ideas of all the other perfections; for this cause could not make me able to comprehend them as joined together in an inseparable unity without having at the same time caused me in some measure to know what they are [and in some way to recognise each one of them].

Finally, so far as my parents [from whom it appears I have sprung] are concerned, although all that I have ever been able to believe of them were true, that does not make it follow that it is they who conserve me, nor are they even the authors of my being in any sense, insofar as I am a thinking being; since what they did was merely to implant certain dispositions in that matter in which the self—i.e., the mind, which alone I at present identify with myself—is by me deemed to exist. And thus there can be no difficulty in their regard, but we must of necessity conclude from the fact alone that I exist, or that the idea of a Being supremely perfect—that is of God—is in me, that the proof of God's existence is grounded on the highest evidence.

It only remains to me to examine into the manner in which I have acquired this idea from God; for I have not received it through the senses, and it is never presented to me unexpectedly, as is usual with the ideas of sensible things when these things present themselves, or seem to present themselves, to the external organs of my senses; nor is it likewise a fiction of my mind, for it is not in my power to take from or to add anything to it; and consequently the only alternative is that it is innate in me, just as the idea of myself is innate in me.

And one certainly ought not to find it strange that God, in creating me, placed this idea within me to be like the mark of the workman imprinted on his work; and it is likewise not essential that the mark shall be something different from the work itself. For from the sole fact that God created me it is most probable that in some way he has placed his image and similitude upon me, and that I perceive this similitude (in which the idea of God is contained) by means of the same faculty by which I perceive myself—that is to say, when I reflect on myself I not only know that I am something [imperfect], incomplete and dependent on another, which incessantly aspires after something which is better and greater than myself, but I also know that He on whom I depend possesses in Himself all the great things towards which I aspire [and the ideas of which I find within myself], and that not indefinitely or potentially alone, but really, actually and infinitely; and that thus He is God. And the whole strength of the argument which I have here made use of to prove the existence of God consists in this, that I recognise that it is not possible that my nature should be what it is, and indeed that I should have in myself the idea of a God, if God did not veritably exist—a God, I say, whose idea is in me, i.e., who possesses all those supreme perfections of which our mind may indeed have some idea but without understanding them all, who is liable to no errors or defect [and who has none of all those marks which denote imperfection]. From this it is manifest that He cannot be a deceiver, since the light of nature teaches us that fraud and deception necessarily proceed from some defect.

But before I examine this matter with more care, and pass on to the consideration of other truths which may be derived from it, it seems to me right to pause for a while in order to contemplate God Himself, to ponder at leisure His marvellous attributes, to consider, and admire, and adore, the beauty of this light so resplendent, at least as far as the strength of my mind, which is in some measure dazzled by the sight, will allow me to do so. For just as faith teaches us that the supreme felicity of the other life consists only in this contemplation of the Divine Majesty, so we continue to learn by experience that a similar meditation, though incomparably less perfect, causes us to enjoy the greatest satisfaction of which we are capable in this life.

Meditation V. Of the Essence of Material Things, and, Again, of God, that He Exists

...But now, if just because I can draw the idea of something from my thought, it follows that all which I know clearly and distinctly as pertaining to this object does really belong to it, may I not derive from this an argument demonstrating the existence of God? It is certain that I no less find the idea of God, that is to say, the idea of a supremely perfect Being, in me than that of any figure or number whatever it is; and I do not know any less clearly and distinctly that an [actual and] eternal existence pertains to this nature than I know that all that which I am able to demonstrate of some figure or number truly pertains to the nature of this figure or number, and therefore, although all that I concluded in the preceding Meditations were found to be false, the existence of God would pass with me as at least as certain as I have ever held the truths of mathematics (which concern only numbers and figures) to be.

This indeed is not at first manifest, since it would seem to present some appearance of being a sophism. For being accustomed in all other things to make a distinction between existence and essence, I easily persuade myself that the existence can be separated from the essence of God, and that we can thus conceive God as not actually existing. But, nevertheless, when I think of it with more attention, I clearly see that existence can no more be separated from the essence of God than can its having its three angles equal to two right angles be separated from the essence of a triangle, or the idea of a mountain from the idea of a valley; and so there is not any less repugnance to our conceiving a God (that is, a Being supremely perfect) to whom existence is lacking (that is to say, to whom a certain perfection is lacking) than to conceive of a mountain which has no valley.

But although I cannot really conceive of a God without existence any more than a mountain without a valley, still from the fact that I conceive of a mountain with a valley, it does not follow that there is such a mountain in the world; similarly although I conceive of God as possessing existence, it would seem that it does not follow that there is a God which exists; for my thought does not impose any necessity upon things, and just as I may imagine a winged horse, although no horse with wings exists, so I could perhaps attribute existence to God, although no God existed.

But a sophism is concealed in this objection; for from the fact that I cannot conceive a mountain without a valley, it does not follow that there is any mountain or any valley in existence, but only that the mountain and the valley, whether they exist or do not exist, cannot in any way be separated one from the other. While from the fact that I cannot conceive God without existence, it follows that existence is inseparable from Him, and hence that He really exists; not that my thought can bring this to pass, or impose any necessity on things, but, on the contrary, because the necessity which lies in the thing itself, i.e., the necessity of the existence of God determines me to think in this way. For it is not within my power to think of God without existence (that is, of a supremely perfect Being devoid of a supreme perfection) though it is in my power to imagine a horse either with wings or without wings.

And we must not here object that it is in truth necessary for me to assert that God exists after having presupposed that He possesses every sort of perfection, since existence is one of these, but that as a matter of fact my original supposition was not necessary, just as it is not necessary to consider that all quadrilateral figures can be inscribed in the circle; for supposing I thought this, I should be constrained to admit that the rhombus might be inscribed in the circle since it is a quadrilateral figure, which, however, is manifestly false. [We must not, I say, make any such allegations because] although it is not necessary that I should at any time entertain the notion of God, nevertheless whenever it happens that I think of a first and a sovereign Being, and, so to speak, derive the idea of Him from the storehouse of my mind, it is necessary that I should attribute to Him every sort of perfection, although I do not get so far as to enumerate them all or to apply my mind to each one in particular. And this necessity suffices to make me conclude (after having recognised that existence is a perfection) that this first and sovereign Being really exists; just as though it is not necessary for me ever to imagine any triangle, yet, whenever I wish to consider a rectilinear figure composed only of three angles, it is absolutely essential that I should attribute to it all those properties which serve to bring about the conclusion that its three angles are not greater than two right angles, even although I may not then be considering this point in particular. But when I consider which figures are capable of being inscribed in the circle, it is in no wise necessary that I should think that all quadrilateral figures are of this number; on the contrary, I cannot even pretend that this is the case, so long as I do not desire to accept anything which I cannot conceive clearly and distinctly. And in consequence there is a great difference between the false suppositions such as this and the true ideas born within me, the first and principal of which is that of God. For really I discern in many ways that this idea is not something factitious, and depending solely on my thought, but that it is the image of a true and immutable nature; first of all, because I cannot conceive anything but God himself to whose essence existence [necessarily] pertains; in the second place because it is not possible for me to conceive two or more Gods in this same position; and, granted that there is one such God who now exists, I see clearly that it is necessary that He should have existed from all eternity, and that He must exist eternally; and finally, because I know an infinitude of other properties in God, none of which I can either diminish or change.

For the rest, whatever proof or argument I avail myself of, we must always return to the point that it is only those things which we conceive clearly and distinctly that have the power of persuading me entirely. And although amongst the matters which I conceive of in this way, some indeed are manifestly obvious to all, while others only manifest themselves to those who consider them closely and examine them attentively; still, after they have once been discovered, the latter are not esteemed as any less certain than the former. For example, in the case of every right-angled triangle, although it does not so manifestly appear that the square of the base is equal to the squares of the two other sides as that this base is opposite to the greatest angle, still, when this has once been apprehended, we are just as certain of its truth as of the truth of the other. And as regards God, if my mind were not pre-occupied with prejudices, and if my thought did not find itself on all hands diverted by the continual pressure of sensible things, there would be nothing which I could know more immediately and more easily than Him. For is there anything more manifest than that there is a God, that is to say, a Supreme Being, to whose essence alone existence pertains?

And although for a firm grasp of this truth I have need of a strenuous application of mind, at present I not only feel myself to be as assured of it as of all that I hold as most certain, but I also remark that the certainty of all other things depends on it so absolutely, that without this knowledge it is impossible ever to know anything perfectly.

25.2 PASCAL'S WAGER

Some of the most influential arguments for the existence of God are practical arguments, insisting that belief in God is rational. The best-known such argument for God's existence is Pascal's wager, developed by Blaise Pascal (1623–1662), a French philosopher and mathematician who was a contemporary of Descartes and a member of the Port-Royal

Academy. Pascal, despairing of any attempt to prove God's existence theoretically, thinks of the person trying to decide whether or not to believe in God as someone about to make a bet. You must place your bet under conditions of total uncertainty; you cannot know whether God exists or not or even where the probabilities lie. And you cannot refuse to bet; you must believe in God or decline to believe in Him. What should you do?

Here is the situation facing you:

	You believe	You do not believe
God exists	Heaven, Virtue	Hell
God does not exist	Virtue	Nothing

If you believe, and God exists, you earn the eternal rewards of Heaven. If God does not exist, you still benefit, for believing in God develops virtues, whether or not God exists. If He exists, it additionally yields the infinite benefit of Heaven. There is nothing to lose and everything to gain. (This assumes that God admits believers into Heaven even if they believe for self-interested reasons and behave despicably.)

Failing to believe, in contrast, can result in no benefit whatever. If God exists, it earns one the eternal punishments of Hell. If God does not exist—or if the traditional picture of Hell is mistaken—then it yields nothing: no reward, no punishment. There is nothing to gain and everything to lose.

Placing a bet that God does not exist, then, cannot win, and placing a bet that God exists cannot lose. Pascal concludes that faith in God is rational, even if God's existence cannot be given rational proof.

Critics counter that belief is not voluntary in the way Pascal thinks; you cannot bet on what is not for you a "live option," to use the words of American philosopher William James. Others say that Pascal has the wrong idea about religious options available as well as the consequences of believing or not believing.

25.2.1 Blaise Pascal, from *Thoughts*

Section III. Of the Necessity of the Wager

184. A letter to incite to the search after God.

And then to make people seek Him among the philosophers, sceptics, and dogmatists, who disquiet him who inquires of them.

185. The conduct of God, who disposes all things kindly, is to put religion into the mind by reason and into the heart by grace. But to will to put it into the mind and heart by force and threats is not to put religion there, but terror; *terrorem potius quam religionem.* ["Terror which is more powerful than religion."]...

195. Before entering into the proofs of the Christian religion, I find it necessary to point out the sinfulness of those men who live in indifference to the search for truth in a matter which is so important to them and which touches

Source: Blaise Pascal, *Thoughts.* Translated by W. F. Trotter. New York: P. F. Collier & Son, 1910.

them so nearly. Of all their errors, this doubtless is the one which most convicts them of foolishness and blindness and in which it is easiest to confound them by the first glimmerings of common sense and by natural feelings.

For it is not to be doubted that the duration of this life is but a moment; that the state of death is eternal, whatever may be its nature; and that thus all our actions and thoughts must take such different directions, according to the state of that eternity, that it is impossible to take one step with sense and judgement unless we regulate our course by the truth of that point which ought to be our ultimate end.

There is nothing clearer than this; and thus, according to the principles of reason, the conduct of men is wholly unreasonable if they do not take another course.

On this point, therefore, we condemn those who live without thought of the ultimate end of life, who let themselves be guided by their own inclinations and their own pleasures without reflection and without concern, and, as if they could annihilate eternity by turning away their thought from it, think only of making themselves happy for the moment.

Yet this eternity exists, and death, which must open into it and threatens them every hour, must in a little time infallibly put them under the dreadful necessity of being either annihilated or unhappy forever, without knowing which of these eternities is forever prepared for them.

This resting in ignorance is a monstrous thing, and they who pass their life in it must be made to feel its extravagance and stupidity, by having it shown to them, so that they may be confounded by the sight of their folly. For this is how men reason, when they choose to live in such ignorance of what they are and without seeking enlightenment. "I know not," they say....

198. The sensibility of man to trifles, and his insensibility to great things, indicates a strange inversion.

199. Let us imagine a number of men in chains and all condemned to death, where some are killed each day in the sight of the others, and those who remain see their own fate in that of their fellows and wait their turn, looking at each other sorrowfully and without hope. It is an image of the condition of men.

200. A man in a dungeon, ignorant whether his sentence be pronounced and having only one hour to learn it, but this hour enough, if he knew that it is pronounced, to obtain its repeal, would act unnaturally in spending that hour, not in ascertaining his sentence, but in playing piquet. So it is against nature that man, etc. It is making heavy the hand of God.

Thus not only the zeal of those who seek Him proves God, but also the blindness of those who seek Him not....

233. Infinite-nothing.—Our soul is cast into a body, where it finds number, dimension. Thereupon it reasons, and calls this nature necessity, and can believe nothing else.

Unity joined to infinity adds nothing to it, no more than one foot to an infinite measure. The finite is annihilated in the presence of the infinite, and becomes a pure nothing. So our spirit before God, so our justice before divine justice. There is not so great a disproportion between our justice and that of God as between unity and infinity.

The justice of God must be vast like His compassion. Now justice to the outcast is less vast and ought less to offend our feelings than mercy towards the elect.

We know that there is an infinite, and are ignorant of its nature. As we know it to be false that numbers are finite, it is therefore true that there is an infinity in number. But we do not know what it is. It is false that it is even, it is false that it is odd; for the addition of a unit can make no change in its nature. Yet it is a number, and every number is odd or even (this is certainly true of every finite number). So we may well know that there is a God without knowing what He is. Is there not one substantial truth, seeing there are so many things which are not the truth itself? We know then the existence and nature of the finite, because we also are finite and have extension. We know the existence of the infinite and are ignorant of its nature, because it has extension like us, but not limits like us. But we know neither the existence nor the nature of God, because He has neither extension nor limits.

But by faith we know His existence; in glory we shall know His nature. Now, I have already shown that we may well know the existence of a thing without knowing its nature.

Let us now speak according to natural lights.

If there is a God, He is infinitely incomprehensible, since, having neither parts nor limits, He has no affinity to us. We are then incapable of knowing either what He is or if He is. This being so, who will dare to undertake the decision of the question? Not we, who have no affinity to Him.

Who then will blame Christians for not being able to give a reason for their belief, since they profess a religion for which they cannot give a reason? They declare, in expounding it to the world, that it is a foolishness, *stultitiam* [I Cor. 1. 21.]; and then you complain that they do not prove it! If they proved it, they would not keep their word; it is in lacking proofs that they are not lacking in sense. "Yes, but although this excuses those who offer it as such and takes away from them the blame of putting it forward without reason, it does not excuse those who receive it." Let us then examine this point, and say, "God is, or He is not." But to which side shall we incline? Reason can decide nothing here. There is an infinite chaos which separates us. A game is being played at the extremity of this infinite distance where heads or tails will turn up. What will you wager? According to reason, you can do neither the one thing nor the other; according to reason, you can defend neither of the propositions.

Do not, then, reprove for error those who have made a choice; for you know nothing about it. "No, but I blame them for having made, not this choice, but a choice; for again both he who chooses heads and he who chooses tails are equally at fault, they are both in the wrong. The true course is not to wager at all."

Yes; but you must wager. It is not optional. You are embarked. Which will you choose then? Let us see. Since you must choose, let us see which interests you least. You have two things to lose, the true and the good; and two things to stake, your reason and your will, your knowledge and your happiness; and your nature has two things to shun, error and misery. Your reason is no more shocked in choosing one rather than the other, since you must of necessity choose. This is one point settled. But your happiness? Let us weigh the gain and the loss in wagering that God is. Let us estimate these two chances. If you gain, you gain all; if you lose, you lose nothing. Wager, then, without hesitation that He is. "That is very fine. Yes, I must wager; but I may perhaps wager too much." Let us see. Since there is an equal risk of gain and of loss, if you had only to gain two lives, instead of one, you might still wager. But if there were three lives to gain, you would have to play (since you are under the necessity of playing), and you would be imprudent, when you are forced to play, not to chance your life to gain three at a game where there is an equal risk of loss and gain. But there is an eternity of life and happiness. And this being so, if there were an infinity of chances, of which one only would be for you, you would still be right in wagering one to win two, and you would act stupidly, being obliged to play, by refusing to stake one life against three at a game in which out of an infinity of chances there is one for you, if there were an infinity of an infinitely happy life to gain. But there is here an infinity of an infinitely happy life to gain, a chance of gain against a finite number of chances of loss, and what you stake is finite. It is all divided; whereever the infinite is and there is not an infinity of chances of loss against that of gain, there is no time to hesitate, you must give all. And thus, when one is forced to play, he must renounce reason to preserve his life, rather than risk it for infinite gain, as likely to happen as the loss of nothingness.

For it is no use to say it is uncertain if we will gain, and it is certain that we risk, and that the infinite distance between the certainty of what is staked and the uncertainty of what will be gained equals the finite good which is certainly staked against the uncertain infinite. It is not so, as every player stakes a certainty to gain an uncertainty, and yet he stakes a finite certainty to gain a finite uncertainty, without transgressing against reason. There is not an infinite distance between the certainty staked and the uncertainty of the gain; that is untrue. In truth, there is an infinity between the certainty of gain and the certainty of loss. But the uncertainty of the gain is proportioned to the certainty of the stake according to the proportion of the chances of gain and loss. Hence it comes that, if there are as many risks on one side as on the other, the course is to play even; and then the certainty of the stake is equal to the uncertainty of the gain, so far is it from fact that there is an infinite distance between them. And so our proposition is of infinite force when there is the finite to stake in a game where there are equal risks of gain and of loss and the infinite to gain. This is demonstrable; and if men are capable of any truths, this is one.

"I confess it, I admit it. But, still, is there no means of seeing the faces of the cards?" Yes, scripture and the rest, etc. "Yes, but I have my hands tied and my mouth closed; I am forced to wager, and am not free. I am not released, and am so made that I cannot believe. What, then, would you have me do?"

True. But at least learn your inability to believe, since reason brings you to this, and yet you cannot believe. Endeavour, then, to convince yourself, not by increase of proofs of God, but by the abatement of your passions. You would like to attain faith and do not know the way; you would like to cure yourself of unbelief and ask the remedy for it. Learn of those who have been bound like you, and who now stake all their possessions. These are people who know the way which you would follow, and who are cured of an ill of which you would be cured. Follow the way by which they began; by acting as if they believed, taking the holy water, having masses said, etc. Even this will naturally make you believe, and deaden your acuteness. "But this is what I am afraid of." And why? What have you to lose?

But to show you that this leads you there, it is this which will lessen the passions, which are your stumbling-blocks.

The end of this discourse.—Now, what harm will befall you in taking this side? You will be faithful, humble, grateful, generous, a sincere friend, truthful. Certainly you will not have those poisonous pleasures, glory and luxury; but will you not have others? I will tell you that you will thereby gain in this life, and that, at each step you take on this road, you will see so great certainty of gain, so much nothingness in what you risk, that you will at last recognise that you have wagered for something certain and infinite, for which you have given nothing.

"Ah! This discourse transports me, charms me," etc.

If this discourse pleases you and seems impressive, know that it is made by a man who has knelt, both before and after it, in prayer to that Being, infinite and without parts, before whom he lays all he has, for you also to lay before Him all you have for your own good and for His glory, that so strength may be given to lowliness.

234. If we must not act save on a certainty, we ought not to act on religion, for it is not certain. But how many things we do on an uncertainty, sea voyages, battles! I say then we must do nothing at all, for nothing is certain, and that there is more certainty in religion than there is as to whether we may see tomorrow; for it is not certain that we may see tomorrow, and it is certainly possible that we may not see it. We cannot say as much about religion. It is not certain that it is; but who will venture to say that it is certainly possible that it is not? Now when we work for tomorrow, and so on an uncertainty, we act reasonably; for we ought to work for an uncertainty according to the doctrine of chance which was demonstrated above.

Saint Augustine has seen that we work for an uncertainty, on sea, in battle, etc. But he has not seen the doctrine of chance which proves that we should do so. Montaigne has seen that we are shocked at a fool, and that habit is all-powerful; but he has not seen the reason of this effect.

All these persons have seen the effects, but they have not seen the causes. They are, in comparison with those who have discovered the causes, as those who have only eyes are in comparison with those who have intellect. For the effects are perceptible by sense, and the causes are visible only to the intellect. And although these effects are seen by the mind, this mind is, in comparison with the mind which sees the causes, as the bodily senses are in comparison with the intellect.

Section IV. Of the Means of Belief

270. Saint Augustine.—Reason would never submit if it did not judge that there are some occasions on which it ought to submit. It is then right for it to submit when it judges that it ought to submit.

271. Wisdom sends us to childhood. *Nisi efficiamini sicut parvuli.* [Matt. 18. 3. "Except ye become as little children."]

272. There is nothing so conformable to reason as this disavowal of reason.

273. If we submit everything to reason, our religion will have no mysterious and supernatural element. If we offend the principles of reason, our religion will be absurd and ridiculous.

274. All our reasoning reduces itself to yielding to feeling.

But fancy is like, though contrary to, feeling, so that we cannot distinguish between these contraries. One person says that my feeling is fancy, another that his fancy is feeling. We should have a rule. Reason offers itself; but it is pliable in every sense; and thus there is no rule.

275. Men often take their imagination for their heart; and they believe they are converted as soon as they think of being converted.

276. M. de Roannez said: "Reasons come to me afterwards, but at first a thing pleases or shocks me without my knowing the reason, and yet it shocks me for that reason which I only discover afterwards." But I believe, not that it shocked him for the reasons which were found afterwards, but that these reasons were only found because it shocked him.

277. The heart has its reasons, which reason does not know. We feel it in a thousand things. I say that the heart naturally loves the Universal Being, and also itself naturally, according as it gives itself to them; and it hardens itself against one or the other at its will. You have rejected the one and kept the other. Is it by reason that you love yourself?

278. It is the heart which experiences God, and not the reason. This, then, is faith: God felt by the heart, not by the reason.

279. Faith is a gift of God; do not believe that we said it was a gift of reasoning. Other religions do not say this of their faith. They only gave reasoning in order to arrive at it, and yet it does not bring them to it.

280. The knowledge of God is very far from the love of Him.

281. Heart, instinct, principles.

282. We know truth not only by the reason but also by the heart, and it is in this last way that we know first principles; and reason, which has no part in it, tries in vain to impugn them. The sceptics, who have only this for their object, labour to no purpose. We know that we do not dream, and, however impossible it is for us to prove it by reason, this inability demonstrates only the weakness of our reason, but not, as they affirm, the uncertainty of all our knowledge. For the knowledge of first principles, as space, time, motion, number, is as sure as any of those which we get from reasoning. And reason must trust these intuitions of the heart, and must base them on every argument. (We have intuitive knowledge of the tri-dimensional nature of space and of the infinity of number, and reason then shows that there are no two square numbers one of which is double of the other. Principles are intuited, propositions are inferred, all with certainty, though in different ways.) And it is as useless and absurd for reason to demand from the heart proofs of her first principles, before admitting them, as it would be for the heart to demand from reason an intuition of all demonstrated propositions before accepting them.

This inability ought, then, to serve only to humble reason which would judge all, but not to impugn our certainty, as if only reason were capable of instructing us. Would to God, on the contrary, that we had never need of it, and that we knew everything by instinct and intuition! But nature has refused us this boon. On the contrary, she has given us but very little knowledge of this kind; and all the rest can be acquired only by reasoning.

Therefore, those to whom God has imparted religion by intuition are very fortunate and justly convinced. But to those who do not have it, we can give it only by reasoning, waiting for God to give them spiritual insight, without which faith is only human and useless for salvation.

25.3 LEIBNIZ AND THE PROBLEM OF EVIL

Gottfried Wilhelm von Leibniz (1646–1716) put the cosmological argument in a form that shows Averroes's influence. It rests on a basic principle of Leibniz's rationalistic philosophy, the principle of sufficient reason:

> ...nothing happens without a sufficient reason; that is to say, that nothing happens without its being possible for him who should sufficiently understand things, to give a reason sufficient to determine why it is so and not otherwise.

This principle is very broad, implying that every event has a cause; that nothing happens purely by chance; that everything can be explained; and that the universe is ultimately intelligible, existing for a reason.

> Now this sufficient reason for the existence of the universe cannot be found in the series of contingent things, that is, of bodies and of their representation in souls; for matter being indifferent in itself to motion and to rest, and to this or another motion, we cannot find the reason of motion in it, and still less of a certain motion. And although the present motion which is in matter comes from the preceding motion, and that from still another preceding, yet in this way we make no progress, try as we may; for the same question always remains. Thus it must be that the sufficient reason, which has no need of another reason, be outside this series of contingent things and be found in a substance which is the cause, or which is a necessary being, carrying the reason of its existence within itself; otherwise we still should not have a sufficient reason in which we could rest. And this final reason of things is called God.

By the principle of sufficient reason, everything exists for a reason—including the entire series of contingent causes. Take the entire history of the universe, finite or infinite, and ask why it exists. Why is there something rather than nothing? Why is this particular history actual? There must be a sufficient reason for the entire universe. And that is God. It cannot be the universe itself or anything material, since matter is indifferent to existence or nonexistence. It must be something outside the realm of the material, temporal world that explains the existence of everything else. There must, in other words, be something spiritual that explains the existence of everything, spiritual and material. And that can only be God.

Leibniz is most famous for his response to the problem of evil. He uses the term *theodicy* for that area of philosophic theology intent on explaining evil on theistic assumptions, that is to say, theology that would justify God's lovingness in the face of evil. The word is also used for any theory that would explain evil while maintaining the reality of God (or the like), and Leibniz himself formulated a theodicy that is in fact an early version of *process aesthetic theodicy*, that God is in the process of perfecting the world. Another contribution of Leibniz's facilitates discussion. He distinguishes three kinds of evil: (a) metaphysical evil, the evil of anything in comparison with God, who is the most valuable entity (even morally perfect angels are evil in this sense); (b) moral evil, evil done intentionally by human beings or other moral agents, for example, Hitler's crimes; and (c) natural evil, evil in the universe for which no moral agent (other than perhaps God, the Creator) is responsible, for example, disease, old age, and death. (These, you may recall, are the evils identified by the Buddha-to-be according to Buddhist tradition.)

Leibniz reasoned that since (1) God is the omnipotent Creator of everything and (2) God is omnibenevolent, or all-loving, then (3) this, the universe that God has created, is the best of all possible worlds. In other words, the conclusion (3) that this is the best of all possible worlds is entailed by the truth of premises (1) and (2), propositions that themselves follow from a definition of God as the perfect being along with the supposition that God in fact exists. Now if it follows from (4) there is evil that (5) this is not the best of all possible worlds, then there is incompatibility between (a) the existence of God as perfect (as both omnipotent and omnibenevolent) and (b) the reality of evil. So there is either no evil or no God.

But surely there is evil of some type or other, Leibniz reflected. There is metaphysical evil just in there being a universe at all. Thus God as omnipotent and omnibenevolent is compatible, he reasoned, with metaphysical evil: God out of God's omnibenevolence would create a universe just to let creatures have, so to say, their day in the sun. So metaphysical evil should be expected given an all-loving Creator. Thus metaphysical evil is not just compatible with an all-loving God, it is explained by God's all-lovingness as what we would expect from God.

Now, moral evil brought about by agents other than God also presents no problem, inasmuch as a precondition of moral action, namely, free will, is itself something good. It is, say advocates of "free-will theodicy," indeed a most valuable attribute of a creature. God does something good in creating beings who are free. Thus given a God who is omnibenevolent and the assumption that it is likely some with free will will sin, then moral evil is to be expected, too. Most critics of theism have accepted this line of reasoning, although there are some that question the assumption whether freedom need mean that any are likely to sin. However, on all accounts the main problem is natural evil, disease, old age, and death.

25.3.1 G. W. Leibniz, from *Theodicy*

Some intelligent persons have desired that this supplement be made, and I have the more readily yielded to their wishes as in this way I have an opportunity again to remove certain difficulties and to make some observations which were not sufficiently emphasized in the work itself.

Source: Gottfried W. Leibniz, *The Philosophical Works of Leibniz*. Translated by George M. Duncan. London: Tuttle, Morehouse & Taylor, 1890.

I. Objection. Whoever does not choose the best is lacking in power, or in knowledge, or in goodness. God did not choose the best in creating this world. Therefore, God has been lacking in power, or in knowledge, or in goodness.

Answer. I deny the minor, that is, the second premise of this syllogism; and our opponent proves it by this.

Prosyllogism. Whoever makes things in which there is evil, which could have been made without any evil, or the making of which could have been omitted, does not choose the best. God has made a world in which there is evil, a world, I say, which could have been made without any evil, or the making of which could have been omitted altogether. Therefore, God has not chosen the best.

Answer. I grant the minor of this prosyllogism; for it must be confessed that there is evil in this world which God has made, and that it was possible to make a world without evil, or even not to create a world at all, for its creation has depended on the free will of God; but I deny the major, that is, the first of the two premises of the prosyllogism, and I might content myself with simply demanding its proof; but in order to make the matter clearer, I have wished to justify this denial by showing that the best plan is not always that which seeks to avoid evil, since it may happen that the evil is accompanied by a greater good. For example, a general of an army will prefer a great victory with a slight wound to a condition without wound and without victory. We have proved this more fully in the large work by making it clear, by instances taken from mathematics and elsewhere, that an imperfection in the part may be required for a greater perfection in the whole. In this I have followed the opinion of St. Augustine, who has said a hundred times, that God has permitted evil in order to bring about good, that is, a greater good; and that of Thomas Aquinas that the permitting of evil tends to the good of the universe. I have shown that the ancients called Adam's fall *felix culpa*, a happy sin, because it had been retrieved with immense advantage by the incarnation of the Son of God, who has given to the universe something nobler than anything that ever would have been among creatures except for it. For the sake of a clearer understanding, I have added, following many good authors, that it was in accordance with order and the general good that God allowed to certain creatures the opportunity of exercising their liberty, even when he foresaw that they would turn to evil, but which he could so well rectify; because it was not fitting that, in order to hinder sin, God should always act in an extraordinary manner. To overthrow this objection, therefore, it is sufficient to show that a world with evil might be better than a world without evil; but I have gone even farther, in the work, and have even proved that this universe must be in reality better than every other possible universe....

VII. Objection. Whoever gives only to some, and not to all, the means which produces in them effectively a good will and salutary final faith, has not sufficient goodness. God does this. Hence, etc.

Answer. I deny the major of this. It is true that God could overcome the greatest resistance of the human heart; and does it, too, sometimes, either by internal grace or by external circumstances which have a great effect on souls; but he does not always do this. Whence comes this distinction? it may be asked, and why does his goodness seem limited? It is because, as I have already said in answering the first objection, it would not have been in order always to act in an extraordinary manner and to reverse the connection of things. The reasons of this connection, by means of which one is placed in more favorable circumstances than another, are hidden in the depths of the wisdom of God: they depend upon the universal harmony. The best plan of the universe, which God could not fail to choose, made it so. We judge from the event itself; since God has made it, it was not possible to do better. Far from being true that this conduct is contrary to goodness, it is supreme goodness which led him to it. This objection with its solution might have been drawn from what was said in regard to the first objection; but it seemed useful to touch upon it separately.

VIII. Objection. Whoever cannot fail to choose the best, is not free. God cannot fail to choose the best. Hence, God is not free.

Answer. I deny the major of this argument; it is rather true liberty, and the most perfect, to be able to use one's free will for the best, and to always exercise this power, without ever being turned aside either by external force or by internal passions, the first of which causes slavery of the body, the second, slavery of the soul. There is nothing less servile, and nothing more in accordance with the highest degree of freedom, than to be always led toward the good, and always by one's own inclination, without any constraint and without any displeasure. And to object therefore that God had need of external things is only a sophism. He created them freely; but having proposed to himself an end, which is to exercise his goodness, wisdom has determined him to choose the means best fitted to attain this end. To call this a need is to take that term in an unusual sense which frees it from all imperfection, just as when we speak of the wrath of God.

Seneca has somewhere said that God commanded but once but that he obeys always, because he obeys laws which he willed to prescribe to himself: *semel jussit, semper paret.* But he might better have said that God always commands and that he is always obeyed; for in willing, he always follows the inclination of his own nature, and all other things always follow his will. And as this will is always the same, it cannot be said that he obeys only that will which he formerly had. Nevertheless, although his will is always infallible and always tends toward the best, the evil, or the lesser good, which he rejects, does not cease to be possible in itself; otherwise the necessity of the good would be geometrical (so to speak), or metaphysical, and altogether absolute; the contingency of things would be destroyed, and there would be no choice. But this sort of necessity, which does not destroy the possibility of the contrary, has this name only by analogy; it becomes effective, not by the pure essence of things, but by that which is outside of them, above them, namely, by the will of God. This necessity is called moral, because, to the sage, necessity and what ought to be are equivalent things; and when it always has its effect, as it really has in the perfect sage, that is, in God, it may be said that it is a happy necessity. The nearer creatures approach to it, the nearer they approach to perfect happiness. Also this kind of necessity is not that which we try to avoid and which destroys morality, rewards and praise. For that which it brings does not happen whatever we may do or will, but because we will it so. And a will to which it is natural to choose well merits praise so much the more; also it carries its reward with it, which is sovereign happiness. And as this constitution of the divine nature gives entire satisfaction to him who possesses it, it is also the best and the most desirable for the creatures who are all dependent on God. If the will of God did not have for a rule the principle of the best, it would either tend toward evil, which would be the worst, or it would be in some way indifferent to good and to evil and would be guided by chance: but a will which would allow itself always to act by chance would not be worth more for the government of the universe than the fortuitous concourse of atoms, without there being any divinity therein. And even if God should abandon himself to chance only in some cases and in a certain way (as he would do, if he did not always work entirely for the best and if he were capable of preferring a lesser work to a greater, that is, an evil to a good, since that which prevents a greater good is an evil), he would be imperfect, as well as the object of his choice; he would not merit entire confidence; he would act without reason in such a case, and the government of the universe would be like certain games, equally divided between reason and chance. All this proves that this objection which is made against the choice of the best perverts the notions of the free and of the necessary, and represents to us the best even as evil: which is either malicious or ridiculous.

25.4 PALEY'S ARGUMENT FROM DESIGN

Thomas Aquinas advanced an argument from design that convinced few. In the hands of William Paley (1743–1805), however, the argument took on new life. Paley graduated Cambridge at 20 and joined the faculty just five years later. He published an influential work on ethics, tirelessly advocated the abolition of the slave trade, and wrote *Natural Theology; or, Evidences of the Existence and Attributes of the Deity* to argue for the existence of God.

Paley compares the universe to a watch found on the heath. The structure and success of the watch would lead us to conclude that it is an artifact; it had a designer, a maker. The universe, like the watch, is highly structured; its parts succeed in working together predictably, according to laws. We have every reason, then, to ascribe to it a designer, a maker. But who could be brilliant and powerful enough to design a universe? Only God.

Paley's argument, in outline, is simple. But *Natural Theology* goes through the organization of nature in great detail, to demonstrate at a small-scale level the intricacy of divine design. Among those who took Paley seriously was Charles Darwin (1809–1882), who undertook to show in equal detail how naturalistic, evolutionary explanations could replace theological ones in accounting for the structure of the natural world.

25.4.1 William Paley, from *Natural Theology*

Chapter I. State of the Argument

In crossing a heath, suppose I pitched my foot against a stone and were asked how the stone came to be there; I might possibly answer that, for anything I knew to the contrary, it had lain there forever: nor would it perhaps be very easy to show the absurdity of this answer. But suppose I had found a watch upon the ground, and it should be inquired how the watch happened to be in that place; I should hardly think of the answer which I had before given, that, for anything I knew, the watch might have always been there. Yet why should not this answer serve for the watch as well as for the stone? why is it not as admissible in the second case as in the first? For this reason, and for no other, viz. that, when we come to inspect the watch, we perceive (what we could not discover in the stone) that its several parts are framed and put together for a purpose, e.g., that they are so formed and adjusted as to produce motion, and that motion so regulated as to point out the hour of the day; that, if the different parts had been differently shaped from what they are, of a different size from what they are, or placed after any other manner, or in any other order, than that in which they are placed, either no motion at all would have been carried on in the machine, or none which would have answered the use that is now served by it. To reckon up a few of the plainest of these parts, and of their offices, all tending to one result:—We see a cylindrical box containing a coiled elastic

Source: William Paley, *Natural Theology; or, Evidences of the Existence and Attributes of the Deity*. London: Printed for J. Faulder, 12 ed., 1809.

spring, which, by its endeavour to relax itself, turns round the box. We next observe a flexible chain (artificially wrought for the sake of flexure), communicating the action of the spring from the box to the fusee. We then find a series of wheels, the teeth of which catch in, and apply to, each other, conducting the motion from the fusee to the balance, and from the balance to the pointer; and at the same time, by the size and shape of those wheels, so regulating that motion as to terminate in causing an index, by an equable and measured progression, to pass over a given space in a given time. We take notice that the wheels are made of brass in order to keep them from rust; the springs of steel, no other metal being so elastic; that over the face of the watch there is placed a glass, a material employed in no other part of the work, but in the room of which, if there had been any other than a transparent substance, the hour could not be seen without opening the case. This mechanism being observed (it requires indeed an examination of the instrument, and perhaps some previous knowledge of the subject, to perceive and understand it; but being once, as we have said, observed and understood), the inference, we think, is inevitable, that the watch must have had a maker: that there must have existed, at some time, and at some place or other, an artificer or artificers who formed it for the purpose which we find it actually to answer; who comprehended its construction, and designed its use.

I. Nor would it, I apprehend, weaken the conclusion, that we had never seen a watch made; that we had never known an artist capable of making one; that we were altogether incapable of executing such a piece of workmanship ourselves, or of understanding in what manner it was performed; all this being no more than what is true of some exquisite remains of ancient art, of some lost arts, and, to the generality of mankind, of the more curious productions of modern manufacture. Does one man in a million know how oval frames are turned? Ignorance of this kind exalts our opinion of the unseen and unknown artist's skill, if he be unseen and unknown, but raises no doubt in our minds of the existence and agency of such an artist, at some former time, and in some place or other. Nor can I perceive that it varies at all the inference, whether the question arise concerning a human agent, or concerning an agent of a different species, or an agent possessing, in some respects, a different nature.

II. Neither, secondly, would it invalidate our conclusion that the watch sometimes went wrong, or that it seldom went exactly right. The purpose of the machinery, the design, and the designer, might be evident, and in the case supposed would be evident in whatever way we accounted for the irregularity of the movement, or whether we could account for it or not. It is not necessary that a machine be perfect in order to show with what design it was made: still less necessary where the only question is whether it were made with any design at all.

III. Nor, thirdly, would it bring any uncertainty into the argument if there were a few parts of the watch concerning which we could not discover, or had not yet discovered, in what manner they conduced to the general effect; or even some parts, concerning which we could not ascertain whether they conduced to that effect in any manner whatever. For, as to the first branch of the case; if by the loss, or disorder, or decay of the parts in question, the movement of the watch were found in fact to be stopped, or disturbed, or retarded, no doubt would remain in our minds as to the utility or intention of these parts, although we should be unable to investigate the manner according to which, or the connexion by which, the ultimate effect depended upon their action or assistance; and the more complex is the machine, the more likely is this obscurity to arise. Then, as to the second thing supposed, namely, that there were parts which might be spared without prejudice to the movement of the watch, and that we had proved this by experiment,—these superfluous parts, even if we were completely assured that they were such, would not vacate the reasoning which we had instituted concerning other parts. The indication of contrivance remained, with respect to them, nearly as it was before.

IV. Nor, fourthly, would any man in his senses think the existence of the watch, with its various machinery, accounted for by being told that it was one out of possible combinations of material forms; that whatever he had found in the place where he found the watch must have contained some internal configuration or other; and that this configuration might be the structure now exhibited, viz. of the works of a watch, as well as a different structure.

V. Nor, fifthly, would it yield his inquiry more satisfaction to be answered that there existed in things a principle of order, which had disposed the parts of the watch into their present form and situation. He never knew a watch made by the principle of order; nor can he even form to himself an idea of what is meant by a principle of order distinct from the intelligence of the watch-maker.

VI. Sixthly, he would be surprised to hear that the mechanism of the watch was no proof of contrivance, only a motive to induce the mind to think so:

VII. And not less surprised to be informed that the watch in his hand was nothing more than the result of the laws of metallic nature. It is a perversion of language to assign any law as the efficient, operative cause of anything. A law presupposes an agent; for it is only the mode according to which an agent proceeds: it implies a power; for it is the order according to which that power acts. Without this agent, without this power, which are both distinct from itself, the law does nothing, is nothing. The expression "the law of metallic nature" may sound strange and harsh to a philosophic ear, but it seems quite as justifiable as some others which are more familiar to him, such as "the law of vegetable nature," "the law of animal nature," or indeed as "the law of nature" in general when assigned as the cause of phenomena in exclusion of agency and power; or when it is substituted into the place of these.

VIII. Neither, lastly, would our observer be driven out of his conclusion, or from his confidence in its truth, by being told that he knew nothing at all about the matter. He knows enough for his argument: he knows the utility of the end: he knows the subserviency and adaptation of the means to the end. These points being known, his ignorance of other points, his doubts concerning other points, affect not the certainty of his reasoning. The consciousness of knowing little need not beget a distrust of that which he does know.

Chapter II. State of the Argument Continued

Suppose, in the next place, that the person who found the watch, should after some time, discover that, in addition to all the properties which he had hitherto observed in it, it possessed the unexpected property of producing, in the course of its movement, another watch like itself (the thing is conceivable); that it contained within it a mechanism, a system of parts, a mould for instance, or a complex adjustment of lathes, files, and other tools, evidently and separately calculated for this purpose; let us inquire what effect ought such a discovery to have upon his former conclusion.

I. The first effect would be to increase his admiration of the contrivance, and his conviction of the consummate skill of the contriver. Whether he regarded the object of the contrivance, the distinct apparatus, the intricate, yet in many parts intelligible mechanism, by which it was carried on, he would perceive, in this new observation, nothing but an additional reason for doing what he had already done,—for referring the construction of the watch to design and to supreme art. If that construction without this property, or which is the same thing, before this property had been noticed, proved intention and art to have been employed about it; still more strong would the proof appear when he came to the knowledge of this further property, the crown and perfection of all the rest.

II. He would reflect that though the watch before him were, in some sense, the maker of the watch which was fabricated in the course of its movements, yet it was in a very different sense from that, in which a carpenter, for instance, is the maker of a chair; the author of its contrivance, the cause of the relation of its parts to their use.

With respect to these, the first watch was no cause at all to the second: In no such sense as this was it the author of the constitution and order, either of the parts which the new watch contained, or of the parts by the aid and instrumentality of which it was produced. We might possibly say, but with great latitude of expression, that a stream of water ground corn: but no latitude of expression would allow us to say, no stretch of conjecture could lead us to think, that the stream of water built the mill, though it were too ancient for us to know who the builder was. What the stream of water does in the affair is neither more nor less than this, by the application of an unintelligent impulse to a mechanism previously arranged, arranged independently of it, and arranged by intelligence, an effect is produced, viz. the corn is ground. But the effect results from the arrangement. The force of the stream cannot be said to be the cause or author of the effect, still less of the arrangement. Understanding and plan in the formation of the mill were not the less necessary for any share which the water has in grinding the corn: yet is this share the same as that which the watch would have contributed to the production of the new watch, upon the supposition assumed in the last section. Therefore.

III. Though it be now no longer probable that the individual watch, which our observer had found, was made immediately by the hand of an artificer, yet doth not this alteration in anywise affect the inference that an artificer had been originally employed and concerned in the production. The argument from design remains as it was. Marks of design and contrivance are no more accounted for now than they were before. In the same thing, we may ask for the cause of different properties. We may ask for the cause of the colour of a body, of its hardness, of its head; and these causes may be all different. We are now asking for the cause of that subserviency to a use, that relation to an end, which we have remarked in the watch before us. No answer is given to this question by telling us that a preceding watch produced it. There cannot be design without a designer; contrivance without a contriver; order without choice; arrangement without anything capable of arranging; subserviency and relation to a purpose without that which could intend a purpose; means suitable to an end, and executing their office, in accomplishing that end, without the end ever having been contemplated or the means accommodated to it. Arrangement, disposition of parts, subserviency of means to an end, relation of instruments to a use, imply the presence of intelligence and mind. No one, therefore, can rationally believe that the insensible, inanimate watch, from which the watch before us issued, was the proper cause of the mechanism we so much admire in it;—could be truly said to have constructed the instrument, disposed its parts, assigned their office, determined their order, action, and mutual dependency, combined their several motions into one result, and that also a result connected with the utilities of other beings. All these properties, therefore, are as much unaccounted for as they were before.

IV. Nor is anything gained by running the difficulty farther back, i.e., by supposing the watch before us to have been produced from another watch, that from a former, and so on indefinitely. Our going back ever so far brings us no nearer to the least degree of satisfaction upon the subject. Contrivance is still unaccounted for. We still want a contriver. A designing mind is neither supplied by this supposition nor dispensed with. If the difficulty were diminished the further we went back, by going back indefinitely we might exhaust it. And this is the only case to which this sort of reasoning applies. Where there is a tendency, or, as we increase the number of terms, a continual approach towards a limit, there, by supposing the number of terms to be what is called infinite, we may conceive the limit to be attained: but where there is no such tendency, or approach, nothing is effected by lengthening the series. There is no difference as to the point in question (whatever there may be as to many points) between one series and another; between a series which is finite and a series which is infinite. A chain composed of an infinite number of links can no more support itself than a chain composed of a finite number of links. And of this we are assured (though we never can have tried the experiment) because by increasing the number of links, from ten for instance to a hundred, from a hundred to a thousand, etc. we make not the smallest approach, we observe not the smallest tendency, towards self-support. There is no difference in this respect (yet there may be a great difference in several respects) between a chain of a greater or less length, between one chain and another, between one that is finite and one that is infinite. This very much resembles the case before us. The machine which we are inspecting demonstrates, by its construction, contrivance and design. Contrivance must have had a contriver; design, a designer; whether the machine immediately proceeded from another machine or not. That circumstance alters not the case. That other machine may, in like manner, have proceeded from a former machine: nor does that alter the case; contrivance must have had a contriver. That former one from one preceding it: no alteration still; a contriver is still necessary. No tendency is perceived, no approach towards a diminution of this necessity. It is the same with any and every succession of these machines; a succession of ten, of a hundred, of a thousand; with one series, as with another; a series which is finite, as with a series which is infinite. In whatever other respects they may differ, in this they do not. In all equally, contrivance and design are unaccounted for. The question is not simply, How came the first watch into existence? which question, it may be pretended, is done away by supposing the series of watches thus produced from one another to have been infinite and consequently to have had no-such first for which it was necessary to provide a cause. This, perhaps, would have been nearly the state of the question, if no thing had been before us but an unorganized, unmechanized substance, without mark or indication of contrivance. It might be difficult to show that such substance could not have existed from eternity, either in succession (if it were possible, which I think it is not, for unorganized bodies to spring from one another) or by individual perpetuity. But that is not the question now. To suppose it to be so is to suppose that it made no difference whether we had found a watch or a stone. As it is, the metaphysics of that question have no place; for, in the watch which we are examining, are seen contrivance, design; an end, a purpose; means for the end, adaptation to the purpose. And the question which irresistibly presses upon our thoughts is whence this contrivance and design? The thing required is the intending mind, the adapting hand, the intelligence by which that hand was directed. This question, this demand, is not shaken off by increasing a number or succession of substances destitute of these properties; nor the more by increasing that number to infinity. If it be said that, upon the supposition of one watch being produced from another in the course of that other's movements, and by means of the mechanism within it, we have a cause for the watch in my hand, viz. the watch from which it proceeded. I deny that for the design, the contrivance, the suitableness of means to an end, the adaptation of instruments to a use (all which we discover in the watch) we have any cause whatever. It is in vain, therefore, to assign a series of such causes, or to allege that a series may be carried back to infinity; for I do not admit that we have yet any cause at all of the phenomena, still less any series of causes either finite or infinite. Here is contrivance, but no contriver; proofs of design, but no designer.

V. Our observer would further also reflect that the maker of the watch before him was, in truth and reality, the maker of every watch produced from it; there being no difference (except that the latter manifests a more exquisite skill) between the making of another watch with his own hands, by the mediation of files, lathes, chisels, etc. and the disposing, fixing, and inserting of these instruments, or of others equivalent to them, in the body of the watch already made in such a manner, as to form a new watch in the course of the movements which he had given to the old one. It is only working by one set of tools instead of another.

The conclusion of which the first examination of the watch, of its works, construction, and movement suggested was that it must have had, for the cause and author of that construction, an artificer who understood its mechanism and designed its use. This conclusion is invincible. A second examination presents us with a new discovery. The watch is found, in the course of its movement, to produce another watch similar to itself; and not only so, but we perceive in it a system or organization separately calculated for that purpose. What effect would this discovery have, or ought it to have, upon our former inference? What, as hath already been said, but to increase, beyond measure, our admiration of the skill which had been employed in the formation of such a machine? Or shall it, instead of this, all at once turn us round to an opposite conclusion, viz. that no art or skill whatever has been concerned in the business, although all other evidences of art and skill remain as they were, and this last and supreme piece of art be now added to the rest? Can this be maintained without absurdity? Yet this is atheism.

Chapter III. Application of the Argument

This is atheism: for every indication of contrivance, every manifestation of design, which existed in the watch exists in the works of nature, with the difference, on the side of nature, of being greater and more, and that in a degree which exceeds all computation. I mean that the contrivances of nature surpass the contrivances of art in the complexity, subtility, and curiosity of the mechanism; and still more, if possible, do they go beyond them in number and variety; yet, in a multitude of cases, are not less evidently mechanical, not less evidently contrivances, not less evidently accommodated to their end, or suited to their office, than are the most perfect productions of human ingenuity.

25.5 HUME'S COUNTERARGUMENTS AND REFUTATIONS

Classical Western rational theology has its most influential critic in the English philosopher David Hume (1711–1776) and his *Dialogues Concerning Natural Religion.* ("Natural religion" means rational theology in Hume's usage.) We shall review here mainly the teleological argument, or argument from design, though there is an atheistic argument from evil in the text which we shall rehearse briefly.

There are three principal characters in the work: Cleanthes, an advocate of the design argument and of an empiricist approach to religion; Demea, a traditional Christian of piety who voices a negative theology and who is distrustful of Cleanthes' arguments; and Philo, usually taken to speak for Hume himself, who is skeptical, like Demea, about Cleanthes' arguments, but who also, unlike Demea, has little patience with religious beliefs.

Cleanthes argues that so many features of the world—the human eye, the correspondences of the sexes, etc.—appear designed that we are forced to accept a designer, God, namely. In other words, the world seems to be an artifact. All artifacts have artificers. Thus the world has an artificer, namely, God.

Philo objects that the cause of the appearance of design in the universe need not be supposed to be similar in nature to a human being in the role of artisan. There are many disanalogies between natural effects and artifacts. Moreover, such a line of reasoning as Cleanthes' could not establish God as traditionally conceived, as infinite, single, simple, etc. We have no experience of anything infinite.

At the time Hume was writing, Charles Darwin (1809–1882) had not yet revolutionized biology with his evolutionary theory. Evolutionary biology seems to put the final nails into the coffin of the teleological argument. The origin of an instrument such as the human eye can be explained through natural selection, Darwin argues, without reference to conscious intention.

Hume also finds in the world's evil an argument against God's existence. God has to be either unwilling or unable to prevent evil, because evil exists. But if God were omnipotent and entirely good, then God would be both willing and able to prevent evil. So the existence of evil shows that God does not exist. Of course, from the theist's perspective, this simply shows the urgency of theodicy as a task.

Philo concludes with a generally skeptical form of argument. In the absence of data, many hypotheses are possible (variability), and we have no way to choose (undecidability). Hume thus leaves us with skepticism concerning our ability to prove God's existence.

25.5.1 David Hume, from *Dialogues Concerning Natural Religion*

Part 5

Now, Cleanthes, said PHILO, with an air of alacrity and triumph, mark the consequences. First, by this method of reasoning you renounce all claim to infinity in any of the attributes of the Deity. For, as the cause ought only to be proportioned to the effect, and the effect, so far as it falls under our cognisance, is not infinite, what pretensions have we, upon your suppositions, to ascribe that attribute to the Divine Being? You will still insist that, by removing him so much from all similarity to human creatures, we give in to the most arbitrary hypothesis, and at the same time weaken all proofs of his existence.

Secondly, you have no reason, on your theory, for ascribing perfection to the Deity, even in his finite capacity, or for supposing him free from every error, mistake, or incoherence in his undertakings. There are many inexplicable difficulties in the works of nature, which, if we allow a perfect author to be proved a priori, are easily solved and become only seeming difficulties, from the narrow capacity of man who cannot trace infinite relations. But according to your method of reasoning, these difficulties become all real; and perhaps will be insisted on as new instances of likeness to human art and contrivance. At least, you must acknowledge that it is impossible for us to tell, from our limited views, whether this system contains any great faults, or deserves any considerable praise, if compared to other possible, and even real systems. Could a peasant, if the *Aeneid* were read to him, pronounce that poem to be absolutely faultless or even assign to it its proper rank among the productions of human wit, he, who had never seen any other production?

But were this world ever so perfect a production, it must still remain uncertain whether all the excellences of the work can justly be ascribed to the workman. If we survey a ship, what an exalted idea must we form of the ingenuity of

Source: David Hume, *Dialogues Concerning Natural Religion*, 1779.

the carpenter who framed so complicated, useful, and beautiful a machine? And what surprise must we feel, when we find him a stupid mechanic who imitated others and copied an art, which, through a long succession of ages, after multiplied trials, mistakes, corrections, deliberations, and controversies, had been gradually improving? Many worlds might have been botched and bungled, throughout an eternity, ere this system was struck out; much labour lost, many fruitless trials made; and a slow, but continued improvement carried on during infinite ages in the art of world-making. In such subjects, who can determine where the truth; nay, who can conjecture where the probability lies amidst a great number of hypotheses which may be proposed and a still greater which may be imagined?

And what shadow of an argument, continued PHILO, can you produce, from your hypothesis, to prove the unity of the Deity? A great number of men join in building a house or ship, in rearing a city, in framing a commonwealth; why may not several deities combine in contriving and framing a world? This is only so much greater similarity to human affairs. By sharing the work among several, we may so much further limit the attributes of each, and get rid of that extensive power and knowledge, which must be supposed in one deity and which, according to you, can only serve to weaken the proof of his existence. And if such foolish, such vicious creatures as man can yet often unite in framing and executing one plan, how much more those deities or demons whom we may suppose several degrees more perfect!

To multiply causes without necessity is indeed contrary to true philosophy: but this principle applies not to the present case. Were one deity antecedently proved by your theory, who were possessed of every attribute requisite to the production of the universe, it would be needless, I own, (though not absurd) to suppose any other deity existent. But while it is still a question whether all these attributes are united in one subject or dispersed among several independent beings, by what phenomena in nature can we pretend to decide the controversy? Where we see a body raised in a scale, we are sure that there is in the opposite scale, however concealed from sight, some counterpoising weight equal to it; but it is still allowed to doubt whether that weight be an aggregate of several distinct bodies or one uniform united mass. And if the weight requisite very much exceeds anything which we have ever seen conjoined in any single body, the former supposition becomes still more probable and natural. An intelligent being of such vast power and capacity as is necessary to produce the universe, or, to speak in the language of ancient philosophy, so prodigious an animal exceeds all analogy and even comprehension.

But further, Cleanthes, men are mortal, and renew their species by generation; and this is common to all living creatures. The two great sexes of male and female, says Milton, animate the world. Why must this circumstance, so universal, so essential, be excluded from those numerous and limited deities? Behold, then, the theogony of ancient times brought back upon us.

And why not become a perfect anthropomorphite? Why not assert the deity or deities to be corporeal, and to have eyes, a nose, mouth, ears, etc.? Epicurus maintained that no man had ever seen reason but in a human figure; therefore the gods must have a human figure. And this argument, which is deservedly so much ridiculed by Cicero, becomes, according to you, solid and philosophical.

In a word, Cleanthes, a man who follows your hypothesis is able perhaps to assert, or conjecture, that the universe, sometime, arose from something like design: but beyond that position he cannot ascertain one single circumstance; and is left afterwards to fix every point of his theology by the utmost license of fancy and hypothesis. This world, for aught he knows, is very faulty and imperfect, compared to a superior standard; and was only the first rude essay of some infant deity, who afterwards abandoned it, ashamed of his lame performance: it is the work only of some dependent, inferior deity; and is the object of derision to his superiors: it is the production of old age and dotage in some superannuated deity; and ever since his death, has run on at adventures, from the first impulse and active force which it received from him. You justly give signs of horror, Demea, at these strange suppositions; but these, and a thousand more of the same kind, are Cleanthes's suppositions, not mine. From the moment the attributes of the Deity are supposed finite, all these have place. And I cannot, for my part, think that so wild and unsettled a system of theology is, in any respect, preferable to none at all....

Part 6

...To render it still more unsatisfactory, said PHILO, there occurs to me another hypothesis, which must acquire an air of probability from the method of reasoning so much insisted on by Cleanthes. That like effects arise from like causes: this principle he supposes the foundation of all religion. But there is another principle of the same kind, no less certain, and derived from the same source of experience; that where several known circumstances are observed to be similar, the unknown will also be found similar. Thus, if we see the limbs of a human body, we conclude that it is also attended with a human head, though hid from us. Thus, if we see, through a chink in a wall, a small part of the sun, we conclude that, were the wall removed, we should see the whole body. In short, this method of reasoning is so obvious and familiar that no scruple can ever be made with regard to its solidity.

Now, if we survey the universe, so far as it falls under our knowledge it bears a great resemblance to an animal or organised body, and seems actuated with a like principle of life and motion. A continual circulation of matter in it produces no disorder: a continual waste in every part is incessantly repaired: the closest sympathy is perceived throughout the entire system: and each part or member, in performing its proper offices, operates both to its own preservation and to that of the whole. The world, therefore, I infer, is an animal; and the Deity is the Soul of the world, actuating it, and actuated by it.

You have too much learning, Cleanthes, to be at all surprised at this opinion, which, you know, was maintained by almost all the theists of antiquity, and chiefly prevails in their discourses and reasonings. For though, sometimes, the ancient philosophers reason from final causes, as if they thought the world the workmanship of God, yet it appears rather their favourite notion to consider it as his body, whose organisation renders it subservient to him. And it must be confessed that, as the universe resembles more a human body than it does the works of human art and contrivance, if our limited analogy could ever, with any propriety, be extended to the whole of nature, the inference seems juster in favour of the ancient than the modern theory.

There are many other advantages, too, in the former theory which recommended it to the ancient theologians. Nothing [was] more repugnant to all their notions, because nothing more repugnant to common experience, than mind without body; a mere spiritual substance, which fell not under their senses nor comprehension, and of which they had not observed one single instance throughout all nature. Mind and body they knew, because they felt both: an order, arrangement, organisation, or internal machinery, in both, they likewise knew, after the same manner: and it could not but seem reasonable to transfer this experience to the universe; and to suppose the divine mind and body to be also coeval, and to have, both of them, order and arrangement naturally inherent in them and inseparable from them.

Here, therefore, is a new species of anthropomorphism, Cleanthes, on which you may deliberate; and a theory which seems not liable to any considerable difficulties. You are too much superior, surely, to systematical prejudices, to find any more difficulty in supposing an animal body to be, originally, of itself, or from unknown causes, possessed of order and organisation, than in supposing a similar order to belong to mind. But the vulgar prejudice that body and mind ought always to accompany each other, ought not, one should think, to be entirely neglected; since it is founded on vulgar experience, the only guide which you profess to follow in all these theological inquiries. And if you assert that our limited experience is an unequal standard by which to judge of the unlimited extent of nature; you entirely abandon your own hypothesis, and must thenceforward adopt our mysticism, as you call it, and admit of the absolute incomprehensibility of the Divine Nature....

Part 7

But here, continued PHILO, in examining the ancient system of the soul of the world, there strikes me, all on a sudden, a new idea, which, if just, must go near to subvert all your reasoning, and destroy even your first inferences on which you repose such confidence. If the universe bears a greater likeness to animal bodies and to vegetables than to the works of human art, it is more probable that its cause resembles the cause of the former than that of the latter, and its origin ought rather to be ascribed to generation or vegetation than to reason or design. Your conclusion, even according to your own principles, is therefore lame and defective.

Pray open up this argument a little further, said DEMEA, for I do not rightly apprehend it in that concise manner in which you have expressed it.

Our friend Cleanthes, replied PHILO, as you have heard, asserts, that since no question of fact can be proved otherwise than by experience, the existence of a Deity admits not of proof from any other medium. The world, says he, resembles the works of human contrivance; therefore its cause must also resemble that of the other. Here we may remark that the operation of one very small part of nature, to wit, man, upon another very small part, to wit, that inanimate matter lying within his reach, is the rule by which Cleanthes judges of the origin of the whole; and he measures objects, so widely disproportioned, by the same individual standard. But to waive all objections drawn from this topic, I affirm that there are other parts of the universe (besides the machines of human invention) which bear still a greater resemblance to the fabric of the world, and which, therefore, afford a better conjecture concerning the universal origin of this system. These parts are animals and vegetables. The world plainly resembles more an animal or a vegetable than it does a watch or a knitting-loom. Its cause, therefore, it is more probable, resembles the cause of the former. The cause of the former is generation or vegetation. The cause, therefore, of the world, we may infer to be something similar or analogous to generation or vegetation.

But how is it conceivable, said DEMEA, that the world can arise from any thing similar to vegetation or generation?

Very easily, replied PHILO. In like manner as a tree sheds its seed into the neighbouring fields, and produces other trees, so the great vegetable, the world, or this planetary system, produces within itself certain seeds, which, being scattered into the surrounding chaos, vegetate into new worlds. A comet, for instance, is the seed of a world; and after it has been fully ripened, by passing from sun to sun, and star to star, it is at last tossed into the unformed elements which everywhere surround this universe, and immediately sprouts up into a new system.

Or if, for the sake of variety (for I see no other advantage), we should suppose this world to be an animal; a comet is the egg of this animal: and in like manner as an ostrich lays its egg in the sand, which, without any further care, hatches the egg and produces a new animal, so ...

I understand you, says DEMEA: But what wild, arbitrary suppositions are these! What data have you for such extraordinary conclusions? And is the slight, imaginary resemblance of the world to a vegetable or an animal sufficient to establish the same inference with regard to both? Objects, which are in general so widely different, ought they to be a standard for each other?

Right, cries PHILO: This is the topic on which I have all along insisted. I have still asserted, that we have no data to establish any system of cosmogony. Our experience, so imperfect in itself, and so limited both in extent and duration, can afford us no probable conjecture concerning the whole of things. But if we must needs fix on some hypothesis, by what rule, pray, ought we to determine our choice? Is there any other rule than the greater similarity of the objects compared? And does not a plant or an animal, which springs from vegetation or generation, bear a stronger resemblance to the world than does any artificial machine which arises from reason and design?

Part 10

... Ask yourself, ask any of your acquaintance, whether they would live over again the last ten or twenty years of their life. No! but the next twenty, they say, will be better:

And from the dregs of life, hope to receive
What the first sprightly running could not give.

Thus at last they find (such is the greatness of human misery, it reconciles even contradictions), that they complain at once of the shortness of life and of its vanity and sorrow.

And is it possible, Cleanthes, said PHILO, that after all these reflections, and infinitely more, which might be suggested, you can still persevere in your anthropomorphism and assert the moral attributes of the Deity, his justice, benevolence, mercy, and rectitude, to be of the same nature with these virtues in human creatures? His power we allow is infinite: whatever he wills is executed: but neither man nor any other animal is happy: therefore he does not will their happiness. His wisdom is infinite: He is never mistaken in choosing the means to any end: but the course of Nature tends not to human or animal felicity: therefore it is not established for that purpose. Through the whole compass of human knowledge, there are no inferences more certain and infallible than these. In what respect, then, do his benevolence and mercy resemble the benevolence and mercy of men?

Epicurus's old questions are yet unanswered. Is he willing to prevent evil, but not able? then is he impotent. Is he able, but not willing? then is he malevolent. Is he both able and willing? whence then is evil?

You ascribe, Cleanthes (and I believe justly), a purpose and intention to nature. But what, I beseech you, is the object of that curious artifice and machinery which she has displayed in all animals? The preservation alone of individuals, and propagation of the species. It seems enough for her purpose if such a rank be barely upheld in the universe without any care or concern for the happiness of the members that compose it. No resource for this purpose: no machinery in order merely to give pleasure or ease: no fund of pure joy and contentment: no indulgence without some want or necessity accompanying it. At least, the few phenomena of this nature are overbalanced by opposite phenomena of still greater importance....

Admitting your position, replied PHILO, which yet is extremely doubtful, you must at the same time allow that if pain be less frequent than pleasure, it is infinitely more violent and durable. One hour of it is often able to outweigh a day, a week, a month of our common insipid enjoyments; and how many days, weeks, and months, are passed by several in the most acute torments? Pleasure, scarcely in one instance, is ever able to reach ecstasy and rapture; and in no one instance can it continue for any time at its highest pitch and altitude. The spirits evaporate, the nerves relax, the fabric is disordered, and the enjoyment quickly degenerates into fatigue and uneasiness. But pain often, good God, how often! rises to torture and agony; and the longer it continues, it becomes still more genuine agony and torture. Patience is exhausted, courage languishes, melancholy seizes us, and nothing terminates our misery but the removal of its cause, or another event, which is the sole cure of all evil but which, from our natural folly, we regard with still greater horror and consternation.

But not to insist upon these topics, continued PHILO, though most obvious, certain, and important, I must use the freedom to admonish you, Cleanthes, that you have put the controversy upon a most dangerous issue, and are unawares introducing a total scepticism into the most essential articles of natural and revealed theology. What! no method of fixing a just foundation for religion unless we allow the happiness of human life, and maintain a continued existence even in this world, with all our present pains, infirmities, vexations, and follies, to be eligible and desirable! But this is contrary to everyone's feeling and experience: it is contrary to an authority so established as nothing can subvert. No decisive proofs can ever be produced against this authority; nor is it possible for you to compute, estimate, and compare all the pains and all the pleasures in the lives of all men and of all animals: and thus, by your resting the whole system of religion on a point, which, from its very nature, must for ever be uncertain, you tacitly confess that that system is equally uncertain.

But allowing you what never will be believed, at least what you never possibly can prove, that animal, or at least human happiness, in this life, exceeds its misery, you have yet done nothing: for this is not, by any means, what we expect from infinite power, infinite wisdom, and infinite goodness. Why is there any misery at all in the world? Not by chance surely. From some cause then. Is it from the intention of the Deity? But he is perfectly benevolent. Is it contrary to his intention? But he is almighty. Nothing can shake the solidity of this reasoning, so short, so clear, so decisive; except we assert that these subjects exceed all human capacity, and that our common measures of truth and falsehood are not applicable to them; a topic which I have all along insisted on but which you have, from the beginning, rejected with scorn and indignation.

But I will be contented to retire still from this entrenchment, for I deny that you can ever force me in it. I will allow that pain or misery in man is compatible with infinite power and goodness in the Deity, even in your sense of these attributes: what are you advanced by all these concessions? A mere possible compatibility is not sufficient. You must prove these pure, unmixed, and uncontrollable attributes from the present mixed and confused phenomena, and from these alone. A hopeful undertaking! Were the phenomena ever so pure and unmixed, yet being finite, they would be insufficient for that purpose. How much more where they are also so jarring and discordant!

Glossary

A posteriori proposition A proposition or statement whose truth value can be known only through experience.

A priori proposition A proposition or statement whose truth value can be known independently of experience.

Absolutism (or objectivism) The thesis that we can speak of statements, assertions, or beliefs—in a given language and given context—as objectively true or false, period, without reference to a speaker, society, or interpretive community.

Academic skepticism The view that knowledge is impossible.

Accident A property that is not essential, that is, not necessary to a thing or kind of thing.

Actual object (*alambana*) The cause of a perception; support; in Dignaga, atoms.

Actual obligation Something I really am, all things considered, obliged to do.

Act-utilitarianism A moral theory that judges individual actions directly by their effects on the amount of good.

***Advaita* (or Non-Dualism)** The classical Indian view that the self (*atman*) is in reality nothing other than Brahman and that in the mystical knowledge of Brahman one knows only the One, the sole true Existent, whose nature is perfect being, consciousness, and bliss.

Agent One who consents to and participates in an act (1) freely—without coercion; (2) voluntarily—that is, having the competence to make the decision to consent and participate; and (3) in an informed way, without being deceived.

***Ahimsa* (Noninjury)** The thesis that one should not kill or injure any sentient being, popularized in modern times by Mahatma Gandhi and propagated in ancient and classical India foremost by Jains.

Ahimsika One who practices *ahimsa*.

***Alambana* (actual object)** The cause of a perception; support; in Dignaga, atoms.

Aloneness (*kaivalya*) The goal of mystical insight and bliss in yoga according to the *Yoga-sutra*.

Analogy A similarity, in certain respects, between distinct things. A source of knowledge whereby we can acquire new vocabulary, according to Nyaya.

Analytic method A philosophical method of seeking to understand complex wholes and concepts by analyzing them into their parts.

Analytic philosophy The style of philosophy that has dominated the philosophical community in Britain and the United States throughout the twentieth century but extends back to Plato and Aristotle, centering on breaking down complex problems into simple parts.

Analytic statement A statement true or false by virtue of the meanings of its words.

Ananda Bliss, spiritual ecstasy; the nature of Brahman considered affectively, according to Vedanta.

Anatman The thesis that there is no self (*atman*); an important position in Buddhist philosophy.

Anekanta-vada Non-absolutism, positive perspectivalism, the "doctrine of many-sidedness"; the metaphysical stance of Jain philosophers.

Apatheia Nonreactiveness, passionlessness, imperturbability, or unresponsiveness.

Appearance A thing as it is known to us.

Argument A discourse that starts with some assertions and tries to justify a thesis.

Argument by analogy An argument inferring a similarity from other similarities.

Argument from design The argument that the universe, like a watch or other machine, shows such a beauty and coordination of parts that it must be the product of a creator. Also called the *teleological argument.*

Argument from error (or illusion) The argument that people make mistakes (dream things we know not to be real; misperceive things; misjudge situations; draw the wrong conclusions; etc.). People are wrong when things are not as they appear to them. Therefore, there is a difference between appearance and reality.

Argument from evil The argument that, if God were omnipotent (all-powerful), omniscient (all-knowing), and entirely good, God would be both willing and able to prevent evil. So the existence of evil shows that God does not exist—or, at least, that God does not have the properties usually attributed.

Argument from thought The argument that God exists, because only God could be the source of our idea of God.

Arhat In Buddhism, especially Southern Buddhism, a saint, who loses all individual personality in *nirvana.*

***Artha* (internal object)** What a perception is (or appears to be) a perception of.

Artificial nature (*yu de*) In Daoism, a defect exhibited by anything that strives to be something other than what it is.

Asana Poses and meditational postures taught as part of some disciplines of yoga.

Asat Nonbeing, bad.

Atheism The view that there is no divine being.

Atman Self; the Upanishadic term for our truest or most basic consciousness; universal Self.

Autonomy Living by the rules we establish for ourselves.

Avidya Spiritual ignorance; in much Vedanta, lack of direct awareness of Brahman, the true self or God.

Bhagavad Blessed, divine.

Bhakti Devotional love.

***Bhakti* movement** A medieval group of Hindu thinkers, including Akka Mahadevi, Janabai, Lalla, and Mirabai, stressing *bhakti* yoga.

Bhakti-yoga Yoga of love and devotion.

Bodhisattva "One whose essence is enlightenment," one who is capable of a final extinction of individual personality in an ultimate Nirvana but who retains form out of compassion for sentient beings; the yogic ideal of Mahayana Buddhism.

Brahman In Vedanta, the Divine Absolute; the One; God; the key concept of the Upanishads.

Brahma-vidya Knowledge of Brahman, the Absolute or God; the *summum bonum,* according to Vedanta.

Buddha "The Awakened"; an epithet of Siddhartha Gautama, the founder of Buddhism, after his enlightenment, or *nirvana.*

Buddhi Rational intelligence.

Buddhism A world religion founded by Siddhartha Gautama, the Buddha, or "Awakened One," who taught that a supreme felicity and end to suffering occur in a special experience called *nirvana* and who laid out a way or ways to attain it.

Buddhist idealism The thesis that everything is mind dependent.

Buddhi-yoga Discipline for the higher intelligence.

Categorematic expression A word or phrase that refers to something.

Categorical imperative An "ought" statement without an "if," applying universally, without regard to circumstances, goals, or desires.

In Kant, the categorical imperative is the highest moral axiom from which other moral imperatives can be derived.

Category In Aristotle and Nyaya, a general kind of thing to which linguistic expressions refer. In Kant, a pure concept of the understanding; an innate cognitive ability of a very general kind; a possible logical form of an object.

Causal-role functionalism The view that types of mental entities and events correspond to causal roles that physical entities and events can play.

Charvaka Also called *Lokayata*, a term meaning "those attached to the ways of the world," a group of ancient Indian philosophers who are materialists, empiricists, and skeptics.

Chi **(material force)** In neo-Confucianism, something akin to matter, but with the dynamic character of force or energy. Chi is also used for material objects, that is, concrete, tangible things.

Chitta Thought and emotion, mind-stuff.

Cogito "I think"; the foundation of all knowledge, according to Descartes.

Coherence theory of truth The theory holding that a sentence or belief is true if it coheres with a comprehensive theory of the world or reality, that is, that it is true if it explains, or is explained by, other statements or beliefs within the comprehensive system.

Coherentism (or antifoundationalism) The thesis that justification does not require a foundation or level of ultimate justifiers but rather an explanatory relationship within a circle or web of beliefs.

Communitarianism The view that the good of the community does not reduce to the good of its members.

Complex ideas Compounds of other ideas.

Concept empiricism The view that all concepts come from experience.

Concept rationalism The view that there are innate concepts—that we have concepts that we do not derive from experience.

Conceptualism The view that universals are mind dependent.

Conclusion The thesis an argument tries to justify.

Consciousness-only A Buddhist school in China that develops from Buddhist idealism, which maintains that only consciousness exists.

Consequentialism The view that all moral value rests ultimately on the consequences of actions.

Contextualism A method that stresses understanding things in the contexts in which they occur.

Contingent proposition A proposition that is neither necessary nor impossible—that is, that could be true and could be false.

Contradictory (or impossible) proposition A proposition that cannot be true.

Copernican revolution in philosophy Kant's view that the laws governing the realm of experience are not in the objects themselves but in us: "We can know in things a priori only what we ourselves place in them."

Correspondence theory The theory of truth holding that a sentence (or statement or belief) is true if it corresponds with reality—if, that is, it corresponds to some fact. It is false if there is no corresponding fact.

Cosmological argument The argument that God exists as a first cause of the universe, or as a necessary being on which all other beings depend.

Counterexample To an argument: An argument of the same form with true premises but a false conclusion. To a principle: An particular case in which the principle gives the wrong result.

Dao In Confucius, the Way or Path; the proper way to live. In Laozi, the way the universe works; the One, which underlies everything but admits no description.

Daoism A world religion founded by Laozi, stressing the *Dao*, the underlying unity of the universe.

Darshana Worldview or philosophy, a "viewing"; a school of thought in classical India including Hindu, Buddhist, Jain, and other philosophies.

De A thing's power, force, nature, character, or virtue; Dao embodied in a particular thing.

Deductively valid argument An argument in which the truth of the premises guarantees the truth of the conclusion.

Deism The view that God exists and created the world but has had no further interaction with it.

Deliberative virtue The ability to recognize the properties of the results of actions; foresight.

Deontological theory A moral theory holding that moral value rests at least in part on something other than the consequences of actions, usually duties.

Designated matter A specific bit of matter, for example, "this flesh and that blood."

Dharma (1) Duty, right way to live; (2) quality or state of awareness; (3) the aggregate of qualities or states of consciousness; appearances; (4) property.

Dhyana Meditation (proper).

Dialectic (also called *Socratic method*) Socrates asks what piety, or courage, or friendship, or justice is. Someone answers. Socrates analyzes the proposed definition by asking questions, leading the parties to the conversation to see that the definition cannot be right. Sometimes, the definition is unclear; sometimes, it includes too much; sometimes, it does not include enough. Someone then proposes another definition, and the process continues.

Dialectical premise A premise advanced as a hypothesis or as an assumption to be reduced to absurdity.

Differentiae Differences; what differentiates something from other things of its kind.

Direct realism The thesis that sensations can justify beliefs about physical objects without themselves constituting knowledge.

Divine command theory The view that God distinguishes right from wrong. What God commands is obligatory; what God allows is permissible; what God forbids is wrong.

Dogmatic empiricism The view that we can know something about the world as it really is, beyond the reach of the senses, even if all knowledge depends on experience.

Dualism The view that there are two kinds of thing: for example, form and matter, or mind and body, or, in theistic Vedanta, God and individual.

Dukkha Pain, suffering.

Dzogchen "Great perfection." In Tantric Buddhism, the original, undifferentiated, intrinsic awareness natural to every sentient being.

Eightfold Noble Path In Buddhism, the route to the supreme good: right thought, resolve, speech, conduct, livelihood, effort, mindfulness, and concentration.

Eliminativism The view that we can and should, in principle, give up speaking of ordinary objects and mental states, replacing this talk with the language of science.

Empiricism The view that all knowledge of the world comes from experience.

Emptiness The Buddhist thesis that everything lacks a reality of its own; that nothing has an essence beyond its relations to other things.

Enlightenment (1) A movement, reaching its height in Europe in the eighteenth century, stressing the importance of reason in discovering truth and producing progress. (2) A state of self-awareness or awakening achievable through meditation and other means.

Epistemology Theory of knowledge, studying what we know, how we know it, and principles of knowledge and justification.

Equivocation An ambiguity in a word or phrase. Also, an argument relying on such an ambiguity.

Error theory The view that ordinary, commonsense views are literally false, even if we cannot do without them.

Esoteric doctrine A doctrine that can be transmitted only by direct personal contact.

Esse est percipi To be is to be perceived; a primary thesis of Berkeley.

Essence The properties necessary to a thing without which it would not be what it is.

Essential property A property necessary to a thing (or kind of thing); without the property, it would not be that thing (or kind of thing).

Eternal law The law of nature, established by God, that governs the entire universe, according to theists. Everything in the universe obeys eternal law, and does so necessarily. Science investigates eternal law and tries to describe it.

Ethical intuitionism The view that conscience is the only reliable practical guide to what to do.

Ethics Theory devoted to the nature of the difference between right and wrong acts and good and bad character.

Eudaimonia Happiness; flourishing; living well. In Aristotle, happiness is the only thing desirable for its own sake, never for the sake of something else.

Excess nature (*yu de*) In Laozi, a defect exhibited by anything that strives to be something other than what it is.

Existentialism The view that existence precedes essence, that the lived life and first-person perspective (existence) trumps all theory (essence).

Externalism (1) In epistemology, the view that knowledge is true belief resulting from a source or reliable means of knowing. Externalism distinguishes knowledge from other mental states by invoking relations between mental states and the world. Those relations are not necessarily transparent to the knower; you may know something because your belief is true and has arisen through a reliable process of belief formation—such as perception—without being able to give any justification yourself. (2) In ethics, the view that moral imperatives do not necessarily give reasons for acting.

Fallibilism The thesis that no view or belief is absolutely certain.

Filial piety (*xiao*) Obedience, reverence, and service to one's parents and elders.

Flying man In Avicenna, a hypothetical person who has no sensory experience but could nevertheless know of his own existence.

Formal reality In Descartes, the reality of objects in the actual world.

Forms Abstract universals, in Plato, that exist independent of us. They make things what they are, and they enable us to think about things as they are.

Foundationalism The thesis that knowledge rests on a foundation consisting of basic items that are perceived or otherwise known directly.

Four Noble Truths The four chief theses of Buddhist ethics and religious teaching: (1) Life is painful. (2) The root of pain is desire. (3) It is possible to eliminate pain by eliminating desire through *nirvana* experience. (4) The way to this good is the Eightfold Noble Path.

Fraternal submission Service and trustworthiness to one's equals.

Functionalism The thesis that we must understand things in terms of the functions they play in a larger whole.

Geist "Spirit," "mind"; a primary concept in Hegel.

Genus Kind.

Gita Song.

God (classical Western concept of) A being who is almighty (omnipotent), all-knowing (omniscient), eternal, omnipresent, transcendent, and compassionate (omnibenevolent).

Golden Rule The moral principle that one should treat others as one would like to be treated: "Do unto others as you would have them do unto you."

Great Ultimate In the *I-Ching*, the *Dao*, the underlying unity of the world.

Guna (1) "Strand" or mode of nature, according to Samkhya: *Sattva* (light, clarity, intelligence); *rajas* (passion, dynamism); and *tamas* (darkness, inertia, stupidity); (2) quality, property; twenty-four are enumerated in the early Nyaya-Vaisheshika literature.

Guru Teacher, venerable person.

Haecceity Individual essence; "this-ness."

Henotheism The view that there is one God who takes many forms. There are various gods and goddesses, but all are forms of a single God.

Heteronomy Following someone else's command.

Historicism The thesis that truth is relative to a culture or historical epoch.

Holism (1) The thesis that we must ultimately evaluate beliefs by evaluating their coherence with a comprehensive system of beliefs; coherentism. (2) The view that all of reality is interconnected.

Humanism The view that value is to be defined in purely human terms.

Hypothetical imperative An "ought" statement, such as "You ought to work hard if you want to succeed," containing an "if," whose truth depends on circumstances or someone's goals and desires.

Idealism The thesis that reality is mind dependent.

Illumination In Augustine, what enables us to know the forms. God illumines the intelligible world, making it intelligible to us.

Immediacy The given; a sharp divide between sensibility and understanding or between perception and conceptual activity.

Imperfect duty A general obligation allowing an agent choice about when and how to fulfill it.

Impossible (or contradictory) proposition A proposition that cannot be true.

Inaction (*wuwei*) In Laozi, the policy of letting nature take its course.

Individualism The view that the good of the community is nothing but the sum of the goods of its members.

Individualizer Something that differentiates ultimate particulars or atoms and individual selves or souls.

Infinite regress A pattern in which trying to solve one problem generates another with no end.

Inherence The relation between a property and the thing that has it.

Innate Inborn; not acquired or derived from experience.

Inner sense The progression of sensations, thoughts, and, in general, representations that constitutes our ordinary, empirical consciousness of the world.

Instrumental goods Things desired as means to other things.

Intellectual virtue An excellence of rationality or thinking.

Intelligible world The realm of platonic forms.

Intentional object An object of thought.

Intentionality The property of being about something.

Interdependent origination The Buddhist thesis that everything is interconnected.

Internal object (*artha*) What a perception is (or appears to be) a perception of.

Internalism (1) In epistemology, the thesis that knowledge is true belief for which the knower can provide a justification. Internalism distinguishes knowledge from other mental states in terms of the characteristics of that state and its relations to other mental states, including sensations. Roughly, for an internalist, knowledge is justified true belief—where beliefs are justified either intrinsically (in which case they are self-justifying or self-evident) or by following from other justified beliefs. (2) In ethics, the view that moral imperatives necessarily give reasons for acting.

Intrinsic goods Things desired for their own sake.

Intuition In Kant, sensation or reflection.

Intuitionism In ethics, the view that goods differ in kind; that they can conflict with one another; and that there are no universal rules for resolving these conflicts. Instead, we must rely on conscience, a faculty of moral intuition closely related to feelings.

Ishvara God, the "Lord"; viewed as the equivalent of Brahman in theistic Vedanta.

Jainism An ancient Indian religion founded by Mahavira, c. 500 BCE, who, like the Buddha, propounded a "supreme personal good" and insisted on noninjury (*ahimsa*).

Jnana Cognition, consciousness.

Jnana-yoga Yoga of meditation.

Judgment empiricism The view that there are no synthetic a priori truths. That is, a judgment empiricist holds that only analytic truths, "trifling propositions," can be known independent of experience; anything that really yields content about the world can be known only through experience.

Judgment rationalism The view that some of our knowledge of the world is innate. A judgment rationalist believes that we can know some synthetic truths a priori—that is, that we can know independent of experience some truths that are not merely linguistic or verbal, that are not automatically true or false because of the meanings of the words that constitute them.

Junzi Superior person; literally, "child of a ruler." In Confucius, one of noble character.

Justice (*yi*) A virtue akin to piety, correctness, and justice in ancient Chinese thought, stressed especially by Mencius and Mozi.

Kaivalya Aloneness or independence: the summum bonum according to the Samkhya and the Yoga of the *Yoga-sutra*.

Karma (1) "Action"; (2) habit; the psychological law that every act creates a psychic valency to repeat the act; (3) sacrifice, ritual karma-yoga, yoga of action and sacrifice or giving.

Koan A Zen paradox, puzzling question (sometimes with responses), meant to break down rational thought and force the mind to recognize its true nature.

Land ethic The view that the land, soil, or, broadly, environment are intrinsically valuable.

***Li* (principle)** In neo-Confucianism, something (akin to form) prior to and independent of material force.

***Li* (propriety)** The observance of proper rites, ceremonies, and principles.

Liar sentence A sentence that asserts its own falsehood (for example, "This sentence is false").

Lila Play, sport; as a concept belonging to Vedanta, the world as Divine play.

Lokayata "Those attached to the ways of the world," an epithet for Charvaka philosophers.

Madhyamika Buddhist "school of the Middle" (avoidance of extremes), founded by Nagarjuna and stressing skepticism.

Mahayana Buddhism The "Great Vehicle." The Northern branch of Buddhism popular in China, Korea, and Japan, taking the Bodhisattva as its ideal.

Manas Sense-mind, the inner sense, the internal organ, the conduit of sensory information to the perceiving self, soul, or consciousness, according to several classical Indian schools.

Manifest image The world as revealed to consciousness, the world as it seems to us prereflectively. The world consists of things that have shape, color, and texture. Things have goals and purposes. We ruminate, make decisions, and act on the basis of reasons. In this consists our freedom. Life is at the center of our concerns. We see things as being meaningful; the world is full of value. There is good and evil, right and wrong, virtue and vice.

Mantra Verse of the Veda; words or sound with occult power to aid meditation, open chakras, etc.

Mantrayana "Lightning" or "Diamond Raft," a tradition in Buddhism (also known as *Vajrayana* or Tantric Buddhism) that stresses techniques for accelerating enlightenment.

Material force (*chi*) In neo-Confucianism, something akin to matter, but with the dynamic character of force or energy.

Materialism (or physicalism) The view that there is only one kind of stuff, which is material or physical.

Maxim "A subjective principle of action," a rule an act falls under that reflects the agent's intention but that abstracts from morally irrelevant details.

Maya Illusion; cosmic illusion, according to Advaita Vedanta; according to Vedantic theists, "(self)-delimitation" (from the root *ma*, "to measure or delimit").

Maybeism The Jain thesis that every view should be regarded as right, maybe ("*syat*," "in some respects"). There is at least a grain of truth in every position; the "maybe" directs us to find and appreciate what is correct in what an opponent is saying.

Mental causation The relation between a thought, such as an intention, and an action it brings about.

Metalanguage A language expanded to include a truth predicate for another language.

Metaphysics The study of what there is and how those things relate to each other.

Mimamsa "Exegesis"; long-running school of classical Indian philosophy devoted to defending the scriptural revelation of the Veda.

Mind/body problem How is it possible that the brain give rise to consciousness? If body and consciousness are separable, how can they interact?

Mishna Saying of a rabbi; an entry in the Talmud.

Moism An ancient Chinese version of consequentialism developed by Mozi to oppose Confucianism.

Monism The view that there is ultimately only one kind of thing.

Monotheism The view that there is exactly one God.

Moral (or felicific) calculus Bentham's method of computing the moral value of possible actions.

Moral argument The argument that morality compels belief in God; recognizing injustice, we must think God exists and will right these injustices in an afterlife.

Moral sense A faculty that enables us to perceive the moral qualities of things.

Moral virtue A good trait of character; an excellence in activity.

Mukti In Hinduism, "liberation"—freedom from desire—enlightenment; the highest value.

Mysticism The view that one can know God or ultimate truth by way of a special kind of experience.

Natural law The law, ordained by God, that prescribes what things should do and be, according to theists; the manifestation of God's eternal law in creatures capable of rationality.

Natural virtue The quality of being disposed to pursue the right ends.

Nature The whole of the physical universe. What makes a thing what it is; that by virtue of which a thing is what it is—a human, a river, a building, or whatever. The nature of a thing not only explains why it is what it is, it is also what we grasp in thinking about the thing.

Navya-Nyaya "New Logic," a school that developed from *Nyaya*, "Logic," founded by Gangesha.

Necessary proposition A proposition that cannot be false.

Nihilism The view that there is no ultimate meaning to life.

Nihsvabhava In Nagarjuna, "without a reality of its own."

Nirvana A universal, impersonal, unconceptualizable bliss; extinction (of suffering); enlightenment; the experience of the "Void" (of desire and attachment); the highest good in Buddhism.

Noble Eightfold Path The Buddha's recommended way of living: right thought, right resolve, right speech, right conduct, right livelihood, right effort, right mindfulness, and right concentration or meditation.

Nominal essence In Locke, the quiddity of a thing or kind of thing, that is, what a definition of it would express. A definition of nominal essence generally makes use of secondary qualities.

Nominalism The view that universals do not exist at all—everything is particular.

Nonabsolutism The Jain view that no metaphysical claim should be taken as absolutely true.

Non-Dualism (or *Advaita*) The view that the self (*atman*) is in reality nothing other than Brahman and that in the mystical knowledge of Brahman one knows only the One, the sole true Existent, whose nature is perfect being, consciousness, and bliss.

Noninjury (*ahimsa*) The thesis that one should not injure or kill any sentient being, popularized in modern times by Mahatma Gandhi and propagated in ancient and classical India foremost by Jains.

Nonreductive materialism The view that a translation of ordinary talk of objects and mental states to scientific terms is impossible, even in principle, but that microparticles and their properties nevertheless determine what is true of ordinary objects and mental states.

Normative statement A statement or proposition that deals with the way the world ought to be, not merely with the way the world is.

Normative term A term such as "ought," "should," "good," "bad," "may," "duty," "responsible," or "obligation," that speaks of how things should be or what ought to be done.

No-soul (in Sanskrit, *anatman*; in Pali, *anatta*) The thesis that there is no self or soul.

Noumenon A thing-in-itself; a thing as it really is, independent of our faculties of knowledge.

Numinous The holy.

Nyaya "Logic"; a school of realism and common sense prominent in India throughout the classical period, from the Nyaya-sutra (c. 200) on, developing out of canons of debate and informal logic; explicitly combined with Vaisheshika in the later centuries beginning with Udayana (c. 1000); focused on issues in epistemology but also defending yoga practice.

Object language A language without the predicate "true."

Objective reality In Descartes, the reality of the contents of our ideas—their objects, what our ideas are about. Since we now call things objective when they do not depend on our own states of mind, Descartes' usage is confusing. When he attributes objective reality to something, he means to say it is an object of thought, an intentional object.

Objectivism (or absolutism) The thesis that we can speak of statements, assertions, or beliefs—in a given language and a given context—as objectively true or false, period, without reference to a speaker, society, or interpretive community.

Ontological argument The argument that God, being perfect, must exist necessarily, for necessary existence is better than contingent existence, which is better than nonexistence, and God is that nothing better than which can be conceived.

Ontology The study of what there is.

Padartha "Types of things to which words refer"; categories.

Paramita Virtue or perfection; six moral and spiritual perfections are exhibited by a Bodhisattva, according to Mahayana Buddhism: (1) charity, (2) uprightness, (3) energy, (4) patience, (5) concentration (*samadhi*), and (6) wisdom.

Participation The relation between things and forms, according to Plato. A thing is tall, for example, if it participates in the form of tallness.

Particular A thing that cannot have multiple instances.

Pascal's wager The argument that it is rational to believe in God, for the believer wins all if God exists and loses nothing if there is no God.

Patriarch A handpicked successor of the Buddha.

Perfect duty A specific obligation to specific people corresponding to rights those people have that the duty be performed.

Perspectivism The thesis that one can say whether something is right or wrong or true or false only relative to a perspective, standpoint, or point of view.

Phenomenology The study of phenomena, that is, appearances.

Phenomenon Appearance; something known to us.

Philosophical theory of truth A theory that tries to go beyond accounting for inferences involving the word "true" by explaining what makes true sentences true.

Philosophy of mind The branch of philosophy that seeks to understand the mind and consciousness and their relation to reality.

***Phronesis* (practical wisdom)** The ability to find the mean between extremes and thus to act virtuously.

Pluralism The thesis that morality rests on goods, values, principles, or feelings that differ in kind.

Polytheism The view that there is more than one god.

Practical argument An argument with a practical conclusion, that is, a conclusion about what ought to be done.

Practical wisdom (*phronesis*) The ability to find the mean between extremes and thus to act virtuously.

Pragmatism The view that meaning, truth, and value depend on practice.

Pragmatist theory of truth The theory holding that truth is "the opinion which is fated to be agreed to by all who investigate."

Prajna Wisdom; spiritual insight; one of the "perfections," *paramita* or marks of a Bodhisattva, according to Mahayana Buddhism.

Prakriti Nature conceived as operating mechanically; in Samkhya, one of two irreducible elements.

Pramana A source of knowledge or justifier; according to Nyaya, there are four: perception, inference, anology, and testimony.

Prameya An object of knowledge.

Pratitya-samutpada Interdependent origination; the Buddhist doctrine that each event comes to be in interdependence with all other events.

Pratyeka-buddha An *arhat*, a "solitary Buddha" who achieves enlightenment. But the term, used in Mahayana literature, is pejorative; the *arhat* does not display the virtues of the *bodhisattva* but seeks a personal enlightenment.

Premise One of the initial assertions of an argument, used to justify the conclusion.

Prereflective experience "Clear mind": experience without thought or self-awareness. The clear mind is like a mirror, reflecting the world just as it is.

Prescriptive term A term, such as "ought," "should," "good," "bad," "may," "duty," "responsible," or "obligation," that speaks of how things should be or what ought to be done.

Prima facie obligation Something I am obliged to do, all other things being equal, if nothing intervenes.

Primary quality A property inseparable from body; the qualities matter has according to the atomic theory of matter.

Principle (*li*) The principles of harmony implied in rites and ceremonies.

Principle of individuation What makes one object differ from another; in Aquinas, designated matter.

Principle of utility The thesis that we ought to maximize good; the sole axiom of morality, according to utilitarians.

Problem of evil The problem posed by the argument from evil: How can God let bad things happen to good people?

Problem of the criterion A skeptical argument based on variability and undecidability: There are many ways of seeing things, and no way to decide which way of seeing things is the right way. One might try to defuse the argument by seeking a criterion for distinguishing correct from incorrect perceptions. But where could we get such a criterion?

Propriety (*li*) The observance of proper rites, ceremonies, and principles.

***Pu* (uncarved block)** In Laozi, something that is what it is and does not try to be anything else.

Purusha The conscious being; in Samkhya, one of two irreducible elements.

Pyrrhonian skepticism A refusal to assert anything, even that knowledge is impossible.

Quiddity From the Latin *quidditas*, literally, "whatness," which in turn is meant to capture the Greek phrase meaning "what it is." A quiddity is what, in reality, a definition corresponds to; it is a definition in the thing. The quiddity of x is what corresponds to x's definition in the world.

Rajas The strand (*guna*) of passion and activity.

Rationalism The view that we can attain some knowledge independent of experience.

Real essence In Locke, the nature of a thing; that which makes it what it is. It stems from the real internal constitution of the object or kind.

Real internal constitution In Locke, the internal structure of a thing or kind according to the atomic theory of matter.

Realism (or platonism) (1) The view that universals are real and mind independent. (2) The thesis that human thought can discover the nature of objective reality. (3) The view that something exists independent of mind.

Reductionism The view that our ordinary ways of speaking are true, because such talk is reducible to scientific language. Reductionists hold that, in principle, it would be possible to translate talk of tables and chairs and people—and of mental entities and events such as thoughts, beliefs, desires, intentions, and so on—into talk of particles and their relations to one another. Each type of mental entity or event corresponds to some type or complex of physical entities or events.

Reflective experience Experience that involves thought and self-awareness.

Relativism The thesis that there are no universally valid truths about the world.

Ren In Confucius, virtue, humanity, benevolence; it involves both being true to the principles of our nature and acting benevolently toward others.

Response-dependent quality A quality that consists in generating a certain kind of response in a perceiver.

Righteousness (*yi*) A virtue akin to piety, correctness, and justice in ancient Chinese thought, stressed especially by Mencius and Mozi.

***Rinzai* (*Linji*)** Founded by Yixuan, the most radical of the ninth-century Zen schools, which stresses the "lightning" method of shouting and beating to prepare the mind for enlightenment.

Romanticism A movement, reaching its height in the nineteenth century, stressing the significance of passions over reason.

Rule-utilitarianism A moral theory that judges particular actions indirectly, by appeal to rules that are themselves justified as maximizing the good.

Samadhi Yogic trance; the ability to shut off mental fluctuations.

Samkhya Analysis of nature; an early school of Indian philosophy according to which the "supreme personal good" is achieved through psychological disidentification; the view that reality consists of two irreducible elements: nature (*prakriti*) and the conscious being (*purusha*).

Samsara Transmigratory existence, the wheel of birth and rebirth, worldly existence.

Samskara Disposition; mental disposition, memory, or subliminal impression.

Santana Stream of psychological elements (*dharma*) said by Buddhist philosophers to comprise personal identity.

Sanzen Consultation; Zen can be passed only from person to person.

Sapta-bhangi Seven styles or truth values, according to Jaina philosophers, i.e., seven combinations of three truth values: truth, falsity, and indeterminacy.

Sat Being; good.

Satori Enlightenment; the goal of Zen.

Sattva *Guna* or strand of intelligence and purity in Samkhya.

Scholasticism The method of dialectical reasoning used in medieval universities in Europe, consisting of examining a question, surveying various possible answers, finding points of disagreement, and using logic and analysis to resolve the dispute.

Secondary principles In Mill, commonsense rules, such as "Do not murder" and "Do not steal," that give us moral guidance and follow from the principle of utility.

Secondary quality Effects of primary qualities on our sense organs and nervous systems.

Self-evidence Self-justification. A self-evident belief justifies itself.

Semantic theory of truth A theory that gives an account of the meaning of the word "true" by accounting for inferences we make involving that word.

Sense-center consciousness A kind of consciousness that coordinates information from the five senses and, according to some, forms concepts.

Shastra An individual science or craft; a scientific textbook.

Shunyata Emptiness; Void vibrant with compassion, according to Mahayana Buddhism.

Silver Rule The moral principle that one should not do to others what you would not want done to you.

Simple ideas Ideas that are not compounds of other ideas.

Skandha Band, aggregate of psychological elements, i.e., grouping of qualities (*dharma*), according to Buddhist philosophies.

Skeptical rationalism The view that we can know something about the world independent of experience, but not beyond the bounds of experience, and not about things-in-themselves.

Skepticism The view that beliefs of certain kinds are unreliable or unjustified.

Socratic method (also called *dialectic*) Socrates asks what piety, or courage, or friendship, or justice is. Someone answers. Socrates analyzes the proposed definition and begins asking questions, leading the parties to the conversation to see that the definition cannot be right. Sometimes, the definition is unclear; sometimes, it includes too much; sometimes, it does not include enough. Someone then proposes another definition, and the process continues.

Sound argument A valid argument with true premises.

Statement A sentence asserted that can be true or false.

Storehouse consciousness In Buddhist idealism, a collective unconscious where collective karma is stored, accounting for people's projecting in common what they take to be external objects such as chairs and trees.

Strands (*Gunas*) *Sattva* (light, clarity, intelligence); *rajas* (passion, dynamism); and *tamas* (darkness, inertia, stupidity).

Supererogatory act An act that goes beyond the call of duty—in a utilitarian context, doing more for the happiness of the community than morality requires.

Superimposition In Shankara, "The apparent presentation, in the form of remembrance, to consciousness of something previously observed, in some other things.…[In other words,] the apparent presentation of the attributes of one thing in another thing."

Superior person (*junzi*) Literally, "child of a ruler." In Confucius, one of noble character.

Sutra "Thread"; a philosophic or another type of aphorism.

Syad-vada "Maybe"ism, perspectivism; the view that each opposing philosophic position has some validity, championed by Jain philosophers.

Syat "Maybe," "in some respects," "from some perspective."

Syncategorematic expression A word or phrase that does not refer to an object.

Synthetic statement A statement not true or false by virtue of the meanings of its words.

Talmud The discourses of the rabbis, compiled in Jerusalem and Babylon in the fourth and fifth centuries.

Tamas Strand of dullness and inactivity.

Tanha Selfish desire; craving; coveting; in Buddhism, the cause of suffering.

Tantra Systematic instruction; "web" or (more literally) "woven fabric" of belief; family of related religious and philosophic systems using feminine imagery in ceremonies and stories, a movement valuing nature as an expression of the Goddess.

Tantric Buddhism A tradition in Buddhism including the Lightning or Diamond Raft (also known as *Mantrayana* or *Vajrayana*) that stresses techniques for accelerating enlightenment as well as the feminine imagery, etc., characteristic of Tantra more broadly.

Tattva Reality, "that-ness"; principle of being or reality.

Teleological argument The argument that the universe, like a watch or other machine, shows such a beauty and coordination of parts that it must be the product of a creator. Also called the *argument from design.*

Theodicy An explanation of how it could be possible for evil to exist in a world created by an all-knowing, all-powerful, and entirely good God.

Theravada Buddhism An important school within the Southern branch of Buddhism, popular in Southeast Asia, which takes the *arhat* as its ideal.

Thing-in-itself A thing as it really is, independent of our faculties of knowledge.

Three evils In Buddhism, disease, old age, and death.

Token-identity theory The view that individual mental entities or events are identical with physical entities and events, but there is no way to generalize about all entities or events of a given kind.

Torah The first five books of the Hebrew scriptures—Genesis, Exodus, Leviticus, Numbers, and Deuteronomy—that constitute the Law.

Transcendence The thesis that knowledge is capable of extending beyond experience to the supersensible; alternatively, the thesis that existence extends to the supersensible.

Transcendental apperception The transcendental ground of the unity of consciousness (that is, the imperceptible "I" that ties consciousness together) in Kant.

Trifling proposition In Locke, a statement in which the predicate is the same as the subject ("A soul is a soul") or part of the subject ("Lead is a metal").

Uncarved block (*pu*) In Laozi, something that is what it is and does not try to be anything else.

Undesignated matter Matter in general, for example, "flesh and blood."

Unity of the virtues The Socratic view that courage, wisdom, self-control, justice, piety, and so on are really the same thing.

Universal An object that may be multiply instantiated, that is, have instances at different times and places.

Universalism The view that we must consider the consequences of an action on everyone it affects.

Upanishad "Secret doctrine" or "mystic teaching"; various prose and verse texts (appended to the Vedas) with mystic themes centered on an understanding of the self and its relation to the Absolute or God, called Brahman; the primary sources for classical Vedanta philosophy and the first texts advocating yoga practices.

Utilitarianism The view that we ought to maximize good.

Utu In East African thought, humanity or goodness; what makes us human and humane.

Vaisheshika Atomism; a classical Indian philosophy focusing on ontological issues, sister to *Nyaya.*

Vajrayana Lightning or Diamond Raft, a Tantric tradition in Buddhism (also known as Mantrayana Buddhism) that stresses techniques for accelerating enlightenment.

Vasana Mental disposition or *samskara* that spans lifetimes, generalized subliminal impression and force; karma.

Veda "(Revealed) Knowledge"; the four Vedas, comprising principally hymns to gods and goddesses; the oldest texts in Sanskrit.

Vedanta Originally an epithet for the Upanishads ("end of the Veda"); school of classical Indian philosophy basing itself on the Upanishads and the *Brahma-sutra* and centered on a concept of Brahman, comprising several subschools, Advaita and theistic Vedanta in particular.

Vedantin theism The dualist view that the individual and God are meaningfully distinct.

Veridical state A state (a perception or belief, for example) that is accurate.

Via negativa The "negative way" of presenting the nature of God by saying what God is not.

Vice A bad character trait.

Virtue A good character trait.

Virtue ethics A system of ethics taking the issue of virtue and character as central.

Warrant The property of a true belief that makes it knowledge or at a minimum sanctions assertion whether true or not.

Weakness of will Knowing the better and doing the worse; knowing what you ought to do and nevertheless not doing it; acting against one's better judgment.

***Wuwei* (inaction)** In Laozi, the policy of letting nature take its course.

***Xiao* (filial piety)** Obedience, reverence, and service to one's parents and elders.

Yama (Ethical) restraints: (1) *ahimsa* (noninjury), (2) *satya* (telling the truth), (3) *asteya* (not stealing), (4) *brahmacarya* (sexual restraint), (5) *aparigraha* (nonpossessiveness), according to the *Yoga-sutra.*

Yana Religious career, vehicle for salvation.

***Yi* (righteousness)** A virtue akin to piety, correctness, and justice in ancient Chinese thought, stressed especially by Mencius and Mozi.

Yin/yang Basic forces of the universe in Chinese philosophy. Opposing yet complementary, they comprise the distinction between passive and active, dark and light, feminine and masculine, night and day.

Yoga Psychological discipline with the goal of mystical insight and bliss, self-realization, or union with God or Brahman.

***Yu de* (excess or artificial nature)** In Laozi, a defect exhibited by anything that strives to be something other than what it is.

Zazen Seated meditation.

Zen A branch of Mahayana Buddhism whose goal is *satori*, enlightenment.

Zhong Reciprocity (sometimes translated "altruism" or "likening to oneself"): "What you would not have someone do to yourself, do not do to others" (Confucius).